Treating Drinkers and Drug Users in the Community

Treating Drinkers and Drug Users in the Community

Tom Waller, MBBS, DObstRCOG
Suffolk County Specialist in Substance Use

Daphne Rumball, MB, ChB, DRCOG, FRCPsych.
Consultant in Addiction Psychiatry

Blackwell
Science

Addiction
Press

Editorial offices:
Blackwell Science Ltd, 9600 Garsington Road, Oxford OX4 2DQ , UK
   Tel: +44 (0) 1865 776868
Blackwell Publishing Inc., 350 Main Street, Malden, MA 02148-5020, USA
   Tel: +1 781 388 8250
Blackwell Science Asia Pty Ltd, 550 Swanston Street, Carlton, Victoria 3053, Australia
   Tel: +61 (0)3 8359 1011

First published 2004

Library of Congress Cataloging-in-Publication Data is available

ISBN 0-632-03575-7

A catalogue record for this title is available from the British Library

Set in 10 on 12 pt MEhrhardt
by Kolam Information Services Pvt. Ltd, Pondicherry, India
Printed and bound in India using acid-free paper
by Replika Press Pvt. Ltd., Kundli 131 028

For further information on Blackwell Publishing, visit our website:
www.blackwellpublishing.com

We would like to dedicate this book to all the colleagues and service users who have taught us so much, and to the memory of Dr Arthur Banks whose compassion, drive and sheer humanity have been an inspiration.

TW
DR

Contents

Series Foreword

Addiction represents one of the most significant challenges to modern society. Addiction to cigarettes is currently estimated to cause some 3 million deaths in the world per year, and this figure is set to rise to 10 million in the next decade. Alcohol dependence is believed to account for more than a million premature deaths each year while dependence on opiates and illicit stimulants, with its associated crime, is a scourge which affects the lives of all of us directly or indirectly and the problem is not receding – if anything it is growing.

Our knowledge and understanding of what addiction is and what can be done to mitigate the problems has also increased in leaps and bounds in the past 50 years and important new findings are emerging all the time. Addiction Press encompasses the Society for the Study of Addiction's journal *Addiction* and a new book series, of which this book is the second volume to be published. Addiction Press was set up with the express purpose of communicating current ideas and evidence in this expanding field, not only to researchers and practising health professionals but also to policy makers, students and interested non-specialists.

The study of addiction involves many academic disciplines including psychology, psychiatry, public health, epidemiology, pharmacology, physiology, genetics, sociology, history and so on. Therefore this series is, of necessity, multi-disciplinary in scope and style. No artificial constraints have been imposed on the type of book that will be included – if the idea is fresh and there is a need for a volume of a particular type, it will be considered to form part of the series.

The series is intimately linked with Blackwell Publishing's major journal in the field, *Addiction*, and it is hoped that my involvement in the editorial staff of the latter will help with developing ideas for topics and authors for the former.

Finally, it is my fervent hope that the series will do more than communicate ideas in this important field; it will be part of the process for generating and stimulating thought and debate and so play some role in taking the field forward.

Robert West
Series Editor
University College, London

Foreword

Alcohol and drugs cause both major and minor problems for individuals and for society, and there can be no doubt that planners and practitioners need guidance on more effective responses to these problems. The trouble is that most existing textbooks just don't fit the bill – either they become too broad and societal in their scope or, alternatively, they become preoccupied with the specific characteristics of the different drugs and hence become like a primer in pharmacology. Whilst probably valuable in other ways, such books fail to address the needs of the busy practitioner who wishes to develop more sensitive antennae to detect problems at an early stage, more perceptive investigative skills to explore existing problems, and more competent intervention skills to prevent and treat the drug and alcohol problems which they encounter in their everyday practice.

And so this book by Tom Waller and Daphne Rumball is a breath of fresh air. It breaks the mould which has shaped so many previous books on this subject. It avoids a narrow blinkered 'alcohol' or 'drugs' perspective, except when important distinctions need to be made. It moves between prevention and treatment, recognising that they are not competitive – indeed it is crucial for them to be complementary. It examines abstinence and mechanisms for achieving and maintaining this new state, and it also examines harm reduction at personal and societal levels. It embraces a wide range of talking therapies, Twelve-Step work, relapse prevention and brief interventions, as well as general and drug-specific prescribing interventions. Above all, the reader is given a framework within which to understand and examine an individual's alcohol and drug use in the context of that individual, in his or her personal and family circumstances, in the prevailing social and political setting.

It is a particular pleasure to explore a book that covers the wide range of different interventions that competent practitioners should have within their intervention toolbox. The authors guide the reader to understand that, as outlined by the US Institute of Medicine in the book *Broadening the Base of Alcohol Problems*, a wide range of interventions can be valuable for different people with different types of problem at different stages of their involvement with alcohol (or drugs). As the authors point out, 'the old battles of abstinence-oriented treatments versus maintenance and harm reduction are battles based on ignorance and grounded in the last century'. The authors emphasise that it is important for practitioners to be focused in their pursuit of health gain and benefit, reminding us that benefit to the individual should be the primary objective of treatment.

In conclusion, there are two particularly important messages which are promoted within this book. First, there is the importance of a proactive approach to prevention and treatment – the focus on 'doing it' – doing it more broadly than we had previously been doing. Second, there is the importance of increasing competence and effectiveness of the interventions that are applied – the focus on 'doing it well' – doing it more effectively than we had previously been doing. My advice, therefore, to the prospective reader echoes these two recommendations with two similar messages of 'read it' and 'read it well'.

Professor John Strang
Director
National Addiction Centre, London

Preface

One main aim of this book has been to produce a practical and unified approach to drugs and alcohol, integrating effective treatments and putting these into a meaningful text that can be used in a practical way by those working with all substance users. A combined service approach to alcohol and drugs is not a new concept, and there is a growing literature on the subject, but there is little to read which covers the issues in a thoroughly rounded way. Although some drug and alcohol services have combined, sometimes this may be for administrative reasons only. But those working on the clinical side with drinkers with problems or dependence have much to give those who deal only with drug users. There is a comprehensive 30-year evidence-based literature on different treatments for alcohol problems and dependence. The literature on the treatment of drug users is in general more recent and often tends to be very medically oriented, focusing on prescribing issues. Nevertheless, there is much that those working with drug users can give to aid those giving help to people with drink problems. We hope that this book fulfils a need for a comprehensive text which unifies treatments for all substance use.

There are other ways in which it helps to view substance use as a single whole. Not only is there the common pitfall that those abstaining from drugs readily become overwhelmed with a drink problem, there is also the question of polydrug use and those who have a combined drug and drink problem and use drink as just another drug. Polydrug use and dependence on several drugs is increasingly common. Some experts talk of the complexities of a web of dependence and focus on the substance-specific factors, the fact that illicit drug use is not strictly interchangeable, and that users have prefer-ences for some drugs and not others (Gossop, 2001). We accept these concerns but believe them only to be interesting theoretical issues. From the point of view of treatment interventions to aid behaviour change, we need to focus on the person rather than the substance. This book is concerned with the practicalities of interventions that help sustain behaviour change away from dependence and problem substance use. From that viewpoint addiction is a concept which crosses the boundaries between substances.

We have tried to write the book so that it can either be read from beginning to end or dipped into and used as a reference work. The concept of the book and the initial planning and writing was undertaken by Dr Waller. The chapters Assessment, Prescribing Interventions, and Physical Health Issues were jointly written. Dr Rumball wrote the chapters Women, Parents and Children, and Substance Use and Mental Health. She gave valuable help with editing suggestions for the remaining chapters, which Dr Waller wrote.

We have, of necessity, included smoking in relation to pregnancy, prevention in young people and physical health but have reluctantly omitted it else-where. There is a strong case for its inclusion throughout the book. Alcohol and tobacco use are strongly linked, and few drug users are non-smokers. Nicotine use by tobacco smoking is prob-ably the major gateway drug to other substance use. The adverse health associations and consequences of substance use would be greatly reduced in the absence of tobacco, which itself poses many health problems. Smoking reduction or cessation is in-creasingly on the UK national agenda, but so far has had little impact in the drug and alcohol field. This is true of many countries, although the specialist addiction treatment services in Canada, and a slowly increasing number of other places, now cover drugs, alcohol and smoking. It could be argued that the collusion of services in the assumption that smoking is too difficult to include is yet another facet of stigma and limited expectations which deprive our clients of valuable interventions. All may helpfully be addressed together, but size constraints to this book would not allow us to do this at this juncture.

The other main aim of the book is to portray the very wide range of interventions that should now be available to all substance users but, in most cases, are only available in part. In 1990 a very important and influential document was published by the American Institute of Medicine (IOM) entitled *Broadening the Base of Alcohol Problems* which helped the alcohol treatment field move away from a 'one-treatment-suits-all' approach (IOM, 1990). Almost all of the interventions promoted in that publication have subsequently been shown to be appropriate for people with drug-related problems and dependence. The IOM treatment framework differed from the one we suggest in that it recommended that all those with significant to severe alcohol problems or dependence should be referred by professionals working in the community to a specialist unit. In contrast, we recommend that generic professionals in the community, particularly GPs and probation officers, should be encouraged to become involved in the treatment of those with more severe alcohol and drug problems. They may be aided in this work by means of shared care arrangements, court orders, networking or other formal working relationships, and in some cases additional payments should be made available. Alcohol and drug use is now so extensive and so interlinked with other presenting problems that it cannot be left solely to be covered by a small number of specialist services.

Each person develops his or her own drink or drug problem in a unique way, and a thorough understanding of the forces that led to this through the eyes of that person is essential. Knowing the difficulties that are currently faced, the harms that have been entailed in the past or may appear in the future and how to reduce them is equally important. We believe that the concept of harm reduction, in its widest possible interpretation, should be extended and that it should be considered the essential part of individual treatment. We also stress the importance of applying harm reduction to the individual. Interventions that seek to reduce harm to the community but in doing so increase harm to the individual drug user or drinker are invariably counterproductive to all.

In order to develop an appropriate care plan, those undertaking an assessment should look carefully at the harm substance users face from associated problems and how to reduce or overcome it. Thus harm reduction as treatment should be the basis of care planning. But this is only one side of the coin. Understanding the inner strengths of the individual and ways to harness them is the other side which may need attention. Most substance users overcome the harm from alcohol- and drug-related problems through their own personal resources. Some, however, need additional help to enhance their psychological and social functioning before they are able to do this. Care plan interventions should not seek to resolve all problems that are associated with substance use as many of these problems will be resolved by the substance user in time without professional help. Treatment interventions should therefore address only the most important problems which are holding up the recovery process, although sometimes personal strengths need to be enhanced first.

We view recovery as an incremental process, which generally takes place slowly, beginning well before abstinence. The twelve-step approach undeniably is a very useful method of helping people once they have decided abstinence is the right way forward and are ready and prepared to embrace the programme. Some people listen at twelve-step meetings and are encouraged enough by what they hear to try the programme for themselves. Others attend but let everything drift over their heads. Help can be given by agencies and concerned professionals to increase motivation and prepare people for change. Within the twelve-step movement itself, former beliefs that the programme is the only way forward is ending. Many now recognise that enhanced motivation, improved social support, housing, methods of coping with difficult psychological and family problems and many other interventions can be helpful ways of anticipating abstinence and augmenting the twelve-step programme. Yet the twelve-step method does not suit everyone and Cognitive–Behavioural Therapy and Motivational Enhancement Therapy have been shown to be equally effective ways of promoting abstinence for dependent drinkers (Project MATCH Research Group, 1997).

Abstinence must not be seen as the only goal or way of progressing. The old battles of abstinence-oriented treatments versus maintenance and harm reduction are battles based on ignorance and grounded in the last century. People can achieve positive change without becoming abstinent. Improvement to the quality of life is important, as is reducing the harm to the individual and to local society. Improvement should have a rightful place as the primary objective of treatment.

It is also important that the individual substance user makes the final decision as to treatment goals and which treatment interventions are given. Those who work in the addiction treatment field soon learn to accept that treatment is only successful if the drinker or drug user wishes it to be so. It is they who hold the reins. At times addiction treatment reaches the level of high art. Skilful treatment providers above all need to be empathetic with the users to understand why they became vulnerable to substance use at a particular time, what has been helpful in the past, and what is the nature of the current forces that deepen dependence and problems from substance use. They must learn how to accelerate motivational change in a beneficial way, and how to harness a person's strengths to help bring about positive change. In doing so a thorough knowledge of the environmental forces which are open to change is necessary. But in thinking beings, the milieu interior is just as important as the milieu exterior in shaping behaviour and behavioural change. Quite correctly, high focus is currently given to the co-morbidity of psychiatric illness and substance use, but psychological dysfunction impeding the recovery process is commonly ignored. We seek to rectify this omission.

This book has sections on evidence base and theory, prevention, assessment, and treatment. Ways to help the family and concerned others and methods of self-help are also included. The overlap between prevention and treatment, especially in young people, is important, but the main focus of the book is on the practical aspects of treatment. It is disturbing to see how many people confine their concept of the treatment of opiate use merely to a substitute prescription. Opiate users of many years duration, who have fought long and hard against ignorance and prejudice in order to obtain a maintenance prescription, may be excused the problems of such limited vision. But treatment service providers need a much wider view. In the alcohol field recent expertise states: 'There is a growing recognition that (1) alcohol problems are best characterised as environmentally responsive behavioural health problems and (2) current systems of care for alcohol problems are often unresponsive to the fact that the affected population is diverse on every dimension relevant to intervention (problems, resources, treatment preferences, goals, motivations, and behaviour change pathways)' (Humphries & Tucker, 2002). We suggest that this is equally true for all substance use problems.

We hope that all those working in the drug and alcohol fields will find this book of practical help with a current authoritative evidence base. It includes up-to-date information and advice on a wide range of issues relating to substance use, including hepatitis C and other blood-borne pathogens. We hope it will be useful not just to specialist workers in the field but to any professional involved in helping drug users and drinkers, including psychiatrists, GPs, psychiatric nurses, psychologists, social workers, probation officers, health educationalists, health visitors, practice nurses and other primary care staff, and will provide service planners and commissioners with an up-to-date evidence base to enable them to make correct decisions regarding the planning and commissioning of services. We also hope that the text will be accessible to people with substance problems themselves and to their families and will encourage and inform them of the interventions which may be beneficial.

Some readers may find the issues complex. We make no excuse for this. By its very nature, addiction is complicated. Most people have complex needs, although commonly many of these are overlooked by service providers. Addiction needs to be addressed holistically, through an assessment of all the problems associated with substance use and the need to look at them in a thoroughly rounded way.

The term *treatment* has broadened to include psychological and environmental as well as medical interventions, a true biopsychosocial construct. A suggested treatment framework has been portrayed which integrates harm reduction with abstinence, and Twelve-step Facilitation with Cognitive–Behavioural interventions. This should fit easily with specialist and generic professional services already being provided, but it is open to adaptation and change according to local circumstance. There is often a need for different treatment interventions to vary according to the stage of readiness to change or other factors. With the right professional advice, choosing appropriately from the broad range of interventions available will help prepare people for a state of achievable sustained behaviour change, rather than allowing them to remain in a cycle of dependence.

A word must be said about terminology in the book. When we talk of substance use we refer to both alcohol and drug use. In the hope of reducing stigma in the field, we have abandoned the terms *misuse* and *misusers*, *abuse* and *abusers*. We do this in spite of recognising that *abuse* is an official DSM-IV term with an accepted definition, and apologise to our North American colleagues if this causes them difficulty. Many of our clients take exception to these stigmatising descriptions, which in their own right can be harmful, encouraging discrimination. In their place we use the terms *drug users*, *alcohol users* and *drinkers*, unless we are specifically quoting someone else's terminology. Instead of *problem drinkers* or *problem drug users* we use *drinkers and drug users with problems or dependence* or a similar phrase. This is not an attempt to be politically correct, but is a way of avoiding terms which enhance social exclusion.

All case examples quoted to illustrate points in the text are pastiches of several different real-life situations. Many are mixtures of the activities of three or more clients. All names given have been changed. Any apparent true reflection of any past client is purely coincidental.

Overall we have tried to address evidence base, theory and practice in one volume – a difficult and time-consuming task. The book has taken ten years to write. It has an emphasis on 'what works' and 'how to do it', but reading it must not be seen as a substitute for attending training programmes to develop specific intervention skills. We hope the result provides a sound base for future effective services, promotes good practice for a wide range of professionals, and aids the fusion of drug and alcohol services.

Publisher's Note

We are sad to report that Tom Waller died unexpectedly on 27 November 2003,
soon after completing his work on the book.
He had been ill for a number of years and we will miss him.

RIP

Acknowledgements

Many people have helped in the preparation of this book to a greater or lesser degree as individuals, often with deep insights. Like most other people working in this field we have both learnt most from the insights our clients have given us. It is a privilege to have worked with so many wonderful yet needy people and to be given the opportunity to understand life from their perspective – each one so individual and different. We are indebted to them. We are also most grateful to Richard Miles and Annie Choong from Blackwell Publishing who have given such encouragement during the writing of this book and tolerated numerous extended deadlines. We also acknowledge the helpful comments of the external assessor.

We would like to thank, too, all those friends and colleagues whose work covers this area and whom we have listened to, harangued with and generally been inspired by throughout our working lives. They are too many to single out by name, but Dr Waller would like to include Dr Arthur Banks, Professor Gerry Stimson, Dame Ruth Runciman, Dr Lenka Speight, Dr Bob Speight, Lorraine Hewitt, Dr Chris Ford, Gary Sutton, Dr Roy Robertson, Professor John Strang, John Reading, Grant McNally, Adrian Kirkby, Carey Godfrey, Chip Somers, Vicky Patterson, Dr Martin Mitcheson, Derek Harper, Sue Cox, Professor Graham Foster and Giampi Alhadeff. He would also like to include all those who worked with him in the early days at City Roads and, more recently, all those with whom he worked in Suffolk, from the East Suffolk Community Drug Team, and the West Suffolk Drug Advisory Service. NORCAS and FOCUS also deserve special mention.

Most particularly Dr Waller would like to thank Dr Daphne Rumball who has been a magnificent co-author. Her enthusiasm, expertise, clarity of vision, attention to detail and commitment to the book have been a beacon of light. At times of darkness, when there seemed no end in sight, she showed the way forward. Writing a book of this nature is a huge undertaking. She has made it an enjoyable and rewarding experience.

Dr Rumball, above all, would like to thank her co-author who has been the originator, driving force and inspiration for this work. A brief conversation on a train concerning a wish to write about this field, which has interested her so deeply for the past two decades, led to an involvement in a project which she never imagined undertaking. For this, she thanks Dr Tom Waller whose faith in her ability to deliver something interesting and useful has been both humbling and inspirational. The process has brought a great enrichment at a personal and professional level.

It is our confident hope that our joint work in producing this book will engage the interest of many more professionals in working with people with alcohol and drug problems, bringing professional fulfilment and a great deal of benefit to many individuals.

Dr Rumball would like to pay tribute to the team with whom she currently works in Norwich and to all the colleagues and trainees who have helped develop the thriving Bure Centre service which is the backdrop to all other endeavours. A great debt is owed to Dr Joyce Riding who encouraged an interest in psychiatry, including alcohol-related illness, from undergraduate days and became a valued teacher and mentor over many years. Also to Professor Ilana Crome who has always given helpful counsel and friendship. The long list of people to thank includes Professor John Strang, Dr Michael

Farrell, Dr Judy Greenwood, Dr Bruce Ritson, Professor Hamid Ghodse, Roz Brooks, Christine Skinn, Dr Nick Seivewright and Dr Mervyn London.

Lastly but most importantly we would like to thank our families. Dr Waller would particularly like to thank his wife, Rosa, for her helpful and detailed editorial suggestions for the book and for the unstinting support which she and their three sons, Jack, Laurie and Harry, have given during its writing. Dr Rumball would like to thank her family, Chris, Katrina and Tony, and her parents, for their encouragement and support at all times. Without all these people the book would never have been completed and we are vastly grateful to them.

Tom Waller
Daphne Rumball

The Authors

Dr Tom Waller worked as a general practitioner (GP) in central London from 1973 to 1988. He was a GP trainer, a tutor for four London medical schools, and Lecturer in General Practice at UCH/Middlesex Medical Schools. He developed an interest in helping drug users when he became the first Medical Adviser to City Roads (Crisis Intervention Ltd), a short-stay hostel for drug users in crisis, and worked there from 1978 to 1983. It was not long before he started utilising this experience in his own general practice. In 1983, he co-authored with Dr Arthur Banks, a GP from Essex, a booklet for GPs on the treatment of drug users, *Drug Addiction and Polydrug Abuse: The Role of the GP*. This was published by the Institute for the Study of Drug Dependence and was the first publication for GPs on the subject. In 1988 the pair co-authored the first full-length book for GPs, *Drug Misuse: A Practical Handbook for GPs*, published by Blackwell Scientific Publications in association with ISDD. Dr Waller was GP representative on the Advisory Council on the Misuse of Drugs (ACMD) from 1983 to 1988 and from 1993 to 1996. In 1988 he moved to general practice in Suffolk and started to work with the drug services there. In 1991 he was appointed to the post of Specialist in Substance Misuse working with the West Suffolk Drug Advisory Service. In 1996 he became Suffolk County Specialist for Alcohol and Drug Problems. He chaired a national campaigning group 'Action on Hepatitis C' from 1999 to 2002, and was a founding director of the UK Harm Reduction Alliance (UKHRA). In 2002 he was given an award for his work in harm reduction by UKHRA, who named the annual award after him.

Dr Daphne Rumball, MB, ChB, DRCOG, FRCPsych., studied medicine at Liverpool University gaining an undergraduate prize in psychiatry. She obtained a variety of postgraduate training including general medicine, paediatrics and obstetrics and a traineeship in general practice before undertaking psychiatric training in Liverpool and East Anglia.

An enduring interest in primary care has shaped her psychiatric practice and her specialisation in substance use. She enjoys working closely with, and providing training for, GPs and is a keen trainer for psychiatric specialists in drugs and alcohol as well as GP registrars, other doctors and professionals of many disciplines. She has been strongly involved in the field of substance use with the Royal College of Psychiatrists over many years, being Honorary Secretary of the Faculty and a contributor to a wide range of working groups including syllabus development and practice guidelines. Other interests include teaching and writing. She is Academic Adviser and Honorary Senior Lecturer, School of Medicine, Health Policy and Practice, University of East Anglia. Her writing interests include training issues, young people and substance use and opiate detoxification.

Clinical work is at the core of her interests. She is a consultant psychiatrist in Norfolk Mental Health Care NHS Trust, specialising in drugs and alcohol, and working with a thriving multidisciplinary team in a large urban and rural service.

Part I
Theoretical Considerations

Chapter 1
An Overview

Theory and Evidence Base Underpinning a Broad and Unified Treatment Approach for Drinkers and Drug Users

Introduction

Most people working in the substance use field wonder from time to time why services for alcohol users are so often separate from those for drug users. Is this really only because alcohol is legal and drugs are illegal? Some substance use services are combined and there are different ways of doing this, but is one way better than another? What can those in the alcohol field learn from those in the drug field and vice versa? If alcohol and drug services do combine at a clinical level in the most cost-effective way, would this change the practicalities of current working practice for both services? Ten years ago questions such as these prompted a search that moved on to become an illuminating journey of discovery. This book is the fruition of that journey.

This chapter examines the evidence base for a unified approach. Terms that are common to the alcohol and drug fields are defined, and the development of alcohol and drug service provision is viewed from its own unique historical context.

What is treatment?

When they talk about treatment for drug and drink problems and dependence, many people think solely of interventions to achieve sustained abstinence or purely about medical prescribing interventions. Considering what enables people to recover from problematic substance use, a much broader concept of the term *treatment* must be encompassed and addressed as a complex construct with biopsychosocial parameters. In the medical field the inter-

play of biological, psychological and social aspects of a person's life is known to be instrumental in the development of health and illness (Engel, 1980; Schwartz, 1982). Thus when biopsychosocial influences are harmful to the individual's health and well-being, this interplay is instrumental in the development of problems from the use of, or addiction to, drugs and alcohol. Conversely when biological, psychological and social influences reinforce each other in a positive way, they protect people from developing such difficulties, or, if problems and dependence are already established, positive biopsychosocial interventions will aid an individual's ability to overcome them. The evidence that this is so, and the way to use these influences and interventions to aid those who seek help, is to be found throughout the pages of this book.

So-called *natural recovery* normally entails recovery from dependent and problem substance use without any professional help. Those who do this harness constructive biopsychosocial influences themselves. This probably happens more frequently than is generally realised, particularly for those with mild to moderate drug or alcohol dependence. The number of persons who recover naturally without medical or other interventions may be as high as those who recover following treatment (Klingeman, 1994).

When professional help is sought, a working strategy that is unashamedly holistic in both intent and practice is required. A broad-ranging needs assessment should be undertaken and from this a care plan can be drawn up comprising the most effective pharmacological, physical, psychological and social interventions.

Who should be offered treatment?

Services should be concerned with both the prevention and treatment of dependence, and with the prevention and treatment of medical, social, psychological and legal problems associated with substance use. In most countries considerably more financial and human resources are directed towards those who already have an established chemical dependency than on prevention. This is in spite of the fact that treatment is much more costly than prevention, both in human and resource terms, and successful treatment is much more difficult to achieve than prevention. However, services are slowly becoming more proactive with time, and prevention services are beginning to become established.

Treatment for those who are not alcohol or drug dependent

Treatment services will encounter people at all stages of a drug or alcohol addiction problem. There will always be opportunities for prevention and these must be given as much priority as those people clamouring for help with an already established drink or drug problem. When prevention initiatives are appropriate, those who come in contact with treatment services may be given structured advice or other evidence-based interventions to enable them to reduce the risk of harm to themselves and others. For drug injectors and those considered to be at risk of injecting, this should include harm reduction advice about injecting and the sharing of injecting equipment and paraphernalia. Harm reduction advice should also be given to binge drinkers. Regular drinkers who drink at hazardous or harmful levels should be given structured advice about keeping within so-called *safe limits*.

For those who have not yet reached the stage of dependent use, a *brief*, or just a 10-minute structured *minimal* intervention may be all that is necessary to stop them becoming addicted or accruing other problems at a later date. As drinking alcohol by adults is legal, it is relatively easy to access adult heavy drinkers before dependence is fully established or when it is at an early stage. However, all too often opportunities are wasted and unstructured general advice is given by services, and structured brief or minimal interventions, which are known to be highly effective, are disregarded.

A brief or minimal intervention given in a structured way to heavy drinkers before they become dependent (or even when they are mildly to moderately dependent) can prevent years of addiction problems. There would be enormous cost savings if widespread government-funded screening programmes were established to identify people drinking to excess, and those so identified given structured brief interventions to prevent them developing serious problems later in life. But surprisingly little of this type of work is undertaken either for those who seek advice or proactively by screening and accessing populations at risk.

In the drugs field there has been less research to show that brief interventions are helpful, although the evidence is starting to accumulate. This is probably because it is less easy to access those who use drugs recreationally. The illicit nature of most drug use leads both to concealment and to an expectation that workers will be compelled to advise complete abstinence. As a result, drug use is less likely to be volunteered before problems are encountered. Sometimes, however, drug problems stem from the overuse of prescribed drugs. Here there would be no difficulty in providing structured brief interventions, if this were felt to be the right way forward.

Youth and outreach workers may advise interim goals to illicit drug users, such as cutting down or moving from injecting to oral use. But others, particularly probation officers, might feel they were breaching their professional responsibilities if they were to do this, because they would seem to be advising the continuance of an illegal activity. It is proposed that all concerned professionals legitimately recognise the value of interim goals for drug users and intervene accordingly. A hierarchy of goals to reduce harm from the spread of blood-borne viruses (BBVs) has been accepted for many years as a valuable way forward, and modern methods of outcome assessment look holistically at improvement rather than just abstinence as the only good outcome.

There are other reasons, too, why disclosure of all types of substance problem tend to be deterred. These include an individual's expectations of stigmatisation, and a failure of professionals to be alert to the symptoms and signs of drinking and drug-taking in the context of other health and social problems. A different but very promising avenue for the prevention of drug and alcohol dependence, which does not rely on disclosure, has been the identification of groups of young people who are *vulnerable* to (i.e. at very high risk of) developing addiction problems. Much research has been done in this area since the early 1990s, particularly in the USA, and several evidence-based interventions have been published. It is clearly a very useful way forward, and will be described in more detail in Chapter 3.

Treatment for those who have established alcohol or drug dependence

There is no clear dividing point between dependent and non-dependent substance use. But once people have crossed over from regular use to drug or alcohol dependence they have much more difficulty in moving away from it. It no longer remains completely within their voluntary control. As a result of help-seeking, the main body of treatment work for specialist agencies is with those who have become drug or alcohol dependent. In most places services are overwhelmed with requests for help. Dependent drinkers, drug users and those with multiple problems are generally offered an assessment followed by a care plan involving various interventions according to the complexity of the presenting problems and the needs of the individual (see Chapter 5).

What is alcohol and drug dependence?

The dependence syndrome

A major step forward in our understanding of dependence came in the mid-1970s when the concept and provisional description of the dependence syndrome was first suggested (Edwards & Gross, 1976). The evidence backing it was summarised ten years later (Edwards, 1986). It was flexible and non-stigmatising. Not all the constructs needed to be present. There was truly 'no one "level of explanation" nor the hegemony of any scientific discipline' in the dependence syndrome, for no single parameter dominated the others. Its importance was recognised by the World Health Organization (which had contributed to early discussions on the syndrome) and it became rapidly accepted. Today it forms the basis of the requirements for a diagnosis of both alcohol and drug dependence in the tenth edition of the *International Classification of Diseases* (ICD-10) and its US counterpart, the fourth edition of the *Diagnostic and Statistical Manual of Mental Disorders* (DSM-IV). DSM-IV (Frances *et al.*, 1994) is the current standard US work elaborating the necessary criteria for diagnosing mental illnesses. DSM-IV applies to all westernised societies. Its international counterpart, ICD-10 (WHO, 1992), is used more widely throughout the world and is applicable to developing as well as developed countries.

Although the dependence syndrome was fully defined by Edwards and colleagues (1977) as a socially learned, biologically based, and psychologically mediated concept for alcohol dependence, similar criteria are now used to diagnose all chemical dependencies. As it is not a fixed entity, the interplay between the various biological, sociological and psychological parameters shifts according to the degree of dependence. In turn, this varies with time and circumstance for each individual.

The term *syndrome* was used because it denoted a recognisable grouping of social, biological and psychological constructs, and encompassed degrees of severity. The alcohol dependence syndrome is comprised of the following elements:

- a narrowing of the drinking repertoire
- the salience of drinking
- an increased tolerance to alcohol
- repeated physical withdrawal symptoms, comprising tremor, sweating, nausea and mood disturbance
- the relief or avoidance of withdrawal symptoms by further drinking

- the subjective awareness of a compulsion to drink
- reinstatement after abstinence

Challenges to the dependence syndrome

There are two main challenges to the concept of the dependence syndrome. Both are centred on the dominance of one particular dimension. The first challenge comes from the twelve-step movement, which originated with Alcoholics Anonymous (AA) and views chemical addiction as a disease. This biological explanation as a dominant dimension of addiction forms the very basic belief underpinning the twelve-step approach and is the main *level of explanation* underlying the approach. It contrasts with the lack of hegemony of the dependence syndrome.

The twelve-step construct requires acceptance by the individual. It is a fixed entity from which all dependent drinkers are presumed to suffer. Those who will not accept that they suffer from the disease *alcoholism* and continue drinking are anticipated to progressively worsen. They lose control after only one drink. The only way to halt the progressive downward path is by stopping drinking completely. One drink leads to drunkenness. Edwards (1987) counters these arguments with two responses:

(1) If the therapist cannot recognise *degrees* of dependence, he will not be able to fit his approach to the particular patient, and sometimes he may retreat into seeing 'addiction to alcohol' as a fixed entity from which all patients with drinking problems are presumed to suffer.
(2) It is unclear whether the experience is truly one of losing control rather than one of deciding not to exercise control. Control is probably best seen as variably or intermittently impaired rather than 'lost'.

In support of this last statement, Marlatt has shown that a single lapse *can* often be controlled and that practising how to do this can help prevent a lapse progressing on to a full-blown relapse. He says that the AA maxim 'One drink – one drunk' becomes a self-fulfilling prophecy because the expectation is that control will be lost. Those who lapse do not attempt to stop any further drinking because they believe that they have lost the ability to do this. He called this the Abstinence Violation Effect (AVE) (Marlatt & Gordon, 1985).

In the second challenge, the scientific discipline of psychology is put forward as the hegemony that overrides all other explanations. Here dependence is perceived to be primarily psychological in nature, and as such is open to change. With professional psychological help some people can relearn how to control their drinking (Heather & Robertson, 1981; 1997).

Edwards (1987) highlights how it is the less dependent drinker who is able to achieve this, at least for a period of time:

> The coherence of the dependence picture is such that the patient who is highly dependent will be able to swing his drinking repertoire only between bouts of heavy dependent drinking and intervening periods of total or near-total abstinence. The less dependent person will have bouts with hazier edges, and intervening periods of non-dependent drinking which gradually edge again towards establishment of dependence.

The implication is that, with help, mildly to moderately dependent drinkers may increase these naturally occurring non-dependent drinking phases. Although exceptions are recorded in the literature, e.g. Booth (1990), it is almost always within this group of mildly to moderately dependent drinkers that success is achievable in moderating consumption to low-risk levels. However, this success may not be sustained in the longer term. In the severely dependent there appears to be a permanent change where drinking is no longer controllable except by abstinence, as has been demonstrated by long-term follow-up studies (Edwards *et al.*, 1983).

Thus the severity of dependence is important to measure. There may be mild, moderate or severe dependence according to the extent to which the criteria of the dependence syndrome are met. Physical and psychological features of the dependence syndrome can be used to assess the severity of dependence on alcohol or a number of drugs by means of a standardised questionnaire specific to the drug used, e.g. the Severity of Alcohol Dependence

Questionnaire (SADQ) (Stockwell *et al.*, 1979), the Severity of Opiate Dependence Questionnaire (SODQ) (Sutherland *et al.*, 1986), which was designed to be comparable with the SADQ and bears a close resemblance to it, or the Severity of Amphetamine Dependence Questionnaire (Churchill, 1993). But it is easier to use a scale designed to measure severity of dependence across a range of substances such as the Leeds Dependence Questionnaire (Raistrick *et al.*, 1994) (Appendix 7).

DSM-IV diagnostic criteria for dependent substance use

The official DSM-IV definition of dependent substance use is as follows:

A maladaptive pattern of substance use, leading to clinically significant impairment or distress, as manifested by three (or more) of the following, occurring at any time in the same 12-month period:

(1) tolerance, as defined by either of the following:
  (a) a need for markedly increased amounts of the substance to achieve intoxication or desired effect
  (b) markedly diminished effect with continued use of the same amount of the substance
(2) withdrawal, as manifested by either of the following:
  (a) the characteristic withdrawal syndrome for the substance
  (b) the same (or a closely related) substance is taken to relieve or avoid withdrawal symptoms
(3) the substance is often taken in larger amounts or over a longer period than was intended
(4) there is a persistent desire or unsuccessful efforts to cut down or control substance use
(5) a great deal of time is spent in activities necessary to obtain the substance (e.g. visiting multiple doctors or driving long distances), use the substance (e.g. chain-smoking), or recover from its effects

(6) important social, occupational, or recreational activities are given up or reduced because of substance use
(7) the substance use is continued despite knowledge of having a persistent or recurrent physical or psychological problem that is likely to have been caused or exacerbated by the substance (e.g. current cocaine use despite recognition of cocaine-induced depression, or continued drinking despite recognition that an ulcer was made worse by alcohol consumption)

Specify if:
With physiological dependence: evidence of tolerance or withdrawal (i.e. either item 1 or 2 is present)
Without physiological dependence: no evidence of tolerance or withdrawal (i.e. neither item 1 nor 2 is present)

ICD-10 criteria for dependent substance use

In the official ICD-10 definition there are six criteria instead of seven, but again three or more answers must be in the affirmative. The criteria are:

(1) a strong desire or sense of compulsion to take the substance
(2) difficulties in controlling substance-taking behaviour in terms of its onset, termination, or levels of use
(3) the substance is often taken in larger amounts or over a longer period than was intended
(4) any unsuccessful effort or a persistent desire to cut down or control substance use
(5) increased amounts of time necessary to obtain or take the substance or recover from its effects; also progressive neglect of alternative pleasures or interests
(6) persisting with substance use despite evidence of overtly harmful problem consequences

The ICD-10 differs from DSM-IV in that the first four criteria focus on control of substance use and the social dimension is excluded because the ICD must be applicable to a wide range of cultures. Social problems differ so widely between cultures that it is difficult to define social criteria that have uniform transcultural application. For example, any use of alcohol in a Muslim country can lead to major adverse social consequences, whereas in Western societies alcohol use is integrated into the social fabric.

Substance abuse and problems related to substance use

Although social harm is missing from the ICD-10 classification of harmful use, there is a commonality for the criteria laid down in these two classification systems for substance use, which is connected with the harm caused by problems associated with substance use. In the DSM this is termed drug or alcohol *abuse*. In the ICD this is classified under *harmful use*. Although DSM-IV gives as its criterion for *abuse*, 'continued substance use despite having persistent or recurrent social or interpersonal problems caused or exacerbated by the effects of the substance', under the ICD-10 classification of *harmful use* this is limited to 'clear evidence that the substance use was responsible for (or substantially contributed to) physical or psychological harm, including impaired judgment or dysfunctional behaviour'.

What is problem drug and alcohol use?

Drug or alcohol dependence can occur without any associated problems. Conversely, problems can occur in the absence of dependence. It is clear, therefore, that dependence should be assessed separately from associated problems and the harm they generate, although chemical dependency can be considered a problem in its own right. The concept that problem alcohol use constitutes a separate dimension from dependence on alcohol was first put forward by the same WHO Scientific Group that helped define the dependence syndrome (Edwards *et al.*, 1977). Later this idea was taken up by British experts in the drugs field who defined problem drug use as 'social, psychological, physical and legal problems related to intoxication and/or regular excessive consumption and/or dependence as a consequence of the taking of drugs or other chemical substances (excluding tobacco)' (ACMD, 1982).

Problem drug use is one of the key forces behind help-seeking and motivation to change.

DSM-IV diagnostic criteria for substance abuse

The word *abuse* is avoided in the UK and some other parts of the world because of its derogatory implications. In the USA, however, substance *abuse* is a commonly used term with a precise definition in DSM-IV. It covers significant substance use which does not meet the criteria laid down for the diagnosis of dependence, but nevertheless is having an impact on peoples' lives through the problems that are generated:

A. A maladaptive pattern of substance use leading to clinically significant impairment or distress, as manifested by one (or more) of the following, occurring within a 12-month period:

   (1) recurrent substance use resulting in a failure to fulfill major role obligations at work, school or home (e.g. repeated absences or poor work performance related to substance use; substance-related absences, suspensions or expulsions from school; neglect of children or household)
   (2) recurrent substance use in situations in which it is physically hazardous (e.g. driving an automobile or operating a machine when impaired by substance use)
   (3) recurrent substance-related legal problems (e.g. arrests for substance-related disorderly conduct)
   (4) continued substance use despite having persistent or recurrent social or interpersonal problems caused or exacerbated by the effects of the substance (e.g. arguments with spouse about consequences of intoxication, physical fights)

B. The symptoms have never met the criteria for substance dependence for this class of substance.

Tolerance

Tolerance is usually operationally defined as either the reduced effect of the same dose of a drug on subsequent administrations, or as a need to increase the dosage in order to maintain the same level of effect (Lader, 1988). It is a reflection of the biochemical and/or neurological changes which accompany repeated exposure to a substance, following which the individual is able to tolerate larger doses. This may be driven by the subjective desire for a more intense pharmacological effect from the substance, or by the need to consume greater amounts to maintain the same subjective effect and to avert withdrawal symptoms. This is an important concept in the understanding of drug-using behaviour and in the field of risk reduction. The concept of loss of tolerance is the reverse process.

Metabolic tolerance is classically seen in heavy drinkers. Here the enzyme alcohol dehydrogenase, which breaks down alcohol, is increased in liver cells by the P450 cytochrome system. This enables alcohol to be metabolised faster so that larger amounts need to be drunk to have the same effect.

Neuroadaptation is a more important form of tolerance. Here the neurones undergo physiological change. If a drug is given in high doses over a prolonged period, changes in the number and affinity of receptors occur. Receptor density is increased so that more drug is needed for a given pharmacological effect. Neuroadaptation is inextricably linked to the physiological changes that constitute rebound withdrawals and the abstinence syndrome of physical drug dependence.

Tolerance and the adaptations of rebound and physical dependence are not limited solely to drugs of addiction, but are widespread phenomena (Haefely, 1986). Metabolic tolerance and neuroadaptation are probably both basic defence mechanisms to help organisms survive in toxic conditions.

Environmental and genetic influences

Although the modern day view is that alcohol and drug dependence is a biopsychosocial syndrome, comprising biological, psychological and social parameters, it would be more correct to talk of *environmental* rather than *social* parameters. Similarly it would be better to talk of environmental rather than social problems because the term environmental has wider connotations. It encompasses social parameters within its meaning, together with all influences that are external to the person, including housing and financial issues, advertising and the media, the availability of substances, and regulation or restrictions on their use (see 1988 ACMD definition in Chapter 13).

Just as the ecosystem of the rainforest is delicately balanced and sensitive to small changes, so too is the human ecosystem. Influences on this human ecosystem may be healthy and positive, or negative and destructive. Drug use and heavy drinking adversely affect this human ecosystem and are associated with problems that generate harm. But removing all negative influences by removing all the associated problems may not always be enough to overcome a drink or a drug problem. Individuals may need additional help in a positive direction like the following example of John C.

CASE STUDY

> John C. was made redundant and became unemployed for several months. He had no close friends and lived in a deprived area of a northern UK town. He felt trapped by his poverty, unable to move away from the area. Depression and boredom set in. He started drinking heavily and regularly came home in the evenings drunk and angry. John eventually found another job but continued to drink heavily. After a few more months his long-suffering partner left him. John C. was devastated. He was now completely isolated. His ability to make and keep close friendships had always had limitations. His depression worsened and he contemplated suicide.

First of all John C. needs an assessment as to why he continued to drink. It may be that he has developed depression as a psychiatric illness requiring treatment and this is acting as a trigger to his drinking. Yet tackling this problem alone may not be enough. Indeed, in spite of reducing as far as possible all the overt and covert problems that are associated with substance use, John C. may still remain entrenched in drug or drink use. Some people need additional help. This may be given by harnessing the strengths which they already have, or by helping them improve their psychosocial functioning so that they function better in society. We already know that John C.'s 'ability to make and keep close friendships had always had limitations'. Social skills training may help him gain friends and the support and respect of others, and enable him to extricate himself from the dominance of problem substance use.

Drug availability and social acceptability of drug use are important factors in the development or resolution of drug and alcohol problems. The wider availability and social acceptability of the licit drug alcohol have no doubt contributed substantially to higher prevalence rates of drink problems compared to drug problems in Western society. But, for both alcohol and all drugs, the effect of environmental changes has been shown to have general applicability for all types of substance use (Griffiths *et al.*, 1980; Henningfield *et al.*, 1986; Higgins, 1997). Common environmental factors for all types of substance use also include financial determinants of choice. Bickel and colleagues (1993), analysing the demand for alcohol and drugs, showed that demand can be accurately described with the same analytic tools that apply for all commodities, and can be regarded as just another commodity. This observation has led to the new approach of behavioural economics and the study of factors that govern choice to use substances, which is described in greater detail in Chapter 7.

Many biological and psychological influences on substance use and dependence are general across all substances, but individuals need not have any exceptional or pathological characteristics in order to engage in substance use or develop dependence. The bell can toll for anyone. Nevertheless, both genetic and acquired characteristics (e.g. family history of alcohol dependence, and psychiatric disorders) do increase the probability of developing alcohol or drug problems and dependence, although they are not necessary preconditions for them to emerge (Higgins, 1999). The genetic liability for the development of both alcohol and drug problems and dependence appears to predominate in men (Reich *et al.*, 1998), whereas both sexes appear to be equally influenced by environmental factors.

Social Learning Theory and the development of the cognitive–behavioural approach to treatment

The way behaviour is learned is known as *learning theory*. Addictive behaviour is learned according to the same principles as all other learned behaviour, and there have been significant developments in our understanding of this area.

Early focus of learning theory rested on the behavioural principles of classical conditioning through a study of stimulus and response. A *stimulus* is any internal or external event which changes an organism's behaviour, and the change is known as the *response*. Any favourable outcome which results from a response is known as *reinforcement*, as it increases the probability that the response will be repeated.

Learning theory changed when Lewin (1951) showed that responses are subject to influence from an interaction between a person and the environment. Schoolchildren behave differently in the classroom and the playground. Cognitive processes are the main factors influencing this change and, instead of stimulus–response (SR) learned behaviour, the model became stimulus-organism-response (SOR). This had important practical implications for professionals seeking to aid behaviour change. Whereas behavioural therapy works on the SR model, Cognitive Therapy (CT) focuses almost exclusively on the O of the SOR, and Cognitive–Behavioural Therapy (CBT) covers the complete SOR model. Although the origins and acceptance of the cognitive model can be traced back 2000 years, when CT and CBT were widely adopted in the 1980s it was regarded as a revolution in thinking.

In the meantime the psychologist Albert Bandura (1969) took the SOR model forward another step by stating that learned behaviour could occur through observation of the behaviour of another person, without necessarily having to perform it oneself. In other words, there can be a short cut in the process if people model their own behaviour on others whom they admire. He called this *Social Learning Theory* (SLT).

As a theoretical base underpinning behaviours that lead to the development of both alcohol and drug problems and/or dependence, SLT has been extremely influential. Bandura advanced the original theory substantially, and in his books published from 1969 to 1986 (Bandura, 1969; 1977a; 1986) outlined the four main elements of SLT. These are *differential reinforcement, vicarious learning, cognition* and *reciprocal determinism*.

Differential reinforcement states that conditioned learning is dependent upon environmental influences, as these determine the consequences of the learned behaviour. However, as some environmental influences are stronger than others, there will be a differential reinforcement according to the degree of influence. For instance, drinking at a party where there is social approval and enjoyable social exchanges will be reinforcing, but drinking at work may earn the disapproval of peers and supervisors, and could potentially lead to termination of employment. Negative effects like this would reinforce behaviour not to drink.

Vicarious learning (or modelling) is behaviour that is acquired through the observation of others, or through spoken or written communication. Bandura argued that virtually everything that can be learned from direct experience can also be acquired, and that vicarious learning is a far more efficient way to acquire and regulate behaviour patterns than by doing things by trial and error – a fact that the advertising industry has been quick to exploit.

Cognitive processes include encoding, organising and retrieval of information that help determine future behaviour. Expectancies and self-efficacy (the self-perception of a person's ability to achieve a desired outcome) are two important cognitive processes in the drug and alcohol field, as they may be key factors in the development and maintenance or resolution of drug and alcohol problems. If you expect alcohol to have a relaxing effect you will tend to drink in situations that are anxiety-provoking. On the other hand, many people do reach a point of recognising that the overall effect of their substance use has become negative and therefore decide and act to discontinue their use. Nevertheless, if after many failed attempts they come to believe that they are incapable of ever becoming drug-free, they may give up trying however well motivated they are to stop.

Research has shown gender differences in expectancies. Women tend to be seen, by both males and females, as more sexually responsive while under the influence of alcohol (Leigh, 1990). Expectancies are also important predictors of treatment outcome. Negative alcohol expectancies predict more successful treatment outcomes in dependent drinkers both in the short term (three months) (Jones & McMahon, 1994), and long term (two years) (Connors *et al.*, 1993).

Other cognitive processes are also important in recovery. These include self-regulatory functions, through which individuals arrange environmental incentives, produce cognitive supports and generate consequences for their own actions. Mark and Linda Sobell's *Problem Drinkers: Guided Self-Change Treatment* (1993) is an example of the way in which self-regulatory functions can be used successfully in treatment.

Reciprocal determinism is a concept that Bandura continued to develop with each of his three books on SLT. He first introduced the concept in 1969. At this time he interpreted reciprocal determinism to mean that although behaviour may be determined by the environment, it may also in turn alter the environment so that both become mutually reinforcing. In 1977 he introduced a third factor, the person, so that the person, the environment and the behaviour become 'interlocking' (Bandura, 1977a). In 1986 he renamed the term *triadic reciprocality*. Here there is a continual interaction of the environment, the person and behaviour in an open system in which each factor is mutually affected.

A review (Maisto *et al.*, 1999) of Bandura's SLT has confirmed that a very substantial body of research now supports his theoretical constructs. Bandura's first book in 1969 applied SLT to enhance our understanding as to how alcohol disorders develop and are maintained. He put forward a coping deficits model and suggested that, for a large proportion of individuals with an alcohol problem, skills training should be one component of treatment.

Bandura's work was particularly important to the substance use field because it led on to the development of the *cognitive–behavioural approach* for the treatment of drug and alcohol problems, and also included elements drawn from other fields such as social psychology. In 1985 Marlatt and Gordon published their classical work on the prevention of relapse for those addicted to drugs, drink and/or smoking based on SLT and its practical application through the cognitive–behavioural approach. Their cognitive–behavioural perspective created a new way of understanding the development and maintenance of substance use disorders and helped establish a sound theoretical and practical approach to treating all addictive behaviours relating to alcohol, drug and tobacco use. The theoretical aspects of the cognitive–behavioural perspective to substance use disorders has been summed up by Maisto and colleagues (1999) in the following statements:

- Addictive behaviours represent a category of 'bad habits' (or learned maladaptive behaviours). Biological factors may contribute to predisposing an individual to substance use problems, but specific patterns of use are learned.
- Addictive behaviours occur on a continuum of use; i.e. behaviour such as problematic alcohol use is not seen in a categorical way (e.g. present or absent), but rather exists on continua of quantity and frequency of occurrence.
- All points along the continuum of addictive behaviour are influenced by the same principles of learning. Therefore, the same mechanism that may be applied to explain harm-free alcohol and drug use can be invoked to explain substance use disorder.
- Addictive behaviours are learned habits that can be analysed in the same way as any other habit.
- The determinants of addictive behaviours are situational and environmental factors, beliefs and expectations, the person's family history and prior learning experiences with the substance or activity. Emphasis also is placed on the consequences of addictive behaviour to understand its reinforcing and/or punishing features.
- Besides the effects of alcohol (or other substance or activity in question), it also is important to discern the social and interpersonal reactions that the individual experiences before, during and after engaging in the addictive behaviour. Social factors are important both in the acquisition and later performance of the addictive behaviour.

- Frequently, addictive behaviours are exhibited under conditions that are perceived as stressful. To that degree, they represent maladaptive coping behaviours.
- Addictive behaviours are strongly affected by the individual's expectations of achieving desired effects of engaging in the addictive behaviour. Furthermore, self-efficacy expectancies (i.e. expectations of being able to use behavioural skills to cope with a situation without engaging in the addictive behaviour) are important. If self-efficacy in a situation is low, and the individual believes (expects) that engaging in the addictive behaviour would help cope with it, then the likelihood of engaging in the behaviour increases.
- The acquisition of new skills and cognitive strategies in a self-management programme can result in changes in addictive behaviour to new, more adaptive behaviours that come under the control of cognitive processes, awareness and decision-making. Accordingly, the individual can assume and accept a greater degree of responsibility for changing the addictive behaviour.

Thus SLT and the cognitive–behavioural approach to treatment suggest that a unified system for the treatment of drug and alcohol problems could be beneficially implemented. But in addition to cognitive–behavioural interventions there are a growing number of treatment interventions which have been shown to work across the spectrum of substance use. For both drug users and drinkers, outcomes can be improved by Motivational Interviewing (MI) (Miller & Rollnick, 1991; 2002); family therapy (O'Farrell, 1993); employment facilitation (Hall et al., 1981; Azrin et al., 1982); social support (Moos et al., 1990; McLellan et al., 2000); social and coping skills training (Monti et al., 2002) and relapse prevention (Marlatt & Gordon, 1985). A wide range of treatments should be available for drinkers and targeted to individual need (IOM, 1990). There is no evidence to suggest that the psychological, social and medical needs of those suffering from alcohol dependence are any more disparate than people who have problems and/or dependence related to drug use. Strategies and interventions similar to those undertaken for dependent drinkers should be applied to those who are dependent on drugs, including such pharmacologically disparate groups as opiates, stimulants and benzodiazepines.

Dealing with problems across the spectrum of substance use

Those who develop problems associated with alcohol or drug use may cope with the problems in similar ways irrespective of which substance has been used. People tend to resolve problems in one of two ways. Either they try to find ways of dealing with the problem and resolve it – this is known as problem-focused coping – or they try to deal with the emotional distress that is caused by the problem. The latter is known as emotion-focused coping. In general, studies show that problem-focused coping is healthy and adaptive but that, even when problems are easily resolvable, some people have a tendency towards emotion-focused coping and this is maladaptive. Of course some problems, such as the death of a loved one, cannot be resolved by problem-solving techniques. In such circumstances helping people deal with their difficult emotions through coping skills training is far healthier than suppressing these emotions by the use of alcohol or drugs. It is now well established that suppressing emotional responses first highlighted by Bandura (1969) in his so-called *coping deficits model*, commonly occurs in substances users (Cooper *et al.*, 1992; Evans & Dunn, 1995).

In the coping deficits model people use drugs and alcohol in ways that are unique to them from both a biological and psychological standpoint. Often they self-medicate to treat distressing symptoms by utilising the pharmacological properties of a drug, e.g. by taking amphetamines to relieve depression, alcohol to relieve anxiety or heroin to stop opiate withdrawals. But in seeking chemical relief for a psychological problem, availability of the drug may take precedence. Indeed at such times the substance use may bear no resemblance to the pharmacological properties of the drug, but more to the expectancy that any drug will do. Thus if central nervous system (CNS) depressants are not available, stimulants are sometimes used to cope with anxiety. Similarly if cocaine or amphetamines are not available, alcohol and benzodiazepines may be used as an aid to cope with depression, even though the pharmacological effects of these drugs would be expected to compound the problems they are being used to alleviate. Thus expectancy responses appear to be fulfilled even when pharmacologically inappropriate. It is as if taking a drug to deal with a psychological problem on a regular basis leads to a conditioned response, the effects of which are to ease the psychological problem, and once this is established any drug will do.

The interventions that work and those that do not, both to prevent the onset of substance use problems or dependence and to treat individuals who already have established problems or dependence, are now relatively well known. Almost all are aimed at treating the person rather than the drug. There are still some gaps in the available knowledge base, however the following section looks in depth at the way integrated programmes, tailored to individual need, might work in the most constructive way.

The case for integrated drug and alcohol programmes

Programmes which are equally suitable for drinkers and drug users are numerous. The Minnesota Model was developed during the 1950s in Minnesota as a twelve-step inpatient programme for alcoholics at Hazelden and Wilmar. It has since expanded to many different centres for those with *chemical dependency* problems (a term originally applied to cocaine users but later changed to cover alcohol and all drugs). Other methods of treating clients followed whatever their substance of use. Following Marlatt and Gordon's demonstration (1985) that the same psychological techniques and approach to prevent relapse were equally appropriate for drug users, drinkers and smokers, Beck and colleagues (1993) developed Cognitive Therapy for all substance users. At about the same time Ellis and colleagues (1988; Ellis & Dryden, 1999) developed *Rational–Emotive Therapy* (RET). This is another form of Cognitive Therapy and has been applied equally successfully to people with alcohol and drug problems. Miller (1983) originally devised Motivational Interviewing to enhance the motivation of drinkers to change, and this was later rolled out to motivate drug users both to tackle their drug problem and to take steps to reduce the risk of HIV infection (Miller & Rollnick, 1991) (see Chapter 8 for an in-depth description of these counselling approaches). Isoo Kim Berg has described the use of Solution-Focused Therapy (SFT) as a brief intervention for both drinkers and drug users (Berg & Reuss, 1998) (see Chapter 10).

Some counsellors have developed their own combined service programmes for users of alcohol and other drugs: Kaufman (1994) uses his integrated psychotherapy treatment for drug users and drinkers; Denning (2000) links a counselling service for all substance users with harm reduction; and Rotgers and colleagues (1996) and Margolis and Zweben (1998) have described several different treatment modules which can be integrated for anyone with a drug or drink problem. These include group therapy, family therapy, behavioural therapy and Cognitive–Behavioural Therapy, network therapy and problem-solving.

With an awareness of the similarities of approach of other treatment interventions apart from twelve-step work, an increasing number of substance use services have become integrated, but there is still considerable variation between and within countries. Some of the earlier joint programmes included an integrated outpatient service for drug users and drinkers at the Washton Institute in New York (Washton, 1995), and a comprehensive and integrated system for treating alcohol and drug problems in Alberta, Canada (Blumenthal *et al.*, 1993). In the UK, although there have been some joint alcohol and drug services for many years, most substance use services remain separate. Where integration has occurred it has helped rectify the disproportion in funding between the two types of service. Throughout Wales in the 1990s it became policy to approach alcohol and drug issues as one problem, with all the Community Drug Teams (CDT) combining with the Community Alcohol Teams (CAT).

In some countries such as Australia and Canada alcohol, drugs and also smoking are generally dealt with by a single agency at local level and there is unified strategic planning. In others, such as England and Scotland, for historical reasons alcohol problems are often dealt with by a completely different agency and national strategy is devised by a completely different group. In spite of this there has been some progress over a number of years in developing joint treatment facilities and joint treatment models in the UK that are appropriate to aid recovery from both alcohol and drug problems.

There is over 30 years research into the effectiveness of treatment for those with drink problems and/or dependence. Unlike treatment research in the drugs field, which has concentrated its efforts on looking at the effects of different substitution therapies, research studies on those with alcohol problems have focused on psychological and social interventions that have been found to aid good outcomes. The drugs field is beginning to learn from the alcohol field and vice versa, and people are discovering that we are dealing with two faces of the same basic condition. This lesson is also being taught to us by service users who increasingly present with the use of alcohol or other drugs in combination or serially.

Although in the past there were more distinct differences, alcohol and drug users are no longer two distinct groups. There is blurring of the boundary between them as a result of an ageing population of drug users, the greater availability of illicit drugs, the greater use of alcohol by young people, and the fact that alcohol is used as just another drug taken by polydrug users. Within the recommended structure of combined alcohol and drug services it is possible for services to combine but still partially keep drug users as a separate group from drinkers if this is felt to be appropriate. Even in the UK where alcohol and drugs treatment services have traditionally been separate, national drugs policy for both Scotland and England have 'shown one way in which different sectors can be encouraged to work together to a common purpose in dealing with alcohol and drug misuse' (Raistrick *et al.*, 1999). For example, it would be possible, for the same staff to give the same interventions but in separate venues for drinkers and drug users. This would be cost-efficient administratively. Substance use workers are able to provide outreach to a wider range of locations, e.g. GP surgeries, Community Mental Health Teams

(CMHTs), Child and Adolescent Mental Health Teams (CAMHTs), Accident and Emergency (A&E) departments or the courts, if each worker addresses both drugs and alcohol. There are other advantages of combining these services. It would be easier to provide cover at times of staff shortages and only one senior manager is required to attend the various planning and management forums. Joint training programmes can be provided, and clients who have both an alcohol and a drug problem are more easily cared for by the same worker.

Abstinence versus harm reduction – two different philosophies of treatment

Those who are more severely dependent will most often need specialist help in some shape or form, but the help given by services appears to polarise into two seemingly very different camps, each with ardent enthusiasts. These are:

(1) treatment where the overriding purpose is to achieve abstinence
(2) treatment where the primary aim is to reduce harm

Although lip service is given to the use of other interventions, in the drugs field many treatment services in the UK and elsewhere mainly limit their role to substitute prescribing for opiate users together with general supportive counselling. In keeping with this, abstinence-oriented treatment is sometimes termed *use reduction*, confining it to a drug-only narrow vision of treatment where the end result is abstinence. The 'use reduction versus harm reduction' argument then becomes one of dose reduction programmes versus maintenance substitution therapy. People often become heated in support of their belief for one of these issues against the other, and it sometimes becomes a tussle between prohibitionists and libertarians.

Use reduction is usually promoted by those who see stopping substance use as the primary solution. This is an easy trap to fall into as service users and their families often equate all their problems with substance use. Sadly, the removal of the substance does not usually remove all the other accrued or antecedent problems. These require careful assessment and, when necessary, appropriate interventions.

Use reduction and harm reduction can and should be complementary and reinforcing rather than opposing approaches. The aim of both use reduction and harm reduction is to help the individual function well in society. Professor Gerry Stimson, one of the great champions of harm reduction in the UK, has argued that all psychoactive substance use interventions aim in some way to prevent harm to individuals and communities. Some do this by aiming to reduce the use of psychoactive substances, while others attempt to reduce the risks associated with their use (Stimson & Fitch, 2000).

In some circumstances use reduction can actually increase harm. For instance, if use reduction is attempted before the person is prepared to embrace this, early relapse is to be expected, and this in turn may lead to depression, rejection by relatives and friends, and a false belief that abstinence is not achievable. Sometimes the harm is even more serious. Occasionally death from overdose can occur in opiate users who lose their tolerance after relapsing.

The UK National Treatment Outcome Research Study (NTORS) has shown that more severely dependent opiate users are best treated by maintenance therapy rather than aiming for abstinence. They are retained better in treatment and use less street drugs on top of their prescription (Gossop *et al.*, 2001a).

Interventions designed solely to achieve and maintain abstinence

Twelve-step programmes

Worldwide the most common form of help for people with drink or drug problems is through the twelve-step self-help programmes of AA and Narcotics Anonymous (NA). When twelve-step structured programmes are utilised within day or residential rehabilitation settings, they are no longer entirely strictly self-help but are facilitated usually by people who have overcome past drink or drug problems themselves through the twelve-step approach. This process is generally known as

Twelve-step Facilitation Therapy (TFT) (see Chapter 19 for further details).

Twelve-step programmes follow a highly structured method to achieve and sustain abstinence. The philosophy underpinning modern twelve-step work is that chemical dependency is generally progressive. Although other factors contribute, recovery will only be achieved if the process is arrested and people accept they are able to control their substance use by abstaining completely, following the twelve-step programme of reparation and improvement, and working it for themselves. This involves the individuals concerned accepting that they suffer from the illness or *disease* known as *alcoholism* or *chemical dependency*, and that complete abstinence from all substance use is the only productive way forward. It involves working at each of the twelve steps of the programme in turn.

AA is the original twelve-step programme founded in the USA in 1935. It is now estimated that nearly two million members currently attend AA meetings worldwide in nearly 99 000 groups in over 140 countries. A large number of other *anonymous* programmes in the chemical addictions field are based on the twelve-step approach, including Cocaine Anonymous (CA), Al-Anon (for the families of drinkers), Al-Ateen (for the teenage children of drinkers), Families Anonymous (FA) (for the families of drug users), and there are an increasing number of similar programmes for people with problems that are not chemical addictions.

For many years twelve-step work was not evaluated, perhaps because it involves a belief system rather than a specific intervention, but also because there are few people with alcohol dependence who have never attended an AA meeting. However, several outcome studies have now been undertaken and a metanalysis of 107 studies on AA suggests that 'professionally treated patients who attend AA during or after treatment are more likely to improve drinking behaviour than are patients who do not attend AA, although the chances of drinking improvement are not overall a great deal higher' (Emrick *et al.*, 1993).

Twelve-step self-help and facilitated programmes are most appropriate when abstinence has been achieved. They may also be begun prior to abstinence, particularly for those detoxifying on substitute prescriptions. Many drinkers and cocaine users for whom substitute prescribing is not indicated will also benefit from these interventions. Although self-help meetings are often attended by those who are still drinking and taking drugs, and who hope to find inspiration and support from abstinent attenders, abstinence is needed in order to work these programmes successfully.

Substitute prescribing as an aid to abstinence

Substitute prescribing can be used to promote abstinence through a reducing prescription. There is an extensive evidence base that specific pharmacotherapies which substitute for opiate dependence, such as methadone and buprenorphine, are useful treatment tools, but there is recent evidence (Gossop *et al.*, 2002) that slow detoxification programmes given over several months are generally unsuccessful and it is better to prepare carefully and then to detoxify at a fast rate (see Chapter 11). Oral methadone mixture (1 mg/ml) and high-dose sublingual buprenorphine are most often the treatment of choice with regard to substitute prescribing for opiate users. The evidence of the benefit of substitute prescribing for other drug groups is starting to grow.

Abstinence-oriented substitution prescribing treatments have traditionally been subdivided into short detoxification (10 days to 3 weeks), medium detoxification (3–6 months) and long-term detoxification programmes (more than 6 months). The latter includes maintenance with a view to abstinence, with an interim goal of progress towards abstinence from illicit substance use through the use of psychosocial interventions. Current advice is now to choose either a period of maintenance or move to short-term detoxification (Gossop *et al.*, 2003). There are several effective methods for this (see Chapter 11).

Other medication to assist detoxification

The withdrawal stage can be assisted by the use of other medication to reduce the direct biochemical effects of withdrawal, such as lofexidine for opiate withdrawal, or by medication to treat the symptoms of withdrawal and to reduce the risk of complications. This may include the use of night sedation and antidiarrhoea medication during opiate withdrawal and anticonvulsant drugs for alcohol withdrawal. The use of such treatments enables the withdrawal to be more comfortable and less aversive. This is important for the future as the likelihood is that the individual will need to undergo detoxification more than once before reaching lasting abstinence. In practice, the relapse situation is dominated by recollections of the pleasant effects of the substance, and an unpleasant withdrawal experience will undermine intention to overcome the withdrawal process again, leading to unnecessary prolongation of dependence.

Medication to assist abstinence

There are three modes of medical treatment used as an adjunct to remaining abstinent: receptor blockade; enabling; and aversive drugs. Naltrexone is an example of receptor blockade. Being an opiate antagonist, it binds to opiate receptors, displacing other opiates, but without having any subjective opiate effect itself. If other opiates are consumed, they are unable to access the receptor and are thus pharmacologically ineffective. Some abstinent opiate users find naltrexone helpful against impulsive relapse and studies show that the rate and duration of abstinence is enhanced. However, patient compliance has been shown to be a problem in almost every study undertaken (Tucker & Ritter, 2000). Because it displaces other opiates from receptor sites, naltrexone also accelerates the withdrawal process and can be used to facilitate ultrarapid opiate withdrawal. Acamprosate is an example of an enabling medication which seems to have an indirect effect of reducing craving or appetite for alcohol. Naltrexone can also be used in this manner for drinkers. Disulfiram is an example of an aversive drug, causing unpleasant symptoms when alcohol is taken. These approaches have some risks of their own, especially the temptation to attempt to override blockade or aversive medication and thus risk overdose and toxicity. The blockade and aver-

sive approaches do not alter desire or craving. They can, however, enable the individual to have a substance-free time in which to master alternative coping strategies and build self-esteem, especially if combined with other therapeutic interventions.

Interventions to reduce harm

McLellan and colleagues (1993) have shown that *harm reduction initiatives* will enhance prescribing outcomes. They randomly assigned 92 opiate addicts to receive either

(1) methadone maintenance alone, without psychosocial services;
(2) methadone maintenance with standard psychosocial services, which included regular individual meetings with a counsellor; or
(3) enhanced methadone maintenance, which included regular counselling plus access to specific psychosocial interventions including help with psychiatric, medical and employment problems, and family therapy, in a 24-week trial.

In terms of drug use and psychosocial improvement, the best outcomes were seen in the enhanced methadone maintenance group (3), with intermediate outcomes for group (2) and the poorest outcomes for methadone maintenance alone. In other words, for optimal progress a broad-based approach is needed, comprising psychological/psychiatric counselling, physical health and social interventions. Rounsaville and Kosten (2000) have shown that methadone treatment alone results in poorer outcomes than methadone plus counselling and psychosocial support.

What is harm reduction?

There is currently no accepted definition of harm reduction. One working definition is: 'an attempt to ameliorate the adverse health, social or economic consequences of mood-altering substances without necessarily requiring a reduction in the consumption of these substances' (Heather *et al.*, 1993).

Lenton and Single (1998), in a review of the subject, proffer the following definition, which is in three parts:

A policy, programme or intervention should be called harm reduction if, and only if:

(1) the primary goal is the reduction of drug-related harm rather than drug use per se;
(2) where abstinence-oriented strategies are included, strategies are also included to reduce the harm for those who continue to use drugs;
(3) strategies are included which aim to demonstrate that, on the balance of probabilities, they are likely to result in a net reduction in drug-related harm.

This does not try to define what they mean by harm, but the first definition by Heather and colleagues does. Yet at first sight Heather's vision of harm appears to be fairly restricted, risking the interpretation that psychological and legal harm should be omitted. However, taking the WHO definition of health as 'a state of complete physical, mental and social well-being, and not merely the absence of disease and infirmity', this does widen the concept of *adverse health consequences* to include psychological problems and impaired physical, psychological and social functioning. Additionally other environmental problems, such as housing difficulties, are not included in Heather's definition. The definition becomes all-encompassing if harm is defined as resulting from environmental, psychological, physical and legal problems and any impaired physical, mental and social functioning associated with substance use.

The other problem with Heather's definition is that it only talks of harm as a consequence of mood-altering substances. It is clear that some problems precede drug use and then become intrinsically tied to it. For instance, if drugs are taken to blot out thoughts related to past sexual abuse, it cannot be called psychological harm as a consequence of drug use. Quite the reverse, the drug use is a consequence of the psychological harm. It is better to talk of alcohol and drug-related harm, than harm which is a consequence of mood-altering substances. Lenton and Single's definition does this.

Improving public health and community safety from crime through harm reduction

Harm reduction as an officially backed policy was given great impetus by national responses to address the HIV epidemic in the 1980s, and is still seen by many people today to be solely a public health approach to prevent the spread of HIV and other blood-borne infections. Those who view harm reduction in this way see, as the most important treatment goal, the prevention of harm to communities and the wider public. Harm reduction can in practice be applied at an individual level, or to families, communities and wider society. But it is important to recognise that the key to success is to ensure that harm reduction initiatives take effect at an individual level. This is because some harm reduction initiatives aimed at reducing harm in society have the ability to increase harm to the individual, and when this happens the harm filters out from the individual to families, communities and wider society negating any previous beneficial effects. But if harm reduction at an individual level is the starting point, it has the potential to benefit everyone.

Even though the intention is to reduce it, one example where community harm reduction initiatives actually increase harm is through legislative measures that are associated with supply reduction. This is particularly the case for those countries that have more punitive legislation. Being tough on drugs does not make a country more effective in reducing drug use, and it often increases the harm sustained by individuals, families and wider society. For instance, prison sentences may protect wider society for a time, but then cause damage to individuals and their families, and later cause harm to the wider community through the spread of BBV infections in prisons. Prisons are multipliers of BBVs, and the wider community may sustain considerable harm from these viruses after a prisoner's release (ACMD, 1988).

Needle exchange was introduced as a harm reduction initiative by Holland, the UK and Australia as a pragmatic initiative to respond to the HIV epidemic in the 1980s, before there was evidence of its effectiveness. It has since been demonstrated to be effective in reducing BBV spread among injecting drug users (IDUs) (Stimson, 1995b; Des Jarlais *et al.*,

1998). Although it has become an important public health initiative to protect communities and wider society from BBV infections, it does so through a primary focus on individual drug injectors.

Maintenance prescribing

For dependent opiate users, although other substitute medications are sometimes used, methadone has been the most commonly prescribed drug since Dole and Nyswander (1967) demonstrated the effectiveness of methadone maintenance in the 1960s. Dole argued that opiate addiction was not a personal weakness which only abstinence could *cure*, but a medical disorder that could be treated with methadone. It was the success of this treatment which first gave legitimacy to maintenance substitute prescribing.

Not all chemically dependent individuals will be aided by substitute prescribing, but it can be usefully given to prevent some of the harmful effects of physical withdrawals. For example, epileptic convulsions that some people are prone to as a result of alcohol withdrawal can be prevented by a short-term benzodiazepine prescription. On a long-term basis, methadone maintenance prescribing will prevent harm and will help retain people in treatment. By prescribing oral methadone mixture to street heroin injectors, services can reduce harm by helping limit illicit drug use (Ward *et al.*, 1998), reduce the spread of BBV infections (Ball *et al.*, 1998), lower deaths from overdose (Caplehorn *et al.*, 1994) and improve community safety by reducing criminal behaviour (Hall, 1996).

The fact that methadone maintenance prescribing can improve community safety through a significant reduction in criminal behaviour was first recognised and utilised in the USA (a country not generally noted for its harm reduction approach) in the 1970s and was a key part of US drugs policy under the Nixon administration. Since the end of the 1990s the reduction of criminality also appears to be the main political reason for the promotion of oral methadone prescribing in the UK.

Retention in treatment through long-term prescribing keeps the client in regular contact with professional services, and this can enable the treatment process through regular discussion with a drug or alcohol worker and aid the delivery of specific psychosocial and medical interventions. Before coming into treatment many clients spend most of the day thinking about drugs or drink, raising money, often through illegal means, and finding ways to satiate their addiction and thus prevent withdrawals. On a substitute prescription their time can be spent more constructively.

Substitute medication is usually reserved for dependent opiate users and for dependent drinkers likely to suffer severe withdrawals. Mild to moderate alcohol dependence and dependence on stimulant drugs are associated with a relatively mild withdrawal syndrome for which substitute medication is not traditionally given. Similarly cocaine users are not generally given substitute medication, although antidepressants are sometimes used to combat withdrawal depression. Substitute medication with dexamphetamine for amphetamine users is a relatively controversial treatment, although undertaken for several years by some doctors. Evidence that amphetamine prescribing may be beneficial is now starting to accumulate (e.g. Shearer *et al.*, 2001).

Harm reduction should be a broad concept

Differing concepts as to the meaning of harm reduction have led to some confusion in the literature. Harm reduction should not be limited to methadone maintenance prescribing and initiatives to prevent the spread of blood-borne pathogens. The original policy of harm reduction which began in the Netherlands was based on reducing harm to individuals from their social and economic problems. The term now should properly include a wide variety of substance-related problems. Examples of harm reduction initiatives for the prevention of problems relating to alcohol include interventions to reduce violence or injury in public houses, and legislation and educational measures to reduce road traffic accidents (RTAs) as a result of alcohol impaired driving skills. Harm reduction for all substance use should aim to limit or reduce psychological, psychiatric, physical, environmental and legal problems.

There is also confusion in the literature over the use of the terms *harm reduction* and *harm minimisation*, which are often used interchangeably. A US author states that 'the harm reduction model is known in the United Kingdom as harm minimization' (Marlatt, 1998) and many UK government documents bear this out by using the two terms synonymously. Harm minimisation carries the implication that harm has been reduced to the lowest possible level. It is difficult to be sure that harm has been minimised, but much easier to establish that it has been reduced. The term harm minimisation is avoided in this book.

Risk reduction

As well as reducing actual harm, harm reduction interventions can also be used to prevent harm occurring. In this capacity *risk reduction* is a better term to use. Stimson and Fitch (2000) state that the total amount of harm from substances in society is a function of the level of use and the degree of risk attached to that use [use × risk = harm]. Examples include the prevention of BBV infections and the so-called British System of 1926, which promoted doctors' maintenance prescribing to morphine addicts to help the patient lead a normal and useful life.

Harm reduction with an emphasis on reducing risk has been used for several years as a method within school education in Australia. In the USA Marlatt (1998) describes a classical example of how this should be done when he wrote about his experiences educating high school students in Seattle about drink problems:

> When we met with members of the senior class (with no teachers present), we asked them what they thought we were going to talk about. One young woman, with a bored expression, replied: 'Another "just-say-no" lecture. Well, while you're doing that, I'm going to be daydreaming about the big party coming up on Friday night.' After we explained that we were there to talk about drinking and its risks and benefits (as we did with college freshmen), the attitude shifted to one of animated discussion. All but one stu-

dent in the class of 20 revealed that they were active drinkers; these students spoke freely about their experiences with alcohol, both positive and negative. In this interactive discussion, students raised numerous questions that could easily be addressed within the framework of harm reduction (e.g. how to respond to peer pressure to get drunk, how to help a friend who has overindulged, how males and females respond differently to alcohol, how alcohol affects sexual activity, etc.).

After a further description of the content of the educational approach, Marlatt went on to say:

> Following this introductory meeting, school officials invited us to put on several harm reduction workshops for the graduating class. This program was found to reduce harmful drinking patterns significantly over the course of the school year.

Harm reduction as treatment

When individuals have tussled for many years with drink or drug dependence, their substance use usually becomes deeply entwined with multiple adverse problems, poor personal and social functioning, and is compounded by the harm related to this. Such problems occur at different levels, and one such harm is to complicate and interact with the process of changing addictive behaviour (Prochaska & DiClemente, 1984).

Reducing problems and the harm they generate is of course beneficial in its own right, not only for the individual, but also for his or her family and friends, the local community and the wider society. However, there is poor recognition of the importance of doing this to facilitate the treatment of dependent substance use in spite of the fact that treatment outcomes are known to be better if these problems are addressed (McLellan *et al.*, 1993; Myers & Smith, 1995; DiClemente & Scott, 1997). Indeed reducing harm from alcohol and drug problems should be the basis on which the care plan is formulated.

There are many examples of the way in which harm reduction is effective as treatment. Several studies have shown that high levels of psychiatric disorder typicallly predict worse outcomes (Carroll *et al.*, 1993). When co-occurring psychological or psychiatric disorders are effectively treated addiction treatment outcomes may be improved (Woody *et al.*, 1990; Kranzler *et al.*, 1994) (see Chapter 14). Social factors often play a key role in an individual's treatment success or failure (see Chapter 13). Attempts to achieve abstinence when you are homeless, depressed, with other complex problems and little or no social support are unlikely to be successful. One of the best predictors of long-term recovery is whether or not the person concerned has a job (Carver & Dunham, 1991). Helping a client with legal or housing problems, helping them sort out financial problems, and treating medical problems such as hepatitis C are important aids to the recovery process. Indeed for some people progress will not be made unless some complex needs are addressed and harm reduction initiatives undertaken.

Assessing treatment outcome in terms of harm reduction

To try to define success by abstinence criteria alone is full of pitfalls. Is someone who has only one slip in a year a failure? If someone is drinking every day but is employed, holding together a family, and contributing to society, is he or she more of a failure than someone who drinks four times a week but is committing crimes and is unemployed, socially excluded and aggressive? Outcome research is now usually measured in holistic terms rather than looking at substance use alone, and researchers focus on the ways people function in society rather than to what degree abstinence is achieved. Tackling problems such as homelessness, debt, social isolation and unemployment, which are all commonly associated with drug use and drinking, enables clients to function better in society and improves outcomes.

It is difficult to make a comprehensive assessment of harm. Newcombe (1992) has suggested that it is better to narrow assessment down to desired goals and measure harm reduction objectives from within a specified framework of type, level, time dimen-

sion, severity and so on. The Maudsley Addiction Profile (Appendix 13) was developed in the UK to assess outcomes associated with reducing harm through the treatment of substance use (Marsden *et al.*, 1998). It was designed as a core research tool and a resource for treatment services wishing to undertake outcome studies. It takes about 12 minutes to complete and measures problems in four domains: substance use, health risk behaviour, physical and psychological health, and personal/social functioning. It is being widely used by services and may become the standard method of clinical outcome assessment in the UK.

Unfortunately few specialist services in the UK or elsewhere offer anything like the range of services which should be available to optimise the progress of drug users and drinkers, and many people remain unnecessarily stuck in the revolving wheel of dependence.

Is maintenance prescribing harmful?

Some commentators point out that almost all the harm caused by illicit drug use is due to its illegality, and that if it were not illegal this would be of major benefit in terms of harm reduction. Others take a different view. For example, Negrete (2001) writes:

> [H]ow can anyone suggest that drug-reward slavery is not, by itself, one of the most damaging risks incurred by users of addicting drugs? The life of people who depend on drugs is driven by the urge to re-experience their effects – either because of a yearning which has become nearly insatiable, or because of an inability to withstand the discomfort of an increasingly altered brain physiology. Thus, drug-taking acquires for them paramount importance, and is usually given top priority over all other interests, concerns and obligations.

This statement may sound prejudicial, but the term *drug-reward slavery* does contain more than an element of truth, and those who have broken free are invariably and rightly proud of their achievement.

There are other difficulties that arise from being on a prescription, e.g. of methadone. There may be trouble obtaining a driving licence and car insurance. If an accident occurs and the prescription has not been declared, most insurance companies will refuse to honour their insurance obligations. There is the inconvenience of having to attend doctors, drug workers and pharmacists regularly to ensure a regular supply of substitute medication. Obtaining enough supplies to travel abroad is also sometimes a problem. Methadone may cause trouble through constipation. Loss of libido may adversely influence intimate relationships. Methadone can, and often does, impair fertility, but if a woman does conceive there will be all the problems resulting from drug use in pregnancy, possible social services involvement, and the problems surrounding neonatal respiratory depression and opiate withdrawals.

On the other hand, Gossop and colleagues (2000) in the UK NTORS confirmed the benefits of prescribing methadone to reduce high BBV risk behaviour. Criminality was reduced to 11% of intake levels, and there were substantial reductions in the use of illicit opiates, stimulants and non-prescribed benzodiazepines. Whether the aim was methadone maintenance or reduction, there were substantial improvements in these and other areas. Interestingly there was no difference in the mean starting doses of methadone or in the dose received at one year. This rather unexpected finding suggests that those who were recruited into UK methadone reduction programmes end up receiving de facto some form of maintenance with considerable improvement.

The study subdivided the samples by cluster analyses into four groups according to the severity of problems. Outcomes showed one group with a poor response. This is consistent with US studies (Gerstein & Harwood, 1990), where about one in four individuals enrolled in the programmes does not improve. One NTORS problem group continued low rate use of illicit drugs, but two of the groups showed significantly improved response rates. Unfortunately, as is consistent with other studies, there was no improvement in heavy drinking and alcohol problems within any of these groups of drug users. This may be related to the way that for many UK services alcohol is an entirely separate domain from drugs, and some authors have suggested that drug treatment programmes pay insufficient attention to drink problems (Klingeman & Hunt, 1998).

Although many people on UK methadone detoxification programmes end up being maintained, this is not the case for users of other substances, nor necessarily for those prescribed methadone in other countries. In the USA gradual methadone reduction treatment has been provided in the form of 90-day and 180-day detoxification programmes, which differ from those in the UK in their origins, goals and methods. A balance needs to be struck. Treatment should not neglect abstinence, even though it may take a long time – sometimes several years – to achieve. To place an opiate-dependent client on methadone maintenance will help remove much of the harm, and reduce the risk of further harm occurring. But it should not relieve clinicians of the responsibility of concern for the problems caused by continued prescribing and the necessity of enabling abstinence when appropriate.

A new approach is needed which includes a wide range of treatment approaches and interventions

Although a reading of much of the literature suggests that treatment packages aim to be either abstinent-oriented or geared towards harm reduction, this is not necessarily the case. These two very different approaches can be combined.

The twelve-step facilitation method of treatment, which focuses on stopping substance use alone, may effect change in substance use but have little effect on associated psychosocial problems. Yet, as might be expected, the severity of problems at treatment admission is a significant predictor of treatment outcome – the greater the problem severity, the worse the outcome (McLellan et al., 1997). To overcome this difficulty, if abstinence-oriented treatments and harm reduction are combined according to assessed need, the resultant package of care should improve outcomes.

Further improvements can occur with additional interventions. For instance, the BRENDA approach, devised in the USA by Volpicelli and colleagues (2001), is one of the few broad-spectrum approaches which combines medication and psychosocial treatments for people with drug and alcohol problems. It emphasises the importance of empathy and constructive feedback and provides targeted cognitive–behavioural interventions, referral to twelve-step self-help groups, and attention to the problems and needs of the individual. It has been shown to improve outcomes in 80% of alchol-dependent patients (Kaempf *et al.*, 1999). BRENDA is an acronym which stands for:

Biopsychosocial evaluation;
Report to the patient on assessment;
Empathetic understanding of the patient's problem;
Needs expressed by the patient that should be addressed;
Direct advice on how to meet those needs; and
Assessing responses/behaviours of the patients to advice and adjusting treatment recommendations.

In addition, both maintenance prescribing and abstinence approaches can be combined with a wide range of other treatment interventions that both reduce harm and improve addiction outcomes through a number of different mechanisms as demonstrated in Chapter 9. What works and what does not work is now relatively well known.

Structured counselling for ongoing client contact

An examination of the literature on the effectiveness of different treatments for alcohol problems by Miller and colleagues (1998) showed that unstructured 'general alcoholism counselling' was the second worst of all possible treatment interventions, with an overall negative impact. In the drugs field, a task force to review the effectiveness of drug services in England (The Task Force to Review Services for Drug Misusers, 1996) similarly concluded: '[T]here is no strong evidence that an inadequately trained counsellor offering only information and advice significantly impacts on drug misuse outcomes.' These findings should come as no surprise, as general supportive counselling with no formal structure or framework had previously been shown to be ineffective when it had been undertaken by social workers (Fischer, 1973; 1978) and probation officers (Lipsey, 1992).

Unfortunately counselling interactions where there is no framework or formal identifiable counselling approach are commonly undertaken by workers at specialist substance use services. If such general unstructured counselling is of no therapeutic value, what type of formal counselling approach should be used?

Insight-oriented psychotherapy for the treatment of drug dependence has now been largely superseded by other approaches that address problem behaviours rather than looking for underlying serious emotional problems as a primary way forward. Even Kaufman (1994), who utilises insight-oriented psychodynamic psychotherapy successfully, achieves this by integrating it with twelve-step work and a variety of specific targeted interventions including CBT and structured family therapy.

There has been a failure of many other types of psychotherapy used to aid the addiction recovery process. Controlled studies of group and individual psychotherapy for alcohol problems have yielded negative findings with remarkable consistency, often despite the predictions of investigators. When Miller and colleagues (1998) compared the efficacy of exploratory psychotherapies to other treatment modalities, the only exception appeared to be client-centred therapy, based on the writings of Rogers (1951), which compared favourably with alternative approaches in three or four studies.

However, there is one circumstance when insight-oriented psychotherapy is helpful. This is its use as a specific treatment intervention when drinking or drug use is undertaken in order to suppress thoughts of painful past experiences. When suppression has occurred over a long period of time and becomes an established way of coping, it can be difficult to make progress towards recovery without tackling the issue with the help of insight-oriented psychotherapy. But such psychotherapy should only be given when stability has been attained and where there is good social support.

We now know that there is a small number of effective counselling approaches for ongoing client contact with substance users. These are outlined in Chapter 8. Some of the fundamental elements underpinning the useful Rogerian counselling approach were taken up by Miller (1983) when he described a method of interviewing clients to enhance motivation, known as Motivational Interviewing or MI. Instead of Rogerian counselling, this is now widely used to good effect by workers in the alcohol and drug use fields.

In MI the use of empathy and an avoidance of confrontation help cement a constructive therapeutic relationship. In addition, highlighting discrepancies between where the drinker or drug user wishes to be and the present situation is used to enhance motivation. Motivation is not a fixed entity that people either do or do not possess. Even the most highly motivated clients have periods of temptation and ambivalence. If specific MI strategies are needed during initial sessions with substance users who are *contemplators*, these can be given as needed. MI has the benefit of being readily learned by staff and empowers service users. It helps facilitate collaborative working within a multi-disciplinary team and its effect is increased if it is used in conjunction with other interventions.

The care plan: the importance of a wide spectrum of biopsychosocial treatment interventions

Research has confirmed the importance of including a wide spectrum of biopsychosocial interventions in the care plan for people with substance use problems (Miller & Wilbourne, 2002). These are:

(1) *Biological treatment interventions*
  - *Substitute prescribing.* Marie Nyswander, Vincent Dole's partner and a skilled psychotherapist, spent many frustrating years 'beating her head against a wall' trying to counsel heroin users. She eventually rejected psychotherapy in favour of methadone maintenance. The pioneering work which she and Vincent Dole undertook in the early 1960s showed that methadone treatment of heroin addicts was a more effective way of reducing psychological harm than psychotherapy. The majority of clients did not require the latter once they had stabilised on methadone, as most stopped showing signs of serious emotional problems (Dole & Nyswander, 1967).

  - Attending to *physical health needs* including the prevention of the spread of BBV infections.

(2) *Psychosocial interventions*
When Dole and Nyswander (1976) reviewed their work after ten years, they recognised that methadone maintenance on its own had limitations, and that additional psychosocial rehabilitation was important to help opiate addicts re-enter productive living. Modern day psychosocial rehabilitation involves not only the use of evidence-based structured counselling but also a large number of targeted interventions known to be effective. They comprise psychosocial treatment interventions for the care plan which promote positive outcomes and enhance forward movement in the cycle of change. Prochaska and DiClemente (1984) have classified the helpful psychological factors into ten *processes of change*, which are outlined in Chapter 9. Although they are reclassified under different headings, they include:
  - Targeted *behavioural therapy* (Drummond *et al.*, 1995), *Cognitive Therapy* (CT) (Beck *et al.*, 1993) and *Cognitive–Behavioural Therapy* (CBT) (Marlatt & Gordon, 1985). Cognitive–behavioural interventions which are targeted to the needs of the individual to help resolve specific psychological problems that are associated with substance use have been shown to be a particularly useful aid to recovery (Kadden *et al.*, 1990). They can be undertaken to relieve psychological harm and aid the process of recovery before abstinence has been achieved. For example, the dysfunctional use of drink or drugs as an attempt to control anxiety or depression can be supplanted by personal management of these difficult emotions using CBT. CBT is being used increasingly and to good effect in the substance use field.
  - *Brief Treatments* (BTs) to help achieve abstinence or stability quickly and in a highly cost-effective way. These are best reserved for individuals with a substance use problem where there is good social support, only mild or moderate dependence and few associated problems.

- *Family therapy* and *marital/couples therapy* (O'Farrell, 1993).
- *Relapse prevention interventions*, including avoiding high-risk situations and coping with craving (Marlatt & Gordon, 1985). Relapse prevention initiatives can be used to help stop street drug use while still on substitute medication, or after abstinence has been attained. These interventions are equally effective in preventing relapse for smokers, dependent drinkers and heroin users. Relapse prevention interventions focus on achieving abstinence through two basic strands of care:

(a) taking steps to reduce the opportunities for substance use
(b) using and improving personal re- sources/strengths to stop or reduce substance use in situations where sub- stance use is likely

Whether or not further treatment is re- quired to overcome a substance use problem or dependence, relapse prevention should be given to all help seekers.

- *Psychological and social harm reduction* can be achieved by:

(a) *Targeted reduction of harm by directly addressing and overcoming the environ- mental/social problems associated with substance use.* These include accommo- dation, financial, interpersonal and other similar problems.
(b) *Targeted reduction of harm by overcom- ing the psychological problems associated with substance use.* Although there is a need for some workers in the addiction field to be trained and accredited psy- chotherapists, in order to help, e.g. those who drink or take drugs to sup- press extremely painful thoughts, most specialist drug and alcohol workers do not need this degree of expertise.
(c) *Harnessing the clients' strengths* (as op- posed to addressing their problems directly) is another way forward. Dis- covering these strengths and finding

ways to harness them is the remit of Solution-Focused Therapy (SFT). SFT is a relatively brief therapy (though not as brief as most other brief interventions) found to be particularly helpful in the addiction field. Berg and Reuss (1998) have written a useful treat- ment manual for alcohol and drug users entitled *Solutions Step by Step*.

(d) *Improving psychological and social func- tioning.* Some individuals jog along in society and get by with relatively poor psychosocial functioning. Although an average person without a drink or drug problem can do this, a drinker or drug user with poor or borderline psycho- social functioning who has been socially ostracised will have the added difficulty of overcoming a *wall of social exclusion* (Buchanan & Young, 2000) (see Chap- ter 14). Additional help may be needed. This may entail attaining better self- control particularly over emotions, or enhancing the substance user's ability to communicate and socialise well, for instance, by becoming good at starting conversations and being able to read emotions in others or express empathy. Much of this can be attained through interpersonal social skills training and intrapersonal coping skills training (Monti *et al.*, 2002).

- *Adaptations of Motivational Interviewing* (AMIs). Ideally, MI should be used by the care manager as an ongoing method of relating to those with alcohol or drug de- pendence (Miller & Rollnick, 1991; 2002; Jarvis *et al.*, 1995), but in many specialist units effective structured counselling methods are not used. As a result motiv- ation can decline. To counteract this, spe- cific time-limited adaptations of MI known as AMIs are added to the care plan to en- hance motivation. Most of these are based on the FRAMES approach [an acronym for **F**eedback, **R**esponsibility, **A**dvice, **M**enu of options, **E**mpathy, **S**elf-efficacy] (Miller, 1995). *Motivational Enhancement Therapy*

(MET) [MI + FRAMES] (Miller *et al.*, 1992) is one such AMI.

(3) *Other interventions*

These include *criminal justice system interventions*, interventions to improve *physical health*, *twelve-step* self-help groups and *Twelve-step Facilitation Therapy* (TFT). Other forms of self-help are *Rational Recovery* (RR) groups and a number of *miscellaneous interventions*, such as Sobell and Sobell's guided self-change and Behavioural Self-Control Training (BSCT), which combine features of self-help with a professionally led intervention.

Taken together these interventions comprise a formidable array of different treatment approaches to be considered when formulating a care plan. Although all should be considered, they do not all need to be included. To give every possible effective treatment intervention would be expensive and unlikely to be cost-effective. Appropriate selection is important and the challenge is to integrate the most appropriate treatments with best practice (Rawson *et al.*, 2000).

Differing tiers of service provision

In order to clarify the most appropriate approach and use of the large number of potentially useful treatment interventions to enable progression with a substance use problem, it is helpful to separate service providers into different tiers. These will be determined initially according to the professional skill of the worker in dealing with substance use problems, tier 1 being generic workers with no additional skills in dealing with drug users and drinkers and tier 2 those that have had some additional training. The specialist substance use services are categorised as tier 3 and residential/inpatient/highly specialised services are tier 4.

A skilled assessment process aided by multidisciplinary discussion and targeted to meet the needs of the client in the most cost-effective way is essential. It should be an integral component of the therapeutic framework which should be flexible

enough to adapt to a wide variety of different situations and conditions.

Who really controls the treatment process?

It is pointless and even destructive to insist that someone become abstinent before they are ready and prepared for this. The result will be failure with early relapse and loss of personal belief in ability to change. Some opiate users may agree to a treatment detoxification regime devised by professionals to ensure a substitute prescription for the present, knowing that they are not ready to detoxify. Ensuring that people are ready for various proposed treatment interventions is important for their successful delivery. A full discussion ensuring complete understanding as to what is entailed and informed consent for any treatment plan is essential. The final decision as to whether any treatment intervention is given should always rest with the individual drug user or drinker.

In keeping with other research into help-seeking, Thom (1987) has shown that alcohol treatment utilisation is often motivated more by the individual's interest in resolving alcohol-related problems than in stopping drinking. There must be no inherent assumption that those entering treatment want to stop drinking or taking drugs. Some people say that they want to stop because they think that this is what those working in alcohol and drug services want to hear, or they worry that help might not be offered if they admit that they want to continue drinking or taking drugs. Yet, when they say they want to stop most clients are not lying. All are ambivalent at least to some degree. They do want to stop, but they also want to continue. That is what addiction is all about. It is the balance between the two forces that is important. When the desire to stop outweighs the desire to continue, then a client is ready to prepare for action, whether this is a move away from street drug use to a maintenance prescription or whether it is abstinence-oriented treatment.

In the not-too-distant past the only criterion used to assess whether someone needed help was their motivation to stop drinking or taking drugs. If people were considered to be unmotivated, they were refused help. Hopefully these attitudes are now obsolete. Motivation is a variable entity and can change. It is also linked to specific facets of behaviour as well as to an ultimate goal. How professionals can help move people forward when they are unsure of change or not even considering it is better understood now. There should be a full discussion of the possible benefits of various interventions. If advice is rejected it can be reconsidered at a later date if no progress is being made.

Opiate users should participate in the decision as to whether the aim of treatment is abstinence or maintained substitute prescribing, and drinkers and other substance users about whether they should aim for controlled use or abstinence. In either case the risks and benefits should be clearly considered along with help to reduce potential harm. Some people need considerable additional help before they are ready to contemplate abstinence. Others will attempt it before they are prepared for it. If a worker feels the decision that has been made is inappropriate, he or she should advise against it, but if the client insists on moving in a direction that is against this advice then the best way forward is often that they should be given clear boundaries and the opportunity to try their choice out for a limited period. If additional interventions are assessed as being required before abstinence, this is an ideal time to offer them.

Conclusion

As has been seen, the evidence base for treatment is effectively the same for all substance users. Later it will be demonstrated that alcohol and drug users can be helped using similar assessment procedures (Chapter 5) and an identical treatment framework (Chapter 6). The basic groundwork is there for combining services for all substance users, and this has many clinical and administrative advantages.

Abstinence is neither the beginning nor the end of the treatment process. For most with moderate to severe dependence, recovery involves a combination of short- and long-term influences that slowly change over a period of years (Tucker *et al.*, 1997). Incremental progress can be made whether or not substance users are ready to embrace abstinence. The care coordinator should advise on an appropriate care plan and arrange for appropriate interventions to be given. However, it is important to ensure that the drug user or drinker is ready to undertake the various treatments which are recommended. There are many interventions which have the potential to aid the recovery process and these are described in greater detail later in this book. Almost invariably their effectiveness and ability to aid progress with a substance use problem is determined by their ability to reduce harm. Harm reduction focused on the individual is the foundation stone of effective treatment. There is, however, one complicating factor which does not always take account of the evidence – involvement of politicians.

Part II
The Political Dimension

Chapter 2
Different National Approaches

One could be forgiven for thinking that there is a right way and a wrong way to treat people with problem and dependent drug and alcohol use, and that treatment, in the broadest definition of the term, would vary according to individual needs. In the real world there is another factor which profoundly influences the treatment process. This is the influence of politicians.

Politicians in a democratic society can be elected or defeated according to the way they tackle the illicit drug situation. They therefore take this issue seriously. However, they are not usually elected according to the way they tackle drinking disorders. Indeed if they were to deal with problem drinking by reducing the availability of alcohol, which is known to be highly effective (Edwards *et al.*, 1994), it would significantly reduce the income to the public purse. Perhaps this is one reason why drug and alcohol treatment programmes remain separated in many countries. Certainly it could be said that in most non-Islamic countries, problem drinking and alcohol dependence, although recognised to be major social issues, are not generally tackled by politicians with the same vigour as drug use. The exception to this was of course the failed US policy of prohibition.

Differing national drug policies and strategies

National drug policies tend to go one of two ways:

- hard-line supply and demand reduction typical of a war-on-drugs approach or
- harm reduction

Some national strategies vehemently advocate reducing the use of psychoactive substances through an emphasis on *supply reduction* by police and customs and *use reduction* by harsh penalties for drug users. Others, such as those in Australia, attempt to reduce the harm from substance use. However, it has been argued that if the morals and rhetoric of these two different positions were ignored, a constructive synthesis would be possible (Stimson & Fitch, 2000).

The politics of harm reduction

Although the term *harm reduction* was not to be used for nearly six decades, the aim of the first UK national drugs policy, the Rolleston report in 1926, was to reduce the harm from drug use (Report of the Departmental Committee on Morphine and Heroin Addiction, 1926). The Rolleston committee report outlined two indications when substitution prescribing could be undertaken. These were:

(1) if the person was being gradually withdrawn, and
(2) if, after attempts at cure had failed, the patient could lead a normal and useful life when provided with a regular supply, but ceased to do so when the supply was withdrawn.

Thus, if attempts at achieving abstinence failed repeatedly, the harm of opiate use could be reduced by a regular controlled prescription. This became known as the British System and was envied by doctors in other countries, particularly the USA.

In the UK the number of patients who received substitute heroin or morphine maintenance prescriptions from their personal physicians via the British System remained stable (400–600) from the late 1920s until the early 1960s. But during that time most of the people who were dependent on opiates were not members of a subculture sharing injecting equipment with like-minded peers, and hardly any indulged in criminal behaviour. The great majority had become dependent on prescribed opiate drugs, which their doctors had given them for pain relief, and because these drugs also helped them cope with anxiety, depression or other emotional problems, they had found them hard or seemingly impossible to stop. In almost every case of addiction to prescribed drugs there was an associated vulnerability of this sort, which made people susceptible to psychological dependence. Thus when they were no longer in pain they still felt a need to continue these drugs. This problem can still be encountered today in people who become dependent on prescribed opiates.

The early 1960s marked a time of change in the UK. The category of people using drugs began to differ, and the number of people becoming drug dependent began to increase rapidly. Instead of middle-aged, middle-class professional people, who had been prescribed opiates for analgesic purposes, and who had serendipitously found these drugs also helped their psychological problems, those now using drugs were young, unemployed, and were taking them (at least initially) for enjoyment. The number of these young drug users increased substantially and continued to expand. Many of them became drug dependent.

This new problem was deliberated by a government Interdepartmental Committee chaired by Sir Russell Brain. It originally reported in 1961 that the drug situation in Britain gave little cause for concern (UK Interdepartmental Committee, 1961). However, in the light of repeated press reports of an escalating UK drug problem, the Interdepartmental Committee was reconvened. The second Brain Committee (UK Interdepartmental Committee, 1965) came to a very different view from its predecessor. It reported that, although some street heroin originated from the Golden Triangle near the Burmese border, the great majority of drugs taken at that time were prescription drugs and

malprescribing by general practitioners (GPs) was seen to be at the root of the problem. The outcome was that GPs were to be discouraged from prescribing such drugs. Instead a number of psychiatrists, specialising in illicit drug use and working from special Drug Dependence Units (DDUs), were to be employed to contain the problem (UK Interdepartmental Committee on Drug Addiction, 1965a). These clinics were set up from 1968 to 1970.

The majority of DDU attenders were opiate users and injectable methadone and pharmaceutical heroin were regularly prescribed as substitute drugs. There was concern in some quarters that this would increase black market supplies. However, it was not the case. Instead it led to an increase in the cost of both pharmaceutical and illicitly manufactured opiate drugs available on the street, indicating reduced availability.

Some politicians had the rather naive expectation that if substitute prescribing continued to be readily available through the clinics, street drug use would gradually fade out altogether. This did not happen. In fact it was not long before the DDUs became crammed with people on maintenance prescriptions. This was the first indication that, as well as aiding individual drug users, harm reduction measures may also inadvertently pose some difficulties for treatment services which need to be addressed. Soon the specialist psychiatrists in the DDUs were so overloaded that they were no longer able to cope with the ever increasing number of people requesting help. This was in spite of the fact that they had already stopped substitute prescribing for amphetamine and cocaine users by the beginning of the 1970s.

At the end of the 1970s some psychiatrists began comparing their own work with that of specialists in the USA, where rigid abstinence-oriented detoxification programmes were the rule for opiate users, and questioned the efficacy of the British System of long-term prescribing regimes (Mitcheson, 1994). Also at that time some British research was undertaken comparing a control sample of DDU attenders who continued their pharmaceutical heroin and injectable methadone prescriptions with those who were refused this but given oral methadone

(Mitcheson & Hartnoll, 1978; Hartnoll *et al.*, 1980). As a result the prescribing of injectable drugs, particularly heroin, was abandoned in favour of oral methadone.

By the early 1980s almost all the UK DDUs had moved over to a pattern of prescribing that was comparable to their US counterparts. Detoxification and reduction towards abstinence were the norm, although generally supplemented by counselling. The flexible British System of maintenance prescribing had been almost completely abandoned, and with it the reduction of harm had all but disappeared. But still this did not contain the problem in the UK. Specialist psychiatrists continued to find themselves struggling to treat increasing numbers of drug users, many of whom had been detoxified but relapsed. A different approach was tried, and from the early 1980s GPs began to be encouraged once more to be involved. As the historian Virginia Berridge (1993) states, harm reduction, either in principle or in name, has been a feature of UK drugs policy for many decades, although during that time 'it has periodically faded before surfacing again'.

Holland was the first country to promote harm reduction by name in official national policy. In the early 1980s drug use was seen by the Dutch as a complex recurring behaviour from which many people naturally recovered. Reducing the medical and social harms that arose from drug use while awaiting natural recovery was important to achieve and became a main plank of Dutch policy (Buning, 1990).

In the UK, the Advisory Council on the Misuse of Drugs (ACMD) first used the term harm reduction in 1984 when it redefined prevention as

(a) reducing the risk of an individual engaging in drug misuse, or
(b) reducing the harm associated with drug misuse.

But it was not until 1988, when a response was needed to combat the HIV epidemic, that the term harm reduction developed international significance and meaning.

At times forces at an international level have worked to suppress harm reduction initiatives. Politically many countries have taken a high moral stance aimed at totally banishing all drugs of recreational or dependent use and escalating far-reaching law enforcement measures. These include the International Opium Convention in 1912, the 1961 United Nations Single Convention on Narcotic Drugs and the 1971 United Nations Single Convention on Psychotropic Substances. However, this has not contained the international drug problem, and member states which ratified these conventions have produced increasingly severe sentences for transgressors as they repeatedly failed. In the 1980s the reality of this failure began to be voiced at international level (United Nations, 1987). It became clear that, whatever governments may wish, few young people had been deterred by the threat of punishment. Clearly a hard-line moralistic approach had been ineffective.

Other national and international forces have worked to promote harm reduction. In the 1980s the Dutch harm reduction model was extended to encompass a reduction of medical harm from blood-borne viruses (BBVs). The first needle exchange was opened in 1984 in Amsterdam as a result of the Junkibonden's (the drug users union) concern that an inner-city pharmacist's decision to stop selling syringes to injecting drug users (IDUs) would result in an outbreak of hepatitis B. By 1986 there were 11 Needle Exchange Programmes (NEPs) in Amsterdam. In 1985 the Dutch policy of *normalisation* was developed to counteract moralistic discrimination which had in the past led to the development of harmful social problems. The government memorandum, Drug Policy in Motion (ISAD, 1985), clearly defines this. It means that drug addicts should be treated as *normal human beings* on whom *normal* demands should be made and to whom *normal* chances for living should be offered, e.g. equal chances for drug users to obtain housing.

Australia also joined the Netherlands to be one of the first countries to officially embrace the concept of harm reduction. The election of the Labour federal government in 1983 created an opportunity to re-evaluate what had previously been a draconian drugs policy. In 1985 the Australian government started to pursue an official policy of harm reduction which has been a major and beneficial influence on the way drug and alcohol services have developed.

The influence of HIV/AIDS on national harm reduction policies

The 1980s was also the decade when HIV/AIDS was first recognised by several countries to be a potential public health disaster. Because many drug users became involved in prostitution and others were known to have multiple sexual partners, there was a realistic concern that HIV could be spread through the sharing of injecting equipment and initiate a secondary wave of heterosexual spread into the wider community. HIV was first identified in 1983 and Moss (1987) pointed out in an article in the *British Medical Journal* that three quarters of those who have contracted AIDS heterosexually in the USA had done so from index cases who were IDUs.

Measures designed to protect communities from contracting the virus from IDUs were recognised to be urgently required, and harm reduction was identified as the best way to block this route of transmission (Des Jarlais & Friedman, 1993). It was a practical approach which targeted individual drug users and led to a complete change in the way most drug services worked. It emphasised a more flexible, user-friendly approach, which included working with those who were not motivated to achieve abstinence, in order to attain an urgent and essential goal – the prevention of HIV. As well as recognising this necessity, service providers from many countries embraced this method of working which did much to enhance professional–client relationships. Soon an international harm reduction movement was established to promote its development.

Although the philosophy of reducing the harm of drug use was not new, it was clear that harm reduction as a public health response to prevent an AIDS epidemic required specific measures. These were first laid out in the recommendations of national advisory committees to the governments of Australia (NACAIDS, 1987–88), the UK (ACMD, 1988) and the USA (USGPO, 1988). Quite independently, these committees set up working parties at almost exactly the same time to examine the combined problems of drugs and HIV/AIDS, and, without any collaboration, the three working parties reached remarkably similar conclusions. These included:

- promoting safer use of injecting equipment;
- advice to all drug users to reduce the risk of HIV from injecting and sexual behaviour;
- needle exchange and free condoms for drug users;
- education about HIV;
- widespread availability of community-based treatment services. In the UK this included encouragement to GPs to be involved in the treatment process, and providing back-up support for them by establishing Community Drug Teams (CDTs) in every health district. The Americans recommended immediate access to treatment;
- outreach services to maximise contact with drug users;
- easy access for opiate addicts to substitution prescribing with oral methadone; and
- a hierarchy of treatment goals before abstinence, the first and foremost of which was the cessation of sharing injecting equipment.

This opened up a new era. In the Netherlands and Australia maintenance prescribing became the norm. In the UK and the USA it was still national policy to aim eventually for abstinence, but this was at the end of a long line of intermediate goals which could be facilitated by methadone maintenance. Success could now be measured incrementally and could be linked with the progressive attainment of a hierarchy of goals. Those running treatment programmes, who had become so dispirited by the revolving door of rigid detoxification and relapse, changed their sights to more achievable ends. In the UK, the stated hierarchy was

(1) to stop sharing injecting equipment
(2) to stop injecting and move to oral drug use
(3) to reduce the quantity of drug consumed
(4) abstinence (ACMD, 1988)

A new more realistic phase had begun. Although abstinence is given here as the final goal, in order to achieve the primary aim of stopping the sharing of injecting equipment, those working in the field have to be prepared to engage with IDUs who appear to have little or no motivation to stop using drugs.

The advice which was given by the Australian National Advisory Committee on AIDS

(NACAIDS, 1987–88) and the British Advisory Council on the Misuse of Drugs (ACMD, 1988) was heeded and acted upon by the governments of Australia and the UK in 1988. However, in the USA, the advice of the US Presidential Commission on the HIV Epidemic (USGPO, 1988) was rejected, showing the importance, not just of knowing what is needed, but also of engaging politicians into accepting and implementing any new approach.

There was, however, a downside to harm reduction. Although the shift in policy facilitated a more inclusive approach within specialist treatment services, the general public perceived an associated powerful negative threat to public health from the drug-using population. This further stigmatised drug users and has been a challenge to practitioners. There are similar problems with the improvement of public safety from reduced drug-related crime as a harm reduction goal. Policy effectiveness may be greatly reduced by the marginalisation of the target population unless steps are taken to overcome this problem, such as the Dutch policy of normalisation.

In the UK political backing for harm reduction as a public health response to the potential AIDS epidemic ensured new funding to establish and develop outreach services, enhance substitute prescribing and needle exchanges, and facilitate health promotion with service users and the wider community. Accessible treatment was needed, and CDTs were set up in the late 1980s throughout the UK, with the intent of involving mainstream generic services in the treatment of drug users, particularly sharing care with GPs. However, most CDTs also became locally based specialist service providers (ACMD, 1998), as they were also obliged to fill the gaps in service provision when GPs did not wish to be involved in the treatment of drug use.

In some parts of the world harm reduction was more than a public health approach to counter the spread of HIV. The Netherlands continued their holistic concept, embracing socio-economic interventions and the policy of normalisation. In the UK the harm reduction service in Merseyside also included the reduction of social harm through economic advice and a negotiated relaxation of the rigid hard-line approach of the local police.

The contrast between services in those countries which embrace harm reduction and those with a rigid abstinence-oriented approach is still seen today in a relatively extreme form in Sweden and the USA. In these and some other countries *zero tolerance* and a *war on drugs* still rage to the distress of many enlightened professionals working there. To counter this an international harm reduction movement began to develop, beginning with a series of international conferences on harm reduction, the first being held in Merseyside.

The estimated cost savings of those countries which have embraced harm reduction have been impressive. The original public health harm reduction drug programmes, pioneered successfully in the Netherlands, the UK and Australia, were accompanied by a fall in HIV infection among IDUs (Feachem, 1995; GG & GD, 1996; Stimson, 1996) and a very substantial saving of public funds. In Australia in 1991, only three years after the implementation of their HIV/AIDS harm reduction strategy, it was estimated that the Needle Exchange Programme (NEP), which cost about A\$10 million, prevented 3000 HIV-1 infections with a resultant saving of A\$270 million (Feachem, 1995).

In contrast, Lurie and Drucker (1997) used modelling techniques to estimate the number of HIV infections associated with the US government's opposition to NEPs. They estimated that by 1996 between 4000 and 10 000 IDUs would have been prevented from becoming HIV positive if NEPs had been put in place. They concluded that this had cost the US health care system US\$250 million to US\$500 million.

Harm reduction has been an extremely successful public health measure in containing the spread of HIV, and there is good evidence that this is also the case for hepatitis C (Judd *et al.*, 1999) and that this has led to both human and financial cost savings. In retrospect it is now clear that, even before the introduction of harm reduction measures in the late 1980s, hepatitis C was numerically a far bigger problem in IDUs than HIV, although this was not recognised at the time as there was no specific test for it. Furthermore, because of the considerably longer time period between infection and the appearance of overt disease, those infected with hepatitis C have not yet died in great numbers and reduced the pool of those infected, in the way they did with HIV. Indeed the total pool of hepatitis C infection within the general population is probably still being added to, albeit more slowly since the introduction of HIV prevention measures. Although the pragmatic provision of NEPs and other public health harm reduction measures may have reduced the number of new cases of hepatitis C virus (HCV) entering the total pool of infected people, the HCV epidemic is still a growing public health disaster. Although the prevalence rate within the drug-using population has fallen following the introduction of needle exchange and other measures to contain HIV in the 1980s, the virus is still endemic among drug users. The consequences of the HCV epidemic will be reaped in ensuing years.

Harm reduction and legislation

Many people believe that the greatest drug-related harm of all has been caused by the legislation enacted by the Western industrialised nations against illicit drug use and that one of the best ways of reducing harm would be to legalise all current illicit drug use. Consequent to the signature and ratification of international treaties, many countries took a hard-line approach to drug use, resulting in fines and imprisonment for those who transgress the law. All the major industrialised nations of the West are among the 109 signatories to the 1961 United Nations Single Convention on Narcotic Drugs which obliges signatories to make possession and other drug-related activities involving a range of drugs (heroin, cannabis, cocaine, etc.) 'punishable offences'. However, close examination of this and subsequent UN conventions reveals that there is considerable flexibility over the way they may be interpreted, particularly with regard to possession. An increasing number of countries now impose only minor penalties for possession, effectively decriminalising at least some drug use. There has been considerable international support for decriminalising cannabis for several years. Between 1968 and 1972 the UK, Canada and the USA concluded that the medical evidence did not justify the severity of the penalties for cannabis possession. Later the Dutch took decriminalisation a step fur-

ther by separating cannabis from hard drug use and allowing its sale in coffee houses.

More recently, Spain and Italy have given a liberal interpretation to the possession of hard drugs, either giving minor fines, cautions or *administrative sanctions* whereby the users may have their driving licence confiscated or penalties will be waived if they agree to attend for treatment. In the UK cannabis has been downgraded from class B to class C and from 2003 those caught in possession once or twice will usually only have the drug confiscated and receive a formal caution. However, a third offence could mean more serious charges. Consideration continues to be given to making possession of class C drugs an imprisonable offence. This would counter the well-argued Police Foundation Report (2000) which recommended reclassifying several drugs in order to reduce harm.

In 1990 nine European cities signed the Frankfurt Resolution stating that

(1) the criminal law should only be used to repress drug-trafficking;
(2) neither the consumption nor the possession of drugs for purely personal use should be prosecuted;
(3) help should not be linked only to abstinence – survival assistance should be the first priority;
(4) there should be a separation in law between cannabis and other illegal drugs;
(5) the use, purchase and possession of cannabis should be decriminalised;
(6) trade in cannabis products should be placed under legal control; and
(7) prescription of drugs to addicts under medical supervision should be considered.

National approaches to legislation rarely take a middle road but seem to oscillate between harm reduction and zero tolerance and between increasingly severe penalties for drug offences versus relaxation of national drug laws.

Hard-line approaches to supply and demand

Many politicians believe they will get more votes if they are seen to be tough on drugs, and promote zero tolerance and abstinence. A few politicians like to be recognised for their humane approach to those caught up in a drug use problem, promoting harm reduction, normalisation and social inclusion. But in doing so they run the political risk of being labelled *soft on drugs*.

When HIV/AIDS surfaced, the tension first became apparent between the public health need to prevent this virus from spreading from drug users into the general population and the need to try to contain the drug problem. In some countries needle and syringe exchanges have been seen politically as condoning and encouraging drug use. In others they are seen as the solution to the problem. In those countries where HIV/AIDS was seen as a greater threat to the community than drugs, needle and syringe exchanges have been set up and people are encouraged to come for help with their drug problem, and there is a user-friendly atmosphere. Those countries which deliberately avoid the public health approach and instead promote a war on drugs, not only socially exclude more drug users but have very different styles of drug services from those which advocate and support harm reduction.

Community safety approaches view the treatment of the individual drug user as aiding the general public by reducing criminal behaviour through methadone prescribing. The effectiveness of this approach was demonstrated with the rapid expansion of methadone clinics in the USA from 1969 to 1974 when Nixon was president. In 1968 fewer than 400 addicts were enrolled in US methadone programmes. Within five years this figure had increased to 73 000. During this period drug arrests dropped from 40 000 to 15 100 and complaints to the police for drug-related crimes such as robbery, burglary and larceny fell from 350 000 to 273 000 (US Department of Health and Human Services, 1993). Ball and Ross (1991) in the USA have also demonstrated that methadone maintenance treatment packages result in a dramatic reduction in the crime rate. Other community safety interventions may be seen, e.g. in the UK, but do not have such a sound evidence base of effectiveness.

Thus different countries deal with drug users in different ways, and sometimes newly elected politicians may totally alter the accepted ethos of drug treatment within their own country, as happened in the UK. Political influence often determines drug strategy, and the implementation of national strategic thinking has a major impact on the treatment process. At both a national and an individual level this has a direct effect on the harm that local communities, drug-dependent individuals and the families of drug users sustain. In turn this can affect the overall national prevalence rates of substance use, BBV infections and criminality within that country, either by reducing or increasing them. How the political dimension to drug use has been handled in different ways by the Netherlands, Australia, the UK and the USA is described below.

Netherlands

In many ways the Dutch system exemplifies harm reduction as has been described. It developed in the following way. The principle of reducing harm to the individual became a central focus of Dutch drugs policy in 1972, when the recommendations of their Narcotics Working Party (1972), entitled *Backgrounds and Risks of Drug Use*, were published. Underlying these recommendations was the basic premise that drugs policy should aim to control the risks of drug use in order that harm can be avoided. The likelihood of harmful effects of drug-taking were categorised by the Working Party according to which substances are taken, the social background of the drug users, and the circumstances in which the drugs are taken. Soft drug use was considered to be less damaging than hard drug use. Cannabis, the only drug to be classified as *soft*, was considered to be less damaging than the criminal proceedings against cannabis users. This led the Working Party to set out to achieve a strict separation of the illicit drug markets for hard and soft drugs, which later was put into effect through a new Opium Act in 1976. Through this Act the penalties for trafficking heroin and cocaine were increased. Although, as a result of international obligations, cannabis remained controlled by Dutch criminal law, it was effectively decriminalised because the Opium Act empowered Dutch prosecutors to refrain from instituting criminal proceedings in the greater public interest. Thus Dutch policy was enabled to move away from punitive legislation to the social control of cannabis.

The open sale of cannabis became allowed in coffee houses, and this turned out to be highly profitable for the owners, partly because the European Court would not allow the Dutch Ministry of Finance to impose purchase tax on their proceeds. The number of coffee shops expanded quickly, but by 1991 concerns were raised about the potential abuse of the system and the 'noise and other annoyance' that was caused to the general public. In addition, a small but increasing number of people were seeking help for problems with cannabis. The Amsterdam City Council decided to halt the proliferation of coffee shops and took steps to restrict the *nuisance*, which was found to be caused mainly by drug tourists (Korf, 1994). At this time there were 400–500 coffee shops selling cannabis in Amsterdam and a total of 1200–1500 coffee shops throughout the Netherlands. In addition, there were estimated to be 700–2200 cannabis dealers in private houses, and 500–1000 in community centres.

The Dutch police agreed to take no action if certain basic rules were followed: that cannabis should only be sold on a small scale; that no hard drugs were allowed; that there was to be no selling of drugs to juveniles; and no price lists were to be displayed in the shops. Coffee shops were also forbidden to advertise and those which did not follow these rules were closed down. However, complaints continued and in 1995, in response to international pressure and continuing public opposition to drug tourists, the Dutch Ministry of Public Health reduced the maximum quantity that coffee shops could sell to an individual from 30 to 5 g. This was an attempt to reduce the number of tourists becoming suppliers of the drug, and, although small-scale home-grown cannabis of up to ten plants for personal use was allowed, large-scale production became prosecuted. This policy has paid off. There is now little evidence of organised crime in the coffee shop operations, and virtually no violence associated with the domestic trade of cannabis in the Netherlands.

What effect has the action taken in 1976 to decriminalise cannabis had on the consumption of this drug? In spite of assumed increased availability, a number of surveys indicated that there was a fall in cannabis use in the general population between 1983 and 1987 (de Zwart, 1989). However, at the end of the 1980s, a 5% increase was reported in the subpopulation using cannabis (Driessen *et al.*, 1989), and later publications have reported an increase in both lifetime and past-month prevalence in the general population (de Zwart & Mensink, 1996), which now comprises an estimated half-million customers. There are many variables that can affect the prevalence of cannabis use in a country, and we are some way off from saying that the decriminalisation of cannabis results in a higher or lower use of the drug by the general population. Nevertheless, comparisons with countries which have not decriminalised are encouraging, for the increase in cannabis use in the Netherlands since the 1976 Opium Act is considerably less than that found in the UK and the USA over the same period.

A more important question is whether the purposeful separation of markets for hard and soft drugs has reduced the demand for hard drugs. Again, of course, there are many other variables which may influence the prevalence of hard drug use in what the Dutch consider to be their *great experiment*. Regular estimates of hard drug use (heroin, cocaine and amphetamine) have been undertaken in Amsterdam and in the Netherlands as a whole. Surprisingly there are marked differences. In Amsterdam itself, hard drug use reached a peak in 1984 with an estimated 8000–10 000 users. Although the estimated number of heroin users has remained stable at 4000–5000 from the mid-1980s (Korf & Buning, 2000), since 1987 there appears to have been a steady decline of hard drug users in total. In 1989 there were estimated to be between 5800 and 7500 hard drug users, and in 1996 the Amsterdam Municipal Public Health Service referred to the hard drug problem as 'vanishing' (GG & GD, 1996). In addition, the average age of hard drug users in Amsterdam has been rising, the proportion of drug users up to 21 years has decreased, and those who inject drugs for the first time tend to be older (van Brussel & Buning, 1988). Some other Dutch urban areas have also shown a decline in hard drug use. These are very encouraging signs.

The Dutch have operationally defined harm reduction as: '[W]hen a drug user is not (yet) willing or capable of stopping drug use, he or she should be assisted in reducing harm caused to himself and others.' The key to this definition is the acceptance of the drug users own perception of whether they have a drug problem and whether they want to do anything about it. If a person wishes to continue taking drugs, this is accepted. Instead of attempts to persuade the user away from active drug use, he or she is offered various forms of sociomedical care (Buning & van Brussel, 1995).

Thus in the Netherlands, education, *safer use* and needle exchange facilities form one aspect of socio-medical care, with the aim of preventing overdose and reducing BBV transmission and tuberculosis. Reduced involvement in drug-related crime is another objective. For those who request help to come off drugs, inpatient abstinence-oriented treatment is available if needed or there is outpatient treatment centring around methadone. However, most methadone treatment involves maintenance prescribing. Methadone became the cornerstone of treatment during the 1980s and has remained in that position. The recognition of an HIV/AIDS epidemic prompted the Dutch public health approach. It aims to make contact with as many addicts as possible through outreach work, through a special project for addicted prostitutes, by visiting addicts in police stations and hospitals, and by setting up NEPs and low-threshold methadone programmes.

Although hard drug use in Amsterdam is falling, this is not the case for the Netherlands as a whole. Here hard drug use and polydrug use are on the increase, although at a seemingly lower rate than the rest of Europe. Estimates for the whole country stabilised at 15 000–20 000 during the mid- to late-1980s but rose slowly to 28 000 in the mid-1990s, although in the under-21 age group the numbers are low.

Taking a simplistic view, the difference between what is happening in Amsterdam (and some other urban areas) and the rest of the country would suggest that there are local factors to account for a reduction in the demand for hard drugs. It is impossible to know the precise cause, but it is more likely to be associated with local service provision than national policy issues. Certainly service provision for drug users is particularly good in Amsterdam and much better than that in the provinces.

Although outreach programmes, NEPs and low-threshold methadone programmes began in the inner-city areas, nowadays they are widely available throughout the Netherlands. For those who have trouble attending clinics, in Amsterdam, there is also supervised consumption of methadone from special methadone buses which take daily supplies to opiate drug users who are enrolled on a central registration programme and have regular contact with a doctor. Through these channels the Dutch claimed that by 1989 they were in contact with 60–80% of hard drug users in Amsterdam (Engelsman, 1989). However, they consider that they are in contact with a higher proportion of hard drug users in less urbanised regions (van Brussel & Buning, 1988). It is thus questionable whether the amount of contact alone accounts for the disparity between Amsterdam and much of the rest of the country.

One part of service provision which is easier to apply in urban areas, particularly in Amsterdam, is the Dutch philosophy of normalisation or social inclusion. This is very different from the UK concept of normalisation as described by Parker and colleagues (1998), who talk of the high prevalence of drug-taking by young people in the UK making it 'normal' for a young person to be offered and to take illicit drugs. The Dutch normalisation policy is one of *encirclement*, *adaptation* and *integration* into normal society. It may be considerably easier to do this in urban areas than in rural communities where everyone knows everyone else's business, but one factor which aids its facilitation, and which appears to be unique, is the presence of several social care oriented counselling centres throughout the Netherlands.

The emphasis on normalisation and social care now means that a Dutch addict more resembles an unemployed Dutch citizen than an alien endangering society, and illicit drug users tend to be treated more like users of socially acceptable drugs, such as alcohol, tobacco, caffeine and cannabis. Integration does not mean acceptance of drug use, but it does mean the destigmatisation and acceptance of the drug user within normal society. The Dutch normalisation policy, with its emphasis on social care and overcoming social exclusion, is perhaps the main candidate to explain the fall in hard drug use in Amsterdam and other Dutch urban areas.

Australia

Until the 1960s Australian GPs undertook maintenance prescribing to morphine and heroin addicts as they did in the UK. This is not surprising given the ties between the two countries.

In the 1960s the international political arena became particularly concerned about increasing levels of illicit drug use in many countries and a developing international trade in these drugs. Heroin was highlighted as a drug which easily led to addiction and many other problems. The Australian federal government responded by banning heroin importations from abroad, and individually the Australian states banned the manufacture of heroin. Increasingly heavy legal penalties were brought into force to deter illicit drug use. In spite of these measures the drug problem in Australia continued to grow.

The 1980s saw the introduction of Australia's first national drugs policy, a National Campaign Against Drug Abuse (NCADA), and the advent of HIV/AIDS as a major new problem. Prime Minister Hawke, whose daughter had developed a heroin problem, was a major supporter of initiatives to counter drug use. The Drug Offensive targeted public information campaign of NCADA was wisely broad based and included alcohol and tobacco.

The Australian National Drug Strategy of 1985 introduced the concept of harm reduction as a central component and this was reaffirmed in 1992. The strategy also encompassed alcohol and tobacco. The key goals laid out in the strategic plan were

- to minimise the level of illness, disease, injury and premature death associated with the use of alcohol, tobacco, pharmaceutical and illicit drugs;
- to minimise the level and impact of criminal drug offences and other drug-related crime, violence and antisocial behaviour within the community; and
- to minimise the level of personal and social disruption, loss of quality of life, loss of productivity and other economic costs associated with the inappropriate use of alcohol and other

drugs (Ministerial Council on Drug Strategy (MCDS), 1993).

With regard to alcohol, in 1989 the MCDS, which represents federal, state and territory interests and has oversight of the NCADA, called for a reduction of harm with particular reference to underage drinking, hazardous drinking, and drinking and driving. Recommendations for responsible drinking behaviour were put forward (National Health and Medical Research Council, 1992), and in some states legislation was introduced to limit the number of liquor licences and outlets.

Analyses of national survey data in Australia (Stockwell et al., 1996) pointed to the importance of high-risk drinking patterns, particularly binge drinking or consuming alcohol to the point of intoxication, and reflected analyses of data from Canada (Single & Wortley, 1993; Room et al., 1995) and the USA (Midanik et al., 1996). Public drunkenness, which had been a criminal offence, was repealed in all Australian states because jailing offenders was considered to increase harm. In Australia Roche (Roche et al., 1997; Roche, 1998) suggested that harm reduction alone is not a global panacea to alcohol and drug problems and proposed an integrated model combining harm reduction and use reduction. This approach supplemented the already established Australian national policy shift away from a reduction of total consumption within the population to harm reduction which focused on high-risk drinking patterns and specific types of harm. Other commentators suggested that both total volume consumed and the drinking pattern need to be considered in alcohol research and policy (Rehm et al., 1996; Stockwell et al., 1996). This had happened in New Zealand, and Australia was to follow suit.

The Australian national recommendations in 1992 were for men to drink less than 29 drinks per week (1 Australian drink = 10 g alcohol) and less than 15 drinks per week for women. This became known as 4 & 2 (i.e. an average daily rate of 4 drinks for men and 2 for women). In 2000 the weekly limit was continued, but the maximum upper limit in any one day was changed to 6 & 4. Australian alcohol policy continues to be based on harm reduction, but has taken into account national and international research data.

UK

The fact that political memories are short and few take account of national and international research or have a sound evidence base of effectiveness is demonstrated by the UK's most recent drugs policy. By the late 1990s, when the success of the UK harm reduction policy had shown a major decline in drug users infected with HIV, UK drugs policy swung away from a public health approach to one that focused on reducing criminality and improving community safety by coerced and legally enforced treatment for those who came in contact with the criminal justice system.

From the late 1990s a raft of measures was introduced in the UK which reoriented drugs policy away from health issues, locating it clearly within the domain of the criminal justice system. These included

- the establishment of new *gateway* services such as Arrest Referral Schemes
- mandatory drug-testing in prisons
- Drug Treatment and Testing Orders (DTTOs)
- Drug Abstinence Orders enforcing abstinence-oriented treatment, which have become an option for the courts, for those who have committed drug-related crimes
- a register of those who have been convicted of supplying drugs
- the CARAT (Counselling, Assessment, Referral, Advice/information and Throughcare) scheme for drug users within the prison system

Many of these initiatives have enabled and coerced users into valuable episodes of treatment. However, those who transgress face legal punishments, which may lead to imprisonment or, for those already in prison, delayed release.

In spite of making social inclusion a prominent stated feature of British policy and setting up a UK national social exclusion unit, to date this has played only a small role. The political focus on criminality has served to further ostracise illicit drug users.

Some UK politicians started to talk openly of a war on drugs, and political speeches became littered with words and phrases like *tough new powers*, *crack down*, *the drug threat*, *this menace* and *a scourge*, with harm reduction hardly mentioned by officials. The UK national policy stance appeared to have converted to a position more akin to the American System. However, this punitive policy stance changed after the advent of the new millennium to encompass 'harm reduction', although the reduction of harm appeared to be translated purely in terms of the criminal justice system and community safety.

In the words of Virginia Berridge, harm reduction is surfacing again. In 2000 the UK Harm Reduction Alliance (UKHRA) was formed. The international harm reduction movement had by now been established for some years, most notably in the USA and Europe, and had started to influence movement away from zero tolerance and a war-on-drugs approach. By other countries' standards UKHRA was late coming, probably because previously the UK had not needed it. Following this, a Home Affairs Select Committee was established to review UK drugs policy and came out strongly in favour of harm reduction. Politicians stopped talking of a war on drugs, although criminal justice issues remained top of the agenda. At the time of writing there is a push within the UK to expand treatment services making them more accessible to drug users and reduce waiting lists. Perhaps lessons have eventually been learned from the US Nixon administration that this is the best way of reducing criminality.

UK alcohol policy

The UK was the first country to recommend *safe limits* to drinking and the medical profession had only just reinforced their recommendations regarding weekly limits (Report of a Joint Working Group of Royal Colleges of Physicians, Psychiatrists & GPs, 1995) when the government set up another group to re-examine drinking guidelines. Although it was termed an interdepartmental group, the working group was dominated by representatives from the drinks industry. When it became clear that the guidelines were going to be revised upwards, Professor Griffith Edwards, who represented the medical profession, walked out. The report of that committee, *Sensible Drinking* (DH, 1995), recommended that there should be daily rather than weekly limits, and instead of a recommended safe limit of 21 units per week, there was now to be a recommended safe limit of 3–4 units per day. Additionally in 2001 legal moves were made to extend the opening times of pubs and make them much more flexible. No one would be surprised if the result of these two initiatives were to increase both drinks sales and the government revenue from it.

USA

The prohibition of alcohol and 'zero tolerance'

There have been two serious attempts to prohibit the drinking of alcohol in the USA, both fuelled by the temperance movement. In 1855 there was a brief and unpopular spell of prohibition which, through individual state controls, affected about one-third of all Americans. In most states the legal measures taken were rapidly reformed in the wake of the civil war and new moral commitments occupied the thinking of politicians, such as the abolition of slavery.

The second and more successful attempt, in spite of its ultimate failure, lasted from 1920 to 1933. It became enshrined in statute in the Eighteenth Amendment to the Constitution, and was endorsed by both houses of Congress and all but 2 of the 48 states. By 1934 per capita consumption fell to the lowest recorded level in US history. Eventually the policy failed because of lack of popular support. Many otherwise well-respected citizens became officially labelled as criminals, and articles on boot-legging filled the newspapers. The economic depression of 1929 helped provide a powerful incentive to stop prohibition when it was argued that revival of the drinks industry would provide many jobs and at the same time boost the economy through tax revenues from legal alcohol sales. In this time of Al Capone and other notorious gangsters, it was recog-

nised that prohibition had not stopped the nation drinking. Instead it had fuelled crime and made many criminals rich at the expense of the state.

States such as California and Texas still do not allow people to buy alcohol to consume until they have reached the age of 21. This compares with 18 in other countries such as the UK, and some people regard it as a relic of the temperance movement and prohibition.

Following in the footsteps of the prohibition of alcohol, and in contrast to the tolerant Dutch policy and the alternating, polarised policies of the UK, the USA has conducted a consistently prohibitionist stance on drugs. US policy is one of zero tolerance, ostracising drug users from a place in society, sustaining a vehement war on drugs, and aggressively resisting calls for a harm reduction approach (Reuter & MacCoun, 1995). In the words of one authority, 'The aim of twentieth-century social policy in the USA, which has drugs policy at its core, is to tame the untamed, regiment, restrain and inhibit the marginalised and excluded.' (Mac-Greggor, 1999)

Historical perspectives of the 'war-on-drugs' policy

The Federal Anti-Drug Abuse Act of 1988 with a policy goal of a drug-free USA was perhaps the formalisation of the US war-on-drugs approach. But in reality this policy was only building on successive prohibitionist policy approaches, beginning in 1911 with the Opium Exclusion Act, which was stimulated by concern that Chinese nationals involved in the opium trade were using the drug to seduce white women. Unlike the flexible British System of 1926, which encompassed maintenance prescribing for those addicted to opiates, doctors in the USA were prohibited by the 1914 Harrison Narcotics Act from maintenance prescribing to dependent drug users. When this Act became law, heroin maintenance clinics were closed across the USA and the moral revulsion formerly directed at drug users was vented on the physicians who were seen to pander to narcotic addicts. By 1922 many US physicians had been arrested under the Harrison Act. It was not until the late 1960s that maintenance prescribing started again in the USA, after the pioneering work of Drs Vincent Dole and Mary Nyswander clearly demonstrated the value of the synthetic opioid methadone. It finally gained full official favour after this, when it was found to substantially reduce criminal behaviour. Current US legislation rests with the Controlled Substances Act of 1970 and its subsequent amendments.

NEPs have been extremely slow to develop in the USA, and in many areas this has become a heated political and moral issue. There is still substantial political support for those ideologues who oppose, restrict and inhibit AIDS prevention programmes. From 1986 to 1989 there was only one small NEP in operation in New York, and this was closed down in 1990 by the new mayor. However, bigoted officials have not always got their own way. When the governor of California vetoed the NEP, local authorities declared a public health emergency which enabled them to override the veto. Needle exchange services still remain relatively few in number in the USA, but sense is now beginning to prevail, at least at a local level, although progression has been slow. In 1997 there were 113 NEPs in a total of more than 60 US cities (Update, 1998) – a similar number to those which were set up in England in 1988 when needle exchange was first given official encouragement to expand there. In 1998 there were 131 US programmes (Update, 2001). Many of the US schemes have been initiated through private funds, and have been officially illegal. Yet, in spite of this, many are now supported by local government authorities, although the US Congress has closed its mind to the wealth of evidence showing the effectiveness of NEPs, and has consistently and vehemently voted to ban any funding for them.

The relative lack of a welfare benefit system in the USA has compounded the problems of those at the receiving end of zero tolerance. The combination of the two has led most illicit drug users and many drinkers to become so deeply entrenched in poverty that they have formed an excluded subculture, where the only possible way out is through repeated acquisitive crime.

Part of the reason for the tough US stance resulted from the influential writings of Charles Murray. In 1984 he argued that US post-war welfare policy had encouraged the growth of a non-productive underclass dependent on welfare payments. This fuelled the Reagan administration's unsympathetic and tough approach to the US Welfare Benefit System (Murray, 1984). Ten years later Murray jointly authored *The Bell Curve* with Herrstein and made even more controversial statements. In this book the two authors suggested that many of the social problems of the USA were due to low intelligence, and it was argued that black people, on average, have lower IQs than white people and often fall into a deprived and dangerous underclass. This underclass, the authors said, is characterised by pathological behaviours, teenage pregnancy, single motherhood, male unemployment, crime and drug abuse (Herrstein & Murray, 1994). Wilson (1987), another influential US sociologist, praised what he saw as the need for sociologists like Murray to describe cultures honestly, as he had done in his first book on US social policy, and not be afraid of speaking out about cultural realities for fear of being labelled racist. In a later book (Wilson, 1996), backed up by extensive research in Chicago, he emphasised the importance of employment by highlighting the formation of ghettos in black neighbourhoods where there is extensive joblessness and weak social organisation. The vacuum left behind, he said, sucks in drug-taking, drug-trafficking and crime which is often violent.

The tough American System of *three strikes and you are out* has led to overcrowding in prisons at immense cost to the public purse. Currie (1993) commented:

> Today the United States incarcerates a larger proportion of its citizens than any other country, having surpassed South Africa and the Soviet Union by the end of the 1980s – an achievement partly propelled by the escalation of the criminal justice response to drugs, both 'hard' and 'soft'. The massive imprisonment of the disadvantaged young that has accompanied this trend means that nearly one in four black men and one in ten Hispanic men between the ages of 20 and 29 are behind bars, on probation or on parole. In New York two young black men are in prison for everyone in college.

This trend has continued. A report published in 1998 from the National Center on Addiction and

Substance Abuse at Columbia University showed that the number of prisoners in the USA had more than tripled since 1980, and that illegal drugs and alcohol had helped lead to the imprisonment of four out of every five inmates (Wren, 1998).

In spite of huge numbers of drinkers and drug users filling the jails, crime in North America has not receded in the way it has in the Netherlands. On the contrary, there are many areas where it is now unsafe for ordinary people to go. This is also in spite of very large sums of money that have been spent on policing for many years in the USA. Drucker (1992) illustrated the point in his description of the work of Special Weapons And Tactics (SWAT) squads:

> Heavily armed SWAT squads block off both ends of the street and make a sweep taking every young male and some young females. They spread-eagle them up against the walls and search them for drugs. These are all black and Hispanic neighbourhoods, of course, and the police deliberately do this in full view of everyone in the neighbourhood – a shock tactic meant to convey a strong message. In New York last year we spent US $169 million on SWAT teams, which made around 9500 arrests. That works out to about US $17 000 per arrest – more than the annual cost of most residential drug treatment centres.

In the ensuing years these policies have continued. In spite of the fact that Congress has voted to shift funds over from supply reduction (police and customs) to demand reduction (treatment), this has not occurred. All the indications are that a war-on-drugs approach is expensive and handles the drug problem badly, but political forces ensure that it still continues in the USA.

Conclusion

These four countries are examples of the ways in which use reduction, harm reduction and zero tolerance have or have not been applied through individual national drugs and alcohol policies. There are other examples of tough, essentially counterproductive policies (e.g. Sweden). For those politicians who have open minds there are clear lessons to be learned. There is increasing evidence that harm reduction works.

Zero tolerance and use reduction must not be seen as the only way forward, particularly when it is coerced. Coerced abstinence-oriented treatments may work in some cases, but generally only if the user really wants this. The narrow concept, held by many people outside treatment services, that the term *treatment* is limited to prescriptions and/or medical advice, must be abandoned and replaced by a range of biopsychosocial interventions which reduce substance-related problems and associated harm.

The aim of a broad and wide-ranging harm reduction programme has a major role in the treatment process. However, harm reduction which promotes the recovery process can also be facilitated through national policy, such as the Dutch policy of normalisation, and other initiatives such as easing legislation, although the latter remains a controversial area which properly rests with politicians. Both local and national politics have a role to play in either facilitating or blocking positive change. Harm reduction is now very firmly on national and international agendas for consideration. Although not an official policy everywhere, the accumulated evidence on harm reduction overwhelmingly supports its use.

Part III
Prevention and Treatment

Chapter 3
Prevention and Treatment Services for Young People

Prevention and Treatment – Not Separate Issues but Part of a Continuum

Background

The need to experiment and to rebel against authority, especially when a particular activity is condemned, are normal features of growing up. Smoking, drinking and experimenting with drugs are part of this. Primary prevention (preventing people from taking any drugs at all, or drinking before they are legally able to do so) is thus difficult to achieve, but it is still important to try. Our knowledge of the most effective ways of doing this is improving.

Secondary prevention (preventing the onward move from recreational to problematic substance use) is also now more clearly understood. The longer substance use continues, and the greater the quantities of substances taken, the more likely it is that significant adverse health, social, psychological and legal consequences will result. Furthermore, dependence may occur and, when it does, is often so difficult to treat that it is sometimes described as a chronic relapsing condition. The secondary prevention of chemical dependence and drug and alcohol problems is of particular importance. It is more achievable than primary prevention and compared to the treatment of problem substance use or dependence, it is considerably more cost-effective. For this reason the main focus of this chapter is on personally appropriate and effective secondary prevention interventions for vulnerable young people who are considered to be at high risk of developing drug and alcohol dependence and the problems that accompany substance use.

In a primary prevention programme outcomes are usually considered to be effective if a reduced percentage of young people admit they have taken drugs, or begun to drink alcohol, or if drug-taking and under-age drinking is delayed. Primary prevention is generally delivered to young people by the school education system and community education programmes.

Both primary and secondary prevention can be enhanced in a universal way by 'healthy public policies, in (for instance) . . . housing . . . (and) education' (Brundtland, 2001) aimed at promoting stable families, communities and neighbourhoods, and providing curricula for children that act to promote success, particularly amongst the least academic (HAS, 2001). Government policies that effectively tackle poverty, social exclusion and inequality will also help prevent substance use problems and dependence. In addition, recent advances in our understanding of the vulnerability of specific groups have aided our ability to deliver prevention services in more targeted ways. A considerable amount of recent research has centred on secondary prevention by identifying vulnerable groups of young people, and delivering targeted interventions to individuals from those groups to prevent substance use problems and dependence. In the USA, Canada and the UK special youth drug teams are being set up to work specifically for these vulnerable young people.

Dependence in young people clearly does occasionally occur, although this has been questioned (Fulkerson et al., 1999; Ridenour et al., 2002). Ridenour suggests that existing classification schemes which have been developed from data collected from adults do not generalise to adolescents (Ridenour et al., 2002). Fulkerson and colleagues have suggested combining DSM-IV abuse and dependence criteria for adolescents. Several questionnaires have been developed for the assessment of substance use in adolescence, but as yet there appears to be no ideal screening or assessment instrument. Until our understanding deepens, where there is any history of substance use, assessments should be supplemented by questions on frequency, duration, age of onset, antecedents and problem severity. Failure to seek and obtain such information may lead to inadequate care plans, and to missed opportunities for health promotion.

Various adolescent screening and assessment questionnaires have been commissioned from a number of sources to attempt to find some useful screening and assessment tools for young people. These include:

- Substance Abuse Module (SAM), which is a revised and expanded version of the section Substance Abuse in the Composite International Diagnostic Interview (CIDI) and was commissioned by the US National Institute of Mental Health;
- Structured Clinical Interview for the DSM (SCID), which was first devised for DSM-III and has been adapted for DSM-IV and ICD-10 for the assessment of drug and alcohol diagnoses in adolescents;
- Diagnostic Interview for Children and Adolescents (DICA) and
- Adolescent Diagnostic Interview (ADI), which are both designed to be used by lay people;
- Diagnostic Interview Survey for Children (DISC) and
- Children's Interview for Psychiatric Syndromes (ChIPS), which are both questionnaires designed for studies on children's psychiatric diagnoses;
- Pictorial Instrument for Child and Adolescent psychiatry (PICA-III-R) questionnaire, which was developed to assess DSM-III-R disorders in children and adolescents using pictures to illustrate the symptoms that are queried; and
- Assessment of Liability and EXposure to Substance use and Antisocial behaviour (ALEXSA), which is a questionnaire to assess the risks and protective factors for later substance use, abuse and dependence in 9–12-year-olds.

There appear to be no good validation studies or reliability estimates reported for substance use disorders for any of these questionnaires. None of these questionnaires can be used to adequately diagnose dependence or its severity.

A recent study comparing screening tools for alcohol problems in under-age drinkers attending emergency departments concluded that the Alcohol Use Disorders Identification Test (AUDIT) was the most effective tool (Kelly *et al.*, 2002). Screening can be undertaken with individual contacts by means of careful enquiry, adapting format to individual comprehension and exploring disclosures. The opportunistic individual approach is more readily applied by professionals and is more acceptable to service users. This contrasts with less acceptable population screening methods involving reaching out to sections of the general public.

Those who progress to dependent substance use usually continue to have the same problems which made them at high risk in the first place, and those problems still need to be addressed. As a result, interventions which are useful to prevent progression to substance use–related problems and dependence are commonly the same as those needed to treat established problems and dependence. Prevention and treatment merge together as part of a continuum and the distinction is not of great importance in young people.

Primary prevention

In theory there is a clear dividing line between primary and secondary prevention. In practice this line is blurred because primary prevention education programmes in schools are always done in group settings, and drug use and excessive drinking are often concealed. Usually some members of the group will already have experimented with illicit drugs, or will have broken their country's laws with regard to the age when they may drink or purchase alcohol. In the USA legal constraints vary from state to state. In California and Texas drinking alcohol under the age of 21 is illegal. In England it is an offence to purchase alcohol under the age of 18. There is some evidence that age of first use and legal constraints with age limits for legal use help to improve primary prevention and reduce the harm from alcohol-related problems, including longer-term problems such as drink-related road traffic accidents (RTAs) and hazardous alcohol use (Holder *et al.*, 2000). However, these advantages are counterbalanced at least to some extent by harm from interactions with the criminal justice system.

Education in schools

The lessons of research are commonly overlooked or forgotten. This, unfortunately, is all too often the case with approaches to drug education for children and young people in schools. In 1975 a well-constructed controlled study of three different types of educational interventions involving 1035 schoolchildren aged 14–16 from 50 classes in 20 different schools was conducted in Rotterdam (de Haes & Schuurman, 1975). The results are as relevant today as they were at that time. The three different approaches used were:

- a warning or mild horror approach, which stressed the dangers and moral dimensions of substance use;
- a factual approach, which aimed at improving personal knowledge so that children could make informed decisions about drug use; and
- a problem discussion approach, which did not focus on drugs at all, but consisted of ten weekly 1-hour classes discussing the problems of adolescence with the hope of helping resolve behavioural problems.

The first two approaches were given by outside *experts* and lasted for about 1 hour. The third approach was given informally by the children's usual teachers. Follow-up showed the expected increase in experimental drug-taking over time. At three months the control group, which had not been exposed to any of the above three interventions, showed a 3.6% increase in experimental drug use. The *mild horror* and *factual* approaches both made things worse, with results showing a 7.3% and 4.6% increase in drug-taking respectively. The only approach which successfully achieved the aim of reducing illicit drug-taking was the person-focused rather than drug-focused intervention, which only showed a 2.6% increase.

This work has been endorsed by the relatively poor results of the Drug Abuse Resistance Education (DARE) programme in the USA (Ennett *et al.*, 1994). This is a programme delivered by the police, which is a mixture of factual information about drugs (some warnings), although it does also contain some life skills work, and resistance training to resist peer pressure to take drugs. In the USA the DARE programme remains the main form of drug education, even though it is at best only marginally successful, and considerably less effective than Botvin's life skills training approach (Botvin *et al.*, 1995).

In a long-term follow-up study of nearly 6000 children from the seventh grade (who also had booster sessions in the eighth and ninth grades), Botvin has shown his programme to be effective in reducing the expected prevalence of smoking, alcohol use and cannabis use six years after the initial baseline assessment. In contrast, in the UK the government's key objective is 'to ensure that schools offer effective programmes on drugs education, giving pupils the facts and warning them of the risks'. In the UK certain aspects of drugs education have been a statutory requirement for 5–7-year-olds, 7–11-year-olds and 14–16-year-olds since 1995. Life skills training has not traditionally been part of this. Britain now has more young people taking drugs than anywhere else in Europe.

Although advice on its own is not an effective substance use deterrent, accurate information about the effects and potential problems of drugs and alcohol is important for all to know so that people can make their own decisions about substance use and if they do drink or take drugs are enabled to do this safely. Good advice will be used by some people, particularly if there is a two-way interchange with the advisor. Accurate advice should not just address abstinence, but should include harm reduction advice regarding intoxication, blood-borne virus (BBV) transmission, strategies in clubs (e.g. chill out areas, appropriate fluids replenishment, etc.), advice on overdose, and related sexual or physical health advice.

During the 1970s and 1980s drugs education in US schools and elsewhere moved on from just giving information about drugs to providing training to resist approaches from peers. 'Just say no' was promoted originally by Nancy Reagan, the wife of the president, and developed into what became known as resistance skills training. However, on its own it was not effective. The importance of overcoming peer pressure was at that time probably overestimated. It ignored the fact that young people choose their peer group, and that vulnerable, risk-taking, potentially deviant people seek out like-minded peers. From the 1990s US educational programmes involving resistance skills were expanded to incorporate a comprehensive system approach. The most effective preventive programmes teach adolescents the following comprehensive package:

- social communication and assertiveness skills to help them develop positive peer relationships
- problem-solving skills for dealing with environmental demands
- behavioural and cognitive skills for managing stressors
- resistance skills for withstanding peer pressure to use drugs and alcohol

This type of work changes attitudes, enhances social competence, reduces alcohol and drug use, decreases negative behaviour and fosters academic attainment. Botvin's work (Botvin *et al.*, 1995), which is along these lines, has been extensively evaluated and gives the best results so far. It should be the standard against which all new preventive educational work is measured.

The importance of education at an early age has also been demonstrated by a small UK study on children aged 8–12 years in two primary schools of a deprived London borough (Hurry & Lloyd, 1997). This was another life skills drugs education programme. Follow-up four years later demonstrated that, although there was no long-term gain in knowledge, there was a positive effect on attitudes. Outcome studies showed a significant reduction in smoking and illicit drug use.

Community education

Community education initiatives and community action programmes often span the divide between primary and secondary prevention, and many

(e.g. drink driving education programmes) may be specifically designed for those who have already indulged in substance use and therefore clearly come into the category of secondary prevention. Detached youth workers and drug and alcohol outreach workers may work educationally on a one-to-one basis with those who are perceived to be at risk. Alternatively community education programmes may be designed for groups of young people, some of whom may not have used drugs. Yet with the normalisation of illicit drug use and under-age drinking among young people, this work increasingly has become secondary, rather than primary, prevention. Whole population approaches, such as fiscal measures, using local policy to affect the drinking environment, regulating local retail outlets more closely through law enforcement, mobilising community support for controls and increasing drink drive enforcement can include components of specific relevance to young people and children such as reducing the sale of alcohol to minors (Holder, 2000). This may be more acceptable and effective than interventions aimed at young people alone.

Secondary prevention

The majority of young people who drink and take drugs come to no harm. Many people therefore believe that, although experimental or social drug use and under-age drinking cannot be encouraged, we should not spend our time worrying about all young people who experiment with drugs or who occasionally drink. Rather, we should concentrate resources on detecting the minority whose drinking or drug use is likely to escalate and become entrenched, and find successful ways of intervening. In order to do this we must first understand how problem substance use in adolescence develops.

Theories and models for the development of problem and dependent substance use in young people

A number of theories and models have been put forward to explain problem drug use and drinking in adolescence. They mainly fall into four different types.

Hereditary models

Genetic factors may influence levels of drug and alcohol consumption, incidence of substance-related problems and the onset of physical dependence. Research into behavioural genetics shows that both alcohol dependence (Lester, 1988) and drug dependence (Grove *et al.*, 1990) are inheritable disorders, but generally only in men.

Recent research has focused on alcohol and the human genome. Two large-scale US family studies, the Collaborative Study of the Genetics of Alcoholism (COGA) (Reich *et al.*, 1998) and a study by the Neurogenetics Laboratory of the National Institute on Alcohol Abuse and Alcoholism (NIAAA) on US American Indians, have provided evidence of genetic loci for those at risk of alcohol problems and dependence. For mild alcohol dependence the loci are situated on chromosomes 1 and 7, and there is a locus for those at high risk for severe alcohol dependence on chromosome 16. Research from the NIAAA (Long *et al.*, 1998) has shown genetic linkage to alcohol dependence on chromosome 11. Both studies show there is also a protective locus on chromosome 4q from nearby genes related to alcohol metabolism (the enzymes alcohol dehydrogenase (ADH) and aldehyde dehydrogenase (ALDH)). In some Asian families the gene encoding an isoenzyme known as alcohol dehydrogenase 3 is situated here. This enzyme is known to protect against alcohol dependence because of the rapid rate at which it metabolises alcohol to aldehyde. The build-up of aldehyde lowers tolerance to adverse flushing effects (Chen *et al.*, 1996).

A positive family history of alcohol dependence (Chassin *et al.*, 1996) or substance use disorder in at least one parent (Milberger *et al.*, 1999) is associated with increased drug and alcohol use during adolescence. There is a four- to ninefold risk of alcohol dependence in male offspring of alcohol-dependent parents (Cloninger *et al.*, 1981; Russell, 1990). However, such studies do not separate out the influences of heredity and environment. To try to do this, various twin and adoption studies have been conducted.

One large-scale twin study (Tsuang *et al.*, 1996) indicated that the hereditability of any drug abuse is about 34%. A Stockholm adoption study (Cloninger *et al.*, 1981), confirmed by later research (Zucker & Gomberg, 1986; Jang *et al.*, 1997), shows that for male drinkers there is a genetically influenced subtype (Cloninger type 2) characterised by a pattern of early alcohol use, persistent childhood conduct problems and criminal behaviour. However, Cloninger type 1 (milieu limited), which affects both males and females, rarely involves criminality and is usually mild. This type is less hereditary and more influenced by the environment (milieu). Thus men have a greater risk than women of developing a substance use problem or dependence. COGA investigators have found that Cloninger type 2 alcohol dependence is also associated with more than twice as much drug use, lower adaptive function, lower socio-economic status and earlier onset of drink problems than type 1.

Inherited temperament and developmental disorders

- *Attention-deficit/hyperactivity disorder* (ADHD) is a developmental disorder which is significantly related to problem drinking among adolescents and adults (August *et al.*, 1983) and illicit drug use in adolescence (Fergusson, 1993), but only when it co-occurs with conduct disorder.
- Cadoret and colleagues (1995) have shown that *impulsive–aggressive behaviour* in adopted children is a genetically transmitted personality trait which acts as a risk factor for substance use.
- *Sensation-seeking* (another heritable temperament deviation) together with social influences may account for heavy drinking (Arnett, 1992), substance use (Wills *et al.*, 2000) and other risky adolescent behaviours.
- COGA studies demonstrate that *novelty-seeking* is an important temperament factor for alcohol problems, and twin studies show its hereditability to be about 50% (Stallings *et al.*, 1996). Polysubstance use has also been most consistently associated with novelty-seeking. Cloninger and colleagues (1988) have shown that high novelty-seeking and low harm avoidance are the

most highly predictive personality traits for early onset alcohol use.

- Temperament can also act as a protective factor. Werner and Smith (1982) report that a *cuddly, affectionate temperament* in infancy and early childhood is associated with a decreased risk for alcohol-related problems in adolescence and adulthood.

Inherited differences in pharmacological effects of alcohol

- There are individual differences in the ability of alcohol to *reduce stress and produce a euphoric effect*. Many sons of alcohol-dependent parents have a reduced alpha rhythm activity on electroencephalogram (EEG) recordings indicating a poor capacity for relaxation, but following the consumption of alcohol, alpha rhythms increase dramatically suggesting a euphoric state (Pollock *et al.*, 1983).
- There may be individual differences in the initial *sensitivity to the effects of alcohol*. People with a family history of alcohol dependence report less feelings of intoxication after a dose of alcohol, have less body sway after ingestion of alcohol and show less deterioration in performance on psychological tests than controls (Schuckit, 1995a; 1995b). However, it is possible that this could be related to tolerance due to earlier onset of use.
- Some Asians inherit a low activity enzyme known as aldehyde dehydrogenase 3 and experience a *flushing response* to the ingestion of alcohol due to elevated aldehyde levels. High levels can give a toxic reaction. This genetically influenced flushing response is associated with reduced alcohol use and a reduced risk of alcohol dependence (Thomasson *et al.*, 1993).

Interpersonal models

- Brook and colleagues (1990) have proposed a *family interactional framework*. A strong parent–adolescent bond, characterised by strong identification, lack of conflict, affectional warmth and parental involvement in adolescent concerns, acts as a strong protective factor against adolescent problem substance use. But the framework is extended beyond the

immediate family to include cultural and school influences, together with personality and behavioural traits that may affect family functioning.

- It is a mistake to assume that *peer pressure* accounts for much substance use. Peers are selected, and the main influences on drug and alcohol use appear to operate via both initial selection processes and reciprocal socialisation processes (Reed & Rountree, 1997).

Biopsychosocial models

- Huba and Bentler (1982) have suggested a biopsychosocial model comprising biological, intrapersonal, interpersonal and sociocultural factors.
- Jessor and colleagues (1991) view adolescent drinking and drug use from the point of view of problem behaviour theory. Their model, which is similar to Bandura's concept of reciprocal determinism (1977a), comprises three systems that interact with each other to predict the expression of substance use in adolescence:

  (1) *personality system*, which includes motivation (e.g. valuing academic achievement), personal beliefs (e.g. self-esteem) and personal control (e.g. attitude towards deviant behaviour)

  (2) *perceived environment system*, which comprises distal (e.g. parental support and control) and proximal structures (e.g. friends' approval of deviant behaviour)

  (3) *behaviour system*, which includes both problematic and conventional behaviour patterns

Models associated with adverse life problems

These models focus on the interrelationship between life problems and substance use. They tend to view variations in consumption of alcohol and drugs and changes in associated problems as variables which can alter with development across the lifespan and give reciprocal feedback (Zucker *et al.*, 1995). They emphasise the disruptive influence which substance use can have on normal development, such as the successful striving for independence.

- Huba and Bentler's biopsychosocial model (1982) does vary with age, and adverse inter- and intrapersonal factors together with age-appropriate sociocultural factors may interfere with normal development and lead to substance use.
- Life history theory is an evolutionary approach which views risky drinking and other high-risk behaviours in relation to the need to reproduce the species. High-risk behaviours are not seen as deviant or pathological, but as related to high-risk high-gain situations where caution may mean total exclusion from reproduction. Success is only achieved by taking great risks. Environmental instability and adverse ecological factors only intensify high-risk behaviour to achieve social and economic resources to aid the survival of descendants. Virtually all studies report a gender difference with higher risk-taking by males. A typical study of high-risk behaviour in Greek adolescents (as defined by the non-use of seat belts, smoking, drinking, driving after drinking, riding with a drunk driver and non-use of contraceptives or condoms) shows the strong inverse relationship between risky behaviour and socio-economic status (Petridou *et al.*, 1997).

Vulnerable young people (at high risk of developing a drink or drug problem)

Considerable work has been done since the early 1990s to detect young people at high risk of developing a drink or a drug problem and/or dependence, particularly in the USA and Canada. No dominant single factor has emerged. Rather constellations of factors tend to group together in the prediction of problematic outcomes.

Young people at high risk of developing a serious drink or drug problem/dependence

Those who require priority for screening, and if necessary further assessment and help, can be identified through membership of the following high-risk groups (HAS, 2001):

- young offenders
- all receiving mental health assessments
- runaways/street or homeless children
- all those in the *looked-after system* or any contact with social services
- those with educational problems, significant change of grade or absences from school, and those who are dropouts or excluded from school
- those with substantial and recurrent disruptive behavioural patterns
- those with recurrent contact in Accident and Emergency (A&E) departments or primary care for trauma or drug- and alcohol-related incidents
- any child or young person presenting with family contact or disruption
- those with any significant change in behaviour
- children of substance-using (alcohol and drugs) parents
- children presenting to A&E and other services with incidents of deliberate self-harm

The 2001 Health Advisory Service (HAS) report recommends screening everyone who falls into one of the above vulnerability groups. In this context, the term *screening* must be taken to mean an opportunistic individual careful enquiry, given the lack of an adequate screening questionnaire for adolescents together with the problems of performing urinary substance use screens in this age group. Work with vulnerable young people will require an assessment of individual needs and a decision as to how those needs may be met. Meeting any current needs, whether or not these appear to be related to the use of drugs or alcohol, is perhaps one of the best ways of helping prevent the future development and escalation of substance use.

With regard to accessibility for appropriate interventions, it is helpful to take a simplified view and say that there are basically two groups:

(1) young people with conduct disorders, particularly those with abnormally aggressive behaviour patterns
(2) accessible groups of young people with other (sometimes multiple) risk factors promoting the development of problem drinking or

drug-taking, and few resiliency factors to counter this effect

Young people with conduct disorder and/or high aggression

Conduct problems in adolescence are a strong predictor of elevated alcohol and drug use in young adulthood (Windle, 1990; Capaldi & Stoolmiller, 1999) and about 25% of children with conduct disorder later become antisocial dependent drinkers. In addition, young people with conduct disorders also have an increased likelihood of engaging in criminal behaviour in the future (Farrington *et al.*, 1990). Throughout the world it has been shown that the same risk, vulnerability and protective factors that apply to problem drug use and heavy drinking also apply to antisocial behaviours such as conduct disorder (Kazdin, 1995), delinquency and criminality (Thornberry *et al.*, 1995). Thus young people who are in one of the vulnerable categories for problems relating to substance use are also, quite independently, at high risk of becoming involved in criminal behaviour. This is particularly the case for those who are excluded from school (Powis *et al.*, 1998), are homeless (Weller *et al.*, 1987) or have experienced parenting problems (Velleman *et al.*, 1997).

Commonly antisocial behaviour patterns and substance use coexist. In most cases of coexisting delinquency, however, delinquent behaviour typically predates drug use (Collinson, 1996). Velleman and colleagues (1997) have reviewed the parenting factors that predispose a child to develop conduct disorder and substance use problems. They concluded:

> [A] low level of communication between parent and child, poorly defined and poorly communicated expectations of a child's behaviour, excessively severe and inconstant discipline, and high levels of negative interaction or family conflict have all been found predictive of increased risk of substance abuse, delinquency and conduct disorders.

Thus identification of children at risk and intervention at an early stage has a double benefit. It not only aids the prevention of later substance use problems but also helps prevent delinquency and criminal activity. Some authorities feel that to be maximally effective the timing of appropriate interventions should ideally be before adolescence. This is because, for an average population of young people, there is a sharp increase in the frequency of delinquent acts and substance use at this age, and this frequency peaks between the ages of 15 and 17 (Loeber *et al.*, 1993).

Although childhood antisocial behaviour, rebelliousness and anger are all predictive of adolescent substance use (Windle, 1990), aggression is a particularly useful identification marker for a number of future problems. Chronic aggressive behaviour also has the advantage that it can often be picked up at a very early age. Longitudinal research has shown that aggressive behaviour from childhood through to early adulthood is, along with intellectual functioning, among the most stable psychological characteristics of children (Olweus, 1979). It is recognised as a broadband risk marker commonly leading to a variety of negative outcomes including conduct disorder, delinquency and substance use (Loeber, 1990), poor school adjustment and dropout (Tremblay *et al.*, 1992), and criminal behaviour (Farrington *et al.*, 1990; Tremblay *et al.*, 1992).

Biederman and colleagues (1999) have demonstrated that effective treatment of childhood behaviour disorder reduces the risk of substance use disorder in adolescence. However, regular or repeated substance use at a young age is a risk factor in its own right for the escalation to drug and alcohol problems and dependence in young adulthood (Robins & Przybeck, 1985), which in turn can lead people into criminal activity. Thus if substance use in a young person from a vulnerable group has already begun, it should be taken very seriously as the risks of later substance use problems and criminality will be increased. Indeed the younger the age of onset of substance use, the greater the probability that a person will develop an alcohol disorder in his or her lifetime (Grant & Dawson, 1998). When those who developed an alcohol disorder before the age of 20 were compared with those who developed a disorder after that time, the early onset group was twice as likely to have been incarcerated for crimes related to physical violence, three times more likely to be depressed and four times more likely to have attempted suicide (Buydens-Branchey *et al.*, 1989). Substance use by young people can also undermine the achievement of academic, occupational and relationship goals which are crucial for adaptation to adulthood (Yamaguchi & Kandel, 1985). It is therefore important that every effort is made to help adolescents from these groups minimise their substance use as well as provide appropriate interventions to prevent future conduct disorder or reduce vulnerability to substance use.

Normally, physical aggression among peers increases in very young children from the age of six months until they are two years (Restoin *et al.*, 1985). Aggressive behaviour towards other children then usually declines in frequency between the ages of two and seven (Strayer *et al.*, 1986). Some children are *early starters* beginning their antisocial careers between the ages of six and eight (Patterson *et al.*, 1992). Moffitt (1993) prefers to use the phrase *life-course persisters* to denote the fact that these youths are at high risk of adult antisocial behaviour throughout their lives. Children with chronic high aggression can be identified with reasonable reliability from the age of seven (Strayer *et al.*, 1986). Half of all aggressive children of this age will commit violent or other antisocial acts in adolescence, and many will engage in substance use, or become Cloninger type 2 alcoholics or drug dependent.

Risk factors and protective factors

Not all risk and protective factors are open to change but, where this is possible, help can be given to vulnerable young people by reducing risk factors and enhancing protective factors (Smith *et al.*, 1995; HAS, 1996; 2001). The factors may be categorised as follows:

(1) *Societal and cultural risk factors*
   - the law and social norms (e.g. social norms of heavy drinking/drug use among young people)
   - substance availability
   - poverty
   - neighbourhood disorganisation

(2) *Individual and interpersonal risk factors*
   - physiological factors
   - attitudes favourable/tolerant to substance use
   - family criminality
   - unemployment
   - history of childhood, sexual/physical/emotional abuse
   - adult sexual abuse/involvement in sex industry
   - use of substances by parents
   - poor or inconsistent parental management
   - inappropriate parental academic expectations
   - family conflict and breakdown
   - early and/or persistent behaviour problems
   - poor academic attainment/learning disability
   - low commitment to school
   - mental health problems
   - alienation by society/peer rejection
   - association with peers who use drugs
   - early onset of drug or alcohol use

(3) *Protective factors (social)*
   - attachment to teachers/commitment to education
   - educational attainment
   - parental supervision
   - pro-social peers
   - strong parent–child attachment
   - a supportive family environment
   - a social support system that encourages personal efforts
   - a caring relationship with at least one adult
   - expectations of gender role (e.g. societal sex role expectations help girls to be more resistant in early childhood, and boys to be more resilient in adolescence)

(4) *Protective factors (personal)*
   - positive *easy going* temperament
   - intellectual ability
   - self-efficacy
   - the ability to be realistic and differentiate between the possible and the impossible
   - possessing social problem-solving skills
   - a sense of responsibility, direction and mission
   - empathy

- an enduring interest or hobby
- humour
- adaptive distancing, particularly for children of dysfunctional, substance-using or psychiatrically ill families

(5) *Other risk and protective factors*

Alcohol expectancies. Expectancies of drug or alcohol use can play a large part in the future development of substance-related problems. Adolescents are capable of differentiating alcohol expectancies in a manner similar to adults. Expectancies that are socially learned are moderately to highly correlated with subsequent drinking behaviour. They include expectations of enhancing or impeding social behaviours, improving cognitive function, enhancing sexuality, increasing arousal and promoting relaxation (Christiansen *et al.*, 1982). Stacey and colleagues (1992) have shown that adolescent expectancies predict substance use nine years later.

Self-esteem. Low self-esteem is commonly associated with problems related to substance use, but programmes that focus on building self-esteem through counselling by helping people see their personal strengths are less likely to be helpful than equipping them with needed competencies. The development of self-efficacy is likely to foster sobriety, enhanced self-esteem, good feelings and positive self-awareness, and this is often the best and most appropriate way forward (Bandura, 1997).

Religiosity. Religiosity has been identified as a protective factor for the early onset and progression of substance use (Bahr *et al.*, 1993).

Coping strategies. Good problem-focused coping is inversely related to alcohol use and alcohol problems (Windle & Windle, 1996). Furthermore, in a study of coping skills among adolescents treated for alcohol and drug problems, Myers and Brown (1990) found that adolescents with fewer problem-solving coping strategies, when faced with a hypothetical high-risk relapse situation, had the poorest relapse outcomes.

Family factors. Parental nurturance or level of emotional warmth and support has been consistently inversely related to levels of adolescent alcohol use (Barnes, 1990). Higher levels of parental monitoring, or establishing and enforcing reasonable rules and boundaries, are also inversely related to adolescent

alcohol use. There is a similar inverse relationship with regard to higher levels of time spent together with parents, and good parent–adolescent communication. There is a statistically significant association between alcohol use by adolescents and alcohol use by their older siblings (Needle *et al.*, 1986).

A web of causation

Risk factors for progression to problematic use are additive, and Lloyd (1998) highlights the way in which many risk factors are related to each other:

> A key feature of the risk literature is its interconnectedness – the deeper one goes into attempting to identify specific factors that are associated with problem drug use, the clearer it becomes that they are all interrelated. Factors relating to the family (including genetic predisposition) and possibly the environment are more fundamental factors that then feed in to the other, largely interconnected factors relating to early behaviour, schooling, peer relationships, mental health and the onset of drug use. While there is a natural tendency for researchers to separate out these variables and ignore their developmental nature, this is likely to be an artificial process which will obscure the processes underlying the development of problem drug use.

Young people are

> likely to have multiple and complex problems that traverse a variety of agencies with major cost implications for all involved. Traditional services are generally provided along historical development lines with little co-ordination between adult and child services, addiction and adolescent mental health services, and with varied philosophies, ethos, staff characteristics and expertise (Gilvary, 1998).

There is 'a need for qualitative work which might better address the complex interactive nature of some of the factors referred to above' (Lloyd, 1998). This includes the integration of training in drug and alcohol assessment and interventions across a wide range of professions (Crome *et al.*, 2000).

Thus, although, for ease of identification, a reductionist approach has been used with regard to isolating single factors that place a young person at high risk of developing problematic substance use, it should not be used with regard to the assessment or interventions employed. It would be very wrong, for instance, to say that since being homeless places a young person in a vulnerable category, all one has to do is provide some accommodation and this will prevent them developing a future drink or drug problem. Almost every young person who is homeless has a number of underlying problems that are likely to have contributed to their homeless state, and these problems may also place them at risk of substance problems and dependence. For instance, in the UK 30% of single homeless people have been in care, both factors making them vulnerable. Similarly *looked-after* children are ten times more likely to be excluded from school than their peers, and 75% of young people leaving care have no educational qualifications (Polnay & Ward, 2000). (The term *looked-after* was first introduced in the UK 1989 Children Act to cover all children in public care, including those in foster or residential homes, and those still with their own parents but subject to care orders.)

Thus each young person must be viewed holistically with the aim of minimising risk factors and maximising protective factors. Sometimes it may be most appropriate to work through the parents or carers, as well as working directly with the young person. This is particularly the case for younger children. However, some parents themselves may have major problems, may be difficult to work with and require additional resources.

Interventions

Intervening with children with conduct disorder, aggression and other antisocial behaviour who are at risk of developing drug and alcohol problems and/or criminal behaviour patterns

Work that has been done in this area has varied from improving neighbourhood facilities for children and young people in an attempt to have a non-specific but wide impact, to focusing on conduct disordered young people and those from other high-risk or vulnerable groups to reduce the risks and strengthen resiliency. This is further explained as follows.

Reducing social and environmental risk factors
Two good examples of the non-specific approach are seen in the Better Beginnings, Better Futures Project from Canada or the Comprehensive Child Development Program from the USA (see Chapter 11).

Training programmes for parents of young children who are behaviourally disturbed
Longitudinal studies in the USA by Anastopoulos and colleagues (1993) and McMahon (1994), and similar research in Canada by Tremblay and colleagues (1996) have shown that if the parents of children with conduct disorder, aggression and other antisocial behaviour are given appropriate professional help, many of those children can be prevented from developing substance use problems and criminal behaviour in later life.

Intervening directly with young people in later childhood and adolescence
Engaging young people in positive long-term relationships is probably as important as any specific treatment intervention, for without it no intervention is likely to be successful.

Services should be *child-centred* and should respect each young person's own priorities for goal-setting, whether or not these appear to be relevant to any intended treatment programme. There is no one set of interventions that will work with all young people, and this must be taken into account when monitoring effectiveness. Effectiveness of treatment will depend upon a good assessment of the young person's needs, and an appropriate care plan that will meet those needs.

One intervention that is often helpful is Cognitive–Behavioural Therapy (CBT). CBT for young people is essentially similar to CBT for adults (see Chapter 6). The basic premise for both is that it is the underlying thoughts and beliefs which lead to the emotions which we feel; that often these are distorted or irrational; and that the way of overcoming difficult emotional states is by changing the way we think, and challenging these underlying beliefs. This needs to be done in a way that will appeal to young people, working with their specific beliefs, and any examples used need to be relevant.

The assessment process for young people usually involves obtaining the story from both the parents/carers and the young person, but doing this separately. Where possible information from other sources, such as friends or school, should be sought. Care must be taken not to break confidentiality. Some assessment instruments have been made specifically for young people, e.g. the Reynolds Child Depression Scale (Reynolds, 1991).

In later childhood and adolescence, CBT can be a helpful way of improving behavioural disturbance, particularly to reduce abnormal and recurrent aggression, a known risk factor for drug and alcohol problems and criminality. Lochman and Wells describe an Anger Coping Programme which has been used at the transition into middle school and early adolescence, and results in reduced aggressive behaviour. In the longer term it has also been shown to be effective in reducing aggression in a three-year follow-up, and also producing significantly lower rates of marijuana, alcohol and drug involvement (Lochman & Wells, 1996). The boys who had learned to cope with anger were functioning at follow-up within the range of a non-aggressive comparison group. These anger-coping boys also maintained an associated improvement in self-esteem and in social problem-solving skills. Delinquency however was not improved (see Chapter 14).

Intervening with children and adolescents from other vulnerability groups who are at high risk of developing drug and alcohol problems and/or dependence

Assessment

Bearing in mind that the client should be choosing his or her own goals, the assessment can be subdivided into the following parts:

(1) the identification of any current drinking or drug-taking behaviour
(2) the identification of risk/vulnerability factors

(3) an assessment of the current impact of these risk factors
(4) an assessment of protective (resiliency) factors

Collaborative care planning is required to

(1) identify ways to reduce the impact of identified risk factors, and thereby minimise the harm, and
(2) identify ways to enhance protective factors.

Assisting natural recovery for young people by reducing the harm from substance use–related problems

This seems to generally involve two processes:

(1) displacing drugs from their central place in the individual's life
(2) learning different ways to deal with underlying problems and stress

Finding a new peer group is often a major part of natural recovery for adolescents.

Reducing the harm from alcohol- and drug-related problems and allowing natural recovery processes to take place occur across the spectrum of biopsychosocial problems and across the lifespan. A typical example is the reduction of mental health problems associated with substance use. Intervention to address such factors and treat existing mental illness can reduce severity of substance use.

Young people with a psychiatric illness have an increased risk of substance use. It is a particularly important source of concern because mental health problems comprise one of the risk factors for later substance use and any young person who undergoes a mental health assessment is now classified as vulnerable to, or at high risk of, developing a substance use problem. For those that do suffer from associated mental health problems other difficulties are commonly present. Often the risk factors are multiple and the needs complex. For example, there is a strong link between homelessness and poor mental health. One study of homeless young people (Klee & Reid, 1998) showed the following results: '...82% reporting psychological symptoms such as depression (62%), aggression (49%), anxiety (43%) and paranoid delusions (34%). Nearly half (47%) said that loneliness was a problem....' The same study showed that self-medication with drugs was common, 71% self-medicating for depression.

Shared vulnerability factors such as early trauma, separations, genetic loading and social disadvantage may explain co-morbidity of mental illness and substance use better than the self-medication model (e.g. postulating symptomatic relief of depression by taking stimulant drugs). (See Chapter 16 for more details.)

Increasing motivation for quitting drug use or moderating drinking

Few adolescents will be motivated to tackle their substance use problems. Indeed most will not be willing to recognise that they have a problem. The way forward is not by confrontation, but to view each young person's situation holistically. Drugs or drink will almost invariably be only one of many problems, and helping a young person tackle those other problems in whatever order of priority they wish will indirectly help a substance use problem. Yet this should not prevent the worker making a professional assessment of the client's needs rather than wants, nor should it stop working in partnership with the client to prioritise goals. Of key importance in this process is the early establishment of a sound relationship with the young persons, in order to be able to empathise with them, and see life through their eyes. Without this basic step any needs assessment will be distorted.

As they begin to mature many young people do become more receptive to tackling a drug or drink problem. In a survey of US college students (Martin *et al.*, 1983), four reasons were found to be the most common causes for quitting:

(1) health reasons
(2) mental and emotional reasons
(3) dislike of the effects of the drug
(4) simple loss of interest in the drug and its effects

Interventions with young people can be subdivided into

- direct interventions to reduce risk factors or heighten resiliency and
- interventions through their parents.

Intervening to heighten the resiliency of young people and adolescents

Common resiliency factors and useful coping strategies that help protect young people in the vulnerable or high-risk categories have been demonstrated in a variety of studies. These include research findings from British children at risk because of severe family dysfunction (Rutter, 1985), American children of mentally ill parents (Beardsley & Podorefsky, 1988), a 30-year longitudinal study of a multiracial cohort of children born on the island of Kauai, Hawaii (Werner & Smith, 1982), young people coping with diabetes (Schwartz *et al.*, 1989) concentration camp survivors (Moskowitz, 1983), children of alcoholic families (Berlin & Davis, 1989), Columbian street children (Felsman, 1989), survivors of cancers (Beardsley, 1989) and young people from the inner city living in poverty (Luthar, 1991). The identification of their resiliency factors and beneficial coping strategies enables them to be transposed to other circumstances, to help young people identified as being in one of the vulnerable groups avoid becoming enmeshed in criminal or substance use behaviour patterns.

According to Albee (1985), there are seven ways in which the goals of prevention of substance use problems can be met, three being reduction efforts aimed at decreasing the degree of organic risk factors, stress and/or exploitation, and four methods being promotion efforts aimed at improving coping skills, competency, self-esteem and/or social support. The following categories of interventions can be identified to aid this process.

Accurate information and advice is essential (Shiner & Newburn, 1996) in order to aid behaviour change. This is in spite of the fact that a review of the literature (Botvin & Botvin, 1992) and meta-analytic studies (Bangert-Drowns, 1988) confirm that arming adolescents in the classroom with appropriate information and providing young people with activities designed to serve as alternatives to drug use when they are not regarded as being at high risk are both ineffective from the point of view of preventing drug use. The provision of accurate information and advice has implications for the training of youth workers. Ignorance and misconceptions among young people about substance use are commonplace. Accurate information and advice is important because harm can be done from minimal drug use, particularly from the sharing of injecting equipment. Homeless young people are known to be at particularly high risk of sharing injecting equipment.

Life skills training (social skills and coping skills training) with booster sessions have been shown to be effective in reducing substance use problems in adolescents for two years (Botvin & Tortu, 1988). Unfortunately these programmes have not been evaluated beyond that time.

Enhancing environmental support. Although targeted life skills training for adolescents almost certainly helps enhance protective factors, it seems that programmes that include community-level components for high-risk or vulnerable youths are the most effective (Meyer, 1995). Such components might include improving social support, helping establish an alternative peer group, finding accommodation for the homeless and working with the family. Often enlisting the support of one responsible adult to befriend and guide the young person can be of great help. Occasionally a teacher may be in a position to act in this way.

Changing expectations of gender roles and sexuality. Although gender itself is not open to change, expectations of the gender role by society, by family members and by the individual himself or herself are open to adaptation. The most resilient girls appear to come from households that encourage risk-taking and independence. In contrast resilient boys tend to come from households characterised by structure and rules and by encouragement of emotional responsiveness. Expectations relating to sexuality are essential to address as traumatic situations related to their sexuality may precipitate emotional illness and substance use in young people.

Education for young vulnerable people excluded from school. Those who have been suspended and later excluded for conduct disorder, drug use or repeated failed school attendance fall into a vulnerable group at high risk of future drug problems and dependence. This is the most difficult group to treat. Nations vary as to their attitudes underlying school exclusion. US policy tends towards zero tolerance of conduct disorder, whereas Australia and the UK are more flexible. Some young people who have been excluded are placed in special schools, some in other mainstream schools and some have dual enrollment. In the UK there are special pupil referral units for some excluded young people. However, like helping provide accommodation for the homeless, the answer is not simply the provision of schools.

Although this high-risk group is relatively easy to locate, studies show that most young people excluded from school tend to be anti-authority, inattentive, and trying to cope with a range of other problems in their lives. Interventions should be realistic and take account of the age of the young person and the fact that school and the young person have mutually rejected each other, and give priority to the other multiple apparent problems that are almost always present. The majority of excluded young people are from low-income single-parent families. Many are already involved in serious crime and drug use. Many are disaffected and marginalised. Their conduct disorder and that of their classmates makes academic achievement difficult or impossible. Diversionary activities for older young people are generally unhelpful. Some adolescents can be placed in work experience or a similar placement according to the interests they specify in assessments. However, in the UK if they are at an age when they are ready to leave the system and do not wish to turn up for follow-up, they do not have to. Working jointly with the families of younger children and schoolteachers to aid school academic performance or to develop a good relationship with one adult at an earlier stage is perhaps the most constructive way forward. Both of these factors help protect young people from later substance use problems.

Multisystemic therapy (MST)

MST has been developed by Henggeler and colleagues and an overview of the research conducted (Henggeler, 1998) has demonstrated it to be an effective treatment for serious juvenile offending, antisocial behaviour disorders and drug use in young people. Studies of MST show its efficacy in preventing future drug use (Henggeler *et al.*, 1992) and drug-related arrests (Henggeler *et al.*, 1997). It is also an effective treatment for serious juvenile offenders, including violent and chronic juvenile offenders in both urban (Henggeler *et al.*, 1992; Borduin *et al.*, 1995) and rural (Henggeler *et al.*, 1997) locations. Research into the use of

MST with juvenile sex offenders has also demonstrated beneficial results (Borduin *et al.*, 1990), and it is a useful treatment for the parents of those who face child abuse and neglect (Brunk *et al.*, 1987).

MST entails a series of community-based behavioural treatment interventions focusing on the family, peer group and school. Although closely allied to the Community Reinforcement Approach (CRA), it is theoretically grounded in general systems theory and the theory of social ecology. The Washington State Institute for Public Policy reported in 1998 that MST was the most cost-effective of a wide variety of treatments to reduce serious criminal behaviour. Henggeler and colleagues (1998a) describe the methods they have developed in their book, *Multisystemic Treatment of Antisocial Behaviour in Children and Adolescents*.

Assessments for MST are conducted in the natural environment of the young person and his or her family (e.g. school, home and community) and involve gathering information from a number of sources. Family functioning is assessed according to the degree of warmth and control of parent–child interactions and to parenting style.

MST interventions through the parents
The aim of *intervening with the family* is to help parents develop an authoritative parenting style where there is not only a warm relationship responding to the reasonable needs of the child, but also expectations and well-defined rules. (See Chapter 15 for more details.)

Other MST interventions
Other MST interventions include *changing relationships with peers* and *finding new peer groups*. Some children are neglected or rejected by their peers and become socially isolated. Those who are neglected tend to internalise their problems, becoming anxious and/or depressed. Those who are actively rejected by their peers tend to externalise their problems, and are at risk of school failure and delinquency (Hoza *et al.*, 1995).

Interventions focus on social skills training (where this is appropriate), enhancing association with pro-social peers and reducing or stopping association with deviant peers. Interventions to encourage association with pro-social peers and discourage association with deviant peers are usually best facilitated through parents, who are encouraged to provide opportunities for social contact outside the family and, while supervising such contact, manage the interactions of the children with their peers. This may be aided by rewards for associating with pro-social peers and disincentives for associating with deviant peers.

If emotional and behavioural disturbance is apparent only in the home environment, *school-related interventions* may be unnecessary. However, the usual scenario is that difficulties extend across both home and school settings, and the parents and school need to collaborate to provide a consistency of approach, with the parents assuming responsibility for the bulk of the work, if success is to be achieved.

Where the youth's poor academic performance is linked with low intellectual ability, there should be less effort at raising grades and more effort at sustaining reasonable efforts and developing other skills. This may involve redefining parental expectations. After years of academic frustration and failure to live up to parental requirements, many young people rebel in a destructive manner. In such cases the primary task is to find ways of capitalising on the young person's strengths in order to promote long-term vocational success. It is important to overcome feelings of incompetence, which tend to occur if the family emphasises academic achievement. Effort rather than results should be rewarded. However, the importance of fostering academic achievement is not always recognised by parents, particularly those with little formal education themselves. Academic achievement helps protect children against subsequent substance use problems or other behavioural difficulties (HAS, 1996; 2001).

The MST professional's role is to help plan meetings with the school personnel, give advice regarding behaviour problems where appropriate, develop a system for monitoring interventions and provide feedback regarding outcomes.

Parents/carers themselves may need help

Although the emphasis of family-focused interventions is to reduce or eliminate antisocial behaviour in young people, such as offending and drug use, individual factors affecting the parents themselves can sometimes act as barriers preventing positive change. For instance, sometimes the parents' own irrational beliefs may prevent them from supporting or helping their children in the most productive way, and some parents need to be offered appropriate individual interventions before positive change can occur.

Depression, anxiety or mixed anxiety/depressive disorders in one or both parents are common when they are trying to cope with an unremittingly stressful home environment due to long-term behavioural problems of the children. Substance use in a parent may underlie, or alternatively be a dysfunctional response to, behavioural disorders in the children. A good professional worker will therefore take time to assess the parents' own irrational beliefs and psychological functioning. Parents and carers may themselves benefit from a number of interventions including CBT to help with the management of depression, assertiveness training, anger management skills, and coping skills or social skills training.

All assessments of young people must therefore be broadly based to include the functioning of families and significant others. By working with the family as an interactive system, family systems therapy may help the individual substance user through the reduction of the problems which parents and carers themselves face. In addition, the assessment process can be used as a vehicle for health promotion to the whole family. Although most young people eventually reduce their substance use without family therapy or other professional intervention, the opportunity of imparting relevant information to family members during the assessment process should not be overlooked. All family members should understand the importance of harm reduction initiatives, especially in relation to the spread of BBVs.

Sometimes simple concrete interventions, e.g. increased social support, or help with debt management, may make a considerable difference to parenting ability and be all that is required to remove the barriers to progress. There is no single or best approach to treatment. A good assessment, clearly recording strengths and substance-related problems and outlining the initial goals of treatment, helps clarify complex cases.

Brief or minimal interventions may be beneficial in some cases, but more intensive long-term treatment programmes should also be available as part of a comprehensive service. Where it is possible to use parents/carers to help decide on and prioritise goals and homework, this can be helpful, particularly when implementing a behavioural modification plan, although the final decision should be left to the substance user.

Young people and dependence on alcohol or drugs

In 1990 when Brown and colleagues first questioned whether dependence occurred at all in young people, tolerance to the substance was generally mild or absent and physical withdrawal syndromes rarely occurred, particularly for alcohol dependence. However, since that time patterns of teenage substance use have changed considerably and the presentation of young people requiring treatment for substance dependence, in the context of complex other problems, is now a major focus of concern. An assessment of the needs of young people with problems from, and/or dependence on, substance use should now be a crucial part of service provision. Treatment services for young people who require medical intervention should be separate from adult services and should incorporate specialist components and liaison applicable to young people's needs. A tiered approach to services has been advocated (HAS, 2001).

Dependence, when it occurs, is usually mild to moderate in adolescence, although earlier onset of experimental and regular use, and changes in the pattern of use towards heroin and cocaine are altering this situation. Adolescents are more likely to be polysubstance users and have higher rates of psychiatric co-morbidity than adults. The nature of presenting problems is often more complex and challenging than amongst adult users of similar substances. The long-term duration of drinking required to produce certain medical conditions (e.g. alcoholic liver cirrhosis and serious neurological damage) means that these markers of severity are not seen in adolescents.

Brown and his colleagues (1990) also raised concerns about the appropriateness of adult twelve-step programmes for adolescents as they advocate total abstinence as the goal, whereas in young people this is often not required. In one study using DSM-IV criteria (Fulkerson *et al.*, 1999), a total of 78 800 students aged 14–18 years were surveyed, and data analysis was carried out on two groups of students, the first sample totalling 9490 and the other 9313. All the students in each of these samples had reported substance use and at least one substance use disorder diagnostic criterion. Analysis of the first sample showed that a single-factor model and correlated two-factor model had similar parameter estimates and fitted the data better than the competing two-factor model. These findings were confirmed in the second sample with the conclusion that DSM-IV substance abuse and dependence criteria may be more optimally structured as a unidimensional construct for those under the age of 18, suggesting that dependence may not occur in adolescence. However, the authors pointed out that a unidimensional structure does not mean that there is not a severity continuum of substance use disorder behaviours in adolescence. Furthermore, it is interesting to note that over half the sample were using three or more substances and that diagnostic criteria endorsement has been found to increase in polydrug users (Harrison *et al.*, 1998). However, this study observed social behaviours in an epidemiological framework and the findings are unlikely to be transferable to populations requiring therapeutic intervention. When dependence is present in those who are under the age of 18, it is more likely to be of a low degree and therefore more open to self-directed change or psychosocial interventions, but this is by no means always the case.

There have been earlier and later studies which do demonstrate dependence in adolescence (Hubbard *et al.*, 1989; Crome *et al.*, 2000). Evaluation showed that heavily dependent adolescent drug users and drinkers were able to reduce substance use and improve psychosocial functioning as a result of treatment, including the use of medical treatments such as substitute prescribing and detoxification following careful assessment to establish the degree of dependence and associated needs.

Those categorised as *good outcome* were more likely to have had supportive parents who were together, to have been in school, training or employment, and to have passed examinations. They are less likely to have had episodes of self-harm and a psychiatric or criminal history (Crome *et al.*, 2000). Other factors predictive of a positive outcome include the use of specific interventions according to need, rather than general supportive counselling, and substitute prescribing in adequate doses. Some doctors, being naturally reticent to prescribe for detoxification or engage in medical treatments of adolescent substance use, hold back too far and prescribe less than is required, with adverse results. There is clearly a need for specialist advice from experienced physicians, integrated with multifaceted services, to address the complexities of adolescent substance dependence.

Those categorised as *poor outcome* are more likely to have had episodes of self-harm, a positive psychiatric history, a family history of substance problems, familial dysfunction and a forensic history, and to have left school early (Crome *et al.*, 2000).

Help for young people with dependent/problem substance use

Young people have needs that are distinct from adults. However mature and streetwise they might feel or appear, young people are vulnerable and reliant on adults for care and guidance. For many, such adult guidance is not available in their personal lives. Professionals therefore have a great responsibility to enable appropriate care.

From a practical viewpoint adolescent drinkers do not as a rule accept or respond to advice that they should stop drinking completely. Indeed when the problem is clearly either non-dependency or a low level of dependency, it may be more appropriate to help them drink more moderately, or to aim for a temporary period of abstinence, than to aim for abstinence on a long-term basis. This supports Brown's view that the twelve-step approach, which focuses on abstinence as a way of life, may not generally be appropriate for adolescent drinkers (Brown *et al.*, 1990). Harmful binge drinking which is strongly reflected in the current UK drink culture is a particular challenge for therapeutic intervention.

However, in the USA twelve-step programmes are advocated for adolescents. One US study (Winters *et al.*, 2000) on the effectiveness of use of the Minnesota Model in the treatment of adolescent drug abusers found that 53% of adolescents who completed the programme of treatment reported either abstinence or a minor lapse for the 12 months following treatment. For those who did not complete the programme the figure was 15%, and for the control group on the waiting list it was 28%. Although most US research has focused on abstinence, some studies have looked at other outcome criteria.

Brown and colleagues (2001) reported four-year outcomes from a twelve-step drug and alcohol treatment centre. There was considerable variability in patterns of substance use. The greatest reduction was in stimulant use, some reduction in alcohol and cannabis use, but little change in tobacco use, which continued at 75%. Deas and Thomas (2001) reported on ten controlled studies since 1990, with positive effects noted for family therapy. Studies using behavioural therapy and CBT were associated with improvements in drug use, school and work attendance.

There is evidence that the longer an adolescent remains in treatment, the better the outcome (Kaminer, 1994). Where follow-up has been undertaken, relapse rates are high (35–85%), and relapse is usually in response to social pressure (Doyle *et al.*, 1994).

The characteristics of those who work with adolescent substance users also have a bearing on treatment outcome. It is clear that the amount of professional experience, the competence of workers in taking a problem-solving approach and the availability of volunteers to interact with the adolescent clients, all have a beneficial effect on outcome (Friedman *et al.*, 1989). However, the employment of staff with past addiction problems to work with adolescent substance users does not appear to have a beneficial effect (Catalano *et al.*, 1990–1991).

Family therapy and CBT have been shown to be particularly useful for adolescents with substance use disorders. If the family is involved, there is an increased likelihood that the adolescent client will complete the treatment programme. It has also been shown that family therapy reduces problem behaviour during treatment (Barrett *et al.*, 1988).

It is clear that many adolescent substance users have poor social skills and limited social networks, and that these clients are at very high risk of becoming dependent on alcohol or drugs in later life. Many approaches using CBT, including relapse prevention, have been shown to be just as useful for adolescents with drink and drug problems as they are for adult substance users (Kaminer, 1994). Adolescent substance users in receipt of CBT show improvements in family functioning, school adjustment, peer and other social relationships, legal problems and psychiatric disturbance.

There are a few specialist residential rehabilitation centres for drug-dependent adolescents in the USA (some are very confrontative and one has been described as a boot camp). There is only one residential rehabilitation centre for adolescents in the UK. Residential rehabilitation houses for adults with substance use problems should not, and indeed most do not, accept young people under 16 years. It is better for a young person to go to an establishment for young people which is not specifically designed to accommodate substance users.

The treatment setting – whether as an inpatient, residential or outpatient – appears to be less important than the treatment programme (Hubbard *et al.*, 1989). However, it may be appropriate for some early teenage substance users to be placed in a residential setting in order to provide an alternative social framework. One of the most important interventions is to provide adequate social support.

For those under 16 who require medical treatment for dependence, especially substitute medication, a multi-disciplinary approach should be adopted and parents involved wherever possible. The prescription of substitute drugs such as methadone will be appropriate and needed in some cases (Crome *et al.*, 2000). Such prescribing should always be on a short- to medium-term basis. No long-term prescribing should be undertaken for this age group. Few young people require alcohol detoxification. It is believed to normally take about ten years of regular heavy drinking to establish a true alcohol dependency and there is therefore a greater window of opportunity for non-medical interventions compared to nicotine or opiate dependency. If adult services are not to be used for those young people who do require substitute prescribing/detoxification, a few general practitioners (GPs) may wish to be involved in treatment provision, but should only do so with expert guidance. Services with expertise in both drugs and young people and with multi-disciplinary resources are the ideal. Links with adolescent psychiatry, education, youth offending services and primary health care are all important components of young people's treatment services.

Conclusion

There is a need for services for young people with problematic use of drugs and alcohol which are separate from adult substance use services. They should be differently resourced and integrated with other sources of help for young people. Generic young peoples' services should focus on preventing substance use problems in later life in those at high risk of becoming alcohol or drug dependent. Services should work with a broad-spectrum approach, addressing the whole young person and his or her problems. A comprehensive specialist service for young people should include outreach, access to primary health care, day care, and community drug and alcohol staff who provide widely based assessments and specific interventions that are appropriate for young people. In addition, there should be provision for appropriate outpatient and inpatient detoxification, and for residential rehabilitation where necessary.

Generalisation of adult models risks the over-diagnosis of dependence though this undoubtedly does occur in young people. When dependence has developed it is usually mild in degree, and many young problem/dependent drinkers are able to drink in a controlled way later in life. Twelve-step therapy for most young dependent drinkers is therefore inappropriate, although twelve-step therapy for young drug users does have a place. Family therapy and multisystemic therapy have an acknowledged place in treatment. A problem-solving approach and Cognitive–Behavioural Therapy, involving social skills training and coping skills training, are known to be particularly useful for young people. Social interventions, particularly those which help structure and stabilise young people's lives such as housing, stable relationships and education/employment, are of paramount importance.

Chapter 4
Prevention and Treatment Services for Adults

Prevention

Background

Adult prevention services mainly centre on alcohol rather than drugs, and the structure of this chapter will reflect this. There are few adults who develop a drug problem for the first time without having taken drugs or even developed a drug problem as a young person. However, it does happen and appears to be increasing as the prevalence of primary drug use extends into an older age range. Some environments, such as prisons, are increasingly likely to expose people to the opportunity for drug use for the first time in adulthood. Sometimes an adult will develop an alcohol problem and then move on to opiate or other drug use, but this is unusual. This may be the result of ready availability of alcohol, the fact that it is legal to drink as an adult, and the fact that most of the effects that are looked for by those who eventually develop a substance use problem can be obtained through drinking alcohol.

Prescribed and over-the-counter (OTC) medicines are also legally and readily available for adults, although community pharmacists are well aware of the dangers of selling these. There is general agreement among UK community pharmacists not to sell codeine-based cough linctus or other opiate containing medicines on a repeat basis because of their potential to generate and maintain opiate dependence. Some adults are more likely than others to become dependent and may inadvertently become dependent on opiates or benzodiazepines in the course of medical treatment. Some may seek help from specialist services or be referred by their doctor. Just as those who were prescribed through the British System developed a psychological gain to opiate analgesia, so, too, does the psychological side of the dependence syndrome predominate in this group.

The balance of risk and resiliency factors which may help determine whether or not a young person develops problem substance use and dependence continues into adulthood and throughout the lifespan whilst the environmental triggers may increase or decrease. For adults additional new risk factors may emerge such as unemployment, social exclusion, social isolation, depression and prison, but in turn these can be balanced by the emergence of additional resiliency factors, or strengths, particularly gainful employment, good problem-solving and coping skills, and the support of friends and family. Good psychosocial functioning facilitates this. It is easier to make friends if you are a good conversationalist, and you are more likely to have a successful job interview if you are good at presenting yourself. Sometimes the balance of risks versus strengths changes in adult life and when this happens problem drinking and sometimes problem drug use may occur as is shown in the following case study.

CASE STUDY

Client C was physically and sexually abused in childhood by his stepfather and so was at risk of developing a substance use problem. However, in spite of initial relationship difficulties, he settled down with a supportive partner and they had two children. All went well for a time, but when he was 36 the relationship broke down and client C left the household to live on his own. He became lonely and depressed and every evening started going to his local pub where he drank heavily. One day he met a woman in the pub and struck up a relationship with her. It was only after they had moved in together that he discovered she was a regular heroin user. Client C was horrified but stayed with her and encouraged her to stop taking drugs. One day he tried some heroin just to see what it was like. It was not long before he, too, was addicted.

A prevention service for young people in one of the *vulnerable* groups should help prevent many adults developing drink or drug problems at a later stage in life but, like client C, not all will be identified. Many who are identified will remain at high risk. In practice, if substance use problems or dependence emerge, reducing the risks and heightening resiliency is often not adequate and additional treatments become necessary.

Primary and secondary prevention initiatives for adults

The primary prevention of adult substance use implies interventions aimed at stopping any substance use at all, and around the world it varies according to culture and creed, but primary prevention initiatives are generally focused on young people and mainly delivered in the classroom. Although adults are encouraged never to use drugs, most secondary prevention initiatives are focused on alcohol. They are aimed at older age groups, with the goal of preventing harm by advocating drinking only at levels where there is a low risk of endangering health, or generating other problems and dependence.

Because in most countries prevention initiatives are concentrated in schools, many adult men and women have received no education about *safe* or *low-risk limits*. Apart from a few leaflets in doctors' surgeries, and interventions through the probation service, such as educational groups for those convicted of a drinking and driving offence, there is relatively little in the way of community education for adults about drug use and drinking. However, heavy drinking and some drug use commence in adulthood and some adults develop problem drug

use and dependence. In the UK, for instance, some men go to the pub every night with friends and drink four or five pints of strong lager, not realising that it may lead to potential problems. It is now known that initiation in drug use as an adult often occurs in the prison setting and the associated risks from this are not always understood. Correct factual information is important for adults to enable them to make decisions about their lifestyle and the amount of alcohol they consume. Research studies have yet to confirm that in practice this is a useful undertaking for the prevention of substance use problems and dependence (Humphries & Tucker, 2002). However, as a treatment intervention for those who are already dependent, an analysis of research studies shows that the delivery of factual information through education, lectures and films does not improve outcomes (Miller & Wilbourne, 2002).

Some shock horror television advertisements about drinking and driving do appear to have been beneficial, suggesting that adults may respond in a different way to young people. However, without questioning the responses that might be obtained, politicians have advocated the use of horrific advertisements against drug use on television and posters. These have been evaluated by market research and are said to have reached the target group. Whether it has made things better or worse in the longer term is another matter. Life skills training is well accepted to be helpful in preventing drink and drug use problems in young people (de Haes & Schuurman, 1975; Botvin *et al.*, 1995), and may well have a role in their prevention in adults.

Many adults appear to develop drink or drug dependency problems following an adverse life event such as job loss or loss of a partner, suggesting that inadequate coping skills may lead to a dysfunctional use of alcohol or drugs. For the prevention and treatment of dependence in those cases where regular daily substance use is a consequence of the need to cope with difficult life events or negative emotions, coping skills need to be enhanced. Left with inadequate coping skills, previous patterns of substance use will surface again as soon as the person stops drinking or taking drugs. It may take ten years of excessive drinking to develop alcohol dependency. Yet there are clearly some people who become alcohol dependent in a much shorter time frame. In such people there is always substantial initial psychological gain from drinking, such as drinking to relieve anxiety or low mood, which reinforces a pattern of heavy daily use and of distress in withdrawal.

Some drugs are more prone than alcohol to induce physical dependency, causing tolerance and powerful withdrawal effects. Some people are more able to tolerate physical withdrawals than others. Thus there is a complex interaction between a person's ability to tolerate abstinence effects and the degree of severity of the withdrawal syndrome, which in turn is influenced by the type of drug used and the quantity that is normally consumed. A person's inability to tolerate the physical withdrawal syndrome may lead to drug-taking to alleviate withdrawals and consequent regular daily substance use. Because most people find the opiate withdrawal syndrome so difficult to tolerate, it normally takes only three or four weeks of regular daily heroin use for dependency to become established. On the other hand, because withdrawal symptoms from cannabis are so mild, dependence on this drug is uncommon, despite the fact that many people smoke cannabis on a regular daily basis for several years. When dependence on cannabis does occur it is almost always tied up with marked psychological gain from smoking it.

However, there are many people who develop a habit of consuming regular large quantities of a drug such as alcohol, more as a way of life than as a method of coping with difficult psychological problems. Such people are at risk of developing medical, social, psychological or legal problems, and in addition may develop a dependence on the drug. Alcohol is the prime candidate for early intervention to stop problems and/or dependence occurring, because it is so widely consumed in excessive amounts and because there is a window of opportunity of several years before dependence is established. Opportunistic Brief Interventions (OBIs) are an extremely cost-effective way of preventing future alcohol problems and dependence when targeted at heavy drinkers who are still capable of controlling their alcohol consumption. In spite of this they have been very little used in the UK or elsewhere – a situation which should be a priority to correct. There have been attempts to use similar brief interventions in the illicit drugs field, but research in this area is not well developed, so that it is not possible at the time of writing to draw conclusions from this work. Their use in the prevention of harm from drug-using behaviours is an area for likely benefit. Brief interventions are described in more detail in Chapter 10.

Historical issues and their influence on current practice

Reducing the risk of harm from volatile substance use

In 1979 in the UK the Institute for the Study of Drug Dependence (ISDD) actively promoted various techniques to reduce harm for those sniffing glue and other volatile substances. Over 40% of deaths from this activity in the previous decade had been due to indirect causes such as accidents and injuries from sniffing in dangerous situations, or suffocation from plastic bags. It is an indicator of the ease with which public opinion can misinterpret advice to reduce harm to the extent that ISDD was severely criticised for condoning volatile substance use when it suggested that if people were going to sniff, they should not do it alone and should avoid dangerous places like rooftops, and canal and railway embankments. If they had given this advice ten years later when reducing harm was widely accepted as the way forward for the drugs field, it is unlikely there would have been such a vociferous response.

Reducing the risk of harm from drugs

The redefinition of prevention to embrace the concept of risk reduction from the use of illicit drugs within its historical context has already been explored in Chapter 1. The widening of the concept from harm reduction to public and individual health, to encompass community safety, and the social and psychological aspects of harm reduction has stimulated the development of harm reduction initiatives in the alcohol field.

Reducing the risk of harm from alcohol

The reduction of harm began increasing in importance in the alcohol field in the early 1980s when a change in thinking allowed many alcohol agencies to promote controlled drinking as an attainable treatment goal for some clients (Heather & Robertson, 1981). This particularly applied to those with a low severity of alcohol dependence and lesser levels of alcohol-related problems (Sobell & Sobell, 1995). New measures of success apart from abstinence became needed and, in view of the immense harm brought on by excessive drinking, the reduction of harm was an obvious candidate.

The link between the level of alcohol consumption and harm to individuals and society became accepted. It has been known for many years that, as increasing amounts of alcohol are consumed, there is an increasing likelihood of harm to the individual (Wilson, 1980) and society (Bruun *et al.*, 1975).

Harm from accidents
In the past the amount of harm engendered by alcohol use through accidents has been underestimated. Studies indicate more than twice as much mortality and morbidity occurs than had been previously estimated. About one-third of all accidental deaths in Canada are known to be due to alcohol, with 22.1% caused by motor vehicle accidents, 6.1% by falls, 1.8% by fire and 1.3% by other accidents. Alcohol deaths by both drowning and suicide (1.2% and 13.7%, respectively) have been shown to be more than twice the previous estimates (Single & Wortley, 1993).

Drunk driving has now been identified as the largest single cause of alcohol-related deaths in the USA (Harwood *et al.*, 1998) and Canada (Xie *et al.*, 1996). The effects of alcohol on driving performance can begin with the first drink and become measurable at Blood Alcohol Concentrations (BACs) of 20 mg% (Mann *et al.*, 1998). Collision rate is significantly increased at BACs above 50 mg% (Zador, 1991). The use of alcohol has strong associations with psychiatric morbidity as both cause and effect of consumption (see Chapter 16 for details). Attention to the recognition and treatment of depression and other mental illnesses can form an important part of accident prevention strategies.

Effect of alcohol on health

Over time the level of drinking that has been regarded as relatively safe has been modified, and there is now a better understanding of the health benefits of low-level alcohol consumption in older age groups. These benefits have also been underestimated. At low levels of alcohol consumption older men and women are protected from heart disease and strokes. Canadian research has shown that, taking into account the overall drinking levels of the Canadian population, alcohol prevents more deaths than it causes. In 1992 alcohol prevented 7401 deaths in Canada (5162 males and 2239 females). This included deaths due to ischaemic heart disease (4205), stroke (2965), heart failure and ill-defined heart conditions (183), and from various other causes (48) (Single *et al.*, 1996).

However, excessive drinking can be anticipated to cause harm to health if it is continued. The health of women is more easily damaged than that of men because women have less body water than men, so at a cellular level the alcohol is more concentrated, making the bodily tissues more prone to damage.

The preventive paradox and binge drinking
The first British attempt to define a *safe drinking limit* was in 1979 when the Royal College of Psychiatrists (1979) put forward 50 UK units per week as the safe limit for men, with 26–50 units categorised as *moderate drinking*. However, Kreitman suggested that there was no *safe limit*, as many people who drank less than 50 units per week also developed alcohol-related problems. Furthermore, although these problems occurred considerably less frequently than in those above this limit, the majority (85%) of all alcohol problems occurred below 50 units per week for men and below 35 per week for women because so many more people drank at this level (Kreitman, 1986). This became known as the *preventive paradox*. It was argued that all drinkers are at risk and a population strategy to reduce alcohol consumption at all drinking levels would be more productive than a strategy to direct preventive efforts towards high-risk drinkers.

Later Stockwell and colleagues (1996) combined Kreitman's data with their own to show that the preventive paradox disappeared when episodes of binge drinking, instead of average consumption, were used to predict the occurrence of alcohol-related problems. Their analysis showed that 84% of those in the *low average consumption* group should be redefined as being in the high-risk category when consumption was measured in terms of alcohol intake on the heaviest drinking day. This demonstrated clearly the importance of binge drinking.

Later still Skog (1999) contended that the findings of Stockwell and colleagues seemed to 'harbour a second-order preventive paradox' for binge drinkers. Taking as his criterion drunkenness rather than heavy alcohol consumption, he suggested that most episodes of drunkenness might be found among drinkers with a low average consumption because these drinkers became drunk more easily. In a survey of the population of Norway he showed that although 83% of all respondents with a high average consumption of alcohol reported at least one episode of high intake compared to 27% of low average drinkers, 76% of all cases of intoxication were to be found in this low average drinking category. He concluded that the 'preventive paradox had reappeared'.

The works of both Stockwell and Skog have subsequently been confirmed by Gmel and colleagues, who conducted telephone interviews on 1256 current drinkers in Switzerland. Using a quantity–frequency instrument to determine overall consumption and a cut-off point of average daily consumption of 20 g for women and 30 g for men, people were divided into moderate or hazardous drinkers. Binge drinking was defined as taking four or more drinks on an occasion for women, and five or more for men. Binge drinkers reported more problems than non-binge drinkers confirming the work by Stockwell and colleagues, and binge drinkers were more numerous in the moderate drinking group, which constituted the majority of drinkers, in accordance with Skog's view (Gmel *et al.*, 2001).

Gmel made considerable progress towards overcoming a major criticism of the preventive paradox – that the severity of alcohol problems should be considered within the analysis. It is clear that the preventive paradox is a reality and that, in addition to average consumption, binge drinking is an important factor in the development of alcohol problems. Policy makers need to reconsider prevention messages and targets in the light of these research findings.

A redefinition of 'safe' drinking levels for healthy adults in the UK

For some people any alcohol is potentially harmful, e.g. those with chronic hepatitis C, but for ordinary healthy adults there is a recognised weekly limit which is considered not to endanger health although it can lead to other problems like impaired driving, poor emotional control and so on. The overall weekly consumption now considered to be *safe* (better termed *low-risk limits* than *safe limits*) was redefined in the UK in 1987. The previous definition of safe drinking limits of 50 units for men and 35 for women was abandoned and redefined in a unified view between the Royal Colleges of Psychiatrists, Physicians and GPs. These colleges also determined the drinking level considered to be definitely *harmful*, and the level which was believed to be *hazardous* but which did not always cause harm. Each of the three Royal Colleges produced documents detailing the harm that can occur through excessive regular alcohol consumption (Royal College of GPs, 1986; Royal College of Psychiatrists, 1986; Royal College of Physicians, 1987) and stating the new drinking limits. These were:

50 units per week or more for men and more than 35 units per week for women	*Harmful drinking* (will cause harm)
21–49 units per week for men and 14–35 units per week for women	*Hazardous drinking* (may cause harm)
up to 21 units per week for men and up to 14 units per week for women	*low-risk limits* (considered safe to drink at this level)

(In the UK one unit or standard drink contains 8 g of alcohol.)

The introduction of daily rather than weekly limits
In view of the fact that lower levels of alcohol consumption were shown to give some benefit to the cardiovascular system by preventing coronary heart disease (Marmot & Brunner, 1991), the three Royal Colleges (Report of a Joint Working Group of Royal Colleges of Physicians, Psychiatrists & GPs, 1995) and the British Medical Association (1995) reviewed the above limits but recommended that they should be continued.

However, shortly after this a government report, entitled *Sensible Drinking* (DH, 1995), gave advice to men over 40 and women of post-menopausal age, who are the two groups likely to benefit from a reduction in coronary heart disease by moderate drinking. They suggested that women should continue to be advised to drink at lower levels than men but that the units of alcohol should be cast in daily rather than weekly terms for both men and women. The guidance for men was that there is a health benefit of drinking one unit per day, but the maximum health advantage lay between one and two units per day. The report stated that regular consumption of three or four units per day will not accrue significant health risks, but that consistently drinking four or more units per day does carry a progressive health risk. For post-menopausal women the report recommended that the major part of the health benefit can be obtained by drinking one unit of alcohol per day, with the maximum health advantage lying between one and two units per day. Regular consumption of between two and three units per day will not accrue significant health risks, but consistently drinking three or more units per day does incur a progressive health risk. The report also recommended that after an episode of heavy drinking, it is advisable to refrain from drinking for 48 hours to allow tissues to recover.

The change of advice from weekly to daily limits of consumption, helping to moderate the harm from binge drinking, is in some ways a favourable move. New Zealand and Australia have gone one stage better and given specific advice for maximum weekly and maximum daily consumption. Unfortunately in the UK the DH's own press release totally misrepresented the 1995 report. The first sentence stated:

A government report published today says that there should be a small increase in the present recommended drinking levels.

It led to outbursts of incredulous anger by commentators. This was followed by rejection of the UK revision from weekly to daily units by the medical establishment (Edwards, 1996; Marmot, 1996). The end result has been confusion rather than clarification.

International variations

International variations in nomenclature

To add to this confusion there are national differences over what constitutes a standard drink and the way alcohol concentration is defined. A single measure of spirits in Scotland and Northern Ireland is one and a half times that in England and Wales (the latter being classified in the UK as one unit). If someone says he or she had a single glass of wine, or a bottle or can of beer, the amount of alcohol consumed may vary greatly. A pub wineglass holds 125 or 175 ml, but the large tulip glasses seen in fashionable restaurants contain 250 ml. Some pubs will serve a large tulip glass when the request is for a single glass of wine. A pub glass of thin Rhine wine might contain 11 g alcohol, but your host's generous glass of stronger Pouilly Fuisse may contain 40 g. Similarly a small bottle of weak beer may contain 8 g alcohol, but a large can of strong beer may hold 35 g.

Different countries may define concentration in different ways. Concentration is expressed as percentage alcohol by volume (ABV) or % v/v in Europe, but in the USA it is expressed as percentage proof. In the USA 100% proof is 50% v/v (50% ABV), but in the UK 100% proof is 57% v/v (57% ABV) which is the concentration able to ignite gunpowder. Concentration can differ widely among apparently similar drinks:

- the strengths of beers are often around 4% but vary from 3.4% to 9% ABV;
- red and white wines, commonly about 12% ABV, range from 8% to 13%; and
- spirits range from 37.5% to 57.3% ABV.

Furthermore, the amount of alcohol in one unit, or standard drink, varies from country to country. In the USA it is 14 g; in Canada, 13.6 g; in New Zealand and Australia, 10 g; and in the UK, 8 g.

The evidence from Canada and the USA confirm that the UK safe limit advice of four UK units per day, if consumed regularly, carries with it a significant health risk. Canadian data suggest that 25% of the population experience two or more adverse consequences of drinking over a period of one year if the regular daily consumption level is at the level of two and a half US or Canadian standard drinks per day (totalling 35 and 34 g, respectively) (Room *et al.*, 1995). Additionally, there is a serious risk of alcohol dependence in those who regularly have three standard Canadian drinks a day (totalling 40.8 g) [which is roughly equivalent to five UK standard drinks per day]. Midanik (1995) has shown that 20% of North American men and women who drink an average of three drinks per day (totalling 42 g) were, according to ICD-10 classification, alcohol dependent.

The national differences in definition as to what constitutes a unit or standard drink is not just confusing for travellers – as most large drinking firms are multinationals, and beers, wines and spirits are imported and exported everywhere – it confuses everyone and has led to some misinterpretation in the literature. There needs to be urgent international agreement as to what constitutes one standard drink and how to express concentration. If this were achieved and the labels on bottles stated clearly how many agreed international units are contained within each bottle of beer or wine, public health messages would be more effective and people would be able to more readily avoid alcohol-related harm to themselves and others.

International comparisons of health problems from drinking at high levels

On current criteria, international comparisons of per capita consumption suggest that the UK has been drinking less and experiencing lower rates of alcohol-related problems than the majority of European countries, Australia and the USA,

although the USA has been drinking less than the UK per capita since 1993. Traditionally deaths from hepatic cirrhosis have been taken as an indicator of alcohol consumption at harmful levels both for different countries and different professional groups within each country. However, this must now be reviewed in the light of hepatitis C. The USA has a very high cirrhosis death rate, but also has one of the highest national prevalence rates for hepatitis C. Better indicators of harmful drinking are now required if reliable international comparisons are to be made.

Alcohol consumption and pregnancy

The risks to the foetus from heavy drinking in pregnancy are portrayed in Chapter 18. They were first recognised by French researchers in 1968 when special characteristics of infants born to alcoholic mothers were noted and described (Lemoine *et al.*, 1968). However, it was not until the *Lancet* published an article five years later (Jones *et al.*, 1973) that the medical establishment accepted the condition now known as the foetal alcohol syndrome.

Harm reduction approaches have not been overwhelmingly successful in preventing the foetal alcohol syndrome in any country. Although there is no scientific evidence that it can be caused by low levels of drinking, the Health Education Authority in the UK originally recommended that pregnant women should stop drinking alcohol altogether. This was later moderated by the UK government's 1995 *Sensible Drinking* advice, which was that women who are pregnant or trying to become pregnant should not drink more than one or two units of alcohol once or twice a week and should avoid episodes of intoxication (DH, 1995). In general this advice appears to have been heeded by moderate drinkers. Those who have an already established alcohol dependency quite understandably have a problem in controlling their drinking at the recommended levels. Thus, although many of those at the very heavy drinking end of the spectrum have reduced or impaired fertility, this advice may go unheeded for those to whom it is most important.

National warning labels on bottles

Similarly, in the USA attempts to reduce drinking in pregnancy by the introduction of warning labels on drinks has only been effective with low-risk drinkers (Hankin, 1994), although there is evidence that most heavy drinkers have read and understood the warning. The US warning label, which came into force in 1989, also warns about drinking and driving or operating machinery. It reads:

GOVERNMENT WARNING
(1) According to the Surgeon General, women should not drink alcoholic beverages during pregnancy because of the risk of birth defects.
(2) Consumption of alcoholic beverages impairs your ability to drive a car or operate machinery, and may cause health problems.

Studies as to the usefulness of this warning label suggest that an increasing number of people become aware of the content of the label over a four- or five-year period. After this time the curve flattens off. After five years about half of all drinkers had become aware of the label and were being reached by at least some of its messages, while more than 80% of heavy drinkers were aware of the label and its contents after only three and a half years. Thus target groups, such as those who purchase, handle and drink large quantities of alcoholic drinks, and who are more at risk of problem drinking, are seeing the label and its content at an earlier time. In spite of the fact that labelling legislation is justifiable to both officials and the public on a right-to-know basis, and can be achieved at extremely low cost for both government and industry, alcohol warning labels are, at the time of writing, mandatory only in Mexico, India and the USA.

National and local strategies to prevent harm

National strategies

In the UK efforts to reduce alcohol-related harm changed when a public health perspective was first promoted by Bruun and colleagues (1975) in a very influential book entitled *Alcohol Control Policies in Public Health Perspective*. This concentrated on preventing harm to populations, and showed evidence that lowering the overall per capita consumption of alcohol within a population by fiscal, legislative or other means was associated with a reduction in alcohol problems. This principle became widely accepted. In the UK the document *Drinking Sensibly* (DH, 1981) stated:

> The experience in other countries tends to confirm the link between total alcohol consumption and harm. What this implies is that, when total consumption increases, the increase is distributed, to some extent at least, in increased consumption at every level of drinking, with some who had a previously high, but tolerable, level of drinking becoming problem drinkers.

The work of Bruun and colleagues had a marked impact on alcohol consumption and alcohol policy at a national level throughout the world. Subsequently, in most industrialised Western countries drinking has declined, in some cases substantially.

However, it was not until 1994 that the concept of harm reduction entered the alcohol literature, with the spotlight on drinking patterns, when work from national survey data from Australia (Stockwell *et al.*, 1994), Canada (Single & Wortley, 1993) and the USA (Midanik *et al.*, 1994) showed the importance of focusing on the prevention of harm from heavy drinking occasions. It was this concentration on drinking patterns, and in particular binge drinking, rather than overall consumption that enabled the reduction of harm to take on a wider meaning for drinkers with recommendations which moved away from quantities of alcohol consumed per week to measures that could be taken to reduce problems that accrue from drinking binges.

In 1994 the evidence base of useful ways to influence drinking in society by both national and local initiatives was thoroughly reviewed by experts in another book called *Alcohol Policy and the Public Good* (APPG) (Edwards *et al.*, 1994). Although the evidence for reducing overall per capita consumption was endorsed, much of what was new in this later book centred on interventions aimed at reducing the harmful consequences of drinking

(Single, 1995). APPG included a comprehensive assessment of the scientific evidence on everything that governments could utilise to reduce the harm from drinking through a public health approach, from fiscal measures, individual per capita units of consumption through to education via warning labels on bottles.

Local strategies

Tether and Robinson (1986) from the UK highlighted local initiatives which also could be highly effective in the prevention of drink problems. Their book focused on methods of reducing alcohol consumption within local communities by attention to education, advertising, media presentation, licensing and alcohol policies in the workplace.

More recent harm reduction approaches have focused on local drinking contexts and environments, with the aim of reducing harm from violence. Examples include the use of safety glasses to reduce the risk of injury, guidelines for servers of alcohol, the design of drinking venues, designated non-drinking drivers, the use of trained door staff at nightclubs and some public houses, and controls over drinking in public places such as town centres, shopping precincts and football matches.

Safety glasses
The substitution of tempered glass was suggested by Shepherd (1994) because some of the more severe injuries from bar fights are caused by using broken glasses or bottles, and these injuries could be reduced substantially by the universal use of toughened glass in bars and clubs. The glasses most implicated are the straight-sided one pint (568 ml) capacity, however there are risks from all types of glassware, and some authorities believe that attention should be given to the more general issue of the potential use of any bar artefact as a weapon (Plant *et al.*, 1994). In England and Wales between 3500 and 5500 violent offences involving bar glass injury were recorded by the police each year (Shepherd *et al.*, 1990), although the actual number was known to be considerably higher because of underreporting. Tempered glass was and still is slightly more expensive than annealed glass, but the small

price differential is more than offset by the fact that it lasts up to 50 times more cycles of use than ordinary annealed glassware of the same design (Evans, 1987). A number of local authorities in the UK will not now grant a Public Entertainment Licence unless an operator uses toughened glass. As well as drinking glasses, glass bottles have the potential to be used as weapons. In many pubs and clubs servers have stopped selling drinks in bottles.

Food availability
Food availability is associated with a reduced risk of aggression in bars (Graham, 1985). One possible explanation for this is that food is known to slow the rate of absorption of alcohol, reducing the blood alcohol level (Wedel *et al.*, 1991), but it may also be that bars which serve food tend to have less aggressive patrons than those where the focus is solely on drinking. Understanding the benefit of taking food while drinking may be an important harm reduction intervention.

The training of bar staff
As another local initiative, the training of bar staff and other servers should include the degree to which the behaviour of patrons is acceptable. An overpermissive attitude towards a number of different behaviours has been shown to be associated with aggressiveness and violence (Homel & Clark, 1994). These include swearing, sexual activity among patrons, prostitution, drug use, drug-dealing, male rowdiness, male roughness and bumping, and drunkenness. The same study showed that if the bar staff did not attempt to control the patrons' behaviour, and did not themselves act in a responsible way (e.g. serving underage customers), this was related to a high incidence of aggressive behaviour. There is an increasing likelihood of aggression with increasing blood alcohol levels (Graham, 1985). Server intervention training, non-aggressive responses to provocation, new licensing policies and a better enforcement of existing policies are helpful ways to reduce aggression (Stockwell *et al.*, 1995). In England and Wales, under Section 174 of the Licensing Act 1964 (or Section 79 of the Licensing (Scotland) Act 1976), licensees may refuse to admit and may expel anyone who is drunk, violent, quarrelsome

or disorderly. In Scotland the charge of breaching the peace can be interpreted very flexibly as it is intended to cover any type of conduct which involves disorder. In many areas of the UK pubwatch and clubwatch schemes operate. These watch schemes are often highly effective in preventing the occurrence of violent affrays and creating a safer drinking environment. They are essentially a communications network between licensees and the police, which provides all parties with an early warning system to prevent the escalation and spread of trouble.

Door staff

Door supervisors are no longer exclusively male, and the emphasis has shifted from muscle power to persuasion. For many years door staff have been employed in nightclubs, but are now increasingly used by public houses and fast-food outlets. They are the public face of the nightclub or public house management and should be welcoming and trained to deal with different kinds of situation, including fire and public safety, drunkenness, drug use and drug-dealing in a skilled and professional manner. If they are trained to work in a non-aggressive style, there are less likely to be violent incidents. Some UK licensing authorities will only grant Public Entertainment Licences if doormen are registered so that controls can be applied on their training and behaviour. In some cases there have been concerns regarding incidents of drug-dealing among door staff, but local registration can be an effective tool to prevent such behaviour. The training of door staff should encompass legal issues regarding licensing and powers; social skills (to defuse conflict and understand body language); restraint techniques; first aid; drugs recognition; age recognition; safe departure home; and fire safety.

It is not just door staff who require training. The majority of UK companies that own premises where alcohol is sold or served organise induction and career development training for their managers, and this is also happening in many other countries to a greater or lesser extent. In England and Wales most licensing committees expect applicants for liquor licences to possess the National Licensee's Certificate or an equivalent qualification showing that they have successfully completed an appropriate training course. Management skills and approach have more influence on the levels of violence in pubs than any other factor.

Reviewing local initiatives

Thus local action can also instigate public health and community safety initiatives to reduce the harm from drinking. Thom and colleagues (1997) published a review of local action on alcohol problems in England in the ensuing ten years after Tether and Robinson's book. They concluded that although there had been a policy shift towards prevention in the 1970s which had continued in the 1990s, only a narrow range of prevention interventions were utilised at locality level with little emphasis on changing social environments or drinking contexts that encouraged risky drinking behaviour. In other words the recent emphasis on the prevention of harm from heavy drinking episodes was not generally being enacted at locality level. Furthermore, there was an apparent lack of evaluation of many projects, a lack of a good system of dissemination of information about projects and project evaluations, and there was conceptual confusion surrounding the definitions of *prevention* and *harm reduction*.

Treatment

As with many other areas of health care, prevention is cheaper and easier to achieve than treatment. Opportunistic Brief Interventions, particularly Minimal Interventions, are some of the most cost-effective ways of preventing progression from heavy drinking to problem use and dependence. However, if dependence and/or serious problems have developed, treatment for adults may require a wide range of possible interventions. For the more stable with few problems and good psychosocial functioning, a Brief Treatment, perhaps utilising personal and environmental strengths, maybe all that is needed. For others, reducing the harm that has accrued through serious and often multiple substance-related problems may be much more difficult to achieve. The problems that are generally associated with drinking and drug use commonly interfere with the recovery process to a degree that consideration should be given to treating these problems as a priority. For some people these problems may be environmental, such as homelessness, for others personal and social functioning may need to be improved.

Substitute prescribing can be an extremely helpful way of stabilising individual substance users, retaining them in treatment and enabling the delivery of psychosocial interventions. Abstinence should not be disregarded as the final goal, although it may take a long time to be achieved or may never be realised. Relapse prevention techniques and coping skills training will help reduce the frequency of lapses and relapses. Motivational Interviewing (MI) as a background counselling style will help keep the individual moving through the cycle of change, or alternatively one of the other talking therapies described in Chapter 6 together with a stand-alone motivational enhancement intervention may be used.

Harm reduction as treatment

Treatment outcomes are better if problems associated with substance use are addressed, and harm reduction at an individual level aids the recovery process. Conversely it has been known for some time that alcohol- and drug-related problems can delay or impair the recovery process. For instance, psychiatric and family or social problems are recognised to be consistent predictors of poor response to treatment and worse post-treatment outcomes (Moos *et al.*, 1990). Those who are unable to utilise their own strengths either through natural recovery or the use of a brief intervention may need to build up their personal resources (strengths). An alternative way forward is to reduce the harm from the social, psychological, physical and legal problems associated with substance use.

Research indicates that professionals should advise in many instances interventions may be needed to enhance social stability before encouraging abstinence (Wille, 1983). McLellan and colleagues (2000) have shown that the incorporation of interventions to address social problems improves outcome in methadone maintenance therapy. Some of the most effective interventions to enhance the

recovery process are those which counter social problems. For example, a stable partner provides emotional and social support countering social exclusion and isolation. Employment is highly therapeutic and for many a fundamental need for economic reasons. For those trying to resolve a substance use problem, it structures time, enhances self-esteem, and provides a new identity and potential new acquaintances and friends who do not have a drink or drug problem.

In 1979, when Miller and colleagues undertook what was to be the first really comprehensive literature review to compare the effectiveness of different alcohol treatments (Miller & Hester, 1980), they were surprised to find that Hunt and Azrin's Community Reinforcement Approach (CRA) (Hunt & Azrin, 1973) was probably the most effective method of treatment for drinkers. Yet in 1986 Miller commented: 'the Community Reinforcement Approach remains little known and seldom used' (Miller & Hester, 1986a) – a situation which had not changed greatly since that time. The CRA employed specific behavioural measures together with interventions to address social needs in order to reinforce sobriety in a community setting. A number of other papers expanding the approach were published later. Among other things the CRA countered social harm by increasing social support through the establishment of drink-free clubs and behavioural marital therapy. Also in the CRA, with the help of employment training, facilitating employment became a helpful intervention to aid recovery, rather than just being a beneficial outcome of treatment. Those whose life has revolved around drinking may find that their only friends are drinkers and will be socially isolated if they stop drinking. The consequent lack of helpful social support may delay or prevent recovery. Reducing social harm by targeted interventions, e.g. by providing non-drinking volunteer *buddies* to befriend the socially isolated client, is a helpful and appropriate aid to recovery.

Psychological problems associated with substance use, such as anxiety, depression, temper outbursts, poor motivation or lack of self-efficacy (the perception of a person's own ability to overcome difficulties), have also been recognised for many years as harms which can prevent a person overcoming a drink or drug problem. Psychological interventions to reduce these harms are thus important ways of helping someone with a substance use problem move forward. For instance, the treatment of depression and moves to counter poor self-efficacy are both important ways to improve outcomes through reducing psychological harm. Motivational Interviewing, which Miller (1983) devised to improve a client's motivation, has been demonstrated to aid recovery, even when only used as a brief intervention (Saunders *et al.*, 1995).

Although Bandura (1977a) in his original work on Social Learning Theory (SLT) concentrated on the negative reinforcing effects of alcohol (e.g. drinking to relieve anxiety or depression), it became clear that he had underestimated the extent to which positive reinforcement also contributes to the development of repeated drinking and subsequent dependence. The euphoria of stimulant and opiate use and the physiological sensations of warmth and relaxation produced by the effects of alcohol can be extremely pleasurable and as a consequence they can be positively reinforcing, particularly in the early phases of a drinking or drug career. In a similar way the intensely pleasurable 'rush' that drug injectors and smokers get from a sudden bolus of the drug into the system is highly positively reinforcing. Although many drug users are positively reinforced by the 'high' of the oral route, it has a more gradual onset and therefore is less reinforcing than smoking or injecting because of the time it takes for the drug to be absorbed. However, later, as problems develop, the pleasurable aspects are often lost and drinking is undertaken to stop withdrawals. Many chronic heavy drinkers who have progressed to dependency and many longer-term drug users will often say that they no longer get any pleasurable effects from the drug and only use it to stop withdrawals or for its other negatively reinforcing effects.

Attention to the physical health and any outstanding legal problems of individual substance users should also be a key feature of any treatment plan. All drug users should be offered screening for hepatitis B and C and HIV, given appropriate counselling, and offered hepatitis A and B vaccination when appropriate. Assessment of blood-borne virus (BBV) high-risk behaviours must be treated as a priority and regularly reviewed. Attention must be given to any current health problems such as injection abscesses. The reduction of harm in the areas outlined is likely to be highly therapeutic and an important part of the recovery process.

Those with multiple and complex needs generally require a lot of help to reduce the harm from problems associated with substance use. However, apart from current acute health problems and legal difficulties, it is a useful rule of thumb to give only as much help as is needed to overcome a drug or drink problem. The substance users themselves can resolve other problems at a later date.

The degree of outcome success can be monitored to a large extent by recording substance-related problems with the help of an instrument such as the Addiction Severity Index (ASI). Progress can be seen to be made over a period of time as it is sensitive enough to measure small improvements in each of the life problem areas, and drug and alcohol use are part of such an assessment. But the ASI does not measure other important factors such as high-risk BBV behaviour, personal and social functioning, and health symptoms. It also takes a long time to complete and therefore is not professional-friendly. From these points of view the Maudsley Addiction Profile (MAP) (Appendix 13) or the Christo Inventory for Substance-misuse Services (CISS) (Appendix 14) are better instruments for clinical situations and the ASI is better retained as a research tool. The quality of life, the ability to contribute positively to society and the reduction of substance-related harm should be an important part of assessment of progress as these are of more importance than to be completely free of chemicals.

A holistic approach is particularly well suited to those working in the community and community-based specialist drug and alcohol services sharing care with generic professionals such as GPs are well placed to intervene (Waller, 1993). Many substance-related problems are obvious but for those clients where further progress is needed, covert medical, environmental, criminolegal and psychological difficulties may need to be actively sought out. This may include looking for hidden problems like depression. If, having done this, no further impediments to progress can be found, other avenues such as utilising strengths and enhancing psychosocial functioning may be necessary for recovery.

The value of treating clients in their own local community

Some authors believe that treatment of substance users in their own community is the key to success with almost all drink and drug use problems. Here they will have to face all their previous triggers for substance use. Miller and Hester have highlighted research showing that milieu therapy (inpatient as opposed to outpatient treatment) is not cost-effective and suggested that treatment should minimise hospitalisation and residential care and focus primarily on intensive outpatient treatment, oriented towards the prevention of relapse (Miller *et al.*, 1995). Residential programmes, including hospital inpatient treatment, clearly have an important place and independent evaluation has shown them to be an effective resource where there is a clinical need (Gossop *et al.*, 1999). However, for most drinkers and drug users, treatment in their own local community is more appropriate, more desirable and cheaper. Associated environmental problems, such as inadequate housing, debt management, unemployment and family difficulties, can sometimes only be resolved when a person is residing in the community. Reintegration into mainstream society can also only occur in a community setting. For many people recovery from substance use is a slow process and interventions focusing on social and coping factors are best done in the local community, where the psychological associations and triggers of drug use can be tackled head-on. One of the earliest examples of this approach was at the Addicts' Rehabilitation Center in Harlem, New York, where the principle of not breaking links between people and their old habitat was adopted. The stated philosophy of the Center was

> that an addict is not really cured until he can survive in his own drug-ridden neighborhood without falling prey to the environment, and

that his rehabilitation should be accomplished in the same kind of environment that he will have to face when he goes back into the world (*A New Life for You*, 1964).

However, for many people there is insufficient help available to achieve recovery in such stressful situations, and a degree of relocation or social change is a useful prelude to progress.

The relationship between problems, individual functioning and strengths

Harm reduction may allow people to reach a stage where they function normally in society, but dependency is a difficult problem to overcome. Healthy people with normal levels of support, adequate housing, a supportive family, cleared debts and even a job often still find difficulty moving away from dependent use. Many people with average coping skills will slip backwards without further help if they do not have a sufficient combination of internal and external resources to overcome their addiction. People normally have difficulty in coping with adverse irreversible life events or negative emotions. Some manage to come through relatively unscathed, others do not. What may be needed instead of reducing the harm associated with substance use is to help clients consciously strengthen their own internal and external resources to enable them function well enough to cope with almost any adversity. Moos and colleagues (1990) see improving the client's coping and social skills as being particularly relevant, and have listed three treatment approaches for strengthening social support systems in the community: family-oriented treatment, coping skills training and community reinforcement programmes.

The functioning of the individual both at a personal psychological level and at a social level is important to assess. The more fully an individual is functioning at a personal and social level, the more able he or she is to cope with problems when they arise. Functioning well at an individual level enables a person to deal successfully with the environmental, physical health, legal or psychological problems he or she encounters in life. It requires good coping and social skills. Functioning and coping are therefore closely related, and functioning will deteriorate if a person is using alcohol or drugs in a dysfunctional way to help him or her cope with psychological or other problems. Over a prolonged period of time the ability to cope with adverse circumstances or negative emotions, such as sadness, loneliness, anger, boredom, awkwardness and discomfort in social situations and so on, without taking a substance may seem to be lost altogether. As a result when such people become abstinent they feel unable to cope. This harmful and maladaptive way of functioning is a common cause of relapse for all substance users. Lapses and relapses are frequent in those who first become abstinent. Improving normal functioning by skills training has been known since the late 1970s to significantly improve outcomes for both drinkers (Chaney et al., 1978) and drug takers (Platt & Metzger, 1987). Since that time others have confirmed that dependent drinkers who successfully abstain use coping responses to help them maintain abstinence (Allsop & Saunders, 1989; McKay et al., 1999), and have found that cocaine users with better coping skills are more likely to avoid relapse. In a follow-up study of heroin users who had attended residential rehabilitation programmes, Gossop and colleagues (2002) found that those who remained abstinent reported making greater use of cognitive, avoidance and distraction coping responses than those who have lapsed or relapsed, and used these coping techniques more frequently than they had at intake. Together these findings suggest a need to develop and strengthen relapse prevention and relapse coping skills among all substance users whose goal is abstinence.

Functioning is also related to belief in personal ability to do things, or self-efficacy. If someone comes to believe that they are unable to do something, they will either not attempt to do it or will fail if they do try. In turn self-efficacy is related to a person's sense of self-worth and whether he or she has some influence over the environment and his or her future destiny. Sometimes the negative thought processes resulting from depression can adversely affect the perception of self-efficacy, and as a result impair personal or social functioning. Self-efficacy is thus not a fixed entity, but like coping and social skills, if improved, will promote personal and social functioning.

Thus drug and alcohol workers should not just look for an absence of problems and assume that everything is going well. They need to take a rounded view which takes account of strengths as well as weaknesses. Personal functioning may be an indicator of good client strengths, but all individuals have some strengths which they can use to their advantage. Discovering and utilising them, perhaps with the help of Solution-Focused Therapy (SFT), can be a faster route to recovery than sorting out entrenched problems. Cultural aspects (particularly in relation to the drug subculture), personal values and motivation can all be strengths or weaknesses that influence individual functioning, and the extent to which someone is included in, or excluded from, mainstream society may be improved with skilled help. A broad treatment approach is needed for success to be attained.

The historical development of a broad treatment approach

For several years there have been increasing attempts to broaden the treatment approach for both drinkers and drug users. The call from the USA by the Institute of Medicine (IOM, 1990) for 'a broader base to the treatment of problem drinkers' was at that time visionary, even though it was the culmination of many previous attempts to do this. The IOM examined in detail more than 600 outcome studies in the field of alcohol treatment. It took the view that, although no one treatment approach works for all individuals, the provision of appropriate, specific treatment modalities can improve outcome. The effect of alcohol on all aspects of the human body was highlighted as the consistent part of alcohol problems, which in turn are deeply and profoundly modified by a multiplicity of other factors that are highly relevant for treatment. The focus of the IOM's report was on the totality of the context in which drink problems occur. A central feature was the vision of a broad, community-wide network of assessment, referral and case management to undertake differential diagnosis, match patients to appropriate treatment and monitor progress. The IOM recognised that such treatment has proven to be more effective when it is oriented towards ongoing life circumstances and when it addresses attendant life problems and includes such techniques as social skills training, marital therapy and stress management. The conclusions of the IOM's report, *Broadening the Base of Treatment for Alcohol Problems* (IOM, 1990), included the following:

(1) There is no single treatment approach that is effective for all persons with alcohol problems.
(2) The provision of appropriate, specific treatment modalities can substantially improve outcome.
(3) Brief interventions can be quite effective compared with no treatment, and they can be quite cost-effective compared with more intensive treatment.
(4) Treatment of other life problems related to drinking can improve outcomes in people with alcohol problems.
(5) Characteristics of the professionals working with the drug user or drinker are partial determinants of outcome.
(6) Outcomes are determined in part by treatment process factors, post-treatment adjustment factors, the characteristics of the individuals seeking treatment, the characteristics of their problems, and the interactions among these factors.
(7) People who are treated for alcohol problems achieve a continuum of outcomes with respect to drinking behaviour and alcohol problems, and follow different courses of outcome.
(8) Those who significantly reduce their level of alcohol consumption or who become totally abstinent usually enjoy improvement in other life areas, particularly as the period of reduced consumption becomes more extended.

It is important that the content and recommendations of this valuable and well-researched report are not forgotten.

Matching therapeutic interventions to the needs of the client

A closer look at Project MATCH

Prior to Project MATCH – the largest alcohol trial ever conducted – it had been postulated that different types of people who were alcohol dependent would respond selectively to a wide range of different types of treatment (IOM, 1990). An extensive literature base suggested that Cognitive–Behavioural Therapy (CBT) would be more effective for patients with more severe alcohol problems, cognitive impairment and sociopathy, Twelve-step Facilitation Therapy (TFT) for high alcohol dependence and meaning-seeking, and Motivational Enhancement Therapy (MET) for those people with a high conceptual level (i.e. those who are more independent, empathetic and cognitively complex) but with a low readiness to change. Project MATCH was set up to give a final answer to the question 'To what extent is matching necessary?'

Contrary to expectations large matching effects in predicted or other areas did not emerge and all three interventions showed remarkably similar results. All were highly effective (Project MATCH Research Group, 1997). The results were so unexpected that publication was delayed. One concern was that the results would be interpreted as recommending that treatment interventions should not be matched to the individual's needs. New research should never be viewed in isolation, particularly new research findings which appear to run in a contrary direction to the recommendations of a group of well-respected experts who have based their views on 600 previous accepted studies (IOM, 1990). It is important that the findings of Project MATCH are clearly explained, interpreted and fully understood. In order to do this the methodology of the trial needs to be examined in greater detail to determine to what extent it can be criticised and to what degree it differed from routine clinical practice.

The methodology of the trial is above criticism. Extreme care had been taken in the assessment, delivery of interventions and monitoring of the trial. The previous literature on addiction repeatedly recognised that substance use problems are multidimensional and influenced by a wide range of factors. The need for broad-spectrum diagnoses had been repeatedly stated, suggesting that treatment programmes should be multidimensional, and that treatment outcome studies should take account of a multiplicity of factors (McLellan *et al.*, 1981; Babor *et al.*, 1988). It was also recommended that if clients are to be matched to appropriate therapeutic interventions, there must be a broad-based multidimensional assessment of the client's problems and needs. The assessment procedures of Project MATCH were appropriately broad based. However, in other ways it was clear that Project MATCH differed substantially from the normal clinical practice. The type of matching was one way in which it differed. There are two different types of treatment matching: *foresight matching* and *hindsight matching* (Miller & Cooney, 1994). Foresight matching is tailoring treatment interventions to meet assessed needs. This type of matching has been shown by McLellan and colleagues (1983; 1997) to improve outcomes in many problem areas, including family relations, employment, medical condition, legal status and drug use. This is the way that all matching is done in clinical practice. The spread of factors which need to be considered for foresight matching is wider than might be apparent at first sight. Marlatt (1999) has highlighted some of these:

> When therapists consider matching someone to treatment, other matching criteria are also involved over and above the nature of the treatment type itself. Such factors as credibility of the therapist ('I think you would work particularly well with this therapist') and the potential for therapeutic alliance are critical. Other factors include perceived need for group support (self-help groups may be recommended for this reason), the existence of other life problems besides alcohol or drug abuse, and coexisting mental health problems. In addition, there are such practical factors as access to treatment, cost and reimbursement, legal constraints, as well as a host of other individual client factors (age, gender, ethnic identity, motivation to change, etc.).

However, in Project MATCH the matching process was very different. It comprised hindsight

randomised matching to selected client characteristics (Project MATCH Research Group, 1997).

Project MATCH was an eight-year multisite trial and involved a total client sample of 1726 people. The three alternative treatments were:

(1) twelve sessions of Twelve-step Facilitation Therapy designed to help patients become engaged in Alcoholics Anonymous (AA);
(2) twelve sessions of Cognitive–Behavioural Therapy; and
(3) four sessions of Motivational Enhancement Therapy, designed to increase motivation for, and commitment to, change.

As Project MATCH was designed purely to compare and contrast the three different treatment approaches with a view to their potential for matching, there was no control sample. There were two settings for the trial: 952 outpatients and 774 aftercare (immediately following inpatient or intensive day hospital treatment).

Although the three different interventions were determined first, the client characteristics were selected for Project MATCH as a result of general agreement as to their expected importance. The principle outcome measured was severity of alcohol involvement. However, other issues examined were: cognitive impairment; conceptual level; gender; meaning-seeking; readiness for change; psychiatric severity; social support for drinking; sociopathy; typology classification (type A–type B); alcohol dependence; anger; antisocial personality; assertion of autonomy; psychiatric diagnosis; prior engagement in AA; religiosity; self-efficacy; and social functioning.

The fact that the principal outcomes measured were limited to the extent to which drinking had been curtailed has been an understandable focal point for criticism. Glaser (1999), who almost a decade earlier had chaired the IOM's report, *Broadening the Base of Treatment for Alcohol Problems*, commented:

> In the widespread appreciation of such concepts as discontented sobriety and the multifaceted nature of treatment outcome, the study's reliance upon two measures of alcohol consumption as its principle outcome criteria is unconvincing.

Another commentator (Peele, 1998) states:

> [P]erhaps the biggest heresy that MATCH supports – inadvertently so – is the value of reduced drinking as a goal in alcoholism treatment. The MATCH organisers chose to present their success in terms of the number of drinking days and the amount imbibed on those days.

Yet, even though the main outcomes measured had such a narrow focus, the unexpectedly good results of the study surprised almost everyone. After one year the three treatments were shown to be almost equally effective. There was only one exception to this. In the outpatient study, clients low in psychiatric severity had more abstinent days after TFT than after CBT (Project MATCH Research Group, 1997). After three years a matching effect was demonstrated in just two areas: those high in anger did best after MET, and those clients whose social circles were highly conducive to drinking did best with TFT (Project MATCH Research Group, 1998). Even so we cannot be completely certain that these are true hindsight matching occurrences. In spite of the size of the trial and its rigorous methodology it is still possible that, out of the many opportunities for matching that could have taken place, the matching effects could have been chance associations.

Patients in all three treatment categories showed major improvement, not only on drinking measures but also in many other areas of functioning. Before treatment, clients averaged about 25 drinking days per month. The frequency of drinking decreased fourfold to fewer than six days per month after treatment. The volume of drinking also decreased fivefold from an average of 15 drinks per day to three drinks per day. Furthermore, after 39 months, follow-up of the outpatient sample indicated continued maintenance of these reduced drinking rates. In the authors' words (Project MATCH Research Group, 1998):

> Although the efficacy of the three treatments cannot be demonstrated directly since the trial did not include a no-treatment control group, the striking differences in drinking by clients from pretreatment levels to all follow-up points suggest that participation in any of these treatments will be associated with substantial and sustained changes in drinking.... One important conclusion of this trial is that individually delivered psychosocial treatments embodying very different treatment philosophies appear to produce comparably good outcomes.

Part of the success and the lack of matching may be attributable to the fact that there was extensive overlapping of AA attendance across the three treatment conditions, particularly the aftercare arm. In addition, the clients in nearly half (44.8%) of this sample had already received some treatment as a hospital inpatient. If all interventions demonstrate a very high degree of success, it is difficult to highlight which interventions are better as improved response rates due to accurate matching tend to be ironed out. This may be the root cause of the failure of Project MATCH to demonstrate any close matching. However, TFT, CBT and MET appear to give equally good results with regard to reduction in drinking, if these therapies are delivered by skilled therapists and there is regular follow-up and good compliance.

Another factor which may have improved the outcome was the length of the assessment process for the trial, which took an average of 8 hours to complete. Assessment itself can be highly therapeutic (see Chapter 5) and may well have contributed significantly to the success of the trial. In the clinical situation community alcohol workers normally expect to spend much less time than this assessing their clients. Additionally considerable effort was expended in achieving good compliance for Project MATCH: clients were called between sessions; reminder notes were sent; and collateral sources contacted. Clients were also paid as an incentive to return for follow-up. This is over and above the normal clinical practice. Finally the therapists themselves were highly trained, closely supervised and regularly checked to ensure that they did not deviate from the therapeutic programme.

Looking in greater depth at the content of the CBT programme, one finds that instead of being tailored to individual need, everyone had the same core programme which was delivered on an individual basis. The programme itself contained a very comprehensive set of interventions. Relapse prevention work (coping with cravings, assessing high-risk situations, managing thoughts about alcohol, problem-solving, drink refusal skills, coping with a lapse and seemingly irrelevant decisions) took up eight sessions. Then another four sessions of CBT were chosen from the following interventions: social skills training (including starting conversations, non-verbal communication, assertiveness training and receiving criticism); enhancing social support networks; provision of job-seeking skills; coping skills training (including anger and depression management); and couples/family involvement.

Although the methodology of Project MATCH is above criticism and the findings of the trial considered reliable, the way the trial is constructed differs considerably from normal clinical practice. The results should not lead those who work with substance users in the community to abandon the practice of matching clients to appropriate treatment interventions.

Twelve-step Facilitation Therapy and Cognitive–Behavioural Therapy – opposing or integrative therapies

Some of those working in the field may feel confused by the fact that these are two approaches to treatment, which, at times, appear to oppose each other. Yet it is quite possible to integrate these two apparently different forms of treatment. One major difference between them is the strong belief by AA and its relatives (Narcotics Anonymous (NA), Minnesota Model, etc.) that there is an illness called *alcoholism* or chemical dependency that is incurable; that those who have it generally go on drinking or taking drugs until they hit their own rock bottom when they become motivated enough to stop; and that the only way of arresting the disease is by complete abstinence. They believe that once the first drink has been taken, the ball starts rolling with the almost inevitable result that a full-blown relapse will occur which may go on for days or weeks, and from which there may be no recovery. If there is adherence to the AA/NA programme, it is extremely successful and many thousands of people owe their lives to it.

The alternative underlying paradigm of Social Learning Theory (SLT) is that chemical dependence results from repeated use of alcohol or drugs as a social habit, has psychological, physiological and social components, and varies from being a mild to a severe condition. The continuum of problems that develops from substance use closely parallels the quantity of alcohol or drugs consumed. There is no specific point within that continuum when someone can be identified as being *alcoholic* or being overtly dependent on drugs, and there is no specific disease entity called *alcoholism*. The severity of dependence can vary. Those that follow this school of thought believe that some dependent drinkers can slide back up the continuum and learn to control their drinking. There is evidence to support this in mild to moderately dependent drinkers (Heather & Robertson, 1997). From SLT framework, people do not necessarily have to hit rock bottom to become motivated enough to stop drinking (many people in AA/NA now accept this), and single *slips* or lapses can be controlled and prevented from becoming full-blown relapses.

This difference in opinion can be particularly confusing for recovered substance users working in the addictions field, if they themselves have a firm belief that the AA/NA programme is the only way forward. Yet if the choice is left to the individual, two treatment options are available instead of one with individuals exercising their choice for abstinence-oriented treatment or harm reduction through substitute prescribing or controlled drinking. If a client does not believe that abstinence is the right way forward, or does not like the spiritual aspects of AA/NA and wishes to attempt to control his or her substance use, he or she should be helped to do this. This should be on the understanding that for many people this is the harder option and that if it does not work out an abstinence-oriented goal can be attempted at a later stage. In this approach, the role of the counsellor, if advising abstinence, is based on a clinical assessment of relapse risk. Such advice should be based on individually oriented informed opinion and evidence, and not on treatment philosophy.

If the choice is abstinence-oriented treatment it is quite possible, and often advisable, for Cognitive Therapy (CT) or CBT to be integrated with TFT in a combined approach. There is thus no need to be forced into an *either–or* situation. Thus whether the ultimate aim is abstinence or controlled drinking/substitute prescribing, a holistic assessment can still be undertaken, and where necessary a specific treatment package enacted to reduce harm and improve individual functioning.

Conclusion

By the time adulthood is reached it is increasingly rare to find a person who has never tried drinking alcohol or taking drugs. Prevention services for adults should therefore be aimed at secondary prevention and the prevention of harm.

Harm reduction initiatives to limit weekly and daily alcohol consumption to safe levels have been recommended in the UK. Unfortunately the amount of alcohol in a standard drink or unit varies from country to country, so there is no uniform international advice.

The recognition of a public health perspective to alcohol consumption, both from a national and a local perspective, points the way to reduce harm. Nationally measures can be taken to lower overall alcohol consumption through fiscal and other measures. Locally harm reduction can be achieved by the use of advice on safer limits, safety glasses, food availability, training of bar staff and employment of doormen.

There is considerable overlap between the prevention and treatment of substance use problems and dependence. Underlying difficulties that move people towards drug use and heavy drinking commonly remain when problems and dependence have developed. Often progress cannot be made until these have been confronted and overcome. Also problems that arise as a result of drinking or drug use compound and entrench adverse substance use behaviour. Reducing the harm from these problems is an important step forward towards recovery and should be tackled at an early stage. Many psychosocial interventions are known to be effective for the treatment of alcohol problems and dependence and these can be equally well used to aid the recovery process in users of other substances.

In addition to harm reduction interventions to resolve problems and the harm they generate, many other cost-effective treatments can be used. These include brief interventions, medical interventions, such as methadone maintenance, and a wide range of other non-prescribing interventions. Treatments should be targeted to individual need. Good longitudinal outcome studies are required to inform the most cost-effective treatment choices (McLellan *et al.*, 1999).

Part IV
Assessment

Chapter 5
Assessment

Introduction

People who have a problem related to drugs or drink, or who are chemically dependent, are generally easiest to help if they are accessed at an early stage. However, the stigma often prevents them or their families from seeking help before difficulties and dependence have become firmly entrenched. Some even die before they reach this stage. Others cause chronic distress to themselves and their families over many years and risk or actually harm their own health and safety and that of their local community. Good case finding techniques are therefore important so that effective risk reduction and harm reduction measures can be put in place. Opportunistic case finding is the most acceptable

Case finding

The need for accuracy and acceptability

Accuracy and acceptability are key to effective case finding. If a questionnaire is unacceptably long it will not be useful, particularly in a clinical situation where opportunistic screening is undertaken. Accuracy is important as false positives waste time and people may be alienated by inappropriate questions and investigations. Clinical case finding methodology should aim for the same high level of accuracy as research. A 5% confidence interval (i.e. 95% accuracy) is considered acceptable for most research methodology. In most clinical laboratory tests, e.g. liver function tests (LFT), a degree of error is acceptable. However, some laboratory tests may require 100% accuracy and when this is necessary a positive result is normally confirmed by the la-

boratory using different methodology. The blood test to diagnose HIV is a good example.

Such high levels of accuracy are most easily achieved when there is a single criterion being researched (e.g. a positive or negative test result, or the number of heavy drinkers who die of cardiac disease). However, things are not always as clear as they may initially appear. For many years deaths from liver failure due to cirrhosis of the liver has been considered to be an accurate marker of the extent of drinking, both between countries and between professional and other groups within a particular country. Comparisons have been made and changes recorded from year to year. Unfortunately these figures are now known to be distorted by a previously unrecognised high prevalence of chronic hepatitis C within the general population, and this varies from country to country and between different groups of people.

Where there is more than one criterion, accuracy is compromised. For example, accurate assessment as to the extent heavy drinking is detrimental to physical health is not possible because of the many different types of physical health damage which may occur. As we have seen in Chapter 4, in order to overcome this difficulty, the substance use field relies on a consensus of statements made by experts from three Royal Colleges. Similarly a Department of Health (DH) committee made a statement in their *Sensible Drinking* report as to the extent of daily alcohol consumption that, in their view, would impair health (DH, 1995).

In some clinical situations it is so important to have an indication as to what is happening that compromised accuracy is acceptable. Assessing outcomes holistically and accurately in a clinical situation is impossible. Again several criteria are involved. The broad-ranging outcome assessment questionnaires known as Maudsley Addiction Profile (MAP) and Christo Inventory for Substance-misuse Services (CISS) (Appendices 13 and 14) give an indication as to what is happening, but they are not accurate tools.

Screening for hazardous and harmful drinking

Most of the standard laboratory indices that can be raised by problem drinking, such as mean corpuscular volume (MCV), alanine aminotransferase (ALT), aspartate aminotransferase (AST), and gamma-glutamyltransferase (GGT), are not specific enough to be useful as screening tools, either alone or in combination, although any abnormalities should be investigated (Hoeksema & De Bock, 1993). Carbohydrate-deficient transferrin appears to be a better laboratory marker available for screening purposes, but is not much better than MCV. Thus laboratory tests cannot be relied upon to identify heavy drinkers in general practice. One of the largest known studies on detecting alcohol problems in a general practice setting has confirmed that 'conventional laboratory tests are of no use in detecting alcohol abuse or dependence in a primary care setting' (Aertgeerts *et al.*, 2001).

The first screening questionnaires aimed at identifying those who are alcohol dependent were highly successful. The Michigan Alcohol Screening Test (MAST) and its progeny had sensitivities exceeding 95% in detecting alcohol dependence, but were much less useful as instruments to detect patients with hazardous or harmful drinking patterns. CAGE is a shorter commonly used questionnaire to detect drink problems. This has only four questions and its brevity and non-intimidating approach make it a well-liked screening and case-finding tool (Lawner *et al.*, 1997). The four questions are:

(1) Have you ever felt you should Cut down on your drinking?
(2) Have people Annoyed you by criticising your drinking?
(3) Have you ever felt bad or Guilty about your drinking?

(4) Have you ever had a drink in the morning to get rid of a hangover? (An Eye opener)

However, in a primary care setting CAGE's sensitivity of 62% at the cut-off point >1 is unacceptably low, and it is even lower in female patients, although the specificity is 81%. There is little doubt that it should now be abandoned as there are better alternatives.

The need to find an easy-to-use questionnaire which would pick up people at an earlier stage of a drink problem appeared to be fulfilled by the Alcohol Use Disorders Identification Test (AUDIT), that was developed by the World Health Organization (WHO) in a six-country collaborative project as a screening instrument for hazardous and harmful alcohol consumption (Saunders *et al.*, 1993). It has been used widely and is more accurate than other questionnaires in detecting heavy drinkers and those who are alcohol dependent. MacKenzie and colleagues (1996) compared sensitivities of the AUDIT, CAGE and Brief MAST. Sensitivities for the identification of weekly drinking over recommended limits were 93%, 79% and 35% respectively, and 94% of those who were drinking within recommended limits had a negative AUDIT score result. Later Daeppen and colleagues (2000) showed that the sensitivity and specificity of the AUDIT questionnaire to detect alcohol dependence in health care settings was 91.7% and 90.2% respectively. This ten-item questionnaire, which covers the domains of alcohol consumption, drinking behaviour and alcohol-related problems, provides a simple method of early detection of problem or dependent alcohol use in health care settings and is the first instrument of its type to be developed on the basis of a cross-national study. Each item is scored 0–4 giving a maximum total of 40. A score of 8 or more indicates problem and/or dependent alcohol use. The AUDIT questionnaire is given in Table 5.1.

However, as AUDIT is a ten-item questionnaire, it is not as easy to administer as CAGE and so is less acceptable in clinical practice (Seppa *et al.*, 1995). Some researchers have modified it in an effort to make it simpler to use. Seppa and colleagues (1998) used the last three CAGE items and the first two AUDIT items for their *five-shot questionnaire*,

Table 5.1 The Alcohol Use Disorders Identification Test (AUDIT)

Please circle the answer that is correct for you

(1) How often do you have a drink containing alcohol?

Never   Monthly or less   2–4 times a month   2–3 times a week   4 or more times a week

(2) How many drinks containing alcohol do you have on a typical day when you are drinking?

1 or 2   3 or 4   5 or 6   7–9   10 or more

(3) How often do you have six or more drinks on one occasion?

Never   Less than monthly   Monthly   Weekly   Daily or almost daily

(4) How often during the last year have you found that you were not able to stop drinking once you had started?

Never   Less than monthly   Monthly   Weekly   Daily or almost daily

(5) How often during the last year have you failed to do what was normally expected from you because of drinking?

Never   Less than monthly   Monthly   Weekly   Daily or almost daily

(6) How often during the last year have you needed a first drink in the morning to get yourself going after a heavy drinking session?

Never   Less than monthly   Monthly   Weekly   Daily or almost daily

(7) How often during the last year have you had a feeling of guilt or remorse after drinking?

Never   Less than monthly   Monthly   Weekly   Daily or almost daily

(8) How often during the last year have you been unable to remember what happened the night before because you had been drinking?

Never   Less than monthly   Monthly   Weekly   Daily or almost daily

(9) Have you or someone else been injured as a result of your drinking?

No   Yes, but not in the last year   Yes, during the last year

(10) Has a relative or friend, or a doctor or other health worker been concerned about your drinking or suggested you cut down?

No   Yes, but not in the last year   Yes, during the last year

(From Saunders, J., Aasland, O., Babor, T., *et al.* (1993) Development of the Alcohol Use Disorders Identification Test (AUDIT). WHO collaborative project on early detection of persons with harmful alcohol consumption. II. *Addiction*, **88**, 791–804. With permission from Blackwell Publishing.)

which is easy to use in a specialist or general practice setting and has reasonable sensitivity for both male and female patient populations in the latter setting. It has a sensitivity of 74% and a specificity of 81% (for men) and 95% (for women) at its cut-off point. Another shorter questionnaire is the AUDIT-C, which comprises just the first three AUDIT questions (Bush *et al.*, 1998). Its simplicity coupled with its high sensitivity and specificity make it an efficient screening instrument for heavy or binge drinking men, up to 35% of whom, through a brief intervention, may be prevented from developing problematic or dependent use. The AUDIT-C questionnaire has a sensitivity of 78% and a specificity of 75%. Unfortunately the detection, by this method, of female patients who drink excessively is not so good. The AUDIT-PC, which uses AUDIT questions 1, 2, 4, 5 and 10 (Piccinelli *et al.*, 1997), has a low sensitivity of 68%, although its specificity is 84%.

As short acceptable tests, the five-shot questionnaire which detects a high proportion of people with drink problems and dependence and AUDIT-C which detects excessive regular or binge drinkers, both appear to be reasonably good short screening tools. At its cut-off point of >2.5 the five-shot questionnaire detects more than twice as many patients who have alcohol problems or are dependent drinkers as those detected by an average general practitioner (GP) asking in an unstructured way. Nevertheless, two out of three patients who screen positive will not have an alcohol problem. AUDIT-C combines brevity with better performance. Its simplicity means that clinicians should have no difficulty memorising both the combination of screening questions and the simple coding system. Regular use of AUDIT-C should lead to the identification of approximately 75% of patients who drink to excess or are alcohol dependent.

More recently a four-item questionnaire has been developed to be of use particularly in medical settings and has undergone successful trials in Accident and Emergency (A&E) departments, fracture clinics, primary health care, and a dental hospital. Known as the Fast Alcohol Screening Test (FAST), this questionnaire has good sensitivities and specificities across a range of settings, with sensitivities ranging from 91% to 97% and specificities from 86% to 95%. Over half of all people with alcohol-related problems or dependence (63% of men and 56% of women) can be identified by just using question 1. The four questions of the FAST questionnaire are given below.

Thus the best brief screening tool suitable for both men and women in health care settings would appear to be the four-item questionnaire, FAST. However, if a single question is preferred, the first FAST question has the potential to be extremely useful.

Whichever method is used, a positive screening test should prompt professionals to take a more detailed history to explore the role of alcohol in the individual's personal, social and professional life. Following this, drinkers can be offered a brief intervention or, if necessary, referred to their GP or a specialist unit for further investigation and treatment.

Screening populations for illicit drug use

Drug use is common and for the great majority of young people it is a short-lived phase for which population screening is unhelpful. Because the incidental discovery by families that young people are using drugs throws up such enormous and unnecessary problems, other approaches are preferable, the most fruitful of which appears to be targeting those groups of people recognised to be *vulnerable* or at very high risk of developing substance use problems. Such populations include young people with serious psychiatric illness, children and young people who are looked after, and young offenders.

Assessment of those seeking help

The interrelationship between assessment and treatment

There is no clear dividing line between the assessment of those with chemical addiction problems and the provision of their treatment. The process

---

The Fast Alcohol Screening Test (FAST)

(1) Men: How often do you have eight or more drinks on one occasion?
Women: How often do you have six or more drinks on one occasion?
Never   Less than monthly   Monthly   Weekly   Daily or almost daily

(2) How often during the last year have you been unable to remember what happened the night before because you had been drinking?
Never   Less than monthly   Monthly   Weekly   Daily or almost daily

(3) How often during the last year have you failed to do what was normally expected of you because of drinking?
Never   Less than monthly   Monthly   Weekly   Daily or almost daily

(4) In the last year has a relative or friend, or a doctor or other health worker been concerned about your drinking or suggested you cut down?
No   Yes, on one occasion   Yes, on more than one occasion

[Score questions 1–3: 0, 1, 2, 3, 4.   Score question 4: 0, 2, 4.
A score of ≥3 indicates probable hazardous drinking.]

(From Hodgson, R. S., Alwyn, T., John, B., *et al.* (2002) The Fast Alcohol Screening Test. *Alcohol and Alcoholism*, 37(1), 61–6. With permission from Oxford University Press.)

of looking formally into the detail of the development and extent of a drug or alcohol use problem with a client can be highly therapeutic in its own right. If the assessment is done well, the client starts to order and make sense of what previously may have appeared to be a series of unrelated events. Such insights are important. Information about substances and risks, particularly those from blood-borne virus (BBV) infection and overdose through loss of tolerance, should be given during assessment contacts, which may be the only opportunity for intervention for some time. This is a crucial time when the relationship between worker and client can be made or broken. A really good relationship with the client where the worker is seen to express accurate empathy is one of the most valuable therapeutic tools. Assessment, a two-way process, thus merges and interlinks with treatment. This is as true for those who require just brief information, reflection or advice as it is for clients who need prolonged in-depth treatment with a wide variety of interventions. Furthermore, during the treatment process the professional working to help a substance user will all the time be informally monitoring and reassessing the client. The alert professional may be thinking: 'How is he coping with problems?' 'Does this negative statement suggest an underlying depression?' 'Is this client's motivation declining now that she has a prescription?' Thus informal reassessment is ongoing throughout the treatment process.

Nevertheless, there are specific times when a more or less formal assessment or reassessment should be undertaken. These are:

(1) preliminary assessment
(2) initial assessment and care plan
(3) assessment of effectiveness of interventions given
(4) reassessments – regular checks on progress
　　(a) achievement of goals
　　(b) clinical outcome audit
　　　　• periodic reassessment and reformulation of goals
　　　　• an in-depth assessment if failing to progress
(5) assessment for residential rehabilitation

Treatment needs

The ultimate aim for every type of formal assessment or reassessment will be to help the individual successfully overcome his or her substance use problem. This will entail an assessment of client *needs* at that particular point in time. This type of needs assessment differs from a social services needs assessment in that the needs are not necessarily social needs, they are treatment needs. They are as many or as few of those things a client requires in order to overcome his or her substance-related problems within a biopsychosocial treatment construct. Thus, they also include psychological needs and those relating to physical and mental health. To meet the assessed treatment needs, a care plan will be developed that may vary from just a single brief intervention to prolonged in-depth treatment to maintenance prescribing without any formal psychosocial interventions.

Choice of goals

Clients may well have many other things which they wish to achieve that are important for them in defining the sort of life they wish to lead. Most drinkers prefer to select their own goals (Sobell *et al.*, 1992a), and achieving, or making progress towards achieving, these personal goals usually enhances the motivation of clients, their self-esteem, and their sense of self-efficacy and self-identity. Personal goals are a valuable aid to the treatment process and should be discussed with clients, listed and prioritised according to their wishes. Goals should be realistic. Unachievable goals, and those that are difficult to achieve, should be discussed with the client and where possible modified. Goals should be defined separately from treatment needs, although there is often an overlap. Indeed many of the things that clients often give as their personal needs and goals, such as overcoming housing problems, unemployment, poverty, and social isolation, are some of the most useful treatment interventions when it comes to overcoming an addiction problem. Also treatment is most effective when it is compatible with the client's choice between controlled drinking and abstinence (Orford & Keddie, 1986).

Miller and colleagues (1988) suggest that clients are more likely to comply with any treatment procedure when they view themselves as having made the decision to pursue a particular strategy. They hypothesised that goal self-selection would attract more people to treatment, reduce the attrition rate and enhance the likelihood of a successful outcome. From the standpoint of self-efficacy theory it is preferable that the individual attributes the accomplishment to himself or herself. With self-established goals a client cannot easily rationalise failure or blame the therapist, and the issue of appropriateness can be confronted directly. Failure to attain a goal not only allows discussion as to whether the goal should be changed but also enables discussion about commitment and motivation. Although it is helpful if the drinker or drug user has the final say in choosing goals, professionals do have a role to ensure that these goals are realistic and not used to justify drink- or drug-related behaviours that are likely to cause problems.

What happens when the drinker or drug user does specify limits that are inconsistent with professional advice? This is an important area to define. In practice it is unusual for those who attend for professional help to go directly against the advice of professionals particularly with regard to harm reduction or other interventions which are clearly beneficial. For example, few people will reject help to obtain more appropriate housing accommodation. Some people, however, just want a prescription and nothing else. If a prescription is appropriate, other treatment interventions should not be forced upon the substance user. The care coordinator should continue to see the individual and over a period of time, with the aid of Motivational Interviewing (MI) or other ways of enhancing readiness to change, many individuals do alter their views and take on board the need for additional interventions.

When discrepancies between professional advice and the client's treatment goals arise it is better to know that the person does not intend to follow advice than to agree to limits the client has no intention of keeping. For example, knowing that someone is intending to drink more than is recom-

mended opens up interesting opportunities for discussion. The question is why drinking at a particular level or frequency is important enough to risk potentially damaging problems.

Assessment and care planning

Preliminary assessment of substance use

When someone telephones, attends or is referred for help the decisive factor as to whether they need a full assessment and treatment hinges upon whether or not they have a significant substance-related problem requiring in-depth assessment and treatment and whether one of these problems is alcohol or drug dependency. A significant problem or dependency should generate the need for a full initial assessment. In theory a full assessment is not required for everyone who approaches the specialist substance use services for help, but in practice the help seeker's recognition that help is required suggests a significant alcohol or drug problem. Thus every substance user approaching these tier 3 services is almost always offered a full initial assessment. Families and concerned others may just be offered advice, but all those who ask for help for themselves are fully assessed and a care plan formulated.

However, when those who attend tier 1 service providers (ordinary generic professionals, such as social workers, GPs and probation officers, who have no special expertise or training in problem substance use) are discovered opportunistically to have a drug or alcohol problem, there needs to be a brief preliminary form of assessment to determine whether a secondary referral should be made to the specialist services for a full assessment or whether, as the American Institute of Medicine recommended in 1990, a brief intervention should be given by the tier 1 service provider. There are therefore a number of different scenarios according to the tier of service provision approached. These are:

(1) The client/patient has a significant drink- or drug-related problem (e.g. lost employment through drinking) or has complicating aspects of need such as pregnancy or psychiatric illness (note: these may not all be recognised by the service user as problems).

Response of the tier 1 service provider: A referral is made to tier 3 services for a full assessment and care plan.

Response of the tier 2 service provider (generic service worker who has special expertise): A referral is made to tier 3 services for a full initial assessment and care plan. In addition, an arrangement may be made for shared care if the tier 2 service provider is a GP.

(2) (a) There are no obvious drink- or drug-related problems. The client/patient admits to heavy drinking and recreational drug use and does not think he or she is dependent.

Response of the tier 1 service provider: The heavy drinker is given an Opportunistic Brief Intervention (OBI) regarding alcohol consumption and harm reduction advice about recreational drug use and is asked to attend for follow-up.

Response of the tier 2 service provider: Dependence is excluded by the use of the DSM-IV questionnaire (Appendix 1). The heavily drinking client/patient is given a similar OBI and asked about other substance use. Appropriate harm reduction advice is given and the client/patient is asked to attend for follow-up.

(b) At follow-up the client/patient has not resumed a normal drinking pattern and/or continues high-risk BBV behaviour.

Response of the tier 1 service provider: He or she is referred to the specialist drug and alcohol services for specialist help to reduce heavy drinking/high-risk BBV behaviour.

Response of the tier 2 service provider: Reasons for failure to change are explored. Structured advice is repeated and appropriate literature regarding heavy drinking and high-risk BBV behaviours is supplied. This is followed up on each occasion the client is seen.

(3) There are no obvious drink- or drug-related problems. The client/patient admits to heavy drinking or recreational drug use and thinks he or she is dependent.

Response of the tier 1 service provider: The client/patient is referred to the specialist drug and alcohol services for full initial assessment and care plan.

Response of the tier 2 service provider: Dependence is confirmed by use of the DSM-IV questionnaire. The client/patient is referred to the specialist drug and alcohol services for full initial assessment and care plan. An arrangement may be made for shared care if the tier 2 provider is a GP. The summary of action taken by generic service providers (tier 1 and tier 2) is shown in Table 5.2.

All injecting drug users (IDUs), whether or not they are dependent and have substance-related problems, should be given harm reduction advice concerning BBV transmission and overdose, and receive appropriate written material from both tier 1 and tier 2 generic professionals. They should also be provided with details of local specialist service provision including needle exchange.

In the case of young people seeking help, an OBI may also be needed. They may be at high risk of developing a substance use problem and/or dependence in later life and it is important that they should be deflected from this course. They should be taken under the wing of the young people's drug service, which should be separate from the adult drug services.

Full initial assessment and care planning
The initial assessment should be holistic. It should cover the extent of past and present drinking and drug-taking, any associated problems from medical, social, psychological and criminal justice domains that accompany it, and strengths, in particular psychosocial functioning, together with the degree of motivation of the client to overcome his or her drink or drug problem. People should not be refused treatment because of a lack of motivation for abstinence. There are now good ways of helping people motivate themselves and move on from contemplating change to being prepared for it. Treatments will differ according to the stage of change. It is important that people should not be detoxified before they are ready to stop drinking or taking

Table 5.2   Summary of action taken by generic service providers

Problems/dependence	Tier 1 service provision	Tier 2 service provision
Problems but no dependence	Refer to specialist services for full assessment and care plan.	Refer to specialist services for full assessment and care plan. An arrangement may be made for shared care.
No obvious problems or dependence but heavy drinking/recreational drug use	Give brief intervention/harm reduction advice.	Dependence excluded using DSM-IV questionnaire. Explore risk behaviour. Give brief intervention/harm reduction advice.
At follow-up still heavy drinking/recreational drug use	Refer to specialist drug and alcohol agency for help to reduce drinking/high-risk BBV behaviour.	Refer to specialist drug and alcohol agency for full assessment and care plan. An arrangement may be made for shared care.
No obvious problems but dependence	Refer to specialist drug and alcohol agency for full assessment and care plan.	Refer to specialist drug and alcohol agency for full assessment and care plan. An arrangement may be made for shared care.

drugs as relapse rates will be high and this will increase the risks of BBV transmission or accidental overdose later. It will also tend to deter them from seeking help in the future.

A medical assessment, a psychosocial assessment, and an assessment for legal purposes, such as a pre-sentence report, are often done by separate individuals. An assessment by a probation officer may have different objectives from an assessment by a social worker, and both these workers may have different objectives from a doctor. A probation officer may be primarily concerned to prevent recidivism and to divert clients, where possible, from custody; a social worker's concerns will often centre around child-care; and medical practice may be directed towards preventing or treating physical illness such as HIV and hepatitis.

The service use patterns of people with complex needs and multiple diagnoses have been highlighted by Keene (2001). People with alcohol and drug problems make frequent use of social workers, housing shelters, A&E departments, community health services, other National Health Service (NHS) facilities, probation services and non-statutory organisations. They become patients or clients whose problems are defined in different ways according to differing professional views and objectives. The assessments and interventions different professionals offer will differ. Commonly the interventions recommended are short term. Their appropriateness for the client is rarely questioned as it is a matter of professional judgement. The ways clients see their own problems are often ignored. If a client fails to accept or progress with the specified treatment, he or she is in danger of being labelled non-compliant, and when they return to seek treatment with the same problem at a later stage they are labelled *revolving door* clients, taking up a disproportionate amount of resources and not using services efficiently. The apportionment of blame towards the client is often caused by a failure of the service provision through an unduly narrow focus of the treatment plan; by omitting to discuss the clients own goals; or by an inability to engage the service user when formulating the care plan.

To overcome these problems, the initial assessment is usually best done by modifying the mental health Care Programme Approach (CPA) where the different professionals involved do their own individual initial assessments and then come together to discuss the case and devise a care plan. In the specialist substance use services the initial assessment is normally done by one worker completing a standardised assessment form. Most community alcohol and community drug teams have devised their own semi-standardised initial assessment forms (e.g. Appendix 2). That worker then generally brings the initial assessment to a multi-disciplinary team meeting for discussion, together with a draft care plan recommending specific evidence-based interventions matched to individual need.

Some authorities feel that structured initial assessments that are impossible to change are of limited value when it comes to formulating a care plan. It has been suggested that these should be excluded and that it is far more valuable to do an assessment which has been specifically designed with regard to future interventions. Hayes and colleagues have emphasised the extent to which such an assessment can contribute to better outcomes by enhancing the planning of interventions. They called this the 'treatment utility of assessment' (Hayes *et al.*, 1987).

Although certain past events or personality traits may be impossible to change, they are important to take into account because of their impact on the client's subsequent behaviour. For instance, if someone has been sexually abused, they cannot change the event but with appropriate counselling they may be enabled to lessen its impact and move on from substance use as a method of blocking painful thoughts. Thus a client's reactions to an event and his or her subsequent behaviour can be modified, even though the event is impossible to change. It is therefore important to do a full initial assessment which takes account of those things that cannot be changed.

The full initial assessment should determine the nature, length and severity of drug and alcohol use, understand how and why it arose, and discover the reasons and circumstances for any significant gaps in substance use. There should be an assessment of the physical, psychological and social harms associated with substance use, and the extent of involvement with the criminal justice system. In addition, there should be an assessment of the strengths and weaknesses of the client by way of individual psychosocial functioning, and the degree of motivation or readiness to change.

The objective of the initial assessment is to produce an individual treatment or care plan to aid the client in the most fruitful way in his or her efforts to overcome addiction to drugs and/or alcohol. When devising a treatment plan the professional should remember that, at best, he or she has only a facilitatory role. It is the client, not the professional, who will achieve success. A client cannot be made to get better. The initial assessment should therefore be used as a mutual planning process between the client and the professional worker involved for a draft care package consisting of targeted and prioritised specific treatment interventions and goals. The worker should suggest things that might be helpful from his or her professional knowledge base and from knowing what is locally available. After further discussion at a team meeting a final care package of specific interventions and goals can be suggested to the client. Thus a care package with treatment interventions tailored to the individual is drawn up.

The relationship between client and professional is most vulnerable at the first interview. From the client's point of view the air will be charged with emotion. Defences will be ready to set in place, and there will be ambivalence. It will usually involve a swallowing of pride, feelings of guilt, anger at a relative or close friend who may have been applying pressure, worry about problems that have occurred, worry that the interviewer may be judgemental and, in addition, there may be a crisis to contend with. It is helpful if the interviewer can imagine what it is like to be in the client's position. If the interviewer is clumsy and lacks empathy, it will lead to the strengthening of defences by the client and in turn an inaccurate history may be given. The drinker or drug user will then be seen to adhere to the stereotype who tells lies and cannot be trusted, and from that poor beginning the relationship may continue to spiral downwards.

The way in which the interviewer presents to the client is crucial if an accurate story is to be obtained. The contents of the care package rely on valid self-reports not just at the initial assessment but at all forms of assessment. The reliability of self-reports can also vary with the type of drug evaluated, symptom investigated, and diagnostic system employed (Cottler *et al.*, 1989). Despite such variability, when factors are conducive to honest and accurate client reporting 'alcoholics do not systematically deny or minimise their drinking and related behaviour' (Maisto & O'Farrell, 1985) and drinkers have been found, in general, to give reliable reports regarding drinking behaviour (Babor *et al.*, 1987). A similar process of accurate information, being dependent upon the ability of the professional to express accurate empathy, is likely to occur with drug users against whom prejudice may be even greater in some circles. However, extreme caution must be exerted when it comes to believing a drug history which may be under- or overstated for a variety of external reasons, including the anticipated level of substitute prescribing.

Testing for drugs and alcohol

The spectrum of illicit drugs consumed is normally determined by taking a good history and examining the client, with further assessment by urine testing. This serves to assess not only the veracity of reported use but may also reveal other drugs which were not disclosed in the history, perhaps because the client had not recognised their significance. Confirming the presence of alcohol is not generally helpful as it will often be found in the urine in the context of normal consumption patterns. With regard to drugs, although no single method of routine laboratory testing is 100% reliable, testing to confirm the presence or absence of cocaine, opiates, amphetamine, benzodiazepines and methadone is helpful. Testing for cannabis is optional and best reserved for those complaining of cannabis dependence. It is possible to have a positive test result from passive smoking of cannabis.

The techniques in routine practice are qualitative, not quantitative. To be certain of the presence of a particular drug, a second test by a different method is necessary (e.g. opiates by antibody testing confirmed by thin layer chromatography). If both show the same result, this will be acceptable in a court of law. Mass spectrometry is the only single method of drug-testing which is 100% reliable. It is used forensically but is prohibitively expensive, and for this reason is not used in routine clinical laboratories. Similarly, quantitative testing is also too expensive to be done routinely in a laboratory setting. Thus it is impossible to tell from routine laboratory testing whether someone is tolerant to opiates or not. In view of potential fatal toxicity from an initial dose of opiates for those who have

no tolerance, careful induction procedures are essential for all those starting opiate substitute prescriptions.

Other methods of testing include analysis of sweat, oral transudate, blood and hair. Oral transudate analysis detects the recent consumption of the substance itself and not the metabolites and therefore is less valuable in assessing regularity of use. Blood testing is invasive and expensive. Hair analysis has the advantage of showing drug use over a period of time and has a potential place in the assessment of illicit drug use, particularly in methadone treatment and in the assessment of psychiatric comorbidity, e.g. due to unrecognised amphetamine use (McPhillips *et al.*, 1998). It is less reliable for people with blond hair than it is for those with dark hair. It takes 30 days to grow half an inch of hair. It is, however, relatively expensive compared to other methods.

Urine testing is often undertaken by a local laboratory. It may however be undertaken by machine testing or dipsticks at the drug service, which is the cheapest method of assessing whether drug use has recently occurred and has the added advantage that it will give a result at the time of attendance. Urines are sometimes surreptitiously substituted from other sources in order to give a desired result. There is a black market for *clean* urines and for those containing different drugs. In the USA it is even possible to purchase freeze-dried urine on the black market in some places. For these reasons some drug agencies insist on observing the passing of urine which is going to be tested. However, this has been decried in law as a breach of article 8 of the European Human Rights Act – the right to respect for private and family life.

The main reason drug users try to substitute other people's urine is because they believe they will be penalised if the truth is known as it is not unusual for drug agencies to arrange for a reduction in the substitute prescription if the use of street drugs occurs on top of a prescription. If the drug user understands that the aim of finding out if street drug use is still occurring is to confront the problem rather than the person and find ways to overcome the problem, the substitution of urine is less likely. The approximate duration of detectability of selected drugs in urine is given in Appendix 3. A more reliable way is to take an oral transudate test as this cannot be substituted, although it is more costly.

Thus if a drug user insists that he or she has not taken any drugs, this may be the truth even though a urine or other laboratory test is positive. Such tests should not be used to catch people out with a view to punishing them or issuing threats that if they do not do better next time their prescription is likely to stop or their stay in prison will be extended. They should always be used as a clinical tool which is part of an overall plan.

For oral methadone prescribing where titration is undertaken, the starting dose will be independent of the history given, so an exaggerated history will not matter. It is of greater consequence when prescribing without titration for benzodiazepines, amphetamines or injectable opiates, none of which are titrated. The starting dose of these less usual drugs should be generally less than reported use and with a predetermined upper limit.

Different types of assessment

Bearing these things in mind, in addition to the structured initial interview, a fuller assessment of a client's substance use problems/dependence is often necessary. The different types of assessment given in Table 5.3 need to be considered.

It is clear that, even when focusing on those things that are potentially changeable, to assess someone fully takes a long time. It cannot be done in one session, particularly if that session is a 10-minute consultation with a GP. Assessments occur over a period of time in the community, and in complex cases often become mixed in with reassessments and evolve over a period of time, with further blurring of the boundaries between assessment and treatment. This is not in itself harmful as long as all the areas which need to be assessed are covered.

Assessments can be done by more than one person; sometimes several people are involved. For example, a GP might do the physical assessment; a worker in a community drug or alcohol team might do the main assessment; a psychologist might be asked to do a formal psychological assessment; a probation officer and a social worker might be involved; and AdFam or another agency might be helping the family. In this situation there can easily be fragmentation of care, duplication of work, giving of conflicting advice, and disparate goal setting, which can be confusing and counterproductive for the client. It is therefore helpful if one person is selected as a case manager to pull this loose-knit team together, but in order to do

Table 5.3   Different types of assessment

Assessment of substance use
Assessment of dependence
Assessment of motivation and the stage of change
The decisional balance
Assessment of self-efficacy
Assessment of BBV risk behaviour
Assessment of risk of overdose or death
Assessment of harm to self or others
Assessment of personal and environmental factors related to addictive behaviours
Assessment of psychological functioning and its relationship to problems and strengths
Assessment of the different problem domains to formulate a care plan
Physical health assessment
Mental health assessment
Assessment of capacity to consent to treatment
Assessment of role/needs of families, cohabitees and significant others
Assessment of child protection issues
Formal psychological assessment
Assessment for inpatient care, residential rehabilitation and specialist day centre care
Assessment of outcome

this ways need to be found to communicate effectively and in a form that is acceptable to the client. Policies on confidentiality should be able to accommodate this.

Different aspects of the assessment process

Assessment of substance use

A good assessment will include a history of the development of the problem. For drug users there is generally, but not always, sequential use of different drugs, often starting with alcohol or cannabis and almost always underpinned by nicotine at an early age. If there is regular use (by definition an average six days out of seven) requiring treatment, it is helpful to know when use of the presenting drug first started, and whether there was any regular or problematic use of any drug, including alcohol, before this. In the UK it is not unusual to see drug service attenders who have been in a state of continuous problematic substance use stretching back to the age of 13 or earlier. Although they may have experienced a great deal, such clients are particularly needy as they may not have achieved independence to enable them to sort out life's problems, and their emotional reactions may remain childlike.

For many substance users the problem does not go back that far. They have often started experimenting with heavy drinking or illicit drug use with their peers, but, unlike their friends, carried on instead of stopping. The reasons for this may sometimes throw light on which programme of help would be most suitable. It is also helpful to know if there have been any prolonged breaks in substance use and, if so, what were the circumstances leading to these breaks. The knowledge that they have been able to control their use in certain circumstances will often encourage drinkers or drug users to try that method again, anticipating that the chances of success will be greater.

An assessment of current substance use will give secondary evidence of the severity of the drug or alcohol problem. In itself, it will not be the only deciding factor as to whether alcohol detoxification

or substitute drug prescribing should be undertaken. However, if a person proves to be drug dependent and a decision is made that substitute prescribing is required, an in-depth assessment becomes more important in order to define the type and, if titration is not to be done, quantity of the substitute drug that is needed.

Breath testing for alcohol or measuring the Blood Alcohol Concentration (BAC) may help confirm a binge drinking pattern, but in itself is of limited value, although a raised alcohol level in the morning may suggest an alcohol problem. For people with drink problems quantification is usually done either by asking for clarification about what happens on a typical drinking day and then working on a quantity–frequency basis to estimate total consumption in an average week or, more accurately, by asking the client to complete a diary (see Appendix 4). The quantity–frequency approach has been found to yield different results from the diary method, with the nature of the difference varying according to the level of consumption (Webb et al., 1990). However, from a practical standpoint all this may be academic and the method of recording depends on the client's ability to engage with it. Difficulty with reading or written recording should be borne in mind.

For drug users, the day of assessment and the four days prior to that are probably the most important on which to obtain an accurate history for prescribing purposes. This is normally done by going through each of these days in turn and recording accurately what has been taken. Those taking a drug history should not forget alcohol, and those taking a drinking history should not forget drugs, particularly benzodiazepines or other central nervous system (CNS) depressants which may summate with drink.

The diary model is equally applicable to drug users and can assist in offering insights and encouraging the client to take an active part in the assessment, as well as forming a baseline for assessments of outcome or change. It should be remembered that the circumstances surrounding dry or abstinent days (or days when there is no use on top of a prescription) can give insights into client strengths, and it can sometimes be more constructive to take this line than to look for cues and triggers of substance use. It also enables clients to recognise the extent of their drink or drug problem.

Assessment of dependence

Confirmation of the presence of dependence through the use of the DSM-IV questionnaire (Appendix 1) indicates the need for a full assessment and the provision of treatment plans. Those who do not work with drinkers, but whose work is limited to helping drug users, commonly make the mistake of assuming that dependence is present if there is daily use of a particular drug. In practice this is generally true only for those drugs where there is a marked physical abstinence syndrome. Thus, although daily use of heroin is almost invariably associated with a physical abstinence syndrome and dependence, this is not usually the case for amphetamine or cocaine users, nor does it apply to moderate drinkers. Just as people can drink moderately every day without becoming dependent on alcohol, so too can some take amphetamine or cocaine on a daily basis without being dependent.

However, some highly dependent drinkers go without drinking for days, weeks or months in between drinking bouts, and some occasional or *weekend* users of amphetamine or cocaine can also be severely dependent. When assessing drinkers or stimulant users it is therefore important to establish at an early stage whether dependence is present. Substitute prescribing for users of any type of drug should not be undertaken, or even considered, in those cases where there is no dependence.

Yet it is not enough to just say that dependence is or is not present. In Edwards' (1987) words:

> The needed skill is a discriminating judgement which is able, in each case, to sense out the degree of dependence, identify the rational treatment goal for that particular person, and propose the treatment fitted to that particular person's problem.

Dependence may be mild, moderate or severe. While dependence can progress and regress throughout the lifetime of a severely dependent substance user, a return to alcohol or drug use after a period of abstinence generally results in the rapid reinstatement of the pre-abstinent pattern of consumption and other features of dependence (Edwards & Gross, 1976). Furthermore, in the severely dependent, this appears to be a permanent change, as has been demonstrated by long-term follow-up studies (Edwards *et al.*, 1983). This is clinically very important for it lends strong support to the view that severely dependent drinkers will not be able to return to a moderate drinking pattern and should be advised to abstain completely from alcohol.

The measurement of the severity of alcohol dependence by the MAST (Selzer, 1971) and Short MAST (Selzer *et al.*, 1974) questionnaires was first attempted before the dependence syndrome was defined by Edwards and colleagues (1977). Subsequently, features of the dependence syndrome have been incorporated into DSM-IV and ICD-10. The previous version of the DSM (DSM-III-R) included criteria for rating the severity of dependence but DSM-IV does not do this. Instead there are now a number of standardised questionnaires to assess the severity of dependence on alcohol or specific drugs, which are all based on the dependence syndrome. These include the Severity of Alcohol Dependence Questionnaire (SADQ) (Stockwell *et al.*, 1979), the Severity of Opiate Dependence Questionnaire (SODQ) (Sutherland *et al.*, 1986), the Severity of Dependence Scale (SDS) (Gossop *et al.*, 1995) for a range of drugs, the SDS for high-dose benzodiazepine users (De Las Cuevas *et al.*, 2000) and the Leeds Dependence Questionnaire (Raistrick *et al.*, 1994).

The SDS has been validated jointly by British and Australian researchers for heroin, cocaine and amphetamine users (Appendix 5). This short five-item questionnaire was designed to measure severity of dependence of a range of drugs, although it was not designed to measure the severity of alcohol dependence. It was originally developed as a research tool, but the authors now recommend its use in clinical practice. In addition, another application of the SDS has been published. This is an adapted version to assess the severity of benzodiazepine dependence in high-dose benzodiazepine users (Appendix 6). The SDS is primarily a measure of compulsive use. It does not include items to measure tolerance, withdrawal or reinstatement, but it can be completed in less than 3 minutes.

The Leeds Dependence Questionnaire (Appendix 7) is a ten-item questionnaire designed to measure the severity of dependence on both drugs and alcohol. It is recommended because of its universal application and because it is one of the easiest to use, being brief, user-acceptable and a self-completion instrument.

It would be unwise to encourage drinkers with a Leeds Dependence Questionnaire score of 20 or more, which indicates severe dependence, to attempt to control their drinking as this could be expected to result in certain failure. It would also be inappropriate to treat most severely dependent substance users with a brief intervention, and opiate users with a score of 20 or more are best treated with maintenance substitute prescribing.

Assessment of motivation and the stage of change

It should be noted that most substance users are ambivalent and motivation may change. Motivation for abstinence should not be the only criteria looked for. Some people who are not motivated for abstinence may be keen to reduce their risks of other harmful behaviours and thus be ready to engage in therapeutic work. Others may have important personal goals. For example, some substance users may be highly motivated to preserve their relationships or their job; others may be motivated to avoid further arrests or improve their health. Loss of relationships and jobs, being arrested, and health problems all impinge harmfully on the recovery process and are thus important to address. Motivation is thus a multivariate construct and is one of the foundation stones for the recovery process. It should be examined in specific detail from a number of angles.

Although most drinkers and drug users are ambivalent about stopping, they become motivated to take some action about their substance use when they recognise that the negative consequences of their drinking or drug use outweigh the gains. Occasionally they recognise this consciously for the first time when they weigh up the pros and cons of substance use in an objective way with a drug or alcohol worker. Sometimes there is only a chink of motivation to be seen. Yet this can be worked on and increased with skilled help. Alternatively, the degree of motivation to overcome the drink or drug problem may not always be as great as it first appears. Some people seek help under duress and threats from relatives. Most heroin users requesting a prescription for an opiate substitute are less motivated to stop than would appear at first interview. This is not a reason to refuse to prescribe for them. People should not be rejected on the grounds that they are not yet ready to stop. It is better, for instance, to prescribe oral methadone in a stable dose to heroin users so that they can reduce illicit drug use and also the harm they are doing to themselves and to others. It is important at the same time to use MI or other methods to increase their motivation to make positive incremental changes in other areas of their lives.

A stable prescription with reduction or elimination of illicit use will also reduce harm by lessening the chance of death from overdose; the risk of transmitting and acquiring BBV infections; and a considerable amount of acquisitive criminal behaviour. Such interventions should be regularly reassessed.

Although in the great majority of cases, where there is an appropriate level of substitute prescribing for opiate users, illicit substance use declines, occasionally it continues unchanged and there is no motivation to reduce harm through the use of substitute medication. In this circumstance harm reduction is not achieved, dependency increases and consideration may be given to discontinuing the prescription. Other situations where harm may increase include:

(1) Detoxifying substance users before they really want to stop (a sure recipe for failure). Opiate users in this situation should be maintained on a substitute prescription.
(2) Refusing to treat substance users until a crisis occurs may allow them to continue to slide downhill causing increasing harm to themselves and others.
(3) Although approval may have been given by the substance user to go ahead with a particular care plan, he or she may not be ready to implement all the proposed treatment interventions resulting in failure and increased harm.

Assessment of the motivation to tackle different drug- or alcohol-related problems and the correct stage of change for each element is just as important as assessment of motivation to be abstinent.

Prochaska and DiClemente's theory of change is closely linked to motivation and has been most helpful in clarifying this. The theory was conceived by the two psychologists while lounging around a swimming pool in Las Vegas in the late 1970s. They spent the next six years developing, testing, teaching and applying *the transtheoretical approach to change*, attempting to integrate ideas and interventions from different systems of psychotherapy and from their own work. This reached fruition with the publication of their book *The Transtheoretical Approach: Crossing Traditional Boundaries of Therapy* (Prochaska & DiClemente, 1984). In it they separated out three different tiers: the stages of change, the processes of change, and the levels of change.

Identifying the stage of change is particularly helpful when making an assessment as different interventions may be required according to the staging. The processes of change are those interventions which act as an engine to drive change forward by enhancing motivation. The levels of change are used to denote various associated problems which occur at the different psychological levels (e.g. mal-adaptive cognitions or current interpersonal conflicts). These can also increase motivation, but on the whole they block any movement through the stages of change unless they are dealt with.

There were originally six stages of change which Prochaska and DiClemente illustrated in the shape of a wheel to demonstrate the reality that in almost any change process it is normal for a person to go round the process several times before achieving stable change, and emphasising that relapse is a normal occurrence.

Later, however, relapse was no longer regarded as a stage of change, but was seen as an *event* or, alternatively, as a form of regression. Also the stage of determination, which was placed between the stages of contemplation and action, was dropped as it could not be supported by research findings. However, after seven years, research data could only be understood if it were replaced by a new stage of *preparation* (DiClemente *et al.*, 1991) (see Figure 5.1).

- *Precontemplation* is the stage when a drinker or drug taker has no thoughts of changing and is usually unaware of any problems.
- *Contemplation* is the stage when a problem is recognised to exist but the drinker or drug taker has not yet decided to do anything about it.

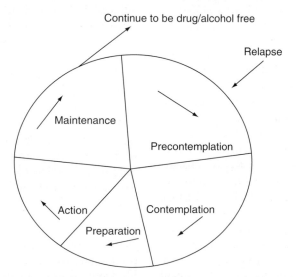

Figure 5.1 The wheel of the stages of change. (Derived from Prochaska, J. O. & DiClemente, C. C. (1984) and DiClemente, C. C., Prochaska, J. O., Fairhurst, S. K., *et al.* (1991).)

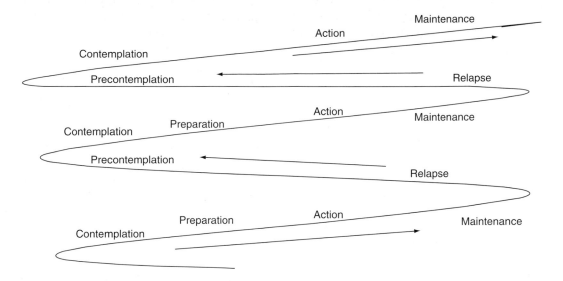

Figure 5.2   A spiral model of the stages of the change. (Derived from Prochaska, J. O., DiClemente, C. C. & Norcross, J. C. (1997) In search of how people change: applications to addictive behaviours. In: G. A. Marlatt & G. R. VandenBos (Eds) *Addictive Behaviours: Readings on Etiology, Prevention and Treatment*, pp. 671–96. Washington, DC: American Psychological Association. Copyright 1997 by the American Psychological Association. Adapted with permission.)

- *Preparation* is the stage when a change has been decided and steps are being taken to prepare for it.
- *Action* is the stage when people change their behaviour.
- *Maintenance* is the stage when change has occurred and is being maintained. It is important that this stage is seen as an active phase and not just the absence of relapse.

More recently Prochaska and colleagues (1997) reconfigured the stages of change into a spiral model to show that people learn from relapses and move on. This is given in Figure 5.2.

Apart from an informal assessment of motivational statements there are a number of structured ways of assessing the stage of change. McConnaughy and colleagues (1983; 1989) developed the University of Rhode Island Change Assessment Scale (URICA), which consists of 32 items shown to reflect four stages of change: precontemplation, contemplation, action and maintenance. Miller and Tonigan (1996) developed the 40-item Stages Of Change Readiness And Treatment Eagerness Scale (SOCRATES). A much shorter scale and one that is commonly used in clinical

practice is the Readiness to Change Questionnaire (Rollnick *et al.*, 1992) (see Appendix 8), although this has been devised for excessive drinkers and is not applicable to drug users.

When Rollnick and colleagues devised the questionnaire they analysed the responses of 141 excessive drinkers, and found a clear structure corresponding to precontemplation, contemplation and action stages of change. No factor corresponding to maintenance could be demonstrated, so this stage was omitted from the Readiness to Change Questionnaire.

Although this has not been validated, the questionnaire has been adapted by some drug agencies in the following way so that it can also be used to assess drug users' readiness to change (questions 1 and 5 have interchanged, but this should not alter the assessment scores as both questions apply to precontemplators):

(1) It is a waste of time thinking about my drug use.
(2) I am trying to use less than I used to.
(3) I enjoy drugs, but sometimes I use too much.
(4) Sometimes I think I should cut down on my drug use.

(5) I do not think I use too much.

(6) I have recently changed my using habits.

(7) Anyone can talk about wanting to do something about drugs. I am actually doing something about it.

(8) I am at a stage where I should think about using less drugs.

(9) My drug use is a problem sometimes.

(10) There is no need for me to think about changing.

(11) I am actually changing my drug-using habits now.

(12) Taking less drugs would be pointless for me.

The scores for precontemplation, contemplation and action are then compiled in the same way.

Over the past 20 years the Stages of Change model has become extremely popular and has had a major impact in the addictions field. Interventions that are appropriate for behaviour change in those who are contemplating change often differ from interventions most helpful for those in the precontemplation stage, and will be again different from those interventions that will be most useful for individuals at the stage of action. The model is intuitively appealing because of its apparent simplicity.

In spite of its importance there have been relatively few outcome studies on the model, and a review of the literature suggests there are a number of problems with the approach which have not received public debate (Bunton *et al.*, 2000). One major criticism is that the model has a tendency to reduce and oversimplify complex sociocultural processes and thereby distorts behavioural change issues (Bunton *et al.*, 1991). We should not be surprised that this model is limited by an intrinsic bias which simplifies complex sociocultural issues as it was devised by psychologists and focuses on psychological theory. As we have demonstrated throughout this book, behaviour change needs to be adequately contextualised within a broad holistic framework of social, cultural and policy processes. These complex biopsychosocial influences interrelate and influence the development of, and recovery from, dependent substance use and need to be tackled. Although oversimplification of the transtheoretical approach model undoubtedly occurs, it

is a useful tool which has proved invaluable in clinical situations.

The Decisional Balance

A way of confirming whether someone is really in the precontemplation, contemplation or action stage is through the use of the *Decisional Balance* (Janis & Mann, 1977) (see Appendix 9). The disadvantages of drinking or taking drugs can be thought of as facilitators of change, and the advantages can be seen as barriers to change (Prochaska *et al.*, 1994). Velicer has demonstrated that for smokers in the precontemplation stage the advantages of smoking outweigh the disadvantages (Velicer *et al.*, 1985). Crossover then occurs during the contemplation and preparation stages. The contemplation stage is high in both pros and cons, whereas the preparation and action stages are high in cons but low in pros. It is the same for all types of substance use.

Although the Decisional Balance applies to all forms of change, it was originally devised out of a recognition that all substance users feel ambivalent about their drinking or drug use. A balance sheet can be drawn up between those factors which promote the desire to continue drinking or taking drugs and the desire to stop. Substance users are asked to list all the pros and cons of drinking or drug-taking, and the pros and cons of stopping. This assessment tool is sometimes also termed *the advantages/disadvantages four square analysis*.

To help ensure that nothing is overlooked, factors that promote and inhibit change are also viewed from their opposite angles. Thus, in the example where one of the boxes is labelled *disadvantages of stopping* as shown in Appendix 9, it helps add a list of those factors which should be included in the *advantages of using drugs/drinking* box as this is a different way of looking at the same thing. Similarly the boxes labelled *disadvantages of using drugs/drinking* and *advantages of stopping* are two different ways of examining the same issue. However, it is not just a case of putting all the factors together which promote and inhibit change and adding up the numerical final totals, because some factors are more important than others. The importance of each item can be assessed by scoring 1 for *not important* to 5 for *extremely important*. This will give a more accurate final score.

If the advantages of change outweigh the disadvantages, the client should no longer be in the contemplation stage. He or she should be ready to prepare for change, although there are one or two exceptions to this rule, such as a lack of self-efficacy as in the following case study.

CASE STUDY 1

Mr A attended his local drug service. Responding to the enquiry as to why he was there he replied, 'My probation officer sent me'. When asked what he wanted to do about his drug problem he said, 'My probation officer wants me to stop'. However, completing an advantages/disadvantages analysis he could only think of one advantage of taking drugs but very many disadvantages. Similarly, there were many advantages of stopping drugs, but only one for continuing to take them. Challenged with this discrepancy, Mr A admitted that he resented being pressurised by his probation officer to attend the drug service, although he knew that he really wanted to sort out his drug problem. He had become so incensed that his probation officer had sent him to seek help to come off drugs without involving him in the decision, and with the lurking threat of a court appearance that would go against him, that his determination to overcome his drug problem had become obscured. In spite of what he had said he was really very well motivated.

Apart from helping to identify the stage of change, there are several other ways in which this matrix can be useful. For instance, it can be used to examine decision-making in those few rough sleepers who do not wish to be rehoused or in IDUs who continue to indulge in injecting or sexual high-risk BBV behaviour. It can also aid decision-making regarding prescriptions. If drinkers are not severely dependent and the Decisional Balance lists a number of advantages of continuing to drink, they may be encouraged to opt for a programme aimed at helping them control their drinking. Similarly heroin users, whose Decisional Balance suggests them to be in the contemplation stage of substance use, might best benefit from methadone maintenance with a view to harm reduction rather than abstinence.

The Decisional Balance can also be used to indicate the client's level of motivation. It is surprising how many people who are deeply embroiled in problematic substance use are very unclear about their motivation to stop. Their ambivalence, which is always present to some degree, seems to confuse them. The Decisional Balance helps clients clarify their thoughts. It often helps if this is included as a fundamental part of the initial assessment. In its own right it is a useful treatment intervention when used in this way.

A further advantage of this versatile psychological tool is that it helps pinpoint the way in which people use drugs or drink for psychological gain. Thus an advantage of using might be described as 'It helps me relax' or 'It gives me confidence', suggesting that the substance is being taken to help the person cope with anxiety, or as an aid in what are perceived to be difficult social situations. Counsellors may then explore these issues further and determine whether their client would benefit from anxiety management skills training or social skills training.

Assessment of self-efficacy

There is one particular situation where Janis and Mann's assessment tool does not apply. However strongly the Decisional Balance indicates good motivation to change, no change will occur if the drug user or drinker does not believe this to be possible, even when the advantages of change far outweigh the disadvantages. Good self-efficacy is necessary for change to occur.

Various questionnaires have been devised to measure self-efficacy. The best of these is the Situational Confidence Questionnaire (SCQ) (Annis & Graham, 1988) which tests the individual's ability to resist drinking when it is sparked by various situational and emotional cues. These cues closely parallel the Inventory of Drinking Situations (IDS) (Annis *et al.*, 1987). There is also an Inventory of Drug-Taking Situations (IDTS) (Annis *et al.*, 1997), a 50-item self-reported questionnaire. There is good compatibility between the IDS and the IDTS.

The three questionnaires have been promoted for use in the clinical situation, but their length and complexity make this extremely difficult. They are necessarily lengthy because efficacy beliefs are multifaceted and involve different types of capability such as management of thought, affect, action and motivation. If self-efficacy beliefs are limited to single-item measures, this fails to differentiate between individuals who differ in their self-efficacy beliefs for higher and lower level tasks. As with the Decisional Balance, efficacy beliefs vary in strength and people should be asked to rate the strength of their beliefs. It is regrettable that there is no validated short questionnaire to assess self-efficacy. The above questionnaires are not used routinely in clinical situations, and the development of a more useful questionnaire for clinical practice is awaited.

Self-efficacy has been shown to be superior to past performance as predictor of future behaviour, and is applicable over a wide range of behaviours associated with chemical dependency (e.g. abstinence, controlled drinking, relapse, BBV high-risk behaviour, etc.). Using a 31-item measure of self-efficacy in smokers, DiClemente and colleagues (1985) have demonstrated its importance. Efficacy judgements are not influenced by a responding bias to appear socially desirable (Velicer *et al.*, 1990). However, a good sense of self-efficacy in one domain is not necessarily accompanied by high self-efficacy in other realms. Highly successful people, who are able to recognise their competence in many other areas may still have a low sense of self-efficacy for overcoming substance use.

There is close interlinking of change, decisional balance and self-efficacy. Prochaska and colleagues (1985) have stated that the stages of change, processes of change, decisional balance, and self-efficacy are all intertwined, and so are interactive constructs that describe and determine behaviour change and the characteristics of the change process.

Assessment of BBV risk behaviour

Assessment of BBV risk behaviour can be considered in three parts:

(1) past risk behaviour
(2) current injecting and sexual risk behaviour
(3) environmental context, cognitive and other internal factors

Assessment of past risk behaviour

Priority should always be given to addressing BBV risk behaviour. Prevention of sharing injecting equipment and injecting should be at the top of a hierarchy of treatment goals because the risk of causing serious harm to other individuals and society is so great.

Although BBV transmission may occur after only one episode of sharing, research conducted on a population sample of 2961 injecting in seven English cities recruited from both drug agencies and the community suggests that BBV infections are not rapidly acquired after initiation into injecting. This was a reversal of expectation. In spite of 42% of current injectors reporting sharing, among those who had been injecting for less than three years, the prevalence of hepatitis C was 7.4% and the estimated annual incidence in those who had begun injecting in the previous two years was below 5% (Hope *et al.*, 2001). These findings suggest there is time to intervene with those who are indulging in BBV high-risk behaviour to facilitate behaviour change.

Because HIV does not survive long at room temperature the original advice given to injectors did not include the spread of HIV through injecting paraphernalia. However, hepatitis C is a much more resilient virus which may survive for several months at room temperature. Thus the assessment of BBV risk behaviour must now include questions about sharing injecting paraphernalia. In Australia, Crofts and his colleagues (2000) have shown that hepatitis C virus (HCV) RNA could be detected on 70% (14/20) of syringes, 67% (6/9) of swabs, 40% (2/5) of filters, 25% (1/4) of spoons and 33% (1/3) of water samples. The authors also postulate that tourniquets may be a source of hazard. These findings confirm that HCV could be transmitted among IDUs through injecting equipment other than needles and syringes, and evidence from behavioural studies suggests that such transmission may not be uncommon (van Beek *et al.*, 1998; Crofts & Aitken, 1997).

A past history of ever-sharing injecting equipment should prompt the worker to offer testing for HIV, and hepatitis B and C, and to ask about current injecting and sexual practice. In clinical practice it is not unusual for a denial of ever sharing any equipment in spite of a positive HCV test result. This may be due to imperfect recall, subconscious denial, the way the question is asked or unrecognised factors. It is thus safest to offer testing to anyone who has ever injected. It is important to ask when sharing last occurred. If it were in the last three months, a retest might be required for HIV and if it were within the last six months, a retest might be needed for HCV. Further information about BBV testing, including pre- and post-test counselling is given in Chapter 17.

Assessment of current risk behaviour

The research definition of current risk behaviour relates to behaviour that has taken place over the past four weeks. A relatively short self-completion questionnaire has been developed in the UK by the Centre for Research on Drugs and Health Behaviour (see Appendix 10). By processes which are similar to those through which drug-using behaviours can be changed, current BBV risk behaviour can be influenced by a variety of personal and environmental factors open to change. Thus positive change can be aided through psychosocial interventions which utilise personal strengths or by reducing environmental and psychological harm. A good assessment enables a care plan to be formed which can be targeted to the treatment needs of the individual.

Assessment of personal and environmental factors that interrelate with BBV risk behaviour

This is based on Bandura's concept of the Triadic Reciprocal Causation of HIV risk behaviour, where the three factors influencing each other are: behaviour, cognition and other intrapersonal factors, and the environment (see Figure 5.3). Bandura's three factors are represented schematically by P representing cognitive, biological and other internal events; B signifying behaviour; and E the external environment (Bandura, 1994).

Thus it is important to assess not only substance use and BBV risk behaviour, but also the compounding environmental and cognitive and other personal factors which influence it, for it is the combination of these factors that dictate the advice and counselling needed. Ignorance sometimes leads to sharing. Some people who have hepatitis C infection think that they will not do themselves or others harm if they share injecting equipment with someone else with hepatitis C. They do not know that they can reinfect themselves with a different type or subtype of the virus and thus worsen their prognosis if they share injecting equipment with someone else who has hepatitis C. Nor do they know that for similar reasons they can worsen the prognosis of others. However, accurate knowledge on its own is often not enough. In Bandura's (1994) own words:

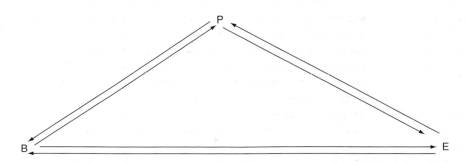

Figure 5.3   Triadic Reciprocal Causation. (From Bandura, A. (1994) Social cognitive theory and exercise of control over HIV infection. In: R. J. DiClemente & J. L. Peterson (Eds) *Preventing AIDS: Theories and Methods of Behavioural Interventions*. London: Plenum Press. With permission from Kluwer Academic/Plenum Publishers.)

Heightened awareness and knowledge of health risks are important pre-conditions for self-directed change. Unfortunately, information alone does not necessarily exert much influence on refractory health-impairing habits. To achieve self-directed change, people need to be given not only reasons to alter risky habits but also the behavioural means, resources and social supports to do so.

For example, in southern Asia, where access to condoms and sterile injecting equipment are limited by both geography and poverty, these environmental factors will dictate a different advice and counselling focus from BBV high-risk behaviour by middle class employed drug users in urban parts of the UK, Australia or the USA.

Less obvious environmental factors also require an adaptable counselling approach to meet the individual's needs to help them move on from dangerous BBV risk behaviour. Thus when asking about the sharing of injecting equipment and paraphernalia, those working in the field should find out whether the sharing is confined to one long-term partner or to casual acquaintances; whether there are practical difficulties in obtaining sterile injecting equipment; what are the circumstances that lead to sharing with current friends and other social contacts; and to what extent drug and/or alcohol use is associated with poor personal organisation.

Assertiveness and the negative thinking associated with depression are particularly important intrapersonal factors. Someone who finds it difficult to assert themselves may feel unable to use condoms or to insist on not sharing *works*. A depressed person may think: 'I don't care whether I live or die. If I died it would solve a lot of problems. I might as well share someone else's works.'

In spite of the differing advice requirements between HIV and HCV over paraphernalia, prevention policies for HIV appear to have an effect in reducing the spread of HCV (Judd *et al.*, 2000) and it is likely that these policies will help reduce the transmission of all blood-borne pathogens. It is therefore essential that the initial assessment of drug users who are seeking help includes an assessment of BBV risk behaviour, and that there are regular re-assessments of all drug injectors in regular contact with services (especially needle exchange services) so that adequate help to reduce the risk of transmission of blood-borne pathogens may be given.

It is important that sexual as well as injecting behaviour is assessed at the first interview as this may be the only time that the client is seen. Some workers find it difficult to ask about sexual habits when a client is initially seen, but difficult feelings about this need to be discarded in the interests of good practice. If sexual behaviour is discussed in a professional way, making clear from the outset the reasons why this is being discussed, there is unlikely to be a problem. When difficulties arise it is usually because an inexperienced worker finds it embarrassing to discuss these matters and this is picked up by the client. Where BBV high-risk behaviours occur, the risk of BBV transmission should be reassessed monthly if possible, as some people take a long time to change their ways and those who do change may lapse back again to high-risk behaviour patterns.

There are two widely held beliefs with regard to the influence of drug or alcohol use on sexual behaviour:

(1) the use of certain substances increases (or decreases) sexual desire and levels of sexual activity
(2) substance use has a disinhibitory effect on safer sex compliance

Yet a critical examination of the literature suggests the evidence supporting these widely held assumptions is thin, and there is little empirical certainty about the causal determinants of either of these two contentions. Instead, of key importance is the finding that individual behaviour and understanding of the use and effects of drugs in relation to sexual behaviour are influenced by a complex interaction between cognition and culture (Rhodes & Stimson, 1994). For example, power and intimacy factors within relationships may be of much greater relevance than the direct effects of the substance itself.

Thus, as with injecting behaviour, insights into Bandura's triadic reciprocity holds the key to aiding sexual behaviour change and there is considerable overlap between the two. For every person who continues to share injecting equipment or practice unsafe sex a full assessment should be undertaken. In order to understand the processes that lead to persistent risk behaviour, these should include the relevant associated personal and environmental influences so that ways can be found to rectify them.

Assessment of risk of overdose or death

From the substance user's perspective, the occurrence of overdose is often accidental. However, there is a school of thought which urges that the term *accident* be avoided in medical literature (Davis & Pless, 2001) as it implies an occurrence which could not be foreseen or avoided. This is clearly very pertinent to the circumstances of substance overdose, which are highly predictable in an actuarial sense though less so in the timing. Overdose is an accident waiting to happen and the rates of opiate-related deaths have been rising significantly (Neeleman & Farrell, 1997; Hall *et al.*, 2000). The professional has an important role in helping the substance user identify and modify risky overdose behaviour and be better prepared in the event of finding someone who has overdosed (Darke *et al.*, 2000). Such interventions are equally applicable in primary care where GPs are likely to find that around half of opiate-dependent patients have personal experience of overdose (Cullen *et al.*, 2000). It has been shown that over 90% of service users have been present when another user has overdosed (Strang *et al.*, 1999) and that they are keen to learn how to respond, including an interest among opiate users for take-home doses of the opiate antagonist naltrexone.

In discussing the risks of overdose it should be remembered that many users are emotionally distressed and may be reckless about their drug use, or ambivalent concerning the outcomes of their use. Neale (2001) found a high incidence of suicidal thoughts in a study of opiate users who had recently overdosed. Working with them to improve self-esteem, treat underlying depression and stabilise relationships can have a significant benefit in terms of risk reduction. The assessment of severity of depression is important. Depression requiring

psychiatric treatment may be suggested by the use of the 17-item Hamilton Depression Rating Scale (Appendix 11) or the 21-item Beck Depression Inventory (BDI-II). These are useful screening tests for anyone aged 13–80. However, the biological symptoms, which are mimicked by the effects of substance use, may load the score towards a significant level and conformation may be required by psychiatric team referral. A seven-item shortened form of the BDI-II may also be obtainable to 'qualified individuals' on the payment of a fee from The Psychological Corporation Europe, 32 Jamestown Road, London NW1 7BY, or online at www.psychcorp.com.

The Advisory Council on the Misuse of Drugs (ACMD, 2000) in its *Report on Drug-Related Deaths* urges that specific attention be given to overdose and other acute risks at the initial assessment stage and repeatedly during treatment, and that this be combined with a care plan to reduce risks. Risk domains include unstable patterns of substance use, chaotic lifestyle, polysubstance use including opiates, benzodiazepines and alcohol, the presence of suicidal ideas or a past history of overdose, current negative life events, or events leading to reduced dose tolerance such as detoxification or imprisonment.

Assessment of harm to self or others

During the assessment it is important to consider the possible risks which the substance user may cause to others. The client may then be encouraged to modify his or her risk behaviour, recognising that the harm which might be caused is rarely intentional. Often the substance user is also at risk from the same behaviour either directly or indirectly. The drugs worker has professional and ethical responsibilities to ensure that appropriate advice is given and necessary action, if any, taken.

Driving of motor vehicles is a common risk domain. The law relating to intoxication, stable medical treatment (maintenance) and other treatments is complex and specific to each country. Workers need to be familiar with the law and should have written information to give to service users. It is wise to make a written record of the giving of such advice and information. On occasions it will be necessary to intervene with a client who intends to drive when clearly unfit to do so. It is helpful to have discussed ways of handling such situations with colleagues.

The issue of risks of violence is unduly emphasised in the stereotyping of substance users. Nevertheless, there are risks which should be anticipated in a structured way. Alcohol and benzodiazepine use produces irritability, stimulants can provoke paranoid and aggressive thinking, and most withdrawal states are associated with anxiety and irritability. Such states are powerful triggers to violence in otherwise calm people. The assessment process can be a good time to discuss such triggers with substance users and to help them find strategies to reduce risks. Discussion about irritable behaviour can be a good introduction to more direct discussion of past offences or other violent episodes. Where there is evidence of high risk to others, it may be possible to access background information of offences and advice about safety through the probation service or the police. Rarely a forensic psychiatric assessment may be appropriate. Such situations may arise urgently. Good pathways and professional links established between services can prove invaluable.

Violence between partners is not uncommon among substance users, and places of safety may need to be considered. The issue of domestic violence can be explored by questions about loss of control or fear of partners. (See Chapter 18 for further details.)

Children in households of substance users are at increased risk of emotional and physical harm, either from direct substance effects or social consequences. Clients should be asked about their own children and any others for whom they have care responsibilities. Again, this should be raised within the constructive framework of enabling the good care and well-being of children. It may become apparent that the service user is not currently able to provide good enough care. Occasionally such concerns are very urgent. Workers should be aware of local procedures for referral and have clear policies for these potential exceptions to normal confidentiality.

The most usual sufferers of harm are still the individual substance users themselves. In this context, deliberate self-harm and suicide may compound the inherent risks of substance use. A history of self-inflicted injury as well as self-poisoning has a high prevalence in clients who have experienced physical or sexual abuse. Inquiry about such behaviours can thus point to sensitive issues to be considered during treatment, mood disorders to be treated and strategies of risk reduction.

Assessment of personal and environmental factors that are related to addictive behaviours

Zinberg (1984) describes the assessment of drug use patterns through the identification of three interrelated factors: drug (substance), set (person) and setting (environment). This has many similarities with Bandura's theory of Triadic Reciprocal Causation, which applies to all types of human behaviour. It can be equally applied to substance-taking and any other addictive behaviour and also to high-risk injecting and sexual behaviour. Thus many personal and environmental factors, including cognitive and cultural influences, that lead to drug use are similar or identical to those that lead to injecting and sexual behaviours that place someone at high risk of acquiring or transmitting HIV and hepatitis. Addressing those influences that were instrumental in the development of persistent BBV high-risk behaviour may help influence a person's whole drug problem beneficially, and vice versa.

CASE STUDY 2

For 16 years client J had been using street heroin. There was no single episode that made client J seek help. He was just fed up with it. He had done many things that he did not feel particularly proud of. He felt badly about some things he had done, but never showed this. He was seen as tough on the streets. Ordinary people avoided him. Even other drug users spent as little time with him as possible, and most of them now seemed much younger than he was. His one close relationship foundered several years before. He did not blame her, although he felt angry at the time. He was isolated and socially excluded. His self-esteem was poor. Although he could handle himself well on the street, he knew there were some things he would never be able to do – like coming off drugs.

Client J had heard that his doctor sometimes prescribed methadone, but he could not face seeing a counsellor and discussing what he had done in the past. One day he went to see his doctor who put him on a methadone maintenance programme. He was offered counselling but refused it. Immediately things got better. He no longer had to spend all day sorting out how to raise the money to support his *habit*. He used heroin occasionally but this got less over the months and years. After two years and a succession of part-time jobs, he got a job in a factory where he felt accepted. He met a girl there whom he liked and who liked him. She had never been involved in drugs but did not reject him when he told her. Eventually they moved in together, and she became pregnant.

His circumstances had changed completely. He had a job and with it a new self-identity. He no longer saw himself, or was seen by others, as a drug user, and he felt loved and supported. He had hopes for the future. He started to feel better about himself and his ability to sort out his addiction problem no longer felt out of reach. Client J decided he would come off drugs and agreed to see a counsellor to help him. He relapsed several times, but with the help of his partner and professionals he carried on and finally achieved sustained abstinence.

Not all cases resolve so satisfactorily but the above example shows how the environment and the person can change to improve and finally overcome damaging behaviour.

Assessment of psychological functioning and its relationship to problems and strengths

Personal psychosocial functioning outlines, and is determined by, the psychological and social strengths of the individual. The psychosocial functioning of individual drug users and drinkers is not easy to assess directly. The psychological side includes self-efficacy, self-esteem, coping skills, problem-solving ability, assertiveness and the ability to deal with negative emotions such as anger, anxiety, depression and so on. The social side includes social skills and the ability to harness environmental resources, such as social support, and overcome adverse social problems like social exclusion and unemployment.

Although they are not easy to assess, in practice, an individual's strengths are suggested by the absence of problem areas. Thus the easiest way is to first assess the problems and difficulties that substance users face, and in the absence of harmful problems to look for strengths. Both strengths and harms are important to assess because harms tend to obstruct the recovery process whereas strengths can be utilised to facilitate recovery. Both are sometimes hidden or easily overlooked. Recognising and highlighting a client's strengths at first assessment will help establish rapport, and lays the foundation stone for a good client–worker relationship.

Research has shown that a high proportion of substance users have multiple and complex needs and are well known to a number of different agencies (Kozarickovacic *et al.*, 1995; Keene, 2001). A study by Keene and colleagues (1999) set out to compare the progress of clients attending two substance use agencies. Differences in outcome between the two agencies were entirely attributable to the number and severity of a range of problems rather than simply to severity of dependence or differences between the agencies. Although the care of dual diagnosis patients (co-morbidity of drink and drug use problems with mental health problems) is primarily the responsibility of health services, substance users commonly have a number of other psychosocial problems, physical health problems, learning difficulties and criminal behaviour which involve a number of different agencies. (See Chapter 16 for further details on dual diagnosis.)

The assessment of a drug-induced psychosis can be difficult without hospital admission to help ensure that the drug is no longer being taken and even with inpatient admission there can be difficulties. For example, amphetamine psychosis generally lasts for about ten days after cessation of use of the drug whereas amphetamine is usually no longer detectable in the urine after 48 hours. So a negative urine test does not exclude the diagnosis. Conversely a positive urine test does not confirm a diagnosis. Carney and colleagues (1984) suggested that there appeared to be more cases of cannabis psychosis among patients discharged from Shenley

Hospital than had been reported previously for the whole of England and Wales.

Newcombe (1992) has demonstrated the complexity of assessing the harm from substance use. He suggests that the evaluation of harm first requires the selection of a subset of desired harm reduction goals from a matrix of potential options. His framework, which can guide the measurement of harm reduction outcomes, offers nine categories of drug-related harm from the dimensions of type (health, social, economic) and level (individual, community, society). These occur within a time dimension (short-, medium- and long-term effects), a duration dimension (temporary, permanent) and a severity dimension (mild, moderate, major). He also states that, as harm reduction goals are hierarchical, assessments need to be made as to the propensity of each for achieving the optimum net reduction in overall harm.

Such detailed assessments are useful for research purposes, but when assessing a substance user in routine practice it is helpful to take a more simplistic view. Some substance users have multiple and severe drink- and drug-related problems which require attention because they interfere with the recovery process. Many of these, such as homelessness and poor social skills, are obvious. Other people have few, if any, problems and do not require interventions to reduce the harm that is present. Generally speaking, but not invariably, if there is no problem present, there is in its place a strength. If someone is socially isolated, it can interfere with the recovery process, but if there is good social support, it is a strength which can help the person overcome a drink or drug problem. The presence of multiple problems suggests that there are few strengths to combat them. Strengths may be internal or external to the individual, psychological or environmental. A person may have good coping skills to help avoid relapse or may have poor coping skills that placed him or her at risk of difficulties from substance use in the first place.

It is important that all harm reduction initiatives are focused on the individual. Those involved in the professional care of people with alcohol and drug problems cannot close their eyes to the harm that is engendered to families, communities and society, through drug- or drink-associated violence, criminality, road traffic accidents (RTAs) and BBV infections. But in practice, if the harm to individual drug users or drinkers is reduced, so will it be reduced to families and local society. Harm reduction to communities should always be facilitated through the individual substance user.

The benefits to community and individual are often reciprocal. Helping drinkers or drug users manage anger, reduce criminality, and improve high-risk behaviour regarding driving and BBV infections are examples where harm reduction aimed at individuals will help protect communities and society as a whole. As HIV has now declined to such low levels in the UK, drug users are no longer perceived as people who are at risk of infecting whole communities, as was the case in the late 1980s. As substance use declines, so too will the associated criminality. Substance users will commit fewer crimes and be involved in fewer RTAs. As individuals they will be viewed to a lesser degree as potentially aggressive criminals who mug people on the street or kill them in RTAs.

If families and communities view substance users as normal human beings, they will become more supportive. Families and communities then become another strength which can be utilised to aid the individual's progress and help prevent further problems developing for the individual substance user. The individual with a solid constructive relationship with a partner and good supportive networks from family, friends and the local community is less likely to indulge in high-risk behaviours than someone who is depressed, has no close friends or family, and whose wife has just said she is going to leave him to live with another man.

It is just as important to take a broad view of strengths as it is of harm. In the UK the definition of problem drug use has been expanded to include 'any form of drug misuse which involves, or may lead to, the sharing of injecting equipment' (ACMD, 1988). This can be interpreted to include all injectors. Understanding the reasons underlying various strengths sometimes helps with their practical application. If a heroin user does not inject, this could be viewed as a strength, but it might be that the individual does not inject because he or she is terrified of needles. This is less likely to be therapeutically useful than some other reasons (e.g. a good friend died of an overdose with a needle in her arm and a decision was made never to inject). Strengths are not just the absence of problems. They need to be used therapeutically. However, the absence of a problem in a particular area does point the way to some possible therapeutically useful strengths.

The assessment process should review as a matter of course all problems that are potentially harmful and all strengths that are potentially useful. A good assessment will highlight the nature and extent of medical, social, psychological and legal problems that are associated with substance use, whether or not the intention is to take action to reduce the harm that these problems generate. Having looked at these problem areas an assessment can then be made of strengths.

Drink and drug problems may occur independently from dependence and sometimes in the absence of dependence. Nevertheless, because by definition severe dependence indicates an impairment of occupational and social functioning, the probability of problems occurring increases as dependence becomes more entrenched. Similarly in the severely dependent there are usually fewer utilisable strengths.

A harm reduction policy which aims to remove as many problems as possible is not generally necessary. Perfection is never achievable. Many people can recover from substance use without reducing every bit of harm from their associated problems. But where these problems and the harm they generate are interfering with the recovery process at least some harm reduction will be needed. As a rule of thumb, harm reduction is generally required to a level whereby personal functioning is no longer dominated by problems or chemical dependence and substance users are able to lead happy and useful lives.

As we have seen, opiate harm reduction initiatives should not be limited to the prescribing of methadone or buprenorphine, although this can, and often does, prevent considerable harm. If, after sorting out some obviously harmful social, psychological, physical and legal problems, no further progress is being made and outcome measurements suggest that someone is stuck, hidden problems can be actively searched out. For example, covert depression may have developed and may be hindering recovery.

Strengths can also remain hidden. However, once trust is gained positive character traits may surface. Sometimes these are hidden purposely because people may feel they have to disguise them in order to protect themselves from being hurt by others in their peer group. Positive character traits such as a caring nature, kindness or generosity make people vulnerable. Often those who feel the most vulnerable protect themselves by toughening up their appearance. Those who present themselves in the most extreme forms, e.g. with facial tattoos, multiple body piercing and extreme hair styles, are quite often those who have been most emotionally damaged in the past, sometimes in childhood. Establishing a therapeutic relationship in such cases takes time and patience. Once trust has been established it becomes possible to discover the hidden assets underlying this vulnerability that can be mobilised to assist the recovery process.

A lack of social support may also remain hidden. The number of friends and acquaintances a substance user has does not always correlate with the degree of social support to help overcome a drink or drug problem. A person can appear to have a lot of friends and acquaintances, yet being unable to make use of them, he or she remains socially isolated with very little in the way of social support.

An assessment, not only of a client's strengths but also of his or her self-efficacy is very important. It takes considerable ability to survive on the streets. For instance, many drug users have highly developed skills in *doing business* – raising enough money in a short time to buy the drugs they require for that day. They know they are competent in this area, but when it comes to coming off drugs they may question their competence.

CASE STUDY 3

> Mr R, who had been dependent on heroin and other opiates for several years, began a methadone withdrawal programme prescribed by his GP. Things had been going well in other areas and he had made a great effort to sort his life out: he had landed a job that he really enjoyed; he had entered into a close and rewarding relationship with a woman who did not take drugs; her eight-year-old son idolised him; and past friends who arrived at the house with any

drugs, including cannabis, were told to leave. Everything seemed set for success, yet every time his dose of methadone mixture reduced to below 50 mg he lapsed. Although he wanted to come off drugs and voiced this, he came to believe that he was incapable of reducing below 50 mg methadone and achieving abstinence. His GP sent him for assessment as to whether he should be maintained on a dose of 50 mg. Mr R was an energetic and competent man. Assessment confirmed that he was highly motivated to achieve abstinence, and that one of his strengths was good self-efficacy in general. Yet he had lost self-efficacy in one small area. When it was realised that his real problem was an erroneous lack of self-efficacy, a way was eventually found to overcome this using cognitive therapeutic techniques. The assessment was the key to his recovery. No one was more pleased than Mr R when he did achieve sustained abstinence.

Early insight of poor self-efficacy can often be obtained by examining the answers given in the advantages/disadvantages analysis of a Decisional Balance. For example, the following answers are given in the advantages box (Appendix 9):

- makes me feel better in myself
- helps blot things out
- stops me feeling depressed, bored, anxious and so on

This indicates potential problems with low self-esteem; inadequate coping skills with possible deep underlying psychological problems; and a poor ability to deal with difficult emotions, respectively.

Further elucidation will be needed before there is a full understanding of the way in which drugs or alcohol have been used. There is no standard pattern. Every person is unique in the way he or she uses the substances of choice. Thoughts that are too painful to confront differ widely, and the way these will need to be handled may vary substantially. An individually tailored care programme can be devised to overcome these problems.

Assessment of the different problem domains to formulate a care plan

Severe problems that are associated with substance use so commonly obstruct the recovery process that it is important that they are removed. The question is whether to remove them directly by targeted interventions or whether the inherent psychosocial strengths of the individual are sufficient to overcome them. Generally speaking those who are able to overcome these problems themselves will have already done this and achieved a *natural recovery*. Some, however, do not recognise their strengths or have not been motivated to do anything about their substance use problems.

Thus many care plans will first seek to target the problem areas and then counter the harm that is emanating from them. If this fails or if the problems appear to be only minor, they will examine the degree of personal functioning and whether it is adequate to overcome the various problems without additional help.

In order to determine an individual's problems and his or her personal strengths, and whether these need to be improved further, it is helpful to formally examine the different problem domains.

(1) *Drug and alcohol use*
   - type of drug(s), quantity/frequency and pattern of use, route of administration, the source of the drug and substitute prescribing needs
   - alcohol use, quantity/frequency and pattern of use (including binge drinking), whether above *safe* level and alcohol dependence
(2) *Social/environmental problem domains*
   The social situation of a drinker or drug taker may or may not be a result of the substance taken. Either way a good assessment of the client's social situation is necessary and, where possible, steps should be taken to improve social stability and social support.
   - Is the client employed? If so, are others at work aware of the drug or drink problem? How do they react to it if they are? If unemployed, does he or she wish to gain employment and how could this be facilitated? Are there opportunities for further training and education?
   - To what extent is there good social support at work and at home? Is the individual excluded from mainstream society and/or socially isolated with few or no friends? Are

there good communication skills? What are the attitudes of partners and *significant others*? Do they drink heavily or take drugs themselves? Is there attendance at Alcoholics Anonymous (AA)/Narcotics Anonymous (NA)? If so, does he or she have a sponsor or telephone numbers to ring if support is needed?

- Is there adequate and secure accommodation or is he or she homeless?
- Are there any large debts or other financial problems?
- What help can be given to reduce the harm from other social problems, including child care problems and domestic violence?

(3) *Psychological problem domains*

- Does the person feel depressed? Are there any other features of a serious depression, e.g. suicidal thoughts or early morning waking? (Depression can be difficult to evaluate in someone who drinks or takes drugs.)
- Does the individual have good social and coping skills? Are drink or drugs taken to help him or her cope with negative mood states such as depression, anxiety or boredom? Because of poor coping skills some people request tranquilliser drugs. For drinkers, apart from the first five to ten days to cover withdrawals, recovery may be delayed if tranquillisers are taken, as their mechanism of action is so similar to alcohol. There is the added risk that, because they *summate* with alcohol, this can be dangerous in the case of a relapse. This is particularly so with chlormethiazole (Heminevrin), which is sometimes prescribed as a hypnotic. Chlormethiazole should never be prescribed as a treatment for alcohol dependence outside of a hospital inpatient setting, as a number of unnecessary deaths have occurred in this way.
- Is there reasonable or poor self-respect, and what is the estimation of the ability to cope with difficulties?
- Is there a history of self-harm?
- Are there any subjective problems or observable aspects to suggest the need for psychiatric assessment?

- Insomnia is a common complaint in both drinkers and drug users. Heavily dependent drinkers often have to wait for three months after stopping drinking before they start sleeping normally. This period may be prolonged if hypnotic drugs are taken. There is also a risk of non-prescribed use or, more often, of transference of dependence. There is a balance to be considered between assisting the person to cope with the anxiety and insomnia and the risk of rapid relapse. Like tranquillisers, hypnotics are best avoided in drinkers and drug takers except during an inpatient stay where there is no self-medication. However, this is a counsel of ideals and sometimes the fundamental achievement of breaking old habits of alcohol and illicit drug use is worth supporting by medication in the short term, even though the full recovery is delayed in chemical terms.

(4) *Physical health problems and strengths to counter-balance them*

- Are there any serious ongoing medical problems? Some medical problems may influence the care plan. Thus it would be wrong to advocate a programme of controlled drinking in someone known to have serious liver disease, as liver damage can be exacerbated even with very small quantities of alcohol. Drinkers and drug users who are medically ill may sometimes be best detoxified in hospital or, if they are being treated in the community, detoxification may need to be done at a slower rate or postponed.
- Are there physical health needs relating to BBV infections or sexual health problems? Is there high-risk BBV behaviour? If there is chronic illness such as HIV disease, good housing (a strength) should be a priority. Providing terminal care to someone with HIV who is homeless has been proven to be exceedingly difficult in New York where this combination of problems is quite common. In the UK there is a strong case for classing someone with chronic progressive hepatitis C or who is HIV positive as *vulnerable* and this is accepted by many housing departments.

- Is there a history of accidental overdose or current practices to suggest increased risk?
- Pregnancy can be a particularly difficult problem in substance users and there is a need to identify pregnant substance users at an early stage in order to reduce risk. Pregnant substance users should be treated as an emergency. However, pregnancy can stimulate a strong desire to change to more constructive behaviour patterns.

(5) *Legal problems and related strengths*
- What legal problems have there been? Are there any outstanding court cases? (If there are and he or she is likely to go to prison, some clients prefer to come off drugs before they are sentenced.) Is a Drug Treatment and Testing Order (DTTO) a possible alternative to prison? Legal problems can often motivate constructive change.
- Do any previous convictions suggest problems of anger management or risk to others?
- Is there a designated probation officer? If so, will permission be given to discuss and communicate current issues?
- Any outstanding fines/charges/warrants?
- Any previous imprisonment/violent offences?

In spite of specifically seeking information about problems and strengths surrounding substance use, many will remain hidden. It may be that the client does not see them as either problems or strengths. Many will come to light in time. However, if alcohol and drug workers make a point of looking at these different domains, a good assessment of personal functioning can be obtained, which is likely to result in a better individual treatment package.

Formal questionnaires for problem substance use
The main research tool for assessing the severity of problem substance use is the Addiction Severity Index (ASI) (McLellan *et al.*, 1980). In some treatment facilities in the USA this continues to be used on an intermittent basis where further assessment of treatment outcome is required. However, it takes 50–60 minutes to deliver and many clinicians believe it is better left as a research tool. It has gone through a number of different editions. The ASI assesses six general problem areas: chemical (ab)use; medical; psychological; legal; family/social; and employment/support. It can be used for either drinkers or drug users and has been validated by comparison with other research instruments. It can be used to measure the extent of harm engendered by substance use. As it was published in 1980 before the emergence of HIV/AIDS, the early versions do not include questions to assess damage from high-risk injecting or sexual behaviour. It has been criticised as being too subjective (Darke *et al.*, 1992; Croft-White & Rayner, 1993), too long and, particularly in the areas of family/social functioning and employment, too orientated towards the US treatment situation (Darke *et al.*, 1992). Severity scores are determined on the basis of the estimates of the interviewer and client regarding problem severity. A more objective research instrument to assess problem severity in opiate users, which has also been used to assess outcomes in a clinical treatment setting, is the Opiate Treatment Index (OTI) (Darke *et al.*, 1992). This has questions on HIV risk-taking behaviour, drug use, social functioning, criminality, health and psychological adjustment. It has been validated and is a quicker means of obtaining reliable and valid data on opiate users undergoing treatment over a range of outcome domains, although it still takes 25–30 minutes to complete. Another problem is that, although it has questions relating to HIV high-risk behaviour, it was conceived before the problems of transmission of hepatitis C via paraphernalia were recognised. Again it is best left as a research tool rather than a clinical outcome assessment questionnaire.

Physical health assessment

The *medical history and examination* is a time-honoured approach that doctors use with a standardised format to elucidate medical problems. In the case of substance users almost any bodily system can become adversely affected. Nevertheless, of particular importance are the liver, pregnancy and HIV disease. The examination includes blood and urine tests (and possibly other laboratory tests).

Blood tests

- Liver function tests (LFT) – (drug users and drinkers).
- Gamma-glutamyltransferase (GGT) – (drinkers).
- A full blood count (FBC) may show raised mean corpuscular volume (MCV) in heavy drinkers or characteristic changes in late HIV disease – (drug users and drinkers).
- Abnormal isotransferrins, a laboratory marker of high alcohol consumption (not as useful as had been anticipated) – (drinkers).
- Tests for HIV, hepatitis B and C if there is a history of injecting – (drug users).
- HIV test (anti-HIV), a positive antibody test that indicates current infection and does not indicate immunity to HIV – (drug users).
- Hepatitis B surface antigen (HBsAg) denotes acute or (if present for six months or more) chronic hepatitis B infection – (drug users).
- Hepatitis B surface antibodies (HBsAb) denote current immunity to hepatitis B and hepatitis D (delta antigen).
- Hepatitis B core antibodies (HBcAb) indicate past immunity to hepatitis B.
- Hepatitis B *e* antigen (HbeAg) denotes current infection with high transmission risk (supercarriers).
- HCV antibodies (anti-HCV) denote current acute or chronic hepatitis C infection – (drug users).
- Polymerase chain reaction (PCR) test for HCV indicates the presence of circulating virus. It is used in those with a positive HCV antibody test to tell the difference between people with past HCV infection and those who have either acute or chronic HCV – (drug users).
- BBV tests must always be accompanied by pre- and post-test counselling.

Mental health assessment

Consideration needs to be given to the possibility of mental illness because of the raised prevalence in substance users and because of the need to incorporate treatment in the care plan. Substance users have often been unable to access effec-tive services and may not themselves have recog-nised their subjective experiences as being due to illness.

There are screening instruments for the recognition of major mental illness (Sheehan *et al.*, 1998) and of the need for psychiatric treatment (Bebbington *et al.*, 1996). Non-specialist staff can be trained to administer these instruments such as the Hamilton Depression Rating Scale (Appendix 11) and the process seems to result in improved understanding of the clients' needs and better care planning. In usual practice the recognition of mental illness by non-psychiatrically trained staff is more intuitive. The recognition of a problem can be difficult for staff to convey and may be followed by difficulty in accessing appropriate services. Effective problem identification is enhanced not only by training but by the confidence of planned routes of liaison and referral with mental health practitioners in drugs teams or psychiatric staff linked to primary care. (See Chapter 16 for further guidance on the assessment and treatment of mental illness.)

A history of psychiatric treatment or suicidal behaviour is linked to all forms of psychiatric illness. Low mood, ideas of despair and loss of drive may point to depressive illness. During inter-views, difficulty in sequencing ideas, abnormalities of the processes of thought, or abnormal thought content raise the possibility of psychosis. Poor attention span or unexplained distractability may be manifestations of hallucinations. The early stages of psychosis, which are most prevalent in younger age groups, are often marked by perplexity and associated with convoluted attempts to find meanings. For the interviewer it may lead to a frustrating feeling or a sense of ineffectiveness. These feelings are not to be ignored and should lead to a request for more expert assessment.

A high index of suspicion may be needed for the recognition of learning disability. Substance users tend to be streetwise and reluctant to admit diffi-culties with literacy or comprehension. Failure to detect such problems can undermine the effective-ness of interventions from the basics of reading appointment letters to the engagement in discus-sion of harm reduction and care planning.

Assessment of capacity to consent to treatment

Technically, treatment begins as soon as any information or advice is given. For most aspects of the process, consent is implied by continuing participation, for instance, in the discussion of a problem or the receipt of a prescription. It is therefore essential to maintain continued assessment of the individual's capacity to understand the process, to be aware of the effects of the interventions and to consent to them.

The law concerning consent from children is largely based on case law and is specific to each country. Indeed the age of adult consent is also variable according to location and to specific matters. In the UK the seminal case law is based on the determination of competence to understand the procedure in question (HAS, 1996). Practitioners are well advised to record an assessment of competence when working with young people and where there is any possibility of learning disability or cognitive impairment.

Assessment of role/needs of families, cohabitees and significant others

Families may need help in their own right. With regard to client treatment the right sort of support and advice to the family should be viewed as an integral part of the client's treatment. Where family therapy is being considered, an assessment of family functioning should be made only if the client gives his or her permission that families, cohabitees and/or significant others may be approached. Any person with whom the drinker or drug taker is living is likely to be his or her main source of support, or occasionally the source of a significant problem. The strain on such persons is likely to be considerable, and the way they react may interfere with the recovery process of the client. They, too, may have a substance use problem which may make it difficult for the client to make progress.

The process of assessment of the family attitudes and dynamics is essential when seeking to involve families. Family assessment should include an understanding of the degree of enmeshment with, or detachment from, the client's problem; and the extent to which members of the family attempt to control the problem themselves, unconsciously reward bad behaviour, and prevent the consequences of substance use affecting the client.

The family themselves may just require support, in which case an organisation such as AdFam or one of the self-help groups may be invaluable, not only for themselves, but also indirectly for the client. On the other hand they may not wish to have this and help should not be thrust upon them against their wishes. Chapter 15 explores in depth appropriate interventions for the family when additional help is indicated. Chapter 18 explores particular aspects of women and families.

The family may not be reliable as a corroborative source of information as to the number of units of alcohol consumed or the amount of drugs taken. If there is a discrepancy between the story given by the client and that given by the family, it is wise to accept the client's view as to the quantities of drugs or alcohol that are normally consumed. The substance user generally knows far better than the family.

An assessment as to the suitability of family therapy may be appropriate in two particular situations:

- when the client has developed a drug or alcohol problem at a young age and is still in the care of his or her parents
- where the whole family is seriously disturbed and is functioning badly and the drug or drink problem appears to stem from this

If the drink or drug problem appears to originate from an unhappy marriage that is still ongoing, an assessment as to the suitability of marital therapy may be appropriate.

If the client's partner also has a drink or drug problem, it will be extremely difficult for the client to achieve control or abstinence. The ideal approach is for the partner also to be assessed and for both to tackle their problems in a coordinated way. Unfortunately this does complicate the treatment process and instead of supporting each other, the relapse of one often leads to the relapse of the other. Occasionally the process of assessment and treatment for each partner requires a separate approach or may not prove possible. The assessment, with the client, of such difficulties may lead to a recognition of the need for relationship changes.

Assessment of child protection issues

Adult and adolescent substance users can have profound effects on all members of their household for good or harm. Substance use itself is not a reason to suppose harm but it is a potential risk factor in the welfare of children. When considering the possible risks to children, the changeable nature of the family groupings and extended social contacts need to be borne in mind. Child protection guidance emphasises the duty of care which adult service providers have towards any children in contact with service users.

A framework for assessment was set out in the guidelines of a collaborative document in 1989 (SCODA, 1989) and still forms a useful tool (see Appendix 12). Further consideration of the assessment of substance use, families and child protection is addressed specifically and throughout topics in Chapter 18.

Formal psychological assessment

For most people a formal psychological assessment by a clinical psychologist will not be necessary. Clinical psychologists can offer further assessment in several aspects, including the evaluation of issues which may underlie a failure to progress in treatment. Formal assessment may include cognitive functioning and the client's capacity to plan and evaluate options for change. This may occasionally encompass personality assessment, especially the salient features of impulsiveness and locus of control. Psychological assessment can be helpful in clarifying the degree of any substance-related dementia and monitoring progress of recovery or decline, and thus enable planning of the level of care required. Clinical psychologists have a range of specific therapeutic interventions for substance users and can offer assessment of the client's needs in respect of such therapy.

Assessment for inpatient care, residential rehabilitation and specialist day centre care

Assessments for inpatient care, residential rehabilitation and specialist day centres form part of the workload of those in the community who work with alcohol and drug users. This helps clarify the individual's need for such services and the motivation to use them. It is important that the service purchased be the most effective service for any individual, rather than the cheapest service, otherwise it is likely to be more costly in the longer term to society and the individual.

Inpatient detoxification is required for all those for whom community detoxification may be clinically dangerous (e.g. drinkers who have delirium tremens or a history of multiple seizures), or for those who are otherwise assessed as needing it. It is also commonly used prior to admission for residential rehabilitation, where that facility does not undertake prescribing. Repeated relapse during a community detoxification programme is another indication for detoxification in a more supported setting. Those who repeatedly return to regular street drug use after community detoxification, or who have such poor environmental and social support that detoxification in the community is unlikely to be successful, may be most appropriately treated with supportive aftercare via residential rehabilitation or specialist day care.

There are a wide variety of treatment approaches within the rehabilitation houses and day centres, which can be targeted to individual need. One solution does not fit all. Assessment should therefore be, not just whether clients need and want residential rehabilitation or specialist day care, but which type of rehabilitation programme is likely to be best suited for their chances of success. Block contracts with one service are unlikely to save money in the longer term.

Most UK day centres provide intensive structured groupwork using a cognitive–behavioural approach, including problem-solving and coping and social skills training. There are also some twelve-step day programmes. There are as yet very few such resources in the UK. Where they are available the Cognitive–Behavioural Therapy (CBT) training groups usually have a rolling programme which new members can join. Thus the membership of the group slowly changes and every group member accesses the entire programme. They are most suitable for those people who have a generalised deficit in social and coping skills, rather than a problem in a single area such as assertiveness. They are also particularly helpful for chaotic substance users who lack daytime social support. Most day centres are unable to accommodate employed substance users and some substance users find it difficult to participate in groups. Thus the need for individual CBT interventions on a one-to-one basis at the specialist drug and alcohol service will remain. There will also be a continuing need for residential rehabilitation. Adequate day centre provision should reduce this need, but will not replace it.

People with serious alcohol and/or drug problems associated with chaotic lifestyles may need fast-track assessments because of recurrent crises. Sometimes, if there is a long delay between assessment and admission, motivation can be lost. Some generic workers and commissioners of services have difficulty in accepting the concept of fluctuating motivation. However, all motivation fluctuates and the window of opportunity can be easily missed. Delays caused by lengthy and complicated assessment procedures, or waiting for beds to become available, or awaiting funding decisions can be associated with a significant deterioration which may carry social, legal and care implications. Occasionally there may be even more serious consequences. Deaths from overdose are known to occur more frequently in those who are unsuccessful in securing the assistance they believe they need (Neale, 2001).

It is, however, important to take time to assess requests for residential treatment. Clients may seek residential treatment for reasons unlinked to readiness to change. Families may think that residential rehabilitation is the only option or may have run out of their capacity to support a family member in the community. The client may be facing a court appearance or just be agreeing to please a partner. An inappropriate placement, for instance, of a client who first needs psychiatric treatment or who feels traumatised by group experiences, can compound a sense of failure and push the individual back into precontemplation. If assessment is undertaken with all treatment modalities in mind, it often becomes clear to client and family that other goals are appropriate, at least for the time being, and could produce the desired change itself.

Assessment of outcome

Interpreting what is or is not a good outcome can be extremely difficult. For instance, if a heroin user stops injecting heroin and moves over to heavy alcohol use, is this a good or a bad outcome? Is one slip-up a treatment failure? If not, where does one draw the line in terms of substance use between success and failure? Individual outcome may be assessed by comparing addiction profiles over time using reliable instruments to track individual change in a range of domains. This approach to outcome assessment informs further care planning and helps avoid the trap of good/bad outcome evaluation or of basing the value of outcome on abstinence. Another approach is to assess remission from dependent substance use. Defining what constitutes a remission can be difficult. One official definition can be found in DSM-IV.

DSM-IV criteria to diagnose remission
- Early full remission: from 1 to 11 months during which no criteria of dependence or abuse are met.
- Early partial remission: from 1 to 11 months during which one or more criteria of dependence or abuse are met but not the full criteria for dependence.
- Sustained full remission: for 12 months or more during which no criteria for dependence or abuse are met.
- Sustained partial remission: for 12 months or more during which one or more criteria for dependence are met but not the full criteria for dependence.
- On agonist therapy: taking an agonist, partial agonist, or agonist/antagonist and no criteria for dependence or abuse are met for at least one

month. (These terms refer to prescribed substitute drugs which mimic (agonists) or oppose (antagonists) the effects of other drugs. Some drugs have both agonist and antagonist properties, which can be clinically useful. For example, the agonist properties of the agonist/antagonist drug buprenorphine enable it to be used as an opiate substitute, and its antagonist properties block the effects of illicit heroin use if lapses occur – see Chapter 11.)

- In a controlled environment: access is restricted by the environment (e.g. locked hospital unit, substance-free jail) for at least the past month.

Even if sustained full remission is attained, how is it to be attributed? For example, is a good outcome from the Minnesota Model due to the treatment regime or to follow-up in AA groups, or is it due to the acceptance of alcoholism as a disease? How does one compare individually tailored care programmes? Do we have the right to say that a programme is successful when it is the individual who should be seen as achieving success? If those in a treatment cohort have differing degrees of severity of dependence, to what extent will results be meaningful?

Academic research
Academic researchers tend to look at three basic designs for outcome evaluation:

(1) pre- and post-treatment comparisons (there is usually no control group)
(2) interval service evaluation, sometimes comparing outcomes with those of service users on the waiting list
(3) longitudinal comparison of the effectiveness of different treatment methods

Many difficulties may confound scientific research to evaluate outcome of treatment for problem substance use. Several studies suffer from a lack of baseline data. Many have problems with client selection, high dropout rates, and varying follow-up times. It is almost impossible to obtain a control population because of the difficulties of doing this, and there is generally very little data on outcomes for untreated populations. As a result most research done in this area is open to criticism.

Outcome evaluation in clinical practice
In practice what is needed most for those working in the field is not accurate statistical research on outcome of all those who attend a particular treatment unit, but a validated outcome assessment tool which can be used to give an indication as to how individuals are progressing. This cannot be done solely in DSM-IV terms of remission. Looking at substance use alone is inadequate. Indeed there is general agreement that all assessments of outcome should always be multifactorial. It is the quality of people's lives that is the most important thing to measure. In practice outcome evaluation involves a baseline assessment followed by interval outcome evaluation using the same questionnaire at regular intervals.

Systems to monitor outcomes were originally developed in the USA and initially have all been research based. From 1980 onwards the first ASI questionnaire (McLellan *et al.*, 1980) and its successors (McLellan *et al.*, 1992) gave a more holistic approach to both initial and outcome assessment than purely abstinence or continuance in treatment. The ASI composite scale scores calculations for physical health, alcohol use, drug use, family/social relationships and psychological health including a core set of the following three questions:

(1) How many days in the past month did the subject experience different types of problems?
(2) What is the subject's own perception of problem severity?
(3) How important is receiving additional specialised treatment to the subject?

The ASI has been used at literally thousands of treatment sites and is well validated, but its main problem is the length of time that is taken to complete the questionnaire. Harrison and colleagues (1996) and Dennis and colleagues (1998) expanded the outcome assessment process further. Harrison and colleagues developed patient profiles for the Minnesota's treatment outcomes monitoring system by utilising the ASI, but also adding questions to collect more information on the consequences of substance use, financial problems, family stressors and HIV risk behaviour. The outcome monitoring systems of Harrison and Dennis are both in-depth assessments that are well validated. They have an all-round holistic approach to outcomes but are time consuming. More recently the emphasis has been to develop a shortened system of outcome audit that may be done at repeated intervals and is thus well suited to monitor progression of outcome. There are two such questionnaires that are in general use in the UK – MAP (Marsden *et al.*, 1998) and CISS (Christo, 2000).

MAP (Appendix 13) measures problems in four domains: substance use, health risk behaviour, physical and psychological health, and personal/ social functioning. CISS (Appendix 14) is based on the seven variables measured by other well-known outcome questionnaires such as the OTI, the ASI, and the MAP, plus three further variables which are highlighted in the literature as having an effect on outcome. The original seven variables are:

- social functioning
- general health
- BBV risk behaviour
- psychological well-being
- occupation
- criminal involvement
- drug/alcohol use

The additional three variables are:

- engagement with ongoing support (counselling, support groups, AA or NA)
- treatment compliance
- worker–client relationship

The relative brevity of CISS and MAP make them both easy to use in the clinical situation. They are both well validated and they can be reused at intervals to assess progress. MAP can also be used as a clinical research tool. It is likely that MAP will become the method of quick regular outcome assessment for all specialist substance use services in the UK. This will not only help unify monitoring systems but it also has the potential to provide a very large database from which ongoing clinical research may be conducted, if required.

Conclusion

A good assessment which results in appropriate targeted goals and treatment interventions is the key to forward movement. A number of different assessments (risk assessment, assessment of the stage of change, assessment for residential rehabilitation, etc.) will be necessary from time to time depending on the clinical situation of the service user. Different professionals within the team will make their assessments based on their own experience and professional training but these may occasionally differ substantially. Good communication and a suitable structure to facilitate this is therefore important. After discussion with a multi-disciplinary specialist drug and alcohol team, the case manager acts as personal professional adviser to the drug user or drinker with regard to formulating the ensuing care package and personal treatment goals.

A full initial assessment should be completed for all those who have significant problems or dependence associated with substance use. Many specialist services have developed their own assessment forms (e.g. Appendix 2). A good initial assessment should include a MAP (Appendix 13) or CISS (Appendix 14) questionnaire to give a baseline score against which regular assessments of outcome can be measured. The content of the care plan will be determined by the assessment process. The care package will only be appropriate and cost-effective if the assessment has been thorough and comprehensive. It will necessitate establishing the severity of problems associated with substance use and also the severity of dependence if the drinker or drug user is dependent. The Leeds Addiction Questionnaire (Appendix 7) is a useful clinical assessment tool. It will help determine whether attempts to control drinking are realistic, whether a brief intervention should be considered, and whether it is appropriate to give opiate users maintenance or abstinence-oriented substitute prescribing.

In order to clearly define the rest of the care package it is helpful to assess various other aspects. Janis and Mann's Decisional Balance (Appendix 9) will highlight the way in which drugs and alcohol are used. (Each substance user has his or her own unique way of using drugs or alcohol.) This will show up most of the important problem areas that need to be addressed by utilising personal strengths or through harm reduction. There may be other problem areas that need attention in order to reduce harm, particularly those relating to social circumstances and to the individual's physical and mental health.

If abstinence-oriented treatment is to be recommended, the stage of change and degree of motivation for this may be assessed using the Readiness to Change Questionnaire (Appendix 8) and/or the Decisional Balance. In cases where there appears to be low motivation it is important that this should not be misinterpreted because of a low sense of self-efficacy or depression.

A full initial assessment does not always have to be undertaken in every case before treatment can begin. Occasionally, if it is clear that substitute prescribing is appropriate this may sometimes be initiated after a short *triage* assessment which highlights the most essential elements of the assessment process. These are whether significant drug- or drink-associated problems or dependence are present and their severity, which stage of change the client has reached, the BBV risk, and the degree and extent of current substance use. Once stabilisation on a substitute prescription has occurred further information can be obtained later, as needed from the client, the client's family (with the client's agreement) and other involved professionals. In this way a full profile can be slowly built up with an in-depth understanding of the problem.

Assessment is a two-way ongoing process between the substance user and his or her professional workers. Assessments become reassessments and merge into the treatment process. Ongoing assessment and reassessments at future interviews may lead to modifications in the treatment package with time.

The addition of personal goals may enhance the prospect of recovery. Others may interfere with anticipated effective treatment (e.g. a goal to control drinking by someone who is severely dependent). But a client's personal goals are important to include where possible and will help maintain motivation.

It is important that there should be good communication between the different parties involved throughout the assessment process. An attempt should be made to prioritise care plan interventions and work them into an individually targeted treatment package. This will go a long way towards enhancing change and consolidating the recovery process.

Part V
Treatment

Chapter 6
The Therapeutic Framework

Introduction

A therapeutic framework needs to be flexible enough to be adapted to suit any local situation. Different countries run their substance use services in different ways but, even within the same country, there are major differences in the way that services for drug users and drinkers are provided. Certain elements of any treatment framework are essential. However, a broadly based therapeutic framework that encompasses multiple interventions demands its own criteria. The framework suggested in this chapter also encompasses a broad range of professionals and others in the community who are in contact with substance users and are able to play a role in a treatment service suitable for both drug users and drinkers. Special groups of substance users place their own distinct requirements on a treatment framework. Young people, ethnic minority groups, women and those living in rural areas each have specific needs. Some needs may be met through groupwork, others on an individual basis. All these things profoundly influence the way in which substance use services are provided. With these issues in mind, a suitable treatment framework must be appropriate, flexible and accessible enough to satisfactorily provide a wide range of treatment interventions by a number of generic and specialist caring professionals, and meet the needs of diverse types of service users, who are at various stages of change, and who have differing severity of problem substance use.

The need for a user-friendly service

A user-friendly service should be an essential element of any treatment framework. However this has not always been the case. It is promoted most in those countries where harm reduction has been given priority. For instance, since 1988, when the UK and Australia understood the importance of attracting drug users into services in order to help them move away from HIV risk behaviour, it became necessary to ensure an empathetic and accessible service, which was attractive to users.

There are other features of modern-day services which have also promoted user-friendliness. Modern-day methods of helping people move through the stages of change by means of Motivational Interviewing (MI) and other motivational enhancement interventions require the whole service to be seen as empathetic, friendly and accessible if maximal success is to be attained.

Empathy and accessibility have remained key features of modern drug and alcohol services. Yet, today, the perception of some politicians, much of the general public, the media and sometimes referrers is more of drug users as potentially violent and antisocial criminals rather than as individuals with important health needs. This is a backward step, particularly when coupled with the promotion of coercive treatments by the criminal justice system, families and employers, which have the potential to increase harm as well as do good.

Although the majority of clients soon establish a good working relationship with specialist alcohol and drug workers, all substance use services have occasional clients who behave badly and need to understand the limits of behaviour in clear and unambiguous terms. Sometimes this may be helped by the use of a well-thought-out contract or by verbal and written warnings. Professionals who are able to define behaviour limits sensitively but firmly will find that this lays the groundwork for a fruitful relationship with their client.

Unfortunately there is still much prejudice against drinkers and drug users. Adverse prejudice can be found in some non-specialist workers, including generic professionals whose work entails professional contact with substance users. Occasionally specialist workers in the substance use field also have prejudices both in respect of service users and other professionals. Much of the ill feeling stems from ignorance, and hopefully will improve as more training becomes available for doctors, nurses, social workers, probation officers and other professionals whose work brings them into contact with drug users. Multi-disciplinary training will help dispel some of the ignorance that relates to the way other professionals work. Such training should help promote a better understanding of the framework within which care is delivered in different agencies and so aid interdisciplinary working with substance users. It is also an important requirement for good advocacy. Knowledge, attitudes and skills relating to problems resulting from substance use should be part of the core training of all professionals whose work brings them into contact with substance users (ACMD, 1990).

In a user-friendly service, thought must be given to ways of making the service attractive to different client groups. For example, to be more attractive to women and more culturally sensitive, alcohol and drug workers of both genders should be available and attempts should be made to employ workers from different ethnic groups, particularly when these form a significant proportion of the local population. Research suggests that many ethnic minority groups are not attracted to existing services although there is some evidence that they may be more willing to consult general practitioners (GPs). There is an identified need for drug services to promote a multiracial image through staffing,

outreach work and service provision generally in order to attract drug users from ethnic minorities (ACMD, 1991).

In rural areas drug and alcohol workers should find ways of taking the service out to the more remote parts, rather than expecting everyone to come in on a regular basis to a central point that may be miles away from their residence. Accessibilty is improved if GPs are involved in substitute prescribing and/or specialist workers from the substance use services provide satellite services at health centres and GP surgeries. Changes such as these, the provision of a crèche, women only clinics, and the recognition that there are a variety of services available which are potentially useful help make services attractive to a diversity of clients. They will help the specialist services break away from a dominant client group of white male drug users in their late twenties and thirties and white male drinkers in their forties and encourage other client groups to attend.

Young people should be provided with their own separate service and not expected to attend adult services where they may forge links that are counterproductive and will not obtain services to fully meet their needs. Where a separate service is not available, the adult specialist services should reach out to them rather than expect them to come into adult clinics. For young people who are already dependent the treatment situation is similar to that for mildly to moderately dependent adults, though the comprehensiveness of the treatment package and continuing flexibility in service delivery is highly important. For young people who are not dependent, but come under one of the *vulnerable* categories and are at high risk of developing a drug or alcohol problem, the treatment options are slightly different. Treatment options for young people who are vulnerable to becoming drug or alcohol dependent should look specifically at reducing risk factors and increasing resiliency factors (see Chapter 3).

The real key to user-friendliness is accurate empathy. In this context it does not mean that those working with drug users or drinkers have to have experienced substance use problems themselves in order that clients perceive they have empathy (although many twelve-step agencies in particular often employ workers who have recovered from substance use). Nor do such workers have to dress in a way that they think will ally them better to clients. The empathy needed to work effectively in this field must be perceived by the client as an expression of warmth and understanding of his or her problems and difficulties. Whatever the differences in age, gender, ethnic group or appearance of the worker, if a professional is perceived as expressing empathy accurately, these differences will be viewed as being of no significance.

Who controls the treatment process?

Treatment decision-making that is likely to be most successful is based on decisions made by the service user. This includes ascertaining if and when the drug user or drinker is ready for significant therapeutic change, including planned reductions in the substance or the prescribed daily dose, finding out their most important biopsychosocial needs, and which biopsychosocial interventions should be given the greatest priority. It is easy to do this when a client is on a maintenance substitute prescription, but may be less easy if he or she is already undergoing detoxification. A full discussion of the fears and concerns of the client may be necessary. No harm will be done if a planned detoxification is interrupted. It is often helpful to plan withdrawal so that reductions may be done under the direction of the client, with resting posts, rather than continuing on fixed plans. This is empowering for the drug user or drinker.

CASE STUDY

> Client A had many problems relating to heroin addiction. His family were threatening to throw him out. Each morning he woke up suffering from opiate withdrawals, and had to work out how he would raise the money to buy some more heroin. He normally did this by shoplifting. He had even stolen from his mother on three occasions, but she was now wise to this. He had been caught shoplifting a number of times and was well known at local stores. He had an outstanding court case and was

likely to be sent to prison. Client A became desperate to sort out his problems from heroin addiction. If he did this everything else would be great, he thought. He contacted the local drug service who found him to be extremely motivated when first assessed and agreed to help by arranging for him to go on a slow methadone detoxification programme. Client A readily agreed and when he started the programme he *honeymooned* – everything was suddenly wonderful. He didn't wake up in the mornings suffering from withdrawals. He didn't have to work out how to raise enough money to fund a supply of heroin and spend the rest of the day doing this. The court was sympathetic as he was on a methadone programme and he managed to avoid a prison sentence by accepting a treatment order. It seemed that all his problems were being solved. But as his prescription was reduced client A began to be concerned. He didn't feel ready to come off drugs. He expressed his concern to the prescribing doctor who was unsympathetic and told him that this was the programme he had agreed to have. He discussed the problem with his specialist worker who encouraged him to continue with the programme. There seemed to be no way out. Client A tried to keep to his script and not use street drugs but started to slip up, and when the prescription stopped he relapsed almost immediately. He had told himself that he knew he could not manage without a script and had planned his return to street drug use.

Therapeutic help does not imply that the therapeutic helper takes over and sorts the problem out. Drinkers and drug users must do this themselves, for this not only increases the chance of a successful outcome, it also helps raise self-esteem, and the empowerment of the individual raises personal belief in his or her ability to overcome problems and dependence (self-efficacy).

Other people, however skilled they might be, never make a drinker or drug user better. It is always the client who does the work. Helping professionals can make assessments, point the way, offer suggestions, provide interventions tailored to meet a client's needs, give appropriate counselling, and do what they can to improve the client's environment, but success, when it comes, always belongs to the client, never to the professional worker.

Who should oversee and carry out the treatment interventions?

It is traditional, appropriate and helpful for services to delegate one person to have ongoing contact and to ensure the care plan is carried out. Various titles have been designated for this role. The Institute of Medicine (IOM, 1990) refers to the *case manager*. Many specialist substance use services in the UK appoint a *key worker* and this person commonly does all the therapeutic interventions. However, with the increasing number and complexity of interventions that are known to be effective, it becomes increasingly difficult for one person to have the skills to do this. It is better to have a *care coordinator*, who is responsible for the day-to-day contact and who will accept responsibility for ensuring that appropriate therapeutic interventions are carried out by those who have the knowledge, skills and training. The ongoing client contact can be utilised to good advantage if the care coordinator is trained in an effective method of counselling such as MI which will increase the prospect of a beneficial outcome (see Chapter 8).

The work of a care coordinator might normally entail

- ensuring good communication between all professionals working with substance users in the community;
- completing a full initial assessment and provisional care plan for those who are dependent on drugs or alcohol;
- discussing the treatment interventions in the provisional care plan with other members of the team and then with the client;
- using an effective method of ongoing counselling with the client;
- arranging for the care plan to be implemented;
- ensuring that other necessary interventions such as blood tests, hepatitis immunisations and hospital appointments are carried out;
- arranging the purchasing of specific treatment interventions such as specialist counselling when these are not within the skills of the team;
- drug-testing and monitoring;
- assessing outcome periodically and revising care plans;

- acting as an early warning system if things start to deteriorate; and
- dealing with crises.

If no specific therapeutic work is being undertaken and the client is not in crisis, ongoing monitoring and support for the client will still be required and he or she will still need to be seen on a regular basis. The time allotted for regular follow-up monitoring might be limited to 10–15 minutes. At these times the care coordinator is needed as a focus of contact for urine (or other) drug-testing to ensure that everything is going smoothly and that structured treatment interventions are properly planned and accessed. From time to time longer interviews will be necessary and this must be catered for if appointments are given. Formal assessment of outcome may need to be undertaken or a crisis may have occurred. If substitute prescribing is being undertaken by a doctor at the specialist services or by a GP, the care coordinator could arrange to see the client just before the doctor. This would aid attendance at appointments with the care coordinator and improve communication between the care coordinator and the prescribing doctor. The doctor would have the benefit of knowing the care coordinator's opinion with regard to progress and the result of any urine tests and so on.

Specialist drug workers can combine the care coordinator's role with a specialist therapeutic interest of their choice if they wish to do so. For example, some may develop a specialism in Cognitive–Behavioural Therapy (CBT) or family therapy. Others may find it rewarding to be the team resource on health issues, advocacy or training. In this model every client will have an accessible named care coordinator who will play a continuing central role to ensure the treatment programme is devised and enacted and that the client continues to make progress. The main difference between a key worker and care coordinator is that the role changes from that of therapist to facilitator.

Under this suggested framework the initial assessment will usually, but not invariably, be completed by the care coordinator. An important part of the care coordinator's role will be to encourage the client to take up what is on offer, and to help him or her find solutions to any practical difficulties in attending services such as transport difficulties or problems with childcare arrangements. The care coordinator should be trained to use a style of counselling which is known to be effective for substance users. Ideally this will be MI, although some other forms of counselling can be helpful to substance users (see Chapter 8). If MI is used, this style of interacting on a continuing basis will help facilitate the client's uptake of treatment, and maintain or increase the client's motivation to change.

Apart from specialist drug or alcohol team workers it would be possible in theory, but not in practice, for a wide range of generic professionals to take on the care coordinator's role. However in practice this is difficult. Probation officers generally see their role as holding probation orders to enhance community safety. They do not see themselves as treatment providers apart from ensuring that Drug Treatment and Testing Orders (DTTOs) are carried out. There are problems, too, for professionals from other services managing the purchasing of treatment interventions. In addition, GPs and other doctors generally do not have the flexibility to be a care coordinator. The only exception is a community psychiatric nurse (CPN) where there is a primary long-standing mental health problem and any associated substance use is a secondary compounding problem. Here the CPN should take the lead and coordinate all necessary treatments for both the mental health problem and substance use. The person who becomes the care coordinator will need to have regular contact and a good relationship with the client. It should be decided at an early stage who should take on this role and the client's views must be taken into account.

As well as acting as monitor, motivator and facilitator of treatment uptake, the care coordinator should also be responsible for completing regular reviews of the client's progress, reassessing treatment requirements and communicating with all other concerned professionals. This may at times be quite demanding on professional time if it is to be done well. It is important that whoever is chosen has the ability to complete the work concerned. In practice, with the exception already mentioned of a CPN when mental health services take the lead, only specialist drug and alcohol workers have the knowledge, skills and flexibility to undertake the role of care coordinator.

A service appropriate for both drinkers and drug users

In Chapter 1 we showed that most substance use interventions that promote constructive behaviour change for drinkers are equally appropriate for drug users, and the psychological and social treatments are aimed at the person and not the drug. Similar observations have been made by other authors. Marlatt has hypothesised that 'there may be common cognitive, affective and behavioural components . . . regardless of the particular substance or activity involved' (Marlatt & Gordon, 1985). Beck (1993a) maintains that the 'same beliefs underlie all addictions'. Nace (1987; 1995) states:

> The condition of being drug or alcohol dependent brings forth a set of phenomena that transcends the pharmacological properties of any specific drug. . . . [These phenomena], together with the affective functions of drug use, polydrug use, and the social aspects of the drug experience transcend any intoxicating drug or class of drugs. Together, these phenomena enable us to consider the substance use disorders in a generic sense.

The evidence that a combined clinical approach is useful has been slowly accumulating. During the 1980s and 1990s an increasing number of specific treatment interventions were shown to be applicable to people who have developed problems with alcohol and a wide range of drugs. The following are examples of psychological or psychosocial treatment interventions that are appropriate for both drinkers and drug users: cue exposure (Dawe & Powell, 1995; Rohsenow *et al.*, 1995), relapse prevention (Marlatt & Gordon, 1985; Annis, 1990; Carroll *et al.*, 1991), coping and social skills training (Chaney *et al.*, 1978; Platt & Metzger, 1987; Monti *et al.*, 2002), the Community Reinforcement Approach (Hunt & Azrin, 1973; Higgins *et al.*, 1993; Myers & Smith, 1995), Motivational Interviewing

(Miller & Rollnick, 1991; 2002), Cognitive Therapy (Ellis *et al.*, 1988; Beck *et al.*, 1993; Ellis & Dryden, 1999) and Brief Treatments (Edwards *et al.*, 1977a; Saunders *et al.*, 1995). Taken together, these and many other therapeutic interventions comprise a formidable array of published evidence that now underpins a combined treatment approach.

Harm reduction interventions are also applicable for all substance users. For many substance-related problems the greatest harm incurred is the perpetuation of active dependence and the prevention of progress to resolve the addiction process. Practical steps taken to reduce the harm from psychological, social and medical problems related to both alcohol and drug use are outlined in this book. When appropriately targeted, these show major treatment benefit for both drinkers and drug users. All substance users will also benefit from relapse prevention strategies and from interventions to improve psychosocial functioning. The twelve-step programmes for Twelve-step Facilitation Therapy (TFT) and the self-help groups, Alcoholics Anonymous (AA) for alcohol and Narcotics Anonymous (NA) for drugs, are virtually identical.

Thus, although the alcohol and drugs fields have been separated historically, they have much to contribute to each other from a clinical standpoint. For many years there have been suggestions that drug and alcohol services should combine (Banks & Waller, 1988; Raistrick, 1988; Dunne *et al.*, 1989) and different treatment units have run their own version of a combined service. The Advisory Council on the Misuse of Drugs (ACMD, 1990) recommended that there should be joint training for drugs and alcohol. An increasing number of drug and alcohol services have joined together.

In many settings, particularly in the USA, the commonality of treatment for drug and alcohol problems is based on a prerequisite for abstinence. In other places treatment interventions are given to continuing drug users and drinkers. Those facilities that work directly with drug users and drinkers in the community are best served by a clinical approach that is able to vary according to the needs of the individual service user whether there is continued use of drink or drugs. A substitute prescription is provided or abstinence is achieved. This enables professionals to work with people at an earlier stage through harm reduction and other strategies such as improved personal and social functioning. Such ways of intervening are also appropriate for polysubstance users who may not be ready to change all their substance use at the same time, but may wish to deal with part of it.

The Dutch model of helping substance users to reintegrate with mainstream society without an initial requirement for abstinence should be accommodated within a suggested treatment framework. The BRENDA approach (Volpicelli *et al.*, 2001), a flexible combination of medication and psychosocial treatments for drug and alcohol dependence, including twelve-step work as appropriate, is one of the few US approaches which does not insist on initial abstinence. It has much to recommend it and a treatment framework that is able to accommodate the needs of people who are still using substances during their engagement is proposed.

The treatment framework should also be able to accommodate separate services if these are required. A liberal national attitude to drug problems does not necessarily lead to integration of drug and alcohol services. In Switzerland, a country which is noted for its tolerant approach of drug users, there is a strict separation of services for drinkers and drug users. Even the provision of identical treatment methods does not always lead to a closer integration of services. In Austria, Canada, Finland, Hungary, Japan, Portugal and Sweden the same types of treatment method are used for both client groups, but in Japan, in particular, services are poorly integrated (Bergmark, 1998).

With these points in mind, it is possible to develop a treatment framework utilising targeted specific interventions that may be used for both drinkers and drug users. It should be possible within that framework to deliver a wide range of treatment interventions via generic caring professionals just as it is via the specialist services. In the event of a clinically focused joint drug and alcohol specialist team being formed, the service users themselves do not need to be amalgamated. Indeed there may be good reasons for some separation based on gender needs, age or problem severity.

There are still differences in the drinking and drug use populations, particularly between older drinkers and young polydrug users, although the age gap between most drinkers and drug users is narrowing as the cohort of drug users becomes older. Some drinkers do not like associating themselves with drug users and prefer to be physically separate and vice versa. Although it can be advantageous to do so, drug users and drinkers do not have to sit in the same waiting room or attend mixed therapeutic groups. There can be one building for drug users and another for drinkers, if this is felt to be desirable. Those working in joint community drug and alcohol teams will be giving a range of biopsychosocial interventions that are equally applicable to drug users or drinkers, wherever they are situated.

Although the treatment framework should be flexible enough to accommodate drug and alcohol services that unite and those that do not, wherever possible we would recommend unification of drug and alcohol services at a clinical level. One of the main benefits of a clinically united specialist drug and alcohol team is that the size of the team covering a given population is increased. A larger team makes absences due to holidays and sickness easier to cover, and specialisation of worker skills is easier if this is desired. Specialist drug and alcohol workers can become experts in particular areas of practice. Besides the range of specialist treatments already mentioned, increased staffing levels might allow the employment of counsellors for adult survivors of sexual abuse, a common problem in female substance users. A larger team also gives better geographical coverage in rural areas, greater availability for specialist workers of the same gender, increased possibilities for the employment of staff from minority ethnic groups and more staff for specialist services for young people. Greater staff numbers will enable a reasonable duty roster to be arranged to cover emergencies, and extra facilities like day programmes and drop-in centres can be run more easily. Life is usually less stressful as more back-up is available, and management and administration costs are cheaper. The essential point is that service providers are skilled to care for drug and alcohol users and that client needs are met in a seamless way.

Those who should be treated by the specialist services

The American Institute of Medicine (IOM, 1990) recommended three functions for community agencies in the treatment of alcohol problems. These are identification, the provision of a brief intervention to those with mild or moderate alcohol problems, and onward referral to the specialist sector of those with substantial or severe alcohol problems. The model we propose differs from this in that generic professionals working in the community not only do the above, but also, when appropriate, become involved with more extensive treatments through shared care arrangements.

In an ideal world some individuals should be treated primarily by the specialist services. The UK national guidelines on the clinical management of drug use and dependence (DH, 1999) give the following list of clinical situations in shared care between GP and specialist services where they feel the expertise of specialist services is necessary:

- Patients with serious risk to physical or mental health or complex needs, e.g. schizophrenia, liver disease, frequent relapses, polydrug use, concurrent alcohol misuse, complications of drug misuse or a chaotic lifestyle
- Patients with a serious forensic history
- Patients not responding to oral substitute prescribing, who may require less frequently used interventions such as injectable opioids, should in most circumstances be managed by a specialist service
- Patients requiring a large element of psychosocial therapy or support for housing, employment and training
- Patients requiring specialised inpatient or day care
- Patients requiring a specialist residential rehabilitation programme

In practice such separation is extremely difficult. Some people refuse to attend anyone else but the GP they know. Others are so ill or so chaotic that they repeatedly fail appointments at specialist centres and can only be seen by community services or, conversely, cannot manage GP or other appointments and are only able to utilise flexible specialist or drop-in services.

Specialist services also need to be accessible for substance users whose GPs choose not to become involved in the treatment process. But, most importantly, specialist services can develop a number of specialist interventions specifically for drug and alcohol users, such as MI and good assessments with care plans most likely to aid a beneficial outcome. These are not provided elsewhere in the community. There must always be a role for specialist services. Their role cannot adequately be provided by members of the primary health care team alone.

Some drug users and drinkers may need to have a specialist intervention in order to progress but may not be ready for it and decline to have it. It is helpful, however, if they continue some contact with a specialist care coordinator, particularly if he or she uses MI as a style of relating to the individual, as this may aid the phase of preparation when the person becomes more ready to accept that particular form of treatment.

Involving others in the community

Professional helpers, particularly generic professionals such as GPs or social workers engaging with their first few clients, sometimes have unrealistic expectations and expect abstinence to be attained and maintained in just a few weeks when the client has a deeply ingrained dependence on drugs or alcohol stretching over several years. Family members may also fail to understand that the process of recovery may take several months or years to achieve. Failure to recognise that dependent substance use is often a persistent, long-term condition may lead to disillusionment and cynicism and, in turn, these negative influences can interfere with the treatment process.

Treatment solutions are not easy. They take time and effort and cost money. Many substance users view themselves as having solely a drink or a drug problem. They do not see the biological, psychological and social problems that run alongside as being relevant and important to resolve. It is true that for opiate users many problems, and the harm

generated by them, are removed just by the provision of a legal substitute prescription of methadone or buprenorphine (Byrne, 2000). The easy solution would be just to provide a maintenance prescription and hope that after a few years the user will have moved away from the circle of drug-using friends, got a job, developed a relationship with someone who does not use drugs, and decided that he or she would want to stop picking up a prescription. This can happen, but not invariably. Some people get stuck on a prescription, when with a bit of additional help they could be moving forward. Almost all those on a maintenance substitute prescription will do better and progress faster if, in addition to prescribing, they have access to structured interventions focused on enhancing motivation, reducing harm, harnessing strengths and improving psychosocial functioning as required.

The multidimensional nature of substance use causes it to impinge upon the work of many different professionals. In addition, drug use has now become so common that treatment can no longer solely be the province of specialists. To have professionals from a wide range of disciplines gaining experience in this field helps increase their awareness of hidden problems and gives better geographical coverage with regard to service provision. The wide range of problems which are experienced by drug and alcohol users makes it important that there be involvement by workers from many different areas.

Many other professionals working in the community may be involved with substance users in the course of their work. These include reception staff at GP practices, Accident and Emergency (A&E) staff, probation officers, midwives, youth workers, community psychiatrists, community pharmacists, clinical psychologists, social workers, community psychiatric nurses, health visitors and district nurses. All should have at least some basic training in substance use problems and dependence. Alert primary health care workers and other professionals working in the community are particularly well placed to pick up a substance use problem at an early stage and respond in a non-stigmatising way. With this in mind the World Health Organization (WHO) has compiled a manual for primary health care workers, with guidelines for trainers (Grant & Hodgson, 1991).

Some of the advantages of involving other professionals working in the community have been highlighted, but this is always dependent on the provision of good communication. Good communication within a community setting can be difficult to maintain and requires organisation and effort. In the UK, occasionally, a GP will make a conscious decision to work alone without involving other professionals. This approach is almost invariably counterproductive giving relatively poor outcomes.

Working together in the community is not easy. It takes time to communicate, and so is particularly difficult for those who are working under pressure. The UK shared care arrangements between GPs and those working in Community Drug Teams (CDTs) has been defined in government literature as 'the joint participation of specialist and other staff, and GPs, in the planned delivery of care for people with a substance misuse problem' and communication is expected to be 'over and above the normal exchange of letters'. The essence of the process is integrated care and skill sharing to the benefit of service users.

Involving family physicians

Many family doctors have now become expert in the treatment of drug users and drinkers, and find the work extremely rewarding. The primary care doctor is in an excellent position to improve physical and mental health through links with already well-established agencies, and improve the social care of substance users. Different ways of sharing specialist and GP care can be seen in different localities of the UK. Sometimes shared care can be provided by a link worker attached to a GP practice. It can also be done through a local CDT or Community Alcohol Team (CAT). It may be through a Voluntary Agency or via the Statutory Sector. Good shared care demands a high level of support, good communication and ready access. Many areas of the UK have now developed local handbooks or guidelines to use in addition to the national guidelines.

Family doctors face special difficulties working with drug users because of their ability to prescribe controlled drugs. Consultations tend to centre around prescribing issues, even when the doctor attempts to move them away from this narrow perspective. Some doctors worry about the possibility of aggression from substance users. Very occasionally a patient may try to obtain a prescription or a higher dose by being aggressive to the doctor concerned or by being disruptive in the waiting room. As with other patients, a polite professional response will often defuse such potentially difficult situations with substance users. In-depth ways of dealing with aggression are described in Chapter 14.

In the UK, from 1983 onwards, a shift in national policy led to increasing encouragement for GPs to take an active role with drug users, and in this respect Britain differs from many other countries. Some countries, such as the USA, are now following this move. In the UK this policy has been very acceptable to drug users, for research showed that most would rather attend their family physicians than specialist drug units for treatment of their drug problem (Hindler *et al.*, 1995).

However, it has been less acceptable to the GPs themselves. Drug users and drinkers generate a heavy workload. In the UK drug users attend 10–12 times more often than the average patient, and their cases are often complex and difficult (Waller, 1993). Although this is now changing, UK family doctors have in the past had little or no training in the treatment of substance use, and often feel unprepared and worried that they may be compromised. More recently with government help this situation appears to have improved. Sometimes additional payments are made to GPs when treatments have a sound clinical base, according to local and national guidelines. This has further advantage of helping raise the quality of care. Additional payments for UK GPs who treat drug dependence in shared care arrangements with specialist community services, after a training programme, began in Glasgow (Scott *et al.*, 1995) and now occurs widely throughout the UK with several organisations, including the Royal College of General Practitioners (RCGP), providing specific training and qualifications.

A possible model for generic worker involvement

Some generic workers have developed considerable expertise in the treatment of substance users and have become specialists in their own right. In 1982 the UK's Advisory Council on the Misuse of Drugs, in its *Treatment and Rehabilitation* report (ACMD, 1982), put forward a possible model for a specialist local CDT, whereby the generic service team members work on a sessional basis with the team but also act as specialists for drug users within their own agencies. For example, a probation officer could be seconded to the specialist team for one or two sessions per week. The rest of the time he or she could work in the probation office utilising generic probation skills, but always with a special interest in drug problems. There he or she would act as a specialist resource within the probation service to develop a more effective probation service response to drug problems. This approach is already being used in a number of services, such as probation, midwifery and general practice, with the development of tier 2 generic providers who have additional training, thereby enhancing their professional work with drug users. This model could be expanded to include provision for service users with problems and dependence from alcohol as well as drugs.

Involving family members

Although the involvement of families in therapy is known to be helpful, in individual cases the help is not always as great as might have been anticipated. A suggestion has been made that this might be because this involvement has not taken into account the stage of change of the addictive behaviour (Prochaska, 1979). Some people may not be ready for change, although their families may be desperate for things to happen. The different ways in which families can work together with professionals both to attain early help-seeking and improved outcomes are described in Chapter 15.

There are of course limits to the extent to which a drinker or drug taker can be influenced by family members. Close family members, cohabitees, and significant others must all learn to cope with their own feelings about the addictive behaviour and its consequences. They must learn to find ways of improving the quality of their own lives, for by looking after themselves and making their own lives as normal and psychologically healthy as possible they will be making it easier when the drinker or drug taker decides to change.

To work with groups or individuals?

When groups work well it can be highly beneficial to the individuals comprising the group. Group interactions such as mutual identification, acceptance, role modelling, and positive peer approval can be extremely helpful. In addition, when a member of the group is making obvious progress, this instils optimism and hope and often inspires self-efficacy for other group members who have a substance use problem. Such advantages are generally unobtainable through other forms of therapy. Thus, groups have the potential to provide a unique form of positive reinforcement for behaviours away from substance use and negative reinforcement for behaviours that are maladaptive.

The public nature of twelve-step group therapy with its associated *confessions* concerning *slips* and transgressions by those who are dependent is also a powerful incentive to avoid relapse. Established group members have a chance to express altruism by taking newcomers under their wing, and at the same time remind themselves how unmanageable their lives were when they first entered treatment. In addition group members can act as buddies and are able to offer continued support outside of the group sessions. In these respects twelve-step self-help groups and TFT can be viewed as group therapy.

However, groupwork is not always appropriate and sometimes it can go badly wrong. Unstructured group therapy is generally unsuitable for those disturbed and vulnerable people who use substances to escape from traumatising thoughts. Such people are best treated on an individual basis. Some may have deep emotional problems which they may not wish to acknowledge in a group setting. Others who have difficulties socialising may feel extremely uncomfortable in groups and may be unable to utilise them.

Although well-run groups are a highly effective form of therapy for appropriately selected clients, it is important that they are not set up in order to save money or because someone in authority believes in groupwork for all clients. However, there is a definite place for focused educational groupwork for all substance users willing to accept it. Groups with specific educational objectives, such as skills training, are sometimes considered to be easy to run because they have preset and well-defined programmes. Day programmes in particular lend themselves to educational groupwork, but some groups may also be run via specialist local drug and alcohol services.

Highly structured educational groupwork focusing on relapse prevention techniques, which include avoiding high-risk situations and learning drink/drug use refusal skills, will be helpful for all substance users. Other educational groupwork like anger management training is not required for all clients and is sometimes best arranged on a one-to-one basis according to individual need or when enough clients can be brought together. Although numbers will vary according to the type of intervention planned, a typical example might be a group with a minimum of six members and a maximum of two therapists yielding at least a threefold increase in the number of clients treated in 1 hour. When it is appropriate to do groupwork, groups can be a very cost-effective means of delivering care to substance users.

As most groups require skilled leadership, only those who are trained should run or co-work groups. Groups that work to a particular focus are generally easier to run and more appropriate for the substance use field than groups set up, e.g. to discuss the psychological difficulties facing a recovering substance user. Considerable time should be spent co-working such groups with a skilled therapist before leadership is accepted. Washton (1995) defines the group leader's role as encompassing the following:

- to establish and enforce group rules in a caring, consistent, non-punitive manner to protect the group's integrity and progress;
- to screen, prepare, and orient potential group members to ensure suitability and proper placement in the group;

- to keep group discussions focused on important issues and to do so in a way that maximises the therapeutic benefit of these discussions to all members;
- to emphasise, promote, and maintain group cohesiveness and reduce feelings of personal alienation, wherever possible;
- to create and maintain a caring, non-judgmental, therapeutic climate in the group that both counteracts self-defeating attitudes and promotes self-awareness, expression of feelings, honest self-disclosure, adaptive alternatives to drug use, and patterns of drug-free living;
- to handle members who are disruptive to the group in a timely and consistent manner to protect the membership and integrity of the group; and
- to educate patients about selected aspects of drug use, addiction and recovery, in order to foster recovery and stimulate meaningful group discussion.

When the group responds as a whole to something, it is said to have *bonded*. Bonding may result in a positive, beneficial and highly therapeutic outcome, or may have negative consequences. The group begins to influence each of its members through what is known as the *group process*. An understanding of group processes is helpful not only in the treatment of substance use, but also in its prevention and diagnosis. Everyone is, at least to some extent, influenced by group dynamics, whether the group they belong to is already in existence (e.g. family groups, friendship groups, workgroups, etc.) or whether the group is specifically set up for a defined purpose (e.g. committees, therapy groups, etc.).

One example of the way informal groups influence the behaviour of the individual is through culture, which can be a major influence on drinking and drug use. In recent years the way that culture is perceived has changed. It is no longer just described as identifiable populations sharing a common set of values, norms, traditions, customs, arts, history, folklore and institutions. A broader concept has emerged. The concept has now expanded to mean that it shapes, and is shaped by, local worlds of everyday experience. Local group attitudes to general life situations are instrumental in this process. Interpersonal communication, interaction and negotiation are all intimately moulded by the group perceptions, cultural attitudes and dynamics found in families, work settings, networks and local communities, and these in turn influence individual decisions about drinking or taking drugs.

As the group process develops, the group may begin to behave in ways which do not always reflect the conscious intent of the individual members. This is known as the group's *mentality*. Quite often the group's mentality is obvious to observers, while remaining hidden from, and unrecognised by, the individual members of the group. Groups have the potential to be greater than the sum of their parts (i.e. greater than the individuals who contrive to overcome their drink or drug problem). Once bonding, group process and mentality have been established they are usually more helpful and more relevant for the client.

Matching the setting to individual need

Consideration according to cost-effectiveness and assessed need should be given as to whether treatment is necessary either as an inpatient or as residential rehabilitation, or whether it can be continued in a community setting. In the USA it is increasingly difficult to obtain inpatient treatment. However, in the UK there is more choice. For those who need additional help in the community, day care programmes or treatment at home can sometimes be provided. Some residential and community treatments are provided within the framework of the criminal justice system.

Residential settings

Expensive inpatient detoxification and further rehabilitation are necessary for some drug users and drinkers, but for most treatment and rehabilitation in the community aided by local community drug and alcohol teams is more appropriate, cheaper and more acceptable. The majority of facilities should therefore be in the community, with inpatient detoxification and residential rehabilitation available only when therapy requires it, as in the following circumstances:

- the proposed treatment is only available residentially
- the client is homeless, chaotic and with little or no social support
- community-based treatment is inappropriate for other reasons

For moderately or severely dependent opiate users for whom treatment in their own communities is the chosen option, maintenance substitute prescribing with psychosocial interventions to facilitate the rehabilitation side of treatment is recommended (Gossop *et al.*, 2001a). However, even for the more severely dependent, a relatively fast intervention package can be made available for service users, particularly those who have few associated problems and good social support. One way of providing this is by using rapid community or inpatient detoxification together with an intensive structured day programme or individual relapse prevention work. In some cases inpatient detoxification, perhaps over 2–3 weeks, for opiate dependence, followed by residential rehabilitation is the chosen option.

Home detoxification

Although many people with severe alcohol dependence might ideally have inpatient detoxification, Stockwell and colleagues (1990) have found that most were unwilling to accept inpatient admission. They suggested a different system in between community and inpatient detoxification. This is *home detoxification* with the aid and support of specialist nursing staff who have clear and effective links with the client's GP and who will ensure that any medication is correctly and adequately supplied. A specialist community alcohol home detoxification nurse would be able to make a thorough assessment for the appropriateness of home detoxification, the extent of likely withdrawal symptoms and an appropriate substitution withdrawal prescribing programme. He or she would also be in a prime position to give specialist advice to patients undergoing home detoxification. Home alcohol detoxification is considerably cheaper than inpatient detoxification and, where this service exists, is now the preferred option for many people. It is equally applicable and has similar advantages when used for opiate users undergoing a rapid 2–3 week detoxification in the community using methadone, buprenorphine or lofexidine.

Treatment provision within the criminal justice system

Drug-related crime is often dealt with by special drug courts in the USA aiding treatment for drug users in order to break the links between drugs and acquisitive crime. Within the UK criminal justice system Arrest Referral Schemes are a useful gateway into treatment at a relatively early phase of drug-using careers whether or not the alleged offence is drug- or alcohol-related. They allow a chance to contemplate change at a time when reflection is heightened. If an offence is so serious that a custodial sentence is inevitable, there may be options for a community sentence linked to treatment as an alternative to prison. The UK DTTO and Abstinence Orders are examples. Defendants who agree to this are given treatment under coercion, but if it helps them stay out of prison harm will be reduced. One of the difficulties is that DTTOs are being increasingly used when prison is not being considered, and drug users may end up going to prison for failing to keep to the terms of the programme, thus increasing harm. Both DTTOs and Abstinence Orders are coerced treatments that commonly rely on abstinence from illicit drugs as a central goal. However, some DTTOs, when appropriately structured, do include the options of short- and long-term substitute prescribing for opiate users as well as detoxification and supported abstinence. Their outcome assessments are increasingly incorporated with those of the specialist services within which DTTO provision is made, thus allowing examination of a range of outcome domains.

Work with those in the criminal justice system includes in-reach into prisons for collaborative early intervention and the availability of treatment on release, including the maintenance of abstinence where relevant and the reduction of risk from overdose.

The Stepped Care Approach (a progressively intensive treatment framework)

Sobell and Sobell (1993) have suggested a progressively intensive treatment framework for drinkers based on the following model, which starts with the anticipated most cost-effective intervention, Brief Treatment, and then, if needed, moves on to progressively more intensive treatment options. It relies on the fact that no one can be certain that a particular treatment intervention will be successful, and therefore recommends starting with the intervention that is considered likely to be the most cost-effective.

After initial matching to the anticipated most cost-effective treatment, progress would be monitored and unsatisfactory progress would result in initiation of more intensive or alternative treatment. Figure 6.1 indicates that treatment increases in intensity, because even switching to an alternative treatment would increase the total amount of treatment delivered.

The Sobells' method is most applicable if the desired outcome is abstinence and this is achievable through a single intervention. If a number of interventions are proposed in the care plan and incremental progress is the desired outcome, it is less applicable. Thus, this method cannot be a universal approach. However, it may be useful to follow their strategy for some clients, particularly those with mild to moderate drug or alcohol dependence who have few associated biopsychosocial problems, good psychosocial functioning and a number of strengths, i.e. those who are most likely to respond well to an Opportunistic Brief Intervention (OBI).

Fitting it all into a practical treatment framework

Drinkers with mild to moderate dependence may be able to control their drinking if boundaries

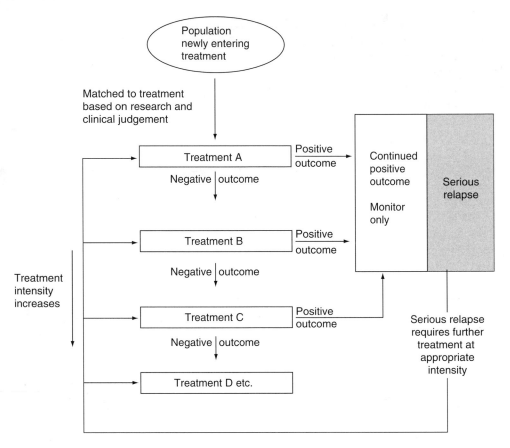

Figure 6.1   Flow diagram of Stepped Care Approach to the treatment of alcohol problems. (Adapted from Sobell, M. B. & Sobell, L. C. (1993a) Treatment for problem drinkers: a public health priority (Ch. 7). In: J. S. Baer, G. A. Marlatt & R. J. McMahon (Eds) *Addictive Behaviors Across the Lifespan: Prevention, Treatment and Policy Issues.* Figure 6.2, p. 150. Beverly Hills, CA: Sage. Reprinted with permission from Sage Publications, Inc.)

are agreed and adhered to. Those who are unable to control it by reducing consumption to within so-called *safe limits* and avoiding binge drinking may be able to attain control by stopping drinking completely. The prospect of no alcohol for the rest of one's life is daunting for most people but for dependent drinkers it can be devastating. A trial period of abstinence, so-called *sobriety sampling*, can be a good way of addressing this. Drinkers with lesser degrees of dependence also may respond to a brief intervention. For heavily dependent drinkers and for drug users requiring treatment, a different treatment framework model is suggested. It is comprised of three-monthly care packages followed by reviews, outcome

audit and goal setting for the next three months. The following example (Figure 6.2) might be appropriate for a severely dependent opiate user.

In other programmes abstinence may take a shorter or longer time to be achieved. Some people are on a substitute prescription for years. Others never manage to stop their substance use. As a general rule maintenance prescribing should not be for any longer than is necessary. Abstinence should not be lost sight of except in the very long-term dependent drug users who are stable and functioning well on maintenance therapy, and who, in spite of prolonged treatment, are not able to change.

A. Initial assessment including BBV harm reduction advice
Ongoing MI + three-month care plan:
e.g.   methadone maintenance prescribing
         harm reduction   help solve
              financial, housing and legal
              problems
         coping skills training
         relapse prevention training

Three-monthly review, outcome audit and goal setting

B. Reassessment including BBV harm reduction advice
Ongoing MI + three-month care plan:
e.g.   methadone maintenance prescribing
         contingency management
         reduce as far as possible any harm
              associated with drug use

Three-monthly review, outcome audit and goal setting

C. Reassessment including BBV harm reduction advice
Ongoing MI + three-month care plan:
e.g.   methadone reduction programme
              initiated
         network with family and significant
              others
         social skills training
         employment facilitation

Three-monthly review, outcome audit and goal setting

D. Reassessment including BBV harm reduction advice
Ongoing MI + three-month care plan:
e.g.   methadone reduction programme to
              be completed
         obtain employment
         continue to network with family and
              significant others for three months

Figure 6.2   Treatment framework model for heavily dependent drinkers and drug users.

A. Initial assessment including BBV harm reduction advice for cocaine users
Ongoing counselling with RET + three-month care plan:
e.g.   harm reduction   help solve financial,
              housing and legal problems
         coping skills training
         relapse prevention training

Three-monthly review, outcome audit and goal setting

B. Reassessment including BBV harm reduction advice for cocaine users
Ongoing RET counselling + three-month care plan:
e.g.   four sessions MET
         contingency management
         reduce as far as possible any harm
              associated with drug use

Three-monthly review, outcome audit and goal setting

C. Reassessment including BBV harm reduction advice for cocaine users
Ongoing RET counselling + three-month care plan:
e.g.   network with family and significant
              others
         social skills training
         employment facilitation

Three-monthly review, outcome audit and goal setting

D. Reassessment including BBV harm reduction advice for cocaine users
Ongoing RET counselling + three-month care plan:
e.g.   attending AA/NA twelve-step self-
              help programme
         obtain employment

Figure 6.3   Treatment framework model for dependent drinkers and cocaine users.

An essentially similar treatment framework might be suitable for a dependent drinker or cocaine user who becomes abstinent at the start of the programme. In the example given in Figure 6.3 the ongoing counselling approach used is Rational–Emotive Therapy (RET) and motivation is prevented from slipping by giving four sessions of Motivational Enhancement Therapy (MET).

Conclusion

The above treatment framework presents a comprehensive and unified approach for all types of substance use. It is flexible enough to accommodate the many different types of treatment intervention considered to be appropriate for a wide range of clients with drink and drug problems and/or dependence.

Chapter 7
Understanding Behavioural and Cognitive–Behavioural Approaches

Introduction

As we have seen there are a number of different ways in which people overcome dependence on drugs or alcohol. For those with problems and/or mild to moderate dependence who do not achieve natural recovery through inherent personal strengths, a professional brief intervention is often the most appropriate way forward. If more intensive intervention is required, face-to-face counselling or support from a key worker or care coordinator together with a number of planned interventions will be necessary. The plethora of biopsychosocial interventions covers the domains of physical and mental health and the environment, and includes self-help and working with families and the legal system. Behavioural therapy and/or Cognitive–Behavioural Therapy (CBT) play a key role for many care plan treatment interventions together with ongoing counselling approaches which are known to be effective. All these interventions are related to unblocking the path to recovery by removing problems that are holding up progress. Many of the problems to be addressed will have accrued in the process of substance use while some will have existed as predisposing factors. Unresolved issues are likely to lead to continuing use. Behavioural therapy and CBT thus contribute to harm reduction as a method of treatment. A sound understanding of these therapeutic methods is essential for all those working in this field.

Classical conditioning

Just as Pavlov's dogs, by a process of conditioned learning, on being repeatedly presented with food at the sound of a bell subconsciously salivate in response to a bell ringing even though no food is present (Pavlov, 1927), so many dependent substance users start to crave when exposed to certain cues. Classical conditioning occurs when there is a pairing of a neutral stimulus, which has no effect upon the response, with an eliciting stimulus, which has an inherent effect. Thus in the example of Pavlov's dogs, on its own the ringing of a bell would not normally cause the dogs to salivate, but, after it has been repeatedly paired with food (the unconditioned eliciting stimulus), at a later date it will do this without the presence of food. When this happens the bell is the conditioned stimulus and salivation is the conditioned response.

BEFORE CONDITIONING
Neutral stimulus (bell) + Unconditioned stimulus
(food) →Unconditioned response (salivation)

AFTER CONDITIONING
Conditioned stimulus (bell)→Conditioned
response (salivation)

The extent to which a given cue leads to a desire or craving for substance use is known as *cue reactivity*. Various factors influence the development of classical conditioned learned behaviour and cue reactivity. These include the timing, frequency and type of cues and responses.

Timing between cues and responses

Immediate and certain responses provide the most potent cue reinforcement. Thus, if a given cue is regularly and closely associated with substance use, dependence, cue reactivity and craving will increase.

Different types of cue and conditioned response in substance users

(1) *External cues.* These are commonly environmental, e.g. the sight of a drug-using friend, or passing an off-licence or drug-using location. Often environmental triggers are easier to overcome than internal triggers. This may be because the timing of the cue in relation to substance use is closer for internal triggers and therefore leads to greater cue reactivity and craving.
(2) *Internal cues.* Negative mood states are common internal cues. The dysfunctional use of drugs or alcohol to help people obtain relief from anger, depression or anxiety negatively reinforce conditioned substance use.
(3) *Agonistic responses.* Stewart and colleagues (1984) have shown that some conditioned responses elicited by drug-conditioned cues resemble the effects of drugs. Pavlov (1927) was the first to describe this phenomenon when he showed that cues which had been reliably paired with the injection of morphine later triggered responses that were similar to morphine itself. Stewart and colleagues (1984) demonstrated that conditioned drug-like states have the potential to trigger drug use and relapse, and postulated that the conditioned agonistic response summates with the actual drug effects and it is this that leads to loss of control. Agonistic drug-like conditioned responses have also been reported in cocaine users, who describe a taste of cocaine at the back of the throat, a faint ringing in the ears, a feeling of excitement and even sexual arousal (Childress *et al.*, 1988).
(4) *Antagonistic responses* (mimicking drug withdrawal effects). Wikler (1948) showed that ex-opiate users who had been drug-free for several months often began to experience signs of opiate withdrawal (sniffing, yawning, eyes running, etc.) when they started to talk about their prior drug use. Siegel (1989) demonstrated

withdrawal-like effects as a conditioned response to drug-taking. More of the drug is needed to combat this state, leading to *conditioned tolerance.* In addition, the antagonistic conditioned response is alleviated by drug-taking, increasing the likelihood of lapses and relapses. Through similar mechanisms, flu-like illnesses and the symptoms of chronic hepatitis C infection, by reminding ex-opiate users of withdrawals, can provoke a relapse as can anxiety in drinkers (as a withdrawal effect rather than an internal cue). Cocaine users commonly describe such experiences on waking from dreaming. Conditioned withdrawal in substance users is common, but occasionally may occur several months after substance use has finished. Weak responses may even occur years later.

(5) *Mixed agonistic and antagonistic responses.* Sometimes there is coexistence of agonistic and antagonistic responses in the same individual to the same cues at different times.

Classical conditioning plays an important role in the development of dependence on alcohol and drugs and in its treatment, but dependence is far more complex than just an example of classical conditioning. It involves cognitive process and is particularly helped by the presence or expectations of rewards.

Operant conditioning

Operant conditioning has been described as a process by which people continue to intensify their substance use behaviour because of its rewarding consequences (positive reinforcement) or relief of withdrawals (negative reinforcement) (NIAA, 1993; Bigelow *et al.*, 1998). It is an important additional mechanism for the development and treatment of alcohol and drug dependence. The pleasurable effects of substance use are perceived through the mesolimbic dopamine system of the brain to be rewarding. Unpleasant consequences have the reverse effect, but the relief of unpleasant withdrawal effects is also rewarding, and this is known as *negative reinforcement.* Thus the neurotransmitter dopamine is implicated in both positive and negative reinforcement, giving rise to the theory that dopamine works by enhancing desire. This is known as 'incentive salience' (Berridge & Robinson, 1998).

A superficial examination of the lives of many drinkers and drug users might suggest that the harm from substance use behaviour, such as progressive loss of friends, family, job, health and self-respect, might be anything except reinforcing. Traditionally this discrepancy has been explained by the concept of compulsion and loss of control. However, a better explanation may be that substance users are themselves powerfully controlled by the immediate reinforcing effects of drug and alcohol use. In addition, substance use often increases exposure to other sources of reward (e.g. changes in social behaviour) and may alter the way other environmental elements change in response to the drinker or drug user to make them more rewarding. Such non-pharmacological consequences frequently contribute to the development and maintenance of inappropriate patterns of drug (Bigelow *et al.*, 1998) and alcohol use (Bigelow, 2001). As a result, operant conditioning is the prime determinant of dependent substance use, and the most effective way to reduce and eliminate it is to provide a competing positive reinforcement which is more rewarding.

Cognitive influences on classical and operant conditioning

Cognitive factors also influence the development of conditioned learning, cue reactivity and the effectiveness of behavioural and CBT interventions. Thus, most conditioned learning with regard to substance use is not only a mixture of operant and classical conditioning, but is still more complex. The reactivity of the conditioned stimulus (cue reactivity) has a conscious cognitive element surrounding both the degree of craving and expectancies or beliefs about substance use.

Cognitive influences will enhance *positive reinforcement* if a person has rewarding beliefs or expectancies associated with substance use. For instance, a businessman may believe that drinking will help him succeed in business deals or individuals may come to believe that their social relationships are enhanced through alcohol or cocaine use. Experiences which positively reinforce substance use lead to expectancies that desirable consequences will occur again in the future.

Similarly cognitive influences will enhance *negative reinforcement* when substance use leads to expectancies that there will be a reduction in the degree of discomfort of an unpleasant situation. Thus many people drink to reduce stress, and research has shown that they drink more when they experience stress at a higher level (Baer *et al.*, 1987). Research has also shown that alcohol reduces tension and improves mood only for the first few drinks; after this the level of anxiety and depression usually increases (Adesso, 1985). Some individuals drink to suppress negative thoughts about themselves (Hull *et al.*, 1986).

Modelling or vicarious learning, where individuals copy the behaviours of others they admire or like, also plays a part in reinforcement (Bandura, 1977). A good counsellor and recovered addicts are capable of influencing substance users' beliefs through modelling.

Conversely, the reactivity of the cues themselves can influence beliefs. Cooney and colleagues (1987) found an increase in self-rated positive outcome expectancies for alcohol use in drinkers placed in high-risk situations, immediately following exposure to alcohol-related cues. Furthermore, there was a significant correlation between the level of positive expectancies and the magnitude of self-reported desire to drink.

Thus, behaviours related to substance use are far more complicated than classical or operant behavioural conditioning models would suggest. The cognitive aspects of substance use – modelling, expectancies, other cognitions, and positive and negative reinforcement – all influence cue reactivity. Rohsenow and colleagues (1995) stress the importance of the complicated nature of cue reactivity in behaviours relating to substance use. They stress the need for a coordinated treatment process to focus not just on behavioural methods but to take into account other mechanisms of action. These should include CBTs that address expectancies, social learning and other cognitive influences on the operant conditioning process. Treatments that ignore the cognitive aspects of cue reactivity are likely to be less effective than those that include them.

Needle fixation

Needle fixation is an example of a more complicated substance use behaviour than simple conditioning alone, although conditioning does play a role. McBride and colleagues (2001) describe semi-structured interviews with 24 injecting drug users (IDUs) from South Wales who fell into two groups. The first group were those in which the process of injecting was directly related to the effects of the drug. Perseverance in trying to find a vein, the search for that elusive *rush* as experienced early on in the injecting career, the use of substitutes and the ritualisation of the process of injecting can all be seen as conditioned responses to the rewarding effects of injecting psychoactive drugs. Some of those interviewed gave stories suggestive of classical agonistic conditioning:

> When you are new to injecting you start to sort of feel the hit as soon as the needle hits your skin even though it cannot have possibly entered your blood stream or hit your brain, you do feel it and they call that 'needle buzzing'. It is so strong; it is like the buzz itself before it actually hits you.

One appeared to use the agonistic effects of several injections with a small amount of the drug to increase the overall drug effect even though this removed the rush:

> I get maybe say three or four hits out of the one little wrap. Whereas before it would just be chuck it on you know, and also whatever fun it is that I get that I cannot really explain, out of injecting it as well, it's more opportunity for sticking a needle into my arm. I am not getting much of a rush, if any. I am still getting the effect of the drug but you do not get the rush.

The second group were those in whom the process of injecting had some secondary gain. These included sexual pleasure, the production of pain for masochistic reasons, the release of deliberate self-harm and the social status. McBride and colleagues

suggest that for this group *chaining* might occur. In the operant conditioning model, chaining consists of sequential component behaviours where each component acts as both a cue for the next behaviour in the chain and a reinforcer for the preceding one (McMurran, 1994).

Failure to recognise the complexity of issues surrounding injecting may deter progress in helping people move away from injecting behaviour. In view of the importance of this to aid the prevention of the spread of blood-borne viruses (BBVs), further research on this subject is urgently required. At the time of writing (2003) there is not even an accepted definition of needle fixation.

Measurement of cue reactivity

Agonistic and antagonistic conditioned responses are difficult to measure objectively, but some researchers include changes in the substance user's physiology. For example, changes in heart rate, electrical skin resistance and skin temperature can be monitored. For the psychological component of cue reactivity, subjective measurements are commonly recorded on a scale of 1:10 in order to assess the degree of drug high, craving and subjective withdrawal effects.

Behavioural economics

The relatively new science of behavioural economics has important therapeutic implications. It is the study of operant conditioning reinforcers and cognitive influences that govern the choice of alternatives to substance use. It is based on the recognition that animal and human behaviours share the same essential features as behavioural decisions that derive from the allocation of economic resources. It sheds new light on decisions taken to instigate, continue or move away from damaging levels of alcohol and drug use.

In terms of behavioural economics, alcohol and drug behaviours can be studied utilising concepts such as demand, elasticity of demand and unit price (Vuchinich, 1997). There is a close relationship between use and availability of drugs and alcohol.

This has generality across substances, normal and clinical populations, and different environments. However, financial and other environmental restraints to reduce access to substance use, such as increasing the price of drugs or alcohol, usually intensify drug-seeking behaviour and associated criminal activity unless valued alternative activities are provided (Carroll, 1996). The price of substance use encompasses more than financial restraint. It entails the use of financial resources plus the physically, socially and psychologically adverse events experienced in consuming and recovering from substance use. All these environmental influences have a bearing on choice and are often major factors in postponement of detoxification and abstinence. Choice also implies the concept of alternative opportunities lost consuming alcohol or drugs, which in turn affects demand and elasticity of demand.

The extent to which heavy drinkers and people with substance use problems appear to go for *smaller sooner* rewards (SSR) (e.g. less alcohol at an earlier stage) and discount *larger later* non-chemical rewards may predict future drink and drug dependence. This is a consistent finding in substance users. Individuals prone to discount *larger later* rewards (LLR) are more likely to develop substance use problems, and once they have developed a substance use problem they are less likely to resolve it (Vuchinich & Tucker, 1998).

However, LLR may sometimes predict positive change. A study of people attempting to resolve their drink problems without professional help showed that the extent to which they organised their behaviour around delayed outcomes when they were drinking heavily predicted successful maintenance of abstinence or controlled drinking for a year or more. This group also drank less and saved approximately ten times more than those who resumed problem drinking (Tucker & Vuchinich, 1997a).

Individuals also vary as to whether they repeatedly choose to engage in readily available substance use or whether they engage in alternative behaviour patterns, which over time increase access to more valued but delayed non-drug activities. The salience and value of alternatives decrease as severity of dependence increases. Heavy drinkers and those with drink problems tend to discount the value of money at a higher rate than light social drinkers (Vuchinich & Simpson, 1998). Opiate-dependent drug users also discount the value of money at a higher rate than non-drug-using controls (Madden *et al.*, 1997). Such discounting gives preference to SSR over LLR so that SSR are more readily chosen (Figure 7.1).

The study of behavioural economics is a scientifically credible way of understanding the choices made in drug-seeking behaviours. It provides a metaphor on which to base constructive thinking

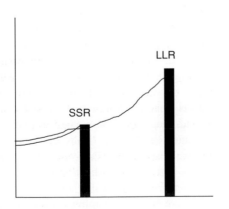 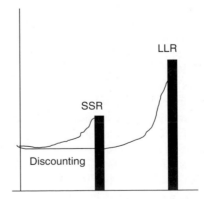

Figure 7.1 Smaller sooner versus larger later rewards.
(Adapted from Vuchinich, R. E. & Tucker, J. A. (1998) Choice, behavioral economics, and addictive behavior patterns. In: W. R. Miller & N. Heather (Eds) *Treating Addictive Behaviors*, 2nd edn. Figure 1, p. 97. New York: Plenum Press. With permission from Kluwer Academic/Plenum Publishers.)

than one of a disease process, and opens the door to a broad base of alternative interventions, the factors which govern their adoption, such as timing and availability, and their intrinsic value as well as their actual cost. In so doing it throws new light on ways to enhance the choice of effective treatment alternatives to substance use.

Behavioural therapy

Classical conditioning plays an important part in several potential therapeutic interventions. These include contingency management, covert sensitisation, aversion therapy and cue extinction. Contingency management is the use of operant conditioning as a therapeutic endeavour by providing a system of rewards for behaviours that avoid substance use. It is particularly effective when used in the precontemplation and contemplation stages of change. Aversion therapy attempts to associate unpleasant happenings, such as drug-induced vomiting or electric shocks, with substance use so that it is no longer rewarding. Although effective, it was not popular with the client group and led to an impaired relationship with caring professionals and therefore has been abandoned. It has been superseded by covert sensitisation where the unpleasant associations are imagined rather than real. Cue desensitisation leading to loss of cue reactivity and eventual extinction removes the rewards that are associated with specific cues. A substance user is exposed to a drug- or drink-related cue without the follow-up of substance use. Each person has their own unique way of using drink and drugs, and most dependent drinkers and drug users have a large number of cues which trigger cravings for substance use. However, it is currently unclear whether the focus of treatment should be more on pure cue exposure or on practising coping skills in the presence of cues (Monti et al., 2002).

Those who achieve abstinence will of course gradually desensitise themselves of all the cues that trigger craving. Hence it becomes easier to maintain abstinence the longer it goes on. In practice, those who attend Alcoholics Anonymous (AA) and Narcotics Anonymous (NA) meetings say that the three-month mark is a danger point when people become overconfident and lower their guard making it easier to slip up at that time. One advantage of using substitute medication that is long acting, such as oral methadone mixture (1 mg/ml) which can be given once a day, is that the psychological associations, not only of injecting but also the other triggers of street drug use, will be broken. Opiate users on oral methadone do their own behavioural therapy both for illicit drug use and injecting if they expose themselves to cues in their local environment without taking other substances.

Cognitive–Behavioural Therapy (CBT)

Although behavioural therapy and CBT can be easily distinguished, in clinical practice Cognitive Therapy (CT) and CBT cannot be readily separated as it is impossible to undertake CT without any reference to behaviour. Most people, therefore, use these latter two terms interchangeably. CBT may be used as a formal counselling approach for ongoing client contact and is an effective way of aiding progress for substance users. It is also an integral part of a number of stand-alone treatment interventions which may be included in the care plan. As a category of care plan interventions, CBT encompasses Brief Treatments, e.g. covert sensitisation; broad-spectrum interventions which take longer to deliver, such as coping skills training; and Beck's CT for the treatment of intercurrent depression, which is even more prolonged. CBT may also be used to aid change for other substance-related behaviours, e.g. high-risk BBV behaviour.

Since 1980 there has been an increasing acknowledgement that CBT is of considerable importance in the treatment of substance use. This applies both for drinkers, e.g. through social skills training (Oei & Jackson, 1980) or a cognitive–affective stress management package (Rohsenow et al., 1986), and for drug users (McLellan et al., 1986; Magura et al., 1992), at least in the short term.

Cognitive therapists observe two types of cognitive processing: automatic and non-automatic. Non-automatic cognitive processing requires effort, intentionality and control, is modifiable and relatively slow, and is subject to conscious awareness. Automatic thoughts are believed to be effortless, are performed without intention or control, and are difficult to modify and operate without awareness. However, they can be brought into conscious awareness and modified. Cognitive therapists state that interpretations of personal experience are hypotheses which may or may not be correct to a varying degree. When people hold unrealistic or negative beliefs about themselves or their experiences, an emotional upset will result. If negative thinking is extreme or persistent, it may lead to an emotional disorder.

CBT interventions are also based on the premise that emotion is determined by cognition. Trower and colleagues (1988) advise cognitive–behavioural therapists to teach their clients to take the following steps:

(1) Monitor emotional upsets and activating events
(2) Identify maladaptive thinking and beliefs
(3) Realise the connections between thinking, emotion and behaviour
(4) Test out maladaptive thinking and beliefs by examining the evidence for and against them
(5) Substitute the negative thinking with more realistic thinking

The last two stages can be difficult to achieve without skilled help, especially in the presence of depressed mood.

CBT interventions include coping skills training and social skills training. The basic tenet on which social skills and coping skills training rests is that dependent drinkers and drug users have developed maladaptive ways of coping and socialising by utilising drink or drugs instead of their own innate coping and socialising abilities. Personal skills in these areas have therefore either never developed or have atrophied through prolonged disuse. By means of social and coping skills training these personal skills can be re-attained through a variety of techniques, such as behaviour rehearsal, modelling, cognitive restructuring and didactic instruction.

Behavioural and CBT interventions such as working with families, improving self-efficacy, social and coping skills training, and countering the negative thinking associated with depression are dealt with in Chapters 13, 14 and 15.

Although insight-oriented counselling is generally ineffective as an ongoing treatment for substance use, it can be helpful in certain circumstances as a care package treatment intervention. This might include post-traumatic stress disorder, (PTSD) and/or a history of sexual abuse (Evans & Sullivan, 1995) as long as the client is ready for it. Other formal counselling approaches, including CBT, can also be used. To aid the preparation for psychotherapy it is sometimes helpful to use CBT to improve coping skills and thus help people deal with the thoughts associated with painful past events (Follette *et al.*, 1998). This enables people to face the negative consequences of painful past thoughts before they are asked to gain insights. In so doing they move on from taking drugs or alcohol to 'blot out' these thoughts or as a dysfunctional coping device. There are dangers of intervening with such sensitive issues prematurely. PTSD can be exacerbated in these circumstances.

Conclusion

A good understanding of behavioural and cognitive–behavioural mechanisms facilitates assessment as well as the choice of relevant treatment interventions to enable people to overcome problem and dependent substance use.

Chapter 8
Effective Counselling for Ongoing Client Contact

Introduction

This chapter describes evidence-based structured counselling approaches that may be usefully undertaken by the care coordinator and designed for ongoing client contact. Unfortunately not all specialist drug and alcohol service workers are trained appropriately, and, even when trained in Motivational Interviewing (MI), they do not always utilise their skills in this area, preferring to use unstructured counselling which is not helpful (see Chapter 1). There is considerable confusion in the substance use literature over counselling terminology which, first of all, needs clarification.

Terminology

In the substance use literature the terms *counselling*, *therapy* and *psychotherapy* are sometimes used interchangeably. To clarify matters, the following terminology to differentiate the various counselling approaches will be used:

- When the professional involved does not use a formal counselling approach, the professional–client verbal interchanges will be referred to as *unstructured alcohol and drug counselling*. (Miller and colleagues (1995a) refer to it as 'general alcoholism counselling'.) When used on its own, unstructured alcohol and drug counselling does not improve substance use treatment outcome and may be counterproductive.
- When the professional involved is trained or accredited in a formal counselling approach for

ongoing client contact that is known to improve substance use treatment outcome, it will be referred to as *structured counselling*. Only a few formal counselling approaches for ongoing client contact are known to improve substance use treatment outcome. These will be outlined in greater detail in this chapter.
- The word *counselling* will be retained to describe professional–client verbal interactions where therapeutic work is undertaken, and as a general word to cover both structured and unstructured counselling.
- The term *psychotherapists* will be reserved for those who are trained or accredited in an insight-oriented counselling approach, which includes psychodynamic, psychoanalytic and cognitive–analytic therapy. This type of professional–client contact will be referred to as *psychotherapy*. There is no evidence that these approaches improve treatment outcomes for substance users when used for ongoing client contact. However, they may be helpful as an additional treatment intervention targeted to individual need in the care plan.
- The term *therapists* will be used for those professionals trained or accredited in a formal counselling approach, who provide counselling interventions appropriate for the care plan. Although these counselling approaches will not improve substance use treatment outcome when used for ongoing client contact, they are able to contribute to a positive treatment outcome if they are required to resolve a psychological problem which is blocking progress.

Which ongoing structured counselling approaches aid the resolution of drink and drug problems and dependence?

The fact that someone is trained in and uses a formal approach when interacting with clients does not imply that he or she will automatically aid the resolution of substance use problems and dependence. Few counselling approaches are recognised to be of use in helping resolve drug and alcohol problems. The 146-page Task Force Report (1996) devoted only half a page to specific counselling approaches and divided them into non-directive counselling, cognitive–behavioural approaches, twelve-step addiction counselling and other approaches, which were said to 'include a variety of individual and group psychotherapies such as Gestalt, family therapy, etc.'. McLellan and colleagues were commissioned by the Task Force to review the literature on counselling in the drugs field since 1975 but they were only able to find six articles which included 'any kind of experimental manipulation, formal comparison or controlled conditions'. They concluded that 'a formal review of such sparse literature was hardly possible'. Yet, had they been asked a similar question with regard to alcohol rather than drugs, a very different picture would have emerged.

Over the years various theories have been put forward in an attempt to give people insights into their addictive behaviour in the erroneous hope that this would help them move to more constructive behaviour patterns.

Early theories focused on instincts, drives, the unconscious effects of drugs and the seeking of drugs for pleasure or self-destruction. Sigmund Freud (1954) wrote that masturbation is the primary addiction and that addictions to drugs such as alcohol and morphine are mainly replacements for that primary addiction. According to him, both masturbation and drug use lead to guilt, anxiety and diminished self-esteem, but are also used to relieve those feelings, leading to a continual cycle and hence to addiction. Rado (1960) theorised that all addictions stemmed from the fact that chemically dependent persons have underlying depression, which he termed 'pharmacothymia'. This, in his view makes them vulnerable to the rebound depressant effects of drugs and alcohol, which invariably follow initial elation. Chein and colleagues (1964) characterised substance use as pleasurable oral regression in an attempt to cope with painful feelings and responsibilities. Khantzian and colleagues (1990) described ego deficits in drug users, including an inability to handle emotions.

There is no evidence that psychoanalysis, psychodynamic counselling and other insight-oriented individual psychotherapies are effective when used on their own as a treatment for substance use problems (see Chapter 1). The reasons why psychodynamic psychotherapy is unhelpful have been summarised by Rounsaville and Carroll (1997):

> [D]ynamic psychotherapy is based on an overall conception that explains all symptoms as arising from underlying psychological conflicts that are at least partly beyond the patient's awareness (unconscious). The major goal of this therapy is to help the patient become aware of these conflicts and to seek healthier methods of achieving wishes and aims that have previously been disavowed. According to this view of psychopathology, the actual symptom choice (e.g. depression, phobia, drug abuse) is less the focus of treatment because symptom substitution is likely to take place if the presenting symptom is removed without resolution of the underlying conflict. The process of the therapy relies heavily on discovering one's conflicts through an unstructured, exploratory and anxiety-arousing procedure of attempting to say everything that comes to mind (free association). A major strategy for discovering unconscious conflicts is the analysis of transference, a process by which the patient begins to develop thoughts and feelings about the therapist that are derived from those originally experienced in other, formative relationships outside of the therapy. To facilitate this exploratory process and development of transference, the therapist typically assumes a

neutral, passive stance and provides a minimum in the way of advice, support or instruction.

There are several reasons why this approach was poorly suited to the needs of drug abusers when it was offered as the sole ambulatory treatment. First, the lack of emphasis on symptom control and the lack of structure in the therapist's typical stance allowed the patient's continued drug abuse to undermine the treatment. Therapists did not address the patient's needs for coping skills because this removal of symptoms was seen as palliative and likely to result in symptom substitution. As a result substance use continued unabated while the treatment focused on underlying dynamics. Limit setting by the therapist was to be avoided so as to maintain neutrality, and no clear guidelines were provided for dealing with intoxication during sessions. The major strategy now is to place primary emphasis on controlling or reducing drug use, while pursuing other goals only after drug use has been at least partly controlled. This means that either (a) the individual therapist employs techniques designed to help the patient stop illicit drug use as a central part of the treatment, or (b) the therapy is practiced in the context of a comprehensive treatment program in which other aspects of the treatment curtail the patient's use of drugs (e.g. methadone maintenance, disulfiram for alcoholics, residential treatment).

There are four ongoing structured counselling approaches known to aid the resolution of substance use problems and dependence:

- Ellis' Rational–Emotive Therapy (RET)
- Beck's Cognitive Therapy (CT)
- Person-Centred Therapy
- Motivational Interviewing (MI)

All four counselling methods are still in current use, at least to some extent, and therefore it is helpful to know about them. Unlike insight-oriented psychotherapies, the cognitive counselling approaches devised by Ellis and Beck tackle the way drinking and drug-taking behaviour is perceived by the user. The central tenet of CT was summed up by the words of the philosopher Epictetus in the first century AD when he stated: 'Men are disturbed, not by things, but by the views which they take of them.' In other words, the way people perceive things dictates the way they react to them. Cognitive Therapy developed in the middle of the twentieth century and by 1987 Mahoney had listed 17 different types. The most influential of these have been Ellis' RET, Michenbaum's cognitive–behaviour modification and Beck's CT.

Beck and Ellis both originally trained and worked as analysts, but became disillusioned with the orthodox Freudian tradition of the 1950s. Beck's CT is widely used in the UK, particularly as a treatment for depression. Both have published books on their methods to counsel 'alcoholics' and drug users (Ellis *et al.*, 1988; Beck *et al.*, 1993). Their work is particularly relevant for substance users who, as a general rule, view drugs and alcohol from a basis of distorted beliefs and expectations. This leads to continuing substance use behaviours in circumstances when most people would not drink or take drugs, making problem drug use and dependence more likely. It also holds up the recovery process and promotes relapse. Ellis' RET is widely used in the USA and provides the theoretical framework for the large network of *Rational Recovery* (RR) self-help groups, which are available for substance users who are unable to accept AA and NA self-help groups. At the time of writing there are no RR groups in the UK, although it would be useful if some were established.

Person-Centred Counselling is essentially about establishing a good working relationship between counsellor and client. Research by Luborsky and colleagues (1985) who analysed the determinants of counsellor success in the drug field showed that those who had the best relationships with their clients achieved the best results. The central components of Person-Centred Counselling – accurate empathy, unconditional positive regard and congruence – give value and credence to substance users and are deeply valued by those who have been rejected by society and who have poor self-esteem.

However, in recent years MI has rapidly been taking over as the mainstay of ongoing structured counselling with substance users. There are a number of reasons for this:

(1) It is very successful in helping drug users and drinkers change behaviour.

(2) Training is relatively short. A study by Dunn and colleagues (2001) showed that the number of hours of training provided to MI interventionists averaged 15 hours (range 2–31 hours).

(3) It is not necessary to be an accredited counsellor to practise it.

(4) It encompasses a non-confrontational style, which overcomes the problems of resistance to change, and enables a good relationship with the client.

(5) It has a synergistic rather than a simple additive effect when another treatment intervention is added, amplifying the benefits to a level that is greater than the sum of the individual effects of the two together.

(6) The methods can be integrated into a range of interventions and professional frameworks and are thus suited to multi-disciplinary working.

(7) MI is closely linked with progress through the stages of change – a concept well understood by the multi-disciplinary team working within specialist drug and alcohol services. It can thus provide a helpful, common, easily learned language for describing the needs of service users.

(8) There is a danger that motivation will be lost over time and MI as an ongoing counselling approach will help prevent this.

Rational–Emotive Therapy (RET)

RET was devised by Albert Ellis in 1955. Instead of focusing on past events and unconscious processes, it focuses on the client's *current* beliefs, attitudes and self-statements believing these to be causing or maintaining emotional and behavioural difficulties. According to RET theory, although negative life events are likely to be accompanied by negative emotional states, these events do not directly cause emotional reactions. The process whereby emotions are the outcomes of events is known as the ABC of RET. The A (Activating event) activates B (Beliefs, attitudes, thoughts and self-statements) which in turn lead on to C (various emotional Consequences). The consequence will vary according to the individual's beliefs, attitudes, thoughts and self-statements.

RET should not prevent people being elated by positive emotions, or stop them feeling negative emotions where these are appropriate. The aim of RET is to maximise positive emotions and minimise disturbed or self-defeating negative emotions so that anger and panic are not precipitated. Helping people feel annoyed rather than angry, sad rather than depressed, concerned rather than anxious and regretful rather than guilty, where it is appropriate, is the goal of RET. Reducing the level of emotion to one which is less painful to experience removes interference with the client's functioning, tends to alienate others less and helps motivate clients towards change.

The method of helping a client reduce the level of emotion is generally through a *functional analysis*. This involves helping clients see that their negative emotions are not serving their best long-term interests. Sometimes an intense negative emotion may result in a short-term gain. For instance, an angry outburst may make people feel temporarily better through a release of difficult emotions. The long-term negative consequence of such an outburst, however, is likely to cause considerable distress to the client and to others. People who feel angry usually want events in their lives to change, and very often this is impossible. A functional analysis can show them that, by perceiving events differently, it is possible to downgrade the anger, which is preventing them from functioning properly, to annoyance, which is more manageable and less disruptive. The benefits of downgrading high emotional states can be demonstrated in many other spheres. As most people who have ever taken an exam know, a degree of arousal is helpful, but there is a point above which any further increase will be detrimental to performance.

Inappropriate emotions are usually preceded by irrational beliefs, whereas appropriate emotions are preceded by rational beliefs.

Rational beliefs

- are provable and verifiable;
- are associated with appropriate emotions;
- are associated with more productive and self-helping behaviours;

- are usually logical and consistent; and
- usually lead to desirable, proportional or happy feelings.

Irrational beliefs

- are not accompanied by evidence to support the belief, or the evidence contradicts the belief;
- are associated with inappropriate emotions;
- are associated with less productive and less self-helping behaviours;
- are often illogical and inconsistent; and
- often lead to undesirable or miserable feelings.

Irrational beliefs often have the following ingredients, which are pointers to alert the counsellor:

(1) the client rigidly demands that something must change, often in a grandiose way
(2) the client magnifies the negative side of the activating event of which he or she is intolerant
(3) the client has a low self-opinion and a low opinion of others
(4) the client overgeneralises about the future

The rational–emotive counsellor approaches substance users in the same way as any other client with the premise that it is largely the clients' self-defeating thoughts and their consequent feelings and actions that sabotage their lives. The quality of the interpersonal relationship with the counsellor is important in helping the client achieve and sustain change. In RET the therapeutic relationship is grounded on

(1) an unconditional acceptance of the client by the counsellor;
(2) the demonstration that the counsellor will actively work at understanding the client; and
(3) the demonstration that the counsellor will work at helping the client change.

As counselling continues, the repeated joint setting of realistic goals together with the client will help enhance self-efficacy when these goals are achieved, but changing addictive thinking is the key to success.

The client will need to understand the basic ABC of RET. People with problematic drink or drug use are often completely unaware of the connections between their thoughts, feelings and actions.

Much of their thinking is automatic, at a subconscious level, ingrained and therefore quite resistant to change. Progress is only made when these thoughts and beliefs are challenged in a logical, empirical, philosophical and scientific manner. There are a number of strategies and techniques in RET which help the counsellor successfully dispute addictive thoughts. Ellis and colleagues (1988) list nine *disputation strategies*:

(1) The counsellor disputes the irrational belief to show its logical fallacies.
(2) The counsellor attempts to assume the irrational belief is true, then explores what deductions could be made about the world if it were true and then empirically tests these deductions.
(3) The counsellor helps the client experience the ability of the irrational belief to explain important life events: Does the irrational belief include accurate attribution for events?
(4) The counsellor helps clients review how holding the irrational belief has helped or hurt them.
(5) Steps 1–4 are repeated over and over again to help convince the client that the irrational belief is false and self-defeating.
(6) The counsellor helps the client construct a new rational belief to replace the irrational belief.
(7) The counsellor explores the new rational beliefs for logical fallacies.
(8) The counsellor makes deductions from the rational beliefs and then tests these deductions to see if the rational belief leads to more accurate predictions about the world than do the irrational beliefs.
(9) The counsellor helps the client predict how changing to new rational beliefs will affect his or her behaviour and then examines whether the change in behaviour will be more advantageous than the behaviour that followed from the irrational belief.

Freeman (1987) has listed several *disputation techniques* which can be used to challenge a client's irrational beliefs:

(1) *Questioning the evidence.* The counsellor can examine the empirical or logical evidence that the client's statements are true.

(2) *Decatastrophising*. The counsellor helps the client realise he or she is exaggerating the anticipated consequences.

(3) *Advantages and disadvantages*. Here the counsellor asks the client to list the advantages and disadvantages of holding a specific irrational belief.

(4) *Turning adversity to advantage*. The counsellor actively searches for good things that could come out of a bad event.

(5) *Labelling of distortions*. The counsellor teaches the client to label irrational processes and helps him or her recognise any irrational thinking.

(6) *Idiosyncratic meaning*. Clients often have their private meanings for words. Pointing out that meaning is arbitrary helps wean them off their rationale for believing it.

(7) *Reattribution*. Counsellors help clients develop more accurate explanations for events, thus helping them give up self-blaming ideas.

(8) *Examining the options and alternatives*. Clients can often give up their narrow, rigid thinking if they conceptualise that there are different ways to think and behave in their situation.

(9) *Fantasised consequences*. Often clients believe something terrible will happen to them if they do not drink or take drugs. Asking them to fantasise exactly what will happen helps them realise that this is probably not the case.

(10) *Paradox and exaggeration*. By taking an idea to its extreme conclusion, the counsellor can help clients see how foolish it is.

(11) *Replacement imagery*. Clients can use imagery to practise new cognitive and rational beliefs with troublesome activating events.

(12) *Externalisation of voices*. Clients can play the role of their irrational selves and argue in favour of their irrational beliefs with the counsellor. This often helps them see the lack of support for their position.

(13) *Cognitive rehearsals*. Clients can be told to rehearse rational beliefs and self-statements.

The acceptance by the client that his or her thinking is irrational creates cognitive dissonance. The counsellor then demonstrates that the irrational belief does not solve the client's problems and is therefore dysfunctional. Finally the counsellor helps the client develop a more rational belief, demonstrating that it has more supporting evidence and is more helpful than the irrational belief. Typical irrational thoughts might be:

- 'Drinking is not a problem for me, even if I do lose control once in a while. It's other people who have a problem about the way I drink.'
- 'I need a drink to relax.'
- 'If I stopped taking drugs I'd lose all my friends and be bored.'
- 'One slip and I'm right back to square one. I might as well have never tried to come off drugs.'

The counsellor needs to be flexible but persistent. Disputing irrational thoughts is usually best done close to the time of the event so that they can be remembered accurately. RET counsellors usually begin by observing their clients' reactions, then question them about their feelings at an appropriate juncture and attempt to elicit their thoughts. Later clients learn to identify their own irrational thoughts and challenge them themselves.

Beck's Cognitive Therapy (CT)

Like other forms of CT, Beck's model focuses on teaching clients to identify and modify their dysfunctional thought processes, and shows them that emotions and behaviour are mediated by cognitive processes. Beck emphasised the importance of a client's automatic thoughts through which the counsellor is able to access important core beliefs. He coined the concept of the client's *personal domain*. This is the conglomeration of real and abstract things which are important to the client, such as family, possessions, health, status, values and goals. The more an event impinges on the personal domain, the stronger the subsequent emotional reaction is likely to be. Beck originally focused on emotional disturbance, particularly anxiety and depression, but then moved on to behavioural disturbance by applying his approach to substance use and personality disorder. His work is probably the most intensively researched form of CT. His research into depression led him to postulate that depression was a form of thought disorder in which the depressed person distorted incoming information in a negative way. This is now widely accepted.

There are many similarities between the CTs of Beck and Ellis, but there are also important differences. Beck does not believe that clients should be told that they are thinking irrationally, and feels that this could be detrimental since they believe they are seeing things as they really are. He emphasises the importance of the therapeutic relationship, and by the use of Socratic dialogue and open-ended questions helps clients look for evidence that supports or contradicts their views and hypotheses so that they are able to discover misconceptions for themselves. In contrast, Ellis is confrontative, places less emphasis on a warm personal relationship with the client and views the counsellor as a teacher whose task is to persuade clients that their thoughts are irrational by disputing them logically.

Beck and his colleagues (1993) have stated that, when working with substance users, the special strengths of CT are:

(1) the identification and modification of beliefs that exacerbate cravings;
(2) the amelioration of negative affective states (e.g. anger, anxiety and hopelessness) that often trigger drug use; and
(3) teaching clients to apply a battery of cognitive and behavioural skills and techniques, ways they view themselves, their life and their future, thus leading to new lifestyles.

Person-Centred Counselling

In an analysis of the effectiveness of psychotherapy in the treatment of those with drink problems, Miller and colleagues (1995a) concluded:

> [C]ontrolled studies of group or individual psychotherapy have yielded negative findings with remarkable consistency, often despite the predictions of investigators.... An apparent exception to this general trend is client-centred therapy, based on the writings of Rogers.

Person-Centred Counselling was developed by Carl Rogers, a US psychologist and psychotherapist who made a radical departure from psychoanalysis, the prevailing form of psychotherapy in the 1930s and 1940s. The central insight which Rogers held was that the client knows the best way forward and that client–counsellor interactions should therefore be non-directive, with the counsellor acting as facilitator. This enabled the client to make contact with his or her own inner resources and meaning, rather than accepting the interpretation of the counsellor. This new approach rapidly caught on after Rogers (1951) published his first book on the subject.

The person-centred counsellor works through a relationship characterised by three conditions: empathy, unconditional positive regard for the client and congruence.

(1) *Empathy* is essentially the ability to see the world from the client's viewpoint. The counsellor does not have to have experienced the effects of addiction to drugs or alcohol in order to be truly empathetic. Indeed this could even be a hindrance as sometimes the personal experience of one drug user may be so different from that of another that it may interfere with true empathy. Rogers described empathy as the accurate sensing of the feelings and personal meanings that the client is experiencing and the communication of that understanding to the client. Mearns and Thorne (1988) have described it as

> a continuing process whereby the counsellor lays aside her own way of experiencing and perceiving reality, preferring to sense and respond to the experiences and perceptions of her client. This sensing may be intense and enduring, with the counsellor actually experiencing the client's thoughts and feelings as powerfully as if they had originated in herself.

The fact that empathy correlates with effective counselling has been well established by research (Patterson & Stouthamer-Loeber, 1984), and most counsellors are generally agreed on its paramount importance (Raskin, 1974).

(2) *Unconditional Positive Regard* is an attitude held by the counsellor which needs to be consistent in order to aid the therapeutic process. Here the counsellor deeply values the humanity of the client and is not deflected from this by any client behaviour, even when that behaviour is contrary to the counsellor's own ethical values. It is the continuing recognition and acceptance of the client's intrinsic worth, whatever his or her behaviour. The counsellor is never judgemental about the things that a client says or has done. Rather he or she investigates the meaning of any behaviour and the reasons it has occurred. In such circumstances, the client is generally relieved to still be valued. It is important that the acceptance felt by the counsellor is communicated to the client.

(3) *Congruence* has been described as a state of being of the counsellor when the counsellor's outward responses to clients consistently match the inner feelings and sensations that he or she holds towards them (Mearns & Thorne, 1988). Thus, the counsellor is congruent if he or she is able to express inner feelings generated as a response to the client when these responses are judged to be relevant to the client. Congruence is not the same as self-disclosure. If it is untimely or motivated by the counsellor's own needs or fears, self-disclosure may inhibit the client's presentation of problems and may be perceived as irrelevant. Congruence, however, is perceived by the client as a relevant response. The counsellor is accepted as a real human being who has listened, understood and can be trusted, rather than a distant, expert and powerful person who may be concealing judgemental feelings. Like empathy and unconditional positive regard, congruence makes it easier for the client to trust the counsellor. It enhances the therapeutic relationship and enables the client to become more open and congruent.

It is important that the congruence of the counsellor is perceived by the client. The ability to be successfully congruent does entail acceptance of the client's inner humanity and intrinsic worth, although of course this does not necessitate acceptance of behaviours that are unacceptable. In the event of the counsellor being unable to establish unconditional positive regard for the client, it has been recommended that another counsellor be found who is able to establish a good professional relationship, in order that a constructive outcome can be achieved. If the client has a long history of not being accepted by society, he or she may initially distrust the counsellor's acceptance of him or her and may attempt to test it out.

Person-Centred Therapy with substance users

Drug users and people with drink problems and dependence tend to be highly suspicious of any authority figure, have a low opinion of themselves and are used to people making adverse judgemental assumptions about them. The more they become entrenched in substance use, the more they tend to be rejected by society. It is not surprising, therefore, that many expect to be rejected by doctors, social workers and even drug and alcohol workers. The therapeutic relationship is often made more difficult by the policing role, urine testing and the setting of firm limits on behaviour (which many clients feel obliged to test out).

Overcoming such obstacles is crucial if a person-centred approach is to be successful. This may be achieved by focusing on the importance of seeing things from the client's viewpoint, by deeply valuing the humanity of the client without being deflected by the client's behaviour, and by the counsellor relating as a human being who has listened and can be trusted.

Some workers in the field become deflected by the fact that clients sometimes lie. Trying to get the client to admit the truth may even become an obsession. Yet, lies are so often used as a defence or as a means of coping that for some substance users lying becomes a habit that is difficult to break. It may be easier for some drug workers to accept the client who has taken illegal drugs and committed repeated burglary and other acquisitive crimes than it is for them to accept the client who lies to them. The deceit does not indicate that the relationship between the client and counsellor has broken down or is ineffective, that the counsellor is not trusted, or that the drug user is taking advantage of the system and does not care. Lies told by the client still happen in the very best of therapeutic relationships. They usually reflect the fact that the client still has a long way to go to full recovery. To focus on proving that a client has lied reduces his or her self-esteem and may foster the belief that he or she is being judged adversely by the counsellor, impairing the therapeutic relationship. This does not mean that lies should go unchallenged. The counsellor should be able to accept that lies are a behaviour of many clients and be able to convey to clients that, although this behaviour is regarded in a negative light, they are still respected as people, and that the counsellor still believes in their ability to move forward.

Apart from lying, taking drugs and drinking to excess, other behaviours such as a history of violence, stealing and verbal abuse may lead workers to judge substance users adversely, and indeed clients often hate themselves for these things. They expect others, particularly those in positions of authority, such as doctors, to be judgemental. Overcoming this difficulty is the first task to be accomplished in order to establish a constructive therapeutic atmosphere.

A client's self-hatred may be expressed as anger. Although a good counselling relationship should be able to accommodate occasional outbursts of anger, most community drug and alcohol services have firm limits about verbal aggression and physical violence for their own protection. Having clear boundaries is helpful for clients who have problems with their temper in order to aid their adjustment to socially accepted norms.

One barrier to accurate empathy may be that the client perceives that the counsellor lacks understanding of the drug-taking or drinking subculture. Some clients may feel that if the counsellor has never taken any drugs, he or she will be unable to see things from a drug taker's point of view: 'How do you know what help I need if you have never taken any drugs?' Drug workers who have a history of drug use themselves do have an initial advantage, but their experience of drug use will inevitably differ from that of the client in many respects. Whether or not the counsellor has had past drug experiences is less important than the establishment of a good counselling relationship which forms the basis of all subsequent work with the client.

Motivational Interviewing (MI)

MI is a counselling approach that was originally developed specifically for people who were dependent on alcohol, but has subsequently been shown to improve outcomes for those being treated for drug dependence. In addition it can be used successfully to increase a client's motivation to overcome a number of substance-related problems, including high-risk blood-borne virus (BBV) behaviour and criminal behaviour. As Rollnick (2001) said:

> [It] was developed from the notion that *the way* clients are spoken to about changing addictive behaviour affects their willingness to talk freely about why and how they might change. Hence its definition as a counselling style, rather than a set of techniques applied to or on people . . . using direct persuasion often carries the risk of eliciting resistance.

Like Person-Centred Counselling, MI is also based on Rogers' work and shares many of the features of that approach. Bryant-Jefferies regards it as an application of the person-centred approach. Rather than being strictly client-centred in the non-directive sense of Rogers (Bryant-Jefferies, 2001), the counsellor has a clear goal to change the client's drinking and drug use behaviour and to reduce any problems related to substance use. MI is defined by Miller and Rollnick (1991) as a directive, client-centred style of counselling that helps clients explore and resolve their ambivalence about changing.

MI has rapidly gained acceptance and credibility as an effective counselling tool for substance users and many professionals have been encouraged to develop short adaptations to boost declining motivation. This has become so prevalent that studies on Adaptations of Motivational Interviewing (AMI) now outnumber studies on MI as an ongoing counselling approach. AMIs, e.g. Motivational Enhancement Therapy (MET) (Miller *et al.*, 1992), have features which are common to the approach. All are delivered in a non-confrontational style with a common goal to elicit motivation to change and to encourage the person to take responsibility for decision-making. Three forms have been identified (Rollnick *et al.*, 2002): brief advice, behaviour change counselling and MI.

Brief Advice (BA) generally lasts 5–15 minutes and is mostly delivered as an opportunistic intervention. Its goals are to demonstrate respect, communicate risk and provide information to initiate thinking about behaviour change. The professional interviewer takes on the role of active expert, whereas the substance user remains a passive recipient. It may be usefully applied as an Opportunistic Brief Intervention (OBI) during the precontemplation and contemplation stages of change.

Behaviour Change Counselling (BCC) usually lasts 5–30 minutes. It can either be used opportunistically or with those who are help-seeking. It has the same goals as BA, but in addition aims to establish rapport, identify client goals, exchange information, choose strategies based on client readiness to change and build motivation to change. It is most usefully applied as a brief intervention during the preparation and action stages of change with the aim of improving outcomes.

Motivational Interviewing (MI), when used as an adaptation of the normal ongoing MI counselling approach, may last from 30–60 minutes per session or longer. It is most often used with those in the contemplation stage of change, but is also appropriate for individuals in precontemplation or at the preparation stage. The goals are the same as those for BA and BCC but in addition include

- developing relationships,
- resolving ambivalence,
- developing discrepancy, and
- eliciting commitment to change.

The professional takes on a leading role with the substance user acting as a partner.

For example, AMIs have been adapted as a 1-hour brief intervention for heroin users (Saunders *et al.*, 1995). Another AMI, Motivational Enhancement Therapy, is a brief adaptation consisting of three or four sessions lasting 1 hour each. It was used for drinkers in Project MATCH (see Chapter 10). It can be a highly effective form of treatment. In Project MATCH (1997) 4 hours of MET produced similar drinking outcomes both to 12 hours of CBT and 12 hours of Twelve-step Facilitation Therapy (TFT). When an AMI, consisting of three 60-minute sessions, was applied as an intervention for

marijuana use, the results were comparable to 28 hours of skills training (Stephens *et al.*, 2000).

Motivational Interviewing is an approach Miller had developed, and first described in 1983, while counselling drinkers over a period of eight years. It is entirely client-led. MI has been shown to be helpful for a range of goals. Besides working with heroin users attending a methadone clinic (Saunders *et al.*, 1991), it can be utilised to encourage condom use by those at risk of sexual transmission of HIV (Carey *et al.*, 1997), and to counsel drug users for HIV risk reduction with regard to sexual and injecting behaviours (Baker & Dixon, 1991). In addition, it has been used successfully for reducing smoking (Colby *et al.*, 1998), increasing exercise (Harland *et al.*, 1999), weight reduction (Rollnick, 1996) and the treatment of sex offenders (Garland & Dougher, 1991). It has been described as being particularly useful for professionals working in Community Alcohol Teams (CATs) (Stockwell, 1991) and those working with young people (Tober, 1991). When combined with a flexible prescribing policy for opiate users it is known as motivational milieu therapy (van Bilsen & van Emst, 1986).

The four general principles of Motivational Interviewing (MI)

There are four general principles underlying MI:

(1) Expressing empathy
(2) Developing discrepancy
(3) Rolling with resistance
(4) Supporting self-efficacy

Expressing empathy. The importance of empathy has already been highlighted (see person-centred section of this chapter). Although studies have shown motivation for change to be increased by discussion with a counsellor (Chick *et al.*, 1985; Babor *et al.*, 1987a), counselling with empathy facilitates motivation, and is also associated with little resistance and positive long-term change (Miller & Sovereign, 1989).

Developing discrepancy. Motivation to change behaviour is created when people perceive a discrepancy between their present behaviour and important personal goals (Miller, 1985). However, there are a number of ways in which the perception of discrepancy can backfire and be counterproductive. The first is denial, which is likely to occur if the counsellor is too confrontative. The second is that discrepancy can reinforce feelings of poor self-efficacy and low self-esteem if the client believes that he or she is unable to overcome the problem.

To avoid the difficulties associated with confrontation, instead of the counsellor confronting the client, reflective interventions are used. The client is encouraged to confront himself or herself by voicing thoughts and deeply held beliefs where there is perceived discrepancy. If the pitfalls are guarded against and overcome, cognitive discrepancy will be successful in enhancing motivation towards positive behaviour change. MI helps create and amplify discrepancy between the present state and how the client wants to be with regard to different personal domains, e.g. health, success, employment, family happiness and self-image.

Discrepancy points to the importance of change for the individual and enables a recognition that substance use is preventing this. MI methods seek to accomplish discrepancy within the person rather than relying on external and coercive motivators. Coercion arises when a person is pressured to change behaviour because it is discrepant with someone else's goals or values. MI highlights behaviours which are discrepant with an individual's own goals and values. A number of techniques such as heightening subjective and objective awareness and selective summarisation can be useful ways to increase discrepancy.

Rolling with resistance. Traditional methods of counselling drinkers and drug users were highly confrontative. In MI the counsellor avoids confrontation. If the client says something that the counsellor disagrees with, the counsellor 'rolls with it'. Overtly directive and confrontational counselling styles tend to evoke a response that is highly resistant (Patterson & Forgatch, 1985). Unfortunately families are often highly confrontational over long periods of time, so that when a drug user or drinker eventually arrives for professional help resistance and denial may be already entrenched. In earlier times services did not accept people who they felt were not motivated to change. MI has now changed that.

Sometimes when unstructured counselling is used, therapeutic failure is attributed to the individual's 'denial', 'resistance' or 'lack of motivation', and therapeutic success is commonly claimed as the success of the alcohol or drug worker or of the methods used. Similarly, success in Alcoholics Anonymous (AA) is often said to be due to the quality of the programme, whereas lack of success is attributed to 'failure to use the programme'. This *heads-I-win, tails-you-lose* situation is very comfortable for the professional worker and those within AA, but it does not do much for the drinker's self-esteem or sense of self-efficacy.

When MI is going well, Miller and Rollnick (2002) describe the therapeutic interaction as *dancing* or *consonant*. When it goes badly they term it *dissonant* or *wrestling together*. Although behaviour that is discrepant with goals and beliefs occurs solely within the substance user, dissonance or wrestling is a product of the counselling relationship and not of one person's behaviour. The alert professional will be extremely sensitive to dissonance, will pick it up at an early stage and take appropriate steps to revert to dancing together. Certain client responses, such as change talk and resistance, are markers of consonance and dissonance respectively and are also meaningful predictors of behaviour change.

Supporting self-efficacy. If self-esteem and self-efficacy remain low, this may, in the mind of the drug user or drinker, give justification for continued drinking or drug-taking. Substance users who want to change, but feel that this is impossible, will not try. In such circumstances self-harm and self-punishment may compound the issue. Self-esteem, which is closely linked to self-efficacy, will plummet if the reaction to a counsellor highlighting discrepancy is to attempt to resolve the issue by self-harm or self-punishment. This may be guarded against by promoting self-efficacy and enhancing confidence to change.

Other features of MI

In Miller's original paper outlining MI (Miller, 1983), he included the Rogerian therapeutic concept of *Unconditional Positive Regard*. Later, however, this appears to have been quietly shelved. In the first edition of Miller and Rollnick's book,

Motivational Interviewing, Unconditional Positive Regard is referred to only in the context of missed appointments. If the client has come to like and respect the counsellor, he or she may avoid coming back with reports of relapse or indecision for fear of causing disappointment. As Unconditional Positive Regard communicates acceptance and respect regardless of what the client expresses, it is seen here as the only remedy for such a situation (Miller & Rollnick, 1991). In the second edition the concept appears to have been dispensed with altogether (Miller & Rollnick, 2002). Perhaps this is because the continuing recognition and acceptance of the client's intrinsic worth, whatever his or her behaviour, makes it difficult to set limits on unacceptable substance use behaviours.

The MI model also *de-emphasises labelling*. Again this is in frank contrast to the twelve-step approach, where acceptance of the label *alcoholic* is seen to be important. The first step of the AA programme requires people to accept the statement, 'We were powerless over alcohol – that our lives had become unmanageable.' Confronted with these issues many drinkers exhibit *denial* by saying: 'I am not an alcoholic. I can have an occasional drink.' In fact for many people stopping drinking altogether is often the best way of controlling it with the support of AA. But for those who are not ready or who are unwilling to accept a label, MI provides a useful counselling approach.

Techniques used in MI

Once an empathetic relationship is established between counsellor and client, attempts can be made to start the interpersonal process of increasing motivation by

(1) utilising a number of psychological techniques to heighten subjective awareness;
(2) showing the client objective measures that will further increase awareness; and
(3) selective summarisation. The counsellor selectively summarises all self-motivational statements (which had been picked out through active listening) and repeats these to the client.

Psychological techniques used to heighten awareness. Various techniques and strategies can be employed to aid this process. As Miller (1983) says, 'the

counsellor is not merely a passive mirror reflecting perfectly what the client presents. Rather the counsellor is selective and active.' Thus, those things that help increase motivation are selected by a process of active listening and then reinforced by:

(1) *Reflection.* Here the last few words of a client's sentence are repeated or restated in different words, e.g. 'You really want to stop using drugs', or 'You've been spending a lot of money on drink', or 'Your mother is upset'. The client will then go on to amplify it or explore his or her inner thoughts, feelings and conflicts.
(2) *Reflective restructuring.* Here a statement that is not going to help increase motivation can be restructured in a way that is more helpful. Reflective restructuring will only be non-threatening and helpful if the client perceives the counsellor to be empathetic. Miller (1983) gives an example of restructuring:

> *Client*:   I am not an alcoholic because . . .
> *Counsellor*: I imagine that's confusing for you. On the one hand you can see that there are serious problems developing around your alcohol use, and on the other it seems like the label 'alcoholic' doesn't quite fit because things don't look that bad.

(3) *Eliciting self-motivational statements.* For example, this can be done by asking about problems caused by drink or drugs, and by asking the client what makes him or her believe that he or she should do something about these problems. Self-motivating statements work on the well-known psychological principle that people end up believing what they hear themselves say.
(4) *Using paradox.* Sometimes a paradoxical statement, if used confrontatively, can persuade the individual to take the opposite view. For example:

> *Counsellor*: It sounds as though you really don't want to stop drinking.
> *Client*:   No I really do want to stop.

The danger of paradoxical statements is that they can backfire and may undermine the relationship the counsellor has with the client. For example, the client may have replied: 'You're right I really don't want to stop.' If this occurs it is important to follow it through by focusing on more realistic goals and acknowledging ambivalence.

Showing the client objective measures to further increase awareness. This also increases awareness of problems and their effects. The following are possible examples:

- quantifying alcohol consumption into units and categorising them as within low-risk limits, hazardous or harmful drinking
- liver function tests (LFT), a full blood count (FBC), and for drinkers gamma-glutamyltransferase (GGT) level
- measurement of severity of dependence

The client is then asked what he or she makes of the results.

Selective summarisation. At intervals and again at the end of each interview the counsellor sums up all the client's self-motivational statements, phrasing them as reflections of what the client has said. The client is then asked to comment, 'Is that complete? Is there anything that I have missed?' If the client has expressed doubts during the interview these should be included in the final summary. If they are left out they will only be elicited again. The counsellor must not 'put words in the client's mouth' as this will be detected as a ploy. The goal is an accurate summarisation with special emphasis on the client's self-motivational statements.

Conclusion

Unstructured counselling does not help improve outcomes for substance users. However, outcomes may improve if unstructured counselling for ongoing client contact is combined with other treatment interventions that are known to be effective.

There are four counselling approaches that do have the potential to improve outcomes for problem drug and alcohol use when used for ongoing structured counselling with clients. These are the two cognitive therapies devised by Albert Ellis and Aaron Beck specifically for substance users – Rational–Emotive Therapy and Cognitive/Cognitive–Behavioural Therapy, Person-Centred Counselling and Motivational Interviewing. The fourth, in particular, is a useful ongoing counselling approach. When combined with other interventions it gives better results than the anticipated sum of the two given independently. It also helps prevent motivation from slipping. Usually this combination of MI as a counselling approach for ongoing client contact together with those interventions approved for the care plan is the most effective way of ensuring progress for clients with moderate to severe dependence and with those who have a significant substance use problem.

Chapter 9
The Nature and Timing of Care Plan Interventions

Introduction

The content of care plan relies on a good assessment, which includes examination of potential prescribing issues, and whether or not the client already has the skills to overcome a substance use problem and/or dependence. If the personal resources to do so are present, they may be highlighted and utilised during treatment, either through a brief structured intervention or by a more detailed examination of personal strengths, e.g. through Solution-Focused Therapy (SFT). If substance-related problems are holding up progress, these may need to be addressed.

Which interventions should be included in the care plan?

There are so many ways of helping clients with addiction problems that it can sometimes be difficult for those working in drug or alcohol agencies to know which interventions to use. Substitute prescribing, brief interventions, relapse prevention work, twelve-step therapy, self-help, the reduction of harm, taking steps to improve psychological and social functioning, utilising the client's strengths and motivational enhancement can all influence change in a positive direction. However, using them all would be unnecessary, enormously expensive and time consuming.

Comparisons of efficacy based on different theoretical models have in the past failed to find significant differences in outcome. According to Lindstrom (1992), any one model of alcohol treatment intervention results in a successful treatment

outcome for between a third and a half of cases, and the majority of clients relapse within two years whichever treatment model is used. However, in the Lindstrom study treatments were invariably abstinence-oriented, and most of those treated attended twelve-step meetings. Outcomes were measured by success in maintaining abstinence. Most clinicians have to date used similar treatment methods and it is now clear that those things that have hitherto been regarded as life contexts and non-treatment variables, such as social support and life skills, should in themselves be regarded as treatment interventions. Indeed they influence treatment outcomes to a greater degree than most other treatments (Keene, 1998).

Those who are drug or alcohol dependent should ideally be treated with Motivational Interviewing (MI) as the preferred ongoing counselling approach together with a specific package of planned treatment interventions (see Chapter 8). All substance users, whether maintained on a substitute prescription or aiming for abstinence, will need to avoid relapsing and will benefit from relapse prevention training. Blood-borne virus (BBV) risk reduction advice should also be given where appropriate. In addition, a number of other treatment interventions can be added according to assessed need. These include substitute prescribing, working with families, psychological and social harm reduction initiatives, harnessing an individual's strengths, treating physical and mental health problems, improving psychosocial functioning and addressing problems relating to the criminal justice system. Twelve-step Facilitation Therapy (TFT) or self-help may also be included, either alone or in combination with other interventions.

From this plethora of possible treatments a way forward needs to be found. It helps initially to assess the severity of dependence and base initial treatment decisions according to whether someone is mild to moderately dependent or moderately to severely dependent. Drinkers who are less severely dependent may be able to control their drinking. Treatment interventions for those with mild to moderate dependence should be by the use of a Brief Treatment. For those who are severely dependent, treatment should aim to resolve substance-related problems which are holding up the recovery process. The latter can be achieved either through the use of personal strengths and resources or by targeted harm reduction interventions. If it is possible to use internal strengths, which include problem-solving ability and the ability to manage negative emotions, this is undoubtedly the easiest and most cost-effective solution.

Formulating the care plan

Care plan interventions for all substance users

All substance users should be given relapse prevention training, if possible at an early stage. The risks of relapse apply to each stage of progress and are not confined to maintenance of abstinence. It is also recommended that coping skills training be included (Gossop et al., 2002). This would be most cost-effective if given to groups of new substance users when they first enter treatment.

Similarly an exploration of each client's BBV risk behaviour should be undertaken, and targeted BBV risk reduction advice regarding both injecting and sexual behaviour should be given to anyone who has ever injected illicit drugs or who is believed to be at risk of BBV infection in the future.

Specific care plan interventions according to assessed need

Options
(1) A brief intervention as the sole treatment
(2) A more intensive package of harm reduction treatment may include:

- substitute prescribing
- attention to drink- or drug-related biopsychosocial problems which are obstructing the recovery process

The care plan should be formally reviewed at specified intervals, e.g. every three months, and a new care plan devised with the most important problems being resolved first.

Specific problems which are impeding successful treatment outcomes should be identifiable through the assessment process and *matched treatment given to reduce harm*, e.g. better accommodation, anxiety management skills, family therapy and so on. In some instances personal strengths may need to be enhanced before progress can be made using assertiveness training or other methods. The cooperation of the substance user may be constructively enhanced by the inclusion of the client's own personal goals in the care plan.

Setting goals
In addition to the ascertainment of needs, there may also be *wants*. Clients may wish to achieve certain things which may differ from their defined *needs*. There is usually considerable overlap between a client's personal goals and the assessed needs of the client. Care must be taken not to exclude personal goals, which may be getting a job, regaining access to children, paying off debts and so on. They need to be realistic, and in-depth discussion with an empathetic care coordinator will always be helpful.

Factors influencing the content of the care plan

The severity of dependence or substance-related problems

Those with no significant problems or mild to moderate dependency
If mild to moderate dependence is present and there are no serious associated problems, a structured Brief Treatment in the community may be all that is necessary. At follow-up assessments personal functioning may need to be enhanced or hidden problems may need to be searched out if outcomes do not improve.

Some drinkers with low levels of dependency and few problems, and who are functioning well may achieve *natural recovery* requiring no professional help. With professional help they may respond to a brief intervention and learn to control their use of alcohol. For drug users with few problems and mild to moderate dependency a quick structured intervention package in the community utilising advice and appropriate literature comprising a minimal or Opportunistic Brief Intervention (OBI) may be all that is required. Some may be helped by ready access to supported detoxification or withdrawal at home followed by short-term support. This issue needs further research, but the demands of cost-effectiveness suggest that these should be the initial treatments of choice for those with mild to moderate dependence.

Those with significant problems and/or moderate to severe dependency

If dependency is moderate to severe, a more extensive care package is generally necessary. To ensure that nothing has been missed and that appropriately targeted treatment interventions are put in place, it is helpful, at the end of the assessment, for the assessor to review client needs from the different domains of a biopsychosocial perspective (NTA, 2002) (see also Chapter 5).

Factors influencing the effectiveness of treatment interventions

Although the Mesa Grande (Appendix 15) gives us a useful comparison of effective treatments for alcohol problems and dependence, there are several reasons why we should avoid relying solely on interventions which have positive cumulative evidence scores (CES):

- There are differences between clinically targeted treatment interventions and controlled research studies.
- Some interventions of the Mesa Grande are based on only one or two studies and are therefore open to challenge.
- There may be variations in methodology which affect outcome. For instance, cue exposure for

1 hour is known to be more effective than for 10 minutes (Dawe & Powell, 1995). Sometimes outcomes can be improved if a second intervention is given concurrently. For example, relapse prevention is more effective if it is coupled with coping skills training (Gossop *et al.*, 2002) and there is a strong case to say that it should always be given in conjunction with coping skills training.

- Some interventions lead to better treatment outcomes when matched to a particular stage of change.
- There may be other reasons for the inclusion of care plan interventions apart from effectiveness.

It is therefore important to discover under what conditions a particular treatment intervention is most beneficial and can be most cost-effectively applied. These issues are examined below in greater detail.

Differences between clinically targeted treatment interventions and controlled research studies

It is surprising how little research has been undertaken in the drug field on the use of effective treatment interventions. Although the Mesa Grande's CES scores for the effectiveness of interventions for alcohol dependence have been regularly updated, there is no such table for treatment interventions for dependent drug use, and the research which has been undertaken has not always been applied with adequate regard to the clinical situation. Most of the studies on the efficacy of drug treatment interventions have centred around the issue of substitute prescribing for opiate users. However, where matching of interventions to assessed need has been researched it has been shown that it can be extremely helpful for both drug users and drinkers (McLellan *et al.*, 1980a; 1983a). Research that does not include matching may therefore be underestimating the potential benefit of these interventions.

A closer examination of research demonstrates the difficulties of comparative results. With regard to alcohol, both the Mesa Grande and the Institute of Medicine (IOM) analysed treatment outcomes from several research studies on the efficacy of relaxation training (IOM, 1990; Miller *et al.*, 1995). A comparison of controlled studies shows that behavioural relaxation techniques have no positive treatment effects for individuals with alcohol dependence. However, if the treatment is targeted, a different picture emerges. Biofeedback in particular has been found to contribute to reductions in drinking but only when targeted to individuals with high levels of anxiety (IOM, 1990). Rosenberg (1979) has also shown that if other behavioural methods of relaxation training are targeted by limiting their use to substance users assessed as having high levels of anxiety, outcomes are considerably improved. If cognitive aspects are included, e.g. with cognitive–behavioural anxiety management, it has been shown to be effective both for drinkers (Rohsenow *et al.*, 1986) and drug users (McLellan *et al.*, 1986; Magura *et al.*, 1992). In practice it should be just as important to know all the interventions that are ineffective (Appendix 16) so that their use can be avoided, as it is to know and use those that are known to be effective. However, like relaxation training, it is possible that some of those interventions with negative CES scores may aid treatment outcomes if they are appropriately targeted. More studies of targeted interventions would be particularly helpful.

The influence of ongoing structured and unstructured counselling on care plan treatment interventions

Interventions combined with unstructured counselling
If unstructured counselling is used as the ongoing style of interacting with the client, therapeutic progress can only be made if there are additional stand-alone interventions in the care plan. Using interventions for which there is no evidence of effectiveness together with unstructured counselling must be avoided. Research has demonstrated that, although unstructured counselling for substance use is unhelpful on its own, beneficial outcomes will occur if it is accompanied by behaviourally based treatments (Russell, 1992). For example, Cognitive–Behavioural Therapy (CBT) interventions will improve outcomes from general unstructured counselling when they are given to opiate (Robson, 1992) and cocaine users (Higgins *et al.*, 1993).

Interventions combined with structured counselling
Outcomes that are enhanced. There is evidence that CBT enhances the treatment effectiveness of relapse prevention initiatives and many other treatment interventions giving enhanced positive outcomes for substance users when used as an ongoing structured counselling approach. On its own, however, CBT is not superior to other treatments (Alford & Beck, 1997; Longabaugh & Morgenstern, 2000; Morgenstern & Longabaugh, 2000). In contrast, when MI is used in combination with other stand-alone interventions, it has a synergistic rather than a simple additive effect, improving outcomes to a level that is greater than the sum of the individual effects (Brown & Miller, 1993). This is one reason why MI is recommended as the preferred ongoing structured counselling approach rather than Cognitive Therapy (CT) or Person-Centred Therapy.

Outcomes that are not enhanced. Some combinations of ongoing CBT structured counselling and a stand-alone treatment intervention do not further improve treatment outcome. Cognitive counselling and behavioural classical conditioning interventions separately improve outcomes by reducing the reactivity of cues or triggers to substance use, making it easier to resist drinking or drug-taking (see Chapter 7) and will eventually lead to cue extinction. Unfortunately progress towards cue extinction is not further enhanced when these two interventions are used in combination (McLellan *et al.*, 1986).

Other reasons for variations in outcome

A right to know
Events such as public awareness campaigns or individual education during a study of other interventions can influence outcome. Consciousness raising is one of the *processes of change* which help move people through Prochaska and DiClemente's stages of change. People with substance use problems and/or dependence have a right to be given accurate information whether or not they choose to utilise this. Education through lectures and films is a case in point, even though this has been given a negative CES score (Appendix 15).

Some interventions can be harmful

Although positive and negative contingency management can be a very effective way of helping people overcome a substance use problem (see later in this chapter), negative contingencies have the ability to increase harm and significantly worsen treatment outcome.

Avoiding the trap of potentially harmful treatment interventions. In the view of the authors, negative contingencies, for which failures are punished, should be abandoned even though they have been shown to be effective. Shaner and colleagues (1998) report beneficial outcomes from the contingent use of withholding public benefits from patients with schizophrenia and co-morbid addiction problems. As a consequence of this and similar research (Whitmore *et al.*, 1997; Schumacher *et al.*, 1998), punitive contingency management principles now appear in federal laws in the USA mandating that welfare recipients must have *performance contracts* that require progress towards employment. These contracts often require substance users to be abstinent or to participate in treatment before benefits are given, and failure to provide a urine sample leads to a reduction or withholding of benefits. This withdrawal of the social safety net will worsen treatment outcome by increasing poverty and deprivation, encouraging criminal behaviour and deterring or delaying help-seeking for a substance use problem.

The revoking of early parole from prison as a consequence of the presence of drugs in the urine is another example of punitive contingency management. This harmful intervention occurs in both the UK and the USA, in spite of UK warnings that this is likely to lead to a change in drug use by prisoners from cannabis (which has long-lasting urine metabolites) to heroin, which is detectable for a shorter time (Gore & Bird, 1998). The harm is compounded with drug users being imprisoned for longer, and as a consequence becoming more likely to use injectable drugs and to contract and spread BBV infections.

A further example of an intervention designed to enhance motivation but which has the potential to cause considerable harm is Dr Vernon Johnson's *family intervention* which was developed in the mid-1960s and is still widely used, particularly in the USA. The process relies heavily on what is known as 'the disease model of alcoholism and drug dependence'. Family and friends are 'educated' regarding the disease and its treatment and trained to confront the person with a drink or drug problem. Johnson's concept was to create a situation where potential drug- or drink-related problems are identified and presented in such a way as to greatly increase the pressure on the user. The unfortunate substance user is then given an ultimatum and a time frame so that a crisis is manufactured.

A number of different types of intervention based on this method from the Johnson Institute have been devised (White & Wright, 1998). All have the potential to cause considerable harm. The individual's job may be threatened, the spouse may be ready to leave or financial problems may be mounting. If, for instance, the spouse is ready to leave, the family and friends, who have been adequately trained and prepared, schedule in a joint confrontation session. The addicted individual is not told the nature of the meeting and it is usually necessary to contrive some deception in order to ensure that the addicted person will attend. The intervention session is highly structured and family members know precisely what they will say and when they will say it. The process is designed to convey the love and concern that the family has for the addicted person and to prevent any display of anger or resentment. Each family member takes a turn to briefly state his or her concern, several incidents that have caused that concern and his or her desire for the individual to seek treatment immediately.

Typically the treatment centre will have already been advised of the intervention and the initial admission information provided. The usual placement is a residential programme followed by outpatient group therapy, with the aim of admission the same day. A crisis is preplanned so that if the person chooses not to go to treatment, either the spouse leaves, the job is terminated or some other serious harmful event occurs and the family and friends withdraw their emotional and financial support.

Although these interventions are not designed to punish the individual but to help him or her take some action, inevitably on some occasions things do not go as planned and serious harm accrues.

Matching treatment interventions to individual clinical need

The lessons to be learned from Project MATCH

Although the outcomes from Project MATCH (see Chapter 4 for details) were highly successful, it is neither practical nor cost-effective to give all substance users such an intensive assessment procedure, such an all-encompassing CBT programme or such intensive follow-up as was available for the participants. In the clinical situation cost-effective service provision dictates the need for foresight matching as the initial approach for people with significant dependence on, or serious problems from, drugs and alcohol. Foresight matching allows fewer and more appropriate interventions to be given to the individual according to his or her assessed needs.

Accurate assessment of the main problems which are holding up the recovery process is essential if foresight matching is to be effective. The importance of measuring life contexts and in particular problem areas in the light of a person's characteristics has been known for several years. More than a decade before the publication of the results of Project MATCH, Orford (1985) said:

> Patients' life contexts and coping skills play an ongoing role in the post-treatment course of alcohol abuse. These factors typically explain as much or more of the variance in treatment outcome as do an individual's demographic characteristics and initial level of functioning.

Orford was impressed by the work of Bromet and Moos who showed the importance of *social characteristics* (which would now be viewed as social strengths). Thus the *characteristics* of being married and having a job conferred a favourable prognosis. Also the quality of the associated environment had predictive significance. The lower the degree of marital conflict, and, for unmarried clients, the greater the degree of job commitment and peer cohesion at work, the better the outcome of the drink problem (Bromet & Moos, 1977).

A client's problems and strengths will only be important for treatment purposes if they are linked to substance use. As has already been mentioned, substance-related problems may have led to the development and maintenance of substance use rather than always being a consequence of it. If they are linked in this way, foresight matching ought to improve outcomes. Any assessment process does, however, rely to a large extent on the client's interpretation of events. Although mostly accurate, there are times when the client's views can be misleading. In the well-known *advice* versus *treatment* survey by Orford and Edwards (1977), which first highlighted the therapeutic importance of Brief Treatment with alcohol-dependent clients, those who did well interpreted their success as stemming from improvements in their marriage or job circumstances rather than the advice or treatment received (Orford *et al.*, 1979).

Results from Project MATCH indicated three matching strategies which health care providers might keep in mind when considering referral to Alcoholics Anonymous (AA):

- For drinkers whose social support system supports drinking, AA appears to result in better drinking outcomes than Motivational Enhancement Therapy (MET) or CBT.
- Actively encouraging angry individuals to attend AA may provoke an angry response and lower the chance of a good treatment outcome.
- Inpatients with high dependence on alcohol may benefit more from twelve-step aftercare treatment than CBT.

If matching fails it does not negate the value of an assessment or imply that everyone should be treated in the same way although all clients are likely to benefit from some interventions, e.g. from relapse prevention training. The assessment procedure gives valuable insights into how the problem arose and why it is maintained. A good assessment and uniform treatment programmes, such as twelve-step work, are both valuable treatment interventions in their own right. There are several reasons why matching may fail:

- There may be more than one problem holding up the recovery process. There is considerable individual variation but social issues are particularly important to rectify. Lack of accommodation and inadequate social support should be prioritised. Homelessness may lead to someone sleeping on the floor of another substance user. Failure to resolve this problem may hold up resolution of problems in other areas.

- If there are problems for which targeted treatment fails, there are sometimes other ways of finding an appropriate solution. For instance, structuring the day through employment or education is a good way of overcoming social isolation and has other advantages (see Chapter 13). Failing this, the AA recommendation of 90 meetings in 90 days aids structure and support. So, too, does attendance at a day programme. An exercise in problem-solving skills (Chapter 14) may help find an alternative approach.
- It may be that personal strengths need to be enhanced before progress can be made. This is particularly important where psychological problems predominate. For instance, assertiveness training may be needed to enhance drink and drug refusal skills.
- Not all clients are ready to resolve problems and may need to progress through some of the stages of change before they are ready for action.
- The timing of these interventions is important as some care plan interventions are more effective at one stage of change than another.

Although some interventions treat everyone in the same way, they may still be useful for some people. No doubt Glaser (1980) had this in mind when he made the following comments relating to an earlier research protocol:

> If the population being treated is in fact heterogeneous, but is dealt with as if it [were] homogeneous, those variables which are critical for successful client-treatment interaction ... will tend to be uniformly distributed in the differing conditions of the experiment, and the results in each condition will be the same for that reason.

However, the lesson to be learned from Project MATCH is that some interventions are likely to be beneficial without requiring matching. TFT, MET, a fully comprehensive CBT programme and a number of other treatment interventions still have the potential to give excellent outcomes. If CBT is the chosen option, it may be more cost-effective to try out a broad-based CBT intervention such as skills training as an intermediary step, before referral to a wide range of CBT interventions, as may be available in a local specialist drug and alcohol day programme.

Evidence from research studies suggests that the following categories of unmatched treatment intervention may improve outcomes for some drug and alcohol users and therefore may be appropriately considered for inclusion in the care plan:

- Mesa Grande treatment interventions with high positive CES scores from more than two studies
- broad-spectrum treatments such as social skills training, coping skills training and the Community Reinforcement Approach (CRA)
- programmes comprising a wide range of cognitive–behavioural interventions (Project MATCH)
- MET (Project MATCH)
- TFT (Project MATCH)
- self-help twelve-step programmes

Treatment interventions and the stages of change

There are several ways of helping individuals progress through the stages of change. The psychological interventions which do this have been refined by Prochaska and DiClemente into ten basic *processes of change*. It may be necessary to use one or more of these if clients are still at a stage before they are ready to action certain treatments in the care plan.

The processes of change

Prochaska and DiClemente (1984) in their book *The Transtheoretical Approach: Crossing Traditional Boundaries of Therapy* identified and categorised the psychological *processes* which can initiate change from precontemplation to contemplation through to preparation, action and maintenance, and the situations or psychological *levels* at which these changes occur. Although there are over 200 systems of counselling and psychotherapy, from their research they were able to identify only ten basic processes of change (Prochaska & DiClemente, 1982). Together with biological and social interventions these processes also comprise the driving force for the recovery process for many substance users. The processes of change are classified in the following way:

(1) consciousness raising
(2) self re-evaluation
(3) social re-evaluation
(4) self-liberation
(5) social liberation
(6) counterconditioning
(7) stimulus control
(8) contingency management
(9) dramatic relief
(10) helping relationships

Consciousness raising. This is the most frequently applied process of change. It includes education and information about a problem and giving feedback to increase the information available so that a client can make more effective responses. For example giving serial results of gamma-glutamyltransferase (GGT) levels to heavy drinkers may sometimes stimulate and maintain a change in drinking pattern (although these tests should be interpreted with caution because of their low specificity), or discussing a drug user's HIV risk behaviour may help stop him or her sharing injecting equipment.

Self re-evaluation. This may be prompted by discussion with another person, not necessarily the care coordinator, or sometimes it may be prompted by a change in circumstance, particularly if this leads on to a change in self-identity such as occurs with pregnancy or employment. When this happens instead of seeing themselves as drug users, people may identify their main role in life as changing.

Social re-evaluation. Here the focus is primarily on reappraising the impact that a problem has, not on one's self, but on others. If the family, a cohabitee or children in particular are seen to be affected by a client's drug-taking or drinking, this may be the deciding factor that precipitates change.

Self-liberation. This involves an increase in the client's ability to choose by becoming aware of new alternatives. In order to be able to utilise this process of change a good sense of self-efficacy is necessary. The following case study is an example of self-liberation.

CASE STUDY 1

Client H aged 29 years was a heavy drinker of several years duration. He had also been entrenched in a pattern of petty criminal behaviour since his early teens. One day he met a girl who was very much against his drinking. She believed in natural healing and healthy living. Much to her mother's disapproval the two set up together, living in an old van which she had bought. New opportunities arose. H, who in his childhood had been brought up in the country, encouraged her to leave her job and take off with him to a rural retreat. H's girlfriend, a strong character, defied her mother, who had been mortified by all this and had done her best to stop the relationship, and the two set off together. Life of course had its ups and downs for them, but with regard to H's drinking this was, at least initially, a highly successful course of action. H had always believed that if the circumstances were right he would overcome his drink problem and make a success of his life.

Social liberation. This involves changes in the environment which lead to more alternatives to substance use, or there may be social changes resulting in new groups of people or friends who do not drink or take drugs. Sometimes care coordinators can act as advocates for this, for instance, by encouraging a client to join a sporting club or to go to AA or Narcotics Anonymous (NA). An example where a change of environment influenced client choice is client P.

CASE STUDY 2

Client P was 27 years old and had been a heavy drinker since the age of 15. From 16 he started dabbling with a number of drugs. He lived with his girlfriend in a flat in a market town. Both worked but unfortunately at a time of recession P was made redundant. At first P was confident that he would soon get another job but this was not to be the case. P became quite depressed. He drank his way through all of his redundancy payment and his drug use escalated. He started using money earned by his girlfriend, then he began shoplifting. Rows over his drinking and drug use became more intense and she threw him out. For nearly two years

P was homeless, living in a haze of polydrug use and drink often not knowing one day from the next. At the beginning he slept on friends' floors, but soon he had no friends left. After this he sometimes slept in a night shelter. Often he slept rough. He begged in the streets and when he was given enough money he would buy some strong cider or a variety of drugs. One day he was beaten up and taken to the local casualty department where he met an old friend who got in contact with his parents. They agreed to have him at home for a temporary period as long as he sought help. He attended a local drug service. For the first time in years he was able to think more clearly and made a decision to be admitted for residential rehabilitation.

Counterconditioning. This involves changing conditioned behaviour so that newly learned positively rewarding responses will be preferred and counter a conditioned response to a stimulus which entails drinking or taking drugs. Most drinkers and drug users who are running into problems have developed repeated behaviour patterns which have become ingrained with regard to their substance use. For example, this might involve going to the pub after every evening meal. If playing badminton, running, going to a film, playing cards or some other enjoyed activity that does not involve drinking is substituted on a regular basis, the new pattern of behaviour will start to take precedence, and counterconditioning will start to occur.

Stimulus control. This again deals with behaviourally conditioned responses, but this time the focus is on the stimulus rather than the response. Avoidance is the most common method of stimulus control. For example, the avoidance of known drug-dealing sites or pubs that are often used is an obvious way of reducing stimuli. Perhaps less obvious are the internal stimuli such as negative mood states.

Contingency management. This is a further use of behavioural techniques. It is probably most relevant for those who are living with a drinker or drug taker. Contingency management means changing the contingencies that control problem behaviour. Thus if a certain behaviour, say problem drinking, becomes unrewarding instead of rewarding, it is less likely to occur. There are many examples of useful positive contingencies as treatment interventions.

Not surprisingly surveys have shown that cash payments and take-home medication tend to be the most popular (Amass *et al.*, 1996). Other examples include voucher programmes where vouchers for positive progress or urines free of illicit substances may be exchanged for various retail items (e.g. restaurant coupons, theatre and cinema tickets) (Higgins *et al.*, 1994). Most behaviourists advocate the use of rewards to reinforce good behaviour. Negative reinforcement with punitive sanctions for those who do not comply has the potential to be extremely harmful and leads to worsened treatment outcomes. In addition, punishment tends to suppress troubled behaviour rather than extinguish it. Problem substance use often brings its own punishments and most agencies dealing with families will recommend that you should not stop the adverse consequences of unwanted behaviour from affecting a drinker or drug taker. Rewarding the dry or drug-free days helps maintain a balanced lifestyle and is recommended for the prevention of relapse. It is a useful area for both individual drinkers or drug takers and their families to work on.

Dramatic relief. The belief that catharsis, or the outpouring of emotions, is therapeutic and can evoke change has its origins in the work of Hippocrates and the theatre of Aristotle. Sometimes deeply emotional events, such as separation, the death of a loved one or the birth of a child, can provoke a cathartic state to a degree that the desire to change will be long-lasting and accompanied by appropriate action.

Helping relationships. In some approaches, such as radical behavioural therapy, the therapist is viewed as being of no importance. However, this is an extreme view and there is no evidence to support it. Most counselling approaches view the relationship between counsellor and client as being extremely important. Some, such as client-centred therapy, see it as the essential process that produces change. The helping relationship appears to be of particular importance for substance users and client-centred therapy is one of the few effective ongoing structured counselling approaches that is helpful for this group. These aspects of beneficial treatment were also demonstrated in Project MATCH.

The levels of change

Looking more clearly at what is really provoking change, and highlighting the content of change, Prochaska and DiClemente (1984) have categorised five different levels where these changes occur:

(1) symptom/situational
(2) maladaptive cognitions
(3) current interpersonal conflicts
(4) family/systems conflicts
(5) intrapersonal conflicts

These are hierarchically arranged. Counsellors should intervene at as high a level as possible, starting with the symptom/situational level, because at higher levels change occurs more quickly.

Symptom/situational. This level takes the drink or drug problem and its associated social, medical, psychological and legal problems at face value and attempts to deal with them directly. The various harms that have been engendered can be reduced via a whole person approach, and this does help bring about change in most clients. Following this, if further help is necessary, other interventions at lower hierarchical levels can be considered.

Maladaptive cognitions. These are common in substance users. Utilising the principles of CT can help rectify them. Depression is common in drinkers and drug users and is a common reason why recovery is delayed or not achieved. The negative bias to the thought processes associated with depression not only obstructs motivation and the recovery process but also may lead to and maintain further depression. CT is a particularly good way of overcoming mild depression in substance users because it is a non-chemical way of dealing with the problem. It has been shown to be as effective as antidepressant medication in treating depression (Rush *et al.*, 1977; Beck *et al.*, 1985), and more effective than antidepressant medication when it comes to preventing relapse of depression (Blackburn *et al.*, 1986).

Current interpersonal conflicts. At this level of intervention the therapeutic focus is on communication and power struggles. Therapists who intervene at this level analyse defences from an interpersonal stance. Transactional Analysis (TA)

as outlined by Berne (1964) in his book *The Games People Play* is an example of this.

Family/systems conflicts. If these problems predominate, family or marital therapy can be considered. Cognitive–behavioural marital therapy has also been shown to be helpful, enhancing treatment outcomes in terms of treatment compliance, subjects' ability to cope with drinking, marital stability and satisfaction and individual subjective well-being (McCrady *et al.*, 1991). Family systems therapy is derived from general systems theory and views the problematic behaviour of one family member as an expression of malfunction of the whole family system. The entire nuclear family is offered treatment. Kaufman (1994a) reviewed 68 studies of family therapy for substance users but found only six where there was comparative data with other treatment or control groups. However, four of the six showed family therapy to be superior to other forms of treatment. One of the two studies finding no superiority did use therapists new to family therapy and addiction treatment. Family therapy would appear to be a useful adjunct to other treatments for drug users and drinkers in select cases, and is particularly valuable if the drug user or drinker is a young person.

Intrapersonal conflicts. There are some very vulnerable drinkers and drug takers whose horrendous experiences in early life have led to an inability to cope with adult life. For such traumatised people drink or drug use can be an escape which enables them to 'blot out' painful thoughts. Unfortunately the perceived need to continue substance use prevents progress with a substance use problem unless another way is found to deal with the painful thoughts. Every alcohol or drug treatment service has such clients. One way forward for opiate users with such needs is to stabilise them on a maintained dose of methadone while they start insight-oriented psychotherapy. For drinkers in particular the situation is more difficult. Many psychotherapists will not start with such a client until they have been dry for a number of months. Such clients find themselves in a catch-22 situation where they are unable to stop drinking because of their underlying problems, and they are unable to tackle their underlying problems without stopping drinking. Clearly, attempting therapy with people when they are frankly intoxicated is a waste of professional time as they will have impaired recall, their emotional responses flattened and their thought processes distorted. It also gives an inappropriate message about the need for change and the value of therapeutic time. However, if there is a local psychotherapist who is willing to take on a client as long as the client undertakes to attend sessions sober and this is the approved care plan, the care coordinator should arrange for this service to be purchased. An ideal solution would be for a psychotherapist to be attached to, or employed by, the specialist substance use service.

Linking care plan interventions to the cycle of change

The effectiveness of many treatment interventions may vary according to the stage of change (see Chapter 5). It is thus important to know at which stage of change a particular care package intervention is likely to be most effective. The picture is further complicated by the fact that most substance users spiral several times through the cycle of change and, although this should be viewed as a learning process, they do return to the precontemplation and contemplation stages.

Forward movement can be aided by the ten processes of change. Sometimes the window of opportunity is lost through motivational decline, e.g. if someone waits too long for residential rehabilitation. Motivation may also decline if problems disappear. Sometimes harm reduction initiatives or simply the prescribing of methadone will reduce the problems facing a substance user to a degree that motivation to overcome chemical dependence is lost.

It is important that those who are assessed as needing specific forms of help are ready and prepared to receive the intended care plan interventions. If they are not ready for them, they will be less effective. The interventions must be congruent with the client's stage of change.

The stage of precontemplation
It is unusual for people who attend services not even to consider the idea of changing unless they have been made to attend against their will, e.g. by relatives, friends or a court order. In the UK, court treatment orders such as Drug Treatment and Testing Orders (DTTOs) are being increasingly used for drug-related offences, but almost all of these are on the basis of a choice between prison and the court treatment order. However, people may be at different stages of change for different treatment goals. They may be in the preparation or action stage for the resolution of one problem, but remain in precontemplation or contemplation for another. An example might be a person who is taking action to reduce high-risk BBV behaviour, but has no thought of becoming drug-free.

Many opiate users who are clearly committed to change are correctly given a methadone maintenance prescription if they are severely dependent and many of them will think that a prescription is all they require and are glad to continue with it. Motivation to make further changes is sometimes not present. It is just as important that people are enabled to see their drug problem in holistic three-dimensional terms as their professional helpers viewing it this way. The social and psychological difficulties that are associated with the drug problem need to be recognised by the substance user as an integral part of their drug problem. The onus in helping them do this lies with the families and professionals who are aiding the drug user or drinker. The substance user has to do most of the work if success is to be achieved but will be aided by a variety of motivational strategies. Consciousness raising, the process of change whereby awareness is heightened, may be required so that substance users see first of all that they have a substance use problem and secondly that it is associated with biopsychosocial problems. This may enable them to move on through the cycle of change.

The stage of contemplation
Aided by harm reduction interventions or by utilising their own personal strengths, many clients overcome drink- or drug-related problems which have been blocking the way forward to the next stage – that of preparation. Many people think about giving up drugs or drink, or changing aspects of their behaviour but never plan how to do this. Forward movement may remain blocked, and the potential to

improve outcomes then becomes more difficult as dependence becomes more severe. Without additional help some people remain stuck at the contemplation stage for years or even indefinitely.

Evaluating the pros and cons of substance use and eliciting discrepancy may enable the client to move forward. The client can be asked what will happen if he or she continues to drink or take drugs. As existing and potential health, psychological and social problems are discussed and it becomes clear that these are discrepant with the individual's personal goals, this discrepancy will open up the need for further interventions. Awareness can be further increased by motivational techniques such as reflecting helpful things that have been said.

If the client has decided that change is necessary, he or she should be asked what is the best way forward. It is important to talk about vulnerabilities and how people can make themselves stronger. For example, if the individual concerned needs to be more assertive in order to fend off previous contacts who have tried to sell them drugs or who will offer them drink, assertiveness training may be helpful. Clients need to re-evaluate themselves and their environment: Is their main role in life that of a drug user? What is the impact on other people?

Often clients have tried various avenues before and are very aware of what does or does not work for them. Drinkers need to decide whether to attempt to drink moderately or whether to completely stop drinking and what help they feel is needed to achieve their chosen goal. There is overwhelming evidence that at least some drinkers do succeed in returning to a moderate, non-problematic drinking pattern (Heather & Robertson, 1997). Because it is illegal to take drugs even in moderate amounts, there is an ethical debate as to whether professionals should help drug users moderate their drug consumption. However, if it is seen in the context of a hierarchy of goals, there is really no ethical difference between this and the prescribing of methadone.

The stage of preparation

Once this stage has been reached and the client prepares for action, treatment is more likely to be successful. As an essential part of preparation the care coordinator needs to ensure that the client thoroughly understands the care plan and the best way to implement it. Various methods to enhance motivation may be required to ensure strong commitment to change. It is also important to check that the client has good self-efficacy and that, if necessary, cognitive or other methods are used to ensure that he or she believes himself or herself to be capable of achieving and maintaining change. Relapse prevention strategies are particularly useful if given in the preparation stage.

The stage of action

At the stage of action the individual is ready to embark on the planned treatment interventions, which with adequate preparation and delivery will optimise the treatment outcome. These may be harm reduction interventions concerned with resolving biopsychosocial problems associated with drinking and drug-taking. Others may be aimed at modifying harmful substance-related behaviours in order to reduce the risk of harm.

The stage of maintenance

Ensuring that someone does not slip back and that the gain is maintained after the delivery of an effective treatment intervention is particularly important when abstinence has been achieved. Sometimes a serious problem related to substance use motivates the drinker or drug taker to stop his or her substance use without any preparation. Sometimes a substitute prescription has been started and it is important that in addition to the prescription there is no illicit drug use. If relapse prevention strategies have not been undertaken at an earlier stage, they should be addressed at this point. In addition the gains achieved from various interventions will only be maintained if they are used regularly. Just training someone in a particular approach does not ensure that he or she will use it. Thus, if a person has poor coping skills, there is a danger that he or she may continue with, or revert to, former ways of inadequate coping in spite of being given coping skills training. This will be particularly likely at times of high stress. The care coordinator will be there to help clients through such difficult times until self-efficacy is raised to a level where the client recognises that no further help is needed. Family and peer support, including twelve-step

Table 9.1   Stages of change and associated features

Stage of change	Main characteristics of individuals in this stage	Intervention match	To move to next stage
Precontemplation	No intent to change Problem behavior seen as having more pros than cons	Do *not* focus on change Use motivational strategies	Acknowledge problem Increase awareness of negatives of problem Evaluate self-regulatory activities
Contemplation	Thinking about changing Seeking information about problem Evaluating pros and cons of change Not prepared to change yet	Consciousness raising Self re-evaluation Environmental re-evaluation	Make decision to act Engage in preliminary action
Preparation	Ready to change in attitude and behavior May have begun to increase self-regulation and to change	Same as contemplation Increase commitment or self-liberation	Set goals and priorities to achieve change Develop change plan
Action	Modifying the problem behavior Learning skills to prevent reversal to full return to problem behavior	Methods of overt behavior change Behavioral change processes	Apply behavior change methods for average of 6 months Increase self-efficacy to perform the behavior change
Maintenance	Sustaining changes that have been accomplished	Methods of overt behavior change continued	—

(From Connors, G. C., Donovan, D. M. & DiClemente, C. C. (2001) *Substance Abuse Treatment and the Stages of Change*. New York: Guilford Press. With permission from Guilford Publications, Inc.)

groups, can also be valuable in the maintenance of change.

Table 9.1 summarises movement through the stages of change with matched interventions.

Prioritising care plan interventions

Prioritising needs will help facilitate a hierarchy of treatment aims and goals, including the reduction of harm. These have been summarised (NTA, 2002) as:

- reduction of health, social and other problems directly related to drug misuse
- reduction of harmful or risky behaviours associated with the misuse of drugs (e.g. sharing injecting equipment)

- reduction of health, social or other problems not directly attributable to drug misuse
- attainment of controlled, non-dependent or non-problematic, drug use
- abstinence from main problem drugs
- abstinence from all drugs

A care plan prioritised to meet the client's needs will change with time. Additionally there are some things which all clients need and others which should be targeted to each individual's specific needs and goals. All injecting drug users (IDUs) should have BBV risk reduction advice and every substance user would benefit from relapse prevention initiatives. These should feature in every initial care plan, rather than being used selectively according to cost-effectiveness and assessed need.

The timing and achievability of abstinence

Once stability, which may involve substitute prescribing, has been achieved for the more severely dependent, other treatments can be given to reduce harm, enhance motivation and improve psychosocial functioning. Opiate users who continue on methadone maintenance without using street drugs are enabled to tackle other issues in their lives and most end up functioning extremely well, the quality of their lives becoming excellent. Eventually many become ready to relinquish their prescription and move on to a drug-free life.

The care plan should be formally reviewed on a regular basis. Only a small number of the most important psychosocial harm reduction interventions will normally be recommended for any defined treatment period. Foresight matching should focus on reducing the harm from social, psychological, medical and legal problems associated with substance use. The combination of stable accommodation and the time structured by employment, study or constructive activity commonly forms the social bedrock to build personal recovery. From the psychological side, the way people use alcohol or drugs commonly links the problem with substance use, and also ranks highly in importance. When alcohol or drug use becomes a method of helping people cope with difficult emotions or painful thoughts, other more appropriate and less harmful coping methods need to be found. If these approaches fail, other problems generating harm for the client should be tackled. If all substance-related problems appear to have been addressed and progress is not being made, untargeted interventions should be considered. Here the client will be expected to fit the programme rather than the programme adapting to meet the needs of the client.

Achieving abstinence is a case of either moving forward by degrees or leaping forward by starting with abstinence. Which is applicable will depend on the type of substance and the circumstances. Incre-

mental progress is made by reducing the harm emanating from substance-related problems. Although many problems are secondary to substance use, they are not always resolved by ceasing to drink or take drugs. There is an interrelationship of problems and substance use. As dependency develops, an increasing number of problems lead to substance use and a vicious circle evolves. Therefore it does not follow that merely stopping substance use will resolve all problems, although many will improve.

If abstinence is not achieved at the beginning, another approach would be to resolve some of the problems first before trying again. Some people are so disadvantaged or disabled by their use or their past and have so little constructive social support that it is very unlikely they will make a successful leap forward to sustained abstinence unless some problems are first rectified.

No one should be excluded and categorised as beyond change or hope. There are potential ways of helping anyone, however severe or apparently insoluble the drink or drug problem. The social support provided through twelve-step programmes can enable people to move forward in other areas. Sometimes the only way forward is through the stability, support and help provided by residential rehabilitation.

Conclusion

The care plan is the lynchpin on which progress is made. A good plan will enable people to move forward even when their situation appears to be insurmountable. An indication of the progress being made can be gleaned from regular outcome re-assessments using tools such as Maudsley Addiction Profile (MAP) or Christo Inventory for Substance-misuse Services (CISS) (see Chapter 5 and Appendices 13 and 14), although they are not 100% reliable and should be used in conjunction with regular care plan reviews with the service user.

Chapter 10
Brief Interventions

Spontaneous remission, brief interventions and the recovery process

Individuals who take drugs or drink excessively may be able to utilise their innate personal resources to stop or reduce their substance use if they have good psychosocial functioning. Brief interventions have been shown to aid this process. When recovery appears to happen for no apparent cause it is called a spontaneous remission. Spontaneous remissions are never truly spontaneous and usually involve great effort on the part of the individual, often after a prolonged contemplation period. They will only occur if the individual's assessment of the problems accrued through continued substance use, or likely to accrue in the future, outweigh the gains, and if personal functioning is at a level where control can be exercised.

Good biopsychosocial functioning enables the exercise of personal strengths. These, in turn, not only help people overcome their problems and the harm that is associated with them but also help them perform successfully in all life areas. As health is not just the absence of disease, so strengths are not just the absence of drink- or drug-related problems and the harms that emanate from them. For instance, overcoming the problem of social isolation may not be sufficient to enable a person to benefit from social support. It is the ability to utilise the support of family and friends in times of need which is required, and that will depend on the relationship between the person and his or her family and friends. Similarly, overcoming homelessness may help solve a housing problem, but is usually only one of a number of factors that interfere with the recovery process. If attention is not given to other harmful issues, adequate progress may not be made.

Thus if the new accommodation is inadequate, leading to a constantly stressful situation, or if other significant problems are left unattended, these may also interfere with the recovery process (and indeed the ability to sustain the new tenancy).

Strengths imply good personal psychosocial functioning and the ability to utilise this. It is possible to improve psychosocial functioning (see Chapters 13 and 14). If help is sought, Solution-Focused Therapy (SFT) is one of the structured approaches to the utilisation of strengths. It is regarded as a Brief Treatment in that it takes less time to enable people to utilise their own strengths than it does to help them sort out drink- or drug-related problems. SFT is by no means a minimal therapy and may involve several structured counselling sessions with a total of several hours consultation time. As such, it differs considerably from other brief interventions.

The majority of substance users do not seek help. In the USA the ratio of untreated to treated people with drink problems has been estimated to range from 3:1 to 13:1 (Roizen et al., 1978; Nathan, 1989). Some go on causing harm to themselves and their local communities until they die. Some recover on their own without any help. Others enlist the aid of self-help groups, and a further population seek professional help.

Several studies on *spontaneous* or *natural* remission highlight the importance of social factors or social change. Saunders and Kershaw (1979) stated: '[T]he mechanisms behind the process appear to involve the establishment of new or improved significant relationships, the termination of alcohol-related employment and other changes in life circumstances.' For an effective spontaneous remission, the support received from significant others has been shown to be of paramount importance when disengagement from drinking and stabilisation occurs (Stall, 1983; Brady, 1993).

One study of spontaneous recovery of problem drinking lasting at least three years (Sobell & Sobell, 1992) found that in about a third of all cases remission was immediate and often event-related (traumatic event, health problem or religious conversion). However, the most common way (57%) was by a process they described as cognitive reappraisal, in which the subjects reported that the main factor was an evaluation of the pros and cons of changing their drinking pattern. This suggests that a good professional assessment may in itself be sufficient to lead to remission in many cases. It is a pity that studies such as Edwards' treatment versus advice (Edwards *et al.*, 1977a) and Project MATCH (Project MATCH Research Group, 1997) did not additionally evaluate the therapeutic effect of the assessment process alone. In many cases it is probably the strength to overcome adverse biopsychosocial factors and a cognitive reappraisal of the situation that leads to so-called spontaneous recovery. These two ingredients are clearly important factors when recovery occurs following a brief intervention.

For all remissions, whether spontaneous or with the aid of treatment, it is helpful if families or significant others are supported in their role, either by a self-help group or by a specialist agency such as AdFam. In a study of adult development, Harvard Medical School, from 1940 to 1980, followed up 660 men from adolescence into late midlife. The 660 subjects fell into two groups: 204 in the upper-middle-class college sample, chosen from an elite college; and 456 in the less privileged core city sample, chosen when they were inner-city boys of junior high school age. The data of these mens' lives were then supplemented by information from a third very different group of subjects, the clinic sample: 100 alcohol-dependent men and women followed up for eight years following inpatient detoxification. Taken together, these three samples have yielded an unmatched longitudinal study of alcohol use. In the eight-year follow-up study of the clinic sample, Vaillant (1983) showed that 'as a group, the chronic alcoholics were psychosocial cripples and the stable remissions were employed and were living in gratifying social environments'. He also showed that social stability at the time of seeking treatment is important to sustained abstinence: '[O]ver the short term, social stability is an important predictor of alcoholism outcome. Premorbid marital status, employment, residential stability, first-admission status and the absence of previous drunk arrests, all significantly predicted who would become a stable remission by 1979.' Over the very long term, however, social stability proved not to be such an important predictor of outcome, as the comparison with the other samples (the 40-year follow-up of the college sample and the core city sample) showed. Fifteen years later Vaillant revisited the 1980 findings to add data collected and review the literature since 1980. In reviewing interviews with remitted core city alcoholics, Vaillant (1995) commented:

> [O]ne of the most striking conclusions . . . is that recovery from alcoholism is anything but 'spontaneous'. Rather, the profound behavioural switch from alcohol dependence to abstinence is mediated not by hitting some mysterious 'bottom' but rather by forces that can be identified and understood by social scientists and harnessed by health professionals.

Other studies on spontaneous remission from illicit drug use also stress the importance of social support systems. Blackwell (1983) stresses the importance of utilising the help and support given by family and friends. Graeven and Graeven (1983) pointed out that spontaneous remission from drug use often occurs among individuals who have relatively strong family support and little contact with the criminal justice system. Sometimes positive change in substance use behaviour is seen to be connected to identity transformation through contact with religious and other ideological groups (Waldorf, 1983). Spontaneous remission is not a rare event, but recovery with or without professional help can occur and is much more likely in those with less severe problems and low dependency. Structured brief interventions are particularly useful in such cases. Where professional help is given individuals often respond well to non-intensive interventions (Sobell & Sobell, 1993a).

There has been considerable confusion with regard to the nomenclature of brief interventions. To overcome this problem Heather (2001) suggests that they should be classified into two separate groups:

- *Opportunistic Brief Interventions* (OBIs), which are known to be highly effective in preventing movement towards future problems and dependence. They have been mainly used in the alcohol field and are most suitable for those who are drinking to excess, and/or have only low or moderate levels of dependence. OBIs are normally directed at a goal of reduced moderate drinking rather than total abstinence. Insistence on abstinence would be a major disincentive for behaviour change among the great majority of those targeted and research shows it would be counterproductive (Sanchez-Craig & Lei, 1986). However, in principle it is possible for OBIs to have a goal of abstinence if the drinker prefers it. In the drug field OBIs have been mainly used to reduce the harm from drug use.
- *Brief Treatments*, where individuals who are help-seeking are given a relatively brief form of treatment. One example is Motivational Enhancement Therapy (MET). Project MATCH showed that four sessions of MET were as effective as 12 sessions of Cognitive–Behavioural Therapy (CBT) or 12 sessions of Twelve-step Facilitation Therapy (TFT).

Opportunistic Brief Interventions (OBIs)

Minimal interventions

OBIs encompass a variety of therapeutic interventions which may be given over a period lasting from a few minutes to several hours. Alcohol Concern (1997) first introduced the term *minimal intervention* for interventions lasting approximately 5–10 minutes and combined with simple handouts.

Minimal interventions were first shown to be effective when given by general practitioners (GPs) to smokers. It was found that 5.1% stopped smoking during the first month and were still not smoking one year later. This is a low figure, but, if it

was consistently applied by all GPs in the UK, there would be half a million ex-smokers per year (Russell *et al.*, 1979). Minimal interventions have yet to be comprehensively assessed in drug users, perhaps because the illegal nature of drug use, and the lack of verified safer limits, makes it more difficult. However, they are a particularly appropriate way forward for those who are drinking more than the recommended limits and who are not heavily dependent on alcohol.

As well as being given by tier 3 specialist substance use services, structured advice as a minimal intervention may be given by tier 1 and 2 workers when they encounter clients/patients who are drinking heavily. Minimal structured interventions may also be given to recreational drug users when there are apparent significant substance-related problems or alcohol or drug dependence (see Chapter 5). For drinkers, such advice should be given to those who are binge drinking and/or exceeding the weekly recommended *safe* limit. (This is a maximum of 21 UK units per week and 4 UK units per day for men, and a maximum of 14 UK units per week and 3 UK units per day for women.) Above this level there is a significant risk of medical problems developing. It should be backed up by written advice which also provides details of local service provision.

Some of the confusion surrounding the efficacy of brief interventions stems from the Mesa Grande (Appendix 15) or *big table* analysis of treatment effectiveness. This analysis of brief interventions does not separate out those who are significantly dependent from those who are not dependent but at risk of becoming so. Most of the brief interventions from this survey were OBIs. Of 23 brief interventions studies analysed, only three were Brief Treatments for significant alcohol dependence and the rest were given to a variety of less serious drinkers. One study was for *alcohol abuse*; one was advice given to hypertensive patients; eight more were categorised as *problem drinkers*, of whom two were classified as *early stage* problem drinkers; one was for drinkers *at risk*; one was for mild to moderate withdrawals; seven were for excessive/heavy drinkers; and one was for *first-time-driving-whilst-intoxicated* offences. The samples were drawn from a variety of different settings: outpatients, inpatients, general practice and through postal screening. All the other interventions in the Mesa Grande are treatments for significant alcohol dependence. The comparison of a brief intervention for excessive drinking with other interventions for people with problems associated with drinking and/or who are mildly or moderately dependent drinkers should have excluded them from comparison. However, this discrepancy should not be allowed to undermine the importance of OBIs. They are an underused resource, which, if applied well, could prevent an enormous number of people developing drink problems and dependence, and lead to savings that would pay for the implementation costs several times over. Transferring these principles to the drug use arena need not be confined to interventions about the quantity of the substance used but may also be applied to reducing the harm from associated behaviours. For example, it could be a very cost-effective way of reducing the incidence of overdose and high-risk BBV behaviour.

Some of the best known OBIs are based on the acronym FRAMES, which stands for Feedback, Responsibility, clear Advice, a Menu of options, Empathy and Self-efficacy. Miller and Sanchez (1993) believe these to be the important active ingredients of OBIs as they have been shown by research to induce change in people with drink problems. For those who have been drinking excessively, particularly if they have already experienced medical, social, psychological or legal problems as a result of drinking, FRAMES is a very useful way forward. Feedback is given on the effects of the person's drinking. The client/patient is then told that it is his or her Responsibility to sort things out. He or she should be given clear Advice to drink at levels where there is only a very low risk of harm (the so-called safe limits). The different ways in which this can be achieved, and other ways to reduce harm, should be discussed (the Menu of options). Research spanning 30 years has demonstrated the importance of accurate Empathy, genuineness and respect (Bergin & Garfield, 1994). Self-efficacy is also an important part of the FRAMES. People need to believe that they can achieve it, if they are to be successful. Persuading them is sometimes skilled work, although many people will respond to the 'you-can-do-it' approach if the person

giving the minimal intervention is perceived to be empathetic.

In the following example of the use of an OBI in clinical practice, someone has been newly diagnosed to be hypertensive, and additionally has admitted to drinking to excess. The doctor might apply FRAMES as a brief intervention along the following lines:

- Your blood pressure is high and there is a recognised direct link between high blood pressure and heavy drinking. At present you are drinking at a level likely to cause medical harm. High blood pressure is just one of the medical problems which result from excessive drinking (Feedback).
- Of course no one else can stop you drinking heavily, if you decide that this is what you are going to do. It is your responsibility to take control of your health and sort this out (Responsibility).
- It is important to determine to what extent the alcohol is contributing to this medical problem. I would like you to stop drinking completely and see you in a week's time, when we will recheck your blood pressure (clear Advice). If it is back to the normal range then we will keep it under review with you drinking within the recommended limits. If it remains high then you will need some tablets in addition to drinking moderately otherwise you will be at risk of having strokes, heart attacks and other major medical problems.
- You have a choice of either continuing drinking at the same level and risk damaging your health, or moderating your consumption to recommended levels (Menu of options). If you choose not to moderate your drinking to within these limits then, although you may feel well at the moment, your health is likely to suffer. There are ways of helping yourself keep within these drinking limits. For instance, you could tell your family and friends that this is what your doctor has advised which may make it easier to achieve.
- It is not easy to change a regular drinking pattern. I can see that you will find it difficult and that you are concerned that you may not always be able to stick to these limits (Empathy).

- But I also know that you are a person who, when the chips are down, has the ability to sort things out. You don't shut your eyes and pretend that things haven't happened. You are a person who does cope with whatever life throws at you, and you will be able to cope with this (Self-efficacy).

Although harm occurs from social, psychological and legal problems, the harm from medical problems associated with heavy drinking is particularly well documented. It is estimated that 25% (Chick, 1994) to 40% (McIntosh, 1982) of male hospital beds are occupied by patients who drink at levels likely to cause medical harm. Given the considerable difficulties in treating people once they have become severely dependent, it is reasonable to assume that it should be cost-effective to screen and intervene with medically ill populations. OBIs are of proven value in primary care, Accident and Emergency (A&E) departments and with general hospital inpatients. Research has also shown OBIs to be effective in a number of other settings including hypertension clinics (Maheswaran et al., 1992), obstetric clinics (Chang et al., 1999), social services (Shawcross et al., 1996), the workplace (Richmond et al., 1999), educational institutions (Higgins-Biddle & Babor, 1996) and the criminal justice system (Baldwin, 1990). There have been several papers (Miller & Wilbourne, 2002; DH, 1993; IOM, 1990; Bien et al., 1993) reviewing the literature and highlighting the effectiveness of OBIs, proposing that they should be introduced into routine practice, particularly in the primary health care and general medical settings. Those drinking to excess may also be found by formal screening programmes, informal opportunistic screening and media surveys.

Estimations of the cost-effectiveness of OBIs are impressive. In the Malmo study in Sweden, researchers demonstrated that excessive drinkers who had received a brief intervention showed an 80% reduction in sick absenteeism from work in the four years following the intervention, and a 60% reduction in days spent in hospital after five years, and a 50% reduction in mortality from all causes over a six-year period following the intervention (Kristenson et al., 1983). A US study showed that men in the minimal intervention group reported less than half the total number of hospital days in the 12-month period following the intervention compared to the control group (Fleming et al., 1997). In 1995 it was estimated that for every US$10 000 spent on minimal alcohol or illicit drug use intervention delivered, US$13 500–25 000 would be saved in medical spending for the managed care provider (Holder et al., 1995).

As we have seen, brief interventions comprise a mixed bag of approaches and some are more effective than others. However, their overall cost-effectiveness is unquestioned. A meta-analysis of six reasonably comparable studies reported, with a 95% confidence interval, an 18–31% reduction in alcohol consumption compared to controls (DH, 1993).

Minimal interventions in general practice

GPs are in an ideal position to screen their patients for excessive drinking. Over 98% of the general population in the UK are registered with a GP. Two-thirds of those registered visit their GP within a 12-month period, and 90% do so within five years (Fraser, 1992). In 1989 more than one million consultations with UK GPs were stated to occur each weekday. Furthermore, heavy drinkers visit their GP roughly twice as often as light drinkers (Anderson, 1989). One study (Israel et al., 1996) has shown that 70% of excessive drinkers can be detected in primary care in an unobtrusive and non-threatening way through a screening process where the receptionists handed out a *trauma questionnaire* (Skinner et al., 1984).

Two major UK studies of screening general practice patients for excessive drinking and providing a minimal intervention have been carried out (Wallace et al., 1988; Anderson & Scott, 1992). Although the Anderson study was confined to men, both studies had very similar results leading to a reduction of alcohol consumption in the range of 25–35%, and a reduction in the proportion of excessive drinkers of around 45%. Interventions of longer duration, with follow-up booster sessions, produced higher success rates of up to around 60–70% for proportions of excessive drinkers (Wallace et al., 1988).

Not everyone responds to a brief intervention. In the study by Wallace and colleagues (1988), which used 47 group practices throughout the UK selected from the Medical Research Council's General Practitioner Research Framework, over half (56% of the males and 52% of the females) continued to drink excessively at the 12-month follow-up. Nevertheless, Wallace and colleagues calculated that consistent implementation of their screening and intervention programme throughout the UK would result in a reduction from excessive to low-risk levels of drinking in 250 000 men and 67 500 women each year. Subsequent international research has confirmed the potential of minimal interventions to reduce excessive drinking and alcohol-related harm. The World Health Organization's (WHO) 1992 trial (Babor & Grant, 1992) on 1655 heavy drinkers from ten countries clearly established that a minimal intervention delivered at primary care level, consisting of a 15-minute structured assessment and 5-minute simple advice was effective in reducing alcohol consumption, and had associated improvements in health. No additional benefit was observed from more extended counselling. More recent studies from Canada (Israel et al., 1996) and the USA (Fleming et al., 1997) have confirmed these results, the US study showing significant reductions in alcohol consumption, including frequency of drinking and binge drinking, compared to controls at a 12-month follow-up. Women showed a higher fall in consumption (31%) than men (14%), but the men in the intervention group reported less than half the total number of hospital days compared to the male control group. This provided the first direct evidence that intervention by primary care physicians reduces medical harm and leads to savings in future health care.

In general practice, questions concerning both weekly and daily alcohol consumption should now form part of the initial patient assessment and be part of an ongoing assessment programme. It should therefore be relatively easy to include a brief intervention, perhaps in written form backed up by verbal advice, to those who are binge drinking or drinking quantities per week that are over the lower risk limits. Unfortunately, there is evidence that such good practice is not the norm. A WHO survey (Kaner et al., 1997) of the 430 GPs in the English Midlands with a 68% response rate showed that GPs do not appear to make routine enquiries about alcohol, with 67% enquiring only *some of the time*. In addition, 57% of GPs had requested five or less blood tests in the previous year because of concern about alcohol consumption. The fact that 65% of GPs knowingly treated only 1–5 patients for excessive drinking in the previous year is striking in view of the evidence that approximately 20% of patients presenting to primary health care are likely to be drinking to excess (Anderson, 1993a).

Clearly many heavy drinkers carry on drinking at the same level without being given any advice about their alcohol consumption. Saunders and colleagues (1985) interviewed 156 hospital patients who had newly diagnosed alcoholic liver disease and found that 35% claimed that they had never been advised to reduce or stop drinking, and only 22% had been referred to a specialist clinic for help with their alcohol problem. Regrettably, although there are several enthusiasts, there is a perceived lack of training, confidence and willingness amongst many GPs to do this work. In spite of exhortations from the UK government and Royal Colleges, a study by Deehan and colleagues (1996) showed that this gloomy situation has changed little in 20 years. This is despite the fact that the cost of delivering a minimal intervention to an excessive drinker was estimated in 1993 to be less than £20 (Freemantle et al., 1993). The WHO survey (Kaner et al., 1997) identified the underlying reason for the lack of GP involvement as being a simple lack of time. GPs felt that they were too busy to incorporate screening and a brief intervention into their already fully packed schedules.

A Danish study (Beich et al., 2002) screening for alcohol problems in general practice using the Alcohol Use Disorders Identification Test (AUDIT) questionnaire showed that such screening threw up considerable problems for the GPs concerned. Although the brief intervention lasted only 10 minutes, it interrupted the natural course of consultations and was inflexible. The doctors were surprised at how difficult it was to establish rapport with the patients who had a positive result and ensure compliance. Almost all doctors experienced negative reactions from some patients, ranging from embarrassment to lying about their drinking behaviour to finding another doctor. They felt screening within a general practice setting was an insensitive way of finding alcohol problems. Lack of time and training were important barriers to effectiveness. Although this was a brief intervention, the extra workload was too high. One doctor compared it to having to do a rectal examination on every patient who came to see him. If screening for alcohol problems is to be done successfully within a general practice setting, these issues need to be carefully assessed and ways need to be found to circumvent them.

Minimal/brief interventions for hospital inpatients

Although hospital inpatients are known to commonly have a history of excessive drinking, screening for this and providing effective brief interventions have both proved to be problematic. One study (Barrison et al., 1982) found that junior medical staff failed to record alcohol consumption in 39% of all patients whose medical histories they had taken, and only in 37% of the medical notes studied was an accurate drinking history recorded. Another study of opportunistic hospital screening found that over half of the patients with drink problems were admitted with an illness not typically related to alcohol (Lloyd et al., 1986). However, a greater identification rate of those at risk of future alcohol problems or dependence can be achieved by the employment of a specialist worker (Tolley & Rowland, 1991).

Two studies (Chick et al., 1985; Elvy et al., 1988) of general hospital inpatients drinking to excess, who were counselled by a nurse or a psychologist for up to 1 hour, failed to show a reduction in alcohol consumption in the counselled patients following discharge, compared to controls. However, one of these studies (Chick et al., 1985) was able to show that the counselled patients had improved outcomes on both alcohol-related problems and the results of blood tests or a relative's report. It has been suggested that the poor results were explicable because many of these patients were not at the stage of contemplation and so were not ready to change their drinking habits.

Heather found that heavily drinking men who had been hospitalised showed a significantly greater reduction in drinking compared to controls at a six-month follow-up after a minimal intervention at the bedside when the appropriate stage of change was taken into consideration. Those patients categorised as *not ready to change* did better if they received brief Motivational Interviewing (MI) than if they received skills-based counselling. Using the Readiness to Change Questionnaire (Appendix 8), 73% of such patients were classified as being in precontemplation or contemplation. Compared to the assessment-only control group, those who were ready to change were given skills-based counselling, whilst those who were in precontemplation or contemplation were given brief MI. This resulted in an average reduction in consumption of roughly ten drinks per week, six months after discharge (Heather, 1996).

Minimal/brief interventions at Accident and Emergency (A&E) departments

Excessive alcohol consumption is a recognised risk for accidents and many A&E attenders have problems relating to alcohol use. In a study of patients attending emergency rooms in four hospitals in California, those screened were found to have almost twice the number of injuries related to alcohol use compared to those in the general population (Weisner & Schmidt, 1993). Another study showed that almost half the patients identified as having an alcohol problem agreed to return the next day for advice on drinking (Green et al., 1993). In Finland, Antti-Poika (1988) demonstrated that an intervention consisting of three sessions of counselling from a trained assistant nurse can have an impact on future drinking levels compared to a control group. After six months 45% had either moderated their drinking or abstained completely, compared to 20% of the control group. This was statistically significant and was supported by falling gamma-glutamyl transferase (GGT) levels, which is an indication of reduced liver damage.

Brief Treatments

The minimal and brief interventions discussed so far are secondary interventions aimed at reducing drinking levels to within *safe limits*, with the hope of preventing future drink problems and dependence. It is now time to look more closely at those brief interventions that can be used with help-seekers when significant alcohol dependence is already established.

Recovery from established dependence is often achieved through a complex interweaving of positive forces and a reduction in negative forces, so that the positive outweigh the negative. Sometimes people reach out for help at a relatively early stage when they have only mild or moderate dependence and do not have the degree of damage of long-term severely dependent drinkers. At such times a single brief intervention may be sufficient to initiate successful action, although this is unusual. Most people do not ask for help until they have recurrent problems related to their alcohol use or until they have significant dependence.

For those who have severe dependence a brief intervention alone is less likely to achieve sustained recovery. Patterns of adverse behaviour have often become ingrained, and excessive drinking over several years has often led to considerable harm and undermined helpful support systems. Employment and close relationships may have been lost, and there may be poor psychosocial functioning. Yet in a few cases where there is severe dependency, sufficient underlying psychosocial strengths may have been maintained for a brief intervention to be successful.

Early research suggested that Brief Treatment with those who are more severely dependent on alcohol is as successful as more intensive specialist treatment (Edwards *et al.*, 1977a; Miller *et al.*, 1980a; Chapman & Huygens, 1988). This was followed by a swing towards Brief Treatment and away from more prolonged treatment. Naturally cost comes into consideration. One influential review (DH, 1993) stated:

> The direct cost per brief intervention delivered to a person who consumes above the (lower risk) limits is less than £20. . . . Evidence from clinical trials suggests that brief interventions are as effective as more expensive specialist treatments. . . . Health commissioners and purchasers should consider the routine opportunistic detection and brief treatment of patients in primary care and hospital settings.

This encouragement to purchasers to concentrate their purchasing on brief interventions because the evidence suggests they are 'as effective as more expensive specialist treatments' was originally inspired by the classic work of 'treatment versus advice' by Edwards and colleagues (1977a). However, the cost compared was that of a minimal 10-minute intervention to prevent the development of drink problems and dependence such as is recommended for family doctors to give their patients who are drinking to excess. The cost of a single hospital outpatient appointment, such as was given by Edwards and colleagues, is many times this amount.

Edwards and colleagues recruited a sample of 100 British men from an outpatient alcohol clinic. They all received a 3-hour initial assessment. By randomisation and matching, half of the sample received a single session of *sympathetic and constructive advice*. The other half received the standard treatment package of the time, including an introduction to Alcoholics Anonymous (AA), disulfiram, additional medication for withdrawal symptoms, treatment by a psychiatrist, and intervention with the wife by a social worker. Inpatient treatment was offered to those who failed to respond to outpatient treatment. The group was followed up for ten years and none of the outcome measures used showed any significant difference between the two groups (Edwards *et al.*, 1983).

Orford and Edwards (1977) also categorised those things that they felt were important for a *basic treatment scheme* for dependent drinkers. Their suggestions are still pertinent, but since that time additional treatment concepts such as relapse prevention, MI and the stages of change have entered the literature. Success was initially centred on abstinence, as it should for severe alcohol dependence, and treatment goals were decided in order to make progress in other areas. There was a monitoring programme, but the recommendations as to how those who do not improve with a brief intervention should be treated centred around inpatient admission. The basic treatment framework which Edwards and colleagues put forward is nevertheless useful, and it serves to underline the importance of Brief Treatments as a first line of treatment for alcohol dependence. The following elements were recommended:

- *A comprehensive assessment*, which Orford and Edwards said serves three purposes: first, it establishes a sufficient basis of information to help clients and their families formulate a plan of action. Second, it helps the client (and partner) broadly review the situation, which may in itself be therapeutic. Third, it helps the advisory team establish their credibility and hence their persuasiveness.
- *A single detailed counselling session for the client and, when the client is in a close relationship, for the partner* is the basic treatment but, they said, 'there will be circumstances in which clinical judgement leads to the conclusion that more (or very much more) than the basic intervention is needed'. The single counselling session involves a discussion between the counsellor, client and partner to define a set of goals. The client and partner should see these goals as logically related to their perception of their problems and should be committed to achieving them. Goals should cover drinking, marital cohesiveness, work, leisure, finances and housing, and should be discussed and jointly agreed with the client rather than presented. Counselling should emphasise both the client's responsibilities and the shared engagement of the partner.
- *A follow-up system to check on progress*, which has a therapeutic effect in its own right, but also serves as a safety net for those clients who do not improve or who continue to deteriorate.

The common reasons for going beyond the basic approach depend on clinical judgement, but some of the following situations would be appropriate for a more intensive approach:

(1) brief admission for detoxification when required, e.g. following re-establishment of severe dependence

(2) underlying psychological illness, e.g. depression, or physical illness requiring admission
(3) life-threatening situations or acute danger to the family requiring admission
(4) homelessness, which may require extensive social services involvement and/or a halfway house placement

Although hospital admission will always be necessary for some clients, the trend has been a movement away from expensive inpatient treatment.

Motivational Enhancement Therapy (MET)

MET (Miller *et al.*, 1992) is probably the best known Adaptation of Motivational Interviewing (AMI), and can be appropriately used to enhance motivation when talking therapies other than MI are used for ongoing interaction with clients, or if no structured counselling is used (see Chapter 8). In such circumstances motivation tends to slip as problems become resolved and circumstances improve during the treatment process. MET is a helpful and relatively quick way of intervening to correct this.

MET consists of three or four sessions, each lasting approximately 1 hour. The first two sessions are designed to build motivation to change. The purpose of the second one or two sessions is to strengthen commitment to change. Whenever possible, the client's spouse or another significant other is included in the first two of these sessions. The first treatment session (week 1) focuses on

(1) providing structured feedback from the initial or a subsequent assessment, particularly with regard to problems associated with alcohol and drug use, level of consumption (alcohol only) and drink- or drug-related symptoms. The Drinkers Check-Up (Miller *et al.*, 1988) is a useful tool for this. During this time discussion should also surround goals and future plans, and the decisions relating to substance use that may be needed to achieve those goals; and
(2) building client motivation to initiate or continue change by using the four general principles of MI: expressing empathy, developing discrepancy, rolling with resistance and

supporting self-efficacy, and utilising the techniques to aid MI (such as reflective restructuring and eliciting self-motivational statements) (see Chapter 8).

The second session (week 2) continues the motivational enhancement process. The gap between the two sessions is important. It allows the individual time to contemplate change if the stage of being ready for action is not yet reached. If people are pushed too fast and not given time to think on their own, they will not be ready to move forward and this will impede the change process.

When two follow-up sessions are given, these are normally at week 6 and week 12. Initially at these sessions time is spent evaluating and monitoring progress and confirming a commitment to change. The remainder of the time is then spent achieving the main purpose of these two sessions, which is to reinforce the commitment to change, by utilising the same principles and techniques of MI that were used in the first two sessions. Using a sales analogy this is *moving in to close the deal*. Recognising the point when the individual is ready for change may be aided by the following observations (Miller & Rollnick, 1991):

- the client stops resisting and raising objections
- he or she asks fewer questions; and appears more settled, resolved, unburdened and peaceful
- makes self-motivational statements indicating a decision (or openness) to change (e.g. 'I know I need to do something about my drinking')
- begins imagining how life might be after a change

The complete MET care package should be finished within 90 days.

The largest ever study of the treatment of alcohol problems, Project MATCH, showed little difference in outcomes at either the one-year (Project MATCH Research Group, 1997) or three-year (Project MATCH Research Group, 1998) follow-up points. It suggests that, because MET was the least intensive and a less costly treatment, it may be promoted by managers in preference to more intensive CBT or TFT.

Social Behaviour and Network Therapy (SBNT)

In the UK the finding that MET was as successful as CBT and TFT needed to be replicated to ensure that this deduction was appropriate to the British treatment system. Researchers suggested that there may be other successful Brief Treatments that had not been investigated by Project MATCH. According to various reviews of the literature, treatment modalities with the most favourable results tended to contain strong social or at least interpersonal elements, such as social skills training and the Community Reinforcement Approach (CRA). In the light of this evidence a brief intervention called Social Behaviour and Network Therapy was developed.

The main aim of SBNT was to build *positive social support for a change in drinking behaviour*. Guided by this aim SBNT therapists use a range of cognitive and behavioural strategies to build social networks to support positive change, involving the client and other network members (family and friends).

SBNT is carried out over eight sessions combining core and elective elements. Each session lasts approximately 50 minutes. The components of SBNT have been drawn from network therapy (Galanter, 1993), behavioural marital therapy (McCrady et al., 1991), Unilateral Family Therapy (Thomas & Ager, 1993), social aspects of the Community Reinforcement Approach (Sisson & Azrin, 1989), relapse prevention (Chaney et al., 1978) and social skills training (Osei & Jackson, 1980).

In the largest UK trial of alcohol treatment known as the United Kingdom Alcohol Treatment Trial (UKATT) – a randomised, controlled multicentre trial with blind assessment involving a projected total of 720 clients – SBNT and MET are currently being compared.

Solution-Focused Therapy (SFT)

SFT differs from most other therapies in that its main focus is to promote change by harnessing people's strengths. Because SFT utilises strengths that are already there it takes a relatively short time to complete. This is why it is classified as one of the brief therapies and can be used as a stand-alone intervention. But personal strengths are not always obvious and can remain undiscovered. Instead of asking what is wrong, which is a natural reaction when someone asks for help for a problem, Solution-Focused therapists may ask what is going well. Even when they are aware of their strengths, many people do not use them to their advantage. Thus, it is important, when utilising this kind of therapy, not just to find ways of discovering what strengths each person has, but to find the best way of using them. One way of starting this process is to ask the client: 'What is going on in your life that is good and which you want to continue?' Other strengths will follow as clients think about what changes they would like to make in their lives and how they would achieve them.

Strengths may be personal and internal, such as good coping ability, the ability to have a good conversation, to be in good control of one's emotions, to be laid back and unruffled by difficulties or criticism. Some strengths may appear to be generally used in negative circumstances but can be harnessed for good use. For instance, stubbornness can be reutilised as stamina, persistence and staying power. Stubborn people do not give up easily.

Other strengths may be external to the person, such as a good social support network, a satisfying well-paid job and a nice home. Families and close friends are strong potential sources of help to aid the treatment process. Solution-Focused therapists are emphatic that this source of help should not be lost. It is not uncommon for the family and intimate friends of people with addiction problems to be left out of the treatment process, particularly if they are pathologised and labelled *co-dependent*. In the words of Berg and Reuss (1998):

> Contrary to the pathology view, our experience is that these spouses, both men and women, have enormous capacity to tolerate frustration, and unlimited patience and undying hope for the problem drinker. We have met many spouses and parents who have told us they know their loved one will make it some day. We view these family members as tremendous resources. They have stood by their partner or son or daughter through more detoxifications and attempts to quit than any professional can ever give them credit for. These spouses know more about the drinker's problem pattern, hidden strengths and weaknesses than any professional can possibly know. When we utilize their knowledge, solicit their co-operation and seek their opinion on what they know will work and not work, the treatment can move along quickly.

Of course family and friends should only be involved if the client wishes it, but some services never enquire. Of those people who decline, some have family and several non-using friends but feel unable to enlist their support. They may feel they have to succeed on their own without any additional help. Sometimes clients have had good family support in the past, but have left home and find it difficult to make contact again when they know they are in a mess.

CASE STUDY

> Client G had walked out of home following a row with her mother two years previously and had not made contact with her. Prior to that her mother had been highly supportive and helpful. Now client G was on a substitute prescription for opiate dependence she had thought of returning to see her mother. It was six months before she eventually got round to this, but when she did the support and help she received was highly beneficial.

Finding out what has helped in the past and what the clients want to happen is not always easily determined. Some strengths remain hidden and it may require considerable skill to unearth them. The strengths that each client has will be unique. Finding out what these are and how to utilise them invariably helps progress the treatment process in a positive direction.

Discovering how time was spent before the drink or drug problem arose can often unearth interests, hobbies, sports skills or other positive diversions which the client may like to employ again and that would aid the therapeutic process. Finding diversions to fill the gap left when someone stops drinking or taking drugs can be an extremely helpful way of starting to restructure someone's life in a positive direction and preventing boredom occurring (a common cue for substance use). Often highly valued interests have become neglected as more and more time was spent obtaining and using the substance of choice and recovering from its effects. The quality of people's lives is enhanced when such activities are rediscovered.

Pretreatment and presession change in SFT

Pretreatment change begins long before people first attend for help. Many have been telling themselves on a daily basis for months or even years that they must stop their drinking or drug use. The very first time the thought arrives 'I've got to do something about this' an important pretreatment change has occurred. Looking back to this time and other similar events can be highly constructive. Talmon (1990) was the first to devise a pretreatment home assignment between the first phone call and the first visit. He found that this increased the number of his clients who felt satisfied they could handle their problems on their own after a single session.

Berg and Reuss (1998) suggest using clinical intuition and judgement to include the following questions (Table 10.1) and adapt them to the client's situation when there is a request for services.

Between sessions is another useful time to glean information. The Substance User's Recovery Checklist and Worksheet (see Appendix 17) is a helpful tool for collecting information on presession change. This can be used to discuss initiatives taken towards recovery before getting into the *problem talk* which enhances the client's self-esteem and motivation to become a cooperative partner for therapy (Berg & Reuss, 1998).

Exceptions

There are exceptions to all substance use problems. If anger is a problem, there are times when temper could have been lost but was not. Inquiring about and exploring the circumstances of exceptions helps unearth otherwise hidden strengths and hidden solutions to problems. For each person, the things that help will differ. Everyone has his or her unique solutions to problems, if they can be found. If

Table 10.1   Elucidating client views on initial attendance

When the client is sent to you for help by someone else	When the client requests treatment for self
(1) Whose idea was it for you to see me today?	(1) What needs to happen today so that you can say it was a good idea to come here?
(2) What makes _____ think that you need to come here?	(2) What would be different in your life then?
(3) Do you agree with _____'s idea that coming to see me is a good idea?	(3) Who will notice most that you have made changes?
(4) What would have to happen for _____ to say this has been helpful for you?	(4) What will he or she do differently? What difference will that make in your relationship?
(5) What will _____ do differently when he or she believes you are making these changes?	(5) What else will be different that will let you know you did the right thing by coming to see me today?
(6) How will that be helpful to you?	(6) What can I do to help you get your life in order?
(7) Are there times now when you are making even small changes?	(7) What is the first small step you must take to head in the right direction?
(8) Tell me, how do you do that?	(8) What would it take to keep you going in that direction?
(9) What would it take for you to keep making these small changes?	(9) What will you notice is different in 3/6/9 months?
(10) Suppose you kept it going for 3/6/9 months, what would be different in your life then?	(10) How will these changes today help you then?
(11) What would your _____ say about how your life would be different then?	
(12) What would _____ do differently to let you know that he or she notices these changes?	

arriving late to work is a problem, exploring the circumstances of those times when he or she arrived on time can throw up as much, if not more, help than exploring the factors that led to late arrivals. Looking in detail at exceptions provides a valuable and constructive way of exploring the problems associated with alcohol and drugs.

Special SFT techniques

SFT has developed some special ways, including the following three methods, of unearthing hidden strengths and understanding the degree of their importance.

The miracle question. 'Suppose when you go to sleep tonight (pause), a miracle happens and the problems that brought you here today are solved (pause). But since you are asleep you cannot know this miracle has happened until you wake up tomorrow. What will be different tomorrow that will let you know this miracle has happened and the problem is solved?'

(From Berg, I. K. & Reuss, N. H. (1998) *Solutions Step by Step.* New York: W. W. Norton & Co, Inc. With permission from W. W. Norton & Co, Inc.)

Berg and Reuss recommend that you draw attention to the word 'suppose' through facial expression, modulation and tone of voice. They also recommend using appropriate pauses as indicated in the text. The purpose of this is for the client to 'suspend the daytime reality of the problem for just long enough to believe in a reality where the problem does not exist'.

They consider it important to note that the problem is defined as 'the problem which brought you here today'. It is not confined to one specific problem (such as drinking or drug use). This allows the client to create solutions that are free of restrictions so that the problem-free life that is created does not suffer from unnecessary limitations.

After the question is asked, the questioner should pause for a very long time. This allows time for a lot of thought. If the client says 'I don't know', the therapist should wait a little longer in silence. This encourages the client to think a little harder. If he or she is still unable to answer, the therapist should say 'Guess!' At the Brief Therapy Center at Milwaukee, Wisconsin, they have never had a client who has been unable to guess.

Clients often answer with some unlikely event such as *winning the lottery, finding eternal youth* and so on. Berg and Reuss suggest that the questioner should think of these answers as a way of giving time to imagine truly creative solutions. After a few good laughs, clients usually settle down to describe changes in everyday life, starting with statements that indicate there would be an absence of the problem. To aid this process the questioner can ask 'What will you be doing instead when you are not . . . ?', 'How will you be feeling?' or 'What else?' (Berg & Reuss, 1998).

The miracle question is a highly useful tool to help unearth the hidden strengths of substance users. It can also be used to aid husband and wife, or parent and child, relationship problems where it often helps find new solutions to problems.

The scaling question. 'On a scale of 1 to 10, where 1 represents the problem as bad as it's been for you and 10 represents the time when you are no longer concerned about this problem, where are you today?'

The scale of 1 to 10 is a very flexible and adaptable technique that helps people state clearly their own assessment of their degree of motivation, hopefulness, progress, confidence and a host of other factors relating to drinking or drug-taking. It is more explicit than adjectives like *very* or *extremely* and shows clearly what margin of uncertainty is left. Scaling questions can also be extremely useful when there is a disagreement between people. Berg and Reuss suggest additional questions like 'When you are one point higher on the scale, what will the two of you be doing that you are unable to do now?'

The nightmare question. 'Suppose when you go to bed tonight (pause), sometime in the middle of the night a nightmare occurs. In this nightmare all the problems that brought you here suddenly get as bad as they can possibly get. This would be a nightmare. But this nightmare comes true. What would you notice tomorrow morning that would let you know you were living a nightmare life?'

(From Berg, I. K. & Reuss, N. H. (1998) *Solutions Step by Step.* New York: W. W. Norton & Co, Inc. With permission from W. W. Norton & Co, Inc.)

The nightmare question is saved as a final phase technique to build a solution to a problem, if all other methods have been exhausted and the solution not found. It should only be used in this situation. It was created by Reuss as a response to some clients who were not motivated by seeing possibilities of life improving. Visualising the reality of the worst possible scenario is better than waiting for it to happen, and for some people can be a motivating force which moves people to action.

If the nightmare question is used, its follow-up is similar to that of the miracle question, only in reverse. Whereas most clients end up responding to the miracle question with a positive and hopeful feeling, most respond to the nightmare question with a behaviour (usually drinking or drug use). Follow-up questions should generally concentrate on feelings:

- When your wife sees you drinking in the morning, what will she notice is different about how you feel?
- When she sees you feeling this way, what will you notice is different about the way she feels?
- What else?
- What would it take to prevent this nightmare from happening?

Bridging questions can sometimes help establish a link to possible solutions. 'Are there times now when small pieces of this nightmare are happening?' and 'What is the nightmare like during those times?'

In SFT the only solution that is believed to work is the solution that the client creates. They are not told the solution by professionals: the only person who can really help is the individual drinker or drug user. The professional's role is to help the substance user discover hidden strengths and appropriate solutions to the problem through presession change, by examining exceptions and by using the special techniques of SFT, and to help apply these in practice.

Conclusion

The main purpose of utilising both Opportunistic Brief Interventions and Brief Treatments is to enhance the prevention and treatment of alcohol- and drug-related problems and dependence. In spite of a sound evidence base as to their cost-effectiveness and the relative ease of their administration, there has been little movement towards instigating these interventions widely. Those in a position to effect change should do all they can to promote these interventions, as the savings are potentially vast. Opportunistic Brief Interventions have not been demonstrated as useful when it comes to preventing drug problems and dependence. This may be because abstinence is generally required as the main goal in research settings. Their application to other goals such as BBV risk reduction is worthy of consideration. Brief therapy for both alcohol and drug problems and dependence may be aided by the use of Solution-Focused Therapy and/or Motivational Enhancement Therapy. The results of the UKATT trial on Social Behaviour and Network Therapy are awaited.

Although the most cost-effective interventions should always be chosen for problem alcohol use and dependence, Opportunistic Brief Interventions and Brief Treatments are not always the answer. All those who are assessed as needing more intensive therapy and those who fail to respond to Brief Treatments should be offered a broad range of interventions according to their assessed need. If successful, more intensive treatment will still incur considerable human and financial cost savings. In addition to the recognition of the costs of leaving those who are chemically dependent to continue without treatment, there is now a greater awareness of the high cost of failing to intervene in order to prevent people progressing towards serious dependence when they are drinking excessively or starting to develop problems associated with substance use.

Chapter 11
Prescribing Interventions

Introduction

Prescribing interventions should usually be within a therapeutic framework of other interventions. Medication alone without psychological and other treatments is less likely to be beneficial. Without proper support and monitoring, medication may even exacerbate the risks and severity of problems or, at best, lead to only limited progress compared to a more holistic approach. In the opiate field there is often such an emphasis on the potential benefits of substitute prescribing that the need for other interventions is overlooked and doctors are seen as prescribers rather than therapists. This is potentially compounded by the service user seeking medication as the central initial goal. A careful assessment and plan including a range of appropriate therapy is generally needed.

Engaging service users and their partners or families in keeping a diary of progress can be useful, and families may also help by supportive supervision of medication. Ongoing contact with a worker using Motivational Interviewing (MI) and/or behavioural interventions also enhances the benefit of prescribing interventions.

Interventions for drinkers

Detoxification

For most people with mild or moderate alcohol dependence, detoxification is not required. However, severe alcohol dependence leading to marked alcohol withdrawals may require detoxification and those with a history of withdrawal convulsions or delirium tremens should always be offered a benzo-diazepine withdrawal programme. Anyone exhibiting signs of delirium tremens should be admitted and treated as an acute medical inpatient as this condition is potentially life-threatening. For those without such complications, if prescribing is required and there is adequate social support at home, alcohol home detoxification with the help of a specialist nurse is appropriate. In circumstances where social support is poor or the patient is homeless or has multiple needs, inpatient detoxification followed by residential rehabilitation may be required. Except in an emergency, a thorough holistic assessment is therefore essential before embarking on a detoxification programme.

Although it may have a role in the specialist treatment of inpatients, chlormethiazole should never be used on an outpatient basis because the combination of this drug with alcohol or opiates is potentially life-threatening due to its ability to cause respiratory depression. The two commonest drugs used to help alleviate alcohol withdrawals in the community are the relatively long-acting benzodiazepines, chlordiazepoxide and diazepam. If chlordiazepoxide is used, in most cases, the following regime is appropriate:

> 15 mg chlordiazepoxide four times a day on days 1 and 2
> 15 mg chlordiazepoxide three times a day on days 3 and 4
> 15 mg chlordiazepoxide twice a day on day 5
> 15 mg chlordiazepoxide once a day on day 6

A maximal dose should be

> 60 mg chlordiazepoxide four times a day on days 1 and 2
> 45 mg chlordiazepoxide four times a day on day 3

30 mg chlordiazepoxide four times a day on
    day 4

15 mg chlordiazepoxide four times a day on
    day 5

15 mg chlordiazepoxide twice a day on day 6

15 mg chlordiazepoxide once a day on day 7

If diazepam is used, the maximum recommended
dose is 20 mg four times a day reducing daily and
ending after seven days. In most cases 5 mg diazepam four times a day should be the starting dose.

Oral vitamin B complex should also be prescribed,
or vitamin B_1 (thiamine) 50 mg twice daily. Those
with significant dependence or malnutrition, Wernicke's encephalopathy or Korsakoff's psychosis
should be given high potency thiamine intravenously
or intramuscularly for at least three days as gastrointestinal absorption is impaired in chronic drinkers
and oral treatment is unlikely to be beneficial.

Acamprosate

Once detoxification is complete acamprosate can
help maintain abstinence. It does so by helping
reduce craving. Its use is recommended in conjunction with counselling and it should be initiated as
soon as possible after the alcohol withdrawal period
is complete. The normal dose is 2 tablets × 333 mg
acamprosate three times a day, but for patients who
weigh less than 60 kg the dose should be reduced to
2 tablets at breakfast, 1 at midday and 1 at night.
The recommended treatment period is one year and
the drug should be maintained throughout any brief
relapses. Research indicates that the improved abstinence rates and an improvement of life expectancy from the prolonged use of acamprosate lead to
reduced total lifetime costs that outweigh the costs
of this treatment even under conservative assumptions (Palmer *et al.*, 2000).

Disulfiram

Disulfiram also has a role in helping maintain
abstinence. It inhibits aldehyde dehydrogenase
(ALDH), the enzyme that catalyses the oxidation
of acetaldehyde to acetic acid causing blood acetaldehyde levels to rise. The resultant aversive reaction

(vomiting and severe headache) varies in intensity
according to the dose of disulfiram and the volume
of alcohol consumed. The idea is that when disulfiram has been taken the consequences of alcohol
consumption are so unpleasant that the individual
knows that he or she will not drink on that day.

Disulfiram on its own without any additional
interventions only has a modestly beneficial effect
(see Appendix 15). There does, however, appear to
be a clear placebo effect, which is more pronounced
in those patients who take this drug exactly as it is
prescribed (Fuller *et al.*, 1986). It is said that when
additional methods are used to ensure that it is
taken regularly, this helps stop drinking more reliably, but the evidence to support this is scanty.
Long-term evidence suggests that the benefit is
time limited (Vaillant, 1996).

Chick and colleagues (1992) have shown that
disulfiram 200 mg daily for six months under
the supervision of an individual nominated by
the patient increased abstinent days, decreased
total drinks consumed and lowered gamma-
glutamyltransferase (GGT) levels (a marker of
liver inflammation associated with excessive alcohol
consumption) compared to a placebo. Again, the
use of the drug should be backed up by non-
pharmacological therapies. Azrin and colleagues
(1982) showed that a trial programme of stimulus
control training, role-playing, communication skills
training and recreational and vocational counselling
improved outcomes in disulfiram-treated patients
compared to those receiving placebo.

Disulfiram must never be used without a person's full knowledge of the consequences. It is recommended that treatment should be initiated only
in a hospital or specialised clinic and by physicians
experienced in its use. Its use is contraindicated in
the presence of pregnancy, cardiac failure, coronary
artery disease, previous history of stroke, hypertension, severe personality disorder, suicidal risk, dementia or psychosis. Extreme caution should be
exercised in the presence of renal failure, hepatic
or respiratory disease, diabetes mellitus and epilepsy. It should be avoided in substance users with
indications of progressive liver disease from chronic
hepatitis C. Patients should not have taken alcohol
for at least 24 hours prior to initiation of therapy,
during treatment or one week after cessation of

treatment. In rare cases deaths have been reported following the drinking of alcohol in those taking disulfiram, but this is almost always at levels greater than 1×200 mg tablet per day. The normal maintenance dose is either one or half 200 mg tablet daily.

Naltrexone for alcohol treatment

Naltrexone was first shown clinically to reduce alcohol consumption and relapse to heavy drinking by a double-blind placebo-controlled study by Volpicelli and colleagues (1990; 1992). Following this there have been a number of clinical trials with positive results, including studies from the UK (Litten *et al.*, 1996), the USA (Anton *et al.*, 1999) and Australia (Morris, 1999). Its main value appears to be enhancing coping skills, rather than helping maintain abstinence. A meta-analysis has shown that naltrexone plus coping skills training to be better at reducing drinking than all other treatments (Agosti, 1995).

Animal studies of operant conditioning with alcohol as the reward show that the blocking of opiate receptors by naltrexone progressively decreases drinking and lever pressing for alcohol. Furthermore these benefits persist after the medicine is stopped. In contrast, giving naloxone and naltrexone during abstinence from alcohol has not been found to be useful, tending to increase alcohol consumption by animals (Sinclair, 1990). Earlier research indicated that alcohol causes the release of endogenous opioids and the binding of these opioids to receptors in the brain may be responsible for the positive reinforcing effects of alcohol (Sinclair *et al.*, 1973). As a result of these animal studies it has been hypothesised that blocking the reinforcement from repeated drinking should extinguish craving and reduce consumption of alcohol to normal levels (Sinclair, 1990).

This has been backed up by clinical studies. In human studies no significant benefit from naltrexone was found when the patients remained abstinent from alcohol and it was no better than placebo in delaying the first sampling of alcohol again. However, there was one important beneficial effect, which was to enable controlled drinking by helping

reduce the frequency of relapse to heavy drinking (Volpicelli *et al.*, 1990; 1992). This finding, which is highly suggestive of conditioned cue extinction, has been replicated by several other studies (Litten *et al.*, 1996; Anton *et al.*, 1999). Follow-up studies, e.g. from the Yale trial (O'Malley *et al.*, 1996), have shown that the benefit of aiding controlled drinking is continued after treatment, but there was no benefit, even in the longer term, in the groups where the aim was to support abstinence.

Thus, for drinkers, naltrexone should be used when abstinence is not required, and when the aim of therapy is to control drinking. It is considerably more cost-effective if it is only taken when drinking is expected and it can be taken indefinitely if necessary (Sinclair *et al.*, 1992). (Although it is quite safe to give naltrexone to someone who is alcohol dependent while he or she still drinks, it is not safe to give it to an opiate-dependent person who still takes opiates. This is of relevance to alcohol users who are opiate dependent or who use opiates for pain relief.) Naltrexone has opened the door for more people to be encouraged to attempt to control their drinking, where previously the only solution for them may have been total abstinence.

In a review of the efficacy of medications for the treatment of alcohol dependence based on comparisons of the research carried out, the WHO's Agency for Health Care Policy and Research (AHCPR) supports the use of naltrexone and acamprosate, but states that of the two, the evidence for naltrexone is somewhat better. Disulfiram was given a moderate rating. It concludes that, apart from these three, the scientific evidence did not justify the use of any other medicines in the treatment of alcohol dependence (Garbutt *et al.*, 1999).

Prescribing treatments for opiate dependence

Substitute prescribing

To some people it is an anathema to encourage the prescribing of substitute drugs for those with problem/dependent opiate use, when this approach would be abhorred for drinkers. However, prescribing methadone to heroin users is very different from giving a bottle of whiskey to a dependent drinker and the benefits of methadone maintenance are now well established.

Although any prescribed opiate could act as a substitute, very few are actually used. Long-acting drugs, such as methadone and high-dose buprenorphine, are the most commonly used. These lead to steady blood levels of the drug and can be given once a day. Buprenorphine in fact has a half-life of about 4 hours when circulating in the blood stream, but it becomes so firmly bound to opiate receptors that it need only be given once every 24, or even 48 hours. Drugs that are given infrequently like this help break the psychological associations and cues to regular drug use. Dihydrocodeine is sometimes prescribed by doctors as a substitute opiate drug. The disadvantage is that it is relatively short-acting and has to be taken several times a day, and that the tablets are sometimes ground up and injected. It does not have a research base of efficacy and is not licensed in the UK for treatment of opiate dependency. L-alpha-acetylmethadol (LAAM) is a very long-acting opiate substitute drug, which can be given every two or three days. Unfortunately, it has been linked with a number of serious adverse events and its use can no longer be advocated in the UK.

Methadone is usually given orally in the form of methadone mixture 1 mg/ml. Higher strength preparations are available but are inadvisable as they may lead to overdose deaths if such preparations find their way to the street. Methadone tablets are commonly ground up and injected and so are not now recommended in the UK for normal clinical practice, although there are circumstances when it may be very useful to prescribe methadone in tablet form. This should only be done in a specialist setting after careful consideration.

The UK differs from most other countries in allowing injectable methadone and heroin in its range of opiate substitution therapies. There is a small place for prescribing injectables as some people are clearly addicted to the process of injecting (needle fixation) and will avoid contact with services unless injectables are given. The UK national guidelines on clinical management of drug users (DH, 1999) recommend that injectable opiates should only be prescribed to patients with long, complicated and intractable histories of opioid dependence, and/or who have failed other forms of treatment including oral methadone maintenance therapy (i.e. it should be a treatment of last resort and only prescribed in a specialist setting). The National Treatment Agency (NTA) issued further advice in 2003, emphasising the same points but endorsing the potential benefit of injectable methadone or heroin if provided within an integrated care package. Sometimes it is helpful for suitably experienced practitioners to prescribe injectable methadone as long as the individual concerned converts, using supportive interventions, to an oral preparation after an agreed period of engagement, e.g. 2–3 months. But there will always be a few people who need injectables on a long-term basis.

High-dose buprenorphine comes in the form of sublingual tablets (0.4 mg, 2 mg and 8 mg) which are absorbed by dissolving under the tongue. If swallowed, the drug is not absorbed from the gut. A disadvantage of buprenorphine's high solubility is that it is readily injected and large-scale studies of buprenorphine maintenance treatment in France have shown that 'injection misuse of buprenorphine is . . . inescapable' (Obadia *et al.*, 2001). However, it is generally considered to be a useful drug for people with medium levels of opiate dependence. It is a partial agonist, which means that it has both a direct opiate effect and an inherent opiate blocking antagonist effect in respect of other opiates. Because it has antagonist as well as agonist properties, buprenorphine has fewer sedative effects and is much safer in overdose as there is significantly less likelihood of respiratory depression, although other drugs such as alcohol and benzodiazepines, if taken as well, may lower the threshold at which this occurs. Also because the opiate receptors are blocked at moderate to high buprenorphine doses (16–32 mg) there is no pharmacological high in the short term if the user lapses to heroin or other opiate use. Some clients find this helps extinguish illicit drug use.

Many users report a greater ease of reduction and withdrawal from buprenorphine compared to methadone. Some may seek it for a new episode of treatment for these reasons or because they wish to try a new approach to stabilisation with less sedation. Transfer to buprenorphine for a planned withdrawal of 2–5 weeks is attractive and cost-effective as it can be readily undertaken in the community.

With regard to heroin, doctors are not allowed to prescribe this drug in the USA, and need a special licence to prescribe heroin in the UK for the purposes of treating addiction, although it may be prescribed by any doctor for analgesic or other purposes. Pharmaceutical heroin has to be taken several times a day for the treatment of addiction and is normally given by injection. Several treatment trials have been undertaken and there clearly are some benefits of heroin therapy, particularly a reduction in criminal activity, stabilisation and retention in treatment (Uchtenhagen *et al.*, 1999). These trials were conducted in a highly supported and supervised setting which may not be generally applicable to normal clinical settings. The fact that it is an injectable drug and is relatively short-acting suggests that it should not be given as a first choice for substitute prescribing. As noted above, the NTA (2003) has issued new advice acknowledging a role for heroin prescribing in highly selected cases as part of a new care pathway.

Titration of methadone

Achieving initial stabilisation when someone first applies for help can be difficult and in some cases where high doses of opiates are used there is a risk of overdose death if precautions are not taken to prevent this happening. Unfortunately the fatal dose of methadone for someone who has little or no tolerance overlaps with the therapeutic dose of those who are tolerant. The dose at which this occurs will depend on the sex, body mass of the individual and whether or not he or she is tolerant, but it is well within the normal therapeutic range of someone who has become tolerant. While fatal methadone overdoses commonly involve several drugs, it is potentially lethal to naive adult users at doses over 20 mg (Humenuik *et al.*, 2000; Milroy & Forrest, 2000). Assessments have to rely broadly on the accuracy of a person's statement as to how much drug he or she has been taking. Urine and other drug tests give a qualitative result as to which drug is being used, but the quantity of the drug used is

more difficult to ascertain, and many drug users overestimate the amount of drug that they take.

The safest way of ascertaining the correct starting dose is by titrating the drug against physical withdrawal symptoms. Titration is applicable to most new assessments but a modified approach with less emphasis on withdrawal symptoms should be used in pregnant women. Heroin users and users of other relatively short-acting opiates, who are not pregnant, are asked to have no drugs since midday on the previous day so that they are in a state of withdrawal and the severity of their physical withdrawals are measured. (Because of the longevity of action of methadone, users of illicit methadone are asked to go for 36 hours without the drug.) An objective method of assessing opiate withdrawals can be obtained by using the Objective Opiate Withdrawal Scale (OOWS) (Handelsman *et al.*, 1987) (Appendix 18).

If patients say that they are withdrawing badly, but there are little or no objective physical signs of withdrawal (a score of 0–1 on the OOWS), this implies that they are mainly craving, i.e. experiencing the early, subjective phase of withdrawal, but not in need of substitute prescribing.

- Mild withdrawals relate to an OOWS score of 2–5.
- Moderate withdrawals relate to an OOWS score of 6–10.
- Severe withdrawals relate to an OOWS score of 11–14.

The UK national guidelines (DH, 1999) recommend that for heavily dependent users, i.e. those who are neuroadapted or tolerant, a first dose can be up to 40 mg but it is unwise to exceed this dose. A second dose may follow after at least 4 hours and may be up to 30 mg depending on the persisting severity of withdrawal. It is important that consideration is given to the cumulative effects of administering a long-acting drug such as methadone.

Utilising the OOWS as an assessment tool to determine the severity of the physical abstinence syndrome, an initial starting point of 0–40 mg methadone, usually as methadone mixture (1 mg/ml), may be given, depending on the severity of withdrawals:

- Patients with no physical signs of withdrawal (OOWS score 0–1) should not be allocated any methadone.
- Those with mild withdrawals (OOWS score 2–5) may be prescribed 5–10 mg.
- Those with moderate withdrawals (OOWS score 6–10) may be given 15–25 mg.
- Patients with severe withdrawals (OOWS score 11–14) may be initially prescribed 30–40 mg.

The patient is then asked to return 4 hours after the time when the methadone was consumed. The consumption of methadone must be observed by those supervising and overseeing the titration regime and observations continued for about 1 hour after each consumed dose in case of toxicity or induced vomiting. Patients must not be asked to have these initial doses supervised at the local pharmacist as they will not continue to be observed there and could overdose on the street without medical help being available. After 4 hours the OOWS score is obtained again:

- People who have a score of 0–1 are given no further methadone;
- Those with a score of 2–5 may be prescribed a further 5–10 mg;
- Those with an OOWS score of 6–10 may be given another 15–20 mg; and
- Those with a score of 11–14 may be given a further 25–30 mg.

Again consumption of the drug should be witnessed and the individual concerned should be asked to remain and be observed for an hour. Thus the maximum given on the first day should not be more than 70 mg methadone. Progress should be monitored daily for three days to assess for accumulating methadone levels.

The week following the first day's substitution therapy
Guidelines from the UK Departments of Health (DH, 1999) recommend that patients are reassessed on a daily basis for the first few days. Where doses need to be increased after the first day, the increment should not be more than 5–10 mg on any one day, and the total week's increase should not usually exceed 30 mg above the starting day's dose.

Subsequent increases
Subsequent increases should not exceed 10 mg per week, and the final total should normally be between 60 and 120 mg methadone daily. Underdosing may encourage illicit drug use in addition to the prescribed substitute drug. Although some people do manage well on lower doses, in general better results are achieved when the daily dose is in excess of 60 mg methadone (Hargreaves, 1983). For a few people, doses above 120 mg may be necessary. Saturation of opiate receptors by high doses will help prevent illicit drug use and so enable stabilisation to occur, but care needs to be taken. This may more easily provoke death by overdose due to combined toxicity with other respiratory depressants or following eventual detoxification when tolerance is lost. For most people a ceiling dose of 120 mg methadone daily is adequate.

A decision should then be made as to whether the individual is to be maintained on a steady dose of methadone or whether they are ready to undergo a reduction or detoxification procedure.

In case of opiate overdose
Naloxone 400 µg ampoules should always be readily available in case of serious life-threatening opiate overdose. Equipment for maintaining the airway and giving resuscitation should also be on hand. Initial intravenous (IV) administration of naloxone is the ideal, followed by an intramuscular dose. Alternatively repeated intramuscular doses can be given. If someone has slipped into unconsciousness, professionals should not wait to see if they deteriorate further. If there is any doubt as to whether to give naloxone or not, it should be given. It will usually cause the patient to go into immediate severe withdrawals and should only be used as a life-saving measure in extreme circumstances. Naloxone's duration of action is short, lasting approximately 10 minutes, and the dose may need repeating especially if the overdose is large or the patient is in circulatory collapse. However, this should give enough time for an ambulance to arrive. Preparations should be made to protect the airway from vomiting and to begin cardiopulmonary resuscitation.

Naloxone may be given intramuscularly, intravenously or subcutaneously. All family doctors, doctors involved in treating drug users, and drug clinics should have in-date naloxone ampoules readily accessible as this can be life-saving in cases of opiate overdose. Winstock and colleagues (2000) found that although 80% of the UK drug agencies surveyed had trained staff in resuscitation, less than 25% had access to oxygen or naloxone.

Dose induction for buprenorphine

The antagonist properties of buprenorphine displace other opiates from receptors as treatment commences. For relatively low doses of short-acting opiates such as heroin, this is not such a problem. For higher levels and for long-acting opiates such as methadone, the transition is more problematic. People wishing to transfer from more than 30 mg methadone, or its equivalent if another opiate drug is being taken, are likely to need considerable support but can achieve transition. This may be preferable to attempting reduction to very low doses of methadone with the risk of relapse to illicit use. Opiates with short pharmacological action but long receptor binding such as codeine may also be difficult.

The key to successful induction is to start only when there are marked withdrawal symptoms. For heroin this is 12–24 hours and for methadone 36–72 hours after last use. Induction is staged over three days, commencing with a low dose of 2–4 mg to gauge reaction regardless of former habit and increasing over three days to achieve symptom relief. Because of the mode of action, dose equivalents are not apparent. Doses of 16–32 mg daily are appropriate for heavy users and those wishing to achieve good receptor blockade against other opiates. A lower dose range is appropriate for others, especially if wishing to move quickly to reduction or abstinence. Patients prescribed high-dose buprenorphine should be warned of the blockade effect in respect of analgesia and should carry a card detailing their medication.

Daily dispensing

Giving someone large doses of take-home medication may destabilise them and leave them at risk of life-threatening overdose. In the early phases of treatment daily dispensing helps counter these problems. In the UK special prescription forms enable the prescribing doctor to write a prescription for daily dispensing for up to 14 days at a time. As the individual becomes stabilised a reduction in dispensing becomes appropriate, with patients picking up for two or three days, or a week's supply. Dispensing for longer periods than two weeks is not recommended.

Supervised consumption

Supervised consumption as a means of promoting individual and public safety is used in the USA and now officially advocated in the UK for at least the first three months of treatment (DH, 1999). There are major ethical problems relating to supervised consumption and official recommendations may be counterproductive in many cases, discouraging, for example, employed drug users from seeking treatment. However, the guidance is clear that clinical assessment should be the basis of all decisions concerning initiation and duration of supervised consumption, taking individual health and personal and environmental circumstances into account.

Supervised consumption can help stabilise patients, but it is not always appropriate. For instance, there may be a loss of confidentiality if someone has to drink methadone mixture at a community pharmacy without privacy. It may not be compatible with individual daily needs such as difficult family commitments or working away from home. Blanket recommendations for supervised consumption are never appropriate and it should be undertaken only at the doctor's discretion, taking account of all aspects of clinical need and with the full cooperation of the patient. For a few it is a real benefit, protecting them from harassment and allowing access to daily support and may be continued long term.

Maintenance prescribing

Methadone maintenance has the following advantages (Farrell *et al.*, 1994):

- It helps stabilise the individual. Opiate maintenance does not cause cognitive impairment and an adequate dose of a long-acting substitute drug such as methadone will keep someone stable, holding off withdrawals for over 24 hours.
- A legal prescription allows the individual to stay away from street drugs.
- Money does not have to be found to purchase street drugs and acquisitive crime diminishes.
- A prescription for oral methadone reduces injecting and its associated problems, particularly the transmission of blood-borne viruses (BBVs).
- Those on a legal substitute prescription are less likely to die of a drug overdose.
- Regular professional contact enables the use of other interventions to enhance the recovery process.

Methadone maintenance as opposed to detoxification is usually the best solution for those who are severely dependent on opiates. If such people are detoxified, the common result is relapse and serious problems resulting from drug use including the transmission of BBVs, criminal behaviour and overdose.

The UK National Treatment Outcome Research Study (NTORS) subdivided opiate treatments into abstinence-oriented services and drug maintenance services, and Gossop and colleagues (2001a) showed that

(1) greater severity of dependence is a strong indication for offering maintenance rather than a reduction programme; and
(2) in the UK, dose levels are often below the level needed to control street heroin use.

The 240 patients whose initial treatment plan was maintenance were compared with 111 where the plan was reduction. From six months onwards, retention in treatment was higher in the planned maintenance group, and those retained were half as likely to be using street heroin. Over the first year, only 36% of those in the reduction group actually received reducing prescriptions whereas 70% of the maintenance group were maintained as planned. Results showed that in many cases the doses were

too low, leading to street drug use. For every milligramme increase in dose there was a 2% reduction in the risk of regular heroin use. The more severely dependent the patient, the less well they did if methadone reduction was the planned treatment (Gossop *et al.*, 2001).

Thus those who are severely opiate dependent do far better on the whole if they are maintained on a steady dose of methadone. Nevertheless, it should always be the user who makes the final decision about the timing and reduction or withdrawal. A few are so desperate to stop using drugs that they will not contemplate long-term methadone prescribing and if they wish to be detoxified, this should be respected and acted upon.

All too often, when there is use of illicit drugs on top of a prescription, punitive measures are implemented and harm is thereby increased. Dose reduction is a common punitive response, and repeated use on top is sometimes punished by cessation of substitute prescribing. This research shows that in many such cases the dose is too low and the right response to illicit drug use on top of a prescription should be dose elevation, not dose reduction or cessation of a prescription. A full assessment of interventions required to achieve stability, the adequacy of the dose and whether harm reduction can be achieved by continued treatment should be undertaken before discontinuation on the grounds of ongoing illicit use.

Opiate withdrawal using methadone

Previous and current national guidelines have recommended reduction of the daily dose in the community over the medium- or long-term and slow reduction regimes. For example, a 4–6-month detoxification regime by reducing 5–10 mg every fortnight is recommended in the current version of the national guidelines (DH, 1999). However, current thinking as a result of the NTORS (Gossop *et al.*, 2003) is that slow reduction regimes should be abandoned and the care plan should specify either maintenance or detoxification – not a slow reduction of dose. Before commencing detoxification, it is important that the client understands the greatly increased risk of overdose which will follow loss of tolerance. Methadone is the most commonly used substitute medication, although buprenorphine is being increasingly used for detoxification, usually from lower opiate doses.

Short detoxification programmes in the community using methadone or buprenorphine are usually completed over two or three weeks, but similar detoxification programmes may also be conducted on an inpatient basis. In preparation for short methadone withdrawal programmes, it may be appropriate to reduce the dose in stepped phases analogous to the final detoxification procedure, or to reduce the dose gradually, but this should only be done with detoxification in view and not as a goal in itself.

Detoxification is best done in the community when someone is using only relatively small quantities of opiates (e.g. an eighth to a quarter of a gramme of street heroin or 50 mg or less of methadone). Decisions as to the most appropriate treatment setting should also be based on the severity of dependence and should be informed by the client's readiness to cope with symptoms and the availability of supportive care, e.g. by a caring friend, professional staff or a home detoxification service.

Opiate withdrawal using buprenorphine

As with other opiates, withdrawal using buprenorphine may be via stepped reductions or directly to abstinence with the aid of a detoxification programme. Again, in view of the NTORS findings, prolonged reductions are best avoided. Usually there has been a stabilisation phase of buprenorphine treatment preceding withdrawal, but buprenorphine can be used just for withdrawal following transfer from another opiate.

Detoxification from buprenorphine is usually undertaken over a period of two or five weeks as an outpatient. Inpatient detoxification from buprenorphine is not normally needed unless there are compelling physical or psychological needs. More gradual reductions according to progress are needed for some individuals. As the dose of buprenorphine declines, receptor sites become vacant and the antagonist properties of buprenorphine which block the effects of street heroin and other opiates

disappear. Most opiate users will be aware of this. The problem of relapse to illicit drug use, together with the risks of overdose from reduced opiate tolerance, should always be discussed.

There is now evidence pending publication that transfer to buprenorphine from a wide range of methadone doses is quite feasible with symptomatic treatments such as lofexidine in an inpatient setting and enables a more acceptable final withdrawal phase which may be completed in the community.

Opiate withdrawal using lofexidine

Lofexidine 0.2 mg tablets may be a useful aid in short-term opiate withdrawal and stepped reductions. It is not an opiate, but it does help significantly with opiate withdrawals, although it is unlikely to completely eliminate opiate withdrawal symptoms. Bearn and colleagues (1996) found that at a maximum daily dose of 2.4 mg lofexidine was approximately equivalent to methadone in relieving opiate withdrawals, although the self-rated symptoms were slightly more severe.

Lofexidine is licensed for the treatment of opiate withdrawals and has taken the place of its analogue, clonidine, as it has fewer hypotensive and sedative side-effects. Both lofexidine and clonidine are alpha-adrenergic agonists and act centrally on alpha-2 autoreceptors in the brain and spinal cord, inhibiting the release of the chemical transmitter, noradrenaline. They both suppress the activity of the locus caeruleus, which is hyperactive during opiate withdrawal.

Clinical experience of *short-term withdrawal* suggests benefit in commencing lofexidine before cessation of the opiate and building up the dose every two days (e.g. 2 tablets twice daily for two days, then 2 tablets three times daily for two days, then 2 tablets four times daily) before reducing. The final level may then be maintained for 7–10 days to cover the withdrawal period after stopping methadone. A shorter post-detoxification period of 5–7 days is required for shorter acting drugs such as heroin and dihydrocodeine.

Although it is helpful in reducing opiate withdrawal effects, lofexidine is no panacea. At higher doses than 20–30 mg methadone, clinical experience suggests that the opiate physical abstinence syndrome will start to dominate in spite of its use. Other medication to cope with symptoms such as vomiting, diarrhoea and insomnia may be required for the detoxification period.

Rapid reduction of opiate use without the need for inpatient treatment

The authors have found lofexidine to be very useful in stepped reduction programmes, particularly for people who wish to reduce from high doses of methadone, but who do not wish to be treated as an inpatient. For instance, if someone is prescribed 150 mg methadone daily, the dose of lofexidine could be built up over six or eight days to 12 tablets (200 μg per tablet) per day. After two more days at 12 tablets per day the methadone dose is dropped by one-third to 100 mg methadone per day for three days, then after another three days the dose is dropped by another third to 65 mg methadone per day. In this way the dose of methadone has been rapidly reduced by just over a half of the original dose without the need for inpatient treatment. Many opiate users are greatly encouraged by this and ask if they can continue immediately with further reductions. However, we find that this is clinically not helpful. It is usually better to maintain a steady dose of methadone and after a gap (e.g. of three months) to repeat the procedure, reducing again by one-third at each reduction. Thus, in the example given below, at three months, after the second rapid community reduction, the daily dose will be down to 30 mg methadone and the patient may be thinking seriously of complete detoxification with few if any self-efficacy concerns.

Lofexidine two-week stepped reduction schedule appropriate for application in a community setting:

(1) Build up dose of lofexidine (200 μg/tablet) to 3 tablets four times per day and maintain at this level.
(2) After three days reduce dose of methadone by one-third (e.g. 150 mg down to 100 mg).
(3) After a further three days reduce dose of methadone by another third (e.g. 100 mg down to 65 mg).

(4) After three days reduce dose of lofexidine slowly over six days monitoring BP and pulse rate.

Maintain methadone at this level (e.g. 65 mg). Clinical experience suggests that many opiate users are ready for a further rapid reduction after three months.

The above regime is not just useful when the individual wishes to reduce quickly from high doses of methadone. It is also helpful when someone has relapsed onto illicit drug use in addition to a previously adequate prescription. Rather than increase the dose of methadone, the above regime offers an alternative whereby the illicit use can be discontinued. A number of other clinicians have tried this approach and some have said that it has revolutionised their practice.

- The action of lofexidine is reduced by tricyclic antidepressants and they should not, therefore, be prescribed concurrently.
- Patients may determine their own dose of lofexidine, titrated against withdrawal symptoms, up to the maximum doses shown.
- Blood pressure and pulse should be monitored regularly. When the dose of lofexidine is increasing the blood pressure may be reduced causing faintness. A compensatory tachycardia is sometimes, but not always, apparent when this occurs. Rebound hypertension (raised blood pressure) on cessation of short courses is said to be rare, and is less of a problem than that produced by clonidine. Nevertheless, when it does occur it is potentially more dangerous than hypotension and observations are particularly important during the phase when the dose of lofexidine is declining and stops.

The patient should be advised

- to omit or take less than the maximum dose if giddiness is a problem;
- that once the maximum dose is reached taking more tablets will only increase the side-effects and will not further diminish the withdrawal symptoms;
- that the worst withdrawal symptoms will be experienced on days 1–5 of being opiate-free; and

- that there may be an immediate drop in tolerance to opiates – so if they relapse, the risk of overdose will be high.

Accelerated detoxification programmes using naltrexone

It is important not to confuse accelerated detoxification using naltrexone with similar methods incorporating extreme sedation or anaesthesia. It is also important to consider the effects of patient selection on the safety and viability of accelerated detoxification (Rumball & Williams, 1997). The prospect of going to sleep and waking cured of heroin dependence is extremely appealing but despite extravagant claims by enthusiasts it continues to be a highly controversial treatment. However, UK research indicates that accelerated detoxification using naltrexone and lofexidine without additional measures can reduce the overall severity and duration of symptoms of opiate withdrawal compared to standard lofexidine treatment (Buntwal *et al.*, 2000) and compared to methadone reduction (Bearn *et al.*, 1998). The method confers advantages for patients who have difficulty with prolonged withdrawal or who have limited time to allow for detoxification, e.g. if working. The disadvantages include the expense of inpatient care, and there is a disappointing rate of continuation on naltrexone despite the high rate of completion of detoxification. The place of this form of withdrawal is probably being superseded by the availability of methods using buprenorphine.

Opiate receptor blockade with naltrexone

Unlike disulfiram, naltrexone is not an aversive drug and its use does not lead to tolerance or dependence. It is a very helpful drug for those opiate users who manage to successfully detoxify but recurrently relapse, and for those who detoxify from opiates having been dependent for many years. It works by blocking the opiate receptor so that if another opiate is taken it has no effect. Conditioning plays a large role in the initiation and continuance of drug use, with the euphoric effects of opiates acting as a strong positive reinforcement for further use. Prolonged use of naltrexone enables the extinction of this conditioned response and any associated drug-seeking behaviour and craving (O'Brien *et al.*, 1984). Care must be taken to ensure that other opiates are completely out of the system, otherwise it will cause a very unpleasant intense accelerated opiate withdrawal. This means being completely free of short-acting opiates such as heroin or codeine for seven days, and having not consumed any methadone for at least ten days. Transfer from buprenorphine has the advantage of being achievable after three days due to its partial agonist properties. Occasional side-effects occur as a temporary phenomenon in the early phase of treatment. They are generally mild and include gastrointestinal complaints, such as nausea, diarrhoea and vomiting, headaches, skin rashes, decreased mental acuity, dysphoria, depression and loss of energy. For anyone who has chronic hepatitis C with clinical indications of cirrhosis or cirrhosis from any other cause, naltrexone is best avoided as the drug is potentially hepatotoxic. If someone with chronic hepatitis C virus (HCV) has not had a recent liver biopsy, the likelihood of cirrhosis is high when his or her platelet count is less than 120, or he or she has a raised bilirubin, a high international normalised ratio (INR) or a reduced albumin. For other drug users where the use of naltrexone is being considered, an informed assessment of risks and benefits should be undertaken. This assessment should include liver function tests (LFT) and a full blood count (FBC) before starting the drug, and one week and one month afterwards.

Naltrexone treatment may be initiated 6–7 days after withdrawal from methadone and three days after withdrawal from heroin or buprenorphine. Following confirmation of opiate-free status by urine test and careful questioning, an initial test dose of tolerance of opiate blockade is undertaken with the short-acting antagonist naloxone by injection. This 'challenge dose' avoids the potential problem of giving the long-acting oral drug to a person unable to tolerate the antagonist effect. An initial dose of half a 50 mg tablet naltrexone (i.e. 25 mg) should then be given, to exclude hypersensitivity to the drug and continued daily for one week. After this, one 50 mg tablet is normally taken daily. However, it is possible to take a schedule of two tablets every two days. For many drug users it is best to continue prescribing naltrexone for six months, or longer in some cases. The patient should be warned that other opiates will not be effective analgesics while naltrexone is being taken. The problem of poor patient compliance can be aided by ongoing family support to oversee its continued use (Hulse & Basso, 2000). Naltrexone implants are used in the USA and have been in use on an experimental unlicensed basis in the UK. It is not clear whether they provide adequate serum levels of naltrexone but the psychological effect is likely to be significant.

Patients taking naltrexone should carry a warning card. In a medical emergency the treating doctor will be able to prescribe to overcome the blockade but must act with care due to the rapidly changing tolerance.

Prescribing for cocaine users

The US Food and Drug Administration has not approved any pharmacological agent for the treatment of cocaine dependence. A recent review, studying the presence of cocaine metabolites in the urine as the main outcome indicator, showed no evidence to support the clinical use of carbamazepine, antidepressants, dopamine agonists, disulfiram, mazindol, phenytoin, nimodipine, lithium and NeuRecover-SA, a marketed compound vitamin, mineral and amino acid compound, as a treatment of cocaine dependence (de Lima et al., 2002).

Cocaine use increases intercellular dopamine, serotonin and noradrenaline levels acutely by blocking their reuptake within the central nervous system (CNS), and chronic cocaine use leads to their depletion and down-regulation, thereby explaining post-cocaine use depression and cocaine craving. Antidepressant medication can therefore be anticipated to relieve the dysphoria and craving of cocaine withdrawals (Margolin et al., 1995).

Any discussion of pharmacotherapy for cocaine dependence should be contextualised within a framework of broad psychosocial interventions.

The study of outcomes from a range of psychosocial treatments indicates that they can have a substantial positive impact (Simpson et al., 1999).

There has been an unusually high drop-out rate across all studies, and measures aimed to retain people in programmes should be one important aim of therapy. It may be that substitute prescribing with dexamphetamine or other longer-acting pharmacological agent could play a role in this way just as longer-acting methadone prescribing helps retain heroin users in treatment. A clearer understanding of the aims of treatment, with outcome measures for incremental improvement rather than simply the presence of cocaine metabolites in the urine, would go a long way towards better treatments for cocaine dependence.

Prescribing interventions of a general kind are helpful in acute withdrawal. Acute paranoid states may require minor or major tranquillisers in the short term. The immediate post-withdrawal *crash* during the first 24 hours may be supported largely psychologically, but is followed by an agitated, irritable withdrawal syndrome lasting 2–4 days, during which day and night sedation can be beneficial. Thereafter a choice concerning possible use of antidepressants can be made.

Prescribing for amphetamine users

Similar interventions to those used for cocaine withdrawal are appropriate in amphetamine withdrawal, though this is more gradual in onset (1–2 days) and slower to resolve (4–10 days).

Substitute prescribing is not usually necessary but may be part of the harm reduction approach for intractable users. In an overview of services prescribing for amphetamine users, Myles (1997) states:

> The balance of risks associated with prescribing dexamphetamine when compared with the alternatives – irresponsible injecting behaviour, lack of retention of stimulant users in drug services, unplanned sexual activity and recurrent episodes of psychosis – suggests that a well-controlled prescribing intervention could quite reasonably be recommended.

It is not always easy to distinguish between dependent amphetamine users and those who are using the drug recreationally. Some daily amphetamine users are not dependent, just as some people who drink alcohol every day are not dependent. Although some heavily dependent drinkers only drink on a sporadic basis, amphetamine users who just take the drug at weekends are unlikely to be dependent. Difficulties in the diagnosis of amphetamine dependence are compounded by the fact that dependent amphetamine use is not always associated with a physical withdrawal syndrome. Examination of the seven criteria of dependence from DSM-IV (Appendix 1) backed up by urine testing is generally required to diagnose dependency.

Dexamphetamine 5 mg tablets as substitute medication for people dependent on amphetamines are being prescribed by a number of UK drug services. The total daily dose given by those drug services which do prescribe this drug rarely exceeds 60 mg, and commonly is less than 50 mg. These levels of daily dose are not high enough to cause an amphetamine psychosis. The tablets should be given in divided doses (e.g. 3 tablets three times daily) and the last dose should not be taken after 4 PM or the patient will lose sleep. It is best to take them at set times and not vary the dose unless this is part of an agreed prescribing programme. Dexamphetamine has been prescribed both on a long-term basis and as an aid to withdrawal, enabling a move away from IV use into abstinence. A withdrawal programme might be to reduce the daily dose by 1×5 mg tablet every two weeks. Care must be taken to assess for serious withdrawal depression, monitor the blood pressure and watch for cardiac rhythm disorders. A history of high blood pressure strokes, heart rhythm disorder, heart disease or any other cardiovascular disorder are contraindications for prescribing. It is best to avoid prescribing dexamphetamine to anyone over the age of 50.

Some people taking street amphetamine develop a very high tolerance to the drug. The purity of amphetamine powder is usually much lower than that of heroin or cocaine (street amphetamine is often only around 5% pure with 95% as *filler*). In recent years a stronger form of amphetamine, known as amphetamine base, has been sold as a street drug. This is commonly 60% pure and

generally comes in the form of a paste. Street amphetamine contains two mirror image isomers: dextro-amphetamine (dexamphetamine) and laevo-amphetamine. Laevo-amphetamine is inactive. If someone says they are taking 2 g of illicitly manufactured amphetamine powder per day, only 5% (100 mg) will contain the drug and only half of this will be the active isomer (i.e. 50 mg). Thus a daily dose of 10×5 mg tablets dexamphetamine is an approximate equivalent dose to 2 g of this form of the drug.

Monitoring for illicit amphetamine use may be aided in the UK through regional toxicology services which provide testing facilities for the laevo-isomers, which are more than 95% removed in pharmaceutical dexamphetamine.

There are indications that the recently re-established amphetamine, methylphenidate, which is commonly prescribed for attention-deficit/hyperactivity disorder (ADHD) and was previously taken off the licit market because it was so sought after by drug users, is being diverted to the black market again. A negative urine test result will not exclude the use of this drug.

Despite the practice of prescribing dexamphetamine being widespread in the UK, research is still at a relatively early stage in assessing the efficacy of this intervention. A large study in Wales by McBride and colleagues (1997) showed amphetamine users were retained in treatment and reduced their injecting behaviour when prescribed dexamphetamine. A retrospective study of 220 amphetamine users in Cornwall has shown dexamphetamine prescribing to be reasonably safe and to be associated with improvements in drug use for both oral and IV amphetamine users (White, 2000).

Prescribing for benzodiazepine users

Most illicit benzodiazepine users are polydrug users who take benzodiazepines sporadically and are not dependent upon them. However, some do take high doses of benzodiazepines on a daily basis and are highly dependent on them. Such people would require detoxification, to reduce the dose at least down to 30 mg diazepam daily. Diazepam is the drug of choice for substitute prescribing because of its long-acting nature and anticonvulsant properties and because it is rarely injected. It has an active metabolite, desmethyldiazepam, which has a half-life of 100 hours.

Substitute benzodiazepine prescribing should be supported by evidence of dependence from the history and use is confirmed by urine examination. There is increasing evidence that long-term prescribing of more than 30 mg per day may cause harm. This is the upper limit of British prescribing guidance for therapeutic reasons other than drug dependence. There is no place for long-term prescribing of diazepam above this dose and no evidence of benefit for long-term prescribing for benzodiazepine dependence.

When considering whether or not to prescribe to benzodiazepine users and what initial dose should be given, the prescribing doctor must be mindful of the need to prevent harm (e.g. from withdrawal convulsions), but this must be balanced against causing harm by very high-dose prescribing or by inducing dependence. If substitute prescribing is considered necessary, an equivalent dose of diazepam can be calculated from Table 11.1. In many cases the starting dose will need to be substantially less than the stated daily dose of illicit benzodiazepines taken, if harm is to be reduced as far as possible. The initial starting dose should ideally be no more than 10 mg diazepam three times per day, and in most cases this will be adequate to prevent withdrawal fits. However, where very high doses of illicit benzodiazepines have been used this initial dose may be temporarily increased, particularly if there is a history of epileptic fits. Signs of impending fitting include a fine tremor coupled with a resting pulse of 100/minute or more in the absence of fever (38°C or more). Usually a maximum daily dose of 60 mg is adequate.

The rate of withdrawal is often determined by the ability of the individual to tolerate withdrawal symptoms. A specific benzodiazepine withdrawal reaction occurs in about one-third of longer-term users, even when withdrawing from normal therapeutic doses of the drug. Key symptoms of the syndrome result from heightened sensory perception to the degree that it has become painful or extremely unpleasant and include hyperacusis (hearing that is painful), photophobia (light that is painful), parasthesiae (pins and needles), hyperosmia (unpleasant smells) and hypersensitivity to touch and pain, gastrointestinal disturbances, headaches, muscle spasms, vertigo and sleep problems. In addition there may be derealisation and depersonalisation and rapid, extreme mood changes. These symptoms are often very hard to tolerate. It is very different from simple rebound anxiety and rebound insomnia. The specific benzodiazepine withdrawal syndrome does not often occur severely, but when it does detoxification should proceed extremely slowly. Otherwise benzodiazepines can be withdrawn at a rate varying from one-tenth (at high doses) to one quarter (at lower doses) of the daily dose every fortnight.

Monitoring illicit drug use through urine or oral transudate testing

For most drug use, desktop urine testing kits, laboratory testing of urine or oral transudate testing undertaken at random are the usual ways of checking that the drug prescribed is being taken and that other drugs are not being used in addition. With any of these methods it is possible to distinguish between methadone and opiates, but it is not currently possible to distinguish between prescribed dexamphetamine and street amphetamine, or prescribed diazepam and illicit benzodiazepines. As routine laboratory tests are not 100% reliable, this does give someone a let out if he or she is adamant that they have not used any illicit drugs. However, to obtain two false positives or false negatives in a row would be so unlikely as to be

Table 11.1 Doses of common benzodiazepines equivalent to 5 mg diazepam

Drug	Dose
Chlordiazepoxide	15 mg
Diazepam	5 mg
Loprazolam	500 μg
Lorazepam	500 μg
Oxazepam	15 mg
Temazepam	10 mg
Nitrazepam	5 mg

unbelievable. The possibility of prescribed or over-the-counter (OTC) medication or laboratory error causing unexpected results should be checked with the service provider. Several OTC preparations contain codeine or morphine. Illicit drug use on top of a prescription should be confronted jointly with the client (rather than confronting the client with illicit drug use). For most clients the habit of using drugs every day for several years is difficult to break. Occasional lapses usually do occur, particularly in the early stages of treatment. Punitive sanctions for lapses, particularly prescription reductions, are almost invariably unhelpful. It is better to be flexible and try to determine the circumstances of any lapses that have occurred. What were the cues that led to craving and a *slip*? Could there be a better way of tackling that situation? Persistent illicit use may indicate that the prescribing intervention was not correctly targeted or that it has become inappropriate. The reasons and alternatives should then be explored and the care plan altered accordingly.

Licences

In the UK a Home Office licence is required by individual doctors to prescribe diamorphine (heroin), cocaine and dipipanone (marketed in the UK in combination with cyclizine as Diconal) for the treatment of drug dependence, although these drugs may be used for the treatment of physical illness. In the USA the clinic rather than the doctor is given a licence so that not all doctors are able to treat those with drug dependence. The US doctors in licensed clinics are allowed to prescribe methadone in oral form, but they are not able to prescribe injectable drugs to treat drug dependence.

In England and Wales more than one dispensation of a drug can be arranged by using special prescription forms, whereby general practitioners (GPs) and drug clinic doctors can arrange for up to 14 daily dispensations of opiates/opioids and amphetamines. Regrettably if daily dispensing of a benzodiazepine for two weeks is required, until now this has entailed a very time-consuming procedure of writing up to 14 days prescribing on separate prescriptions. Scotland has been an exception where daily dispensing can be written on an ordinary prescription, and there are plans to introduce prescribing by daily dispensing using a single prescription throughout the UK.

Under UK legislation, prescriptions for controlled drugs (with the exception of benzodiazepines and all drugs in Schedule 4 and 5 of the 1971 Misuse of Drugs Act) must stipulate the daily dose, the total amount in words and figures, and must be signed and dated in the doctors' own handwriting, though exemption from handwriting the other details may be granted by the Home Office.

Conclusion

A range of different prescribing options are available for opiate users and have a well-founded place in treatment. These include detoxification regimes, stepped reductions and maintenance prescribing in appropriate settings. Initial dose assessments, supervised consumption, daily dispensing and their indications for opiate users are described. Occasionally substitute prescribing also has a place for some drinkers, benzodiazepine users and amphetamine users. There are also several adjunctive treatments to help drinkers achieve and maintain abstinence.

Prescribing interventions should not be the sole therapeutic intervention. They should comprise part of a broad-based approach to aid the recovery process from problem and dependent substance use. The importance and need for other therapeutic interventions must not be overlooked.

Chapter 12
Everyone Needs Help to Prevent Relapse

Introduction

Relapse prevention initiatives are important for all clients who are maintaining positive change in addictive behaviour and should be included in every care plan. They are particularly useful for those who wish to stop but who are drinking or using drugs periodically, and for people who repeatedly lapse or relapse to other substance use whilst on a substitute prescription. As good coping skills are an essential element in preventing relapse, consideration should be given to including coping skills training as a routine relapse prevention intervention (Gossop *et al.*, 2002).

Very occasionally there is a massive leap forward in our understanding of a subject. When this happens it is usually accompanied by a different way of seeing things – a paradigm shift in our thinking. The work by Alan Marlatt and Judith Gordon in looking at the recovery of substance users by focusing on the prevention of relapse instead of examining ways to successfully detoxify was, at the time, one of those ground-breaking paradigm shifts. Much of this work is still as important today as it was when their book, *Relapse Prevention*, was first published in 1985. An associated feature of their work was that they drew parallels between dependence on all substances including alcohol, heroin and tobacco and compulsive gambling.

Marlatt and Gordon (1985) highlighted the shared commonality in the relapse of addiction to different substances. This was first clearly demonstrated by Hunt and colleagues (1971) who published a paper which showed a striking consistency between the relapse rates for alcohol, heroin and smoking as shown in Figure 12.1.

The relapse curves, which were virtually identical, were based on multiple treatment outcome studies. For example, the curve for smokers was based on averaging data drawn from 84 separate smoking treatment studies. Criticisms that the curves are based on group averages and do not necessarily represent what is happening to any given individual are justifiable. All other criticisms have been discredited by further statistical analysis. The commonalities are quite clear. Other work has confirmed this study and shown it also applies to gambling and eating disorders (Marlatt & Gordon, 1980) lending further support to the hypothesis that there is a common mechanism underlying the relapse process across different addictive behaviours.

Thus relapse prevention is a self-control programme designed for those who are in the maintenance stage of any phase of treatment progression or who are planning a change in which relapse prevention can be a valuable preparation for change, be it towards control or abstinence from alcohol, smoking and drug use or any other life change. It can, for instance, be used to augment the management of some aspects of psychiatric illness or high-risk blood-borne virus (BBV) behaviour. It utilises a cognitive–behavioural approach which can also be applied as a more general programme of lifestyle change. Both lifestyle change and the prevention of relapse are seen to be key factors in the maintenance of behaviour change. Far more variables are now seen to be influential in relapse than even a decade ago, and in most instances of relapse multiple variables are involved. The original work on relapse intervention focused on individuals who had a substance use problem. Now relatives (or *significant others*), professional caregivers and the system of treatment delivery are all seen to be important

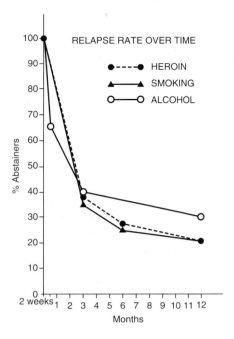

Figure 12.1   Relapse rate over time. (From Hunt, W. A., Barnett, L. W. & Branch, L. G. (1971) Relapse rates in addiction programmes. *Journal of Clinical Psychology*, **27**, 355. Reprinted with permission from John Wiley & Sons, Inc. Do not photocopy.)

extra factors that can influence relapse. It is thus an essential part of treatment programmes.

Assessing high-risk situations

Being able to avoid high-risk situations that may lead to relapse is essential if abstinence is to be maintained, or if someone on a substitute methadone prescription is to avoid relapse to street drug use. As they say in Alcoholics Anonymous (AA), 'If you go to a barber's shop often enough, you are bound to end up with a haircut.' In almost every case, when a relapse has occurred it begins in a high-risk situation. It is therefore important to be able to spot high-risk situations so they can be avoided and other appropriate action taken. The effectiveness of other substance use treatments can be increased by rehearsing behaviours for high-risk situations (Rohsenow *et al.*, 1995).

Relapse can be viewed not only as an event but also as a process in which there are indicators that appear before the relapse takes place (Daley, 1987). To do this, it is not only important to be able to see

and avoid immediate relapse precipitants but also any earlier warning signs. Sometimes warning signs appear some days or even weeks before a lapse occurs. For example, if negative emotional states are an important cue which trigger relapse for a particular individual, these can sometimes be picked up at a very early stage and resolved. Interactions between the individual and certain environments can also sometimes be high-risk situations. The cues will differ for each individual as each person has his or her own unique profile of cues which provoke craving. Marlatt (1985) suggests two techniques for helping identify them:

(1) Ask the client to write a short autobiography describing the history and development of their drinking or drug use with special emphasis on the client's subjective image of himself or herself.
(2) Ask for descriptions of past relapses (if any) and relapse fantasies. These will very often highlight high-risk situations that the client had not previously been aware of. Situations which trigger feelings of loneliness and isolation, self-pity

or powerlessness may be high risk for one person, whereas group activities, social encounters, parties and the need to be seen as attractive by peers may be high risk for another.

As can be seen from Table 12.1, immediate precipitants show similarities between the various addictions, and in almost three quarters of cases there are three main causes: negative emotional states, interpersonal conflict and social pressure.

These findings have been replicated, but one well-designed study of opiate users differed on the importance ascribed to social pressure (Bradley, 1989), leading to considerable debate. However, that study had a much narrower definition for social pressure than given by Marlatt in his work. It is important to note that these studies are based mainly on cues which are consciously recognised, but that there are often cues which lead onto relapse that are not consciously recognised (Ludwig & Wikler, 1974).

The immediate precipitants, which Marlatt subdivided into interpersonal (social/environmental) and intrapersonal (psychological) groups, are conditioned stimuli or cues that provoke craving to drink or take drugs as a simple conditioned response. He found that negative emotional states were the most frequent precipitants for both drinkers and drug takers (see Table 12.1).

Preventing craving and urges to drink or take drugs

Intrapersonal cues

Once there is a good understanding of the various cues which induce thoughts, cravings and urges to drink or take drugs, steps can be taken to prevent this happening by finding other ways of dealing with those cues apart from drinking or drug use.

Often intrapersonal cues, such as difficulties in coping, or anxiety states and depression, are brought on by unresolved problems. Sometimes it is possible to find ways to resolve these difficulties. Some people are better at solving problems than others. For those who are not good at solving run-of-the-mill problems, or for those who have what appear to be huge and unresolvable problems, there are specific approaches that are often effective. *Problem-solving training* programmes (see Chapter 14) have been used successfully for many years in the treatment of addiction problems (Spivack *et al.*, 1976). They should be flexible rather than tied to

Table 12.1   Analysis of relapse situations with alcoholics, smokers, heroin addicts, compulsive gamblers and overeaters

Relapse situation	Alcoholics (n=70) %	Smokers (n=64) %	Heroin addicts (n=129) %	Gamblers (n=19) %	Overeaters (n=29) %	Total (n=311) %
Intrapersonal determinants						
Negative emotional states	38	37	19	47	33	35
Negative physical states	3	2	9	—	—	3
Positive emotional states	—	6	10	—	34	—
Testing personal control	9	—	2	16	—	5
Urges and temptations	11	5	5	16	10	9
TOTAL	61	50	45	79	46	56
Interpersonal determinants						
Interpersonal conflict	18	15	14	16	14	16
Social pressure	18	32	36	5	10	20
Positive emotional states	3	3	5	—	28	8
TOTAL	39	50	55	21	52	44

(From Marlatt, G. A. & Gordon, J. R. (1985) *Relapse Prevention*. New York: Guilford Press. With permission from Guilford Publications, Inc.)

particular situations. However, overt practice is necessary for new learning to occur (Chaney *et al.*, 1978a), both for increased problem-solving ability and for the development of new coping skills. Role-play sometimes helps address the practical application of these programmes.

Often conditionally learned intrapersonal cues for drinking or drug-taking seem to appear without warning, resulting in an emotionally stressful response. In such situations there is no time to develop ways to avert the problem. The problem has already arrived and is leading to the development of stressful negative emotions. The practical acquisition of coping skills to deal with these emotional responses will again be greatly helped by rehearsal. *Coping skills training* such as anger and anxiety management is one of the cornerstones of relapse prevention work. There is a well-grounded research base demonstrating its effectiveness. For example, Chaney, who used an eight-session group programme of skills training lasting 90 minutes per session for 'chronic alcoholics', demonstrated a significant improvement in the number of drinks consumed, days of continuous drinking before regaining abstinence and the number of 'drunk' days (Chaney *et al.*, 1978a).

The use of alcohol or drugs as a method of coping with stressful situations will depend upon the innate coping skills of the individual and the severity of the environmental demands. Stress occurs when there is an imbalance between environmental demands and an individual's resources (Wills & Shiffman, 1985). Some life events, such as sexual abuse in childhood, rape, bereavement and the breakup of a close relationship, are so stressful that anyone would find them difficult to cope with. Yet there are some people who seem to take the most appallingly stressful situations in their stride and seem relatively unruffled by them, while others have difficulty coping with ordinary day-to-day situations which could only be described as mildly stressful by an impartial onlooker. Sometimes these are the proverbial straws which break the camel's back in someone who is shouldering intense psychological stress. Other people appear to be naturally anxious without any obvious deep underlying psychological cause. These people have poor coping skills, and fear that they will be unable to cope. They worry about their anxiety, or panic that they are going to panic.

For some the maladaptive use of alcohol or drugs is for a short time only, but for others such use continues and is reinforced. Many psychologically resilient people use drink or drugs to help them temporarily cope with severe stressful situations such as bereavement. Others may feel the need to take substances to cope with what would appear to be only mildly stressful situations, and have naturally poor coping skills. Some people are not old enough to have developed good coping skills before serious emotional problems occur, and the dysfunctional use of drugs or alcohol to aid coping prevents them from developing mature coping responses. Others never learn to deal with small problems well because they have not had the emotional support of their parents during childhood. It is worrying that many young people are turning to drug use as they find it more difficult to cope with life without drugs, having never fully developed their own coping abilities.

Learning to cope unaided for the first time in your late twenties or thirties is much more difficult than relearning a coping process which you had managed well in the past. Those who find it easiest to break away from intrapersonal cues for drinking or drug use are often those who normally coped well with stressful situations in the past, but who began substance use after a difficult major life event, such as separation or divorce, and continued to reinforce it.

Expectancies are imagined outcomes as advertisers are only too well aware. Expectancies that alcohol will help deal with stressful situations can lead to the use of alcohol as a method of coping. Thus many people expect to relax and unwind when they come home from work by drinking alcohol. The cognitive pairing of alcohol consumption with an imagined reward encourages repeated use, which in turn will positively reinforce the conditioning process making it more likely that drinking will occur again. Those who drink or take drugs expecting them to stop withdrawal effects or dissipate unpleasant emotions will negatively reinforce a similar conditioning process. Such habits easily become entrenched. Thus expectancies are intimately tied to the operant conditioning process, leading on to the establishment of increasingly severe chemical dependency.

Cue specific craving has been highly significantly correlated with positive outcome expectancies in drug users (Powell *et al.*, 1992). The sight and smell of drink has been shown to substantially enhance outcome expectancies of both social and dependent drinkers (Kaplan *et al.*, 1985), and both relapse and the amount of drinking by detoxified 'alcoholics' has been shown to significantly correlate with positive outcome expectancies assessed during detoxification (Cooney *et al.*, 1989). Positive outcome expectancies are therefore of considerable importance in substance use.

Interpersonal cues

Just as avoidance is a common effective way of dealing with environmental cues, so too is it helpful when past substance-using friends are encountered. The thoughts and conversations of such meetings may well lead to cravings which are difficult to control. It is good advice that people should minimise unstructured contact with past acquaintances who are drinkers or drug users and develop and promote friendships with those who do not have a drink or drug problem, or who have overcome such a problem, preferably a long time ago.

Twelve-step groups recommend to members that they find a sponsor with several years of sobriety behind them. The involvement of families and significant others as an official positive support network will reduce the risk of relapse. It produces positive benefits both to the substance user and to themselves (Daley, 1988; Gorski & Miller, 1988). Marc Galanter (1993), an eminent US psychiatrist who works in the addiction field, has devised a method of working which he terms *network therapy* where family members are intimately involved in the treatment process. However, they should be included only with the full consent and cooperation of the drinker or drug user. Family members and significant others who are drug users or have drink problems themselves should be excluded from this method of working.

Unfortunately contact with past friends and acquaintances who use substances cannot always be avoided. Even with the best of intentions chance encounters do occur, and when they do many drug users are not very good at either asserting themselves or using other social skills to extricate themselves from a difficult situation. Social skills training can enable substance users to avoid relapses due to interpersonal cues.

Overcoming and coping with cravings and urges to drink or take drugs

Historical issues

In 1955 the World Health Organization tried to exclude the term *craving* from scientific literature (WHO, 1955). In spite of this, the term is now well established. Craving was originally viewed purely in terms of classical conditioning theory but was later expanded to include cognitive and behavioural elements.

There is evidence that classical conditioned responses both push drug users towards relapse to seek relief from antagonistic reactions (Teasdale, 1973) and pull them towards relapse when the conditioned response is agonistic (Stewart *et al.*, 1984). Research into both opiate drug takers (Childress *et al.*, 1986) and drinkers (Ludwig & Wikler, 1974) has shown that subjective craving is as equally reliably correlated to cue exposure as objective changes in physical state.

Ludwig and Stark (1974) asked 60 alcoholics to define craving in their own terms and classified their responses as either

(1) craving in terms of achieving desired effects of drinking or
(2) craving in terms of a need or desire for alcohol (with no specification or mention of desired effects)

The outcome showed that craving should be regarded as the conscious recognition of subconscious conditioned responses and an expression of the desire to obtain relief from them. This paved the way for the use of Cognitive–Behavioural Therapy (CBT) as a method of countering craving and preventing relapse and extended the range of interventions available to overcome craving.

Beck (1993) has identified four major types of craving:

- response to withdrawal symptoms
- response to lack of pleasure
- *conditioned* response to drug cues
- response to hedonistic desires

All of these have cognitive and behavioural aspects and are open to therapeutic change by the use of behaviour therapy and CBT.

Unfortunately, although a wide set of craving measures have been developed encompassing self-report and non-verbal approaches, none of the measures are appropriate across all settings. Agreement on a unified approach that will cover craving for any substance is needed. This should take account of time, self-reporting bias and whether craving occurs at a subconscious level.

Methods of preventing craving from substance-related cues

Cue reactivity can be reduced by two methods: counterconditioning and cue exposure treatment (CET).

Counterconditioning. This is an early form of behaviour therapy which was originally used in the 1950s. It is sometimes called aversion therapy. One method is for doctors to prescribe the drug disulfiram to make a client vomit on drinking and so associate drinking with punishment instead of rewards. It was modestly successful (Cannon & Baker, 1981) but most clinicians are relieved that we use the drug in a different way today.

The early punitive methods of counterconditioning were highly unpleasant, seriously undermined the relationship between the client and therapeutic staff, and discouraged many from seeking inpatient treatment when they needed it. Thankfully the review of the literature by Miller and colleagues (1995) concluded that two other forms of counterconditioning were not helpful. These were *electrical aversion therapy* where a painful electric shock was given every time the client drank alcohol, and *apnoeic aversion therapy* where a drug was given which caused temporary paralysis and a frightening inability to breathe. These very unpleasant treatments have been long since abandoned. The form of aversion therapy known as *covert sensitisation* which is the induction of conditioned aversion solely by imagined processes is, however, modestly successful, although it is rarely used. A 1998 review of this method by Miller and colleagues gave it a cumulative evidence score (CES) of + 18.

Cue Exposure Treatment. CET can be used with either abstinence or moderation as the treatment goal. Repeated exposure to small amounts of alcohol without drinking reduces craving for a drink, aiding a controlled drinking treatment goal for some dependent drinkers (Laberg, 1990). In allied fields such as agoraphobia, specific phobias and post-traumatic stress disorder (PTSD), passive CET has proved to be a very useful therapeutic tool in reducing unwanted behaviours, and there are many similarities between these behaviours and chemical addictions (Marks, 1990). Typically those using CET to aid moderate drinking are asked to sniff, taste, then drink one to four 30 ml drinks and then try not to drink any more. They are told they could drink more if they could not resist. Most of the research studies reported good outcomes including no alcohol-related absences from work (Pickens et al., 1973) and significantly reduced number of heavy drinking days (Rankin, 1982).

For those aiming for complete abstinence, Blakey and Baker (1980) were able to demonstrate CET also aided this drinking goal during the nine-month follow-up period. Overall CET has not been as successful as had been originally hoped for. In one of the few randomised controlled trials of cue exposure with opiate addicts, cue exposure did not confer any additional benefit over standard inpatient treatment (Dawe et al., 1993). One factor may be that in some circumstances strong conditioned responses can be reactivated several months after becoming drug-free (Wikler, 1948). However, the cognitive aspects of cue reactivity, such as craving, mood and withdrawal symptoms, are all perceived on a conscious level, whereas behavioural extinguishing of the conditioned response by cue exposure only occurs on a subconscious plane. From this point of view CBT should enhance the therapeutic effect of cue exposure as has been demonstrated. Cue exposure has been usefully combined with relapse prevention techniques (Cooney et al.,

1987) and skills training (Monti *et al.*, 1987) in the treatment of people with drink problems. Such combination therapy is an important way forward for both drinkers and drug users.

Later research has shown CET to be more effective than communication skills training and sobriety education (Rohsenow *et al.*, 2001). However, if coping skills such as urge reduction imagery and self-mastery statements are compared with CET, after three months those who had coping skills training show greater improvement (Marlatt & Gordon, 1985). They have a higher incidence of continuous abstinence, a higher number of abstinent days, and tend to have fewer drinks per day than the comparison group. Measures show that from the comparison group there is a decreased urge to drink during treatment. The coping strategies of thinking about the positive and negative consequences of use, in particular, appear to be successfully utilised during the follow-up period. More frequent use of coping skills strategies has been correlated with less drinking during the follow-up period.

Although it shows more reductions in cue reactivity in an assessment of high-risk situations, CET does not seem to work by reducing reactions to substance-using triggers. Its beneficial effects appear to be primarily by allowing clients to practise urge-specific coping skills (Monti *et al.*, 2002).

Self-managed exposure treatment leading to cue extinction is as effective as using therapist-accompanied exposure in anxiety disorders (Marks, 1991), and to some extent a similar process may occur with substance users when they stop drinking or become drug-free in their own environment. However, Powell (1990) has argued that laboratory-based CET will preferentially extinguish conditioned withdrawal responses. He has suggested that extinction of craving through cue exposure is enhanced if this is done under laboratory conditions using simulated heroin, the subject being aware that the substance is inert, as this signals drug non-availability.

It is clear that there are several ways in which CET can be conducted, and discovering the optimum way is crucial if the intervention is to be successful. Some failures of CET are probably attributable to poor treatment design rather than a failure of cue exposure itself as a method of treatment. CET should last for about 1 hour (Childress *et al.*, 1986a; Dawe & Powell, 1995), producing a significant decrease in craving and withdrawal symptoms over 18 sessions (Childress *et al.*, 1986). However, it is probably more important that trial designs are adapted to include treatment for the cognitive aspects of cue reactivity (Rohsenow *et al.*, 1995). Anxiety management skills are particularly helpful because anxiety impairs concentration and interferes with the deconditioning process. Other CBT interventions appropriate to the individual's need can also be used. In addition, cognitive interventions can also be undertaken to empathetically challenge the individual's expectations when exposed to drinking cues and strengthen self-efficacy expectations about ability to resist craving.

Methods of coping with cravings and urges

The most important thing to enable a person to deal with their cravings is to recognise that they are occurring. Although this sounds rather basic, cravings are not always easy to spot. Some people are more aware of their moods and feelings than others. Wanigaratne and colleagues (1990) recommend setting a watch with a bleeper to go off several times a day at which time the wearer has to examine his or her thoughts and feelings thereby increasing awareness of them. Once people can recognise craving and acknowledge the problem, they are in a position to do something about it.

People often talk about not having the will-power to deal effectively with cravings. This may be because they are not approaching this problem in an effective way. There are a number of techniques which can help.

Urge-surfing. When fighting craving it helps to know that the craving will be time-limited. It is most unusual for craving, once it has been initiated by an appropriate cue, to last for more than 1 hour, and during that time it should gradually decline in intensity. The Americans have suggested the term *urge-surfing* to suggest that if you stick it out for 1 hour, the craving should gradually subside and disappear. A number of different strategies can be utilised to urge-surf successfully. These include the use of cognitive coping strategies or avoidance and distraction. The *avoidance* of high-risk situations where triggers and cues precipitate craving has already been discussed. Avoidance of thinking about substance use by purposely thinking of other things can also be helpful. This may be augmented through distraction and cognitive techniques. *Distraction responses* include the use of elastic bands, aversive thoughts, flashcards and visual imagery. *Cognitive responses* where thoughts are consciously managed are also described below. These different types of strategy form the basis of coping skills needed to deal with cravings.

Avoidance and distraction coping strategies. Many simple distraction techniques help clients change their focus of attention away from craving. They include:

(1) Moving away from a cue-laden environment.
(2) Elastic bands. The sub-vocal command STOP and the snap of an elastic band worn round the wrist is a simple and effective way to interrupt craving.
(3) Instructing people to concentrate on describing their surroundings.
(4) Using talking as a distraction. This can include talking to oneself inaudibly using positive self-statements, which may be particularly helpful for those with low self-esteem. It has been shown that in opiate addicts verbal distractions (e.g. oral repetition of a nursery rhyme) during cue exposure will result in a rapid reduction in self-reported craving, but unfortunately this benefit is not sustained. Research has shown that in subsequent sessions craving was reinstated at the original level (Bradley & Moorey, 1988).
(5) Telephoning a friend.
(6) Performing household chores.
(7) Spending time playing games of cards, video games, board games and so on or engaging in other enjoyable activity.

Cognitive coping strategies. These are equally effective in tackling craving and they include:

(1) Aversive thoughts. Most drinkers and drug users rationalise the decision to drink or take drugs by focusing on the positive immediate effects of substance use and ignoring or minimising the longer-term negative and destructive consequences. This is particularly so in high-risk situations. Such thinking can be countered by teaching people to catch themselves thinking about the positive consequences and substitute thoughts of the negative consequences of substance use. Beck and colleagues (1993) recommend rational responses to urge-related automatic thoughts. However, when cravings are strong clients seem to lose their ability to reason.
(2) Flashcards. Cards (e.g. 3″ × 5″ index cards) can be useful to flash through. Suitable coping statements which the individual feels are helpful can be written on each card. A list of advantages of not using that are personally appropriate can also be of great help in getting through the worst of the craving period. In addition some people write down all the reasons that they can think of as to why they should not drink or take drugs. These cards can be carried in a pocket or handbag. When people are troubled by craving they take them out and quickly read them.
(3) Imagery. Some people advise silently saying STOP and then imagining the visual image of a stop sign or a policeman. Others use imagery to help them relax and find this helpful when first experiencing cravings. Imagery techniques include:

• Imagery refocusing. If craving occurs, refocusing to a visual image the worst scenario of what might happen after using is sometimes very helpful.
• Negative image replacement. Clients sometimes report picturing themselves using drugs or drinking, particularly in the first few weeks of abstinence, and seeing these images as a method of coping with their current problems. It is more helpful if they substitute a negative image showing the negative consequences of taking the substance.
• Positive image replacement. Those who use drugs to help them cope with depression are particularly likely to benefit from this. Here a negative image, such as a vision of

the children being taken into care, is consciously replaced by a positive scene.

- Image rehearsal. This is a particularly useful way for clients to prepare themselves when they know they are going to enter a cue-laden environment. Here they imagine and rehearse what they will do to avoid drinking or taking drugs.
- Image mastery. Repeating image rehearsal several times may be necessary before mastery gives a client the confidence to overcome a forthcoming difficult situation.

(4) Managing thoughts about alcohol and drugs by identifying and modifying beliefs that exacerbate cravings. Beck's form of Cognitive Therapy, which focuses on automatic thoughts, underlying beliefs and expectancies associated with substance use, is a particularly helpful way of managing thoughts about alcohol or drugs.

Beck's Cognitive Therapy to aid coping responses to cue-induced cravings

Beck's method of aiding coping responses to prevent relapse involves helping people self-monitor automatic thoughts when they are experiencing unpleasant emotions such as anger, anxiety, sadness or boredom. They are then instructed to undertake homework sessions while experiencing cravings and urges by using the table in Appendix 20 to link their automatic thoughts and feelings, and the questionnaire in Appendix 21 to explore their underlying beliefs. These are discussed later with the therapist.

Thoughts point the way to underlying beliefs and there may be many other beliefs held which differ from those portrayed in Appendix 21. As dependence on alcohol or drugs becomes more entrenched, an increasing number of beliefs are assimilated which will induce craving and they become more irrational and open to challenge. For example, an initial belief 'If I drink I will be like some others in the group and will feel part of it' might progress onto 'I need to drink to be accepted by the group', and later this might become 'I need to drink to relieve my loneliness'. Once the automatic thoughts

that accompany craving are identified, they are open to challenge and modification.

A safe and helpful way to explore the automatic thoughts and beliefs associated with cravings is to ask the individual concerned to imagine various situations (emotional or environmental) that induce craving, e.g. being offered drugs or a drink. The therapist then asks 'How do you feel?' and 'What thoughts are coming into your head?' For example, some persons might state that they feel very tense and they could really do with a drink or really need some drugs, opening the way to work on the belief that drugs override tension and the way this belief infiltrates other areas of their life.

The client is also asked to practise ways of overcoming the craving by urge-surfing, distraction, aversive thoughts and imagery. Beliefs about self-efficacy are important to ascertain and improve as they are essential to the recovery process. Sometimes a poor sense of self-efficacy may be wrongly interpreted as lack of will-power.

Beck and colleagues (1993) were impressed by the commonality of certain beliefs across various types of addiction: from addiction to a wide variety of drugs and alcohol through to the eating disorders. They showed that addictive beliefs could be considered to be a cluster of ideas surrounding pleasure-seeking, problem-solving, relief and escape. Common addictive beliefs are:

- the conviction that a substance is needed to maintain psychological and emotional balance;
- the expectation that the substance will improve social and intellectual functioning;
- the expectation that there will be pleasure and excitement from using;
- the conviction that drugs and alcohol will give energy and increased power;
- the expectation that drugs and alcohol will have a calming effect;
- the assumption that the substance taken will relieve boredom, anxiety, tension and depression;
- the conviction that if nothing is done to satisfy craving, the distress will continue indefinitely and may get worse.

In addition, various permission-giving automatic thoughts are common:

- I've had a difficult time and therefore I'm entitled to use.
- If I have one hit it won't matter.
- I'll give in this time, but next time I'm going to stop completely.

As can be seen beliefs and automatic thoughts are often presented as expectancies. Once the individual is able to identify and modify such automatic thoughts and beliefs with professional help, he or she should be able to continue this process unaided at the time these thoughts occur.

Drink and drug refusal skills

Modelling. Although the process of modelling on the behaviour of another person is clearly instrumental in the development of many socially learned drink problems, it can also be used to reverse the process during treatment. For instance, an alcohol worker can act as a model by demonstrating how to refuse a drink.

Role-play. Individual role-play between substance user and therapist is one of the best ways of enhancing refusal skills. In a group situation individuals can do this in pairs. It is often helpful and enjoyable for drinkers and drug users to practise refusal skills with articles that are not drug related such as a pen or a watch and if possible to video record the role-play. Much can be learnt from the video playback.

Appropriate assertiveness is essential to the process of refusing offers of drinks or drugs. People with addictive behaviours have been shown to be particularly deficient in assertiveness skills (Miller & Eisler, 1977) and some will benefit from formal assertiveness training. Underassertiveness will cause people to be passive and fearful, with the outcome that they will either flee from the situation or more often find it impossible to refuse the offer. Overassertiveness is usually accompanied by aggression, anger and sometimes physical violence. Appropriate assertiveness occurs when the drinker or drug user responds to the offer with self-confidence and confronts the situation directly.

Appropriately assertive behaviour involves appropriate thinking and the correct use of speech and body language. Video-recordings are useful because they enable detailed examination of speech and physical movements. Is the drug user catching the eye of the person making the offer or is he or she looking at the ground? Was the response aggressive? Could the wording be improved? Some people respond by making an excuse for the time being which may encourage more offers in the future. Recordings also enable the therapist to say 'What were you thinking when you said that?'

As people slowly master the process of refusing offers of drink or drugs, their self-confidence and self-efficacy grow. They have learnt to control their lives and the decisions they make are the ones they really want to make. If people fail to be assertive, they come away with negative feelings of anger and frustration, but those who are appropriately assertive and have demonstrated their abilities at drink or drug refusal skills feel good about themselves.

Planning for emergencies and coping with a lapse

Loss of control, lapses and relapses

It is considerably easier to cope with a single lapse than a full-blown relapse, particularly for those with less severe chemical dependence. This factor probably goes some way to explaining why many people with mild to moderate dependence are able to control their drinking (Heather & Robertson, 1981; 1997). There have been a number of rather simplistic attempts to explain why control over a drug or drink problem is easier after a single lapse but after the second and subsequent lapse control rapidly becomes more difficult. Siegel (1983) has suggested that *conditioned tolerance* may have a role in this process. Here the sight, smell and taste of alcohol induces a withdrawal reaction which counteracts the effects of alcohol, reducing the rewards of drinking and increasing craving. He postulated that the craving associated with this withdrawal reaction increases as more is consumed leading to loss of control drinking. The reality is probably far more complex than this for all substance use, and involves not only classical conditioning but, in addition, complex cognitive and biological changes. Expectancy is clearly one of these factors and has been shown to significantly predict the amount of further drinking after the first drink (Rohsenow & Marlatt, 1981).

One of the great controversies in the addiction world centres on the way lapses should be approached. The AA/NA/Minnesota Model maxim that a lapse will inevitably lead to further substance use, if not on that day then later, is one of the foundation stones of twelve-step work. 'One drink – one drunk' is the philosophy, and the only way to control drinking, once you are an *alcoholic*, is to avoid the first drink. Marlatt (1978) suggests that this is true only if you believe it and terms it the Abstinence Violation Effect (AVE). He suggests that those who lapse will tend to carry on drinking partly to help relieve the guilt and inner conflict produced of not sticking to the programme, and partly because the programme has told them that if they slip up once they will continue to drink or take drugs. Their failure is attributed to weakness and there is no expectancy of being able to resist further substance use. It thus becomes a self-fulfilling prophecy.

It is clear that with any form of chemical dependence, if abstinence is the chosen way forward, any lapse is highly dangerous. Nevertheless, if a single lapse has occurred, it is often possible for people to stop themselves going on to develop a much more destructive full-blown relapse. Occasional lapses are so common that some people say they could be considered a normal part of the recovery process. Furthermore, teaching people to practise coping with a single lapse is helpful to the recovery process and is an important part of relapse prevention work. This applies just as much to someone on substitute medication for opiate dependence in preventing lapses into illicit drug use becoming full-blown relapses, as it does to dependent drinkers who have attained sobriety.

The following regime is adapted from the methods for dealing with lapses recommended by Wanigaratne and colleagues (1990) and Marlatt (1985b):

(1) *Stop, look and listen*. When a lapse occurs *stop* what you are doing and think. This is a warning that you are in danger. Think of it as a flat tyre: the driver stops in a safe place to deal with it.

(2) *Keep calm*. Remember, one slip does not make a total relapse. A slip does not mean you are a failure and have no will-power or that you are a hopeless addict. There is no failure, only feedback. It is an opportunity to learn. Let the feeling of 'I have started so I will finish' pass. Avoid the idea 'Well I might as well go for a total bender.'

(3) *Review your commitment*. Recall your decision–balance matrix. Weigh up the short- and long-term benefits of abstinence. Remember how far you have come in the journey of habit change. Do you really believe that a single slip cancels out all the progress you have made to date? Renew your motivation and commitment.

(4) *Review the situation leading up to the lapse.* What events led to the slip? Were there any early warning signals? What was the high-risk situation? You may get new information concerning sources of stress in your life. There may be thoughts and feelings that the effects of the drug taken during the slip are going to overpower you and make it impossible for you to regain control.

(5) *Make an immediate plan of action for recovery*:
- Get rid of all drugs/alcohol.
- Remove yourself from the high-risk situation. Take a walk, leave the scene.
- Plan a substitute activity that will also meet your needs at the moment.

(6) *Ask for help*. Make it easy for yourself. Ask friends, relatives or professionals for help.

It can be seen from Figure 12.1 that, although there are individual exceptions, for most people about two-thirds of all relapses occur within the first 90 days of cessation of use. In practice the reality is that it does appear to be substantially easier for clients to maintain their abstinence after about three months. Indeed there is a danger that some people will drop their guard about this time and relapse as a result!

Seemingly irrelevant decisions

Sometimes the relapse is a last link in the chain of events that happen over a long period of time. Occasionally, choices are made which seem to purposefully lead clients into high-risk situations where a relapse will almost inevitably occur. Sometimes drinkers or drug takers will admit that they purposefully contrived a row with their cohabitee in order to justify taking drugs or drinking. Sometimes a high-risk situation is chosen to see whether they still need to work so hard at abstinence or to test how *normal* they are. Whenever there is a perceived need to justify drinking or drug-taking by someone who is chemically dependent, the justification will almost always contain an element of 'stinking thinking' as AA and NA call it. When therapists hear justifications they should always ask themselves:

- Where is the evidence for that?
- What other explanations are there?
- What would I think if I were him?

Later, people with addiction problems can also learn to automatically ask themselves the first two questions.

A balance of lifestyles

Many workers when they first come into the field see all the problems associated with substance use and overlook the fact that drinking and drug use can be a rewarding experience. But when abstinence has been achieved, the loss of repeated rewards regularly throughout each day can leave a big hole. The same is true for those on long-acting substitute medication. Even the loss of the expectation of rewards makes people feel deprived. Furthermore, the emotional relief that drink and drugs can bring (blotting out problems, relaxation, helping cope with anger, etc.), the pleasure of the *rush*, the relief of withdrawal symptoms and relationships with other substance users form a major part of the lives of many drug users and drinkers. It is often the loss of these, rather than the substance itself, which many drinkers and

drug users find the most difficult, when they first receive treatment and particularly when abstinence is achieved. It helps therapeutically if the balance is redressed by finding other ways of achieving positive outcomes or rewards.

There are other major changes which substance users find difficult when entering treatment and tackling substance use problems. Often at least 90% of the day is spent in activity focused on procuring and using drugs or drink. Again its absence generally leaves a big gap, which if left unaltered can predispose people to relapse. Making the necessary adjustments to achieve a *balance of lifestyle* should be a priority for anyone striving to maintain abstinence.

Marlatt (1985b) has suggested that people should focus on restoring the balance between the demands of life (the *shoulds*) and those activities perceived as pleasures (the *wants*). Paying household bills, performing routine chores and doing menial tasks at work can build up to a lifestyle that is out of balance if no rewards are taken, and in such a case a lapse becomes *justified*. Helping a client find new rewards that are more constructive than drinking or drug-taking should be part of every relapse prevention programme. These might include a fishing trip, lunch with a friend, engaging in some creative task such as painting, seeing a film or a play and so on, or what Marlatt calls 'positive addictions' such as regular exercise or running. It can be helpful to map out forthcoming days in writing to make sure that the shoulds and the wants balance each other. Structuring the day in this way is sometimes known as *activity scheduling* and can help ensure that boredom, depression and other destructive components do not interfere with the maintenance of the recovery process.

Other more extensive changes are needed in the longer term. Some people need to make fundamental positive changes in the way they view themselves, their lives and their future, thus leading to new lifestyles. This should be the ultimate goal of therapy, not just abstinence. Self-identity is highly important, and self re-evaluation is one of the *processes* which helps aid movement through the cycle of change (see Chapter 9). If a person sees himself or herself as a drug user who is not at the moment taking drugs or a drinker who is not drinking, the commitment (and therefore the will-power) to move right away from substance use may be in doubt. This does not mean that those who have become abstinent should be encouraged to forget their past, which could be dangerous. The past cannot be changed and must be accepted. Indeed at AA meetings the first thing the speaker always says is 'I am an alcoholic and my name is . . .' and this is seen as an important and helpful part of twelve-step programmes.

One of the benefits of gaining employment which is often not recognised is that it enables people to change their self-image in a positive way. People are commonly described by their employment. They enter a new phase in their lives by becoming a postman, a secretary or a businessman. Motherhood also enables women to change their self-identity. Becoming a mother rather than a drug user, with all the important responsibilities that go with it, can be a major force for positive change, particularly if enough support is given. A change in self-identity through employment or motherhood also helps improve self-esteem, which is characteristically low in drug users and drinkers.

Although relapse is less likely to happen in those who are well motivated, with a good sense of self-efficacy, and who have good coping skills, it is so common as to be considered a normal part of addictive behaviour. In the words of Prochaska and DiClemente (1984):

> Though individuals experience some of the satisfaction of an addiction-free life for varying amounts of time, most of them cannot exit from the revolving door the first time round. They struggle to maintain their recent success, but they soon find themselves relapsing back into an addictive lifestyle. They want to exit while they are in the realm of non-addicts. Forces unknown to them, however, seem to hold them back, and the momentum of the revolving door seems to shove them back around into an addicted lifestyle again.

Conclusion

With appropriate relapse prevention training at least some of these relapses should be prevented from happening and the chances of successful recovery considerably improved. It may then be possible to refute the old saying that it is easier to come off drink or drugs than to stay off them.

Chapter 13
Reducing Environmental Harm and Increasing Social Strength

Introduction

There is a close relationship between an absence of problems and good functioning of the individual. But, just as good health is more than simply the absence of disease, so good personal functioning is more than just the absence of biological, social or psychological problems. Good personal functioning is a strength which can be utilised in the treatment of substance use problems and dependence. Sometimes further help is needed to enhance personal functioning in order to prevent future substance use problems or to deal with current difficulties like social exclusion which may be holding up the recovery process. In such cases the same interventions to reduce harm will also enhance personal functioning. This chapter deals specifically with those interventions which will both reduce environmental harm and, at the same time, strengthen and improve the social functioning of substance users. Although environmental issues should include working with families, this is of such importance that it is dealt with separately in Chapter 15.

In the substance use field the use of the word *environment* is generally to be preferred over *social*. It is more wide-ranging and has been defined more broadly. In the UK the Advisory Council on the Misuse of Drugs (ACMD, 1998) describes it as

An interactive whole – as the world in all its complexities in which the individual lives, and through which that person moves, not only being influenced by it but also influencing it themselves. Family, school, work, and leisure environments and peer group influences are part of this whole, as is homelessness. Friendship networks, intimacy and social support are

important at all ages. Cultural beliefs and expectations permeate the environment and for many people include spiritual values. Quality of housing and other aspects of the physical environment, and whether the setting is rural or urban can be relevant. The degree of access to education, gainful employment, welfare support, medical care, childcare and justice are further significant aspects. The economic and commercial climate will bear in many ways on the quality of the complex mix of social, cultural, interpersonal and physical factors caught up in this one word.

The study of these complex interrelationships, sometimes termed *social ecology*, has thrown considerable light, not just upon the causation of substance use problems, but also upon their resolution. Some of the most therapeutic interventions for substance users involve the removal of those environmental factors which led to drinking and drug use in the first place, preventing problems from substance use by creating a better environment for those who are perceived to be at high risk.

Distinguishing between race, ethnicity and culture

Despite distinct differences in their meaning, the terms *race*, *ethnicity* and *culture* are frequently used interchangeably. It is important to have a clear understanding of these concepts and the impact they have on those with substance use problems. *Race* refers to the classification of people on the basis of their inherited physical characteristics.

Ethnicity refers to members of a group who share a common identity, including ideals and aspirations. *Culture* is the sum total of life patterns passed on from generation to generation. It also includes values, attitudes, customs and shared beliefs about behaviours shaped by local group attitudes from family, work settings and so on. It influences the way patterns of drinking and drug-taking develop (Straussner, 2001). It plays a major role in determining how substance use behaviour patterns continue in different social settings and in understanding the way such behaviours are viewed. Drinking beer in a Manhattan bar, snorting cocaine in a private house or passing a bottle of wine among a group of unemployed men in a park are all instigated through different cultural mechanisms and all generate different attitudes and reactions according to the culture of the viewer. It is within this environmental context that substance use behaviours are established, and the same context determines the attitudes and reactions of observers to the use of alcohol and drugs.

Local decisions, particularly those concerning police law enforcement in relation to substance use, such as stop-and-search practices, may discriminate against some ethnic groups. The interlinked environmental effects of poverty, unemployment, social exclusion, criminal behaviour and patterns of substance use may negatively influence people's attitudes. Compounding these problems, funding difficulties may prevent specialist drug and alcohol services responding appropriately to their clients' specific ethnocultural needs. If it becomes a policy that the work should be left to *experts*, such as ethnic minority providers, and the service does not have the resources to fund sufficient posts, it may become less accessible to ethnic minority groups (Home Office, 1998).

Informed consent for treatment interventions is more difficult to obtain in certain cultural settings. Interpreters and language barriers may distort the counselling process. All assessments must ensure that clients understand what is being jointly developed and should utilise facilities within existing community networks. Standard good working practices will cover most that is required by racially and culturally diverse groups, although there are many hurdles to address.

Reducing environmental harm

Improving the environment for young people

In Canada some work has been done to reduce social and environmental risk factors in the hope that this will reduce the incidence of a number of emotional and behavioural problems, including problematic substance use. One such programme is the Better Beginnings, Better Futures Project (Peters & Russell, 1996). Here families with young children up to the age of eight, living in 11 socio-economically deprived neighbourhoods in Ontario have been given extra aid in the form of additional pre-school programmes, and enhanced existing aids such as drop-in centres, mother and toddler groups, toy libraries, increased training, other informal supports and improved physical facilities. Longitudinal studies are following the children up until they are in their mid-twenties.

A similar project in the USA, the Comprehensive Child Development Program (CCDP), encompasses 34 separate projects (Pizzolongo, 1996). The CCDP projects concentrate on alleviating the pressing problems faced by low-income families, including inadequate housing, poor health care and nutrition, family breakup, teenage pregnancy, lack of positive role models and growth experiences for children, and poor educational attainment and employment prospects. The focus is more at an individual family rather than local community level. Although the aim of the CCDP is to enhance the assessed strengths of individual low-income families and improve their social conditions, the desired result is the same as projects which enhance community facilities in deprived neighbourhoods. Reduced crime, lower welfare dependency payments, and fewer people with emotional and behavioural problems, including problems relating to substance use are all anticipated outcomes.

Improving the physical environment for adults

Examples such as improved design of pubs, having food with drinks, the training of doormen and bar staff, and the use of shatter-proof glasses are to be found in the alcohol field. In the drugs field better street lighting, CCTV, safer places to use drugs and attention to areas of deprivation will help reduce the prevalence of drug-taking in a particular area.

Overcoming social isolation

Social support by professionals, non-professionals, and family and friends is of great importance if those who have become addicted to alcohol or drugs are to successfully overcome their problem. The benefits of good social support have been outlined by Colletti and Brownell (1982). Good social support helps make someone feel cared for, loved and valued and improves self-esteem. It provides feedback concerning beliefs and values, and if these become distorted, helps rectify them. It also helps provide a sense of belonging, of identity and of being connected to other people.

If present, adequate social support may reduce negative emotional reactions to adverse life events and stresses (e.g. less depression following job loss). Conversely, lack of adequate social support leads to more emotional problems and increased morbidity. Bandura (1977) has pointed out the value of support from others in sustaining goal-directed performance. Social support plays an important role in the maintenance of good mental and emotional functioning and, from this viewpoint alone, can be helpful in the prevention and treatment of drug and alcohol problems. Interestingly it is the perception of a strong support system, rather than the actual existence or availability of support, which is the key to influencing outcome. Whatever the reality, there is a greater likelihood of successful treatment outcome and maintenance of change if a client believes that he or she is well supported (Gordon & Zrull, 1991).

Attention to the ways in which an individual's support system can be strengthened is of prime importance. This may include involving buddies and community support workers, and, where appropriate, working together with partners and concerned others. In some cases couples therapy or family therapy may be necessary. Introducing the person to new social groups by facilitating employment, education and/or sporting activities, and by encouraging the re-establishment of old friendships

with people who are not alcohol or drug users can be an excellent aid to overcoming social isolation.

Some substance users are inhibited from establishing new friendships, or re-establishing old ones, because of poor communication skills. Social skills training helps overcome this problem and should be an integral part of a client's core therapeutic programme where there is perceived to be any difficulty socialising or communicating. Self-help groups such as Alcoholics Anonymous (AA) or Narcotics Anonymous (NA) are also useful sources of social support, and most attenders at the twelve-step meetings freely give their telephone numbers, encouraging others to telephone them at difficult times, e.g. when craving for a drink or for drugs. These meetings always have well-established members who have been off drink or drugs for several years who will act as sponsors for new attenders, accompanying them to further meetings. In some countries, particularly the USA, extra social support is gained through the twelve-step clubs. AA/NA meetings are held in these non-profit-making clubs, which are dedicated to recovery through the twelve-step route. They often have pool tables and other facilities, and members can drop in and socialise in a drink- and drug-free environment. Alcohol-free clubs have been shown to aid the recovery process for drinkers in the UK (Azrin et al., 1982), and are a valuable resource whether or not they are associated with the twelve-step movement.

Although a considerable amount of support may appear to be given, if it is of poor quality, its value may be limited. Personal support may be available but may not be emotionally satisfying. Successes may not be acknowledged. Those in support may not be able to mobilise the drinker or drug user when this is needed, may not be able to empower him or her to call on internal resources and may not be able to provide material resources when this is necessary and appropriate. Thus it is not just the amount of support that is given but the quality of the support which is paramount. Some drinkers and drug users require such intensive social support that a residential therapeutic community rehabilitation programme is their only option.

Billings and Moos (1983) have shown that when clients are maintaining sobriety or have stopped using drugs, social factors (e.g. family stability), exposure to social stressors (e.g. homelessness) and social support are better predictors of recovery than events that occur during the active treatment phase. This suggests that there is a need for increased attention to the environmental and social support systems available in the community when a client is either treated in the community or returns after inpatient detoxification, a prison programme or residential rehabilitation. Families and cohabitees are particularly important sources of social support, but many substance users are separated from their families and are socially isolated. Commonly their only social contacts are other people who drink or take drugs, and often these are acquaintances rather than friends. Volunteer buddies who do not use drugs or drink and community support workers can be invaluable in this situation, at least in the interim before a network of *helpful* friends has been established.

Thus the importance of adequate social support and social care as treatment interventions to help drinkers and drug users overcome their problems should not be underestimated. Some workers in drug and alcohol treatment agencies help clients find a job, sort out their debts, housing problems and so on, and are generally helpful and supportive without understanding that this in itself is an important part of treatment.

Evidence of the importance of social support and the right social environment to aid the resolution of addiction problems can be seen in two astonishing studies by Robins and colleagues on US soldiers who left Vietnam in 1971. In the first study (Robins *et al.*, 1974), 500 men were randomly selected from the 14 000 US army men returning home. Of these 43% had used opiates while in Vietnam, and of these nearly half had taken opiates at least on a weekly basis for six months to one year. One in five reported being addicted to opiates while in Vietnam. Yet 8–10 months after they had returned home, less than 10% reported that they had used opiates, and less than 1% felt they had been addicted since their return.

In the second study Robins and colleagues (1975) selected 500 men from the US army who were known by urine testing to be drug takers. Of these about three quarters were interviewed 8–12 months

after their return. Only 33% had used opiates since Vietnam and only 7% of the sample felt they had been addicted since leaving Vietnam. Social change in these two studies preceded, rather than was the result of, these remarkable changes in drug-taking behaviour – a fact that has been shown to be generally true in drinkers and drug users who successfully sustain change (Wille, 1983).

Buddies

Although it is a potentially useful service development, there is a paucity of research on the use of volunteer or employed buddies to enhance substance use treatment outcome. In their most recent Mesa Grande table of comparative effectiveness of treatments for alcohol disorders, Miller and Wilbourne (2002) identified only one study on the effect of buddies on treatment outcome. They gave it a negative cumulative evidence score (CES) of − 8. However, buddies come in a number of different forms, and some are instrumental in bringing about successful treatment outcomes (Budney *et al.*, 1991).

Where the drinker is in the precontemplation stage, concerned others have been used successfully as a Community Reinforcement Approach (CRA) intervention and here a controlled trial of contingency management as a method of increasing motivation for change and treatment gave 'impressive results' (Sisson & Azrin, 1989). The CRA has also used contingency reinforcement successfully with a spouse, friend or colleague agreeing in advance to engage in some desirable activity, when urinalysis demonstrated abstinence from cocaine (Higgins *et al.*, 1993). An important part of the function of an AA or NA sponsor is to act as a well-informed buddy. Thus there are plenty of examples where buddies can be successfully utilised.

Although AA and NA recommend that sponsors should be of the same sex, there should be no hard and fast rules about the age and sex of buddies. Someone who is in a position to be a mother figure or a father figure can often be very useful as a buddy. However, it may be helpful to ask the drinker or drug user his or her opinion. In the UK it is usually recommended that anyone with a history of problems from substance use should be at least two years drink- or drug-free before contemplating working with others with similar problems.

Like all volunteers, buddies need to be well trained, supervised and well supported in order to work to their greatest effect and prevent burnout. They are not a cost-free option. Some have special reasons why they choose to spend their time working in this area, and may come with a certain amount of emotional need which, if it is neglected or handled badly, has the potential to be quite destructive. Thus it is important that they are well supported by a warm, caring, sensitive and knowledgeable person, who is readily accessible. If such a person is able to give them support, volunteer buddies can be an invaluable aid to the recovery process.

Community support workers

The essential difference between buddies and community support workers is that the latter are paid professionals whose work is specifically to help vulnerable people cope with social and environmental issues. In the UK some housing departments and housing associations employ community support workers to help their tenants with known social problems to stabilise so that they are able to pay their rent. This may include tenants with alcohol and drug problems. Some mental health service or drug and alcohol service managers also employ community support workers to assist community alcohol and drug team workers by dealing with time-consuming and difficult social problems.

Community support workers, often low paid and without formal qualifications, are a very cost-effective option. They generally become very skilled at dealing with difficult social problems, forming close links with community organisations such as housing departments, Citizens Advice Bureau and so on. Community support workers and buddies can sometimes accompany socially isolated substance users for hospital appointments where they are likely to default (e.g. for investigation and follow-up for chronic hepatitis C). Emotional and social support at such times can be invaluable.

Housing and accommodation difficulties

'A "home" implies more than simply a physical structure' and homelessness cannot be equated with rooflessness (Hutson & Liddiard, 1994). The term *homelessness* includes all those people who are sleeping temporarily on the floors of relatives or friends; those sleeping rough; men, women and young people living in hostels and bed-and-breakfast establishments; and those living in squats.

Homelessness and inadequate housing are both recognised to be related to problem drinking and drug use. According to the ACMD (1998) 'poor housing or lack of access to affordable housing is, in many instances, a contributory factor in drugs misuse and, at very least, will hinder drug prevention'. In 1998 Klee and Reid stated:

> The profiles of homeless people today are very different from the traditional stereotype of the aging alcoholic or 'bag lady' [of the 1960s]. Not only are they younger but they are more heterogeneous in the path they have taken into homelessness and the environments they inhabit.

Poverty, unemployment and the breakdown of family relationships are often contributory factors (CHAR, 1994), but a more recent UK Rough Sleepers Unit survey by the National Addiction Centre and Crisis showed that 30–50% of rough sleepers have a mental health problem, half have a serious alcohol problem and 80% have difficulties associated with illicit drug use (Fountain & Howes, 2002). The association between homelessness and mental health and/or substance use problems is well recognised in the UK (Scott, 1993), the USA (Smith *et al.*, 1993) and Australia (Downing-Orr, 1996), but many homeless people do not have professional help for these associated problems.

Substance use can lead to homelessness, which can lead to problem drinking and drug-taking, creating a vicious circle for substance users who become homeless. In a study of 1437 homeless adults in Northern California, the prevalence of problem drinking, illegal drug use and psychiatric hospitalisation when adults first became homeless were 15–33% lower than prevalence studies of these problems after homelessness had become established (Winkleby *et al.*, 1992).

Medical problems have been known for many years to be compounded by homelessness, which also leads to increased risk of illness. In New York the treatment of homeless AIDS patients is more difficult. More have been shown to discharge themselves from hospital. More refused to undergo diagnostic tests and treatment for opportunistic infection. More failed to keep hospital outpatient appointments, had longer hospital stays, lost their prescriptions and became lost to follow-up (Torres *et al.*, 1987). Tuberculosis is higher in those with HIV infection if they are homeless (Stark *et al.*, 1989). In New York blood-borne virus (BBV) high-risk behaviour in drug users has been shown to be 15 times greater among the homeless and those staying transiently in shelters and low-income hostels, than in drug users in more stable accommodation (Joseph & Roman-Nay, 1990). Young homeless people are at particularly high risk of contracting HIV and other sexually transmitted infections, becoming addicted to drugs and being victimised by violence on the street (Kennedy *et al.*, 1990).

The ACMD (1989) made the following comments on the combined problems of homelessness, drug use and HIV disease:

> Adequate secure accommodation is central to the concept of care in the community. It can be difficult or impossible to deliver appropriate care to somebody who is homeless or in poor accommodation. Furthermore, the stress and inconvenience associated with homelessness or poor housing can in itself lead to physical and mental illness. It is therefore important that accommodation requirements are sorted out *before* people with HIV disease become ill.

In the UK housing authorities are not obliged to accommodate those who make themselves intentionally homeless, and it is a common belief that this applies to the majority of homeless young people. In fact most homeless young people have left home against their will. Research on 7500 homeless young people in seven different locations across the UK found that 86% had been forced to leave home rather than choosing to leave (National Report into Youth Homelessness, 1996). Furthermore, a study by CHAR (Housing Campaign for Single People) found that four in ten homeless young women in Britain had suffered sexual abuse prior to becoming homeless (CHAR, 1992).

The provision of stable, satisfactory accommodation is a strongly positive influence in the recovery process for drinkers and drug users, and good, relevant accommodation should be viewed as an important treatment goal in the management of substance use (NIAAA, 1989; Argeriou & McCarty, 1990). Drinkers and drug users have a wide variety of housing needs. These include *wet* and *dry* hostels; accommodation for homeless families and for the single homeless; rehabilitation houses; halfway houses for those who have completed a residential programme but need additional support before transferring completely to the community; supported housing for the mentally ill; and for those with other needs. But a roof on its own, however appropriate, is often not enough. The UK government figures show that about 30% of people who make their way through the hostel system into permanent accommodation end up back on the streets. Many people need additional help to rebuild their lives.

Drug and alcohol rehabilitation houses provide in-depth help for recovering substance users to reintegrate into society. Other ways of helping people rebuild their lives, some while still using substances, may be required. Some housing projects concentrate on improving residents' ability to work or other basic skills. The Foyer system gives 16–25-year-olds affordable accommodation, advice, support and help with budgeting, self-care, further education or job-training under one roof. There are 100 Foyers in the UK offering 5000 homeless young people this sort of help. The Emmaus communities are for previous long-term rough sleepers and insist that residents sign off benefits and work full-time for the community, e.g. in a vegetable garden, coffee shop or furniture-restoring workshop. They give people stability and a sense of belonging. The Cyrenian network is a therapeutic community which teaches homeless people how to manage their lives. St Mungo's concentrates on helping street drinkers and mentally ill and elderly rough-sleepers. Such projects help stop the revolving door of homelessness.

Housing authorities can sometimes be persuaded to consider people with a history of dependent drug use or drinking as being potentially vulnerable, and in priority need of housing. However, some people are clearly more vulnerable than others. Those with mental illness, those with chronic problems relating to their physical health, in addition to a substance use problem, and young people under the age of 25 are particularly vulnerable, the vulnerability increasing as the age is lowered. Those under the age of 18 are probably better housed in supported hostel accommodation, rather than given their own premises, where they may feel unable to resist the demands of drug-using friends.

Appropriate, stable accommodation, particularly when combined with additional support, helps people reintegrate into mainstream society, increases self-esteem and helps the recovery process from problem substance use. However, not all those with a substance use problem are able to make use of it as a springboard to recover without further help. This is particularly so for drinkers who as a general rule tend to be more chaotic than drug users. As already discussed, the recent trend in the UK for the employment of community support workers, either free-floating or linked to housing is a helpful innovation. These workers befriend and help drinkers and drug users with social issues such as Welfare Rights, organising payment of bills, accessing employment training, providing transport for drug clinic and hospital appointments and so on. They provide a very valuable service.

Rehousing substance users can be problematic but so can rehousing tenants who do not have a substance use problem. Some substance users are so chaotic that the rent does not get paid or there may be frequent rows with the neighbours. In some cases drug-dealing occurs. Local authority housing departments and housing associations should review their policies on tenancies, drug use and drug-dealing and consider whether two-way *social contracts* are adequate. Any policy in relation to drug problems should be stated and public, and conveyed to tenants' associations and other relevant bodies.

Some housing departments, housing associations and private landlords have been known to terminate tenancies on minor evidence of drug-dealing, such as a newspaper report of a conviction for supply or possession with intent to supply. However, as virtually all users do from time to time buy drugs for a partner or friend and accept money in return for this, most drug users risk being convicted on this charge at some point in their drug-using career. The conviction of possession with intent to supply drugs is usually made purely according to the amount of drug found and no other evidence. Those who purchase several days supply for themselves, or are heavy users, are at risk of being wrongly convicted of intention to supply. However, major suppliers should not be tolerated by communities. If large numbers of people come for short spells late at night, causing disruption to the peace of the neighbourhood, this should be catalogued and the police informed. If a conviction of supplying drugs is upheld and there are several complaints from neighbours, there are strong grounds to revoke a tenancy agreement. However, in general tenancies should only be removed if there is adequate associated evidence of neighbourhood disruption.

In the USA more extreme action is taken in the form of nuisance abatement orders. Here, instead of criminal proceedings being taken against dealers, a civil action is taken against the owner of the property. Starting in Portland, Oregon, in 1987 this method has now spread to several other states. Some abatement procedures are more severe than others. In Toledo, Ohio, prosecutors seek a two-week temporary restraining order against the property. When this is granted a large team of people, armed with battering rams and search warrants, immediately close and padlock the building on the grounds that irreparable harm is being done to the community. It may remain closed for one year. This makes everyone except the owner feel better, but in reality just shifts the problem elsewhere.

Prisons

Prison is a particularly difficult environment. Apart from the risks to physical health described in Chapter 17, anxiety and depression in prisoners is common. This may be precipitated by the fear of violence from other prison inmates, lack of social support coupled with lack of privacy, separation from families, boredom, lack of exercise and few meaningful social contacts within a prison setting. The prospect of this situation continuing for months or even years compounds the problem. Drugs and alcohol are available within most prisons and, not surprisingly, are highly sought after. It is not unusual for substance use to begin within a prison setting and then to be continued after release. Systems have recently been set up in the UK to help prisoners with drug problems but these are in need of more comprehensive developement. With the cooperation of prisoners, attempts have been made to establish drug-free wings in some prisons with voluntary drug-testing. However, in many of these areas testing is too infrequent to ensure a truly drug-free area. The poor prison environment and the deleterious effect this has on drug problems are good reasons why penalties should be reduced for those who contravene national drugs legislation. Prison experience carries a high risk of making a drug problem worse, though well-developed treatment interventions can provide opportunities for change.

Financial issues

Poverty is intimately linked to drinking and drug use. In the USA poverty is most concentrated in areas where black people and Hispanics live (Jargowsky, 1996), but in Britain the greatest concentrations of poverty occur in the north in white populations (Glennerster *et al.*, 1998).

Those who continue drinking or drug use commonly become impoverished as a result of their addiction. For drinkers there is often a narrowing of drinking repertoire. This is one of the hallmarks of the dependence syndrome, but sometimes it may be as much to do with financial considerations as dependence. Cider, for instance, may be preferred as it is cheaper and stronger than most beers.

For drug users in particular, the difficulties faced every day in having to raise large financial sums, often through criminal activity, in order to purchase drugs, is a frequent underlying reason why many people seek help. Financial difficulties are common major presenting problems of drug service attenders. Many drug users and drinkers become heavily in debt and good debt advice, perhaps by linking in

with the Citizen's Advice Bureau, should be seen as an important part of treatment.

Outcomes for people with drink problems are improved by preservation of their economic resources. Signs of this may occur before any action to change drinking behaviour is undertaken. During the year prior to maintained abstinence or moderated drinking, people with drink problems save about ten times more than those who continue drinking heavily. This happens even when the two outcome groups are similar in their income and financial practices (Tucker & Vuchinich, 1997).

In comparison to the financial resources set aside for the treatment and rehabilitation of drinkers and drug users, the costs of substance use to society are disproportionately high. Society's costs include those of substance-induced illness, law enforcement, the prevention of drug-trafficking, acquisitive crime, road traffic and other accidents, unemployment, absenteeism from work, and media and educational prevention campaigns. Findings from the California Drug and Alcohol Treatment Assessment (CALDATA) report indicate that the cost-benefit of the treatment of substance use averages seven dollars return for every dollar invested (Gerstein *et al.*, 1994). The majority of savings were from crime reduction.

Overcoming employment problems

For many years the links between unemployment and substance use has been well recognised (Faupel, 1988). There is an increased likelihood of job loss for those who use drugs (Kandel & Yamaguchi, 1987) and employment plays a significant role in the rehabilitation process for substance users (Wolkstein & Hastings-Black, 1979; Wille, 1983). Employment also helps prevent addiction problems. In a study of 100 New York heroin addicts and 100 alcohol dependents, Vaillant (1988) showed that the drinkers who were employed at the time of admission, and the heroin users who had been employed for at least four years prior to admission, both had a significant reduction in sustained addiction compared to the rest of the sample. Furthermore, a year of parole (parole in the USA is the equivalent of probation in the UK) was vastly more effective in reducing substance use than either short imprisonment or voluntary hospitalisation, and employment was a key factor in this. Parole helped despite the fact that only the more severe offenders received parole and the past histories of paroled individuals did not contain more favourable prognostic factors. Virtually all the parole successes had previously relapsed after other forms of treatment. Vaillant commented that

> parole was not successful because it punished. Rather parole was useful because it altered the addict's schedule of reinforcement. Parole required weekly proof of employment in individuals previously convinced they could not hold a job. It altered friendship networks. Parole . . . provided an external superego and external source of vigilance against relapse. It was probably no accident that several addicts with no other history of regular employment successfully completed tours of duty in the highly supervised setting of the armed forces. Work provides structure to the addict's life and structure interferes with addiction.

Another study showed that even those who continue to use drugs do so in a more controlled way if they are employed (Zinberg, 1984). Employment is also known to be the most important factor which positively influences criminality when juveniles are under justice system supervision, preventing criminal recidivism in 35% of cases in this population (Lipsey, 1992a).

Prison on the other hand has a detrimental effect on employment. Most people lose their jobs when they go to prison and have increased difficulty in finding employment if they have a prison record. Helping drug users and drinkers find or keep employment is an important treatment goal and should be part of every recovery programme. This is not always an easy task mainly because of discrimination by employers. The old joke of an employer saying 'You've done the right thing telling me about your drug problem, now clear your desk and get out' has more than a ring of truth. Surprisingly, in spite of zero tolerance, the USA is one of the best countries at preventing discrimination by employers against drug users in treatment. The Americans with Disabilities Act makes it illegal for employers to discriminate against methadone patients. Assisting with employment can be particularly difficult where additional psychiatric or medical problems are present. Substance users with severe employment problems have been shown to have high rates of chronic medical and psychiatric problems (McKay et al., 1998). These co-occurring difficulties interfere with alcohol and drug rehabilitation and increase the likelihood of post-treatment relapse.

Unemployment is not only a social stigma in its own right, it is directly associated with, and often leads to, ill-health, substance use, depression and social isolation. Conversely there is an association between abstinence from opiates and increased employment, enhanced social stability and mental health, as well as a reduction in depression and criminality (Lipsey, 1992). An English study showed that the proportion of opiate users working increased from 23% to 44% during the year following treatment (Sheehan et al., 1993). Fujii (1974) collected data from 27 programmes in New York and showed that prior to entry into treatment for opiate addiction about 30% of all clients were employed, but after treatment approximately 65% were employed.

Economic recession has a disproportionately adverse effect on the continued employability of former addicts compared to the rest of the population (Gearing et al., 1978). Drug use leads to the loss of 'the critical years of social maturation' (education, job training and the evolution of productive social attitudes). Early onset of substance use and addictive behaviour is particularly likely to have some impairing effect on physical, social, psychological, educational and employment ability. There may be limited interpersonal and communication skills and inappropriate stress coping techniques. Employability skills are provided through vocational rehabilitation, aided by psychological and environmental harm reduction interventions with goals individually tailored to the needs of the client.

Substantial improvements in the rate of employment for methadone clients can be attained by the introduction of vocational rehabilitation and by vocational training for a specific employment (Metzger & Platt, 1990). There is also evidence which suggests that for unemployed substance users focused counselling to facilitate employment may improve, not just their job finding skills, but also their retention in employment. Such counselling is built into the CRA and was part of a research study by McLellan and colleagues (1997a). Employment not only provides a predictable legitimate source of income it also gives workers an opportunity to develop meaningful and continuous relationships with non-drug-using persons and improves self-esteem by giving a sense of personal identity and achievement. Evidence from training programmes suggests that on-the-job training is more effective than classroom training and work experience (Barnow, 1987).

An example of a vocational rehabilitation programme
In the USA the National Association on Drug Abuse Problems (NADAP) was specifically set up to help those recovering from substance use find work placements. It organises group workshops, which utilise skills building exercises, role-playing, videotaping, and the involvement of employer representatives. The workshops provide clients with opportunities to learn and practise job-related social skills.

For those who have never worked before and who have been living in a subculture pervaded by drugs and drink, the basic social interaction skills necessary for a working environment often need enhancement. Various questions are pertinent:

- Can he or she communicate effectively both by speaking and by listening?
- Can he or she interact appropriately with co-workers, supervisors and employment authority figures?
- Does he or she dress appropriately?
- Does he or she have the skills to ask questions if unclear about instructions, and notify if unable to meet a commitment?
- Is he or she able to portray marketable job qualities and a positive work attitude at interview?
- Can he or she talk about work gaps, a criminal history and perhaps even a history of past drinking or drug-taking in a way that will relieve an employer's fears?

A thorough assessment of the clients' readiness and suitability for job placements should include

- an assessment of the client's ability to work in physical, psychological and social terms;
- an educational assessment;
- an assessment of strengths and abilities by various aptitude tests; and
- a vocational assessment and discussion of employment goals.

Interviewing skills can be enhanced by means of role-play and videotapes. Clients learn from this that the way information is presented is as important as the information itself. They should be encouraged not to volunteer negative things about themselves unless it is specifically requested. Furthermore, they can be taught to couple the admittance of any past negative experiences with at least one positive one.

In the UK there are few employment programmes specifically designed for substance users, although various national courses are available for the unemployed.

Employment and the US Salvation Army programme
Employment is an important feature of the Salvation Army programme in the USA. In comparison to clients in other US treatment programmes, Salvation Army clients have few social or personal resources. They are often homeless with no social support and drinking or other substance use can be a 'total life problem', yet outcomes are surprisingly good. Of the four treatment components that are significantly associated with outcome, two are unique to the programme: Sunday worship and part-time jobs. Moos and colleagues (1990) showed that the number of part-time jobs held was associated with improvement in alcohol consumption, physical symptoms, depressed mood and social functioning.

The work programme operates as a self-sustaining business based on the sale and repair of goods donated by the community, with clients providing most of the labour. It is relatively inexpensive because a substantial proportion of its costs are met by income generated through the residents' part-time jobs. Eighty-seven per cent of the clients worked on at least one part-time job, while 64% worked at five or more. Compared to other treatment programmes, this programme was the most successful in helping clients get back to work in the community at a later date. There was a 22% gain in employment rate from just prior to intake to six months after treatment for Salvation Army patients, compared to an 18% gain for patients from the halfway house programme, and 9% for those from the hospital-based programme.

Dutch employment agencies for substance users

TOPSCORE is an employment agency for drug users in Rotterdam. It is part of the Dutch *normalisation* policy and is subsidised by local government. It gives various jobs to local drug users, which helps them rehabilitate back into society. It is in fact part of a social inclusion programme. Jobs include street cleaning, upkeep of gardens, distribution of leaflets, message delivery and cleaning industrial establishments.

Workplace policies

In 1981 the UK government encouraged companies to adopt workplace policies for their employees who have drink problems to enable them to identify their need and be given help (DH, 1981). Many companies have developed similar policies for drug users, and this is particularly important where there is urinary or other screening for drugs in the workplace. No such screening programme should be started unless an acceptable workplace policy has been installed. The aim of such policies, both for drugs and alcohol, is simple. They are statements agreed by both employer and employees with the aim of discouraging inappropriate drinking or drug use at work and providing help for employees with a drug or drink problem.

In a workplace policy substance use should be viewed as a health problem. Each policy should give an undertaking that those coming forward for help and those identified by disciplinary procedures, will be given appropriate aid and support, and, if they accept this, their job and job rights will be preserved. In those workplaces where there has been no such policy, a number of cases where claims of unfair dismissal have been upheld on the grounds that substance use should be regarded as an illness and that employers should investigate the medical position rather than dismiss the employee.

Workplace policies should not just focus on problem drinking or drug-taking. A good workplace policy will contain three strands:

(1) individual conduct and corporate policy (including hospitality) concerning alcohol and drugs in the workplace
(2) alcohol and drug education
(3) identifying and responding to problem drinking and drug use

The identification of drug takers in the workplace by urinary testing, hair analysis or other forms of screening is still relatively controversial. Where this is already done it is essential that a good workplace policy is already in place to protect the employee. Testing should only be undertaken with the fully informed consent of the employee. Policies should recognise that

- some drugs, such as cannabis, can enter the system passively;
- unless testing by two different methods or mass spectrometry is done, the results cannot be regarded as reliable;
- a positive result showing opiates, including morphine, can occur from a number of over-the-counter (OTC) preparations; and
- a positive test result does not necessarily imply that a drug problem exists, that work is impaired through drug use or that drugs were taken during working hours.

As alcohol is a legal drug the situation is much easier. A good workplace policy for alcohol and drugs will enhance early prevention of, as well as early recovery from, substance use problems in employees. Every policy should be monitored to ensure that it is being properly and consistently implemented and also to gauge its impact.

Facilitating education opportunities for adults

Poor self-esteem is often tied to educational under-achievement and it is not unusual to encounter adult substance users who have serious problems of literacy and numeracy. Some are dyslexic and this may have not been detected even though dyslexia and ways of overcoming it are now better understood. Education and training opportunities for adults are more widely available than before in many countries including the UK, and enrolment on educational programmes will enhance future employment opportunities. Every effort should be made to encourage drinkers and drug users to enhance their chances of future employment through education and training and to establish a new career path away from the *business* of substance use.

Addressing social exclusion

There have been several definitions of social exclusion. It was originally suggested by Townsend (1979) to be the end result of poverty, which he described as

> a serious lack of resources preventing an individual obtaining his or her customary diet; preventing participation in customary activities; stopping normal living conditions; and in effect excluding the person concerned from ordinary living patterns, customs and activities.

Since then the definition of social exclusion has expanded to encompass

> processes (which) are dynamic and multidimensional in nature . . . linked not only to unemployment, and/or to low incomes but also to housing conditions, levels of education, and opportunities, health, discrimination, including discrimination because of skin colour and language barrier, citizenship and integration in the local community (Warburton, 1998).

It is both a condition and a process (Foster, 2000). The authors could have included discrimination against drinkers and drug users. McDermott (2002), himself stable on methadone maintenance for several years, writes:

> Dependent drug users are a heterogeneous population with members from all points on the social spectrum, but if you have a job you want to keep, if you have a mortgage, or life insurance or a driving license, then keep your head down. To reveal that you are an active drug user puts all these in jeopardy.

Smith (2001) describes the effects of social exclusion in the following way:

The inability of our society to keep all groups and individuals within reach of what we expect as a society and the tendency to push vulnerable and difficult individuals into the least popular places. The result is that children living in poverty may enter a cycle of poor educational achievement, unmanageable behaviour, drug misuse, unemployment, teenage pregnancy, homelessness, crime and suicide. This is hugely expensive for society, not only in human but also in economic terms. It can lead to a society that is unpleasant for all.

Social exclusion is a reality for many drinkers and drug users. Buchanan and Young (2000) have described the results of three studies in Merseyside on the self-reported barriers which drug users face and what assistance they need to be able to recover and reintegrate into the wider community:

> When this group were asked how they felt in the presence of people who did not use illegal drugs the answers were quite revealing. Many 'problem drug users' felt rejected and stigmatized by the non-drug-using population. The impact of this discrimination appears to have been deep and intrusive:
>
> 'They [non-drug users] look down on me as scum of the earth and as someone not to be associated with.'
>
> Many recognized the low status they were ascribed as a 'smackhead' and were acutely aware of the negative stereotypical roles attributed to them:
>
> 'They see me as a drug addict, a smackhead and they think I'd rob them.'
>
> Such was the degree of isolation (perhaps initially partly self-imposed because of its illegal nature), but which was now so severe and long lasting, that many now felt uneasy or even unable to cope in the company of non-drug users:
>
> 'I feel the odd one out, I've nothing in common with them. I start to get paranoid.'
>
> Aware and afraid of harsh judgmental attitudes some avoided contact:
>
> 'I used to avoid them like the plague. I used to be scared of what they might think.'

Others believed they were constantly being observed and watched:

> 'I feel nervous in case I slip up, I know they would look at me in disgust.'

The war on drugs has encouraged strong public disapproval of drug-taking and drug users and contributed to the isolation and detachment of drug users. Separate 'worlds' have been created, with little overlap or interconnection.

The process of overcoming social exclusion must begin with harm reduction by addressing the social and psychological problems associated with it, in addition to addressing the drug problem itself. As people overcome social isolation, are rehoused, sort out their financial problems, form relationships with non-drug users and gain employment, their self-esteem and expectations increase and they are more able to identify with mainstream society. Self-care, including attention to personal and dental hygiene, is an important part of the integration process. Once the problems have been overcome the use of personal strengths is necessary if substance users are to enter mainstream society.

Overcoming 'the wall of exclusion'

Although there are degrees of social exclusion, rejection by society can act as a seemingly impenetrable barrier, making it very difficult to break away from the subculture of substance use. Buchanan and Young (2000) have identified a wall of exclusion which prevents many substance users gaining access to wider society and denies them opportunities afforded to other people (Figure 13.1).

If social inclusion is not achieved and a drug user or drinker remains within a drug use and drinking subculture, so that the only friends they have drink to excess, use drugs and are involved in criminal activity, it is likely he or she will also continue these activities. Substance users can only overcome the wall of exclusion by utilising their own inner resources, and this requires good social and psychological functioning. The ability to communicate effectively and form close meaningful relationships is essential. In addition they need good psychological control. People whose behaviour is dominated by anger, depression or anxiety are socially handicapped. Thus, good personal functioning does not just improve the quality of

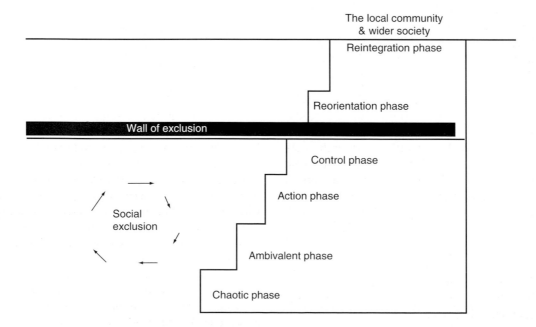

Figure 13.1 Steps to reintegration. (From Buchanan, J. & Young, L. (2000) The war on drugs. *Drugs Education, Prevention & Policy*, 7(4), p. 420. With permission from Taylor & Francis Ltd, <http://www.tandf.co.uk/journals>.)

peoples' lives, it is essential for inclusion into mainstream society and, when this is achieved, it aids the recovery process.

The US psychologist Daniel Goleman has coined the term *emotional intelligence* to describe the abilities, apart from a high IQ, which enable some people to succeed at work or in society in preference to others. It is these factors which come into force to enable those with a modest IQ to do better in life than those with a high IQ (Goleman, 1996). The same factors are needed to overcome the wall of exclusion. Goleman's premise is basically that, in order to succeed, IQ is not the only criterion. Unlike IQ, emotional intelligence can be enhanced with appropriate help. Many drug users and drinkers need such help if they are to overcome exclusion.

Goleman describes emotional intelligence as including good self-control, enabling those who are endowed with this to avoid being at the mercy of their emotions. It also entails being able to motivate oneself, and to have persistence, empathy and the ability to read emotion and the intentions of others. Those with low emotional intelligence, particularly those who have poor control of their emotions, become readily overwhelmed with rage or anxiety and are unable to handle relationships smoothly or communicate effectively. They cannot rein in their impulses or read another's innermost feelings. Their social and psychological skills are poor and consequently they are socially disadvantaged. In contrast, those with good social and psychological skills are personally and socially advantaged, tend to be optimistic and make the best of their experiences and opportunities. In Aristotle's words, to have the ability 'to be angry with the right person, to the right degree, at the right time, for the right purpose and in the right way' is a major personal and social asset. People with these abilities have a wide circle of friends and are often highly successful in life.

Enhancing social functioning

Assessing the need to improve social functioning

Those who do not function well at an individual level and have a low emotional IQ may need interventions to improve personal functioning. An assessment of psychological and social functioning should be undertaken so that the relevant skills needed to achieve social inclusion can be enhanced. Where there are weaknesses, drug and alcohol service workers are well placed to aid social reintegration through social skills training, assertiveness training, family therapy, cognitive help to reassess attitudes, values and beliefs, stress management and coping skills training. All these interventions are known to aid the recovery process of drug and alcohol dependence in their own right. There is thus a double benefit of their incorporation into the care plan.

Social inclusion is not a fixed entity. Just as there is a continuum of harm, so too there is a continuum of social inclusion, which substance users tend to slide up and down. At a low level clients just tick over and function with difficulty. They may manage to cover up their problems but life is a constant struggle. Socially focused harm reduction with substance users will help promote social inclusion. So too will abstinence when this can be successfully achieved and maintained.

When assessing the degree of social exclusion and the need for help to be socially included, workers should enquire about

- current and anticipated future social identity
- the age when substance use first became an important feature of life
- the expectation of support from local society, family and friends

Current and anticipated future social identity
Being identified by others as a drinker or drug user is a common social barrier. Conversely one of the processes of change, which Prochaska and DiClemente (1984) have termed *social liberation* (see Chapter 9), can be a potent aid to social inclusion. Social liberation has many advantages in addition to liberating the individual by expanding the choice of alternatives to substance use. The *liberating* development of a new socially acceptable identity through employment, or by joining a political, sporting, religious, environmental or campaigning group, aids the recovery process in its own right as does the enhanced social support network that is brought with it.

According to Biernacki (1986), the reawakening of old identities or the establishment of new ones is the key to the recovery process. He believes that a decision to stop taking drugs generally comes about when the user's addict identity conflicts with and undermines other identities that are valued both by the user and by normal society. A study of Motivational Interviewing (MI) has already shown us that discrepancies of this nature strongly motivate positive change. The perception of a positive identity by partner, parent or employer is usually greatly valued by substance users. Conversely, its threatened or actual loss and replacement with an identity of drug addict is unacceptable to those who are valued in mainstream society.

Age when substance use began
When substances are used as a coping mechanism from early adolescence, the ability to find and develop normal coping skills may never be attained. Thus the age when people first develop drug or alcohol problems dependence may be a signpost to their own innate ability to function well at a personal level. This is illustrated in the following two cases.

CASE STUDY

Client M first became dependent on alcohol at the age of 45, having drunk heavily for ten years before that time. Until the age of 35 he had been a successful businessman and coped well with life's stresses. Client N, however, started drinking heavily in his early teens and at the age of 16 started taking heroin. Within a few months he was opiate dependent. Even before he was independent of his parents, client N had used alcohol or drugs to help him cope. His own sense of self-efficacy was low, which in turn had led to poor self-esteem. Client N wanted to stop but does not believe that he can handle life without heroin. Client M had inherently good personal functioning in the past, which can perhaps be reawakened. Client N does not.

The expectation of support from society, family and friends
The attitudes of society are important, whether this is at a national or local level. In many places drug users are seen as a threat to the general public. The

media generally portrays them in an adverse light, responsible for violent muggings, and other serious crimes. Countering this is difficult. The Dutch policy of *normalisation* is extremely helpful. In England a voluntary sector project for substance users known as Kaleidoscope in Kingston-on-Thames, Surrey, helps substance users mix with the local churchgoing community and aids the process of social reintegration.

Family and friends are all part of the reintegration package. If family and friends are socially excluded, it is considerably more difficult for a substance user to become socially integrated. Drug and alcohol workers and other professionals can help facilitate social inclusion, which might otherwise take years, or never properly occur. They can do this through their own professional relationship with their clients by their attitudes, warmth and empathy, and by helping drinkers and drug users develop better social skills where this would aid the social integration process.

Overcoming the social exclusion barrier is only the beginning

Readers will note on the social exclusion side of the wall the similarities between the named steps and the cycle of change (Figure 13.1). Overcoming social exclusion is very different from being fully integrated into society. Passing the wall we come on to two new phases: those of reorientation and reintegration.

Reorientation
Long-term social exclusion has an effect on expectations and attitudes (Glennerster *et al.*, 1998). In his book *The Children of Sanchez*, Lewis (1961) describes how familial experiences of poverty can shape attitudes and expectations leaving people trapped and unable 'to take full advantage of changing conditions or increased opportunities which may occur in their lifetime'. Almost 40 years later Foster (2000) describes essentially the same phenomenon in the north of England:

A senior police officer voiced the hopelessness and desperation of residents on the estate which had no constructive expression: 'Increasingly what they lack is any sort of view or expectation of a future... partly because of what they've experienced, and what their parents have experienced, has been an absence of future, and partly because they have no building blocks for the future. They have no concept of my idea, which is to have a job, with a family, have a holiday twice a year.... All they can see is a very short-sighted future. The City will provide me with a house. I might have a girlfriend and I might have a baby. There's no expectation I will live with them. My chances of getting a job are very low, the illiteracy rate is very high and so my expectation of further education is limited. There don't appear to be any expanding job opportunities and so why should I conform? That's my rationale for it. What do I gain by conforming? All the horizons are short term and in the short term they gain by not conforming.

To move out of such a mindset, even with the best help, is not easy. For an individual to change such ingrained thought patterns, when similar behaviour is entrenched within the culture of a community, may seem unrealistic. But it is achievable when it becomes part of a slow process of reintegration. Reorientation and reintegration are perhaps better described as interdependent and entwined processes, rather than a stepwise process of reintegration.

Reintegration

Reintegration involves becoming employed or constructively occupied, achieving better housing conditions, overcoming poverty and isolation, improving education and health, and moving away from crime and illicit drug use. It is a practical process which can be accelerated with appropriate help. Much can be done through interventions which reduce environmental and psychological harm and improve personal functioning in the manner that has been already described.

Social skills training

Some people who become dependent on drink or drugs use these substances because they are not very good at socialising or forming close relationships, and have found that drugs or drink helped them socialise. Such people are not socially phobic, and if they had never become involved in substance use, they would have managed in society, albeit not very well. Others might not be very good at coping with negative emotions. Neither of these two groups would have been high achievers in society. Thus if they develop a drink or drug problem they have great difficulty extracting themselves from it.

By improving communication skills and assertiveness, social skills training enables many clients to increase the quantity of support that they receive from others, and enhance its quality. Social skills deficits have long been recognised in those with drink problems (Hover & Gaffney, 1991) and drug users (Linquist *et al.*, 1979), and may prevent the individual client from obtaining the support from others needed to maintain abstinence and adequately resolve difficult situations. If someone does not have the skills to be assertive with others, he or she may feel unable to refuse if a drink or drugs are offered, even though acceptance is likely to lead on to a major relapse. If someone has been made homeless because of their drinking or drug use, there will be fewer options available for them to deal with homelessness. Those who have good social skills are better at accessing desired resources, including treatment.

Social skills training methods are well established and focus on initiating and developing one-to-one and group relationships. They are useful for enhancing marital, family and work relationships and building up a network of friends who do not use drugs or drink. Monti and colleagues (1989; 2002) have developed a multi-session interpersonal social skills training package for groupwork with those who have drink problems:

session 1:   introduction, group building and problem assessment
session 2:   starting conversations
session 3:   giving and receiving compliments
session 4:   non-verbal communication
session 5:   feeling talk and listening skills
session 6:   introduction to assertiveness
session 7:   giving criticism
session 8:   receiving criticism

session 9:   receiving criticism about drinking
session 10:   drink refusal skills
session 11:   refusing requests
session 12:   close and intimate relationships
session 13:   enhancing social support networks

Other texts are useful for social skills training on a one-to-one level (Nelson-Jones, 1996).

Social skills training has been shown to produce a reduction in drinking over the short term. Eriksen and colleagues (1989) randomly assigned 12 alcohol-dependent clients to receive either eight sessions of social skills training in addition to standard alcoholism group counselling treatment, or only the standard treatment. Those who received social skills training had their first drink on average 51.6 days following treatment compared to 8.3 days for control subjects. They consumed about one-third less alcohol per week than the control group and their consumption was judged by their significant others as being socially acceptable. However, the long-term effects of social skills training on positive treatment outcome for substance users have been questioned (Hawkins *et al.*, 1989).

Variations in success rates are almost certainly related to the way the programme has been constructed. If clients are given the opportunity to observe models, role-play social situations and receive feedback (Oei & Jackson, 1980), and if a cognitive component is incorporated into the training programme (Oei & Jackson, 1982), good long-term outcomes can be demonstrated. Surprisingly, although social skills training has been shown by Monti and colleagues (1990) to be even more efficacious than coping skills training in reducing problem drinking, it is rarely used by alcohol or drug services.

Assertiveness training

Unassertive people are non-threatening and usually get along in normal society, but are not always good at overcoming drink or drug problems. Dependent drinkers who are successful in maintaining abstinence respond to problem situations more assertively and with more effective drink refusal than those who relapse (Rosenberg, 1983). For instance, some people may not be assertive enough to be able to tell old drug-using acquaintances to go away when they knock on the door in the hope of selling some drugs. For such people assertiveness training may be needed if treatment is to be successful.

Assertiveness has been defined by Monti and colleagues (1989) as 'recognising your right to decide what you will do in a situation, rather than acceding to what someone else expects or demands. It also means recognising the rights of the people you deal with, which must be respected.' In this context the word *rights* refers to

(1) the right to inform others of your opinions;
(2) the right to inform others of your feelings as long as it is done in a way that is not intended to be hurtful to them;
(3) the right to request others to change their behaviour if it is affecting you; and
(4) the right to accept or reject anything that others say to you, or request from you.

People differ in their interpersonal styles. They can be passive, aggressive, passive–aggressive or assertive:

(a) *Passive* people tend to give up their rights if it appears there might be a conflict between what they want and what someone else wants. They usually fail to let others know what they are thinking and feeling, bottling up their emotions and are often left feeling anxious or angry, or are depressed by their own ineffectiveness. Because they do not communicate their thoughts and feelings other people have no way of knowing what they want and passive people seldom find that their needs are met. In addition others may come to resent them for not communicating.
(b) *Aggressive* people trample over the rights of others in order to protect their own rights. The immediate needs of aggressive people may be met, but the long-term effects of their aggression are often negative as they leave a trail of resentment behind them.
(c) *Passive–aggressive* people are indirect. They may hint at what they want, be sarcastic or mumble something but they fail to state directly and clearly what is on their minds. They may

act out what they want to say, e.g. by slamming doors, by giving someone the *silent treatment* or by doing a sloppy job. People around them may become confused or angry and the passive–aggressive person then feels victimised or frustrated.

(d) *Assertive* people decide what they want, plan an appropriate way to involve other people and then act on that plan, clearly stating their thoughts and feelings, without making threats, demands or negative statements. Occasionally an assertive person may utilise other responses if it is in his or her best interests (e.g. a passive response to avoid conflict with an insensitive boss, or an aggressive response when someone persistently asks for something that has been repeatedly politely declined). Assertive people are thus able to adapt their responses to fit the situation in order to achieve what they want. Assertive people generally feel pleased with their actions and are usually well regarded by others, as they use the most effective way they know to communicate their thoughts and feelings.

To develop skills in becoming assertive, clients are advised to think before they reply so that assumptions are not made about other peoples' intentions, and also to try to communicate clearly their own thoughts and feelings by being specific and direct. Body language and tone of voice are important and clients should be willing to compromise. If attempts to communicate fail for one reason or another then the message needs to be restated. Assertiveness skills are needed to be able to give and receive criticism, and are essential in order to successfully refuse an offer of drink or drugs. These skills are best developed by role-play and modelling in a one-to-one or group therapeutic situation.

Conclusion

Environmental harm interlinks and may combine with other harm relating to physical and mental health and problems relating to the criminal justice system. Other commentators have also noted how social isolation, unemployment, educational deprivation, substance use, poverty, imprisonment, poor health and homelessness all interlink and compound each other to drag down individuals and communities (Blaxter, 1990; Richards *et al.*, 2002). Interventions to resolve harm reverse this process making individuals stronger. It is an incremental process. If one social harm is removed, the problems that remain become weaker and in turn are more easily dealt with. At the same time personal functioning improves, further facilitating the process of recovery. A gradual lifting of social harm is most difficult at the beginning, but with persistence reaps great rewards. If all harmful problems appear to be removed and progress has halted, further attention to heighten individual functioning and interventions to enhance motivation may move the substance user to a stage where he or she is more able to contemplate abstinence.

Chapter 14
Reducing Psychological Harm and Increasing Psychological Strength

Introduction

Just as environmental harm reduction and enhancing social functioning complement each other, so too do psychological harm reduction and enhancing psychological strengths. Again they are two sides of the same coin because interventions which address the psychological problems associated with dependent and problem substance use simultaneously reduce harm and improve personal functioning.

Chapter 16 describes mental illness and mental health problems where multi-disciplinary working with psychiatric services is of paramount importance. This chapter is concerned with the management of psychological problems of a lesser degree, which nonetheless strongly influence the recovery process from dependent and problem substance use. Psychological problems may underlie and pre-date substance use, or be exacerbated by, or consequent to, it. Many substance users are chronically stressed by poverty, unemployment and social isolation. They have to cope with repeated withdrawals, are rejected by family and friends and are frequently despised by other people for their behaviour. Their self-esteem is generally low. In such circumstances it is unusual not to develop emotional difficulties.

Many quickly find the seemingly double advantage that substance use brings. It helps them deal with both environmental problems and unpleasant negative emotions. If dependence becomes established, further use may help them deal with drug or alcohol withdrawals. Most are aware that this is avoidance coping which in the long term solves nothing, entrenches their chemical dependence, and deskills them from both dealing with life's

problems and with difficult emotions. But life is so complicated that the easiest way of dealing with daily hassles and larger problems is often to drink or take drugs.

Substances themselves may cause chronic symptoms of anxiety, depression or low self-esteem. The depression of chronic opiate use and anxiety of recurrent alcohol withdrawals are examples of this. Raising awareness of these mechanisms of symptom generation is important as it can enable motivation to change. In contrast, continued use of substances to cope with unpleasant negative emotions, such as anger, anxiety or depression reinforces the perceived need to use them again in this way in the future. For some people drink and drug use becomes so entrenched that they cannot conceive of coping without them.

Helping people find other methods of solving problems and coping with negative emotions, and helping improve their self-efficacy in all these areas are important ways to aid drinkers and drug takers in the recovery process. Drug and alcohol service workers, probation officers, and all those working with substance users in a professional capacity need to develop skills in the areas outlined below.

Working with young people

The Anger Coping Programme

This programme is suitable for older children and helps young people deal with anger more effectively. It focuses on the way aggressive children wrongly perceive and misinterpret information which relates to social interaction. These cognitive distortions and deficiencies relating to social information processing have been reviewed by Lochman and Wells (1996). Aggressive children/adolescents:

- attend to and remember hostile social cues more than non-hostile cues;
- rate their partners as being more aggressive than they really were, and rate themselves as being less aggressive than observers rate them;
- have characteristic deficiencies in their social problem-solving skills;
- generate fewer solutions to social problems than non-aggressive children;
- generate fewer bargaining and compromise solutions;
- are less able to accurately perceive other people's motives or create solutions that integrate the needs of both self and other;
- choose aggressive responses because they believe that aggressive behaviour will enhance self-esteem and will not be negatively evaluated by peers; and
- are less aware of their emotions. They tend to minimise emotions that make them feel vulnerable, and report that they feel more anger and less sadness and fear than non-aggressive children. When they reach adolescence they are poorly prepared to cope with their emotions when they encounter situations which typically evoke fear or sadness.

Aggressive children are capable of highly competent solutions when they think in a deliberate, slower manner. Interventions are helpful when they focus on a careful evaluation and planned response. The Anger Coping Programme includes a behavioural management system whereby the children receive points for good group behaviour, abiding by the group's rules, and for positive participation. There is a goal-setting component which is mutually selected every week. A self-instruction component assists children to recognise situations that usually provoke intense feelings and to use inhibitory self-instruction (Stop! Think! What can I do?). There is role-play of certain situations, particularly those that are ambiguous, and discussions with the child of the various intentions that other people might have. Lochman also included a direct focus on parental factors associated with the development and maintenance of the child's aggressive behaviour. The Anger Coping Programme leads to significant reductions in disruptive–aggressive classroom behaviour, significant improvements in perceived social competence, and trends for reductions in teacher-rated aggressive behaviour in comparison to a control group (Lochman, 1992).

Enhancing coping skills

Individual variations of stress reactions

Although ordinary daily hassles are less stressful than major life changes, such as divorce and bereavement, or being made homeless, hassles can be very stressful when they pile up or touch on special areas of vulnerability (Gruen et al., 1989).

The influence of family, culture and religion does not necessarily indicate how any individual will cope with stress. Those who cope badly will develop a stress reaction. This is the emotional response generated when a vulnerable person perceives a stressful stimulus. The perceived ability to cope with the problem (self-efficacy) will influence whether or not there is a stress reaction. The motivation to deal with the problem will influence the need to cope effectively, and the type and intensity of any emotional reaction will vary according to the way the problem is appraised by thought processes. This in turn will be influenced by personality factors.

Personality characteristics found to help people resist the deleterious effects of stress include a sense of self-efficacy (Bandura, 1977; 1997), the ability to think constructively (Epstein & Meier, 1989), hope (Snyder et al., 1991), learned resourcefulness (Rosenbaum, 1990) and optimism (Scheier & Carver, 1987). From a cognitive standpoint, viewing oneself as helpless favours a stress reaction of anxiety and withdrawal, whereas having a sense of power over outcomes favours anger and aggression. Anxiety is more likely to occur and will be stronger when a person has a poor regard for his or her capacity to cope with the world effectively. This idea has been explored substantially by Bandura (1997) via his concept of self-efficacy, and Greenberg and colleagues (1992) have shown that good self-esteem reduces anxiety in the face of a stressor.

Links between thoughts and emotions

Thus the way in which a stressor is viewed influences the type of emotional response, and the emotional response itself can be modified by thought processes.

> If a person appraises his or her relationship to the environment in a particular way, then a specific emotion, which is tied to the appraisal, will usually follow unless the appraisal is changed by cognitive coping processes. And if two individuals make the same appraisal, then they will experience the same emotion, regardless of the actual circumstances (Lazarus, 1991).

Appraisal theory provides a set of propositions about what one should think to feel a given emotion. Lazarus says that it should be possible to understand what a person is thinking from the knowledge of what that person is feeling. Similarly we should be able to predict the emotional reactions if we know beforehand what people are thinking and the environmental stressors they are facing. From a therapeutic point of view, appraisal aids the coping process. It may also be possible to improve or prevent destructive negative emotions, or even replace them with positive emotions, if the thoughts associated with them change. Thus, if someone has difficulty in coping with problems or with unpleasant negative emotions, examining the stressors and accompanying thoughts may sometimes help relieve the intensity of those emotions and aid personal coping without substance use. Lazarus (1991) provides us with the core relational themes for each emotion (Table 14.1).

Emotion can be viewed as a superordinate system whose component parts are comprised of motivation (an individual's goals), stress, cognitive appraisal and coping. Together these form a conceptual unit (Lazarus, 1999).

Different coping methods

Coping has been defined as: 'Constantly changing cognitive and behavioural efforts to manage specific external and/or internal demands that are appraised as taxing or exceeding the resources of the person' (Lazarus & Folkman, 1984). There are many different ways of coping. Denial was once thought to be a harmful coping method, but it can be beneficial under certain circumstances.

Table 14.1   Core relational themes for each emotion

Anger	A demeaning offence against me and mine
Anxiety	Facing uncertain existential threat
Fright	An immediate, concrete and overwhelming physical danger
Guilt	Having transgressed a moral imperative
Shame	Failing to live up to an ego ideal
Sadness	Having experienced an irrevocable loss
Envy	Wanting what someone else has
Jealousy	Resenting a third party for loss or threat to another's affection or favour
Disgust	Taking in or being too close to an indigestable object or idea
Happiness	Making reasonable progress towards realisation of a goal
Pride	Enhancement of one's ego identity by taking credit for a valued object or achievement, either one's own or that of someone or group with whom we identify
Relief	A distressing goal-incongruent condition that has changed for the better or has gone away
Hope	Fearing the worst but yearning for better
Love	Desiring or participating in affection, usually but not necessarily reciprocated
Gratitude	Appreciation for an altruistic gift that provides personal benefit
Compassion	Being moved by another's suffering and wanting to help
Aesthetic experiences	Emotions aroused by these experiences can be any of the above; there is no specific plot

(From Lazarus, R. S. (1991) *Emotion and Adaptation.* Table 3.4, p. 122. New York: Oxford University Press. Used with permission from Oxford University Press, Inc.)

Following a severe life event, such as the death of a loved one, denial (feeling it is impossible to believe that it has happened) is the normal first stage of adjustment and lasts for a few days.

Coping is usually either problem-focused or emotion-focused. A problem-focused person obtains information about what to do and mobilises actions for the purpose of solving the problem. The coping actions may be directed either towards oneself or the environment. Emotion-focused coping is aimed at regulating the emotions tied to the stressful situation – e.g. by avoiding thinking about the threat or reappraising it – leaving the problem unchanged. When conditions of stress are appraised as changeable and within the person's control, problem-focused coping predominates. However, when conditions are appraised as unchangeable, emotion-focused coping predominates (Folkman, 1984). Under certain circumstances emotion-focused coping can be detrimental to health and well-being. However, McQueeney and colleagues (1997) found that those who continue to struggle to change conditions they cannot change, relying rigidly on problem-focused coping are far more troubled in the long term than those who accept the reality and rely more on emotion-focused coping. In reality substance users need to draw on both.

Ways of coping often change with time. For this reason Lazarus (1999) terms coping a process rather than an event. The questionnaire in Table 14.2 has been widely used to determine the general coping methods of individuals, and how they respond given a specific situation.

Helping those with poor or dysfunctional coping methods

Those who cope poorly with one method can be encouraged to try another, or can reduce the difficult emotional consequences of stress by cognitive reappraisal or other methods outlined below. Teaching coping skills can either be given in broad coverage through educational groupwork, e.g. at day centres, or they can be targeted to individuals with specific problems. Most coping skills training packages, such as the ones devised by Monti and colleagues (1989; 2002) or by Kadden and colleagues (1995) for Project MATCH, have been developed for groups of drinkers enabling them to develop basic cognition skills, perceptions, expectations and mood. They are equally applicable for drug users. Those devised for groups generally run briefly through a number of relapse prevention techniques and combine this with problem-solving and some relaxation techniques and basic anger management. They also include social skills training on a broad but rather limited basis. This is enough for many people, but some people are not able to utilise groupwork, or they have deeply entrenched problems in particular areas and need further work on an individual basis. Details of those methods of coping skills training that have not so far been covered are outlined below.

Problem-solving

Problem-solving skills are important for everyone to have, but they are particularly useful for people who have a drink or drug problem. All too often the standard solution to any problem for almost every substance user is to drink or take drugs, and other innate skills for dealing with difficult problems become lost in the process of time. Training clients in problem-solving has been shown to promote positive change in substance users (Platt *et al.*, 1980). Problem-solving skills training was originally devised by D'Zurilla and Goldfried (1971). It involves enabling the client to

- recognise when a problem exists;
- *brainstorm* a variety of potential solutions;
- select the most appropriate option;
- work out a detailed action plan;
- put the plan into action; and
- evaluate the effectivenesss of the option chosen.

Various clues may enable you to recognise when a problem exists. These may be physiological clues (e.g. craving, *butterflies in the stomach*), clues produced by thoughts and feelings (e.g. loneliness, fear, etc.), clues from your own behaviour (e.g. being persistently late for work, neglecting the family), the ways in which you react to other people (e.g. angrily, lack of interest) or the ways in which

Table 14.2 Factors and sample items from the Ways of Coping Questionnaire

(1) Confrontative coping
Stood my ground and fought for what I wanted
Tried to get the person responsible to change his or her mind
I expressed anger to the person(s) who caused the problem

(2) Distancing
Made light of the situation; refused to get too serious about it
Didn't let it get to me; refused to think about it too much
Tried to forget the whole thing

(3) Self-controlling
I tried to keep my feelings to myself
Kept others from knowing how bad things were
I tried not to act too hastily or follow my first hunch

(4) Seeking social support
Talked to someone to find out more about the situation
Talked to someone who could do something concrete about the problem
I asked a relative or friend I respected for advice

(5) Accepting responsibility
Criticized or lectured myself
Realized I brought the problem on myself
I made a promise to myself that things would be different next time

(6) Escape–avoidance
Wished that the situation would go away or somehow be over with
Hoped a miracle would happen
Avoided being with people in general

(7) Planful problem-solving
I knew what had to be done, so I doubled my efforts to make things work
I made a plan of action and followed it
Changed something so things would turn out all right

(8) Positive reappraisal
Changed or grew as a person in a good way
I came out of the experience better than when I went in
Found new faith

other people react towards you (e.g. by avoiding or criticising you). Having recognised that a problem does exist, it helps to have a structure to sort it out.

The Community Reinforcement Approach (CRA), as outlined by Meyers and Smith (1995), utilises a modified version of D'Zurilla and Goldfried's steps (reproduced with permission from Guilford Publications, Inc.):

A. *Defining the problem*
Define the problem as specifically as possible. Separate out any secondary or related problems.
(For example, Problem: my girlfriend is refusing to speak to me. Secondary problems: (a) I recently went on a drinking binge and am feeling rough; and (b) I've run out of money.)

B. *Generating alternatives*
  (1) Use brainstorming to generate potential solutions.
  (2) Do not criticise any of the suggestions offered.
  (3) Go for quantity, the more potential solutions, the better!
  (4) Stay within the problem area.
  (5) State solutions in specific terms.

(If brainstorming is not generating enough possibilities, it sometimes helps adapt a solution that worked before, e.g. in response to the problem defined above, talk to her about why she is giving the silent treatment; do something that you know she likes. Another helpful tip is to change your frame of reference, e.g. imagine you are advising a friend what to do.)

C. *Deciding on a solution*
  (1) Eliminate any solutions that you would not feel comfortable attempting. No explanations are needed.
  (2) Evaluate the feasibility of each remaining alternative while identifying its probable consequences.
  (3) Decide on one solution and describe exactly how you will carry it out.
  (4) Consider possible obstacles to enacting the solution.
  (5) Generate 'backup' plans to circumvent these obstacles.
  (6) Commit to trying the selected solution an agreed-upon-number of times before the next session.
  (7) Decide whether to attempt a second solution as well.
  (8) Go through steps 2–6 for each subsequent solution considered.

D. *Evaluating the outcome*
  • Review the outcome at the next session and give a satisfaction rating.
  • Modify the solution if necessary.
  • If an entire new solution is required, repeat the problem-solving procedure.

Example: insomnia

Defining the problem. How long has it been a problem? Is it caused by anxiety or depression about a specific issue? If so is this issue the real problem, or a secondary one? Is the main problem minor or major? Is it related to past or present substance use? (Sleep disturbance is common for a period of time after abstinence has been achieved. When a client ceases heavy drinking, sleep disturbance commonly continues for about three months.) Does smoking or caffeine use in the form of coffee, tea or cola drinks cause, or at least contribute to, the problem?

Generating alternatives. Brainstorming as many solutions as possible (even those which seem really unlikely) might give the following possible solutions:

(1) Visit general practitioner (GP) to obtain sleeping pills.
(2) Take more exercise during the day.
(3) Stop drinking coffee, tea or cola drinks after 4 PM.
(4) Stop smoking.
(5) Have a warm bath and a milky drink (not tea or coffee) before going to bed.
(6) Install double glazing.
(7) Move bedroom to the back of the house where it is quieter.
(8) Hit partner with pillow when he or she snores.
(9) Buy a new mattress.

Deciding on a solution. The client does not feel comfortable with the idea of stopping smoking so this solution is eliminated. Installing double glazing or purchasing a new mattress is not feasible as they are too expensive; therefore these two solutions are eliminated. Attending the GP and asking for a hypnotic is not an ideal solution, as dependency may well be transferred to the hypnotic prescribed. This was originally the only solution considered by the client, but after discussion with the counsellor it was decided that, although this solution would not be discarded, it would be placed at the end of the list of possible solutions. In this case it was decided to combine a number of the possible solutions to see if this would overcome the problem. The client took up swimming every day and played football twice a week, he stopped drinking caffeine-containing drinks after 4 PM, and had a hot bath and a milky drink before going to bed.

Evaluating the outcome. It is important to evaluate outcomes of problem-solving. Drinkers and drug users need to know that this is a method that works. In the above case the outcome evaluation may have gone the following way.

When the client was next seen after two weeks, the sleeping problem had improved. Although the client still suffered from insomnia, after discussion with the counsellor, he said he would try to manage to live with it, as he knew it would continue to improve and probably disappear completely in three months time. He decided to try to improve things further by moving his bed to the back of the house, and had already been whacking his partner with a pillow every time she snored. His sleeping pattern did in fact return to normal after three months, and he felt very proud of the fact that he managed to contain and eventually overcome the problem in a non-chemical way.

Anxiety management

As already mentioned anxiety reactions tend to be generated in situations where an individual feels powerless over outside forces. Some anxiety is appropriate and can even be life-saving as in *fight or flight* reactions. But some people are overanxious and others use alcohol and drugs dysfunctionally to help them cope with anxiety, thereby deskilling themselves of normal coping methods. Both groups may be helped by anxiety management training.

Cognitive approaches

Cognitive models of anxiety propose that individuals experience anxiety because their beliefs about themselves and the world make them prone to interpret a wide range of situations in a threatening fashion (Beck *et al.*, 1985a). For anxious people most of these beliefs concern issues of acceptance, competence, responsibility and control, and include beliefs about the symptoms of anxiety. They give rise to automatic thoughts which are often a skewed version of reality, tending to catastrophise a situation which other people might view as less threatening. It is these thoughts that generate anxiety. Reappraisal of their situation to enable anxious people to recognise that they do have control over at least some elements of the situation will help reduce fear and anxiety. Appendix 20 can be used as *homework* in between therapeutic sessions, for discussion when the individual is next seen. Subsequently people can use it themselves to continue the recovery process.

Behavioural approaches through relaxation techniques

Behavioural methods of reducing anxiety can also be useful adjuncts to such Cognitive Therapy (CT), although on their own they do not appear to help people with drink or drug problems. These include deep muscle relaxation (Bernstein & Borkovec, 1973), breathing techniques (Clark *et al.*, 1985) and imagery (Lazarus, 1984). Relaxation training is a skill that can be easily learnt and the more it is practised, the better the person becomes at evoking a deep state of relaxation of both body and mind. Deep muscle relaxation involves the systematic, progressive relaxation of various muscle groups. Controlled breathing also reduces the discomfort of emotional distress.

Progressive muscle relaxation. Clients are taught to alternately tense and relax certain muscle groups, starting with the feet. To begin they are instructed to tightly curl up their toes, hold the tension for 5–10 seconds and then let the tension go for 15–20 seconds. The same procedure is then undertaken with other muscle groups working upwards: the ankles (heels down, toes up); the calves (toes down, heels up); the thighs and knees (bring feet under the chair); the stomach (tighten abdominal muscles); chest and back (push chest out); shoulders (shrug shoulders); upper arms (arms bent at elbow, touching shoulders); forearms (arms straight, hands pointing up); fingers and hands (tightly clenched fists); neck (chin buried on chest); jaw (bite down); mouth (lips pursed); eyelids (tight shut); and forehead (wrinkle forehead), each tensing for 5–10 seconds and then relaxing for 15–20 seconds. Clients are encouraged to practise deep muscle relaxation during daily living activities, starting with slow non-stressful activities such as watching TV or reading a book. All muscle groups are allowed to relax apart from the ones that are absolutely essential according to which activity is undertaken. Once this is mastered the client moves on to practise muscle relaxation in muscles not being used during more demanding activities such as waiting for a bus or shopping. Eventually the client can use relaxation skills during highly demanding activities such as talking to an angry person, running to catch a bus or any stressful situation.

Breathing techniques. Here the client is encouraged to take a deep breath and then exhale very slowly. For the next few minutes he or she is asked to continue to breathe slowly and steadily, keeping the body completely relaxed, limp and heavy. Each time the client exhales he or she is asked to slowly and softly say the word 'Relax!' The client is then asked to imagine the word 'relax' each time he or she exhales and to continue to do this for the next 2 minutes.

Imagery. Clients are asked to imagine a scene which will help them relax. The only requirements are that (a) it is relaxing, peaceful and serene; and (b) the client is alone at the scene. Different people find different scenes relaxing. Some can relax and unwind by imagining themselves at a beach, park, lake, or by imagining a walk through the woods, or by picturing themselves fishing on a riverbank, listening to the ripple of the water and waiting patiently for a fish to bite. The more detail there is, the easier it is to visualise and relax. Once a scene has been visualised which is effective in helping the client relax, it can be remembered and recalled at times of stress. Sometimes a word or phrase can be picked out to focus on and associate with the concluding parts of relaxation training so that clients can condition themselves to relax by just repeating the word or phrase at times of stress. Imagery is usually used in combination with deep muscle relaxation or breathing techniques. It is

helpful if clients are taught all three methods of relaxation.

Anger management

Preventing harm to staff

Risk assessment is covered in Chapters 5 and 16 and the need for policies and procedures have been emphasised. Although it is unusual in a well-run empathetic service, aggression from those attending services seems to be increasing. In the course of their working lives, staff working with substance users will encounter anger at the point of potential violence. It is important that buildings are *safe* for reception staff and workers, and that consulting rooms are organised so that workers are nearest the exit point and that there are means of summoning help urgently, if required. No one should work on their own in a building. All staff must know what to do in the face of aggression and should receive training in this.

Averting aggression

In most cases anger can be prevented from escalating to overt aggression by the response of professional staff. Aggression always has an antecedent phase, and if this is handled well violence can usually be averted. The overriding context for aggression is that people experience a series of events in which at some point they begin to see themselves as victims or suffering injustice.

Those who are on the edge of giving physical vent to their feelings are usually desperate for some form of care. Booker (1999) recommends the mnemonic DELIVER CARE. This is a helpful guide for a sound professional response:

DEcide quickly
- whether you stay or leave. If leaving, do it politely if possible. Decide whether you need help, being aware that when you really need it, you may be unable to call. If help is needed call for a colleague (or the police if appropriate). If the picture is complicated by intoxication or

distorted thought patterns, which can be a particular problem with drinkers and stimulant users, the person should be calmly and insistently asked to return when sober. Attempting to work in a cognitive–behavioural way is not likely to succeed in this situation.

LIsten
- If you stay, listen to what is being said as this is calming. Do not respond with evaluative comment. Encourage the other person to tell their full story by the use of short non-verbal prompts and paraphrasing. Show you are paying attention.
- Do not crowd. Allow good personal space.

VERify
- If seeing someone for the first time when they are angry, personalise the situation. Give your name and ask theirs.
- Check out the details of the problem. Ask and listen. Repeat the details to check your understanding.

Concentrate
- This tells the other person you care.
- Ignore the phone/others.

Awareness
- Watch the other person's body language: change tack or retreat if the tension seems to rise. If they speak with a quieter voice and appear less tense, this is a good sign.
- Watch your own body language. It must be assured but non-threatening.

Respond
- Ensure they know that you understand the facts and are able to see things from their point of view. Accurate empathy is very calming. Clarify anything you still do not understand. Do not hide behind your status, and do not begin to suggest that you will hand the problem over to someone else to deal with unless it would meet the client's needs better.

End. Part only after you have
- clarified the concern;
- determined what the priorities are;
- been honest about what you will do;

- advised further action;
- reviewed the situation;
- written down important points (dates/details/action); and
- satisfied the other person (if possible).

Teaching personal anger management

Anger management may be appropriate

(1) for those who persistently avoid anger; and
(2) for those who are chronically angry.

Some timid people need reassuring that it is normal and appropriate to feel and express anger, and this can be done without endangering others. Those who repeatedly suppress their anger may get trampled by more aggressive individuals. Families of substance users often try to avoid being angry with the drinker or drug user after sobriety has been achieved. But this allows resentment to build up and remain simmering under the surface, which can be far more destructive than an angry outburst.

Some people with chronic anger regularly take substances which suppress emotional responses, such as opiates, and their normal anger management skills atrophy. Those who use alcohol or drugs in this way usually have a history of uncontrollable outbursts of anger, which concerns them and may make them a danger to others. Sometimes aggressive behaviours are discovered by disclosure from a partner in treatment. Sensitive inquiry about domestic violence or reasons for anxiety/depression may reveal a third party problem requiring engagement.

Education about drug use
People with poor aggression control must be advised that some drugs will make this problem worse, particularly alcohol, benzodiazepines and stimulants such as amphetamine and cocaine in high doses. Although a person's history is the best predictor of violence, individuals with no history of violence may become aggressive when exposed to both life stresses and one of the above drugs.

As we have shown in Chapter 3 genetic factors may influence aggression (Cloninger type 2). Further research (Graham et al., 1997) suggests that at a biological level there is a relative dysfunction of the neurotransmitters 5-hydroxytryptamine (5-HT) and gamma-aminobutyric acid (GABA). That alcohol-induced aggression might also work through these receptor sites is a promising explanation. There is a clear relationship between diminished 5-HT metabolism in the central nervous system (CNS) and poor control of aggressive impulses. Also, through its inhibitory action on GABA, alcohol inhibits fear and may in turn encourage the expression of aggressive behaviour that is normally inhibited (Gray, 1987). Alcohol also impairs higher order information processing (Peterson *et al.*, 1990) which may also reduce inhibitory control and attention to inhibitory cues. Drinking seems to produce greater aggressive responses in people who easily become aggressive, and this problem is increased by heavy drinking.

Although low doses of benzodiazepines and small quantities of alcohol individually have minimal effects on aggression individually, the combination of the two can dramatically increase aggressive behaviour (Bond *et al.*, 1997). Their disinhibitory effects can also exacerbate the effects on behaviour of a number of other substances.

Learning to cope with anger

A safe environment is necessary if anger management training is to be undertaken. Probation services are normally well set up to cater for this.

Aggression is primarily a social behaviour, and the way in which people appraise a situation will influence how they feel and behave. Thus a cognitive–behavioural approach, utilising the table in Appendix 20 can be a useful aid towards management.

Therapy is usually easiest with those who have a narrow band of anger. The woman who is generally easygoing but rages about her husband's cocaine use, or those who control their anger with women but not men, have anger management skills they are already utilising. Many people have tried various tactics to limit their anger and it is valuable to discover what methods apart from substance use have worked the best. But if you ask people how

they have tried to control their anger, the response 'I never have', has an ominous ring. Are they unaware of their anger? Do they feel it is impossible to control? Or have they been forced to come and see someone against their wishes?

Specific patterns of anger and their underlying thoughts can be identified by use of the Anger Inventory (Potter-Efron & Potter-Efron, 1991).

THE ANGER INVENTORY
Here are 20 statements that people often make about their anger. Read each one of them and then circle a number from 1 to 5.

1 – This statement does not apply to me at all.
2 – This statement is true once in a while.
3 – This statement is somewhat true for me.
4 – This statement is frequently true.
5 – This statement applies to me a great deal.

(1) I try never to get angry.
  1 2 3 4 5

(2) I am very uncomfortable whenever anyone else gets angry.
  1 2 3 4 5

(3) When I get angry at somebody, I may say something about it but not directly to them.
  1 2 3 4 5

(4) People often tell me I'm mad when I don't see any signs of anger.
  1 2 3 4 5

(5) I get so mad sometimes I just explode.
  1 2 3 4 5

(6) I blow up a lot when I get angry.
  1 2 3 4 5

(7) I get mad so I can get what I want.
  1 2 3 4 5

(8) I try to scare others with my anger.
  1 2 3 4 5

(9) I hang onto my anger for a long time.
  1 2 3 4 5

(10) I have a hard time forgiving people.
  1 2 3 4 5

(11) I often feel outraged about what people try to do for me or others.

   1   2   3   4   5

(12) I become very angry when I defend my beliefs.

   1   2   3   4   5

(13) I get angry when someone insults me.

   1   2   3   4   5

(14) I become angry when I feel 'bad' about myself or inadequate.

   1   2   3   4   5

(15) I get angry with people who are more successful than I am.

   1   2   3   4   5

(16) I am a jealous person.

   1   2   3   4   5

(17) I like the strong feelings that come with my anger.

   1   2   3   4   5

(18) Sometimes I get mad just for the excitement.

   1   2   3   4   5

(19) I just can't break the habit of anger.

   1   2   3   4   5

(20) I seem to get angry all the time.

   1   2   3   4   5

(From Potter-Efron, R. T. & Potter-Efron, P. S. (1991) *Anger, Alcoholism and Addiction: Treating Individuals, Couples and Families.* Table 4, p. 83. New York: W. W. Norton & Co, Inc. Copyright 1991. Reprinted with permission from W. W. Norton & Co, Inc.)

This questionnaire throws up the following anger patterns:

questions	1 & 2	anger avoidance
questions	3 & 4	passive aggression
questions	5 & 6	explosive anger
questions	7 & 8	instrumental anger
questions	9 & 10	resentment
questions	11 & 12	moral anger
questions	13 & 14	shame-based anger
questions	15 & 16	envy and jealousy
questions	17 & 18	excitatory anger
questions	19 & 20	habitual anger

Therapy for *anger avoidance* (questions 1–4) may involve helping people express some anger safely, but in all other circumstances this approach should be avoided. Anger management, where anger appears to be excessive because control is poor, involves containment of anger. Ventilation of anger simply rehearses it and ultimately increases overall levels of anger (Tavris, 1989).

Those with *explosive anger* may need help to recognise their feelings and know when to take time out, e.g. by leaving the room. They need to be able to spot when an outburst is coming and find ways of defusing situations which provoke their anger. Clients with antisocial personality disorder are most likely to *use anger instrumentally*, but few will admit that they use anger intentionally as this is not generally acceptable in society. Treatment may focus on the ultimate negative consequences of manipulating others with anger such as a build-up of resentment and values that conflict with the use of instrumental anger. *Resentment* can be viewed as unresolved initial displeasure that has changed into long-term dislike or even hatred. Those that feel powerless to change something may end up feeling this way. *Moral anger* is often a positive force that can be used constructively, but it can be dangerous if it is used to justify aggression. Rage is a common defence against *shame*, giving a strong message that others should stay away. Shame-prone individuals typically show contempt so that others may share their deep humiliation. As self-esteem improves shame-based anger will recede.

Envious people resent the success of others, taking it as a repudiation of their own good qualities. *Jealousy* involves efforts to guard and protect that which is perceived to belong to someone. This includes material possessions and interpersonal relationships. Very jealous people become obsessed with their need to control the object of their jealousy (Othello syndrome) and treatment is extremely difficult. It may be part of a paranoid mental illness requiring expert intervention. *Excitatory anger* has close links with substance use. Some people use anger to get high and feel alive and energised when irate. Their anger excites, exhilarates and even intoxicates them and alcohol or drugs may be used to increase these anger sensations further.

Anger may gain control over people who just wanted some excitement in their lives, and become *habitual anger* – a compulsive and unmanageable behaviour pattern. Many chronically angry people have been the victims of physical, sexual and/or emotional abuse. Substance use to contain anger of any of the above types can also become habitual. Chronically angry people and those with ingrained habits of containing or expressing anger may need long-term help to change their well-established links between thoughts, feelings and behaviour.

Dealing with depression

Depression as a psychiatric disorder is fully dealt with in Chapter 16 but lesser degrees of depression are also important to address because they interfere with the recovery of substance users. Unfortunately milder depression and even major depressive illness are both commonly overlooked by those working with substance users. A psychiatric opinion should be sought for

- those with severe unipolar depression;
- the suicidal;
- those with bipolar mood disorder (see Chapter 16); and
- depression in pregnancy or the post-natal period.

If there is significant depression it is important to ask about a past history of bipolar mood disorder. Specific treatments may be indicated which are different from the management of depression alone. Clients with bipolar mood disorder have a history of episodes of abnormal elevations of activity levels, abnormally elevated self-esteem and mood or other features that can be considered to be the opposite of depression. They swing between a highly excited state known as hypomania, and severe depression. But there may be long periods of months or even years between these phases when they appear well. Milder and more frequent forms of such mood changes are seen in some personalities and can make life difficult and unpredictable. Such attributes are difficult to elucidate in the context of substance use. Learning to recognise mood swings

is important for mobilising appropriate coping responses.

Occasional suicidal ideation is not unusual in those who are depressed, but those who feel there is a serious risk that they might commit suicide warrant immediate urgent psychiatric referral and assessment.

Lesser degrees of depression should not be ignored. The distorted negative thinking and behaviour changes, which are associated with major depressive disorders, also occur in less florid depressive illness. Even mild depression is important in substance users because it interferes with the recovery process. Associated negative thought patterns impair motivation and committed involvement in treatment. Many drug users and drinkers become labelled as being unmotivated (and are occasionally denied help because of this) when in fact they are really depressed. Some people drink to help them deal with depression. Others develop physical symptoms relating to depression. Distorted negative thinking may impair motivation of substance users, stop individuals contemplating change, interfere with the setting of goals and prevent movement towards personal goals that have already been established. If there is no light at the end of the tunnel, most clients will not wish to move forward or work on their problems, and some may even sabotage therapeutic endeavour. Efforts to help substance users with lesser degrees of depression reassess their negative thought patterns are important to the recovery process.

The symptoms of depression

Affective symptoms. Depressed mood or sadness, and loss of interest and pleasure may vary at different times of the day (diurnal variation in mood). Depressed people typically, but not invariably, suffer low mood states in the mornings. At these times nothing seems enjoyable, not even experiences that previously elicited positive feelings, including work, recreation, social interactions, sexual activity and so on.

Cognitive symptoms. Depressed people commonly see themselves as worthless and incompetent and they are critical of their own acts and characteristics. They feel hopeless about the future and view their lives as being bleak and unrewarding. In addition to such negative thinking patterns there is often impairment of concentration (particularly when reading or watching television), and impaired decision-making and memory. Poor concentration may be due to distraction by irrelevant thoughts or by a slowing down of mental processes, which is another feature of depression. Simple decisions are often viewed as mountainous obstacles.

Behavioural symptoms result from the associated apathy and loss of motivation that is characteristically associated with depression. Depressed individuals withdraw from social activities and in severe cases may stay in bed for prolonged periods. Psychomotor changes may occur when movements may be slowed down, faces show little animation, there is poor eye contact, and speech is slowed and monotonous. Agitated depression, however, is accompanied by anxiety when the reverse occurs and, although they are depressed, people are restless, fidget, and make repeated hand movements and gestures. Speech, however, is not increased in agitated depression.

Physical symptoms include poor appetite, reduced energy, a feeling of listlessness and lethargy, and sleep problems. Those who are depressed often report early morning waking – waking up at about 4–5 AM and have difficulty going back to sleep. Other sleep problems may occur, such as difficulty falling asleep, staying asleep or having too much sleep.

Treatment

Psychiatric referral for medication with or without *hospitalisation* is indicated for those whose depression is moderate, severe or unresponsive to other interventions, the suicidal, and those with bipolar mood disorder. Additional psychological treatment using Cognitive–Behavioural Therapy (CBT) may sometimes be of value in unipolar depression (Hollon *et al.*, 1992).

Where depression is a psychological problem not requiring psychiatric services, CBT can be used to effect symptom change from four domains: affect (mood), cognition, behaviour and physical func-

tioning. It may surprise some people to discover that physical functioning is open to change with CBT, but physical symptoms tend to be more intrusive in depressed people or they may be psychosomatic. These adverse effects may be reduced by the use of CT. Physical functioning will also improve as depression lifts. With moderate and mild depression many of these secondary effects will be absent.

Cognitive Therapy for depression
Before the mid-1970s, it was believed that the cognitive and behavioural disturbances associated with depression were the consequences of a primary disturbance of mood, and were thus not appropriate targets for treatment in their own right. The work of a number of psychologists changed this, and Beck's CT (Beck *et al.*, 1979) is now one of the most widely adopted and extensively evaluated of all treatments for depression. This views depression primarily as a thought disorder characterised by a profound negative bias, including expectations of negative consequences of the client's own personal behaviour, and a negative view of self, context and goals. A number of other biological, developmental, social and psychological variables can also influence the development of negative thinking and depressive illness. However, the cognitive and behavioural aspects of depression are the most open to adaptation.

To distort incoming information in line with pre-existing conceptual frameworks is not in itself abnormal (Nisbett & Ross, 1980). Everybody does it at least to some degree. But persistent negative thinking leads to depression, which in turn deepens negative thinking bias, forming a vicious circle. Negative thoughts often appear as spontaneous automatic thoughts, but in fact they are always the end product of inaccurate pre-existing concepts and other influences which distort the thinking process. Early experience commonly moulds such assumptions, and there are usually trigger factors which stimulate the production of negative automatic thoughts.

Some depressed people, including those who have had traumatic past problems such as physical or sexual abuse, may need further help later. While CBT can be a useful treatment on its own for trauma (Follette *et al.*, 1998), it can also be a useful adjunct to other therapies helping those with post-traumatic stress disorder (PTSD) to confront and deal with painful past memories, and preparing them to utilise other appropriate psychotherapy.

Beck's cognitive model of depression has three elements: *'cognitive triad', faulty information processing* and *negative self-schemas.*

Cognitive triad. Part of the process of assessing depression should be to pick up negative thinking in the three areas of the cognitive triad: the clients' views of themselves; their thoughts about the world (including the local environment); and their opinions as to the future.

A negative self-concept may initially arise from past difficulties unrelated to substance use or it may be the direct result of dependence on drink and drugs. If people see themselves as weak or helpless, they are unlikely to even attempt to resist craving or to try to overcome their dependence. If they feel unlovable or a total failure, they may say to themselves, 'What is the use of even trying?' Negative thoughts such as 'I have no friends, nobody wants to know me' may stop people seeking out the extra social support they need to become abstinent. Sometimes negative thinking is coupled with a general lack of self-efficacy, and the perceived inability to deal with ordinary daily living stops people beginning to tackle their chemical dependency. The thought 'I can't handle all these demands on me' is typical.

A negative view of the world and the local environment may equally interfere with the recovery process. It may lead to procrastination and delay in tackling their problems. 'If it wasn't that I'm trapped in this horrible neighbourhood . . . ' or 'If my wife was more supportive, instead of going off with her friends . . . ' or 'If my partner stopped criticising me and watching me all the time . . . I would sort all my problems out'. The negative side of anything that happens in the world is exaggerated and positive attributes and events tend to be suppressed.

A negative view of the future such as 'I will never be able to stop using', 'The future is hopeless', 'There is nothing to look forward to' may prevent someone even trying. A lack of belief in one's own ability to change is common in long-term substance

users particularly if they have tried and failed to become drug-free on a number of occasions in the past. Yet with the right help this, too, is amenable to CT.

Faulty information processing. The mental processing of thoughts and information is commonly biased but depressed people are particularly selective in what they attend to. They commit logical errors by leaping to conclusions that are not warranted. These processing errors occur because of pre-existing beliefs and assumptions. They *see* what they expect to *see*, and believe those things that support their pre-existing beliefs. Thus negative thinking tends to perpetuate and justify itself.

Negative self-schemas. The term *schemas* refers to outline representations in memory that serve as a mental filter, guiding the selection, interpretation and recall of information. All human thought is directed by schemas, whether or not a person is depressed. They are essential to all human information processing, improving the efficiency of sifting vast quantities of information into meaningful interpretations and selectively attending to those bits of information that may be useful. Having selected such information, schemas then help fill in the *missing* bits according to what is expected. For instance, we might recognise a friend by the fact that he is tall and has dark hair and use this information to pick him out from a crowd. However, errors are possible and closer inspection may show that the person first selected was not who we thought it was. In depression mental schemas lead to the selection and interpretation of information that fits pre-existing negative beliefs. Thus only confirmatory negative information is taken in, even when there is a bank of accumulated evidence to the contrary. For instance, depressed people may feel that they are incompetent. Any evidence that supports this belief is selectively accepted and stored. Past mistakes are recalled and highlighted while evidence of competence is ignored, even though it may considerably outweigh the one or two mistakes that have been made.

Challenging negative thoughts

Having identified a negative thought, clients can be taught to ask themselves 'Is this a distortion of what really is happening?'; 'What is the evidence for this?'; 'Is there another way to look at it?'

Challenging interpretations of events and testing beliefs can occur at different levels. A superficial level challenge might be: 'If he didn't telephone it doesn't mean that he doesn't like me', whereas a challenge at the level of core beliefs about self-worth might be: 'If someone doesn't like me it doesn't mean that I'm no good' or 'It's not necessary to be valued by everybody for everything I do in order to be a worthwhile person.' Homework utilising these concepts and asking the client to complete Appendix 20 in the time period between sessions is one of the best ways of helping the client move forward.

Behavioural interventions
CBT for depression may include behavioural interventions such as pleasant events scheduling (Lewinsohn *et al.*, 1982) and the giving of rewards.

Cognitive Therapy for positive outcome expectancies

Beliefs about the positive effects of using substances were originally redefined by Marlatt and Gordon (1985) as positive outcome expectancies. They are often a reason why people continue to drink or take drugs. Like beliefs in other areas, they are open to reassessment with professional help, and various techniques such as 'On a scale of 1–100 how much do you believe that statement?' help demonstrate to people that they do hold areas of doubt. Belief systems are cognitive mechanisms which people commonly use to try to remove doubt from their minds. However, there is always a degree of ambivalence. If areas of doubt are explored sensitively and empathetically, in many cases, positive outcome expectancies will be generated.

A drinker or drug user's positive outcome expectancies such as 'helps me relax' may be identified through Janis and Mann's (1977) Decisional Balance (see Chapter 5 and Appendix 9). A list of positive outcome expectancies unique to the substance user may be found in the complementary boxes 'advantages of using drugs/drinking' and 'disadvantages of stopping'.

Enhancing self-esteem

William James, a well-known nineteenth-century psychologist, stated that good self-esteem has its 'taproot' in efficacy and is earned through competence and achievement of personal targets (James, 1983). But he saw it to be dependent on achievement and competence only in those areas that are personally important:

> I, who for the time, have staked my all on being a psychologist, am mortified if others know much more about psychology than I. But I am contented to wallow in the grossest ignorance of Greek. My deficiencies there give me no sense of personal humiliation at all. Had I 'pretensions' to be a linguist, it would have been just the reverse.

Later psychologists viewed self-esteem from a number of different areas (love and acceptance by others, power, ethical standards, etc.) and dimensions (direction, intensity, stability, etc.), but many are now returning to James' original view.

Certainly self-esteem is unduly low in those who are depressed, and may be open to reappraisal. Self-punishment and self-destructive behaviour are common ways in which poor self-regard becomes manifest. Low self-esteem can block progress. If you do not believe yourself to be a worthwhile person, there may seem to be no point in attempting recovery.

Self-esteem will be enhanced as the individual makes progress towards recovery so long as abstinence is not the only goal. If drug use and drink problems are properly understood in their holistic context, recovery can be viewed as a process during which a number of goals are successfully achieved. During this process, if substance users are given credit for their successes, treated with respect and feel that they are understood, then their self-esteem will begin to rise.

Improving self-efficacy

Effective personal functioning is more than knowing what to do and being motivated to do it. The belief that one has the ability to achieve it is central to whether action is taken. Many long-standing drug users and drinkers have come to believe that they cannot cope with life without drink or drugs, and so will not attempt to stop even when highly motivated to do so. Dependent drinkers with a high sense of self-efficacy achieve a relatively high rate of sobriety (Rychtarik *et al.*, 1992). Similarly the stronger the belief of self-efficacy instilled by treatment, the more successful are opiate users in staying off drugs (Gossop *et al.*, 1990). It is clear that the enhancement of self-efficacy aids the recovery process, but like any deeply ingrained belief system it can be extremely difficult to effect change in this area by cognitive methods alone. Recently a method of enhancing self-efficacy through Motivational Interviewing (MI) has been described (Miller & Rollnick, 2002).

Using Motivational Interviewing to enhance self-efficacy

In a manner similar to promoting motivation to change, MI can also be used to enhance confidence to change thereby improving self-efficacy. Again it is a collaborative exercise between the counsellor and the drinker or drug taker utilising the four MI principles of expressing empathy, developing discrepancy, rolling with resistance and supporting self-efficacy. One might think it strange to include *supporting self-efficacy*, but it is unlikely that the individual feels totally unable to change. In order to enhance confidence, Miller and Rollnick (2002) recommend self-efficacy be treated as an ambivalent issue. Each person has arguments within themselves as to why they could change and why this cannot happen.

There are three major traps to avoid. The first is to take over and tell the individual what to do and how to do it. Information and advice may be given as long as the client is clearly free to take or leave it. Just as MI is a directive counselling approach with a clear goal to change substance use behaviour, so too can directive advice about self-efficacy be given within an MI context as long as there is consonance (dancing together) and not dissonance (wrestling). The second trap is not taking an expressed lack of confidence seriously, responding instead with re-

assurance. The third is to fall into and share the person's perception of helplessness or hopelessness.

Having avoided these three traps, open questions can be used to explore the individual's ambivalence with the aim of eliciting the person's own ideas, experiences and perceptions that are consistent with an ability to change.

> How might you go about making this change?
> What would be a good first step?
> What obstacles do you foresee, and how might you deal with them?
> What gives you some confidence that you can do this?

It can be helpful to ask people to scale their answers numerically from 0 to 10. Another way to enhance confidence is to tap into past successes:

> When in your life have you made up your mind to do something, and did it? It might be something new you learned, or a habit that you quit, or some other significant change that you made in your life. When have you done something like that?

If several examples can be found, this strengthens confidence more. Another route is to ask about personal strengths and resources that may be helpful in making the desired change:

> What is there about you, what strong points do you have that could help you succeed in making this change?

A final method is through brainstorming any possible solution. Past failures should be reframed as attempts. Smokers usually have three or four goes at giving up before they are successful. It is normal to have a number of failed attempts.

If the individual is struggling with the practicalities of self-efficacy, it may be helpful to think hypothetically: 'Suppose this one big obstacle was removed, then how might you go about making this change?'

When MI is used to enhance motivation, one objective is to stimulate the client to talk in a positive way and persuade himself or herself. Just as *change talk* is a meaningful predictor of behaviour change, so *confidence talk* is a good predictor of self-efficacy change. When confidence talk does occur it is important to respond in a way that reinforces it. Reflective summarisation and other methods used to reinforce change talk are equally appropriate for confidence talk. MI is a useful method of enhancing self-efficacy and appears to be a promising new way forward.

Success also enhances self-efficacy

Repeated practice of self-control in the face of strong enticements strengthens efficacy to reduce drinking (Rohsenow *et al.*, 1990–91). As Bandura (1997) points out, this can be interpreted as extinction of conditioned responses by conditioning theorists, but sociocognitive theorists would see it as enhancement of self-regulatory capabilities.

Self-efficacy is often situation-specific. Rist and Watzl (1983) showed that subjects with weak self-efficacy in alcohol-related situations were significantly more likely to relapse than subjects displaying strong self-efficacy in the same alcohol-related situations. Bandura (1982) defined self-efficacy as 'a cognitive evaluation of one's ability to cope with a specific high-risk situation'. It is about belief in the control that people have over their own lives and this may vary according to circumstances. Women may view themselves as good mothers, but may also believe they are unable to cope successfully in a given situation without drinking or taking drugs. Those who are highly successful in several areas apart from their substance use – for instance, the successful businessman and good family man who has a cocaine problem – are often easier to help, because they believe more in their own abilities in other areas. Confidence in handling situations where there is low self-efficacy takes time, but success on one occasion makes people stronger for the next. High-risk situations, where a *slip* can be anticipated, should be avoided by drinkers and drug users who are abstinent and by opiate users on a substitute prescription. At some point, however, a high-risk situation is bound to be encountered, and successfully avoiding a slip-up will further increase the self-efficacy of the drinker or drug user.

The concept of a variable *locus of control* was first described by Rotter (1966). There may be cultural or experiential factors which influence the position of this locus of control. For instance, the fatalistic beliefs of the Hindu religion may lead to a low sense of self-efficacy to change life events. In contrast too high a sense of control over one's own abilities to cope can lead to a destructive downfall. Ideally one's locus of control should be high, but realistic (Figure 14.1).

Someone who has experienced a significant period of sobriety in the past is likely to have good self-efficacy if the circumstances of that time were to be replicated. Sometimes professionals may have unrealistic expectations of the ability of a patient or client to overcome addiction to alcohol or drugs. For instance, it would be completely unrealistic to expect someone with little or no social support and an uninterrupted 14-year history of drug addiction to detoxify successfully in the community over a two-week period. Just as King Canute demonstrated to his subjects that he did not have control over the incoming tide, so professionals should listen to their clients' views about their own self-efficacy and allow them to judge when the time is right to come off a substitute opiate prescription. If they feel the need to continue on methadone maintenance, they should be enabled to do so. Professionals working with substance users will find that if attention is paid to improving other biopsychosocial factors, for most people the time will eventually come when they are ready to detoxify. In some cases a low locus of control caused by poor self-efficacy may hold them up. This may be open to improvement with CT as well as MI. For others it may be an accurate assessment at the time, but later on, given enough support and improved coping skills, self-efficacy will rise. Specific help with coping skills or social skills training in those areas of vulnerability may sometimes be all that is

| Low | | Ideal | High |

Figure 14.1   Locus of control

needed to enable them to achieve success. People become more able to change as they become more competent.

Conclusion

Professionals working with substance users have an important role to help reduce harm from the psychological problems described in this chapter. A good empathetic working relationship with the drinker or drug user is essential. No one should be allowed to attribute past failures to weakness, lack of will-power, moral or other personal failings. They should be advised that success can come to anyone through appropriate changes in thinking and behaviour. The division of necessary tasks into manageable units with achievable goals and the provision of ample positive feedback help individuals gain confidence. Cognitive interventions through reappraisal of automatic thoughts and underlying belief systems when combined with practical help to improve life skills are a potent force for positive change, and should be an essential part of the recovery process for most substance users.

Chapter 15
Working with Families

Introduction

In spite of the fact that many workers in the drug and alcohol field think of substance users as being on their own, unsupported by their families, in fact the reverse is more often true. It has been known for a long time that, compared to others without a substance use problem, drinkers and drug users are more likely to be in close contact with their families. Perhaps this is an indication of the very real concern and distress which families feel about a son or daughter who is drinking heavily or taking drugs. It is also an acknowledgement by substance users that families can help them. In a US study, Eldred and Washington (1976) showed that heroin users rated their families of origin or in-laws as most likely to be helpful to them in their attempts to give up drugs; their second choice was their opposite sex partners. Vaillant (1966) showed that 59% of 30-year-old drug users in New York lived with their parents, or with another female blood relative such as a grandmother or a sister. Similar figures have been demonstrated from other parts of the world: England 62%, Italy 80%, Puerto Rico 67% and Thailand 80% (Stanton, 1982). This situation appears to continue today.

Families that are functioning well are in a prime position to offer the right sort of support to substance users. In a five-year follow-up study of drug users, Levy (1972) found that those who were successful in overcoming their drug problem usually had good family support. In the UK enhanced support for families can be obtained nationally and locally through AdFam, local family support groups and the twelve-step groups Al-Anon (for the families of alcoholics), Al-Ateen (for their teenage children) and Families Anonymous (FA) (for the families of drug users). More dysfunctional families may be best aided by family therapy.

Although working with families can be a very helpful addition to the range of treatment interventions for substance use, there are of course limits to the extent to which a drinker or drug taker can be influenced by family members. Close family members, cohabitees and significant others must all learn how to cope with their own feelings about the addictive behaviour and its consequences. They must learn to find ways of improving the quality of their own lives, for by looking after themselves and making their own lives as normal and psychologically healthy as possible they will be making it easier when the drinker or drug taker decides to change.

There are different ways that families can be involved in the treatment process. They may be able to prevent drug and alcohol problems/dependence developing. But if these have developed:

- they may need support or professional help themselves;
- they may be able to prepare and aid professional help-seeking by the substance user; and
- they may work together with professionals to improve outcomes for the family member who has an alcohol or drug problem.

Many of the self-help groups and support agencies are helpful, not just in giving support, but in helping families function better. This includes reducing guilt, and helping achieve what some agencies term *tough love*, a balance between being too soft and too hard with the substance user. In the early days some groups made the mistake of being too directive, e.g. by telling parents to force their drug-using children to leave home. If parents do this, it is important that it is their own decision to do so, and that they make it clear that they still love their son or daughter but they can no longer tolerate the drinking or drug-taking. Parents should understand that, although forcing their son or daughter to leave might well increase his or her motivation to do something about a drink or drug problem, the reduction in support will also make abstinence more difficult to achieve.

Parenting programmes to prevent young people developing substance use problems and/or dependence

Help for the parents of young children with conduct disorder

When parents of children with conduct disorder, aggression and other antisocial behaviour are given appropriate professional help, many of those children can be prevented from developing substance use problems and criminal behaviour in later life. This has been shown to be the case for behaviourally disturbed children as young as seven years old.

Poverty, parent psychopathology, parent criminality, parent substance use, divorce and parental conflict are all family factors which predict child conduct disorders (Offord *et al.*, 1986; Dodge *et al.*, 1990). Such factors can have a deleterious effect upon the way in which parents handle child conduct disorders. In these circumstances parents often resort to harsh physical punishment and/or are inconsistent in the boundaries that are set. Inconsistent limits may allow a child's whining and refusal to comply to be rewarded by cessation of parental demands, reinforcing non-compliance (Snyder & Patterson, 1995). Sometimes negative parent–child interactions escalate in a stepwise manner, each party becoming increasingly aversive (Patterson, 1982).

Non-compliance may result in the parent exhibiting aggressive behaviour towards the child, and the child may adopt this as a model in later life. The combination of repeated negative parent–child interactions and the social isolation that accompanies poverty, marital separation and lack of

social support can lead to depression in a parent (Webster-Stratton, 1990). The depressed parent is less likely to interact with the child in the positive ways that are required to provide the supportive activities that promote academic readiness, emotional control and other social skills (Greenberg *et al.*, 1991). Hence the high-risk child is not only poorly prepared for the social and academic demands of school but in addition has a well-developed capacity for aggression and non-compliance.

The same conduct disorders occur in the school environment and impair the young person's ability to derive maximal benefit from the education system. This impairment may worsen if there is an absence of family support for good behaviour and successful performance at school. Rejection by the young person's peer group will compound the situation. Repeated negative parent–child interactions at home may result in a misinterpretation of social interactions with peers, and the child may jump to false conclusions about the hostile intentions of his or her peers (Dodge *et al.*, 1990). Rejection by peers is likely to be met with mistrust and more aggression (Dodge & Coie, 1987). Such aggressive rejected children are less likely than their classmates to be supported by their teachers (Campbell, 1991), feeding into an ongoing cycle of poor academic performance, conduct disorder and rejection by both peers and adults. Later this may lead to alienation from the values and standards of mainstream society and social exclusion (Hawkins & Weiss, 1985).

In the USA training programmes for parents of young children with behavioural disturbances have been shown by longitudinal studies to reduce the risk of conduct disorder in the children, both in the short term (Anastopoulos *et al.*, 1993) and in the longer term (McMahon, 1994). In Canada a controlled two-year intervention scheme starting at the age of seven and involving parent training, child social skills training, fantasy play stimulation, television education and teacher support was conducted on 43 families with disruptive boys. Longitudinal studies showed a statistically significant reduction in early adolescence (11–15 years) of gang membership, significantly fewer 15-year-olds reported getting drunk or taking drugs in the previous 12 months, and the frequency of stealing, vandalism and substance use was significantly less from ages 10–15 years. From the age of 13–15 years there were increasing differences in reported arrests, the treated group reporting significantly fewer arrests both of themselves and their friends (Tremblay *et al.*, 1996).

Help for the parents with older children who have conduct disorder or substance use problems

Multisystemic therapy (MST)

MST is a community-based method of delivering behavioural therapy and Cognitive–Behavioural Therapy (CBT) interventions to young people via the family, peer group and school, with the main focus on the family (see Chapter 3). The MST assessment process views family functioning and parenting style from two dimensions – *warmth* and *control*. The *warmth* dimension reflects verbal and non-verbal behaviours that are emotional in tone, ranging from warmth to rejection. Warm parents are relatively accepting and nurturing and use frequent positive reinforcement when they interact with their children. This creates an emotional bond which is protective. Parents who are rejecting and low in nurturance, relatively hostile, and who tend to use criticism and even aggression do not bond properly with their children. These children then have difficulty having positive experiences with others and may develop interpersonal and behavioural difficulties. They may also have difficulty trusting, responding positively to and developing empathy for others.

The *control* dimension teaches children frustration tolerance and socially acceptable behavioural norms. These might include the avoidance of aggression, cooperation with others and respect for authority. If behavioural limits are not taught at home this will encourage the child to adopt social norms that promote aggression and non-cooperation in the child's relationships with peers and other people outside the home (Patterson & Stouthamer-Loeber, 1984). The interplay of the balance of parenting style between these two dimensions has important consequences on child behaviour.

Henggeler and colleagues (1998) identify four types of parenting style: authoritative, authoritarian, permissive and neglectful. *Authoritative* parents have a warm relationship with their children, but they also have well-defined rules. They use inductive methods of discipline only when necessary and appropriate. This style of parenting is associated with positive outcomes, including good academic achievement, social responsibility and positive relationships with peers. *Authoritarian* parents on the other hand lack warmth and are overcontrolling and directive, preventing children making their own choices and decisions. Punishments tend to be severe and often physical. Children have poor self-confidence and are socially withdrawn or abnormally aggressive. *Permissive* parents are warm and responsive but exercise too little control so the child's environment is not structured. The children are impulsive, lack social responsibility, and over-value peer norms. Alcohol and drug use is common in this group. *Neglectful* parents have low warmth and poor control and do not respond to age-appropriate behaviour. It is most strongly related to childhood distress and delinquency.

MST interventions steer parents towards the warmth and age-appropriate control as exhibited by authoritative parents. This is achieved through the use of cognitive–behavioural interventions, discussing parenting difficulties, and enabling parents to categorise their reactions and reinforce normal boundaries of acceptable behaviour from their children by operant conditioning.

Factors which sustain ineffective or inappropriate parenting styles are identified. Permissive parenting styles reward and reinforce inappropriate behaviours. Authoritative parents do not give enough rewards and expect behaviour to be kept within strict limit by the use of threats and punishments. A neglectful parenting style gives no boundaries so operant conditioned learning does not occur.

Parents learn to reward good behaviour and back this up with a warm loving atmosphere. Interventions to promote change are tailored to the particular needs and strengths of the parents and family. Parenting styles are not easily changed but positive progress is achieved incrementally with eventual good results.

Help and support for the families themselves

Families with a substance-using member are placed under considerable stress and not all of them cope with this well. To make matters worse they are often labelled co-dependent and feel blamed or stigmatised.

Some families have other problems including substance use by more than one member. Substance use by parents of young children is a particularly important problem to address. Coping skills training and other methods to improve family functioning can be very helpful if appropriately targeted.

Assessment of the appropriateness of family involvement should be undertaken carefully. Despite the great potential for benefit, there is a significant prevalence of a history of childhood emotional or sexual abuse and it may occasionally become clear that ongoing abuse is occurring which is not amenable to therapeutic intervention. Child protection issues may arise with younger service users and issues of separation may become relevant for others. For the majority of clients the involvement of the family can greatly enhance the experience and outcome of treatment.

Co-dependency

The term *co-dependency* was originally coined by those in Alcoholics Anonymous (AA) for someone, usually a family member, who has let another person's behaviour affect him or her to the degree that they have become as obsessional about controlling drinking as the person who is alcohol dependent (Beattie, 1987). Later this was extended to include the family members of drug users. This clearly does occur, but an unfortunate consequence has been that there is now a substantial literature blaming family members for those in their midst who have drink or drug problems (Blechman, 1982; Emmelkamp & deLange, 1983). It has even influenced some of those working with substance users, making it difficult for them to empathise with family members.

Much of the growing professional and popular literature on co-dependency such as *Women Who*

Love Too Much (Norwood, 1986) can be read to imply that the spouse is suffering from an unconscious need or predisposition which led him or her to select a partner who would develop an addiction problem and becomes entrenched with a need for the substance user to continue to drink or take drugs. Some texts are more blaming than others and describe co-dependency as a neurosis, personality disorder or sickness. This is in spite of a review of the evidence which shows that, in general, spouses of current or recovered *alcoholics* are not characterised by neurotic or disturbed personality traits (Nace, 1982).

In an examination of the literature, Gordon and Barrett (1993) uncovered criticisms of the co-dependency concept from 30 different sources describing it as 'conceptually weak and empirically unsubstantiated', 'therapeutically iatrogenic', 'simplistic', 'ethnocentric', 'insensitive to gender issues' and 'the chic neurosis of our time'. They summed up by stating:

> In a close examination of co-dependency theories and the family, there is a great potential to promote blame, to fuel anger and guilt, to follow a narrow focus on pathology and inadequacy, and to reduce individuality and heterogeneity among families touched by addiction and trauma. Perhaps the most serious issue is that the co-dependency movement may serve to divide family members of alcoholics who have been resilient, maintaining a high degree of social and psychological competence despite significant stress. This is not a model that builds on the strength and integrity of the family, or that examines social interactions in an environmental context, but rather a model that judges family and individual processes from a medical and deviance perspective.

Some unskilled proponents of family therapy still attempt to make family members aware of their co-dependency and their denial of it, even with well-balanced supportive families and partners. Referring to the situation in the USA, Levin remarked: 'Today, if you say hello to your spouse, you may be labeled co-dependent' (Levin, 1995). This confrontative approach has divided families and reduced the support available to the drinker or drug user.

Although most of the published work on co-dependency has been in relation to the families of drinkers, it has been applied equally to the families of drug users. Labelling them co-dependent and confronting them with statements that they themselves have become sick, are consciously or subconsciously making things worse, are gaining from this and are in denial is always counterproductive and exacerbates feelings of guilt. It is better to avoid the term co-dependency, and instead intervene in an empathetic and constructive way through family and couples therapy.

The effect of abstinence on the family

The recovery of the individual when abstinence is attained is a time of great change for the family, and family members often have great difficulty adapting without help. Children in particular may be left with emotional deficits when the drinker or drug user abstains. The bond between couples has often altered and this can influence child development. If during active substance use emotional detachment is used by family members as a coping mechanism, children are not able to learn the normal route of control of boundaries of behaviour through modelling. This may lead to confusion and later to conduct disorder. When abstinence is attained, sometimes all that is left appears to be lack of trust and emotional lability, demonstrated through the anger and hostility of other family members.

Family expectations of the effects of abstinence generally remain unfulfilled and this can lead to difficulties. Brown and Lewis (1999) describe how the lack of intimacy that occurred when a drinker was *lost to alcohol* continued when he was newly abstinent:

> At the end of drinking and the beginning of abstinence Hal was struggling within himself and was not available for an intimate partnership with Maggie.

They continue:

> This is often very difficult to accept, for the couple and the therapist. The reality of separateness, both in the terrible downward slide to the 'bottom' of drinking and the often terrible beginning days and weeks of abstinence, runs counter to everyone's belief about how things should be. In fact neither partner is capable of a healthy, intimate bond at this point.

A return to a state of balanced and healthy family functioning may be enabled by good coping strategies as outlined below.

Dealing with parental substance use

Substance use where the parents themselves also drink or take drugs can be a difficult complicating factor and reactions of partners to this may deter or advance progress not only for their partners but also the children. Children are not only at risk of neglect but they should also be classified as *vulnerable* (i.e. they are at high risk of developing substance use problems themselves) if their parents are drinkers or drug users (see Chapter 3). In families where there are young children and the parents use drugs or drink heavily, the treatment of parental substance use should be given priority.

Family coping skills

Some families clearly cope more effectively with a drinker or drug user than others. Skills training for families with poor social and coping skills has been shown to help the family return to a state of balanced and healthy functioning (Moos et al., 1990; Copello et al., 2000). This will not only help the family directly but also indirectly aid a positive outcome for the substance user. Controlled outcome studies have shown that involvement of the partner in social skills and coping skills training also gives enhanced results for the substance user (Gondoli & Jacob, 1990). Partners who have undergone such training have a better understanding of the issues involved and may help, e.g. by suggesting alternative ways of coping with craving.

Moos and colleagues (1990) demonstrated that a supportive family with effective family coping skills is related to success in maintaining abstinence from dependent drinking. Orford and colleagues (1976) identified ten styles of wives' coping behaviour, some of which were associated with a good prognosis for the partner with a drink problem. Responses that implied some bond between the partners, such as emotional demands, were related to improvement in the husband's drinking behaviour. However, some women increased their work and hobby commitments to avoid contact with their husbands, making their own friends and social plans. Such avoidance coping is associated with depression and physical symptoms (Gorman & Rooney, 1979) and has been shown to be related to poorer treatment outcomes for the drinking partners (Steinglass *et al.*, 1987; Anderson & Sabatelli, 1993; Steinglass, 1994). In the situation where a family member is alcohol dependent, Orford (1990) recommends an integrated model of coping skills therapy and family systems therapy as a particularly helpful treatment combination. This would take into consideration both internal and external stressors, the use of alcohol to cope with stress, and the family's attempt to cope with the stress of living with a drinker. Such an approach would encompass a broad range of family dynamics, incorporating the characteristics of individual family members, environmental stresses and intrafamily stresses, as well as providing insights into the inception and most appropriate treatment of problem alcohol use.

It is not always easy to involve family members. Although no family member can be held responsible for the drinker's or drug taker's substance use problem, in all types of family therapy it is important that the family comes to view drinking or drug use as a family problem which they can help resolve. Individual family members can be enabled to look at their own responses and ways of handling the problem, instead of telling the drug user or drinker what he or she should be doing.

Social support for families

Family support groups
Family support groups need to be planned and structured if they are to be successful. If difficult families are put together without proper planning and with no structure, their situations can deteriorate (Vaux, 1983), causing dissatisfaction and disil-

lusionment. There is a considerable difference between a support group and a therapeutic group, and families need to be clear at the outset that the sole purpose of a support group is to enable group members to give and receive support. This will help offset any anger and disillusionment of those who come to a group looking for solutions. Nevertheless, solutions are almost always at the back of every family member's mind. This may be one reason why support groups for the families of drug users often ask for information about drugs. A lack of knowledge about drugs is associated with feelings of powerlessness, but improving or rectifying the knowledge base does not usually make any member of the group feel more powerful. It is the situation that they find themselves in that makes them powerless, for it does not take long for any family member to discover that the only person who is going to stop the drinking or drug use is the drinker or drug user himself or herself.

Structure and size. Family support groups need structure if they are to function usefully. It is possible for groups to set themselves up and run successfully as self-help groups, particularly where there is a structured programme to work to, as is the case with twelve-step family programmes such as Al-Anon or FA. When support groups do not work to such a programme, structure can be provided through a facilitator, whose function is to guide rather than control the group discussions. Workers from the specialist drug and alcohol services sometimes take on this role. The facilitator must be sensitive to the needs of the individual members of the group. Some group members may wish to sit in a corner and just listen, while others, e.g. members in crisis, come with an urgent need to unload their feelings and talk about their own situation. The facilitator must allow enough flexibility for these things to happen, and yet be able to facilitate group interaction without allowing one person to dominate the proceedings or another to be excluded. Sometimes this is best done indirectly by asking such questions as: 'Has anyone in the group had a similar experience?' or 'What would other people have done in that situation?' Sometimes, in spite of good facilitation, group structure can be impaired if groups subdivide creating informal subgroups. This usually occurs because certain members of a group find that they have a particular affinity for each other. Some members meet together for a drink in the pub after the main group has finished meeting. Others telephone each other regularly between meetings. Such liaisons and subgroups have the potential to be disruptive and alienate other members of the main group, preventing the main group from operating in a supportive way to all group members. A good facilitator will recognise when this is starting to happen and will bring it into the open as an item for discussion before a problem has developed. Yet a balance has to be struck, for it is clearly helpful to have the friendship and support of other members of the group outside of the support group meeting. This aspect should be encouraged as long as it does not interfere with the effective functioning of the main group.

Apart from the need for structure, the size of the group is quite important. Too large a group will lead to poor interaction and group dynamics. Too small a group will also not function well. Even with a group the right size, the formation of subgroups can alter the functional size of the group, and so interfere with group working. The ideal size is perhaps seven or eight members. Groups larger than 14 members have a tendency to split into factions, and effective group working then becomes more difficult. Any partner or nuclear family member of a substance user should be welcome to attend support group meetings and the term *family* should be extended to include significant others who have a close relationship with the drug user or drinker. Although people of both sexes are usually invited to attend, women usually predominate and some support groups are comprised entirely of women.

Planning. At its initial meeting the group should decide whether to be *closed* with a fixed time span and membership, or *open* when new members are able to come and go when they choose to do so. The time and frequency of meetings should be arranged so that all group members are able to attend. The venue should be easily accessible by public transport. Self-referral of family members to open groups should be encouraged by professionals, and commonly a successful group gets advertised by word of mouth. With time old members drop out of open groups and unless the number in the group is balanced out by new entries, the group will go into decline.

Every group is different, and the way a support group functions is determined to a large extent by the personalities of the members. Support is achieved by being together with others who are able to understand and empathise with problems caused by a loved one who drinks too much or takes drugs. The distress felt by one family member will be recognised and shared by other members of the support group. The facilitator may at times need to help members expand on what they have said, or explain more clearly what they mean. Sometimes this is best done by reflective listening, e.g. by repeating the last few words of what has been said or by summarising what has been said. The ventilation of feelings can lead to a reduction of emotional distress which can be very therapeutic. The telling of stories ends feelings of isolation, can relieve hopelessness and lessen self-blame and self-doubt (Gold-Steinberg & Buttenheim, 1993). It is liberating and usually makes the speaker feel better and more in control. The process of sharing stories and feelings with the group helps the process of coming to terms with the difficulties surrounding a substance user in the family. Group members must agree to maintain confidentiality at the outset and there should be no pressure to self-disclose. Members of the group are entitled to privacy if they wish it. There may be some very difficult personal or sexual issues which a group would not handle well, and would be better left to discuss on a one-to-one basis with a professional counsellor. Some families gain so much benefit from attending support groups that they do not need any further input. Others manage to stumble along on their own without any help. Many families, particularly the more disturbed ones, would benefit from family therapy if available. Both family support groups and family therapy, when used appropriately and professionally, will indirectly benefit the recovery of the substance user.

A structured day programme for parents with young children

The beneficial effect that structured help for parenting skills can have on the relationships of drug users with their children is shown by a study of recovering drug users who attended a student-centred structured day programme in Liverpool, England (Buchanan & Young, 1998). Many of these parents were concerned that social services would take their children into care. The structured day programme given in Merseyside appears to have been an effective way of averting this. The data on relationships with partners, parents, friends and children is illustrated in Table 15.1. It illustrates the acute social isolation that is often felt by drug users prior to receiving help. The relationships which the drug-using parents had with their own children may in reality have been worse than admitted, for fear of intervention by the social services. Relationships with parents, partner and friends were all rated as barely *okay*. Three months after completing the course there was a positive impact on all relationships, but the most significant improvement was the relationship of parental drug users with their children. Comments made by one woman in chronological order were:

First interview: 'I was very irritable. I needed to be hospitalised, sectioned. I'd have sold my daughter for crack. I even phoned the police to take her away.'
Second interview: 'Very close. Her teacher phoned me to tell me that no child had come on so much in a month.'
Third interview: 'Fine. I've got more patience with her. I set a timetable with her, it's like coming to a job.'

This type of service to help the children of drug-using parents is a good way to aid *vulnerable* groups of young people. It could be replicated in many local service settings.

Family and couples therapy

Like other treatment interventions in the care package, in order to be most cost-effective, family therapy and couples therapy should be appropriately

Table 15.1 Improving the quality of relationships

Quality of relationships	Average rating 0 = very poor 25 = poor 50 = okay 75 = good 100 = very good		
	6 months prior	On entry	On completion
Partners (*n* = 28)	44	68	74
Parents (*n* = 50)	53	70	76
Children (*n* = 36)	67	67	89
Friends* (*n* = variable)	51	63	76

* A number of students said they had no friends and therefore could not answer the question.
(From Buchanan, J. & Young, L. (2000) The war on drugs: a war on drug users? *Drugs: Education, Prevention and Policy*, 7(4), 409–22. Figure 3, p.416. http://www.tandf.co.uk/journals. Adapted from Buchanan, J. & Young, L. (1998) *The Impact of Second Chance Structured Day Programme for Recovering Drug Users: A Student Perspective*. Liverpool: Social Partnership, Transit. Copyright 2000 Taylor & Francis Ltd. Reprinted with permission.)

targeted. Family therapy should be reserved for the situation when the family needs more help than a simple support group. If both partners use substances, treatment is more difficult, but this should not prevent services working with them jointly or singly. However, couples therapy is most helpful when only one partner is a substance user. An improved relationship, where rewards are more meaningful and aid positive contingency management, can have a constructive outcome for the substance user. However, in spite of the need for family or couples therapy it would be wrong for services to be working with the families or partners of substance users if the drug user or drinker did not want this. The exception to this being Unilateral Family Therapy with the substance user in the precontemplation or contemplation stage of change when the family has professional help to coax the substance user into treatment.

The type of family therapy should vary according to the stage of change

The sort of intervention that may be most helpful for families to give may depend entirely upon the substance user's stage of change (Prochaska & DiClemente, 1984):

(1) precontemplation stage
(2) contemplation stage
(3) preparation and action stages
(4) maintenance stage

Precontemplation stage. The family's role should be to provide information and encourage the individual to seek help, both verbally and by behavioural means. Behaviour therapy is particularly useful when the substance user is in precontemplation, denying that there is a problem, especially when it is done via a partner, as the appropriate use of behavioural techniques can reduce the length of this stage to a few months, while, left unaided, it can go on for several years. It is important that drinkers and drug users are not rewarded as a result of their drinking. Sometimes family members or partners will reward drinkers or drug users by pacifying them when they are angry or protecting them

from the adverse consequences of their substance use.

Contemplation stage. The family can continue to aid positive change through behavioural techniques, which should be continued in this phase with appropriate rewards for sobriety and negative reinforcement through the adverse effects of substance use itself. The emphasis should always be to help, but only when the drug user or drinker has decided which way forward he or she wishes to go. If there is indecision, putting pressure on someone to go in one particular direction for help can be counterproductive. There is usually more than one way to achieve success and it is important that the substance user makes his or her own decisions as to which form of help he or she needs.

Preparation and action stages. The family has an important role by providing further information and feedback, by providing reinforcement of behaviour change, by being supportive and by joining in family or marital therapy if this is recommended. Although it is generally helpful for family members to move away from a caretaking and controlling role, there are times when it is useful for them to be in a round-the-clock monitoring or watching schedule, particularly when home detoxification is attempted or for the supervision of disulfiram use or other medication. Family members can also assist in helping drug users and drinkers keep appointments in a sober state, and facilitate their attendance at AA or NA meetings.

Maintenance stage. The family members should continue to reinforce change and continue to change/monitor their own behaviour.

Different models and approaches to family and couples therapy

Evans and Sullivan's model
One useful way of working with dysfunctional families which has been put forward (Evans & Sullivan, 1990) is to consider the ideal family response as the centre-point between two axes. The first axis has the endpoints of *chaos* versus *rigidity* and the intersecting axis has the endpoints of *enmeshment* versus *disengagement* (Figure 15.1).

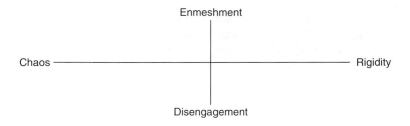

Figure 15.1   The Evans and Sullivan model of family responses to substance use.

Chaotic families are unpredictable, with seemingly inconsistent rules governing their reactions and interactions. In contrast *rigid families* respond in set ways, being inflexible in their responses, even when the situation calls for exceptions. The members of *disengaged families* are emotionally detached from each other and interact as little as possible. *Enmeshed families*, on the other hand, interact too intensely and have poor boundaries. The main therapeutic objectives of family therapy should be to help the family move towards the centre of the two axes, and overcome any other presenting problems of the family. To achieve this family rules need to be consistent but flexible, and family interactions should be caring with clear and appropriate boundaries.

Enmeshment is the most common way in which families of substance users become dysfunctional. It means being trapped by the problem, obsessively searching for solutions. One survey of the families of drug users (Velleman *et al.*, 1993) states:

> The reality for most family members is that they swing from one unsatisfactory position to another; they try one method of coping with what is often an intolerable situation, and then reject that method as 'not working' and try another. Even those who do not swing so violently and attempt to be consistent, have the problem of knowing what to be consistent about. That is, there is uncertainty about whether it is best to engage the problem drug taker or best to disengage and leave him to his own devices; and there is the problem about whether to be 'tough' with the drug taker, or to be 'soft' and caring. Often family members report that it is difficult to get the balance right: i.e. whether to leave or stay, to tell the drug taker to go or not, to continue to

worry about the drug taker or to distance oneself emotionally, to take a tough or a soft line over a variety of issues such as borrowing, helping out in a crisis, coming in answer to a plea for help and so on.

For deeply enmeshed families the Al-Anon suggestion of detaching with love is a helpful way forward. This normally refers to psychological detachment from the problem, rather than physical detachment by throwing someone out.

Disengagement is accompanied by complete emotional detachment. It is the opposite of enmeshment and is equally dysfunctional. It is a form of escape when family members cannot cope with the problems that drinking or drug-taking bring. A degree of detachment may sometimes be helpful, particularly if it enables enmeshed family members to lead more normal lives. However, with complete emotional detachment the rest of the family behaves as if the substance user does not exist. Some families behave in this way even if there is no drinker or drug taker in their midst. It is as if they are neighbours living in large anonymous blocks of flats where no one knows or speaks to any of the others living on the same floor.

For most dysfunctional families there is a combination between two of the axes. *Enmeshed/chaotic* families swing from one emotional extreme to another during their search for solutions. Normal and important family functions are neglected as family members continue to be totally obsessed with the drink or drug problem. Such families are often at their limits of coping and appear to be on the verge of disintegration. Anyone working with an enmeshed/chaotic family will find it an emotionally draining experience. In a *chaotic/disengaged* state the family members have abandoned each other in spite of knowing that other members are not coping with crises. Things are left to get worse. The family members do not interact with each other in any meaningful predictable way and ignore the various crises that occur. *Rigid/enmeshed* families may superficially appear to be functioning reasonably well, but this is a fallacy. By being obsessively controlling and inflexible they stifle any response which could in any way threaten their way of dealing with the substance use problem in their midst, even though they may be making things worse. The *rigid/disengaged* family is no longer a family.

As family members move away from the centre towards the ends of the axes, they become increasingly dysfunctional and inadvertently reinforce drinking or drug-taking behaviour. Homeostasis of the family system at a fixed point near one of these extremes is usually maintained by negative feedback loops between the substance user and the rest of the family. For example, a drinker might say 'I wouldn't be at the pub so often if things were better at home and you stopped criticising me' and family members retort 'We wouldn't be so critical if you didn't go out drinking so often'.

Progress towards the centre of the axes may be achieved by interrupting the negative feedback loops. If this is done by the actions of just one person (e.g. stopping the trips to the pub), it is known as a first order change. If both people involved in the negative feedback loop make changes (in the above example the trips to the pub and the criticisms both stop), it is known as a second order change. First order changes are more subject to relapse, whereas second order changes are more likely to endure because the family system has been strengthened (Anderson & Sabatelli, 1993).

Family systems therapy
Family systems therapy views the drinker's or drug user's problems in terms of a system malfunction of the whole family. The drinker or drug user is just one part of that system. With the help of a trained therapist, the family members focus on their interrelationships and are enabled to make changes which aid the recovery process. Family systems therapy has been known for many years to improve the prospects of recovery of substance users (Orford *et al.*, 1975). It is particularly helpful for young substance users who are still legally under parental control.

If possible several family members should be convened for family systems therapy. If the substance user is an adolescent or a young adult, it can sometimes be helpful to invite senior family members such as grandparents to attend. Sometimes parents resist attending family therapy sessions, fearing that their own use of drink or drugs may be challenged. Indeed they may themselves have a drink or a drug problem and fear discovery, or believe they will be blamed for their son or daughter's behaviour. Guilt is commonly felt by the substance user and by family members. Scapegoating from one to the other is common but this should be countered as it is highly destructive to the therapeutic process. It is essential that the therapist assumes a non-blaming stance towards the entire family and recognises good intentions. It may be helpful to ask other family members to aid recruitment. Family systems therapy should not be undertaken if a drinker or drug user of legal age refuses to attend.

Some family members who have become highly disturbed themselves as a result of the persistent emotional strain that they are under may covertly, or even overtly, sabotage the treatment process. When this happens the way forward is not through confrontation, as this will tend to harden attitudes. The techniques and style of Motivational Interviewing (MI) of rolling with it, but not agreeing with it, should be helpful in such cases. As with MI, accurate empathy is also important.

Other dysfunctional family responses can be approached in a similar way. These may include external referencing, caretaking, self-centredness, control issues, dishonesty, frozen feelings, perfectionism and fear. Family therapy may not only bring relief to the family members concerned, but also indirectly help the substance user instigate positive change. However, overt change does not always occur, and it would be a mistake for the therapist to promote unrealistic expectations of abstinence. The therapist must strike a balance, being positive about the way forward, without blaming current behaviour of any one family member as a cause for the drinking or drug use.

Apart from the useful therapeutic supervisory roles that have been already mentioned, such as facilitating attendance at AA/NA meetings, it is generally helpful for family members to move away from a caretaking and controlling role. The emphasis should always be to help, but only when the drug user or drinker has decided which way forward he or she wishes to go.

When abstinence is finally achieved it often takes a while for the family to accept this. Family members recognise that the chances of relapse are high and may intensify controlling and other dysfunctional behaviours to the disappointment and anger of the drinker or drug user, increasing the risk of relapse or at least providing an excuse for it. Some family members may intentionally provoke relapse, paradoxically to minimise disappointment. If abstinence continues, the next phase is again a difficult one for families. Steinglass and colleagues (1987) describe it as an 'emotional desert'. This applies particularly to enmeshed families who have organised their lives around alcohol or drug use. Such families 'have the sensation of having been cut adrift, loosened from their family moorings, lost in a desert without any landmarks upon which to focus to regain their bearings'. Instead of being joyful they may feel empty and sad, and have been known to say or do things that seem designed to be counterproductive, e.g. 'I liked you better when you were drinking/taking drugs.' Some may even go as far as to buy some alcohol for the abstinent drinker. For this reason it is important that family therapy does not stop when abstinence is achieved.

Behavioural family therapy
Although modern day behavioural family therapy recognises the importance of underlying thought processes as well as behaviours, attention to the modification of the behaviour of family members towards substance users through classical conditioned and operant learning is of crucial importance. The reinforcement of positive substance use behaviour with rewards and the withdrawal of any rewarding reinforcement for negative behaviours have been known for many years to aid the treatment process of the individual substance user in community settings using the Community Re-inforcement Approach (CRA) (Hunt & Azrin, 1973; Sisson & Azrin, 1993). A clear understanding of the principles underlying behavioural therapy by family members so that drinkers and drug users are not rewarded for their substance use is particularly useful in the precontemplation and contemplation stages of change.

Behaviours that make drinking or drug-taking more rewarding include giving more attention or care when substance use occurs, drinking together and engaging in enjoyable activities together during a drinking or drug-taking bout. Billings and colleagues (1979) have shown that in marital relationships where the amount of verbal interaction is low, drinking usually acts to increase the amount of verbal output – an outcome which is rewarding and likely to reinforce drinking behaviour. Sometimes family members or partners will reward drinkers or drug users by pacifying them when they are angry or protecting them from the adverse consequences of their substance use.

More effective ways are required to discourage substance use in a family member. This entails the use of effective rewards by

- helping ensure a good family or marital relationship when the substance user is not drinking or taking drugs.
- withdrawing positive rewarding relationship factors, such as companionship, communication and sex, when the partner or family member concerned is indulging in substance use.
- appropriate timing of rewards. Given at the right time they can help reward success and prevent abstinence being viewed as a punishment. As such they are highly therapeutic contingency management interventions which can help someone move on to sort out their drink or drug problem.
- making drink or drugs more difficult to obtain and avoiding behaviours which enable easier access to substance use.

Conversely behaviours by family members/partners which improve access to drugs and alcohol are counterproductive and will delay the recovery process. Examples include providing more drink during a drinking bout, giving a *hair of the dog* to ease withdrawals or a hangover, providing money for drink or drugs, going out to score drugs or buy drink in order to help ease the substance user's withdrawals.

For most families and partners it is a difficult course to steer. They need to avoid protective and placatory behaviour on the one hand, and punitive and controlling behaviour on the other. Controlling behaviours such as parents 'policing' their sons and daughters to try to keep them away from drink or drugs are very common. Sometimes a family member will provide money to buy street drugs, thinking that it will stop thieving or running up debts with potentially violent criminals. Other counterproductive family behaviours include covering up for the drinker or drug user, searching the house for drugs or bottles of drink and, when they are found, pouring them down the sink or flushing them down the toilet. To do any of these things can prevent the substance user himself or herself from taking responsibility, and he or she may continue to expect someone else to sort out the problem. There may, however, be occasions when the removal of a harmful substance is appropriate to prevent further harm such as overdose or violent behaviour which is a direct risk to the user or to third parties. Other ways of preventing harm such as stopping a family member driving a car when he or she has been drinking is also to be encouraged. Family members should never be criticised for ensuring safety. Such interventions should not be confused with the general principles of a behavioural approach to enable the substance user to change but are part of harm reduction and the setting of meaningful boundaries.

Behavioural couples/marital therapy
Studies have shown that partners can be successfully taught behavioural methods to enhance their relationship (Thomas *et al.*, 1987). In addition McCrady and colleagues (1991) and O'Farrell and colleagues (1992) have shown that behavioural marital/couples therapies which focus not just on alcohol but also on the marital relationship may reduce marital and drinking deterioration during long-term recovery better than individually focused methods. Ensuring a good family or marital relationship when the substance user is not drinking or taking drugs, and withdrawing positive rewarding

relationship factors, such as companionship, communication and sex, when the partner or family member concerned is drinking heavily or starts taking drugs is good contingency management. Care must be taken to ensure that rewards are not given inadvertently at a time when they can be associated with, and thereby reinforce drinking or drug-taking behaviour.

There are other ways, too, that behavioural couples therapy and behavioural family therapy can be useful. Attendance for outpatient follow-up can be improved by behavioural contracting between dependent drinkers and family members (Ossip-Klein & Rychtarik, 1993). Relapse rates can be improved by behavioural marital therapy (O'Farrell *et al.*, 1992; Mattick & Heather, 1993).

Community Reinforcement Approach (CRA) marital therapy
CRA marital therapy is another helpful method with which to reinforce recovery. Typically the partner who is not a substance user reacts in one of two ways: either he or she becomes embroiled in arguments over drink and drugs increasing (albeit negative) communication or begins to withdraw leading to decreased communication. Whichever situation develops it will usually worsen with the passage of time. The substance user often reacts to the stress and tension generated by arguments, or to the increasing isolation and loneliness caused by withdrawal, by drinking or taking drugs. Gradually a vicious cycle develops with progressive dysfunction of the couple's relationship.

CRA behavioural marital therapy works on improving the relationship between cohabiting couples in the hope of breaking this vicious circle and thereby indirectly having a beneficial effect on the substance user. Meyers and Smith (1995) delineate how couples are given positive expectations through CRA marital therapy:

(1) Discuss ways the couple's current aversive communication style creates tension.
(2) Assure them that other couples in similar situations have improved their relationships.
(3) Explain that they will be taught communication and problem-solving skills.

(4) Give specific examples of these skills, such as making requests and tackling problems together instead of dwelling on them alone.

(5) Inform them that as progress is made they will feel less and less overwhelmed by their problems.

(6) Discuss how the initial learning process will take weeks, not years.

Couples are then given the CRA Marriage Happiness Scale (Appendix 22) to complete.

Both partners then discuss together their completed happiness scales. Potential solutions are purposely avoided at this point. After reviewing the completed happiness scales another CRA tool, the Perfect Marriage Form (Appendix 23), is used. With the help of this form couples identify behaviours in which they would like to see their partner engage. Couples are encouraged to talk about the positive aspects of their early relationship and the role their partner played in this. They are told that they can enjoy these good feelings again and instructed to ask for anything they want when completing the Perfect Marriage Form, no matter how selfish it may seem. This 'dream list' becomes the basis for later negotiations aimed at closing the gap between the situation now and where they would like to be.

The therapist should decide which partner responds first, and each category is explored in turn for both partners. The therapist emphasises that this is a wish or dream list for the ideal relationship and each partner is left to discuss and negotiate their wishes and needs for their ideal relationship. In doing so the groundwork is set for behavioural change by each partner in order to improve their relationship together.

Cognitive–behavioural couples therapy
Cognitive–behavioural couple's therapy should not be used to attempt to solve entrenched relationship problems or help marital relationships where there is violence. It is most useful where the partner who does not have a drink or drug use problem wishes to give more constructive support to aid treatment outcome. It focuses on improving communication skills within the relationship and the giving of rewards.

Many substance users have always had inadequate communication skills. Often they have grown up in a family where they never learnt to express feelings, solve problems, deal with criticism or work through arguments (Marlatt & Gordon, 1985). On the other hand, if they were in a family where there were adequate communication skills and learnt these by modelling, they have usually lost these skills as a result of long-term substance use. In either case the results are unsatisfactory relationships and poor coping strategies to deal with feelings of anger and frustration that arise in the normal course of interpersonal relationships. Cognitive–behavioural couples therapy helps substance users and their partners

- express their own feelings;
- communicate the ways in which each partner reacts to the other's behaviour;
- check out the perception of the partner's thoughts and feelings;
- provide feedback; and
- respond to perceived criticism.

These are achieved by the use of the following techniques:

- *'I' messages.* The ability to express feelings clearly is an essential component of any successful intimate relationship. Unfortunately many couples have difficulty expressing their feelings within their relationship, particularly if the level of criticism has been increasing. 'I messages' are a practical way to enable clients and their partners to overcome this problem. They can begin with the simple I-message formula: 'I feel Y when X', or 'When X happens, I feel Y'. For example, they can be asked to complete the sentences 'I feel cross when...', and 'I feel really pleased when...', ensuring that both positive and negative emotions are included.

- The next step is to extend the message so that it refers to the partner's behaviour using the following formula: 'When you...[behaviour], I feel...[emotion] because...[specific reason].' Alternatively the message to the partner can be put round another way: 'I feel...[emotion] when you...[behaviour] because...[specific reason].' For example, 'I feel angry when you leave me to do all the washing up because we should be sharing these household chores.' It is important that non-threatening topics are chosen to practise with, and that positive as well as negative feelings are included.

- *Perception checks.* It is through the complex mixture of verbal and non-verbal information we receive, and our own personal knowledge structures and expectations, that we form impressions and make social judgements about other people. According to Forgas (1985) we must first perceive and interpret other people before we can meaningfully relate to them. Perceptions are thus particularly important in the development and maintenance of close relationships. However, not all perceptions are accurate. It is easy for partners to damage their relationship together by mistakenly assuming they have interpreted each other's motivation or intentions correctly. For example, a wife might think 'You only bought me some flowers to make up for the way you treated me.' A perception check ensures that judgements and interpretations are correct by the insistence that partners ask if their perception is right. It involves

(1) identifying a behaviour;
(2) stating what you have guessed that behaviour means; and then
(3) asking if that interpretation is correct. For example, 'You've gone very quiet over the past few minutes. I think I may have upset you when I was talking about my brother. Am I right about this?'

- *Positive reinforcement.* It has been suggested (Clore & Byrne, 1974) that positive reinforcement accounts to a large extent for the feelings of attraction between two people. The responses and pleasurable feelings which stem from receiving rewards become associated with the provider, or even a third party (such as a family member) who happens to be present when they are dispensed. Dickson and colleagues (1993) list the following outcomes as being associated with social rewards and reinforcers:

(1) promoting interaction and maintaining relationships
(2) increasing the involvement of the interactive partner
(3) influencing the nature and content of the contribution of the other person
(4) demonstrating a genuine interest in the ideas, thoughts and feelings of the other
(5) making interaction interesting and enjoyable
(6) creating an impression of warmth and understanding
(7) increasing the social attractiveness of the source of rewards
(8) improving the confidence and self-esteem of the recipient
(9) manifesting power

Sometimes simply reminding couples to reward one another is sufficient. For others, however, the relationship may have deteriorated to such an extent that it is necessary to help the partners view each other in a positive light before they can give each other any positive feedback. To achieve this it can be useful to ask each partner in turn what it was about the other that initially attracted them. Partners should be encouraged to give verbal and non-verbal messages to reinforce any positive behaviour. Smiles, compliments, hugs or doing something nice for the other person are all positive rewards that reinforce positive behaviour. They should be specific about why they are offering each reward. For example, a person might say, 'I have noticed since you stopped drinking how attractive you look.' Non-verbal rewards need a verbal explanation in order to make them specific. For example, 'That hug is because it's now three weeks since you had any street drugs.' Another example of a non-verbal reward might be for the drug user to prepare a special meal for his partner at the same time letting her know why he did this: 'I made this special dinner because I really do appreciate the fact that you have joined in therapy with me.'

Sometimes couples have blocks which need to be dismantled as they stop the process of reinforcement. Clients should be asked how often they offer rewards to each other for the things that they like, and any fears they have about reinforcing behaviour change should be explored. Some people are afraid that if they reward sobriety their partner will give up trying, having achieved some success, and will relapse. To help clients get started they should be asked what types of things they appreciate being noticed, and they should also be asked to give each other feedback regarding the most effective way to state any positive reinforcement which is given. Noticing and acknowledging spontaneous positive reinforcement helps get this beneficial process firmly established.

Overall couples/marital CBT appears to be a useful way of enhancing the relationship where this has not been severely impaired as a result of long-term substance use by one partner. It can be utilised to reward the substance user who is making positive progress.

Unilateral Family Therapy to help the substance user enter treatment

The Pressures to Change approach
Barber and Crisp (1995) report the success of a *Pressures to Change* approach. This is a programme of interventions hierarchically arranged at different levels of pressure.

Level 1 pressure: feedback and education. Information as the severity of dependence is provided from assessment questionnaires and education about substance use is given.

Level 2 pressure: incompatible activities. This involves the completion of a drink/drug diary. High-risk times are identified and activities incompatible with substance use are planned for these times.

Level 3 pressure: responding. The drink/drug diary is also used to identify cues relating to the family relationship which may reinforce substance use. A number of responses by family members are known to reinforce substance use. These include:

(1) *Hostile or persistent nagging.* Persistently telling the addicted person to cut down their drinking, repeatedly applying pressure to stop drink and drug use, providing warnings of what will happen, or repeatedly bringing up past drinking episodes in argumentative angry tones, is not helpful when done to excess. Couples with the highest hostile and/or coercive verbal inter-

actions prior to treatment have been shown to have the poorest treatment outcomes (Orford *et al.*, 1976). Confrontation without warmth is known to be unhelpful. Nagging can also hinder recovery. In one study 74% of a sample of male drinkers in treatment claimed they sought help when their wives stopped nagging and trying to control their drinking (Djukanovic *et al.*, 1976).

(2) *Behaviours that are intended to control the drinking or drug-taking but instead enable it* (Orford *et al.*, 1975). Examples may include causing embarrassment by sending a friend (or even the children) to the pub to bring the drinker home, taking away a cheque book, and hiding drink or drugs or throwing them away. Such behaviours prevent drinkers and drug users taking control of the problem themselves.

(3) *Behaviours which prevent the consequences of substance use affecting the drinker or drug user.* Such behaviours reduce the influences that might enhance motivation to do something about the problem. Examples might include making an excuse to an employer when the individual is feeling too unwell to go to work, or clearing up the havoc at home that has been created by substance use. It is important that individuals accept responsibility by making their own excuses and doing their own clearing-up. Periods of amnesia associated with drinking binges, during which anything may have happened and may never be recalled, compound this problem through lost opportunities.

Level 4 pressure: contracting. This usually involves negotiating a drinking contract committing the drinker or drug user to abstinence or moderation at high-risk times in exchange for a positive rewarding reinforcer.

Level 5 pressure: confrontation. This involves the use of one of the confrontation techniques developed by the Johnson Institute and the manufacture of a crisis. For example, family members may be asked to write testimonials comprised of three parts:

(1) A declaration of the author's love for the drinker/drug user.

(2) Feedback about the ways in which drinking/ drug use is diminishing their relationship.

(3) A simple unambiguous plea to change or seek help.

It is very unusual to have to resort to Level 5.

Community Reinforcement And Family Training (CRAFT) approach

This involves behavioural approaches by the family that seek to improve family functioning and facilitate change. It is based on the CRA where the involvement of families in the community using operant learning methods has been shown to be successful (Meyers & Smith, 1995). CRAFT does not utilise programmed confrontation nor does it focus on educating concerned significant others (CSOs) about drug or excessive alcohol use. Instead it has some unique components including an emphasis on safety issues, a reliance on the functional analysis of behaviour, a focus on identifying and utilising positive reinforcers for both the drinker and the CSO. CRAFT also relies heavily on skills training. In a trial 76% of resistant drug users and 67% of resistant drinkers were successfully engaged in treatment (Meyers *et al.*, 1998). The basic components of the CRAFT procedures are:

(1) Preparing the CSO to recognise and safely respond to any potential for domestic violence as behavioural changes are introduced at home.

(2) Completing two functional analyses with the CSO, the first to identify the substance user's triggers for using alcohol or drugs, as well as the consequences, and the second to profile the user's triggers for non-using or pro-social behaviour and its consequences.

(3) Working with the CSO to improve communication with the substance user.

(4) Showing the CSO how to effectively use and withdraw positive reinforcement such that it discourages a loved one's harmful using behaviour.

(5) Teaching the CSO methods for decreasing stress in general, and emphasising the importance of having sufficient positive reinforcement in his or her own life.

(6) Instructing the CSO in the most effective ways to suggest treatment to the substance user, and helping identify optimal times.

(7) Laying the groundwork for having outpatient treatment available immediately for the user in the event that the decision is made to begin therapy, and discussing the need for the CSO to support the drinker or drug user during treatment.

Working together with professionals to enhance treatment outcomes

Marc Galanter (1993), a US psychiatrist, has pioneered a form of treatment, which he calls *network therapy*. Here family members and close friends of the client are invited to become members of the treatment team. The network team works closely together and consults at times of crisis. For instance, with each slip the whole team works with the client to understand what drinking cues – situations and emotional states – led to the relapses and how the client would handle those cues when they happen again. By involving the family and concerned others in the treatment process the therapist is in a position to help orchestrate family dynamics in a way that is most beneficial for the client. Although it has been generally promoted in the USA, family involvement in treatment is often neglected elsewhere, in spite of evidence that it 'enhances the accuracy of assessment, increases the chance of successful intervention and helps a patient stay motivated in treatment' (Kaufman, 1992).

Other ways in which the family can work jointly with professionals treating alcohol and drug users have been outlined by Higgins and Budney (1994) and Epstein and McCrady (1998). The current UKATT multicentre alcohol treatment trial of Social Behaviour and Network Therapy (SBNT) (Copello *et al.*, 2002) identifies family members and friends who are supporting the user's efforts and engages them in the treatment process.

Conclusion

In keeping with other comprehensive reviews of the substance use treatment literature, Miller and Wilbourne (2002) found that the treatments which incorporate a social component are among the most efficacious. Working together with families is one important way of achieving and maintaining positive change for the substance user. A good assessment will demonstrate the degree of family/marital dysfunction and family strengths. Those whose relationships are not severely damaged may obtain the greatest benefit from a family support group, whereas those with more dysfunctional relationships may benefit from family or couples therapy.

If the substance user is not ready to be involved in the treatment process, Unilateral Family Therapy with family members, utilising behavioural treatment interventions, has been shown to aid progression through the stages of change and encourage involvement of the substance user with treatment services. Other methods of families working jointly with professionals once help is sought show considerable promise. Family therapy can lessen the harm to family members and others affected, including children.

In spite of the evidence showing the importance of family involvement, this has been a neglected area of treatment by most UK alcohol and drug services who have tended to focus solely on the individual. A few services in North America are leading the way but even here one study has shown that in just 2.8% (5 of 174) of client contacts family members were seen as clients in their own right, and family members were involved in couple interventions in only a further three cases (1.7%) (Fals-Stewart & Birchler, 2001). Working with families is clearly a neglected issue that needs to be rectified.

Chapter 16
Substance Use and Mental Health

Introduction

Practitioners in the drug and alcohol field will be very aware that some service users have mental health problems. Whether drugs or alcohol have caused the illness, made the individual indifferent to its consequences or unable to access care, or the substance use been provoked by the experience of the illness, the practitioner can have a role in enabling assessment and treatment.

It is well recognised that alcohol use, drug use and mental illness are all individually associated with stigma (Farrell & Lewis, 1990; Hayward & Bright, 1998). The association of any combination of substance use and mental illness tends to compound the problem and provides particular challenges for the exercise of advocacy – a need already well known to those working in the field.

The aim of this chapter is to familiarise a wide readership with the range and assessment of mental disorders which may present in conjunction with substance use, noting those that require urgent treatment and describing the specialist mental health services and the routes of access to them. Further information on the diagnosis and treatment of mental illness may, of course, be found in standard psychiatric texts.

Current service provision

The history of the development of substance services and contemporary health and social services have had a considerable influence on the complex situation which now exists for people with combined mental illness and substance use. In the UK the early clinics for drug addicts were largely pioneered by psychiatrists. Some of the clinics included provision for people with alcohol problems. The presentation of major mental illness in such settings was relatively uncommon but was readily addressed by the psychiatric services in which the same staff held responsibilities.

The 1980s saw a diversification of community-based services for drug users, the development of Community Drug Teams (CDTs) and the involvement of primary medical care. Such services were cheaper and more accessible. However, associated with this change, many drug workers specifically distanced themselves from previous links with psychiatry, seeking to advocate the needs of drug users as members of the general community in need of access to treatment without the additional stigma of psychiatric illness. Whilst psychiatrists continued to see patients presenting with mental illness who also had addiction or substance use problems, there was no longer the same integration of drug service provision and mental health services.

Compounding these problems, a significant number of psychiatric professionals have come to see substance use as excluded from their remit, and access to psychiatric treatment is often difficult when need has been identified. It is hoped that the divisions will recede with an increasing awareness of the issues of psychiatric co-morbidity and the provision of comprehensive services for substance users.

The complex needs of those with combined problems are not readily accommodated in acute psychiatric services and are often seen as a threat to the therapeutic aims of a psychiatric ward or team. Psychiatric rehabilitation services do not generally have the skills to cater for those with combined mental illness and substance use, whilst most residential drug and alcohol rehabilitation services have exclusion criteria for mental illness, especially for individuals in need of continuing psychiatric medication or treatment. Historically, many drug and alcohol rehabilitation services were too challenging in style to be appropriate for someone recovering from mental illness, and there was a legacy of regarding concurrent mental illness as a consequence of drug use to be addressed by psychosocial rehabilitation alone.

The advent of care in the community has enabled many people with major psychiatric illness to live at home and engage in treatment with CDTs. Long stays in hospital, particularly by young people, are now very unusual. Community life presents many of the same advantages, challenges, risks and opportunities to all, including the current social influences of alcohol and drugs. As the prevalence of drug use has risen there has been a major rise in the association of mental illness and drug use, especially in young men.

In this context there has been a growing population of socially excluded individuals who present with complex needs, including physical health problems and social deprivation. Many present to treatment facilities via the criminal justice services. This picture should not, however, obscure the needs of those with significant mental illness and addiction who have not accumulated such additional problems, and who will continue to present to primary medical care or to community drug and alcohol services without making any overt request for mental health services. The visibility of such need has, however, been a major factor in the promotion of a response to 'dual diagnosis' and the stimulus to think again about the links between mental illness and the addictions.

Definitions and terminology

The choice of language is of central importance in psychiatry. Labels influence public and professional understanding of a subject as well as being helpful or harmful to the individual.

Dual diagnosis has been adopted as a shorthand term for the co-occurrent diagnoses of serious mental illness and substance use (El-Guebaly, 1990). There are, however, a number of inherent problems (Mueser, 1998). Dual implies that two problems are present. It is much more usual to find more than one substance being used, multiple substance-related problems, along with mental illness, social or personality adjustment difficulties and often a physical health problem. Thus, the term dual diagnosis does not encourage full assessment and problem definition or diagnosis. It is also evocative of a dualist concept of problems, whereby the defined problems exist together but separately, rather than interacting. This is profoundly misleading as will be demonstrated in this chapter. Common use of the term dual diagnosis has latterly come to be an assumed diagnostic term in itself, implying a combination of drug dependence and schizophrenia and identifying a subset of individuals as though they formed a homogeneous group. A term which set out to advocate attention to a particular need is in danger of contributing to narrowed thinking.

Co-morbidity, or more accurately, *psychiatric co-morbidity*, has become the preferred term from the professional perspective. It encompasses the important concept of a relationship between the disorders and does not limit the consideration to two components.

The interface between substance use and the mental disorder may fit several theoretical models. Some mental states are provoked or caused by the drug, such as excitement states provoked by stimulants. Others are a result of abrupt withdrawal such as the delirium of alcohol withdrawal. There is some evidence that drugs may precipitate the onset of mental illness as is postulated with cannabis and schizophrenia. The self-medication model is widely espoused but is not as helpful as an examination of underlying factors which predispose to both disorders.

For most conditions the common factors model is the best fit, encompassing vulnerability and life events as the link. Except in a few conditions, it is a mistaken belief that the withdrawal of the substance will lead to a resolution of the mental illness. In some it may even precipitate or exacerbate illness.

Thus the need for psychiatric assessment encompasses factors of psychological development, of physical health and an exploration of presenting problems, including those related to substance use. Assessment can then conclude with a formulation of individual health and social need, often including the diagnosis of particular illnesses. There emerges a description of '██████████ eeds', although this term in itself is too no██████████ o be helpful. Care planning must be ba████████ ividual assessment and must address the ██████ ychosocial and physical components whic█████████ ately related.

Prevalence

Substance-using populations

In drug and alcohol clinic populations, psychiatric illness and substance use co-occur more commonly than expected by chance. This is a consistent finding from alcohol populations (Hesselbrock *et al.*, 1985; Glass & Jackson, 1988) and drug use populations (Hall & Farrell, 1997).

The large UK National Treatment Outcome Research Study (NTORS) examined the prevalence of psychiatric symptoms at intake. The largely opiate-using population showed a high level of psychiatric morbidity. One in five subjects reported recent psychiatric treatment. Psychiatric symptoms were highest among opiate users who were also users of other substances such as benzodiazepines, alcohol and, in particular, stimulants. Female gender, physical illness and personal relationship problems were more powerful predictors of psychiatric symptoms than substance use (Marsden *et al.*, 2000).

There is accumulating evidence to demonstrate that smokers are not a psychologically well group. Anxiety, depression, schizophrenia and other substance use above general population levels are related to nicotine use.

Psychiatric populations

High levels of substance use have been consistently found in studies of psychiatric inpatients (Crowley *et al.*, 1974; Cantwell *et al.*, 1999). In addition significant links between suicide and homicide, mental illness and substance use were reported by Appleby in the *Reports of the Confidential Inquiry into Homicide and Suicide by Mentally Ill People* (DH, 1992; 2001).

The general population

The same raised prevalence of association of mental illness and substance use is found in general population studies (Regier *et al.*, 1990; Farrell *et al.*, 1998; 2001; ONS, 2002) and cannot therefore be explained by help-seeking behaviour.

The Epidemiological Catchment Area (ECA) study found that alcohol use carries a 36.6% lifetime prevalence of other mental disorder, which is twice the rate for people without alcohol disorder. Drug addiction was associated with a 53.1% lifetime rate of an additional mental disorder. All forms of major mental illness were found to coexist with substance use in greater than expected prevalence.

Prison and forensic populations

The imprisoned population also shows significantly raised co-morbidity of substance use and mental illness. Gunn and colleagues (1991) studying sentenced prisoners found 37% with psychiatric disorders of whom 23% had substance use disorder. In 1999 the UK Office of National Statistics (ONS) recorded a similarly high co-morbidity amongst prisoners (Singleton *et al.*, 1998). Expert reports such as the *Reed Report* (1992) have drawn attention to the need for better integration of services to meet the needs of prisoners with mental disorder and substance use. An analysis of the issues and recommendations for change were also made by the Advisory Council on the Misuse of Drugs (ACMD, 1996) in the report *Drug Misusers and the Prison System*. The prison population is not distinct from the general community in the course of individual drug use. Community-based services can constantly expect to see people following release or pending sentencing who have been exposed to the high-risk environment of prison. This population is particularly vulnerable to suicide as well as the risks of their mental health and substance use–related problems remaining untreated.

The needs of the wider forensic population, including those within secure psychiatric settings has been reviewed by Snowden (2001) who highlighted the high prevalence of co-morbid disorders and the need for better identification and treatment.

A study of the significant links between drug use and psychosis in the prison population provides information of relevance to the general population. Farrell and colleagues (2002) in a large study of UK prisoners found that severe dependence on cannabis and psychostimulants is associated with a higher risk of psychosis, in contrast to severe dependence on heroin which has a negative relationship with psychosis.

Homeless populations

It is not surprising that there are great similarities between the co-morbidity found among homeless people and that in the criminal justice system. There are also echoes of the needs of young people. A large national statistical survey (ONS, 2000) found that 22% of homeless people had been through the statutory care services as young people. The same study found that two-thirds of all respondents were dependent on drugs or had a hazardous pattern of drinking or both, the rate being higher, at 84% in those aged 25–31 years. Nearly one-third (40% in age groups 16–24 years) had attempted suicide at some time in their lives and 44% were assessed as having at least one non-psychotic mental disorder.

Young people

The literature examining co-morbidity in younger people under 18 years is relatively underdeveloped. Large-scale population studies have shown that young people who suffer psychological distress are at increased risk of developing substance use problems. Diagnostic groups are different in predominance from adult populations, with conduct disorder, attention-deficit/hyperactivity disorder (ADHD) and mood disorders, including suicidal behaviour, being more common. Substance use in the context of the early stages of schizophrenia and other psychoses is also significant. A review by Zeitlin (1999) concluded that these disorders are not attributable directly to the effects of the substances used. He found that substance use warranted vigilance in all children presenting with psychiatric disorder and found that early intervention could reduce the risk of subsequent physical and psychiatric disorder. Vigilance is also required in criminal justice services for young people, such as young offender institutes and youth-offending services, where the prevalence of psychiatric co-morbidity is likely to be high.

Problem identification, assessment and access to treatment

Effective treatment can only occur if the components of co-morbidity are identified. Several studies have demonstrated that substance use is not adequately inquired about during primary care contacts although patients are presenting with a wide range of related health and psychosocial problems. Psychiatric illness is similarly underrecognised (Freeling et al., 1985).

The use of standard screening tools developed for use in the general population has been shown to be effective in populations with severe and persistent mental illness. Maisto and colleagues (2000) found good sensitivity and specificity for symptoms and diagnosis using the Alcohol Abuse Screening Test, Alcohol Use Disorders Identification Test (AUDIT) and Drug Abuse Screening Test (DAST-10). Psychiatric screening instruments such as the Beck Depression Inventory (BDI) (Beck et al., 1961), the shortened form (Short BDI-II) (Beck et al., 1996) or the Hamilton Depression Rating Scale (Appendix 11) have been shown to have utility when used in substance-using populations (Steer et al., 1980).

Commander and colleagues (1999) found that alcohol problems were not recognised during routine consultations, even when the nature of the problem had known associations with alcohol. Grant (1997) found that in the general population there was a reluctance to seek treatment for alcohol problems because of fears of rejection and labelling. Specialist substance services are also poor at psychiatric problem recognition, including depression and suicide risk, as highlighted in the NTORS results (Gossop et al., 1997). Low rates of recognition in psychiatric populations occur despite knowledge of high prevalence rates (Ramsay et al., 1983).

Ethnic minorities have particular problems in accessing treatment. Analysis suggests that Asian and black patients are less likely than white patients to have their psychological problems identified in primary care settings (Odell *et al.*, 1997). The prevalence of co-morbid psychiatric illness and substance use is underrepresented in clinical settings. Language and cultural needs are often neglected and there is little outreach to help address social and cultural barriers to service access.

The medical professions have a high morbidity of drug and alcohol and psychiatric problems and yet the identification of doctors and nurses with substance-related illness and their engagement in treatment remains low (Strang *et al.*, 1998; Bennett & O'Donovan, 2001).

Access to treatment is further complicated by professional and public false assumptions of poor treatment response and compliance which inhibit referral and intervention. Farrell and Lewis (1990) found that practitioners with some experience in specialist substance use services are less likely to make such erroneous assumptions.

There are many opportunities for identification of co-morbidity. The health and social risk factors which could prompt enquiry for substance use and mental illness are well known. General practitioners (GPs) are ideally placed to make connections with family history and social circumstances. These opportunities occur in all age groups, including adolescents.

With current knowledge of co-morbid associations of nicotine addiction, other substance use and mental illness (Brown *et al.*, 2000), GPs could also include attention to the likelihood of substance use and psychiatric illness when making interventions on tobacco smoking.

There is thus a major educational task to improve professional skills of enquiry and information gathering and to remove the barriers to problem disclosure and engagement in treatment.

The benefits of treating substance problems

As in other drug- and alcohol-using populations, there is considerable value in treating substance problems in those with co-morbid mental illness. As will be seen, the treatment of substance use can be effective in itself in improving mood, concentration and social stability, thus enabling the delivery of more specific psychiatric treatments where required. Treatment is effective and can be implemented in a wide range of settings and styles. Brief interventions are effective in primary care and within the more complex treatments of specialist psychiatric services.

The importance and difficulties of diagnosis

Early intervention for the treatment of mental illness is increasingly recognised as having importance. It may reduce the risks of suicide in a wide range of conditions and is now known to improve the course of schizophrenia (Larsen *et al.*, 2001). Accurate diagnosis of associated psychiatric illness is thus important for the development of a care plan to incorporate the full range of need, including the implications of prognosis, risk assessment and adequate resource allocation.

The interpretation of studies of the prevalence of mental disorders is confounded by issues of direct and indirect drug effects upon presenting symptoms and thus on diagnosis. This same difficulty comes sharply into focus when individual diagnosis and treatment is considered.

Alcohol and drugs are taken for mood-altering effects and many substances have profound effects upon perception and cognitive functioning. The finding of increased rates of depression, paranoid states and confusional states is thus inevitable in populations still using substances in harmful ways. Substance use influences access to services and thus the opportunity for diagnosis. Diagnosis is also affected by the presence of substance use as a diagnostic criterion for some conditions, e.g. antisocial personality disorder and childhood conduct disorder.

Research models of diagnosis often require a defined period of abstinence from substance use before diagnosis of mental illness. In clinical practice this is desirable but often very impractical or unachievable. As with many branches of medical practice, there is a necessity to commence treatment based on a presumed diagnosis. This approach has elements of risk reduction familiar to drug workers. Such working diagnoses must be regularly reassessed and the goal of resolving the compounding substance use held clearly in focus in the care plan.

In situations where substance use is a direct causal factor, the primary goal must be safe withdrawal and abstinence from the provoking substance. However, continuing substance use should not be a rationale for abandonment of diagnostic assessment and therapeutic planning, a situation that appears to occur all too often and may constitute an avoidance of therapeutic effort in the face of complex need. In all cases, an assessment of risk can be a helpful approach to decisions concerning treatment. It may be helpful to consider two examples of such treatment dilemmas.

CASE STUDY 1

Client J is an elderly woman physically and psychologically dependent on alcohol. She complains of depression and reports a previous diagnosis of bipolar (manic–depressive) illness. Her spouse says she has talked of killing herself and says she often seems confused. An examination reveals a very low mood and a possible alcohol-related dementia. A definitive diagnosis concerning the possibilities of depressive illness and dementia cannot be made whilst she continues to drink heavily.

Client J was seen by the psychiatrist at her local specialist alcohol service but would not give an undertaking to stop drinking at first interview. The psychiatrist offered her inpatient treatment, commenting to a student that he might not have done this had she been a young single man.

The core intervention here is detoxification as neither a definitive diagnosis nor treatment can proceed in the context of ongoing substance use.

CASE STUDY 2

Client X is a male opiate user aged 23. He admitted dependency on heroin, daily use of cannabis and binge drinking. After arrests for burglary and shoplifting offences, he was assessed by a worker from a local Arrest Referral Scheme. This assessment

revealed social decline disproportionate to the severity of his addiction and a constellation of symptoms and behaviours suggestive of schizophrenia.

The history suggested that the abnormal mental state began at about the same time as his drug use and persisted during periods of reduced substance use. Client X was referred for a psychiatric opinion and, despite the possibility that cannabis and alcohol may be exacerbating the condition, a working diagnosis of underlying schizophrenia was made and treatment commenced with antipsychotic medication.

The balance of risk in this case was in favour of commencing medication as experience suggests that the likelihood of an improved mental state would enable progress to be made with the social and medical components of the care plan, including stability of drug use and reduced alcohol use.

The diagnosis of major mental illness must be frequently reviewed to take account of the remaining possibility of the state being drug precipitated or induced, and therefore likely to remit or require less medication in the absence of the substance.

Physical health and psychiatric illness

The association of physical illness with psychiatric disorder is well recorded (OPCS, 1995). This is thought to have a mixture of causes including poor access to primary and secondary care for prevention and treatment as well as factors attributable to personal care, chronic pain, disability and social exclusion. As physical illness is a significant predictor of poor outcome in substance use as demonstrated by data from NTORS (Gossop et al., 1997), there are significant gains to be made by the treatment of associated physical conditions.

Direct physical effects of drugs and alcohol on general health are also important to consider (see Chapter 17). This is further complicated by the myriad of indirect effects of substance use including social effects such as high-risk sexual behaviour, bereavements and trauma, and the effects of poverty, particularly dietary neglect, all of which are likely to be worse in the context of co-morbid mental illness.

One aspect of ill health likely to impact on psychiatric morbidity is smoking and chronic lung disease (Breslau et al., 1991; Brown et al., 2000).

Cigarette smoking is almost universal in substance users. There is also a markedly increased rate of smoking in psychiatric populations (Hughes *et al.*, 1986). Nicotine cessation or partial withdrawal states provoke anxiety, irritability and insomnia. This is an area of intervention that has not been given adequate attention in harm reduction strategies but which may achieve greater interest as the range of interventions for nicotine dependency increases and the rising prevalence of smoking-related lung cancer in women creates a focus for action.

Liver disease is the other major issue in the co-morbid population. Malnutrition may arise from alcohol- or drug-related anorexia, poverty or malabsorption. HIV, chronic hepatitis B and hepatitis C produce a wide range of physical and psychological effects. HIV infection and alcohol use have direct physical effects on the brain and central nervous system (CNS) and can thus cause psychiatric disorders.

These physical sequelae of substance use may thus have a provoking or complicating effect on psychiatric illness. They also have a major effect on the choice of medical treatments, particularly the choice of antipsychotic medication, mood stabilisers and antidepressants. Monitoring of serum therapeutic drug levels and toxic effects is essential for some treatments. Such treatments as lithium for mood disorder or clozapine for schizophrenia may be precluded for practical reasons in people with a history of intravenous (IV) use who have little or no access to peripheral veins. There are also influences on drug substitution treatment and therapies to assist withdrawal and abstinence. Drugs which might worsen the course of chronic liver disease should be avoided if possible and care must be taken to monitor illness-related changes in metabolism which could lead to unexpected toxicity.

The occurrence of hepatitis C virus (HCV) infection amongst drug users who have ever injected is estimated at 43% in the UK (PHLS, 1999) and 52% in the US (NIDA, 2000) clinic populations. This condition is likely to be the most common chronic illness affecting people with current or former substance use problems. Examining the occurrence of depression in this population, Johnson and colleagues (1998) found high levels of depressive symptoms; 57% in HCV positive compared to 48% HCV

negative, the HCV positive group scoring higher on somatic components. Evidence is emerging of brain lesions occurring in hepatitis C which may predispose to depression. The evidence is present in histologically mild hepatitis C and is unrelated to encephalopathy or IV drug use and suggests that a biological process underlies the symptoms of fatigue and depression in hepatitis C (Forton *et al.*, 2001). The same authors have also found cognitive impairment independent of depression, fatigue or IV drug use in HCV positive patients (Forton *et al.*, 2002). The cognitive impairment was associated with abnormal findings on magnetic resonance spectroscopy suggesting a biological cause.

Personality disorder and mental illness

Recognition and appropriate care and treatment of patients with personality disorder and all its effects are core skills of psychiatric services in the substance use field. The main psychiatric issues relating to personality disorder are those of depression, anxiety and conduct (Verheul *et al.*, 2000).

The ECA study (Regier *et al.*, 1990), using a narrow diagnostic approach, found a prevalence of 18% whereas estimates of the prevalence of personality disorder in clinical populations are high; a review by Verheul and colleagues (1995) concluded that the clinical population rate may be estimated at 79%. Seivewright and Daly (1997) suggest a lower figure emerges if all drug types and non-clinic substance-using populations are considered.

Again, the effects of the substance use itself and of social influences make assessment problematic. Personality disorder can have a marked effect of generating adverse life events by means of antisocial behaviours such as aggression and criminality. Emotional responses can seem disproportionate both in terms of severe depression or apparent indifference.

There is an increased tendency to acts of self-harm (Farrell *et al.*, 1996) and an increased prevalence of a range of neurotic symptoms (Tyrer *et al.*, 1990). Thus, this group presents challenges to everyday treatment interventions and major difficulties in terms of risk assessment.

In clinical practice, it is important to try and separate the effects of substances used from those of the underlying personality. For example, the irritability of stimulants, the disinhibiting effects of alcohol or the indifference from benzodiazepine use can mimic severe personality difficulties. Presentation may vary from time to time in the same person. A detailed personal history, ideally with confirmation from an independent source, a forensic history and past psychiatric records can be of help. There may be a record of conduct disorder or ADHD in childhood preceding antisocial personality disorder in adulthood. As with other diagnostic groups, an account of behaviour and mental state during any drug-free episodes can be very useful.

The readiness of professionals to make a diagnosis of personality disorder has fluctuated considerably over recent decades and settings. There remain some pejorative connotations, and associations with treatment pessimism. In the UK there has recently been greater public awareness of the concept of personality disorder and an undue emphasis on associations of dangerousness as a result of a politically driven attempt to define a condition of dangerous severe personality disorder for the purpose of compulsory detention. This may produce a further stigmatising effect.

There are some distinct advantages to the recognition of personality disorder, especially in terms of treating affective (mood) symptoms and the management of associated substance use. There are also several emerging effective approaches to the treatment of personality disorder itself, including Cognitive–Behavioural Therapy (CBT) and dialectical behaviour therapy for borderline personality disorder (Linehan et al., 1999).

Some symptoms may improve with long-term substitution treatment in opiate users (Musselman & Kell, 1995), whilst the use of selective serotonin reuptake inhibitor (SSRI) antidepressants may improve mood and reduce craving (Sellers et al., 1991).

Treatments aimed at opiate abstinence may be less successful in those with personality disorder (Darke et al., 1994) – a finding of some importance in deciding how best to respond to repeated requests for detoxification and to reduce risky behaviour (Gill et al., 1992). A very helpful review of the effects of personality disorder on treatment was undertaken by Seivewright and Daly (1997).

Risk assessment and risk reduction

The assessment of risk and its incorporation in care planning is now an explicit aspect of psychiatric practice. This fits well in the addictions field where there is a philosophy of risk reduction and harm reduction.

With our greater awareness of the extent of psychiatric co-morbidity it is important to have a working knowledge of the particular risks associated with psychiatric illness. The general risks of substance use are discussed in Chapter 5 and the specific risks relating to child protection in Chapter 18.

The importance of multi-disciplinary and multi-agency working cannot be overstated. As will be seen by an analysis of the risks, there are many dimensions which will not be resolved by either medical or social intervention in isolation. They form major barriers to treatment of the substance disorder and are often beyond the resources of drug and alcohol specialist teams alone.

Many aspects of psychiatric co-morbidity need long-term management and support and a higher than usual level of monitoring. It is also necessary to respond urgently in some situations and to have access to specialist mental health assessment with a view to urgent admission which may require compulsion. It should be noted that although compulsory detention under UK Mental Health Legislation (Mental Health Act, 1983) is not permitted for substance use itself, these powers are available for use in the presence of mental disorder posing significant risk to the health of the patient and the safety of others, including mental disorders provoked by intoxication or withdrawal.

As for other forms of risk it is helpful to consider risks to the individual substance user and risks to third parties.

Risks to the individual

Inherent risk factors such as personality, intellectual ability, social skills and learned behaviours contribute to level of risk. So too does knowledge of available services, understanding of risks and capacity to cope with external stress. The presence of personality disorder carries an increased risk of self-harm and other impulsive behaviour and often a reduced capacity to access services. These factors must be borne in mind when assessing other risk domains.

Exploitation may occur in the context of social isolation, depression or with associated cognitive decline or learning disability. It may further contribute to feelings of paranoia and may exacerbate psychotic states.

Self-neglect can often appear to be the result of substance use but may be linked to the lack of drive of depression or the social withdrawal of psychosis. It may also result from the inability to organise personal life which may occur in schizophrenia or, occasionally, in manic states. Addressing social needs can be a valuable and necessary beginning of treatment for both the substance use and the psychiatric problem.

Criminal behaviour is a risk for those who find survival in the community additionally difficult. This includes acquisitive crime, prostitution, drugs offences and assaults. Criminal behaviour may be part of a problem of exploitation to which some mentally ill individuals are prone (Johns, 1998). Probation and social work input is particularly helpful and can enable the engagement which facilitates acceptance of medical treatment.

Disinhibited behaviour can lead to serious problems as can be seen in the context of substance intoxication. Similar states occur in various psychiatric illnesses including hypomania, schizophrenia and dementia. The presentation may be associated with hyperactivity in excitement states and can resemble stimulant, especially cocaine, use.

It is vital to try to differentiate these states from intoxication itself and avoid making assumptions of cause before undertaking a trial of stabilisation or detoxification, if necessary, in hospital. The persistence of disinhibition can lead to sexual risks, drug use risks, fights, loss of accommodation and social isolation.

Overdose by accident is common and carries a significant mortality. Overdose risk may be increased in states of distress when polysubstance use, including alcohol, is a hazard. Depression may lead to indifference concerning risk of death; indeed, the use of substances may be construed as a chronic form of deliberate self-harm or suicide though this is rarely a conscious motivation.

Deliberate self-harm and suicidal behaviour have an increased prevalence in substance users. This relates to commonality of risk factors for substance use and self-harm and the raised prevalence of psychiatric illness. Deliberate overdose using opiates with suicidal intent is more common than generally recognised. In a study of overdose presenting at emergency departments, Neale (2000) found a significant incidence of suicidal ideation and intent in patients who had been assumed to present with accidental overdose. As in psychiatry, it is important for workers in the substance use field to enquire about suicidal ideas when discussing overdose risks with substance users. Some will have depression in need of treatment, or other forms of psychiatric illness or emotional distress. Self-harm by cutting and other methods is common following childhood abuse, among young people in institutional care, in prisons and in homeless populations. There may be formal psychiatric illness to be treated and it can be beneficial to offer therapy to develop other ways of coping with distress.

Exacerbation of existing psychiatric illness may arise through exclusion from services as a result of abnormal mental states. Failure to seek help or engage in treatment for mental illness or substance use may occur as a result of depression, delusions, self-neglect or lack of insight. It can be difficult for the individual to perceive the gradual deterioration in their mental health or to regulate the chaos produced by increasing use of substances. The substance itself can then produce other mental disorders such as confusion, dementia, paranoid psychosis or depression. Specialist drug and alcohol workers have a vital role in problem recognition and in advocacy of access to all relevant services for mentally ill service users.

Physical illness, including liver disease, influences risk in many aspects of mental health. Not only is there an increased prevalence of depression in chronic physical illness, there are greater risks of complications of psychotropic medication. The presence of physical illness also appears to reduce psychiatric problem recognition by professionals (Odell *et al.*, 1997). The converse also applies, with psychiatric illness reducing the recognition of physical illness and reducing access to primary care and specialist physical health care. The presence of mental illness may make it more difficult to take precautions against sexual and blood–borne virus (BBV) infections. In common with substance use itself there is a high prevalence of cigarette smoking and all the associated health risks.

Risks to third parties

Violence related to mental illness is disproportionately publicised. Nevertheless, it is an important aspect of risk assessment which can be missed with awful consequences. The risks of violence associated with mental illness, and delusional thinking in particular, are substantially increased by substance use (Soyka, 2000) and stimulant drugs in particular. Assessment of substance use is an essential component of risk assessment in the severely mentally ill (Scott *et al.*, 1998) and is likely to yield an increasing number of referrals to drug and alcohol services. In forensic settings the risk of violence is increased by co-morbidity as discussed by Snowden (2001).

A history of violent behaviour with or without previous convictions should be enquired for and any findings noted carefully. The rationale given may include abnormal perceptions or beliefs of a paranoid type. If these are held in association with ideas about particular individuals, or in association with a high level of stated intent, there is an urgent need for further assessment and treatment, probably in hospital and possibly with compulsory detention. It is usually mistaken to think that the ideas will go away if levels of acute or chronic drug use are reduced, although the individual may be slightly less inclined to act on such beliefs when the irritability or disinhibition of substance use is removed.

In clinical settings it is important to consider risks related to intoxication, the carrying of weapons such as knives and the association of psychiatric symptoms with the risk of violence. Team policies should be in place to assess and manage the raised level of risk which this population can present. Much can be done to reduce risk and make services safe and pleasant for all concerned if basic precautions and policies are explicit, and staff well trained.

Chronic illness and social exclusion can lead to the acquisition of violent patterns of response to problems. These may be modified by behavioural techniques such as anger management and cue identification, including advice on the important role of intoxication. It can thus be helpful to elucidate the particular triggers for each individual in order to provide the appropriate treatment response.

Domestic violence may be triggered by depression, paranoia and delusional jealousy although the majority of domestic violence is not associated with mental illness in the perpetrator. The mentally ill person may also be at risk as a victim. The risks of domestic violence can be exacerbated by relationship problems and financial tensions due to substance use. Verbal and physical violence between parents or other adults in the home can have a very adverse effect on the mental health of children and may predispose to future substance use. The risk of women experiencing domestic violence is increased during pregnancy when violence may occur for the first time. The consequences of domestic violence on mental health include a significantly raised incidence of depression, anxiety disorder and suicidal behaviour. Services should make routine enquiry and have readily available information on sources of help and safe refuges.

Risks to children should be considered and addressed as with all substance users. Parental depression may exacerbate the risk of emotional deprivation, further increased if suicidal behaviour is present. Rarely, in states of severe depressive hopelessness or delusion, this is an urgent matter of risk to the health or survival of children. Harm prevention measures such as additional domestic support, play therapy and more frequent psychiatric review should be considered when patients with serious mental illness and substance use have care of children.

Young substance users may present child protection concerns in their own right. There are increased risks of suicide, exploitation and neglect. The presence of psychiatric illness can mimic delinquency, and substance use can result in criminal behaviour. There is thus a risk that the psychiatrically ill young person will become involved in the criminal justice services. The risk of suicide by young people in custody is high. Every effort should be made to identify co-morbidity and to alert all relevant staff to the need for treatment and vigilant care.

It is worth noting, as shown by Kendler and colleagues (2000), that childhood sexual abuse is a factor in the development of adult psychiatric and substance use disorders and may thus form part of family pathology.

Public health risks, including the spread of blood-borne infections may be increased by abnormal mental states, particularly those which lead to grandiose or reckless behaviour, and by failure to access services. These risks are compounded by homelessness which is of significant prevalence in co-morbid populations. Social care, easy access to physical health care and psychiatric treatment are likely to reduce the levels of risk.

Specific major psychiatric illnesses and their treatment

Co-morbidity research has tended to focus on epidemiology with relatively little emphasis on the treatment and outcomes for specific illnesses. This certainly reflects the diagnostic difficulties which have already been considered as well as the poor resourcing of research, training and treatment provision in this field (Crome, 1999). This area of practice is complex by definition and does not emerge readily from the textbooks or from an evidence base. Clinical practice therefore relies heavily on consensus, clinical training from experienced practitioners with an interest in the field, and the translation of good practice from the general psychiatry field.

Anxiety

Clinical problem

Anxiety is a ubiquitous symptom and an understanding of causes and treatments is important. Whilst some individuals seem exceptionally immune to anxiety, the majority of substance users will experience and complain of anxiety at least intermittently.

Most substances produce anxiety as a major symptom of withdrawal states. This may present as anxiety or irritability. It is important to recognise the cause as drug related and to give appropriate advice. The anxiety of withdrawal may occur between doses of short-acting drugs such as heroin, and as blood levels fall during reduction in dose, well before the full syndrome of withdrawal occurs. In alcohol treatment programmes, estimates of coexisting anxiety problems tend to be high, varying from 22.6% to 68.7%. From this, Kushner and colleagues (1990) suggested 'Alcohol has the potential to interact with clinical anxiety in a circular fashion, resulting in an upward spiral of both anxiety and problem drinking'. For example, if a drinker temporarily becomes more anxious from alcohol withdrawals, inspite of the fact that any increase in anxiety will disappear when the withdrawal phase is over, it is resolved more quickly by consuming more alcohol. This in turn will heighten anxiety levels further on withdrawal. In addition, as a dependent drinker increases his or her tolerance to alcohol, so anxiety levels on withdrawal will increase. Such symptoms often lead to requests for other medication.

Anxiety disorder has a high prevalence and is often related to formative experiences in earlier life and to adult depression. Childhood emotional, physical and sexual abuse are more common in substance users, as are experiences of separation and bereavement. Regier and colleagues (1998) found the average age of onset of anxiety disorder to be 16 years and that anxiety disorders, especially social and simple phobias of adolescence, were a strong predisposing factor for subsequent major depression and addictive disorders.

Anxiety is a common symptom of depressive illness and may be its presenting complaint. An association with lack of drive, energy and appetite and ideas of guilt or hopelessness suggest a diagnosis of depression. Of course, many of these phenomena occur as direct effects of substance use; a high index of suspicion and enquiry is therefore required.

Treatment

It is not usually appropriate to prescribe minor tranquillisers for the anxiety of intermittent withdrawal symptoms except for short-term treatment of acute withdrawal. It is also important to explain that long-term benzodiazepine use may paradoxically cause anxiety and that gradual withdrawal can be beneficial.

Changing to longer-acting opiates may improve symptoms in heroin users. The stability of methadone maintenance treatment is often associated with an improvement in anxiety symptoms. An explanation of the cause of symptoms and simple coping strategies such as distraction or relaxation can be beneficial. Advice about the nature of panic attacks and instruction on rebreathing techniques usually help reduce their frequency and duration. Cognitive treatments, possibly linked with counselling, may be beneficial and can have lasting gains. Scott and colleagues (1998a) provide a helpful review of treatment of anxiety and depression in the context of substance use.

Depression

Clinical problem

Depression presents with many of the predispositions and symptoms described above and can be equally difficult to diagnose. A dominance of negative ideas such as worthlessness, failure and hopelessness are linked with depression.

It is important to try to distinguish depression due to substance use, particularly alcohol, from primary depression. Studying inpatients in an addictions treatment unit, Charney and colleagues (1998) found a higher rate of symptom resolution and longer abstinence in the group with substance-induced depression.

Treatment

Where substance-induced depression is suspected from the chronology of substance use and symptoms, an attempt to achieve detoxification should precede psychotropic medication.

Improvements to general health and social circumstances can enable recovery in depression of all types but should not be assumed to be sufficient for recovery. Depression responds well to antidepressant treatment in many cases. The SSRI drugs are favoured because of the relatively better side-effect profile and lower toxicity which is important in combination with other substances and risk behaviours. There is also some evidence that they reduce craving for substance use.

The increased risk of suicide in depression may paradoxically further increase as treatment begins to lift mood – probably associated with insight and improved drive. Increased, not reduced, contact is thus required at this stage, with positive encouragement and support.

Post-traumatic stress disorder

Clinical problem

Post-traumatic stress disorder (PTSD) may present with anxiety or depression (Brady et al., 2000) and is characterised by flashback memories, nightmares and avoidance of cues. There is some evidence that recall of traumatic experiences during debriefing can more likely be followed by PTSD, as may subsequent rehearsal, for instance, through formal investigations and court proceedings. Research has demonstrated a high incidence of co-morbid substance use. Najavits and colleagues (1997) showed that the higher rates in women (30–59%) most commonly derive from repetitive childhood physical and/or sexual assault.

The use of substances during or following trauma may have a protective effect and may explain why many service users seem relatively unscathed by their adult experiences. However, modified traumas may emerge following detoxification and should be anticipated as much as possible by careful preparation.

Treatment

The treatment of choice is Cognitive Therapy (CT) augmented by an SSRI antidepressant if depression is significant.

Bipolar affective disorder

Clinical problem

Previously called manic–depressive disorder, the coexistence of this condition with substance use is common and frequently unrecognised. Sonne and

Brady (1999) found that as many as 50% of individuals with bipolar disorder have a lifetime history of substance use or dependence. Brady and Sonne (1995) reported this to be the major psychiatric disorder most likely to co-occur with substance use and found a higher rate of hospitalisation and treatment resistance compared to non-substance users.

The condition has various forms manifesting as unipolar, bipolar, mixed and rapid cycling combinations of excitement and depression. Some of the difficulty in diagnosis lies in the recognition of the altered mood as being illness based rather than substance induced. The presentation of grandiose, excited or aggressive states out of proportion to the use of provoking substances or causing major concern to peers or family should alert to this possibility.

Treatment

In extreme form the manic state is a psychiatric emergency requiring hospital admission because of the risk of exhaustion, disinhibition and aggression. Standard management with lithium is problematic if monitoring is hampered by poor veins or unstable lifestyle. The alternative drugs such as valproate may also be of limited use if liver function is poor. Antipsychotics by depot injection are sometimes an alternative. There is early evidence that cognitive approaches to symptom and trigger management are beneficial.

Drug-induced psychosis and other states

Clinical problem

Although drug-induced psychosis, as formally defined, is a toxic reaction rather than a major mental illness, there may be some diagnostic uncertainty and a need for urgent psychiatric intervention.

The central clinical dilemma lies in the differentiation of true drug-induced states, which generally resolve with the removal of the causal agent, from those with an underlying process illness for which longer-term psychiatric treatment is necessary. The complications in practice often relate to a failure to engage with individuals experiencing psychosis because of erroneous assumptions about the nature of the disorder. Appropriate treatment is thus not

pursued. Drug-induced psychosis usually refers to time-limited psychotic states produced by acute or chronic drug effects. These states typically occur during the period of use such as the paranoid states linked with stimulants and cannabis, and the hallucinatory effects of lysergic acid diethylamide (LSD), solvents, cannabis and Ecstasy. The features of amphetamine psychosis were described in the classical work of Connell (1958).

The onset of drug-induced psychosis is classically acute. Behaviour may be difficult to manage, constituting a risk to the patient or others. There may be an altered and fluctuating level of conciousness. Mood change may be striking and the presentation of hallucinations in all modalities, especially visual and tactile, is much more common than in other psychoses. Recurrent hallucinatory states, sometimes with associated mood changes, may occur in relation to previous use of cannabis or LSD. A condition of chronic hallucinosis with associated delusions is described in chronic alcohol use.

Psychosis also occurs as a phenomenon of acute withdrawal from sedative substances, particularly alcohol, benzodiazepines and barbiturates and is associated with acute confusion and delirium. In a helpful review of drug-related psychotic reactions, Poole and Brabbins (1996) concluded that the evidence for persistent drug-induced psychosis (following withdrawal) is weak. Studies are inconsistent in diagnostic criteria and uncertainties of substance use histories confound the diagnosis. In many instances, the onset of psychosis occurring in association with substance use does not resolve with elimination of the substance. Such states may be better construed as underlying illnesses, provoked or precipitated in onset but not causally related to substance use. First and recurrent episodes or exacerbations of schizophrenia may be triggered by substance use or withdrawal.

It is worth noting that substance use and first episodes of schizophrenia are both at their peak incidence in early adulthood. The conditions are therefore most likely to be coincidental or due to shared or independent factors of aetiology.

Although methodological difficulties persist, the evidence that cannabis use plays a causal role in the development of schizophrenia and depression is growing. In a prospective study, Arseneault and colleagues (2002) found that adolescent cannabis use is a risk factor for schizophrenia even after adjustment for pre-existing childhood psychosis. Patton and colleagues (2002) found a strong association between daily use of cannabis and depression and anxiety in young women which persists after adjustment for intercurrent use of other substances. Pre-existing depression did not predict cannabis use. These studies point to a need for strategies to reduce frequent recreational use in young people.

Persistent substance use may be covert and is not always detectable by intermittent urine testing during psychiatric treatment. In a study comparing hair analysis to self-disclosure and urine drug-testing, McPhillips and colleagues (1997) found that a much higher incidence and duration of substance use was detected by hair analysis. This illustrates the diagnostic problems that occur when potentially causal or provocative drug use is ongoing in association with schizophrenia or other illnesses.

Treatment

Safety is the first priority. Psychosis occurring in association with acute confusion or delirium is a medical emergency requiring urgent investigation and treatment in hospital. A calm and reassuring environment is essential. Full physical assessment should be undertaken as soon as possible to consider any physical causes requiring medical treatment. A sample of urine for drug toxicology is important for diagnostic reasons, obtained as soon as practicable following the onset of symptoms. If psychotropic medication is required for safe and comfortable care of symptoms, doses of antipsychotic medication should be chosen cautiously, and frequent reviews undertaken.

Drug-induced psychosis classically remits within a short time from onset. The persistence of symptoms such as delusions and auditory hallucinations beyond the acute presentation period of 2–3 weeks should raise the suspicion of an underlying schizophrenic illness or the ongoing use of a provoking drug. Where it is suspected that an underlying psychosis is being precipitated or exacerbated by substance use, the primary treatment should, if possible, be the elimination of the substance. In practice

it often becomes necessary to address both the issue of the use of potentially provoking substances and the possibility of an underlying illness simultaneously. This may include the use of an educational approach (harm reduction) and of antipsychotic medication. There should also be judicious reviews of the differential diagnosis especially when the opportunity arises to become substance-free.

Schizophrenia

Clinical problem

The possibility of a diagnosis of schizophrenia should be carefully explored in all cases of guarded, unusually hostile or incongruous presentations. The split (schiz) of schizophrenia applies to the dissociation between thought content and expressed mood but is not present in all cases.

Many missed diagnoses are related to stigma and an erroneous attribution of symptoms to drug-induced causes. These points have been poignantly illustrated in public enquiries into homicides by people with mental illness. Failure to diagnose schizophrenia is reflected in the prison population where there is a need for improved coordination between substance use and psychiatric services. The relatively poor outcomes in studies to date may, however, reflect the retrospective nature of studies in populations for which there was little integrated care.

Diagnosis is facilitated by careful assessment with attention to the chronology of symptoms and substance use and by an environment in which disclosure of symptoms is felt to be psychologically safe. It may thus be demonstrated that symptoms suggestive of psychosis pre-date the substance use.

Fear and suspicion may seem congruent with a precarious lifestyle. However, a diagnosis of schizophrenia should be considered when such fears are expressed in the absence of rationality. Delusional thinking is about the manner in which beliefs are held rather than their actual or possible veracity.

Other significant phenomena are third person auditory hallucinations discussing or commenting on the persons as if they were not present, voices in the form of a running commentary, delusions of external control, abnormalities of boundaries of thought and a form of expression of thought which makes it difficult to follow or understand. The latter is termed formal thought disorder and is a powerful discriminator for schizophrenia. Devising a statistical model to differentiate schizophrenia from substance-induced psychosis, Rosenthal and Miner (1997) found formal thought disorder and bizarre delusions to significantly predict a diagnosis of schizophrenia.

The finding of toxicological evidence of substance use related to onset or exacerbation of symptoms does not negate the possibility of a diagnosis of schizophrenia. Nor should a self-report of drug use; such self-report may erroneously be offered subsequently as a rationalisation of the abnormal subjective experience.

Treatment
The risk of adverse events, including suicide (Kamali *et al.*, 2000), is greatly reduced by treatment. It can be difficult to engage patients in treatment-requiring medication which tends to produce unpleasant effects, especially if past use of substances has been for hedonistic effects. Some studies suggest that patients with associated substance use require higher doses and are more prone to side-effects (Swofford *et al.*, 2000). Further substance use may occur in response to depression or to get high for pleasure even though the negative effects of use are recognised (Addington & Duchak, 1997). Careful attention to negative symptoms and adverse side-effects of medication is thus important.

Admission to hospital for collaborative care with a general psychiatry team can assist diagnosis by a period of stable care and enables supported commencement of neuroleptic medication combined with psychosocial interventions.

The newer neuroleptics are generally better tolerated and can produce striking improvements in patients whose symptoms have failed to improve on other treatments through poor compliance and intolerance of side-effects. However, pre-treatment screening and the monitoring of serum levels and adverse effects necessitating repeated blood tests can limit choice of second line treatments, e.g. with clozapine. For patients with low social stability, the use of depot medication by intramuscular injection often remains the best option. Advice about the propensity of cannabis and stimulants to exacerbate paranoid and other psychotic symptoms should be offered.

Carefully managed methadone maintenance can help control symptoms of paranoid schizophrenia (Brizer *et al.*, 1985). This benefit probably acts by a central effect and may also act by protecting against emotional stress. Some patients are therefore best counselled against detoxification from methadone.

Studying the temporal relationship between substance use and the onset of first episode of schizophrenia, Addington and Addington (1998) found that substance use was associated with an earlier age of onset of symptoms and that current users had poorer quality of life scores but less negative symptoms. This may suggest that although substance use is linked with early onset, it may protect against some of the negative effects of the illness. The study concludes that treatment for schizophrenia should be commenced at an early stage which is in keeping with emerging evidence in favour of early intervention in schizophrenia and in substance use.

Delirium and dementias

Clinical problem
Rapid withdrawal of sedative drugs can cause a state of altered consciousness (delirium) marked by acute confusion, impaired memory, disorientation and vivid hallucinations. The state of delirium may precede the onset of seizures and is associated with underlying brain injury (encephalopathy), possibly causing permanent deficits, and with a significant risk of death. Most typically, this condition presents in alcohol withdrawal but is also seen in withdrawal from benzodiazepines and barbiturates.

Psychiatric symptoms of agitation and hallucination may predominate and can be associated with secondary delusions. There is therefore a risk to third parties as well as the patient and the true cause may initially be missed in the crisis.

Long-term alcohol use causes dementia by generalised toxicity to the brain. However, significant dementia also arises as a result of untreated encephalopathy and may be superimposed on chronic global deficits. The dementia which follows encephalopathy is the specific condition of Korsakoff psychosis, marked by impaired short-term recall and thus causing severe disability, often in very young people. Because of social circumstances and patterns of substance use, prodromal episodes may have passed unnoticed and apparently resolved with resumption of the substance, usually alcohol. Dementia may therefore be the first presenting symptom. States of dementia may also be produced by head injuries, severe infections and other generalised illnesses. Evidence of the neurotoxicity of Ecstasy is emerging including the possibility of long-term impairment of cognitive function (Henry, 1996).

Treatment

The treatment of delirium is a medical emergency and should be undertaken in hospital where urgent anticonvulsant sedation and high-dose injectable thiamine should be given. Dementia occurring with acute onset always requires urgent medical investigation. Full physical examination and further investigation to exclude trauma or infectious causes is essential.

Chronic cognitive deficits make the treatment of substance use additionally complex. Assertive treatment in all cases of suspected delirium and dementia, including acute presentations in emergency departments, is thus essential.

Obsessive–compulsive disorder (OCD) and other disabling neurotic disorders

Clinical problem

Perhaps because a degree of neurotic behaviour is common to us all, the disabling effects of severe forms of these conditions are often unrecognised and seldom come to mind when considering serious mental illness.

Anxiety-reducing substances are often used to reduce the anxiety of resisting obsessive compulsions or the anxiety associated with phobias. A reduction in anxiety can liberate the individual and enable social integration. The power of such learned response can be difficult to address unless the problems produced by the substance use become greater than the substance-induced relief from anxiety. For example, an obsessive–compulsive checker may be able to overcome his or her anxiety in leaving the house after taking alcohol or opiates but may then be overwhelmed by the expense and problems of maintaining sufficient alcohol use as tolerance and dependency develop.

Treatment

It is important to identify the underlying disorder and to facilitate detoxification so that behavioural techniques can address the true anxiety. Whilst some reduction in problems may be achieved without detoxification, perhaps by substitute medication or the treatment of associated depression, the continued use of anxiety-reducing drugs does not allow for fully effective, exposure-based, behavioural therapy. It should also be recognised that the substance itself may be exacerbating anxiety by lowering mood or reducing cognitive efficacy. These compounding effects are common with alcohol and benzodiazepines. Addicted individuals can therefore benefit from careful educational input about the drug effects and be optimistic, rather than fearful of detoxification. Some SSRI antidepressants are licensed for use in OCD and phobias and can be helpful adjuncts to treatment.

Eating disorders

Clinical problem

Alcohol, drug and eating disorders have many causal or provoking factors in common, especially childhood trauma and affective disorders, anxiety states and problems of personality development (Lilenfield et al., 1997).

Substances are powerful regulators of appetite and their use can quickly develop into biochemical dependency. Opiates may be used to suppress appetite. Stimulants are often chosen to increase energy and reduce weight without a drastic reduction in food intake.

There are therefore many associations between eating disorders and substance use. The choice of drug may also reflect underlying mood, personality and opportunity. Alcohol may be part of binge behaviour and may replace calorific intake whilst modifying mood and anxiety. Drug use may vary episodically in response to symptoms such as insomnia and food craving which are common. All patterns of substance use are seen in anorexia nervosa and bulimia nervosa, the existence of which may be concealed over a long time.

Treatment

Eating disorders are easily overlooked. Poor appetite and weight loss may be attributed to the depressed appetite of substance use, poor eating habits and social norms of substance use. Disclosure may not be forthcoming unless careful enquiry is made. Once recognised, referral to specialised counselling is advocated and a careful examination should be made for associated depression or anxiety states requiring treatment. In severe states, urgent referral for physical health care, possibly including supervised substance withdrawal, is essential before initiating psychiatric treatment.

Illness in adolescence

Clinical problems

Relatively little has been written about the psychiatric problems of young substance users. Child and adolescent psychiatric services do not usually have particular skills to respond to young people who use substances, and specialist drug and alcohol services have traditionally been for adults with established addiction. In contrast, younger substance users tend to be non-dependent polydrug users. As the prevalence of use of illicit drugs increases in the adolescent population it is becoming clear that although the presenting symptoms and conditions may differ, the prevalence of co-morbid psychiatric illness is similar to that found in adults (Kandel *et al.*, 1997).

Reviewing studies of psychiatric symptoms in drug-using adolescents, Zeitlin (1999) found that the most common conditions were depression, conduct disorder, ADHD, eating disorder and psychosis. Swadi (1992) found a raised prevalence of behavioural disturbance. As with adult mental illness, a common factors aetiology linking substance use with mental illness is probably the most relevant, with the associated conduct disorder being a common link. The diagnostic criteria of conduct disorder which include substance use are however a confounding issue.

There are some pointers to the links between psychiatric symptoms and subsequent substance use which may also indicate possibilities for early intervention. Kumpulainen (2000) studied psychiatric symptoms and behaviours in a population whose age was 12 years and assessed their alcohol use when followed up at the age of 15. Externalising behaviours and depression were the factors predicting heavy use of alcohol when gender, socioeconomic status and family structure were controlled.

Recent advances in the understanding of ADHD, a developmental disorder, suggest an over-representation among substance-using young people. Diagnosis is difficult due to the similarity of symptoms of polysubstance use.

The early stages of schizophrenia often present diagnostic difficulty but are important to consider. Schizophrenia typically presents for the first time in young adulthood. A prodromal disorder of social disengagement, altered mood and unfocused thinking in adolescence can often be recognised in retrospect. Studying the prevalence of substance use in first episode psychosis (schizophrenic and other), Cantwell and colleagues (1999) found a 37% prevalence, the high rate being especially in young males. Recent research suggests that early intervention, including antipsychotic medication, reduces morbidity and mortality in schizophrenia (Falloon *et al.*, 1998). Withdrawn behaviour, social and communication difficulties and altered mood may present before the occurrence or disclosure of delusions or hallucinations in schizophrenia. Thus it is hard to distinguish from adolescent adjustment and the effects of substances. A high index of diagnostic suspicion is needed. If the presenting behaviour is very different from peers and if mood changes are severe or incongruous, mental illness should be considered. Advice about avoiding potentially harmful substances, especially cannabis (Johns, 2001), is particularly relevant in the prodromal or early stage of schizophrenia.

Depression may commence in earlier childhood and be unrecognised or disabling. Common factors of vulnerability lead to substance use, and mood disorder may underlie the transition to problematic substance use. Depression should be suspected in any young person whose substance use is entrenched or disproportionate to their peer group. Childhood emotional and sexual abuse, bereavements and trauma are risk factors and may require specific interventions. A study of young people who had made serious suicide attempts (Beautrais, 2000) found high rates of psychiatric morbidity including depression, affective disorder (70.5%) and substance use (38.8%).

The risk of suicide currently rising, particularly in males aged 16–24 years, should be recognised and incorporated into care planning, including contingencies for direct access to help for young people in distress. Hawton and colleagues (1993) found that substance use was the best predictor of suicide in a population with a history of deliberate self-harm. It has been suggested that the most significant impact on adolescent suicides would be achieved by prevention and treatment of substance use (Williams & Morgan, 1994).

PTSD in young people has a wide range of causes which are also vulnerability factors for substance use. The approach to treatment should recognise the potential for further trauma inherent in exposure to recall. The practice of debriefing following trauma is not necessarily therapeutic – a finding which is important when meeting the needs of co-morbid illness in young people who are at risk of further adverse events as a result of substance use.

Eating disorders arise in association with depression, OCDs and psychosis or, most commonly, as a primary problem. Treatment of underlying illness is important, as is the direct treatment of eating disorder through individual therapy, the use of support agencies and family therapy. There is a high mortality and morbidity in unresolved illness. The associated factors in respect of substance use are discussed earlier in this chapter.

Interventions

Maintaining contact with younger service users is likely to be complicated by their poor personal organisation and impulsive behaviour, illustrating the need for a more assertive and individually focused approach to treatment. Skills in the treatment of co-morbid psychiatric illness are still predominantly in the field of child and adolescent psychiatry. Close collaboration is thus important.

In responding to co-morbidity in young people, a multiagency and multi-disciplinary approach to treatment is vital in order to address the associated problems which accrue in combination with adolescent psychiatric illness and substance use. Substance use and mood disorders are associated with early educational underachievement requiring specific educational interventions. The involvement of family is important and will sometimes reveal parents with substance use, psychiatric illness or both – these parental factors being known to be associated with higher prevalence in young people (Crome, 1997; Crome *et al.*, 2000). Links between adult and young people's agencies can therefore be very valuable.

Recommendations concerning the optimum therapeutic structures have been described in the Health Advisory Service (HAS, 1996) thematic review of the needs of substance-using young people, revised (HAS, 2001) to take account of rising prevalence and greater awareness of need. The principles of service integration must be combined with a recognition of the need for a child-centred approach, distinct from the services for adults.

Illness in older people

The majority of problematic substance use in older people probably remains undisclosed, unrecognised or untreated. The natural history of addiction in younger people has been thought to be one of resolution of problematic use by mid-life. However, this is not universal, and as social boundaries become less distinct there is an emerging prevalence of illicit drug use, including heroin, in older people. There is also a significant prevalence of the use of other substances including alcohol, prescribed and over-the-counter (OTC) drugs, perhaps replacing the illicit use of earlier life. The issue of whether such use reflects social changes alone or, as in problematic use in young people, reflects additional vulnerability, remains largely unexplored. Clinical experience suggests that older people presenting with substance dependency are likely to have additional psychiatric problems.

Psychiatric disorders of older age include a higher preponderance of depression and dementia and a higher risk of suicide. The depression is likely to have been recurrent from younger life and to be only partially responsive to treatment. Nevertheless, the approach to treatment should be energetic and optimistic. Poor expectations possibly account for some of the poor outcomes in population studies of the health of older people (Crome & Day, 1999).

Alcohol use in association with psychiatric illness remains the most common presenting problem. In later life the associated cognitive decline can reduce awareness on the part of the drinker. Carers may not recognise the significance of the alcohol use or may not be aware of it at all. Episodic use is associated with fluctuating confusion and paranoia, whilst chronic use causes depression, hallucinations and paranoid delusions and increases suicide risk (Crome, 1997). Both patterns of use are associated with dementias, either of the Wernicke–Korsakoff type affecting short-term memory or a global cognitive loss.

Because of the complexity of needs, older at-risk drinkers may need more intense or innovative approaches to help them cut down or stop drinking. Noting this, Blow and Barry (2000) have advocated a range of approaches, including targeted screening and brief interventions, applicable in primary care and specialist care.

Prescribed minor tranquillisers and hypnotics have often first been prescribed in the context of emotional distress or psychiatric illness. They can lead to addiction and are sometimes used problematically by older people. Their effects are potentially similar to those of alcohol but more commonly lead to milder mood instability and cognitive underperformance. Support to withdraw from tranquillisers can therefore be a valuable adjunct to the treatment of psychiatric illness.

Opiates prescribed for chronic pain occasionally become a problem through gradual increase in level of use. The possibility of underlying depression, more common in the presence of chronic pain, needs to be considered. Alternatives for the management of pain by referral to the appropriate medical facilities, combined with gradual dose reductions, treatment of depression and cognitive interventions should all be offered. Antidepressants are recognised as a useful adjunct to the treatment of chronic pain even in the absence of depressive illness.

Intervention in co-morbid substance use in older people requires services to match their multiple needs. Liaison between primary care and specialist services is essential. Treatment of physical health problems can be a helpful link into addressing substance use. Chronic pain, sleep disorders, depression and the range of symptoms linked with substance use may be more easily accepted as the starting point of treatment from which withdrawal of substances may then be approached.

Learning disability and psychiatric co-morbidity

Learning disability may present additional risks to individuals in respect of substance use. Education and prevention strategies seldom take account of this population. Substance use is associated with an increased prevalence of social and psychological disorders of childhood which are likely to impair educational progress. Underachievement at school is known to be linked with increased vulnerability to adolescent and adult substance use although such individuals are often unrecognised as having special educational needs.

The prevalence of major mental illness is increased in learning disability and the course of disorders such as schizophrenia may be more adverse. In addition, the vulnerability to exploitation is increased. For such reasons, the prison population contains many casualties of social and professional inattention to the needs of people with learning disability.

The development of a street-wise demeanour may be misleading. A higher level of awareness of the possibility of learning disability and the complex needs of individuals is therefore required.

Psychiatric service models, collaborative care and primary care

The need for a collaborative approach between substance services and psychiatric services and primary care is clear from all the data on co-morbidity. It has also been clearly demonstrated by enquiries into serious adverse outcomes. Appleby (2000) highlighted the need for better integration of general psychiatry and substance services to enable better detection of the risks of suicide and homicide and better care planning. Reviewing a series of public inquiries, Ward and Applin (1998), in a publication aptly named *The Unlearned Lesson*, graphically illustrated the need to improve collaborative care for people with co-morbidity who are at high risk of harm to themselves and others.

Models of co-morbidity services have largely focused on the interface between psychiatric and addiction services for adults. The leading research on intervention does not always reflect the added important role of the involvement of primary care teams and GPs. The latter are more able and better trained to make integrated health assessments, addressing physical, social and psychiatric needs, and initiating appropriate specialist referrals. This arrangement avoids some of the difficulties of disparity of focus between psychiatric and substance services.

With the exception of alcohol, the drugs which are the most common causes of concern in the treatment of psychiatric illness, i.e. cannabis, benzodiazepines and amphetamines, are not the usual focus of addiction services. The process of collaborative working must address these issues. Similarly, addiction services are not traditionally skilled in the recognition of psychiatric symptoms. Psychiatric and substance services do, however, have skills of risk and harm reduction in common, including social interventions, though expressed in different terminology and with different referral patterns.

Models of good practice essentially seek to share skills through collaborative working and training and to remove the barriers to effective care. The most appropriate service structure for any locality may be determined by issues of local prevalence, population mobility, existing structures, rural or urban setting, the quality of primary care and the willingness of all staff to work together.

The development of link workers to outreach and liaise with other teams is relatively easy to implement but should not be seen as a sufficient solution. Drugs workers may be located in primary care and Community Mental Health Teams (CMHTs), and community psychiatric nurses (CPNs) from primary care and CMHTs similarly linked to addiction teams. All services need to work collaboratively with a psychiatrist who has had specialist training

and experience of working with the complex needs of substance users. Staff who focus on co-morbidity should have a reduced caseload to allow for greater complexity, for assertive follow-up and increased liaison activity which are the cornerstones of effectiveness. Collaboration should include clarity of roles and the identification of the appropriate person to act as overall care coordinator for each individual service user.

As skills develop, liaison staff are increasingly in demand for specialist training of other professionals and can be powerful ambassadors for the needs of this group. All mental health care staff in primary and secondary services require skills to identify, intervene and refer people with substance-related problems. Currently the training of most health professionals does not provide such skills and therefore specialists have an important educational role.

Dedicated dual diagnosis teams may be able to provide effective integrated care for the most severely ill group and to deliver the addiction treatments with greater flexibility than traditional services. They will not be able to accommodate the wide spectrum of co-morbidity of substance use and less severe psychiatric disorders, and their presence does not remove the necessity for such skills to be developed in other teams.

In an analysis of treatment models, Ley and colleagues (2000) found no evidence in favour of any one model, including integrated specialist teams, but noted that improved interventions require additional resources. Reviewing recent evidence of effective interventions, Drake and Mueser (2000) found separate services to be ineffective whilst integrated treatment programmes combining substance use and mental health interventions offered more promise. Successful programmes included assertive case management, motivational interventions for patients who are not able to recognise the need for drug or alcohol treatment, behavioural interventions for those who are trying to maintain abstinence, family interventions, help with housing, rehabilitation and psychopharmacology.

Co-morbidity outreach and specialised skills are vitally needed in the prison and other forensic services (Gunn *et al.*, 1991). Responses to substance users in prisons, as in the UK, have so far tended to address only drug use itself and have not included the recognition of psychiatric co-morbidity. The custodial system contains many young people with highly complex needs and a high mortality from suicide, often linked with substance use. Services urgently need to address this area.

The importance of separate, child-focused services has been repeatedly stressed in analyses of the needs of young substance users. Their needs cannot be provided by adult psychiatric services which do not have the necessary interagency networks or the experience in adolescent mental health. In most localities this population is not currently being referred to, or recognised by, Child and Adolescent Mental Health Teams (CAMHTs) although the prevalence of substance use in young people suggests that many service users with conduct disorder, ADHD and parasuicide are indeed users of drugs and alcohol. There are major training and clinical resource issues to be addressed and much research required to determine suitable treatment interventions and models of best practice. Early experience of assertive liaison work indicates the enormous need and the considerable rewards of working with such needy young people (Crome *et al.*, 2000).

Engaging service users into psychiatric care

The nine principles of effective working described by Drake and colleagues (1993) illustrate the importance of placing service users' needs at the centre of strategy. These principles, which emerge from clinical research, include:

(1) assertive outreach to facilitate engagement and participation in substance treatment
(2) close monitoring to provide structure and social reinforcement

(3) integrating substance use and mental health interventions in the same programme
(4) comprehensive, broad-based services to address other problems and adjustment
(5) safe and protective living environments
(6) flexibility of clinicians and programmes
(7) stagewise treatment to ensure appropriate timing of interventions
(8) a longitudinal perspective congruent with the chronicity of dual disorders
(9) optimism

Perhaps the greatest of these is the optimism without which the energy will not be found to deliver care and influence strategy. Practice based on the principles of assertive care and measured interventions suggests that the previous findings of poor outcome can be modified by changes in practice. As noted by Dixon's review of poor outcomes (1999), the association of substance use in schizophrenia with increased psychotic symptoms, poor treatment compliance, housing instability and homelessness, medical problems including HIV, poor money management and greater use of crisis services illustrates the need to provide more effective care for this population.

Techniques of engagement familiar to the addictions field can be applied to co-morbidity treatment. Motivational interviewing (MI) interventions have been demonstrated to enhance outcomes in terms of engagement in psychiatric treatment (Swanson *et al.*, 1999).

Conclusion

There are many service users with severe and disabling mental illness and substance use who have never received psychiatric assessment and planned care. They can be greatly helped, and enormously pleased, when they find their needs being met and their health improving.

Chapter 17
Physical Health Issues

Introduction

Enabling substance users to minimise the risks to their physical health and to maintain good health are core tasks in this field. A good knowledge of relevant health issues is essential. This knowledge has to be applied in particular settings in order to be relevant to service users. As well as reviewing the physical associations and consequences of substance use, this chapter also takes an applied approach to physical and emotional health, considering specific settings and situations which commonly occur in the course of substance use. Improvements to physical health can be aided by holistic harm reduction and enhanced personal functioning through a bio-psychosocial approach. Aspects of health specific to women, including pregnancy, are considered in Chapter 18. Mental health and psychiatric illness has been considered in Chapter 16. Both mental health and environmental issues closely interrelate with physical health, and substance use is an integral part of this. Improvements to the environment (Chapters 13 and 15) and the use of interventions to relieve psychological distress (Chapter 14) can be key issues which ensure and enhance physical health.

The interrelationship between psychological/ psychiatric issues and physical health

Disorders that are traditionally, and perhaps mis-leadingly, termed psychiatric are highly prevalent in medical populations. At least 25–30% of general medical patients have coexisting depressive, anxiety, somatoform or alcohol-related disorders (Ormel *et al.*, 1994). Because they are so common,

psychological/psychiatric disorders may simply co-exist with physical health problems, but medical disorders may also directly cause psychological/ psychiatric disorders. Similarly, mental health disorders may lead to physical illness. At least one-third of all physical health symptoms remain unexplained, some of which include a phenomenon known as somatisation (Reid *et al.*, 2001). The use of psychological interventions to relieve psychological distress is known to improve physical health outcomes, quality of life and social and work functioning, greater satisfaction on the part of both patient and doctor, and leads to a reduced use of health care services (Kroenke, 2001).

The interrelationship between the environment and physical health

Socio-economic status has long been recognised as an important determinant of ill health and lifestyle-related illness, including poor nutrition, alcohol and drug use (Blaxter, 1990), and people from deprived areas are more vulnerable to disease (Richards *et al.*, 2002). There is a vicious circle between deprivation and vulnerability to ill health. People become more vulnerable when they become unwell. Ill health may itself lead to low income and poverty, unemployment, family disruption, social isolation and in some cases homelessness. Some people are more vulnerable than others to deprivation and the effects of adverse social factors such as social isolation. Lone motherhood is strongly associated with poor health, as is ethnic minority group status and substance use. Health status and outcomes of treatment are known to be profoundly affected by poverty. Ill health following unemployment is common, although more prevalent for men than women. Homelessness is strongly associated with disease and increased mortality. In the UK the life expectancy of rough sleepers is about 30 years and they face a wide range of health problems because of the conditions they experience (Pleace & Quilgars, 1996). This compares to the national average of 74 years for men and 79 years for women. The importance of social interventions in health care cannot be underestimated.

Health risk and behaviour

Health can be improved not only by helping ease adverse environmental and mental health problems, but also by helping people choose behaviours which are less damaging to their health. Many behaviours pose high risks, not only to the health and well-being of the person concerned and those who are closely tied to them, but in many cases there is also a significantly increased risk of loss of life, both in the short and the longer term. Enabling people to change their behaviours is particularly important for young people, drug users and heavy drinkers, and those involved in male or female prostitution. Enabling change does not necessarily mean stopping those behaviours. Many prostitutes, drinkers and drug users either do not wish to stop or would find it too difficult to achieve. Almost all, however, will welcome friendly help and advice to reduce the harm they may do to themselves and others. In particular young people and drug-using prostitutes may engage in high-risk behaviours that are more likely to occur in certain environments, especially prisons.

Access to routine health procedures and facilities should be encouraged. A history of social deprivation in childhood is common in substance users and is linked to poor health. Many substance users have low expectations of health care and have experienced difficulty in accessing services. Poor diet and dental disease is a clear example of a problem compounded by substance use. Damage to teeth from neglect, the tooth grinding of stimulant use, the acidity and sugars of methadone mixture and the effects of trauma result in poor self-esteem, recurrent pain and social disability. These problems are exacerbated by exclusion from access to dental care because of stigma, fear and poverty.

Young people

Initiation to alcohol and drug use is generally at a young age and carries quite serious risks to health. Teenage drinking is often in binge mode and may be reckless. There appear to be quite marked international differences, but teenagers from those countries reporting the highest levels of intoxication in the general population (Denmark, Finland, Britain, Ireland and Iceland) report much higher levels of periodic heavy/binge drinking (Plant & Miller, 2001). The risk of alcohol poisoning and death from binge drinking appears to be little known in most countries. Adolescence and young adulthood is a period of high risk of alcohol-associated accidents, and this is also true of accidents related to other drug use in which alcohol often plays a significant part.

Young people tend to regard themselves as invulnerable to health risks stemming from their behaviours relating to alcohol and drug use, injecting behaviour and sex (Plant & Plant, 1992). Injecting drug use is likely to be unsafe in young people due to inexperience and lack of appropriate equipment. Condom use and knowledge of safer sexual practice is also relatively limited in younger people. This is a challenge for outreach approaches to health promotion, particularly through primary care.

Prostitution and health behaviour

Substance use is linked to prostitution through several powerful mechanisms. Perhaps the most recognised is the issue of selling sex to fund drug use. There are, however, other influences on both male and female sex workers and their use of alcohol and other drugs.

Women and men engaged in sex work for financial gain may find that the stress of prostitution becomes a trigger for alcohol or drug use, thereby producing a complex cycle. The hours and setting may also prompt substance use as a social facilitator or to ease physical discomfort. The use of alcohol and benzodiazepines to overcome the anxiety of street work can be the start of further substance use.

For others, prostitution is a consequence of substance use, being used to fund a habit. Such habits may become increasingly severe and complex as earnings enable higher levels of use. Often the source of supply is linked through pimps and may include threats or actual violence from which it is difficult to escape.

Since the recognition of HIV the gay men's movement has contributed enormously to peer education and policy. Persistent advocacy promoted constructive and effective local and national policy and helped reduce stigma. This has been of considerable benefit to drug users with HIV. However, due to the persistence of separate funding and of different group identities, the integration of health promotion and harm reduction between sexual and substance use risks has not been very successful. It is often overlooked that many substance users are gay and that many others are involved in homosexual sex in risky settings, particularly in prisons and in commercial sex. Some of the messages about safer sex may not be reaching younger gay men and minority groups such as drug users. There is much that remains to be done to enable staff to sympathetically address these issues and to enable service users to receive relevant information and care.

Young, homeless street workers are often entrapped into the drug scene through relationships with older males who initially seem protective. A history of childhood sexual abuse leaves young adults ill-equipped to make judgements about adult relationships and may underlie poor self-esteem and sexual risk-taking.

Whilst condom use has increased among sex workers, they remain at risk from sexually transmitted infection. Studies indicate that the major risks occur through non-commercial partnerships rather than with clients (Ward *et al.*, 1999).

Clients of sex workers bring sexual risks which differ from the prevalence among drug users (Elifson *et al.*, 1999). Whilst drug users, especially intravenous (IV) users, have a raised prevalence of viral infections, their clients bring increased risks of syphilis and bacterial infections as well as HIV and hepatitis.

Cocaine, with its relatively high price, disinhibiting effects and the facility to enhance endurance whilst reducing pain, has strong links with prostitution. One London study demonstrated a higher rate of hepatitis C among crack cocaine users as compared to other prostitutes and postulated that this may relate to transmission through oral lesions from smoking (Ward *et al.*, 2000).

Morbidity and mortality from violence is also a hazard both as a risk factor for primary drug use and as a consequence of prostitution. Research in Liverpool found that 61% of prostitutes reported the experience of violence inflicted upon them by a sex trade client at some point of time, 44% in the previous year, whilst 58% had been raped, 26% in the previous year (Morrisson *et al.*, 1994). A study of attenders at a genitourinary medicine (GUM) clinic in Norwich demonstrated a significantly raised profile of previous sexual assault in childhood or as adults. Assaults which involved penetrative sex, or violence with weapons in childhood, or as a result of sex work were particularly associated with the development of post-traumatic stress disorder (PTSD) and other emotional problems (Matthews *et al.*, 2000). For many the result is likely to be a long-term emotional problem (Bownes *et al.*, 1991). Sexual dysfunction is found to result in approximately half of those whose assaults relate to childhood sexual abuse (Keane *et al.*, 1996).

Studies of street prostitutes have found their needs to include protection from assault, social support, counselling, addictions treatment, job training and medical care (Valera *et al.*, 2001). Males who have commercial sex with men have been found to take greater risks if drug-using. About one-third do not identify themselves as gay, are not in contact with health promotion aimed at the gay community and may also take greater sexual risks in non-commercial and heterosexual activity (Rietmeijer *et al.*, 1998). This group are not very apparent to drugs services. They warrant further research and interventions in harm reduction.

Young people of school age are often overlooked, but a study in Oslo indicated that 1.4% had sold sex. Boys were involved more often than girls. Adolescents who had sold sex were lonely and more often reported symptoms of depression and anxiety than others. There was an association with conduct problems, alcohol and drug use. The majority reported no contact with any helping services, indicating the need for more preventative work and greater knowledge (Pederson & Hegna, 2000).

A wide range of interventions can contribute to harm reduction for substance-using sex workers. Because of the hidden and transient lifestyle of many users, the inclusion of an outreach model is important. This may be through direct street work or via inreach to other organisations. Examples include medical sessions, drugs service outreach workers and needle exchange within an HIV prevention unit (Morrisson & Ruben, 1995) and contact sessions within non-statutory prostitution support services.

Complex social and psychological reasons prevent male and female sex workers from finding the time, motivation and confidence to access traditional services. The attitudes and approaches of staff are of central importance (Hindler *et al.*, 1995). The provision of health services specifically for drug users involved in prostitution can enable the dissemination of health information, male and female condoms appropriate to sex work, referrals for substance use interventions, screening for sexual health–related illnesses and treatment for sexually transmitted infections. Studies have shown a higher rate of cervical dysplasia, indicating a raised risk of cervical cancer in female sex workers (Woolley *et al.*, 1998). Appropriate screening and medication for sexually transmitted infections can reduce HIV seroconversion in prostitutes (Laga *et al.*, 1994). Regular screening has been shown to reduce the incidence of gonorrhoea in female sex workers from 11% to 4% and halved the incidence in their clients (Holmes *et al.*, 1996).

Recognition of the raised prevalence of psychological problems, PTSD and psychiatric illness in substance users due to a commonality of factors and as a result of related experiences indicates the importance of the availability of specialist services as part of interventions with sex workers who use substances.

In summary, although sex industry workers are at high risk of assault, blood-borne virus (BBV) infections, sexually transmitted infections, cervical cancer, long-term emotional problems and substance use, they generally do not access traditional

services. Specific outreach is needed to facilitate harm reduction and treatment initiatives, and to help provide this needy group with needle exchange, social support and housing, counselling, addictions treatment and medical care. Sexual health promotion with all substance users, linked to ready access to appropriate treatment remains a high priority.

Prisons and the health of substance users

Prison is not only an unwelcome and unpleasant environment, it is a very hazardous one in terms of substance use, populated with generally disadvantaged people whose health is characterised by multiple problems. These problems include high-risk injecting drug use, and problem alcohol use.

BBV infections
A national sample of 8% of the UK prison population in 1997 found high lifetime levels of injecting in adult males (24%), females (29%) and young offenders (4%) with a strong possibility that some infections with hepatitis B virus (HBV) and hepatitis C virus (HCV) had occurred in prison (Weild *et al.*, 2000). Of those who had injected while in prison, 75% had shared injecting equipment. Of the 2679 adult males, 645 had a lifetime history of injecting drugs. Of these

- 3 (0.5%) had antibodies to HIV
- 131 (20%) had antibodies to HBV and 5% of these (6–7 people) will have chronic hepatitis B
- 200 (30%) had antibodies to HCV and 80% of these (160 persons) will have chronic hepatitis C

France has similar figures (Hedouin & Gosset, 1998). Cannabis use is detectable in the urine for about two weeks and metabolites of heroin for only two days. Initial concern that mandatory drug-testing of prisoners, used punitively, may encourage prisoners to switch from cannabis use to class A drugs (Gore & Bird, 1996) has been backed by anecdotal evidence. When this happened in Switzerland the pragmatic response was to cease testing for cannabis, thereby averting potentially serious health care consequences.

Because of the absence of needle exchange in prisons and the relative unavailability of injecting equipment, one syringe is usually shared between many prisoners leading to a rapid spread of BBVs. Needle Exchange Programmes (NEPs) have been successfully implemented in Switzerland, Germany and Spain in 17 different prisons (Rutter *et al.*, 2001). In Spain needle exchanges are to be set up in all prisons. In the UK there are no plans to introduce needle exchanges into prisons. Instead disinfecting tablets are being distributed in 11 pilot prisons with plans to extend this to all prisons. It is hoped that this will help people clean their injecting equipment. This may help prevent the spread of HIV, but it may not be effective against hepatitis C, which is a far greater problem. There is evidence from Australia that methadone maintenance treatment within a prison setting reduces HCV transmission (Dolan *et al.*, 2000).

HIV and HBV are also commonly transmitted sexually. Many heterosexual men become involved in homosexual activities whilst in prison, and few UK prisons make condoms readily available. On their release prisoners may spread these two viruses to their partners in the wider community.

Another route of BBV spread is via unsterile tattooing while in prison. A Norwegian study has shown that a history of tattooing independent of injecting drug use has been shown to be significantly related to BBV infections (Holsen *et al.*, 1993). In a prison setting a single needle is commonly used to tattoo many people. In France 44% of prisoners have a history of drug use (Rotily *et al.*, 1998). A similar percentage of Australian prisoners with a history of drug use also receive a tattoo while in prison. In New York 24% of all female prisoners report being tattooed while in prison. These are some of the reasons why prisons have gained a reputation as being multipliers of BBVs.

All prisoners should have access to testing, assessment and treatment services. Those who have developed a BBV infection or other illness should receive the same level of health care available to the general population. The prison environment often provides difficulties. Investigation and treatment may be interrupted by moves between prisons or by release. Visits to hospital require escorting officers and may be cancelled if there are staff shortages. Every effort should be made to resolve such problems in the interest of equity and public health.

Health problems on entering prison
At the point of remand or sentence, drug- and alcohol-dependent prisoners are likely to experience withdrawal. In severe alcohol dependence there is a danger of delirium which requires prompt medical treatment with sedation and IV thiamine to prevent seizures, brain damage and risk of death. Acute benzodiazepine withdrawal from high non-therapeutic doses carries similar hazards of seizures and is associated with severe mood swings and emotional distress. The syndrome is easily missed, being unrecognised by the user and undetected by professionals. Substitution benzodiazepine medication and gradual withdrawal is indicated. Other drugs do not carry the same risks in withdrawal although opiate withdrawal may lead to severe diarrhoea and vomiting and occasionally dehydration and fatal collapse.

During the stay in prison
The main risk of drug dependence occurs in the absence of substitute treatment which, together with the emotional triggers for continuing use, leads to illicit use in a setting with a high probability of sharing of injecting equipment. Substitution treatment is needed in prison either for short-term remand prisoners to enable continuation of treatment commenced in the community, to assist detoxification or to provide maintenance. In the UK, the prison service has stated an acceptance of the principle that health care in prison should be equivalent to that in the community. However, despite overwhelming evidence indicating the benefits of methadone treatment programmes, even within the first month (Strang *et al.*, 1997), in many prisons in the UK and elsewhere such treatment remains unavailable, although the situation is slowly improving.

Prison may be a good time to focus on health improvement with immunisations and screening.

All prisoners with a history of drug use should be immunised against HBV. Attention to mental health is also of great importance with a high prevalence of mental illness, emotional distress and suicidal behaviour.

The efforts of health and social professionals working with prisoners is therefore focused on risk reduction, supporting people through detoxification with symptomatic medication and education about the risks of overdose.

On release

One of the most common times for overdose to occur is in the first two weeks of leaving prison. Whilst in prison tolerance is generally lost or substantially reduced and most prisoners who are also drug users celebrate their release by taking drugs. Often this is at the same level they had been taking before prison. For opiate users in particular there is a high risk of accidental fatal overdose in this circumstance. All drug users leaving prison should be warned of this.

In the UK and a few other countries there are various rehabilitation schemes within prisons for those who seek to be drug-free, sometimes linked with additional privileges. Local drug services should be notified of prisoners needing services following release and aftercare services arranged. Some specialist drug and alcohol services, overwhelmed by the demands of those with current problems, have become relatively unskilled at working with substance-free former users in the community, and may need to provide more relevant aftercare.

Types of physical health risk faced by substance users

The health risks that all substance users face are from

- the substance itself
- the unknown quantity of many street drugs
- the low safety margin of some drugs
- contaminant substances and infections
- the route of use
- blood-borne pathogens

Health risks from the substance itself

Health risks from alcohol use

UK units are measured by 8 g alcohol/unit drink. At low levels of regular drinking (up to 14 UK units per week for women, or 21 UK units for men) there can be a health benefit through the prevention of coronary heart disease by altering the blood fats in a beneficial way. This was originally challenged (Shaper, 1990) because the British Regional Heart Study of middle-aged British men showed that 70% of non-drinkers are ex-drinkers who have high rates of heart disease and high blood pressure. This is sometimes termed 'the sick quitters syndrome'. However, the cardioprotective effects of moderate alcohol intake were subsequently shown to be present even when those with poor health or chronic disease have been excluded from the group of abstainers (Boffeta & Garfinkel, 1990; Jackson *et al.*, 1991). Blood levels of high density lipoprotein are increased, and in turn results in a comparative reduction of the more dangerous low density lipoproteins. It is thought that alcohol may also have an indirect action on platelet stickiness and that these factors combine at low drinking levels to exert their cardioprotective effects.

At higher levels of drinking, blood fats are affected in a different way. There is a rise in triglyceride levels and this has an adverse effect upon the heart, thus explaining the so-called J- or U-shaped curve of initial benefit followed by increasing medical problems as alcohol consumption increases.

Alcohol use over the so-called *safe* limits has the unfortunate distinction of potentially affecting every organ and system of the body from skin to brain and all internal organs. There is a close statistical relationship between levels of weekly alcohol consumption and risk of medical harm – the greater the alcohol consumption, the greater the risk (Anderson *et al.*, 1993). If drinking occurs for long enough above a certain level, harm becomes a certainty. If women continue to drink more than 35 UK units per week, and if men continue to drink 50 UK units per week or more, medical harm will eventually occur. Women are more susceptible to the effects of alcohol mainly because they have less body water than men and so at tissue level alcohol is more concentrated.

More recent research looking at alcohol consumption and mortality shows that age is an important factor as well as gender. Although both non-drinkers and heavy drinkers have a higher all-cause mortality leading to a J- or U-shaped curve, studies on young people show a direct dose–response relationship to medical harm with the beneficial effects of alcohol only becoming apparent in older age. For women aged 16–54 and men aged 16–34 there appears to be a direct dose–response relationship to alcohol with increasing harm and substantially increased risk of all-cause mortality, even in people drinking at lower levels than the officially recommended limits. It is only at ages of 55 years and above for women and 35 years and above for men that a health benefit from drinking becomes apparent. Based on the evidence of this work, White and colleagues (2002) recommended that women should limit their drinking to one unit per day up to age 44; two units per day up to age 74; and three units per day over age 75. Men should be advised to limit their drinking to one unit per day up to age 34; two units per day up to age 44; three units per day up to age 54; four units per day up to age 84; and five units per day over age 85.

With regard to non-medical harm there is no J-shaped curve at any age. Drinking at any level is a contributory factor for accidents and for violent and other behaviours which themselves are hazardous to health, such as drug use, unsafe injecting behaviour and high-risk sexual contact. The short-term physiological effects of alcohol include diminished coordination and balance, increased reaction time and impaired attention, perception and judgement. All of these increase the risk of accidental injury and again there is a close correlation between the amount of alcohol consumed and harm. The more you drink, the greater the likelihood of harm. In the UK alcohol is a factor in approximately 40% of all deaths from falls, 40% of all deaths in fires, 15% of all drownings and 25% of all deaths in road traffic accidents (RTAs). Over a quarter (28%) of pedestrians in accidents have blood alcohol levels over the legal limit for driving.

Preventing trauma from alcohol is more than just the encouragement of a global reduction in drinking patterns. It is encouraging individuals not to drink in specific circumstances by peer pressure, by in-creasing awareness through health education, notices and so on, by legislation (e.g. for drinking and driving, football crowds) and by advertising. Accidents can also be prevented by making environmental changes such as toughened beer glasses and safety barriers. A range of over-the-counter (OTC), prescribed and illegally obtained drugs, particularly sedatives and tranquillisers, can summate with alcohol to further impair judgement and the performance of skilled tasks and are a contributory factor in many accidents.

In the context of health alcohol is a preventable adverse factor in the progression of other diseases, most notably for people with chronic hepatitis C infection. Here alcohol increases viral replication, enhances viral complexity, increases liver cell death, suppresses immune responses and causes iron overload (Vento & Cainelli, 2002).

The brain and central nervous system (CNS) is particularly sensitive to damage from drinking, and chronic heavy drinking leads to cerebral atrophy and overall shrinkage of the brain, delirium, dementia and specific memory impairment of the Wernicke–Korsakoff type. Thiamine, which is needed for the healthy maintenance of nervous tissue, is used up when alcohol is metabolised. In addition many drinkers have an inadequate diet and poor absorption and do not replenish their store of thiamine as it is used up. The treatment of delirium to prevent focal brain damage is a medical emergency requiring IV thiamine.

There may be central or peripheral nerve damage, leading to unsteady gait, numbness and poor coordination. These signs also require treatment and advice about personal care, and should not be confused with the short-term effects of intoxication.

Many mild episodes of brain and CNS damage due to partial withdrawal probably go unnoticed and untreated. Periods in custody or even in hospital are times of risk and the attention of those in charge of such settings should be drawn to the need for treatment. It is also easy in these situations to overlook serious accidental head injury while drunk and confuse the signs of head injury and low blood sugar with inebriation. There have been several instances where drinkers left to *sleep it off* in police custody have been found dead the next morning. The effects of RTAs on those who have been drinking can be worse than anticipated. Alcohol is known to increase the effect of the initial kinetic impact (Marshall *et al.*, 1992) and there is evidence to suggest that it also potentiates the severity of traumatic brain injury in RTAs (Cunningham *et al.*, 2002).

Long-term heavy drinking produces inflammation and fatty infiltration in the liver. Early changes, detectable with blood tests of liver enzymes and by scanning are reversible. The demonstration of biochemical improvement, particularly ongoing reduction of gamma-glutamyltransferase (GGT) levels, can be motivating following withdrawal and is a helpful form of feedback in relapse and during screening. The liver has great powers of recovery. After several years of excessive alcohol use fibrosis of the liver will occur, but this is also reversible in the early stages. However, if damage continues, the next stage, cirrhosis, is irreversible, and, when enough of the liver becomes cirrhotic, the result is liver failure and death.

In people with chronic hepatitis B or C even low levels of drinking can lead to hepatic fibrosis and cirrhosis. Because heavy drinking can cause changes in blood clotting leading to increased hazard with liver biopsy, drinkers with HCV and prolonged clotting time due to alcohol use may be deemed unfit for liver biopsy until they have reduced their alcohol consumption. A period of inpatient treatment for the alcohol problem may facilitate treatment for HCV by allowing clotting times to improve.

Certain cancers are common in drinkers. As most drinkers smoke it has been difficult to determine whether drinking or smoking is the causative factor. A history of heavy drinking is statistically related to cancers of the lip and lower bowel, but we now know that although cancer of the rectum is associated with beer drinking only, both smoking and drinking are independently associated with cancers of the oral cavity, pharynx, larynx, oesophagus, stomach, liver and breast. Because of these strong links, interventions to assist alcohol and drug users to reduce smoking are an important component of harm reduction. The details of treatment aids to help smokers are not discussed in this book, although much of what is written in the text for drinkers and drug users is equally applicable to those addicted to nicotine (see Preface).

In general, however, the greatest bodily harm from alcohol occurs to the digestive system, the brain and the peripheral nervous system. Gastritis with associated morning nausea and vomiting (which is partly also due to a central effect of alcohol) is commonplace in drinkers. Part of the retching is due to an abstinence effect and may be reduced by the consumption of more alcohol. Gastritis usually subsides quickly after intake ceases but in those with a severe drink problem erosions develop to a more serious degree. Gastric or duodenal ulcers are not uncommon and can be a source of serious haemorrhage. One of the most unpleasant illnesses caused by heavy alcohol consumption is acute pancreatitis associated with acute pancreatic cell death 36–48 hours after an alcohol debauch. Pancreatic enzymes are released and literally digest the person's own internal abdominal tissues. It is associated with severe upper abdominal pain and is diagnosed by a raised amylase level of at least 1.5–2 times above the normal range. If it is complicated, e.g. by shock, renal failure, coagulopathy or adult respiratory distress syndrome, the mortality may exceed 30% (Ranson, 1984). For those with a history of heavy drinking for several years chronic pancreatitis can occur and the abdominal pain may become persistent. The liver is one of the prime organs affected by alcohol. Acute fatty liver, chronic fatty liver, alcoholic hepatitis and hepatitis can all be caused by excessive drinking although the relationship of these conditions to each other is not clear.

The reproductive system is affected both directly and by the effects of liver disease on the metabolism of sex hormones. Fertility is reduced in men and women and chronic drinking causes breast enlargement in both sexes. Other abnormalities of the hormonal systems may exacerbate chronic fatigue.

Nutrition is usually impaired, often to a severe degree. The inflammatory effects of alcohol on the stomach causes impaired digestion, but provides a source of calories which reduce appetite. Alcohol withdrawals affect the vomiting centre of the brain and reduce appetite through chronic nausea and discomfort. For those drinkers who have developed an appetite for alcohol in preference to food careful attention to diet and vitamin supplements is needed following withdrawal. There is little evidence of value of oral vitamins in those who continue to drink hazardously but this should not negate efforts to improve nutrition in general.

Drinking even at moderate levels is associated with raised blood pressure and may cause coronary artery disease or disease of the cardiac muscle. Cardiac arrhythmias and cardiomyopathy are associated with prolonged excessive alcohol intake. Red blood cells become increased in size as a toxic effect of alcohol, and deficiencies of clotting factors develop. There is an associated risk of external and internal bleeding including strokes and brain haemorrhage. Chronic bleeding from the stomach or gut may lead to iron deficiency anaemia. In advanced liver disease there is an increase in the circulation relating to the liver and gut known as the portal system, from which catastrophic bleeding can occur – most commonly from dilated veins in the oesophagus (oesophageal varices).

Health risks from naturally occurring opiates and synthetic opioids

Even a low opiate dose that is well within the therapeutic range can be fatal if there is no tolerance to the drug. However, in tolerant individuals, apart from dependence, opiates alone at normal therapeutic doses are unlikely to cause serious medical problems. However, they do cause constipation, suppress the cough reflex which may lead to an increased frequency of chest infections, cause loss of libido for both men and women, and many women have reduced fertility through suppressed ovulation with amenorrhoea lasting several months at a time. Most of the medical harm from opiate use is dwarfed by the harm that accrues from social problems, criminal and legal difficulties or from unsafe injecting practices. These more serious harms, which affect not only the individual but also the wider community, are substantially reduced and often completely removed by the legal prescription of an oral opiate substitute such as methadone mixture, in the context of treatment (Gossop *et al.*, 2001) – a fact which, for many clients, justifies long-term prescribing.

The health risks of CNS stimulant use

These vary in their medical effects from the very mild (e.g. caffeine, pemoline, coca leaf chewing),

through a moderate strength range (e.g. amphetamine sulphate) to potent stimulants (e.g. crack cocaine and methamphetamine). Caffeine and other weak stimulants are unlikely to cause any significant medical problems unless taken to excess. This does sometimes occur.

CASE STUDY

> Patient X attended his general practitioner (GP) complaining of recurrent headaches. A striking feature of these headaches was that they only occurred at weekends. It transpired that the complainant was in the habit of drinking 40 cups of strong coffee each day when he was at work. Realising that this was not good for him, he made sure that he had no coffee at weekends resulting in withdrawal headaches. A simple understanding of the problem was all that was needed, following which he adjusted his weekday consumption to lower levels and his headaches disappeared.

As can be seen from the above example, although physical dependency may be a feature of stimulant use, dependency as a syndrome with social, biological and psychological constructs may be absent in mild, or even moderate strength, stimulant users. Many amphetamine users take their drugs only at weekends, stopping them without difficulty during the week.

However, with regular use and high dosages, dependency on amphetamines clearly does occur and, with the more powerful CNS stimulants, becomes more common. Indeed, Freud, who had made several studies of cocaine and often took it himself, later became so disillusioned with the drug as more reports appeared linking it with dependence, that he eliminated all his studies of cocaine from his autobiography. Yet in spite of this, until the mid-1970s it was widely accepted that cocaine did not produce dependence because a physical abstinence syndrome had not been clearly demonstrated. Since then, with the emergence of crack cocaine and the increased global use of methamphetamine, withdrawals featuring depression, fatigue, irritability, and loss of libido or impotence are commonly encountered.

Methamphetamine (Methedrine) was used by many forces personnel during World War II. Gossop reports that the German Army is said to have found them 'very useful in modern battle conditions when used in mass attacks'. He also states:

Hitler received daily morning injections of what seems to have been methedrine. By 1943 he needed more than just one injection – sometimes as many as five a day. Witnesses at the time described how these made Hitler instantly alert and talkative. In addition to the injections, Hitler also took methedrine tablets. Such prolonged and progressive use of amphetamines takes its toll, and it has even been suggested that Hitler's unrealistic optimism and his fixed, rigid thinking during the battle of Stalingrad and on subsequent occasions may have been due to the adverse effects of his amphetamine abuse. This sort of speculation is interesting but inconclusive, though the irrationality, outbursts of rage, obsessional thinking and persecutory ideas that Hitler showed at that time are known symptoms of excessive use of amphetamines (Gossop, 1993).

Seventy-two million amphetamine tablets were distributed to the British armed forces during the war. There are anecdotal stories of English wartime fighter pilots who died because they fell asleep and crashed their aircraft as the effects of amphetamine use wore off.

In the decade following the war the old war stocks of amphetamine were placed on the open market in Japan. By the early 1950s about 550 000 of the Japanese population were thought to be using the drug. Of these 55 000 had methamphetamine psychosis (WHO, 1997a). In spite of subsequent strictly imposed government controls, a large illicit manufacturing and distribution trade has built up in Thailand, China, Indonesia, Malaysia, Myanmar, the Philippines and Singapore. Methamphetamine use and consequent psychosis is now a major public health issue in the Asia-Pacific region (Farrell & Marsden, 2002).

Other harms that accrue from stimulant use include heart rhythm disturbances, elevated blood pressure, epileptic fits, anxiety and phobias, overheating and drug-induced psychosis. Although these problems are usually temporary in their effects certain individuals may be particularly prone to develop them and sometimes may go on to develop more serious harms. For instance, those with a history of convulsions will be most likely to fit; those who already have a cardiac rhythm disorder may go into heart failure or even cardiac arrest; and those who already suffer from hypertension may develop strokes. These problems occur more frequently as those who continue to use drugs move into old age. The use of crack cocaine has a reputation for being associated with aggression and violence.

Health risks and CNS depressants

Barbiturates, benzodiazepines, meprobamate, alcohol and gamma-hydroxybutyrate (GHB) all fall into this group and cause the same harmful effects which have been described as the 'central nervous system depressant syndrome'. Although sometimes known as *soft drugs* this name belies the very real dangers that can occur through CNS depressant use. The occasional barbiturate user is still seen today but thankfully this is not often. More commonly benzodiazepine users are encountered. Benzodiazepines are safer than barbiturates in that it is much more difficult to overdose on them, although in polydrug users they contribute to some fatal opiate and/or alcohol overdoses. Dependency is, however, now a well-established problem of benzodiazepine use, even at low therapeutic doses. Drug takers often take them at levels that far exceed the therapeutic dose. High doses will impair cerebral functioning, making the user appear drunk and chaotic. Lesser cognitive effects of benzodiazepine use tend to persist, even when the user had habituated to the sedating effects. The capacity to retain important information within short-term memory processes is greatly impaired by benzodiazepine use. Those involved in the treatment of substance users should be aware that this may impede therapeutic endeavours, particularly information-based interventions. GHB (or GBH as it is sometimes dubbed) is an anaesthetic. At low doses it gives the relaxant and euphoric effects of CNS depression. It has been linked with date rape and is used as a dance drug. At high doses nausea, vomiting, muscle stiffening, convulsions, coma and respiratory collapse have all been reported. Luckily it has a very short duration of action and most people who have been hospitalised from GHB use have made a rapid and full recovery.

Withdrawal effects from CNS depressants are also notable for the harm that they can cause. Of particular note are withdrawal convulsions, which, as with alcohol withdrawals and excessive stimulant use, are particularly likely to occur in those who have a history of fitting, and are more likely in polydrug users. Delirium tremens can occur in the withdrawal state from any drug of the CNS depressant group, not just alcohol. As diazepam is a particularly long-acting benzodiazepine withdrawal fits can occur ten days or more after cessation of drug use. Just as with long-term heavy drinkers, CT scans of the brain show a reduction in size of the cerebral cortex associated with long-term benzodiazepine use (Lader et al., 1984). The significance of this is still not clear.

Health risks from inhaling volatile substances
The practice of sniffing glue and other volatile substances varies considerably between localities and over time. The fatality rate has varied in the UK since the 1980s from one to over two per week. These tragedies sometimes occur in those who are sniffing for the first time. About half of all deaths are caused by accidents that occur when intoxicated. The other causes of death from inhaling volatile substances derive from the substance itself. Some substances, such as lighter fuel or aerosol propellants (halons) are more harmful than others to inhale, such as glue. Unfortunately there appears to be a trend away from sniffing toluene (a relatively less harmful solvent found in most glues) to the more dangerous fluorinated hydrocarbons.

Fluorinated hydrocarbons sensitise the heart muscle causing it to overrespond to circulating adrenaline and noradrenaline. If someone sniffing aerosol propellants becomes startled and attempts to run away, an excess amount of adrenaline and noradrenaline is released (the fight or flight reaction). This in turn acts on the sensitised heart muscle leading to heart rhythm disturbances and, in some cases, death. Sensible harm reduction advice for those first encountering someone inhaling a volatile substance is to approach them slowly and do nothing to startle them.

Sensible harm reduction advice for those who inhale these substances is to avoid the most dangerous volatile substances such as fluorinated hydrocarbons and lighter fuel. Also to make sure that they are not in a dangerous place, such as a canal bank or roof, avoid the use of plastic bags to inhale from, and never do it when alone. When advice like this was first issued by the Institute for the Study of Drug Dependence in 1979 there was severe criticism (ISDD, 1979).

The health risks of cannabis use
Cannabis is a *dirty drug* from a pharmacological point of view in that it has more than 50 active compounds known as cannabinoids. Some cannabinoids can have beneficial effects such as hypnotic, tranquillising, antinausea, anticonvulsant and pain-killing effects. Nabilone is a synthetic cannabinoid which has a medical product licence to treat nausea and vomiting in those who are receiving chemotherapy for cancer. In the UK cannabis itself is not currently used therapeutically. It is known to reduce the pressure in the eye, and in the USA it has been used to treat glaucoma following a special case made by someone who was unable to tolerate other medical treatment. There is a claim made by some people with multiple sclerosis, which has yet to be fully substantiated by research, that they benefit medically from smoking cannabis, particularly in respect of muscle spasms and chronic pain.

Looking at the harms and risks to physical health, smoked cannabis resin does contain three times the tar content of ordinary cigarettes. As the inhaled smoke is retained longer than the smoke from a normal cigarette, carbon monoxide levels in the blood of cannabis smokers are on average five times the level of those smoking ordinary cigarettes. Cannabis smokers are at increased risk of respiratory disease, particularly chronic bronchitis. The lung tissues of chronic heavy cannabis smokers show the same histological changes that precede the development of lung cancer in cigarette smokers (Tashkin, 1999).

Other potentially harmful effects of cannabis are a loss of ability to estimate time and space accurately. There may be an associated reduced ability to concentrate, and an impairment of memory, thinking ability and physical coordination. These problems tend to occur at high blood levels of the drug and in this respect cannabis has some similarities with alcohol. From a theoretical point of view high levels of cannabis use are likely to be associated with an increased risk of accidents and this has particular relevance to heavy users of cannabis who drive cars, fly aeroplanes or operate industrial machinery. There are several papers in the international literature showing high numbers of fatal RTAs associated with post-mortem tests for cannabis that were positive. However, most of these have been uncontrolled and are often accompanied by alcohol use. On balance the evidence does suggest that cannabis makes a small contribution to RTAs in its own right (Gieringer, 1988). Its major public health significance may be in exacerbating the adverse effects of alcohol and driving. The majority of cannabis users involved in fatal accidents have used both drugs (Hall *et al.*, 1994). About 3% of the adult population of the USA (Anthony & Helzer, 1991) and Australia (Hall *et al.*, 1999) meet criteria for cannabis dependence.

Health risks and the use of psychedelic drugs
All these drugs are taken orally, with the exception of phencyclidine, which can also be smoked or injected. They are generally classified into synthetically made drugs and those that are naturally occurring. Synthetic psychedelic drugs include: LSD, mescaline, hallucinogenic amphetamines, phencyclidine and analogues. Those that are naturally occurring include magic mushrooms, fly agaric, mescaline, morning glory seeds, grated nutmeg, mace and ergot. LSD is the most powerful of all the psychedelic drugs and because such small quantities are needed it is usually distributed as microdots on paper carrying distinct designs such as Toadstool, Red Heart, Pink Panther, Palm Trees and so on. Although tolerance to LSD may develop rapidly, withdrawal symptoms from the drug have yet to be demonstrated suggesting that perhaps this is metabolic tolerance, causing the drug to be eliminated from the body more quickly, rather than tolerance of the CNS to the drug (neuroadaptation). Dependence does not seem to occur, and these drugs all tend to be used on a sporadic or occasional basis. It is not clear whether psychoses may be precipitated but the phenomenon of flashback is recognised and may be linked to the same risky behaviours as intoxication. Apart from risks to mental health which are discussed further in Chapter 16, the main health risks which stem from psychedelic drug use are from accidents while hallucinating. There have been reports of people who have walked under cars and trains or attempted to fly from a window.

Health risks and hallucinogenic amphetamines
Ecstasy – MDMA (3,4-methylenedioxymethamphetamine) – is a synthetic ring-substituted amphetamine. In spite of its classification this drug is not hallucinogenic at normal doses. Ecstasy, like other stimulants, tends to cause tachycardia, hypertension and constriction of the blood vessels in the skin which, coupled with an effect on the temperature-regulating mechanism of the brain, causes a rise in body temperature. It is commonly used as a dance drug as the increased energy given by its stimulant properties enables prolonged dancing. This in itself causes the dancer to become hot, and in a hot atmosphere there can be further overheating to the point where fatalities may occur. The sale of cold drinks and the provision of a cool area for dancers to chill out will reduce the likelihood of this harm occurring. However, Ecstasy also increases antidiuretic hormone (ADH) release, leading to fluid retention so that drinking too much fluid can be harmful – in some cases even fatal. A reasonable balance is about one pint non-alcoholic fluid consumed per hour. Of the 81 Ecstasy deaths in England and Wales recorded between 1997 and 2000, only six (7%) had occurred when the drug was taken on its own. It has been suggested that other drugs, particularly opiates, were taken to modulate Ecstasy's adverse effects. Typically the deceased took several different prescribed and non-prescribed drugs (Schifano *et al.*, 2003). There is current controversy as to whether Ecstasy causes brain damage. Individuals suffering from heart disease, high blood pressure, glaucoma, epilepsy or mental illness are at particularly high risk of health problems from the use of Ecstasy, stimulants and hallucinogenic (psychedelic) drug use.

Ketamine users can experience hallucinations at normal doses (100–200 mg), and, like LSD users, often experience synaesthesia or a confusion of sensory impulses, so that they see touch or smell sound. Out-of-body flying or floating experiences are common and their combination with anaesthetic drug effects may lead to serious physical injury. Ketamine is used as a dance drug and is the only hallucinogen which can be injected. Impairment of the memory processes continues for at least three days after a single dose, leading to chronic memory problems in regular ketamine users (Curran & Monaghan, 2001).

Another drug of this group, phencyclidine, is commonly used as a street drug in the USA, but not in the UK or Europe. Like ketamine, phencyclidine is a dissociative anaesthetic so that out-of-body hallucinations are also linked to physical injury.

Health risks from anabolic steroids and other drugs taken to promote anabolic processes

Anabolic steroids. Testosterone is the naturally occurring drug of this group from which almost all of the many synthetic anabolic steroids are derived. Some are manufactured illicitly. The medical use of these drugs is limited to only a small number of conditions. Testosterone replacement therapy is given for the maintenance of male sexual drive and characteristics when medical problems such as brain tumours or injury interfere with the body's natural supplies. Currently medical use of the synthetic analogues is restricted to the treatment of aplastic anaemia, and the reduction of itching which accompanies chronic biliary obstruction and terminal liver disease. Their use as a treatment for female osteoporosis has been abandoned.

There is a large illicit market for synthetic anabolic steroids such as nandrolone and stanozolol to boys of high school age, gym users and high performance sports enthusiasts in the hope of muscle building. The claims that steroids make people more aggressive and increase muscle strength have yet to be substantiated, although they do help increase muscle size.

Side-effects such as fluid retention may occur. Some steroid users take a mild diuretic to overcome this problem. The most serious medical problems from illicit steroid use arise from the acquisition of BBVs through shared injecting equipment. Eighty-one per cent of steroid users are thought to inject and about one-third of these have shared injecting equipment (Drugscope, 2001). Hypertension is a common side-effect. Because testosterone analogues compete for the testosterone receptor, their use can allow the feminising effects of the small amount of naturally occurring oestrogen in men to predominate and male infertility and gynaecomastia (enlargement of breast tissue) may occur. In contrast the use of androgenic steroids by women may lead to the development of male secondary sexual characteristics with enlargement of the clitoris, increased body hair, deepening of the voice, amenorrhoea and acne.

Other drugs sometimes taken by body builders because of their believed anabolic effects. Some other drugs are taken in the (usually erroneous) belief that they themselves have anabolic properties. Thyroxine and insulin are widely and wrongly believed to augment anabolic processes by enhancing the body's ability to utilise foodstuffs. Overdoses readily occur through insulin use. An injection with only a slight excess of insulin may rapidly lead to hypoglycaemic coma and death. Body builders should be warned against the use of these drugs. Human chorionic gonadotrophin (HCG) is used by some people in the belief that it will stimulate the production of naturally occurring testosterone when this is suppressed by anabolic steroid use. Growth hormone is used for its own intrinsic anabolic properties and the recreational drug GHB is taken by some body builders in the hope that it will stimulate growth hormone release during sleep.

The unknown quantity of many illicit drugs

Many illicit drugs are manufactured illegally with no quality control or other manufacturing safeguards. In addition filler powders, such as lactose, which look like the drug, are often added at street level before a sale so that low-level dealers are able to make money. Thus street drugs are often of unknown strength and purity, and this is associated with a risk of accidental overdose.

The low safety margin of some drugs

For some drugs there is only a relatively small gap between the therapeutic and lethal dose (the therapeutic index). Barbiturates, which were common street drugs in the UK until the late 1970s, fell into this category. Accidental overdoses were common and in many cases were fatal. Barbiturates are particularly dangerous because tolerance is rapidly built up to the psychic effects of the drug without the development of a similar tolerance to the physical effects. Accidental overdoses from barbiturates in particular occurred with relative frequency because one prominent side-effect is to impair recent memory, increasing the possibility of a double dose. In the mid-1970s barbiturate users would overdose, be taken to a hospital casualty department, wake up, ask for help and then discharge themselves, only to return unconscious with another overdose, often the same day. Lethal overdose would commonly follow. Many opiate drugs, including heroin and methadone, also have a low therapeutic index. As already mentioned in Chapter 11, the normal dose recommended for stabilising people on maintenance methadone may be fatal for those who are not tolerant to such doses. A time of great risk is when people are first introduced to illicit heroin and have no tolerance.

Biological and chemical contaminants

Contaminant substances

Contaminant substances may be purposefully introduced or derived from impurities of illicit manufacture. Recurrent newspaper articles suggest that heroin and other powdered street drugs are cut with lookalike substances which are often more dangerous than the drug itself. One typical example states:

> [Heroin], so benign in the hands of doctors, becomes highly dangerous when it is cut by black-market dealers – with paracetamol, drain cleaner, sand, sugar, starch, powdered milk, talcum powder, coffee, brick dust, cement dust, gravy powder, face powder or curry powder.

In fact the cutting agent is almost always a harmless sugar such as glucose or lactose.

However, purposeful contamination with another psychoactive substance to make a low purity illicitly manufactured drug appear stronger does sometimes occur and may increase the risks of street drug use. For example, barbiturates or benzodiazepines are sometimes added to illicit heroin, increasing the risks of fatal overdose. Occasionally contaminant drugs are produced by mistake in the manufacturing processing. In the USA in the 1980s a designer drug known as MPPP was illegally manufactured for use as a street drug. If too much heat or acid was used in the manufacturing process of this meperidine (pethidine) analogue, a contaminant drug known as MPTP was produced which had the ability to induce an irreversible form of Parkinson's disease. Other less harmful contaminants include tablet filling agents, which may cause sterile abscess formation if tablets are ground up and injected by mistake into the tissues surrounding a vein.

Biological contaminants

Infections may be introduced directly from the environment during the manufacturing process or by injecting with unsterile water. More dangerously, contamination by blood-borne pathogens can occur through contact with other drug users' equipment. Contamination can also occur during transport and storage of illicit drugs, e.g. with pathogens in soil.

From April 2000 there has been a spate of serious illnesses among injecting drug users (IDUs) in Britain and Ireland. One particular form was accompanied by a syndrome of soft tissue inflammation at the site of drug injection, circulatory collapse, leucocytosis (raised white blood cell count), pleural effusions (fluid in the lungs), and soft tissue oedema (swelling) and necrosis (tissue death). Eighty-eight people were affected and 40 died. In several cases *Clostridium novyi* type A was identified in local tissues (GGHB, 2000). This is a bacterium thought to have entered the drug supply from soil contact on the Afghan–Pakistan border where much illicit heroin is manufactured.

Botulism can also occur but is rare. This life-threatening illness is normally associated with the ingestion of botulinus toxin produced by *Clostridium botulinum* when preserved foods become infected in the absence of oxygen. However, infection of wounds can occur and botulinus toxin produced *in situ*. Over 90% of cases of wound botulism have been reported from the USA (75% from California). In the UK and Eire it was first diagnosed in the year 2000, but there has been a cluster of cases in 2002. Temperature remains normal, but there is acute descending paralysis involving autonomic and cranial nerves. Double vision, difficulty swallowing, slurred speech and muscle weakness occur. If untreated, progressive paralysis rapidly develops involving the limbs, trunk and respiratory muscles. Antitoxin is available but botulism is rapidly fatal unless intensive care is given. Artificial ventilation may be required for several weeks.

Fungal endophthalmitis, a rare infection of the internal tissues of the eye, is thought to arise in drug users from contaminants of lemon skin introduced intravenously (Leen & Brettle, 1991).

More common biological hazards are of bacteria from the skin and from the viruses hepatitis C (HCV), hepatitis B (HBV) and HIV. Hepatitis A, B, C, D, E and G are all more common in drug users than in the general population. Hepatitis A virus (HAV) is normally spread by the *faecal–oral route* when the preparation of cold food is associated with poor personal hygiene. However, it has been suggested that injecting paraphernalia contaminated by HAV-infected faeces could give rise to blood transmission of HAV in this group (Sunkvist *et al.*, 2003). The prion causing vCJD (variant Creutzfeldt–Jakob disease) is also in theory likely to be spread by shared injecting equipment, but at the time of writing (2003) a specific test to confirm this is not available.

Bacterial contaminants of the injection site can cause hot, inflamed injection abscesses. Other localised infections may cause clots and obstruct blood supplies causing tissue death, strokes and so on. Septicaemia, an infection of the blood, can be serious and life-threatening, particularly if caused by Gram-negative bacteria. In the presence of congenital heart abnormalities subacute bacterial endocarditis can occur, which commonly leads to slow destruction of heart valves. It is associated with a low-grade intermittent febrile illness and flu-like symptoms and is easily overlooked. Withdrawals are unlikely to cause a raise in body temperature of more than 0.5°C. Higher body temperatures should be viewed with suspicion, prompting a search for signs of septicaemia or other serious infections.

Health risks and benefits according to the route of use

The oral route

Swallowing is the safest route to take drugs, mainly because after absorption from the gut the drug has to pass through the liver before it reaches the general circulation. One of the main functions of the liver is to detoxify poisons and prevent them from harming the individual. About one-third of most drugs are detoxified in this *first pass* through the liver. It is also safer to take drugs orally because it takes 30–60 minutes for most drugs to be absorbed, giving a time safety margin in case of overdose. In addition, the oral route is less likely to be associated with dependence. The reward is paired with the memory of the stimulus (i.e. when the drug was taken) rather than the stimulus itself, and this produces a weaker conditioned response than classical Pavlovian conditioning. Drugs taken sublingually (i.e. under the tongue), e.g. buprenorphine, are absorbed directly into the blood stream of the general circulation, and because of the resultant rapid absorption curve, their safety margin is reduced (although buprenorphine has some inherent protective aspects as described in Chapter 11).

Sniffing/snorting

Sniffing powdered drugs directly or via a straw, or tube of rolled paper bypasses the liver and is also a direct route into the general circulation. Cocaine powder is commonly taken this way if it is not injected. Cocaine acts both as a local anaesthetic and constricts local blood vessels – the combined effect may lead to repeated injury of the nasal septum without the user realising this. Those who have snorted cocaine repeatedly for several years may end up with a perforated nasal septum. Shared straws from cocaine use have also been implicated in the transmission of hepatitis C.

Smoking

Inhaling the fumes from heroin powder ('chasing the dragon') heated on aluminium foil is a common way of taking the drug initially, and may pave the way to dependency and later injecting. There may be an association between heroin smoking and an increased risk of asthma, but this has still to be verified. The smoking of specially prepared cocaine was formerly known as 'freebasing'. Originally this referred to a chemical process whereby cocaine was freed from the hydrochloride part of the molecule by mixing it with a volatile chemical like ether and then heating it up. Later, after a US comedian had blown himself up, a safer method was discovered by mixing cocaine hydrochloride with ordinary sodium bicarbonate and heating the mixture in a microwave. The resultant small pellets or rocks make a cracking sound when smoked. Crack, as it has become known, is not pure cocaine but greater quantities are absorbed by smoking and so the toxic effects of the drug are more common by this route. The drug takes only a few seconds to get into the blood stream and dependency is often quickly established. Although up to one-third of heroin that is smoked may be lost, smoking is a relatively efficient route to absorb a drug. If cannabis is smoked, about three times as much of the drug gets into the systemic circulation than if it is taken by mouth.

Injecting

Drug users' injection techniques vary substantially. Skill does not necessarily correlate with length of experience. Thus some relatively new injectors have extensive scarring, injection site ulcers from drug leakage, bruising and superficial thrombosis or inflammation. The degree of local damage relates to the substance used as well as the actual technique. Women seem to suffer local damage and loss of veins more readily than men.

At that stage, or as a matter of choice to aid concealment of injection sites, some users chose to use the femoral vein in the groin. This is more hazardous due to the proximity of the femoral artery and other structures. There is a high risk of abscess formation and thrombosis (clotting) in the vein.

Thrombosis of a vein produces pain, inflammation, swelling and tissue damage. This is particularly hazardous in larger vessels of the legs where deep vein thrombosis (DVT) may ocur. There is a danger that part of the thrombosis in a deep vein may break away as a small clot and move round the circulation to lodge in a blood vessel in the lung as a pulmonary embolus, causing sudden death. The most common sites for a DVT are the veins within the muscle of the calf. Thromboses of the larger veins in the thigh are seen in groin injectors. The characteristic signs are pain, and tenderness and swelling of calf or thigh muscles. These are often, but not always, accompanied by fluid overlying and swelling the ankle which will indent if depressed with a finger or thumb. If a DVT is suspected, medical help should be sought urgently.

Accidental injection into an artery can lead to spasm of the artery and gangrene of the tissue supplied, sometimes with loss of a limb, particularly with barbiturates which contract the smooth muscle in the arterial wall. If barbiturates are injected into an artery by mistake instead of a vein, there will be a drug-induced prolonged spasm of the artery severely reducing or stopping the blood supply to the tissues supplied with blood by that artery. Gangrene of the leg and ensuing amputation were not unusual consequences when barbiturate use was common. Thankfully they are now not often encountered.

Diconal (dipipanone + cyclizine) if ground up and injected, may precipitate isolated spasm of small blood vessels leading to gangrene of the tissues supplied by, e.g. small branches of the mesenteric (gut) or optic arteries. Since a licence to prescribe Diconal to drug users in the UK became required in 1983 this drug stopped being a common street drug.

Severe inflammatory tissue reactions can occur from injections into local skin tissue if the vein is missed. If barbiturates are injected into the subcutaneous tissues, the resulting tissue reaction will cause sterile abscess formation and later the superficial layer of skin will often slough off, leaving what is termed as a *barb burn*. Diconal injections into the tissues are particularly associated with massive swelling of part or whole of a limb, leading to *boxing-glove hands* or grossly swollen legs mimicking a deep vein thrombosis (DVT).

Diazepam if injected intravenously will often cause a thrombophlebitis, whereby the lining of the vein becomes inflamed and a clot develops within the lumen, with the result that the vein not only becomes sore but also unusable. Perhaps for this reason diazepam in rarely injected by drug users.

Blood-borne pathogens

Human Immunodeficiency Virus (HIV)

Prevalence. The Human Immunodeficiency Viruses HIV-1 and HIV-2 were originally identified in 1983 and 1986, respectively. Both are responsible for a global pandemic. Approximately 99% of infections are caused by transmission of HIV-1, with HIV-2 being found predominantly in West Africa. HIV-2 is less infectious and is less associated with disease progression than HIV-1. It is encountered rarely in injecting drug users (IDUs). In much of Central Africa 20–25% of the population is HIVpositive, with 1 in 300 HIV positive in the USA, and 1 in 1500 HIV positive in the UK.

Injecting drug use has been a major cause of HIV epidemics in different areas of the world (WHO, 1997b). The prevalence of HIV infection among drug users varies considerably between countries according to the extent to which public health harm reduction activities have been implemented. Since their introduction in the UK in 1986 needle exchange and other harm reduction activities have been instrumental in averting an HIV epidemic (Stimson, 1995) and HIV prevalence among IDUs remains low and stable at around 3% in London and 1% elsewhere in the UK (Stimson *et al.*, 1996; Unlinked Anonymous Surveys Steering Group, 1998). In a survey in England none of those injecting for five years or less were HIV positive (Judd *et al.*, 2000). International comparative studies suggest that cities with syringe exchange show a downward trend in HIV prevalence among IDUs compared to cities with no syringe exchange provision, which show an upward trend (Des Jarlais *et al.*, 1998).

Clinical effects. HIV preferentially infects T4 helper lymphocytes, which are necessary to maintain cell-mediated immune responses. Immune function is progressively impaired and opportunistic infections break through.

Transmission. The following routes of transmission apply:

- unprotected vaginal, anal and oral sex
- injecting drug use with shared equipment
- mother-to-baby vertical transmission *in utero*, during delivery or via breastfeeding
- occupational exposure, especially for those involved in invasive procedures such as phlebotomy, surgery and midwifery
- tattooing, acupuncture, ear and body piercing, particularly in countries or environments where poorly sterilised equipment may be used (e.g. prison)
- blood transfusion in resource poor countries who may not be able to afford to screen for BBVs
- blood transfusion/blood products/organ donations prior to 1985 in the UK

HIV is a relatively slow virus taking perhaps 8–10 years before life-threatening disease intervenes. The virus is found in all body fluids, but saliva, tears, sweat, urine and faeces are not infectious unless visibly bloodstained. HIV is easily spread through shared injecting equipment and both heterosexual and male homosexual intercourse, especially if there are multiple partners, and can be spread vertically from mother to baby. Although in sub-Saharan Africa heterosexual spread remains the main route of infection, in much of the Western world the primary route of infection has been firstly via male homosexuals and secondly in IDUs. In 1987 Moss showed that for those who had become infected through heterosexual intercourse, three quarters of all index cases could be traced to IDUs, many of whom were involved with prostitution. This prompted the belief that for many Western countries the key to preventing a third wave of heterosexual spread of the virus would be by effective intervention to stop HIV infection among drug users. In the USA, however, where the introduction of NEPs was strongly resisted, injecting drug use and heterosexual contact became more important as modes of transmission during the 1990s, and the incidence of HIV infection increased among females relative to males (Klevens *et al.*, 1999). Sexual partner mixing and IDU partner mixing are now the two primary forms of contact between infected and uninfected individuals that have determined the spread of HIV/AIDS in the USA (Centers for Disease Control and Prevention, 2000).

Testing. The presence of HIV antibodies denotes current infection and not resistance to the disease. Seroconversion after exposure takes 6–8 weeks to develop and a negative antibody test is only considered confirmatory at more than three months after exposure. Immune competence is measured through the T-lymphocyte cell count. Measurements of viral load indicate viral activity. These indicators allow clinicians to predict prognosis and monitor response to therapy.

In the developed world HIV treatments have meant that AIDS is becoming far less common. AIDS is only diagnosed if certain illnesses are present which are classified as AIDS-defining. For most people there is no single point in time when they move from relative good health to severe life-threatening illness. Instead there is a continuum from HIV infection to HIV disease and advanced HIV disease.

Prevention. Prevention measures have in the past focused on the areas of sexual transmission and shared injecting equipment. These include public health campaigns regarding safe sex, the promotion of condom use with spermicide such as nonoxinol 9, which has the added advantage of viricidal action against HIV, water-based lubricants which reduce condom and tissue damage, needle exchange, the prescribing of oral substitute drugs, and other successful harm reduction measures.

Considerable research is being undertaken to find an effective vaccine. Treatment is being developed for primary HIV infection before seroconversion occurs. During this phase some patients have symptoms and signs of acute retroviral syndrome and can be identified. Post-exposure prophylaxis (PEP) using drug therapy to prevent HIV infection after significant exposure shows promise. Initiatives to prevent the vertical transmission of HIV are making an impact. Since 1994

zidovudine (azidothymidine, AZT) alone has been shown to be effective if given in the last three months of pregnancy. Other effective interventions include caesarian section, and therapy for the baby whilst avoiding breastfeeding. Mandatory antenatal HIV screening in France and the offer of interventions to stop vertical transmission is said to have prevented any French babies being born with HIV in 1997.

Treatment. Drug treatment aims to suppress viral replication by triple therapy and treat any specific HIV/AIDS-related illnesses by specific drug therapy for viral, bacterial, parasitical, fungal infections and cancers. Triple therapy with highly active antiretroviral therapy (HAART) has revolutionised the treatment of HIV disease, which previously had been uniformly fatal. HAART contains

- nucleoside analogue reverse transcriptase inhibitors (NARTI)
- non-nucleoside reverse transcriptase inhibitors (NNRTI)
- protease inhibitors (PI)

Tolerating and managing these complex and toxic combinations is challenging. Difficulties in tolerance to effects and in treatment adherence produce risks of viral drug resistance. During such treatment, careful attention should be paid to mood states and to adjustment of any substitute prescriptions including the possibility of drug interactions.

Hepatitis B virus (HBV)

Prevalence. In the USA an estimated one million people have chronic HBV infection, and each year there are 100 000–150 000 new cases. In many Eastern countries HBV is endemic. In the UK there is a high prevalence in drug users, surveys showing a rise in the prevalence of antibodies indicating past infection concurring with the length of injecting history, being approximately 10% at five years, 15% at 15 years and 40% after 15 years of injecting drugs (Unlinked Anonymous Prevalence Monitoring Programme, 2000).

Clinical effects. The acute infection lasts 2–6 weeks. It may be symptomless, apart from feelings of malaise but 20–50% of patients become jaundiced. The clinical picture is sometimes complicated by joint pains, itching and rashes. Liver function tests (LFT) are elevated. Very rarely a severe acute illness develops with fulminant (overwhelming) liver failure and death.

Chronic HBV infection develops in 5–10% of cases. Normal LFTs do not exclude the possibility of chronic HBV infection. After several years liver biopsy may be required to establish the extent of liver damage. Chronic disease is usually slowly progressive, and may finally result in liver cirrhosis, liver cancer and liver failure.

Transmission. Hepatitis B is mainly spread via the sexual route and through shared injecting equipment. IDUs and the sexually promiscuous, particularly male homosexuals, are at high risk of infection. HBV transmission also occurs through poorly sterilised acupuncture needles, tattoo and body piercing equipment, vertically from mother to baby, needle-stick injuries and, to a much smaller extent, the sharing of toothbrushes and razors.

Testing. The virus multiplies itself by using the reproductive mechanisms of liver cells. Various pieces of the virus are found circulating independently in the blood stream and occasionally a whole virus is seen. The viral elements are identifiable proteins known as antigens. The immune response produces specific antibodies to these antigens. Routine laboratory tests will pick up surface antigen (HBsAg), e-antigen (HBeAg), core antigen (HBcAg) and antibodies to these antigens (anti-HBs, anti-HBe, anti-HBc). The presence of core antibodies indicates past resolved infection and immunity. If surface antigen persists for more than six months chronic hepatitis B is diagnosed. The presence of e-antigen closely correlates with the number of virus particles and the relative infectivity of serum or plasma. Chronic carriers of HBeAg are sometimes termed supercarriers. Conversely the presence of antibodies to e-antigen may indicate low infectivity.

Vaccination. Because HB surface antigen will also combine with the delta agent of hepatitis D to complete the hepatitis D virus (HDV), vaccination against hepatitis B also protects against hepatitis D. This is important because HDV superinfection

can transform mild hepatitis B into a more severe illness. Coinfection of delta agent with HBV is usually clinically indistinguishable from HBV alone, but it increases the likelihood of fulminant acute hepatitis B and of a more aggressive course of the chronic disease. HBV vaccine is not effective in HBV carriers.

To be most effective HBV vaccine should ideally be given in early childhood, or at age 11–15 years in two doses 4–6 months apart. In the USA hepatitis B vaccination has been integrated into infant immunisation schedules. All non-immune adults at risk, including health care workers and IDUs, should receive HBV immunisation, although age, smoking and the male gender all reduce the likelihood of effective uptake of the vaccine.

The question as to whether individuals should be offered testing for immunity prior to immunisation will depend on the local prevalence of HBV infection. If the prevalence is low, it will be cheaper and more effective to offer the vaccine without establishing whether or not immunity is already present. If the drug user is known to have no immunity or his or her immune status is unknown, there are various schedules to consider.

- Standard
  (1) baseline
  (2) 1–2 months later
  (3) 4–6 months after the initial dose with a booster dose at 5 years
- Accelerated version
  (1) baseline
  (2) 1 month later
  (3) 2 months after initial dose, with a booster at 1 year
- Exceptional version
  (1) baseline
  (2) 1 week later
  (3) 3 weeks after initial dose, with a booster at 1 year

The choice of schedule should depend on the circumstances of the patient. The ability to commence and complete the course is more important than the dosing schedule, although the faster schedule produces less lasting immunity. Testing for immunity after completion of the vaccine course should be delayed until 8–12 weeks after the final dose of the initial schedule. If HBV immunity has not been established a further dose can be given, followed by retesting after a further eight weeks. Some people never achieve immunity and a maximum of five doses is recommended. Testing for immunity after completion of the vaccine course should not be neglected. It is important for the patient to be aware that immunity is not automatic after three injections and that they are not fully protected until confirmed immune.

Pregnant women in high-risk groups who are not immune should be offered immunisation during pregnancy. All non-immune women should be offered immunisation following delivery. If acute HBV infection occurs during pregnancy or a pregnant woman is found to be HBsAg positive before any e-markers have developed, both immune globulin and vaccine should be given to the baby within 24 hours of delivery. If the mother is of low infectivity (i.e. anti-HBe positive) the baby will not require immune globulin and should just be given vaccine at the time of delivery, two months later and a booster dose at 12 months.

Treatment. Those with liver cirrhosis from chronic hepatitis B or another cause (see Chapter 11) should avoid the use of drugs which may damage the liver and should abstain from alcohol. Treatment with interferon-2b injections for 4–6 months gives long-term remission in one quarter to a half of patients. Within 6–8 hours of the first dose patients may report a flu-like illness that lasts for about 12 hours. Promising new treatment options are becoming available, but for those with end-stage chronic hepatitis, liver transplant is the only potentially life-saving intervention.

Hepatitis C virus (HCV)

Prevalence. About 170 million people worldwide have been infected with HCV. Injecting drug use is now the most important risk factor for hepatitis C in developed countries (WHO, 1997c). Ever since blood products were heat treated to remove viruses in 1985 and blood transfusions screened for HCV in 1991, almost all new cases in the UK and other Western countries have derived from drug users who share injecting equipment. It is a new

epidemic because injecting drug use was rare before the late 1960s. There was clearly a major surge in infection via this route in the early and mid-1980s when sharing was rife and *shooting galleries* in evidence. However, those countries, like Australia and the UK, which introduced needle exchange and widely available oral methadone as the cornerstones of treatment to reduce the spread of HIV in drug users from the late 1980s, may have fortuitously benefited by also reducing the incidence of HCV by this route (Judd *et al.*, 1999).

Official UK estimates suggest that about 300 000 people in the UK (0.5% of the general population), and about 250 000 in Australia, may be HCV positive. In the USA and other countries which vehemently resisted needle exchange schemes there is now a massive HCV problem, with 1.8% of the general population infected (over two million people) in the USA alone (Alter *et al.*, 1999). American needle exchange provision compares poorly with the UK for accessibility and provision. The estimated 19 million syringes distributed in 1998 from 131 American outlets lags far behind that of the UK where 25 million syringes were exchanged in 1997 from more than 2000 outlets (Parsons *et al.*, 2002).

UK research on drug users in the community suggests an overall prevalence of about 40% HCV positive, but among injectors of less than three years it was estimated to be less than 10% (Hope *et al.*, 2001). There is clearly a window of opportunity for behavioural change. Scottish evidence suggests a more modest fall than the rest of the UK since 1990. The prevalence of HCV in Scottish injectors was 60% overall and over 30% in those injecting less than three years (Taylor *et al.*, 2000), but there are 3–4 times fewer syringe exchange schemes operating in Scotland for the resident population and the number of estimated drug users compared to England and Wales.

Clinical course. Acute HCV infection lasts 1–26 weeks (5–12 weeks in 80% of cases). Symptoms are mild. About 5% are jaundiced, more might feel sick and lethargic and have no appetite, but many people experience no symptoms at all. About 20% of those who have acute hepatitis C appear to recover completely from the infection.

The main problem is that 80% of cases develop chronic HCV. Without treatment about 20% will develop terminal liver cirrhosis, liver failure, and/or primary liver cancer in 20 years, and 30% in 30 years. (Following cirrhotic change hepatocellular cancer develops at a rate of about 3% each year.) The remaining 50% deteriorate more slowly, or reach some sort of steady state, but remain infectious to others. Markers of possible cirrhosis include a platelet count of less than 120×10^9/L, raised bilirubin, high INR and/or reduced serum albumin.

Other organs apart from the liver may become infected with HCV and complicate the clinical picture, leading to depression, extreme tiredness, rashes, joint pains and a higher than normal incidence of associated autoimmune disease such as scleroderma or vasculitis. The tiredness and depression is often of a degree to prevent people working, and may impair the ability to walk short distances or climb stairs. Unfortunately many relatively young drug users who say they are too tired or depressed to be able to work are not always believed by their doctors.

HCV in childhood appears to be a milder disease than in adults, but little is known about the long-term consequences although hepatic fibrosis and cirrhosis do occur. Considerably more research is needed. Children respond as well as adults to current drug treatments.

Transmission. HCV is spread very easily through shared injecting equipment. Some people being treated for end-stage HCV liver disease have injected only once at a party. Haemophiliacs and others who have received blood products prior to 1985, and those who have received blood transfusions prior to 1991, may have become infected from these sources. The other modes of spread are the same for all BBVs, but HCV transmission via the sexual route is rare, although it does occur. HCV may survive for long periods at room temperature and is therefore more likely to be spread through drug injecting paraphernalia, such as acidifiers, spoons, filters, stirrers and shared water from a cup (Crofts *et al.*, 2000). Contaminated hands, particularly the thumbs of injectors used to apply pressure to injection sites, may transmit infection if there is poor hand hygiene. Similarly, lighters, tourniquets and candles used regularly in the injecting process may become contaminated and pass the virus from hand to hand, and on to other people. HCV is also more resistant to disinfection, and although basic hand-washing (if available) using water or alcohol will remove most contaminated material, some is likely to remain. Thus information to drug users about cleaning their syringes with bleach or washing-up liquid, which was helpful in reducing the spread of HIV, is less likely to prevent the spread of HCV. The advice should now be that, although cleaning your injecting equipment may help to some extent, it will not prevent the spread of hepatitis C. New sterile injecting equipment should be used for each injection and great care taken over hygiene. Vertical transmission occurs in about 5% of cases, but, unlike HIV, it is considered safe for HCV positive mothers to breast-feed.

Testing. Prior to 1989 when a specific test was developed for hepatitis C, clinicians were aware of another form of viral hepatitis. This was known as non-A, non-B hepatitis, and over 95% of cases are now known to be due to hepatitis C. Routine laboratory antibody testing for HCV indicates past infection. Seroconversion for hepatitis C takes longer than for HIV infection. A negative test is promising at three months, and fairly certain six months after exposure, but can only be confirmed at one year. For those who test positive, in order to determine whether the disease has become chronic, testing for the presence of circulating virus by polymerase chain reaction (PCR) is necessary. This confirms the presence of circulating virus, although, for those people who are also infected with HIV, one in five have a false negative PCR test (George *et al.*, 2002). As with HBV the presence of normal LFT does not exclude chronic disease, although it may point towards it. Liver biopsy is the only way of determining the extent of liver damage in those with chronic HCV.

Although over 90% of those infected in the UK are unaware that they have a potentially treatable life-threatening disease, which can be readily diagnosed by a simple blood test, screening of the general population is not recommended. Opportunistic testing associated with widespread government publicity campaigns should be the way forward.

Screening antenatal clinic attenders might identify patients when they are receptive to health care interventions. However, combined interferon and ribavirin drug treatment of HCV is contraindicated during pregnancy. There is some evidence (Gibb *et al.*, 2000) that caesarian section may reduce the materno–foetal transmission of HCV but this is a single study and numbers are small. The best way of obtaining prevalence data of HCV positive pregnant women would be by adding anonymous HCV testing to the Guthrie heel prick test on babies, a routine neonatal blood test. Anonymous HIV testing is already done in Scotland by this method. The maternal antibodies for HCV and HIV are both passed over to the newborn baby. There is no case for named HCV testing of babies. But if a woman is known to have chronic hepatitis C, then consideration should be given to testing the baby for the presence of antibodies at one year, by which time antibody transmission from the mother should have cleared. Women who subsequently discover their HCV positive status who think they may have been positive in pregnancy may value referral to a paediatrician to discuss the risks of infection in existing children.

Vaccination. At the time of writing (2003) no vaccination against HCV is available.

Treatment. Preventing deterioration of those who have chronic HCV, specific drug treatments for both acute and chronic HCV, social care and alternative therapies all help complement modern drug treatment interventions.

The deterioration of those with chronic HCV is variable and is closely related to behavioural risks, particularly drinking alcohol, and the presence of superadded BBV infections. Combined HIV and HCV infection carries with it a poor prognosis, resistance to treatment, and rapid deterioration although better treatments are being found. People who share injecting equipment may reinfect themselves with different types or subtypes of HCV and worsen their prognosis. Superadded HAV, HBV, infections on top of chronic HCV will also escalate the problem, as will HDV and HEV. Current recommendations by the UK Public Health Laboratory Service are that all drug users at risk of HCV infection should be immunised against both hepatitis A and B. Those with HBV or HCV who con-

sume more than 50 g alcohol per day show an increased progression of liver fibrosis (Poynard *et al.*, 1997). Those who drink more than 80 g alcohol per day have more than a sevenfold increased risk of developing hepatocellular cancer (Tagger *et al.*, 1999). Potentially hepatotoxic drugs that might lead to deterioration of chronic HCV, including naltrexone and buprenorphine, should be avoided if there is evidence of cirrhotic change (see Chapter 11). Drug users do reduce or stop their alcohol consumption if found to be HCV positive (McCusker, 2001).

If the disease is picked up during the acute phase of infection nearly 100% of patients can be prevented from becoming chronic carriers of the virus by treatment with interferon alfa-2b (Jaeckel *et al.*, 2001).

Treatment of chronic HCV is more difficult. It is currently reserved for those with moderate to severe disease, and more than 50% have sustained recovery if a combination of pegylated interferon and ribavirin is used. Unfortunately in many places current illicit and IV drug users are excluded from treatment. The grounds for this (mainly poor adherence to treatment regimes and possible reinfection) appear to be discriminatory and unfounded and are not supported by evidence (Edlin *et al.*, 2001). In the UK, drug interactions have been added to the reasons for exclusion, but only for those drug users taking drugs intravenously, not orally (NICE, 2000). It therefore seems difficult to justify. Contrary to professional concerns Backmund and colleagues (2001) have shown clearly that current IDUs can be treated successfully with interferon and ribavirin.

The need for a flexible and unified approach to prevent the spread of blood-borne pathogens in IDUs

It is clear that the successful advice given to contain HIV infection is not adequate to contain the spread of HCV, although it has helped. Because of greater stability and enhanced survival of HCV at room temperature, the spread of HCV via injecting paraphernalia is important. In many countries it is illegal to supply clean filters, sterile water, citric acid for preparing IV heroin, and other appropriate harm reduction material. In parts of Australia clean disposable spoons are provided. In the pursuit of harm reduction, legislative change to allow provision and sale of paraphernalia was announced in the UK in 2003.

Advice about hand-washing both before and after injecting is now essential. Many drug users place their thumbs over the injection site to contain the blood flow after withdrawing the needle. Advice about cleaning syringes and blood spills with bleach needs to be refined to take hepatitis C into account. Dilute bleach may not adequately disinfect HCV.

Placing limits on the size and number of syringes distributed at any one time can be counterproductive. In Scotland the Lord Advocate's initial guidance was that no more than five needles and syringes should be given to each drug user per visit. In 1994 this was increased to 15. Used needles and syringes should be returned in a special safety container, but one-for-one exchange should never be insisted upon. Accessibility and an adequate supply of sterile equipment is paramount. Dispensing machines for syringes and containers in public places for disposal of used works is a useful feature of Australian harm reduction practice.

Several manufacturers have tried to make non-reusable syringes. All have some dead space at the end of the syringe preventing a small part of the syringe's contents from being used. As well as being expensive, they are unpopular with drug users who find they are difficult for IV use, and most will not use them.

Needle-stick injuries and other significant exposures

There is a risk of developing a BBV infection if surgeons, professional staff, IDUs or other members of the public are accidentally pricked by a needle or other sharp instrument contaminated by blood. Other significant exposures include contamination of broken skin, and splashes to mucous membranes (e.g. eyes, lips or nose) during an operation or incident. Drug users themselves are at high risk of needle-stick injuries.

Although HIV does not survive long at room temperature, HBV will remain viable for about a week, and HCV for much longer. The approximate risks of infection following a single exposure from a positive source are:

HBV (e-antigen positive)   1 : 3
HCV   1 : 30
HIV-1   1 : 300

Viral load, innoculating dose, depth of injury and immune factors can have a large effect on these rates. The following steps should be taken:

- Ensure the sharp is disposed of safely.
- Encourage bleeding from the puncture wound.
- Wash thoroughly for 5 minutes under cold running water.
- Splashes of body fluids into eyes, nose or mouth should be rinsed with copious amounts of water.
- Cover the wound with a waterproof dressing.
- Report the incident to a senior staff member.
- Medical help should be sought as soon as possible. In the UK this would ideally be at a hospital Accident and Emergency (A&E) department.
- A baseline blood sample is normally taken and stored for future testing for BBV infection. He or she should be routinely offered BBV testing at one month for viral material and antibodies, then at every three months for antibodies for up to one year. If the recipient of the injury has a history of HBV vaccination, the antibody levels should be determined at the time of exposure and appropriate boosters or immune globulin given.

HBV. Treatment given to prevent HBV transmission will depend on the recipient's vaccination history, the donor's infective status if known and the type of injury received. This can range from just a booster to a full accelerated course. Short-term immunity can be conferred by administering hepatitis B immune globulin (HBIG) within 24 hours. The recipient will also require counselling, regular testing and sexual health information.

HCV. Counselling is offered and testing at 3, 6 and 12 months. Recent studies have been suggestive of the efficacy of treating acute hepatitis C with antiviral therapy (Jaeckel *et al.*, 2001) and therefore PCR testing at one month should be considered.

HIV. PEP antiretroviral medication should be offered if the donor is known to be HIV positive or at high HIV risk. It is usually taken for four weeks and ideally should be started within 1 hour of injury. The recipient will also require counselling, regular testing at 3, 6 and 12 months and sexual health information.

Dealing with spillages of blood and other body fluids contaminated with blood

Procedure

- Wear latex gloves and plastic apron.
- Apply chlorine-releasing agent, e.g. sodium hypochlorite 1% solution or 1 in 10 solution of household bleach (hypochlorite solutions should not be used on large urine spills).
- Leave for 2 minutes.
- Mop up with paper towels and dispose of as clinical waste.
- Clean the area with hot water and detergent in order to reduce the corrosive effects of the disinfectant.

Chlorine-releasing agents should not be used on carpets or furnishings. They are highly corrosive and will bleach colour from fabrics. If carpets become soiled, mop up most of the body fluid with disposable paper towels and then clean using a steam cleaner, if available, or suitable disinfectant.

On upholstery and soft furnishings, excess fluid should be mopped up with disposable towels, sponged with cold water, then cleaned with hot soapy water or steam cleaned. If soft furnishings are badly soiled with body fluids, they may need to be considered for disposal. If blood spillages have already dried, apply chlorine granules/bleach solution to a wet paper towel and clean the spillage area before disposing safely. If there are spills on clothing,

- carefully remove clothing. If removal over the head is required, consider cutting away to avoid

contact with mucous membranes of the face. Dispose as clinical waste.
- for other clothing, sponge with cold water (do not leave to soak).
- wash as soon as possible in the hottest wash the clothing will stand.
- ironing the fabric also helps.

BBV pre- and post-test discussion and advice

Offering the test. With the exception of criteria that would exclude them, such as likely self-harm on hearing a positive result, all those who ask for a test should be offered the chance to explore whether this is appropriate for them. If they decide to go ahead informed consent must be ensured (DH guidelines for this: www.doh.gov.uk/consent). Pre-test discussion should be undertaken without judgement and with objectivity in a quiet environment. There should be appropriate literature to support the discussion, and enough time for individuals to ask pertinent questions. Arrangements for venopuncture should be made at an appropriate time for the patient, enabling as short a time as possible before imparting the results.

Pre- and post-test discussion. It should ideally be delivered by the same individual, and face-to-face rather than by telephone. Discussion should include:

- Transmission and how this might apply to the individual.
- Harm and risk reduction strategies appropriate to identified risk behaviours/transmission routes.
- What the test involves. The window period following exposure. What the results mean.
- There should be a short explanation of the natural history of BBVs.
- If the history suggests exposure, potential options and the success rate of treatment can be discussed.
- Time to discuss any specific concerns of the individual including confidentiality, life insurance (guidance can be sought in the UK from the Association of British Life Insurers) and

concerns regarding effects on partners, family and contacts.

Consideration must be given to the clients' ability to cope with the test result. The following questions should be considered:

- Are they depressed? Could the timing of the test be improved? Are there other issues, e.g. worries about drug use, relationship problems, pressure from others?
- Ask how they might feel if the test is positive or negative, and who they might turn to for support.
- Tell them how they will be informed of the result (usually in person by the testing doctor or health practitioner).
- How will they cope with waiting for the results?
- Will there be someone with them when they come for the result?

If the result is negative. Is a confirmatory test needed? Is a repeat test needed at a later stage? Discuss ways of avoiding risk behaviour.

If the result is positive. The patient will be shocked and may not take much in. Allow time for feelings to be individually expressed. All concerns must be identified and addressed. Discussion may include fears of death, stigma and social isolation. What is the patient planning to do in the next few hours and days? Whom to tell and not tell? Natural support systems should be identified, and information should be given about local and national support services.

Pre-test information should be reviewed with them. Reiterate what is known about the natural history of BBV diseases. Encourage helpful lifestyle change, such as giving up alcohol for those who are HCV positive. Again discuss ways of reducing risk behaviour. Make sure the individual knows the next step, including who will take action concerning referral to a hospital specialist. Ensure a default procedure if referral or initial appointment is missed. Confirm they know how to make contact with local support services and have written information if they require it.

Arrangements should be made to see the patient again, and medical follow-up and referral to other agencies discussed. All those with a positive test should be referred to a specialist (gastroenterologist/hepatologist/infectious disease consultant).

The need for a full range of accessible high quality services for testing and for the prevention of BBV transmission

Testing. Widespread and comprehensive testing facilities, including the availability of pre- and post-test discussion, should be available and accessible via appropriate local services. Universally available testing and information facilities should be used to provide opportunistic testing of clients at risk.

Needle exchange. If needle exchange is to be an effective public health measure, good access for IDUs is essential. Each locality should have at least one 24-hour needle exchange and a wide variety of outlets. Provision of needle exchange can operate successfully from non-specialist outlets such as pharmacies. However, generic professionals working in the community who provide needle exchange services need to be adequately supported and appropriate attention must be given to their educational requirements (Sheridan *et al.*, 2000). A full range of services will include needle exchange outlets via community pharmacists, outreach workers, specialist services, hospital A&E departments and, where appropriate, emergency needle exchange packs should be made available for those leaving police custody. Outreach services are particularly important and should not be given lesser priority than reactive services. A survey of UK drug injectors not in contact with treatment services found that over half had shared needles and syringes in the previous four weeks (Hunter *et al.*, 2000). There should be appropriate means for the safe disposal of used equipment. Needle exchange services should be widely publicised and regularly monitored. Regular local needs assessment is required to determine the range and amount of equipment to be supplied.

In UK pharmacy-based exchanges only about one-third of used injecting equipment is returned, a potential area of weakness of schemes. However, return rates of used equipment are higher where returns are pursued, and linked studies show that the remaining two-thirds of equipment may be returned to other needle exchange outlets or other safe disposal methods pursued. Fewer than 15% report disposing of equipment in an unsafe way such as loose in rubbish bins, drains or public places (Sheridan *et al.*, 2000).

Treatment services. The other important foundation stone in helping prevent potential epidemics of blood-borne pathogen disease, which threaten, not just the drug users themselves, but local communities, is locally accessible services for substitution prescribing – particularly oral methadone. Engaging GPs in the treatment of drug use is an important part of this policy in the UK. Recent research has shown 25% of UK GPs doing some substitute prescribing, and 19.8% of GPs involved in shared care with local community drug services (SMMGP, 2002).

Overdose

Accidental overdose is the commonest cause of mortality in substance users (ACMD, 2000). Non-fatal overdose is highly prevalent in substance users and is the cause of considerable morbidity. Australian research found that 69% of heroin users had experienced a heroin overdose, 28% in the preceding year. Of those that had overdosed 79% had experienced at least one overdose-related morbidity symptom, and 14% had experienced overdose complications of sufficient severity to be admitted to a hospital ward. Indirect overdose-related morbidity included physical injury sustained when falling at overdose (40%), burns (24%) and assault while unconscious (14%). Direct overdose-related morbidity included peripheral neuropathy (49%), vomiting (33%), temporary paralysis of limbs (26%), chest infections (13%) and seizure (2%) (Warner-Smith *et al.*, 2002).

Alcohol and fatal overdose. Death from alcohol poisoning alone occurs if alcohol concentration in the blood and consequently the brain, rises rapidly, depressing the respiratory centre or bringing about aspiration of stomach contents into the respiratory tract. Binge drinking leading to death from acute alcohol poisoning can occur in young people and alcohol is a complicating factor in accidental deaths due to overdose of opiates and other substances.

A study of blood toxicology of fatal overdose cases has shown that alcohol consumption is much higher in fatal cases compared to the broader heroin user population (Darke *et al.*, 1997). Excessive use of alcohol has been proposed to be a major factor explaining the low and decreasing life expectancy in Russia (Shkolnikov *et al.*, 2001). Alcohol is a significant factor in the aetiology of suicidal behaviour. It should be remembered that a degree of ambivalence and of suicidal intent has been demonstrated in a high proportion of illicit drug overdoses which appear to be accidental (Neale, 2000) and that an assessment of mood and intent is important following overdose.

Reduced tolerance to opiates a major risk factor. Hair analysis of those who have died of an overdose supports the view that absent or low opiate tolerance is a main contributory cause (Tagliaro *et al.*, 1998; Darke *et al.*, 2002). In the Tagliaro study there was no significant difference between hair morphine concentrations in the fatal cases and incompletely abstinent controls, leading the authors to conclude that most fatalities had recommenced heroin use after a period of virtual abstinence. The study by Darke and colleagues (2002), in which current heroin users had median hair morphine concentrations four times that of the fatal overdose cases, suggested that the fatal cases were also using heroin and other opiates, but at a lower degree of chronic intake.

Abstinence-oriented treatment can lead to higher risk of overdose mortality in case of relapse after losing tolerance to opiates (Magura & Rosenblum, 2001). There is an increased risk of overdose mortality during the first two weeks after entering or re-entering methadone treatment (Buster *et al.*, 2002.) Accumulation of methadone, inadequate assessment of tolerance and concurrent periods of stress or extreme heroin use when entering treatment are possible explanations. Opiate users with help-seeking behaviour are more likely to make a suicide attempt (Ghodse *et al.*, 1985). There is an increased risk of overdose in the first six weeks following release from prison (Seaman *et al.*, 1998) and after any episode of reduced level of use including hospital admission and detoxification. Advice on the risks of overdose should be clearly and repeatedly given in these circumstances. Drug users have been shown to be interested in learning to cope with overdose in their peers and to respond favourably to educational and treatment interventions, including take-home naloxone (Strang *et al.*, 2000).

Other risk factors. IV heroin use is a major risk factor (Darke & Ross, 2000). Overdose mortality is not related to age (Warner-Smith *et al.*, 2001), and is significantly more frequent in males. Women seem to have more chance of surviving an overdose (Buster *et al.*, 2002), and there is a lower overdose mortality risk among married opiate users (Davoli *et al.*, 1993). It is unusual for heroin overdose cases to be enrolled in a treatment programme. In one study three quarters of overdose fatalities had never been enrolled in methadone maintenance (Zador *et al.*, 1996). The recruitment and treatment of at-risk heroin users may substantially reduce overdose mortality and morbidity.

Reducing high BBV risk behaviour

The original HIV harm reduction advice about injecting equipment was accepted and acted upon by IDUs. Many drug injectors continue to clean their syringes with bleach/washing-up liquid and do not share injecting equipment (Nightingale, 2002). Ways need to be found to ensure that updated advice, particularly about the possibility of BBV transmission via injecting paraphernalia, reaches all IDUs. A delicate balance needs to be struck between challenging risky behaviour and maintaining contact in a supportive framework which encourages engagement in treatment. Verbal advice regarding transmission of BBVs and overdose should be backed by up-to-date written information. A hierarchy of goals is needed:

- stop sharing injecting equipment and paraphernalia
- stop injecting

This will help reduce the risks of BBV transmission and overdose.

Although further risk reduction will occur if someone successfully reduces their dose of drugs; if relapses occur, the risks are increased. This applies not only to the risk of overdose, but also to the risk of injecting without a personal supply of sterile injecting equipment and paraphernalia. Thus, for opiate users on substitution maintenance, only when a person is mentally ready and properly prepared, with adequate understanding of the risks involved, should maintenance be converted to abstinence-oriented programmes. At this time the remainder of the hierarchy is:

- reduce quantity of drug
- abstinence

Aiding behaviour change to help stop sharing injecting equipment is difficult to achieve, although individuals may appear superficially willing during discussion. Frequent coverage of the topic is vital.

First time injecting drug use

Most people start illicit drug use through other less invasive routes such as sniffing, smoking or oral use. It has been suggested that first injection is a vulnerable time for BBV transmission (Garfein *et al.*, 1998). First-time injectors may be more likely to inject with equipment belonging to others either because of ignorance, lack of planning or through the influence of their initiators. In one survey nearly three quarters were injected by someone else, in 41% this was by a close friend (Roy *et al.*, 2002).

Homelessness, being male and drug dependency are all linked to high-risk injecting behaviour. Up to 36% of street youth in Canada (Roy *et al.*, 2000) and 42% in the USA (Pfeifer & Oliver, 1997) report ever injecting drugs, and girls were found to be significantly less likely to inject themselves than boys. High levels of heroin dependence as measured by Severity of Dependence Scale (SDS) (Gossop *et al.*, 1995) have been found to be related to both injection (Gossop *et al.*, 1993a) and sexual high-risk behaviours (Gossop *et al.*, 1993). However, one survey of street injectors found two-thirds were not dependent (Garfein *et al.*, 1998), suggesting that other factors play a significant role determining initiation into injecting drug use among street youth. The most common reason reported for first injecting was curiosity (61.6%). Looking for a stronger effect was reported by only 6.6%. Over 30% claimed never to have used the first injected drug before their initiation into injecting. Most used sterile needles and syringes at first injection, but did not use clean paraphernalia. This is of considerable concern regarding the transmission of HCV.

High-risk sexual and injecting practices between established partners

Research suggests that five characteristics of injection partnerships are associated with relatively high-risk behaviour for the transmission of BBV infections.

Sexual relations increase the high-risk injecting behaviour probably because intimacy and bonding often induce a general reduction of precautionary measures in interactions between partners (Williams *et al.*, 1995). Similarly *closeness of the relationship and extent of reciprocity* is associated with increased trust between partners and with a decline in precautionary measures which reduce BBV transmission risk (Neaigus *et al.*, 1995).

Asymmetrical power relations between injecting partners may be especially common in individuals who are dissimilar in gender and age. Older male IDUs sometimes provide financial and other support (especially drugs) to younger women in exchange for sexual services. This pattern is associated with heightened BBV sexual and injecting risk behaviours among young women. In Washington, social service agencies generally grant greater access to low-income public housing to women, allowing older female IDUs to exercise social power in partnerships with younger males. Both types of age–gender asymmetry may increase high-risk behaviour (Johnson *et al.*, 2002).

Crack cocaine and speedball use (heroin with cocaine/amphetamine). Johnson and colleagues (2002) showed that whereas crack use alone increases high-risk behaviour by 50%, the use of crack and heroin together increase risk behaviours by 300%. The increased risk may result from extreme stresses on cognitive functioning from crack smoking, and from the practice of exchanging sex for drugs in the inner city. *Frequency of injection* is a strong indicator of high BBV injection risk behaviour. The increased effect of additional injections on

BBV high-risk behaviour accelerates rapidly in the range between 20 and 40 injections per month (Johnson *et al.*, 2002). It is not clear whether this is linked to unavailability of sufficient sterile equipment or is a marker of highly compulsive use.

Facilitating change away from high-risk BBV behaviour

An important key to establishing effective behaviour change in this area lies in the fundamental insights of the Transtheoretical Model of Change (Prochaska & DiClemente, 1984; Prochaska *et al.*, 1997) that the stages and processes of change are similar, whether they occur inside or outside a treatment concept. They apply to many different forms of behaviour. As with helping people move away from other harmful behaviours (smoking, bulimia, excessive drinking, etc.) the processes of change to reduce high-risk BBV behaviour needs to be appropriate for the stage people are at. The interventions given, and the level at which they are implemented, must be appropriate for the stage. It is no good giving an intervention designed for the action stage to someone still in precontemplation (Table 17.1).

The experiential processes of change (consciousness raising, self re-evaluation, environmental re-evaluation, dramatic relief and self-liberation) are indicated during the stages prior to the action stage. Once the action stage is reached, behavioural processes (helping relationships, contingency management, counterconditioning, stimulus control and social liberation) are the most appropriate interventions.

Services need to be given at an individual level. First of all there needs to be a common understanding as to what constitutes the *sharing* of injecting equipment. Misperceptions are common. It is not good enough just to ask whether or not people have ever shared injecting equipment, or how often they have shared it in the last month. Many drug users do not know that sharing paraphernalia is high risk. Some recognise that sharing filters is high risk but will dip into a shared cup of water which has been, or will be, used by others. Some do not define sharing injecting equipment with a sexual partner

Table 17.1   Stages of change in which particular processes of change are emphasised

Precontemplation	Contemplation	Preparation	Action	Maintenance
Consciousness raising Dramatic relief Environmental re-evaluation				
	Self re-evaluation			
		Self-liberation		
			Reinforcement management Helping relationships Counterconditioning Stimulus control	

(From Prochaska, J. O., DiClemente, C. C. & Norcross, J. (1992) In search of how people change: applications to addictive behaviors. In: G. A. Marlatt & G. R. VandenBos (Eds) *Addictive Behaviors: Readings on Etiology, Prevention and Treatment*. Washington, DC: American Psychological Association. Copyright 1992 by the American Psychological Association. Reprinted with permission.)

as sharing. There are a range of specific practices, such as *front-loading* and *back-loading*, which are methods of sharing drugs by filling syringes, which are high risk but are not always recognised to be so. Clearly some practices are higher risk than others, but enquiries about sharing need to be searching to be accurate. The question 'You don't share, do you?' may supply good figures to present to managers, but is very unhelpful in the longer term. For anyone who is currently sharing, repeated in-depth enquiries should be made on a monthly basis, to help promote eventual behaviour change.

Many drug users accept the fact that they should not share injecting equipment, but are highly resistant to behaviour change when it comes to safer sex. The Stages of Change model is as applicable to condom use as it is to addictive behaviours (Grimley *et al.*, 1993). Condom use and high-risk injecting behaviour can also be improved by Motivational Interviewing (MI) (Baker & Dixon, 1991). MI appears to be particularly useful in the precontemplation and contemplation stages of change.

IDUs can reduce the risks by changing to an oral alternative if at all possible. This is a primary focus of harm reduction work. Hunt and colleagues (1998) have reported a brief intervention aimed at current IDUs raising the awareness of the risks and helping increase consideration and prior anticipation of the possibility of initiation of others into injecting drug use. The goals of intervention are to reduce behaviours that may lead to initiation of

others, increase competence at managing initiation requests and to increase disapproval of initiation, so increasing reluctance to initiate others. They have reported some success with this approach. Official UK policy now includes such an approach to reduce the initiation of others and asks for outcomes to be monitored and evaluated (DH, 2001a). Brief interventions focusing on alcohol consumption will also reduce harm for those who have chronic HCV. Such interventions should include an assessment of risk behaviour, information on risks and clear advice for the individual, often with booklets and details of local services (Wallace *et al.*, 1988). They can be carried out by informed generalist workers in non-specialist settings and are brief and user-friendly. Policy statements on health promotion have emphasised the broadening of action to promote health, stressing partnerships and interorganisational work (WHO, 1996; Davey Smith *et al.*, 1999). UK national policy statements endorse this view (DH, 1999a; 1999b).

For those who continue to inject, and it should be assumed that lapse is likely in former injectors, needle exchange services are vital. The health message must include the avoidance of all forms of sharing including spoons, filters, water and tourniquets, the paraphernalia being estimated to increase the risk of HCV fourfold (Parsons *et al.*, 2002). Users should be given information on the methods of injecting to reduce risks of overdose by gradual injection, of thrombosis by avoiding larger vessels, and of tissue damage by avoiding ligatures and being fastidious about hygiene.

BBV testing is relevant for people who have ever injected. Almost all will have been without symptoms at the time of infection and for many years afterwards. Careful pre-test counselling is essential in order to enable informed consent and to provide the basis of support for one or more complex, life-altering diagnoses.

Environmental influences, such as ease of access to needle exchange, markedly influence BBV high-risk behaviour patterns. Just as environmental influences affect treatment processes, so too do they influence BBV high-risk behaviour patterns. For example, poor access to needle exchange will reduce the supply of sterile injecting equipment so that sharing becomes more likely. Psychosocial problems will tend to increase risk behaviour and personal strengths will promote BBV risk reduction. A practical broad-based approach within a biopsychosocial framework will thus not only aid the recovery from drug and drink problems, it will also benefit associated problems such as high-risk BBV behaviour and will be of benefit, not only to the individuals concerned but also their local communities.

The provision of adequate local facilities is of course crucial. One of the difficulties facing harm reduction initiatives even today is that many people outside the field, with power over funding decisions, do not understand the importance of harm reduction initiatives. The US Senate remains implacably opposed to needle exchange believing it will encourage injecting and cause more harm.

If there is any perceived conflict between movement away from substance use and high-risk BBV behaviour, the harm from BBVs must be prioritised in the interests of public and individual health. It is said that when the ACMD's report *AIDS and Drug Misuse*, Part I (1988) was first given to the UK ministers, 30 minutes of cabinet time was spent discussing the statement in bold type in the overview 'HIV is a greater threat to public and individual health than drug misuse'. The decision to uphold this statement has had a lasting beneficial effect on the health and welfare of the UK population, but the political decision to reject similar advice in the USA has been disastrous.

Promoting good health

The concept of *health promotion* emphasises that there has been a move away from the old rather negative model of preventive care of just preventing illness, towards the more positive goal of achieving good health as well. Education about healthy behaviours has much to do with this. People often drink at levels that they mistakenly believe to be moderate or take drugs believing that they have not incurred any health problems.

Individuals who drink or take drugs knowing that these may be injurious to their health often have low opinions of their own self-worth, poor emotional health and little or no hope for the future. This may be associated with a temporary state of depression or may be more enduring. Either way the promotion of good health involves the interlinking of positive physical, social and psychological parameters. Skin care, diet, personal fitness and dental care are all aspects of health care which can contribute not only to good health but to an improvement in self-esteem, which is important in motivation to change. Those involved in the care of substance users will particularly understand the importance of positive regard, the belief in every individual's capacity for change, the value of exercise, diet and self-care, and other ways in which health promotion may be able to reduce the need for substance use.

Conclusion

The prevention and reduction of harm to physical health and the promotion of good health are an important part of treatment. Attention to these physical health issues not only improves outcomes for people with drug and alcohol problems or dependence, it also interrelates in a beneficial way with psychological/psychiatric issues and with the environment which in themselves also influence outcomes for substance users. Physical health issues are therefore an important aspect of biopsychosocial treatment.

Alcohol in excess, if continued, is capable of having a deleterious effect on virtually every organ of the body, the brain being the most susceptible to damage. Other substance use may also cause harm to physical health either directly or sometimes indirectly, e.g. through BBVs. Needle exchange, safer sex advice and the ready availability of specialist treatment facilities for substance users are essential components of modern day drug services. The prevention of HIV and hepatitis B and C transmission is of prime importance. In the UK, GPs are responsible for the physical health needs of substance users but many UK drug and alcohol agencies also conduct an annual physical health check for service attenders in order to look for already established physical health problems. Others provide an outreach service for the physical health needs of substance users not in contact with the service, e.g. prostitutes. Attention to physical health issues is important and should not be overlooked.

Chapter 18
Women, Parents and Children

Introduction

The needs of women and children, and of men as parents, have often been overlooked in training and research in this field. Several factors are currently raising the profile of consideration. As the prevalence of substance use in general has risen there are more women using services. Drug users are possibly becoming more open about their use, and the rising number of very young substance users is generating a need to consider the whole family. The concept of risk assessment and risk reduction increasingly prompts an assessment of the welfare of any children for whom adult service users have parental or other care responsibilities (ACMD 2003), thus placing emphasis on their status as parents and as carers.

Parents are important role models in preventing substance use and in reducing the risk of problem substance use. Non-using parents have a buffering effect on the influence of peers and a helpful effect on the use of refusal self-efficacy (Chaoyang et al., 2002). Bolstering this constructive role is therefore an important aspect of work with substance users.

Many of the issues of relevance to women, including mental health, general health, domestic violence and prostitution are encompassed in other chapters but will be raised here in the context of a gender specific focus. As the understanding of issues such as parenting and prostitution increases it is clear that a similar gender specific focus should be linked to the needs of men and all aspects of gender. It has been argued that research and services to the whole population can be improved by paying attention to the gender of men as well as women (Broom, 1995). Much more research is needed concerning issues of drug-using men as fathers (McMahon & Rounsaville, 2002). Never-

theless, a focus on the needs of women as a stimulus for service improvement is also advocated (Oppenheimer, 1991; 1994).

The consideration of non-using partners and families of substance users brings the needs of women to the fore (Broom, 1995). The majority of drug users and those who use alcohol harmfully are male and the majority of partners are female. The needs of women who are not themselves using substances should be an important consideration for professionals.

For many years, women in Europe and North America have been prescribed more than twice as many psychotropic drugs as men. It is of interest that this phenomenon inversely reflects the gender ratio of illicit drug use. Reviewing the complex reasons for the high rates of prescribed psychotropic drugs in women, Ashton (1991) noted several possible factors. Women are diagnosed with higher rates of psychiatric disorders such as anxiety and depression and there is an increased likelihood that women complain of psychological distress compared to men. There may be a bias in the readiness of doctors to diagnose psychiatric disorders in women and to respond to women with prescription medicines. Sociological factors include domestic roles and fewer outlets for stress, including social use of alcohol, compared with men. Women also have unique hormonal and health issues which may relate to mood disorders and pain, including pregnancy and menstruation. Ashton concluded that a significant proportion of prescriptions were inappropriate and not closely related to the conditions for which they were prescribed.

There are many factors unique to women which may better inform our interventions. Genetic factors of vulnerability and familial risk are being elucidated and gender-related environmental factors, emotional and sociological, including the high prevalence of childhood sexual abuse, are emerging (Millstein, 1998; Kendler *et al.*, 1999).

Prevalence

In the UK general population studies (Mason & Wilkinson, 1996) and the US Epidemiological Catchment Area (ECA) study (Regier *et al.*, 1990), the estimated ratio of male–female alcohol use was 2:1 and for drug use 4:1. Populations in treatment may have greater gender differences due to differentials in access by women. The differences may become even greater in subpopulations such as women with young children and in older-age women. Predictors of mortality in the general population among people with alcohol problems included unmarried status, depression and medical complications (Lewis *et al.*, 1995).

A large-scale and thorough Australian study of the prevalence of women's substance use was linked to an examination of their treatment needs (Swift *et al.*, 1996). This was a population in treatment who may be regarded as good observers of the changes necessary to attract other women into treatment. There was a high level of psychological distress, and more than one-third had a current physical health problem. Seventy-two per cent had a history of previous physical or sexual violence with 37% reporting sexual abuse, and 21% physical abuse in childhood. This latter group were more likely to have attempted suicide, the overall report of attempted suicide being 55%. Half the women had sought treatment for depression or anxiety and 56% had some form of eating disorder.

The prevalence of social problems was similarly high. Fifty per cent had legal problems related to drug use and 21% had been in prison. Half of the women were mothers. The great majority of the women thought that they could be helped by treatment but reported barriers to treatment access. These included fear of failure, guilt, shame, stigma, lack of childcare and ignorance of treatment options. They reported a need for a safe and pleasant treatment environment into which they could bring children, opportunities to address past abuse,

staff who are skilled and less punitive, and help to overcome shame and stigma through a range of interventions including outreach and rehabilitation.

Women's physical health and substance use

Vulnerability

Women appear to develop dependency to addictive drugs more quickly than men (Anglin *et al.*, 1987). They also experience more severe health consequences from similar habits and have particular health needs for biological reasons. Many substance-using women do not have stable accommodation and therefore do not keep contact with primary care. They tend to miss routine screening and immunisations. Services may be able to inreach to primary care and to deliver primary care in other settings in order to make relevant resources available.

The physical effects of alcohol and drugs are different for women. Both alcohol and drugs will be more concentrated at tissue level in women because of the lower proportion of body water. In addition alcohol and some drugs, such as cannabis, are stored longer in the fatty tissue of women and their metabolism is slower. As a result the effects of alcohol and drugs may last longer and be more pronounced in women than in men. The UK recommended *safe limit* of 14 units per week for women is lower than the advised limit of 21 units per week for men. The prognosis of chronic alcohol-related liver disease is less favourable for women, with a risk of earlier development of cirrhosis as a complication. As a consequence of their increased sensitivity to drug effects, women tend to require slightly lower doses of opiate replacement therapy.

Smoking

Smoking tends to have an early onset and to be almost universal in substance users. Indeed the finding of a urine drug screen result without the presence of nicotine can raise questions about the validity of the sample. Along with alcohol use, smoking is a strong predictor of illicit drug use in adolescence (Best *et al.*, 2000). The difficulty of quitting, the lower profile of risk in terms of legality, and the assumptions of normality make smoking cessation a very low priority for most service users and providers. With the advent of new interventions to aid smoking cessation, these assumptions are finally being challenged, and interventions successfully implemented in methadone maintained patients (Shoptaw *et al.*, 2002).

The toll of smoking on women's health is substantial. Women now have the fastest rising rate of lung cancer and smoking-related disease in the world. Whilst interventions for smoking have not been specifically included in this volume, it would be unthinkable to omit the topic here, especially in the consideration of pregnancy.

Many workers in this field are themselves smokers and feel disempowered to address service users' smoking. Developing workplace policies in respect of smoking, with encouragement and assistance for staff who wish to quit, is probably an essential first step. Providing service users with smoke-free environments and information about opportunities to reduce or stop smoking can produce a surprising level of interest not least because of its novelty. Being aware of the risk of increased cigarette use during detoxification and as mobility decreases in late pregnancy may help women develop alternative coping strategies. As with other interventions in this field, advice on risk and harm reduction, given in a non-judgemental manner and combined with opportunities to change, may enhance motivation.

HIV and sexually transmitted infections

The risks of infection with HIV are increased by coexisting infections with other viruses and sexually transmitted infections. This is a particular concern for those women who take high risks with sexual partners or who are involved in prostitution in conjunction with substance use.

Facilitation of access to screening and treatment for sexually transmitted infection is an important aspect of substance use services, in addition to health promotion, education and prevention and measures such as the availability of appropriate condoms and lubricants. These services require a female-oriented component to supplement their general availability. Helpful introductions to treatment and referral include the provision of privacy at needle exchanges, female-focused literature and the inclusion of female staff in direct access service components.

The association of risky sexual behaviour with genital viral infection, particularly viral warts and herpes infections and the associated risk of cervical cancer places this population at high risk. If the woman's risk behaviour is not known to the general practitioner (GP), she will not be called for adequate rates of cervical smear screening; the advised frequency being every three years in high-risk groups and more frequently if abnormalities have been detected. This screening is best arranged at genitourinary clinics unless the woman is actively engaged in treatment with her GP.

Fertility

Fertility is a complex subject for women substance users. Opiate and stimulant use, poor diet, low weight and chronic alcohol use are all associated with amenorrhoea. Many women wrongly assume that the absence of menstrual periods indicates a lack of fertility, whereas occasional ovulation is likely to continue. They may be aware that pelvic infections reduce fertility, and also assume that a lengthy experience of unprotected sex without conception is indicative of infertility. This assumed sense of loss of fertility and parenting prospects can lead to very ambivalent behaviour, including attempts to become pregnant even though the current circumstances are far from ideal. Women who state clearly that they would wish to be substance-free before conception continue to have unprotected sex while still using substances hazardously. In fact, fertility can resume quickly when general health improves, even when still using opiates, e.g. following the commencement of substitute prescribing or other health care. The risk of pregnancy should be a routine message at the commencement of methadone treatment and other interventions, including detoxification. Working with the ambivalence of women to offer preconception health advice may be a more effective strategy than assumptions that they require contraceptive advice.

Contraception

Substance-using women have particular needs in respect of contraception. Liver dysfunction, alcohol, anticonvulsant medication, antibiotics and other medications alter liver metabolism and may render the oral contraceptive unreliable. This, combined with the unreliability of daily routine and medical appointment keeping, makes an alternative choice of contraception preferable for many women. The importance of condom use for infection risk reduction can be helpfully combined with contraceptive function. This may be beneficial to many couples as it is known that women are less likely to protect themselves in personal sexual partnerships (Klee *et al.*, 1991).

A history of pelvic infection or high-risk behaviour is a relative contraindication for the use of intrauterine devices for regular contraception though they may be useful for post-coital contraception. Information on the availability of the 'morning after' pill is of particular relevance for young women and those likely to experience unplanned exposure. Further information should be available on urgent viral risk management including HIV post-exposure prophylaxis (PEP). Depot progesterone contraception is appropriate for women in stable relationships or where an adjunct to barrier contraception might be important.

Injecting behaviour

Although women are less likely to inject than men, their injecting behaviour may be more dangerous. It is possible that women may be at higher risk of BBV infection than men because they share more often (Bennett *et al.*, 2000). Women seem to have more fragile veins than men and tend to lose injection sites sooner. This may lead to a decision to cease injecting but a severe degree of local tissue damage

often occurs before that decision is reached. The compulsive nature of injecting behaviour for some people, combined with powerful interpersonal factors may make injection cessation very difficult. There may be a search for larger veins such as the femoral (groin) vein which introduces a higher risk of harm through bleeding, thrombosis and infection (see Chapter 17). Some women choose to use the femoral vein in order to avoid the use of publicly visible injection sites, also recognisable by family members and professionals, and thus to conceal their habit.

Women are particularly likely to have been introduced to injecting by a male partner who may continue to inject her rather than the woman acquiring the ability for herself. This may be linked to a range of issues including power and control, intimacy or needle phobia (McBride *et al.*, 2001). The continuation of injecting by a sexual partner is frequently associated with sharing of equipment and increased risks of viral infection (Klee *et al.*, 1990).

Women's mental health and substance use

This section focuses on gender specific issues in mental health. Assessment and intervention in co-occurring substance use and mental health are addressed in detail in Chapter 16.

Help-seeking

Gender differences in help-seeking behaviour, diagnostic thresholds and service utilisation make estimates of true prevalence in this heterogeneous population difficult to establish. Nevertheless, some trends do emerge with implications for service policy and delivery (Alexander, 1996; Crome, 1997a). The UK National Treatment Outcome Research Study (NTORS) data indicates that psychiatric symptom level was higher on all scales in females seeking treatment for opiate dependency (Marsden *et al.*, 2000).

The psychosocial needs of women with severe co-morbid mental illness in residential treatment were studied using a concept of 'level of burden' (Brown *et al.*, 1999). Women were found to require intervention for health-related problems, housing and past physical or sexual abuse. Women with severe mental illness were less likely to remain in residential treatment or to access other services.

Schizophrenia

Studies of gender differences in schizophrenia have found women to have a later age of onset, less debilitating symptoms, fewer hospitalisations and better premorbid and overall functioning. However, when comparisons are adjusted to examine those who use substances, the differences are less marked, suggesting that women with schizophrenia may be especially vulnerable to the adverse effects of substance use (Gearon & Bellack, 2000). Examining a population of homeless people with schizophrenia and substance use, women were found to have higher rates of sexual and physical victimisation, co-morbid anxiety and depression and medical illness than men, but were more socially connected to children and families (Brunette & Drake, 1998). The authors concluded that special attention is required for women in the prevention and treatment of victimisation as well as improved access to medical care.

Post-traumatic stress disorder (PTSD)

PTSD has a high incidence in substance users, and in women it occurs at two or three times the rate in men. It is thought to play an important aetiological role in the development of substance disorders in women. The higher rate in women has been found to be related to repetitive childhood physical and/or sexual abuse (Najavits *et al.*, 1997).

Eating disorders

Eating disorders have a much higher incidence in women and are linked to the use of a wide range of substances including alcohol (Bulik *et al.*, 1997), illicit drugs and over-the-counter (OTC) medications particularly laxatives. There is an association with mood and anxiety disorders and with sexual abuse and PTSD.

Depression

Variations in women's mental health and vulnerabilities for depression occur in relation to hormonal changes, although hormonal effects are not the sole reason for the disorders. Depression, irritability and anxiety are related to the premenstrual syndrome whilst there is a rise in the rate of depression associated with the menopause.

Whilst all forms of mental illness tend, though not universally, to improve during pregnancy, depression and psychosis are a significant risk pre- and postnatally. A recent cohort study demonstrated that symptoms of depression were higher during pregnancy than postnatally (Evans *et al.*, 2001). The presence of depression may be a confounding factor in the reluctance of some pregnant substance users to present for care. The rate of transient depression in the first week post-partum, the so called 'blues', is 50%, and of subsequent depressive illness 10–12%. In impoverished, inner-city pregnant and post-partum women the rates may be doubled (Hobfoll *et al.*, 1995). Post-partum depression may last for many months and has a significant mortality from suicide and occasional infanticide. Post-natal depression can interfere profoundly with infant–mother bonding (Zekoski *et al.*, 1987) and subsequent emotional development of the child (Murray *et al.*, 1999). Depression also affects the mother's ability to cope with existing children and with the quality of the relationship with her partner.

Initial recognition of pre- and post-natal depression can be difficult, being easily explained by tiredness. The guilt of depression may be exacerbated by personal and social responses to substance-using mothers whom society expects to feel guilty. The support of professionals who know the mother can be valuable, enabling recognition of depressive guilt and advocacy of appropriate treatment with psychological and practical support and antidepressant medication. The Edinburgh Postnatal Depression Scale (Cox *et al.*, 1987) is used by midwives and other professionals to assist early recognition.

Post-natal psychosis

Post-natal psychosis is more rare, occurring in 1% of pregnancies, but has a dramatic onset in the first week or two post-partum with predominant features of perplexity, altered motor function (irritability or stupor), delusional ideas and possibly hallucinations. The presentation of psychosis is an emergency posing risks to maternal and infant safety. If the mother has the ability to retain contact with the baby at this stage, contact should be carefully supervised. In substance-using women it is essential to differentiate this condition from drug-induced conditions, especially alcohol or benzodiazepine withdrawal delirium. If there is a diagnostic possibility of alcohol withdrawal psychosis, urgent treatment with high potency injectable thiamine or multivitamins should be given. Sedation with minor tranquillisers will reduce the risk of withdrawal seizures in alcohol and benzodiazepine withdrawal, whereas antipsychotic medication alone to treat psychotic symptoms will increase the risk of seizures; if in doubt, a combination is advisable. The goal of treatment is safe care of mother and infant with facilitation of their relationship as maternal health permits.

Domestic violence

Domestic violence contributes a significant dynamic to the aetiology and course of substance use in women. Women partners of substance users are at increased risk of exposure to violence (Stark & Flitcraft, 1996).

Adult victims of domestic violence, predominantly female, experience increased rates of depression, suicidal ideas and substance use (Scott-Gliba et al., 1995). Attempting to leave may escalate the risk of violence and the woman may feel trapped in a frightening and depressing environment (Walker, 1979) which can lead to an escalation of substance use. Domestic violence is more likely to occur for the first time during pregnancy and should always be enquired about during the care of pregnant women (Mezey & Bewley, 1997). Domestic violence is a significant factor leading to adverse outcome in pregnancy which should be

specifically addressed (Amaro et al., 1990; Bacchu et al., 2002).

Although domestic violence usually refers to violence between adults, it is recognised that children within a violent household are at an increased risk of being assaulted or abused, as well as traumatised by witnessing parental violence (Strauss et al., 1980; Mullender & Morly, 1994).

Domestic violence is an important adverse factor in childhood experience of family life and has an adverse effect on the development of self-esteem and on mental health. There is a raised prevalence of PTSD in childhood (Masten et al., 1990) and an association with conduct disorder. Both these conditions are associated with increased risk of adolescent and adult substance problems. The evidence is that the burden of psychological pathology is high (Black & Newman, 1996). The witnessing of domestic violence during childhood also influences expectations of adult relationships and the recurrent experience of violence across generations.

Women as partners

The need for services to address the concerns of women as partners of substance users should receive more attention. It is more common for a male user to have a non-using partner. Also, the prevalence of substance use is greater in men, thus making the majority of non-using partners female. Primary care teams are often in the best position to begin to address those needs, as are self-help groups.

Conversely, women who use drugs are more likely to have a drug-using partner. This tends to add difficulties to her attempts to address her use. Women are often dependent on partners for substance availability, either directly in terms of obtaining illicit drugs or by means of funding. Other women may themselves be the source of funding for both of them by means of prostitution.

The woman may be in the position of considering her own use whilst also encouraging her partner to change, or facing the problems of his continuing use. Her need to consider change may be precipitated by the wish to become pregnant or the event of a pregnancy. The support of professionals in engaging the partner or supporting the decisions of the woman herself can be vital in enabling her progress.

Support and help for families

Families may include siblings, partners and parents who are themselves using substances as well as the presenting individual. In others, the discovery of the substance use may be a bewildering new experience. Significant harm and difficulty may accrue to family members of substance users (Velleman *et al.*, 1993). Helping reduce such harm is part of the role of specialist services.

Families may be shocked, distressed, angered or profoundly disrupted by the addiction or use of substances by a family member. They are, however, potentially in a prime position to assist recovery. Their reactions may also have the reverse effect, despite the best of intentions. Family responses may vary rapidly between help and rejection as they attempt to cope with a difficult situation. Professionals require patience, skill, understanding and compassion. Supervision and co-working can help workers remain objective and consistent and avoid projection of the family's distress. Labelling the family as 'co-dependent' or to blame is never helpful, however enmeshed or distorted the family has become. Constructive interventions include family therapy, support groups, individual or marital counselling which are addressed in Chapter 15. Much can be achieved by the provision of information about the nature and course of substance problems, together with details of other sources of help, including emergency helplines and self-help organisations such as Families Anonymous (FA).

Adolescent female substance use

The prevalence of female adolescent substance use has risen rapidly in recent years. Adolescents referred to treatment services are distinguished especially by the degree to which girls have internalising symptoms and family dysfunction (Dakof, 2000).

In a recent study of adult drinking patterns, Plant and Plant (2001) reported that by far the highest proportion of women who were high-risk drinkers was amongst those aged 18–24 years, a new trend not reflected in men whose peak of problem use is older. Noting that women are less likely to present to specialist agencies for help, they advise that staff in the type of agencies which young women are more likely to attend, such as well women clinics and primary care, are trained in early intervention.

Younger women are more likely than young men to receive minor tranquillisers from doctors (Golding & Cornish, 1987) and are currently the population in which the prevalence of nicotine use through smoking continues to rise (DH, 1998). With the knowledge that cigarette smoking in young adulthood is the strongest predictor of subsequent illicit drug and alcohol problems, young women should be a target group for early intervention in the specialist field (Bauman & Phongsavan, 1999).

Drug use has been shown to increase the risk of early, unplanned or undesired pregnancy by a factor of four and the risk of abortion by a factor of five (Mensch & Kandel, 1992). These differences occur after correction for personality, lifestyle and biological factors. The authors noted the multiplicity of possible common risk factors and social influences, the potential value of integrating education and prevention of substance use in teenage sexual health strategies as well as the importance of sexual and contraceptive advice and services for adolescent substance users.

The disruption of personal life and the social consequences of substance use may lead to complex social problems very quickly. Young users are very vulnerable to exploitation, particularly if they are homeless, learning disabled or mentally ill and the range of direct access services for women is less than those for men. The need for services to offer social support and protection is clear and may occasionally amount to a need for formal child protection consideration. Problematic substance use is never a solely medical issue and is likely to need multiagency input (SCODA, 1999). Knowledge of such services and a working contact is an important aspect of working with young people. Guidance on working with young people with complex problems is developing and now takes account of the need for service planning, and the provision of treatment as well as strategies for primary prevention (HAS, 2001).

Pregnancy

Engagement in care

Achieving the best health and social outcomes and reduction of risks involves engagement as early as possible in pregnancy. For some women, engagement at all is a difficult matter. Services with clear policies for liaison between all relevant agencies are more likely to be successful in reassuring women of the benefits of engagement both in terms of a coherent policy and in terms of a reputation for effective care.

Some women will present late through lack of recognition of the pregnancy due to the absence or irregularity of menstrual periods related to substance use. Appropriate advice about the improvement in fertility which occurs during treatment is therefore important. Opportunity to present early is also essential for women considering termination of pregnancy. Fears about the effects of substance use may be unfounded and social problems may have solutions. Early referral for treatment with good liaison and aftercare is valuable for women who choose termination.

Early engagement in pregnancy enables treatment of any associated health problems, accurate dating of the stage of pregnancy, reduction of harmful substance use in early pregnancy and the maximum duration in which to achieve abstinence, if desired, before the birth.

A UK study of perinatal maternal mortality (DH, 1998a) highlighted the adverse effects of maternal substance use and maternal mental illness and the importance of engagement in treatment.

An appropriate environment for a baby

Assistance with housing and finances are important for basic health needs such as good diet as well as the opportunity to prepare for the baby. The pur-

pose of interagency child protection planning meetings during pregnancy is to anticipate the emotional and physical needs of the mother and baby. There is now evidence that maternal mental illness, including depression, can adversely affect the development of the baby and impair the bonding of the relationship (Atkinson et al., 2000). Early detection of illness and of emotional or practical difficulties in relating to the baby requires early assessment. The identification of mild learning disability is important in this context. Domestic violence or household conflict also present a risk. The engagement of the woman's partner enables further risk assessment and reduction. Prioritisation of the partner for treatment of any substance use can greatly assist her care.

General health

The focus on substance use should not distract from attention to general health during pregnancy. Use of conventional sources of health advice is reduced among substance users and this probably applies to conventional antenatal health care such as parentcraft, relaxation classes and routine primary care appointments. Expectations of individual health may be low and it can be pleasing to see improvements in overall health in women who are motivated to achieve good health in pregnancy.

Vomiting, which commonly occurs in the first 16 weeks of pregnancy requires special attention in substance users. Alcohol causes gastric inflammation and opiates may cause nausea and vomiting in withdrawal or intoxication. Increased use of these or other substances to overcome vomiting in pregnancy can lead to prolonged symptoms and the incapacity to absorb medication, occasionally leading to severe illness. Early treatment by controlled alcohol withdrawal or long-acting substitute opiates and an explanation of the rationale of treatment can produce improvement. Occasionally hospital admission is necessary.

Dental care has additional importance during pregnancy because of the demands on calcium metabolism and the risks of periodontal disease. Reduced access to dental treatment, poor attention to personal care and diet, and the effects of substances themselves are all factors in the high prevalence of poor dental health among substance users. Stimulant use is associated with tooth grinding and methadone liquids with dental decay due to acidity and sugar content. Advocacy and encouragement are often needed in order to engage in dental treatment. Other issues for attention include skin care, injection sites and breast care, including encouragement to prepare for breastfeeding unless contraindicated.

Mental health is additionally vulnerable in pregnancy. There is a raised prevalence of depression during pregnancy and in the post-natal period as previously noted. Self-esteem may also be vulnerable to ideas of self-blame and to judgemental comment. A clear framework of shared care between the services involved in the care of substance users during pregnancy helps avoid such harm through a collaborative and encouraging framework.

Hepatitis C and B and HIV

Testing for sexually transmitted infections, hepatitis C virus (HCV), hepatitis B virus (HBV) and HIV undertaken in antenatal clinics should be linked to more detailed assessment and risk reduction strategies for women at high risk. In pregnancy and in women who have had children, issues of vertical transmission require advice and active management. There are treatment reasons for knowing HBV and HIV status in pregnancy and although antiretroviral treatment for HCV is contraindicated in pregnancy, women nevertheless find this a helpful time to know their status as part of a new focus on their health. Many women will only become aware of their positive status a long time after the suspected exposure and will then be concerned about whether their existing children have been exposed to the viruses. Services should develop arrangements for parents and their children to obtain advice from specialists in child health and liver/infectious diseases. In the family setting, the viral status of partners is relevant to ongoing risks of transmission. Services can assist by offering advice and testing for partners.

Newly occurring infection with HCV, HBV or HIV during pregnancy may result directly in foetal infection. HBV antibodies appear soon after exposure but for HCV and HIV there is a lag period of around three months. Testing of pregnant women therefore requires a careful history of possible exposure in order to determine the timing of follow-up tests. Among UK drug users who have ever injected, the prevalence of HCV is around 40% in urban and rural communities. (See Chapter 17 for detailed information on BBVs.)

Babies of mothers positive for HBV are at a significant risk of exposure to the virus during delivery, infectivity depending on the viral picture of the maternal infection. Normal delivery is advised with passive immunisation of the neonate and active immunisation of the mother post-partum; hence the importance of testing for HBV in pregnancy.

Exposure to HCV during delivery carries a low risk of infection in the order of 5%. There is no current intervention to reduce risk of HCV transmission in pregnancy or to treat intra-partum exposure.

HIV positive mothers should be treated with antiviral drugs prior to delivery. Transmission to the baby is reduced by caesarian delivery (Ratcliffe et al., 1998). Breastfeeding is not contraindicated in HBV and HCV but is not advised in HIV positive mothers.

The effects of substances on pregnancy

In addition to the adverse psychosocial associations of substance use such as poverty, poor nutrition and lack of health care, there are substance specific effects on maternal health and the foetus. The widespread use of alcohol and tobacco and of poly-substances produces confounding effects on studies of other substances (Little et al., 1989; 1990). Similarly, when alcohol or tobacco is used at high levels there is a likelihood of associated social harms which make direct toxic effects difficult to distinguish. However, there is sufficient evidence to produce a consensus from which to offer advice. The route of use has important implications. Intravenous (IV) use of drugs may produce more marked variations in maternal and foetal drug levels, and if linked to the sharing of injecting equipment or paraphernalia carries a risk of infection.

Alcohol

The level of sensible drinking (see Chapter 4) is difficult to define in pregnancy and thus some women choose to totally abstain. The Department of Health, in its advice on sensible drinking (DH, 1995), advised women who are pregnant or contemplating pregnancy to keep their alcohol intake to substantially below the limits advised for non-pregnant women. Evidence is now accumulating to suggest that even low levels of use may be toxic to the foetus and that the best advice is to consume no alcohol if trying to conceive or during pregnancy.

Binge drinking or irregular or persistent heavy drinking is certainly known to cause adverse effects including spontaneous abortion (miscarriage), foetal growth retardation, facial abnormalities, other physical abnormalities, impaired mental development, behavioural abnormality and physical developmental delay. A spectrum of disorders, known as the foetal alcohol syndrome (FAS), alcohol-related neurodevelopmental disorder (ARND) and alcohol-related birth defects (ARBD) may result from alcohol use.

Diagnosis is made in infancy on the basis of a combination of a characteristic facial abnormality, a history of foetal growth retardation and the presence of central nervous system (CNS) involvement such as neurological abnormality, developmental delay or intellectual impairment. These effects have been difficult to research due to multiple factors including volume of use, timing, peak levels and environmental factors. Low-dose prenatal alcohol exposure is linked to a much wider spectrum of developmental and behavioural problems than is commonly recognised in the UK. The effect has been demonstrated at average levels of exposure as low as one drink per week (Sood *et al.*, 2001).

Recent animal studies indicate that alcohol causes the death of nerve cells at critical stages of synapse development by interference with neurotransmitters, this damage being known as apoptosis (Ikonomidou *et al.*, 2000). The research raises significant avenues of investigation concerning toxic effects of other substances, many of which act on the same neurotransmitters (Olney *et al.*, 2002). Neurological damage in the foetus also appears to be caused by aldehydes (a breakdown product of alcohol). Disulfiram, which works by preventing the metabolism of aldehydes, allowing these toxic substances to build up, should be avoided in pregnancy. Its use may lead to features of FAS, even at low levels of drinking. A similar picture may be produced by other causes such as anticonvulsant drugs.

Tobacco

The harm related to tobacco smoking in pregnancy and infancy deserves a much higher profile in terms of interventions with substance users, especially during pregnancy. Smokers have an increased risk of low birth-weight babies (less than 2.5 kg) and perinatal mortality. Constriction of placental blood vessels due to nicotine reduces placental efficiency and thus foetal nutrition and oxygenation. This is compounded by reduced oxygen in the maternal blood supply of smokers. The latter effect is readily reduced by smoking reduction or abstinence and thus can form a good motivation for reducing and giving up smoking at any stage of pregnancy. There is an increased rate of cot death in smoking households which is in addition to the perinatal risks of low birth-weight babies. Gunton and colleagues (1995) report that smoking cessation programmes for pregnant women could prevent several thousand low birth-weight babies and save numerous deaths each year.

Women struggling with withdrawal from other substances commonly report an increased level of cigarette use. Predetoxification planning should encompass this risk by information and psychological interventions. There may also be a place for careful use of nicotine replacement in reducing doses as a harm reduction intervention as foetal risk is related to the smoke, tars and the carbon monoxide products of smoking as well as the nicotine content.

Cannabis

Cannabis use is usually associated with the use of tobacco and often with other substances. Thus it is difficult to find research data to clarify specific risk. Whilst some studies have suggested a link with adverse outcomes, a large Canadian study (Fried, 1986) which controlled for social deprivation found no significant differences in rate of miscarriage, frequency of obstetric complications, birth weight or physical birth defects even among the heaviest users. Heavy use, defined as smoking more than six joints a week during pregnancy, was associated with a shortening of gestation by about a week. This may be of marginal significance in women with risk factors for prematurity. A review of the effects of cannabis by the World Health Organization did not demonstrate any problems which could be specifically linked to use in pregnancy (WHO, 1997).

Benzodiazepines

These drugs are commonly prescribed and widely used from illicit sources. They may be less obvious to the user or professionals as a source of difficulty and should be specifically enquired about and tested for. Benzodiazepine use is often irregular in quantity, being taken as an adjunct or moderator of other substance use. There are risks to mother and foetus including the risk of maternal seizures following abrupt cessation.

Although chlordiazepoxide treatment appears to be safe in pregnancy, studies have linked the use of other benzodiazepines in first trimester to facial malformation including cleft palate. Risks extend throughout the pregnancy with associations with cardiac defects, pyloric stenosis (a condition of the outlet of the stomach which causes persistent vomiting and requires surgical correction) and impaired cognitive development.

The use of even relatively low therapeutic doses of diazepam has been known in a few instances, when the baby's liver function is immature, to cause prolonged respiratory depression in the neonate. Diazepam tissue levels remain high especially in the liver, GI tract and CNS because the foetus is unable to metabolise it to any appreciable extent (Marselli *et al.*, 1973). Diazepam and its active metabolites may persist for 1–2 weeks post-delivery. Benzodiazepine use is associated with a neonatal abstinence syndrome (Harrison, 1986; Sutton & Hindliter, 1990) which features respiratory depression, poor body tone (floppy baby), irritability (hard to settle), feeding difficulties, hypothermia and raised bilirubin levels (possible jaundice). The onset is usually at 24–48 hours and can delay and exacerbate the symptoms of opiate withdrawal which is a common association.

Cocaine

Cocaine or crack cocaine use is associated with significant harm to mother and foetus at all stages including a hazard of maternal, foetal and neonatal death. Because many studies have not corrected for socio-economic deprivation or lack of antenatal care, the findings have been difficult to interpret. Occasional use may not be as harmful as previously thought while regular use carries high risks. Many of the effects appear to result from the effects of cocaine on the muscle of the uterus and on placental and foetal circulation, with constriction of blood vessels causing restriction of blood supply and oxygen. There is a risk of early and late miscarriage, stillbirth, premature rupture of membranes, premature labour and placental abruption in which the placenta separates from the uterus with catastrophic bleeding. Maternal risks also include cerebral bleeding, hypertension and cardiac disorders. Foetal abnormalities include limb and organ deformities occurring throughout pregnancy, postulated to be due to intercurrent damage to blood supply as well as disrupted organ development. Foetal growth is affected by multiple factors and includes delayed growth of the head making gestational dating more difficult and suggesting an associated effect on brain development (Little *et al.*, 1989). Babies may be born prematurely and tend to be small for gestational age. Withdrawal effects in neonates include easily startled, irritable behaviour, poor sleep and feeding difficulties in the early days. There is an increased risk of sudden infant death although it is not clear how specific this effect is.

Amphetamines

The effects on pregnancy are thought to be non-specific and relate to the suppression of appetite and to the effects on blood vessels. There is an association with low birth-weight and preterm delivery. Maternal risks include hypertension, strokes and abnormalities of cardiac rhythm. There is less written about amphetamine use in pregnancy than cocaine use, but neuropharmacologically they act in a similar way, the main difference being that amphetamines are longer acting. The main risk in pregnancy will be that they cause a rise in blood pressure, and therefore increase the risk of pre-eclamptic toxaemia (PET), a condition of high risk to mother and foetus related to raised blood pressure, intrauterine growth retardation and a much greater risk of ante-partum haemorrhage and placental abruption, foetal death and early labour.

Opiates

The main adverse associations with short-acting opiates, such as heroin, are low birth-weight and prematurity. Growth retardation is described with heroin use and this may, at least in part, be related to its association with adverse social circumstances. There are opiate receptors in the uterine wall which govern the size of the blood spaces (lacunae) and hence the amount of nutrition and oxygen available to the baby. It is clear from past evidence that stabilisation of opiate blood levels through methadone maintenance both enhances foetal growth and prolongs the gestation period (McCarthy *et al.*, 1994), even when given to those living in poverty and adverse social circumstances. There is an association between opiate use, preterm birth and an increased rate of intrauterine and neonatal death. This may relate to intrauterine withdrawal due to erratic maternal opiate consumption as well as social and other health factors contributing to low birth-weight. Opiate users commonly smoke cigarettes. Opiate withdrawal is linked to uterine irritability and foetal hypoxia. However, Hepburn's experience of supervising opiate withdrawal at all stages of pregnancy, and at any rate of withdrawal acceptable to the mother, suggests that the process is not itself associated with adverse outcome (Hepburn & Forrest, 1988).

High maternal blood opiate levels will pass through to the baby and may impair neonatal respiration at the time of delivery. The neonatal abstinence syndrome presents at about 24 hours in heroin use and from about 48 hours with methadone. The latter may be more prolonged. Earlier onset may occur during or soon after prolonged labour if the mother has been deprived of opiates during labour. Signs include tremor, sweating and fever, a high pitched cry, irritability and poor sleep, feeding problems, diarrhoea and vomiting, respiratory distress, and convulsions. In all but the mildest form there is a need for observation in hospital. However, in most cases observation can be done

equally well on the wards with the use of special charts to monitor potential neonatal opiate withdrawal symptoms, rather than the baby being observed routinely in a special care baby unit. Of 200 babies born in Glasgow to mothers using illicit drugs or legal methadone, only 7% required treatment for withdrawal, while even fewer required admission to the special care nursery (Hepburn, 1993).

For those babies who do require specific treatment for opiate abstinence, it is most usual now to use tapering doses of opiates, either morphine or methadone, to prevent withdrawal symptoms and reduce the risk of fitting. Occasionally more intensive treatment with supported respiration is required for respiratory depression or seizures. There is an association of maternal opiate use in pregnancy with sudden infant death syndrome, but this is rare.

LSD, Ecstasy, methamphetamine

There is no clear evidence of specific effects on pregnancy.

Reduction, detoxification and substitute prescribing in pregnancy

Plans for treatment should take a collaborative, harm reduction approach. Access should be without delay and the response to women's needs non-judgemental. Goals of abstinence should be balanced with the importance of retaining honest engagement, the risks of relapse and overdose and therapeutic time to focus on general and obstetric health. For many women, pregnancy provides high motivation to change but for some that change does not include abstinence. Partners, health workers and social workers should be included in care planning wherever possible in order to set mutually agreed goals.

Alcohol

Withdrawal should be strongly encouraged and will require formal medical treatment if dependence is marked. Although benzodiazepines are not recommended in pregnancy, chlordiazepoxide remains the drug of choice for short-term alcohol withdrawal and is of less risk than continued alcohol use. If alcohol-induced vomiting is persistent, this may necessitate inpatient general hospital treatment. Vitamin supplementation and attention to diet is important. Where risk of relapse appears significant detoxification may still be worthwhile, allowing a period of sober choice with a high level of support to enable abstinence. A marked improvement in health may itself enhance motivation to change.

Benzodiazepines

If physical dependence is established, withdrawal should be encouraged at the greatest rate tolerable to the woman. Minimisation of use may be the best achievable option having enabled an informed choice.

Stimulants

There is no specific intervention relevant to pregnancy. Abrupt cessation does not carry any hazard. Supportive inpatient care to cope with the period of craving and irritability which follows the initial 'crash' phase of withdrawal may be helpful. Counselling and support linked to health and social care are particularly powerful interventions in pregnancy. Substitute stimulant prescribing is not advised and may endanger the foetus.

Opiates

Methadone is currently the treatment of choice for reduction or maintenance in pregnancy. Pregnant women should be given fast access to treatment to maximise engagement in care and reduce risks of illicit and of IV use. For women who are using heroin and not severely dependent, symptomatic treatment of withdrawal to achieve abstinence may be acceptable. Severely dependent women may benefit from a supportive inpatient setting to commence treatment. For all women, adequate dosing determined by estimation of dose and frequent follow-up is essential. Classical dose titration requiring presentation in withdrawal and commencing on very low doses may carry risk and is, at least, likely to exacerbate morning sickness making dosing more difficult. Some people believe there is an increased risk of miscarriage from withdrawals in the first trimester. This is difficult to ascertain because the exact statistics of the rate of miscarriage in

the first trimester in people who use or do not use drugs is unknown. Nevertheless, the rate of miscarriage in opiate users in the first three months of pregnancy is probably raised. Interventions which may compound the risk or leave women feeling anxious or culpable are probably best avoided.

Substitution treatment to enable stabilisation and improvement in health should be the starting point. Thereafter, reduction and withdrawal can proceed at a pace acceptable to the woman with regular reviews to enable slowing of pace or maintenance prescribing if necessary.

When opiate dependency is disclosed for the first time during labour it is important to address maternal dependency urgently in order to manage pain relief and to enable the mother to cope with the immediate post-natal period. Breastfeeding is not contraindicated by methadone use.

Buprenorphine is being assessed for use by pregnant women seeking detoxification or maintenance. Currently it does not have a product licence for use in pregnancy and caution is indicated. Animal studies have shown potential foetotoxicity including post-implantation foetal loss. Early clinical results, though limited, are encouraging (Fischer *et al.*, 2000). The neonatal abstinence syndrome is greatly reduced in incidence and severity and maternal stability in treatment has been shown to be good although the population studied was small and highly selected. Potential problems arise in labour due to the partial agonist properties of the drug (see Chapter 11) which interfere with conventional opiate analgesia. Women taking buprenorphine in pregnancy need to be prepared for the use of epidural analgesia and for more complex interventions for any emergencies. However, many women may prefer these arrangements, if available, for the potential neonatal benefits if they are unable to achieve abstinence. The dose transmitted through breast milk appears to be low and is not a contraindication to breastfeeding.

Planning the birth

Good multi-disciplinary care during pregnancy will address all potential complications including those of labour and the post-natal period. Antenatal consultation with paediatric staff and a visit to the special care baby unit will help allay fear if such treatment is needed. Regular liaison between all concerned also reduces stigma and judgemental attitudes as well as setting clear plans and boundaries. Such coordinated care is still unusual but is much appreciated by service users and is enabling to staff (Clarke & Formby, 2000).

A liaison team usefully includes the drug clinic link worker, antenatal clinic nurse or midwife to enable engagement, special care baby unit nurse, community midwife to enable continuity of after-care, GP, social worker and health visitor for family care and subsequent support. It is essential to clarify which person should lead on each aspect of care including child protection, mental health and drug or alcohol treatment. Formal enquiries when things go wrong often comment on the need for clearer communication but this is only effective if skills are present and are effectively shared. Training for all concerned, ideally in a shared interdisciplinary format, is therefore important.

Elements of the birth plan must include analgesia, mode of delivery, access to veins should IV fluids be needed, persons to support the mother and an estimate of time in hospital. Plans for breastfeeding should be explicit as should a plan for review of mental health postnatally.

Analgesia is often a major cause of maternal concern, especially in opiate-dependent women. Anecdotal stories of punitive or fearful attitudes from staff demonstrate the need for active liaison. In general, analgesia will only be effective if withdrawal symptoms and high arousal are first addressed. Doses required can be titrated quickly against symptoms and the hazard of neonatal intoxication anticipated with appropriate staffing. If foetal intoxication or respiratory depression is thought likely to occur, a paediatrician should be asked to attend the delivery to resuscitate the baby if necessary. Babies born opiate dependent who fail to establish respiration should be intubated and their breathing assisted. Only in extreme circumstances where respiration cannot be established by this method should opiate antagonists, such as neonatal naloxone, be given as these will induce severe and dangerous opiate withdrawals in the baby. As IV drug users may have few remaining veins, it may be preferable to obtain an IV line electively at the start of labour rather than have major problems in a crisis.

Post-natal care

Postnatally, the treatment of maternal health needs, including substitute medication, is vital to enable collaborative care of the baby and to avoid problems such as illicit or covert drug or alcohol use in the hospital, or sudden self-discharge. The dose of opiate maintenance treatment may be reduced in the immediate post-natal period as circulating volume reduces but for those who have already withdrawn or minimised their use there is a very real risk of overdose, especially in the context of stress or depression. The mother, her partner and support staff should be given specific information about the risk of overdose. Careful support, including the continuation of opiate maintenance, may enable the woman to succeed in parenting her child and reduce the risks of erratic drug use. Sometimes women who have achieved abstinence in pregnancy for the sake of the foetus are unable to sustain it postnatally in the context of tiredness, depression or other stress. Regular reviews are important with a readiness to resume substitute prescribing if other supportive interventions do not enable sustained abstinence.

Follow-up interventions include contraception, advice on safer sex and drug use, immunisations, family support and mental health care.

Child protection

The care of pregnant substance users and associated aspects of child protection have been well-recognised needs for several years. These considerations are now developing in substance use services to include the context of support, assessment and ongoing therapy to enable good enough, or good quality, parenting at all stages of children's lives.

In the UK the legal framework and the philosophy of social services within the Children Act (1989) requires that the needs of children are considered as paramount to those of adults. Thus, adult carers are explicitly obliged to work to protect their children's interests. The same obligations are placed on professionals who have any contact with parents or carers, even though their primary therapeutic and organisational focus is with adults. This obligation has implications for confidentiality, about which it is important to be explicit with service users. It is particularly helpful to explain child protection obligations to all service users at the outset of engagement.

A statement of policy in waiting area notices and leaflets may enable service users to consider the issues prior to individual discussion. Wording should include a clear commitment to collaborative working, and a focus on best care for the adult service user as well as their children. For example, a statement which has been in use at a Norfolk statutory drug service and has proved acceptable to professionals and helpful to service users is given below:

Your children
   If you think that you may need help with your children, please talk to staff here.

   The team here are committed to child safety. If we or you were ever seriously concerned about the safety of a child, we would ask social services to become involved for the protection of that child. This would always be done with your knowledge, unless circumstances made this impossible.

   Norfolk Social Services have a clear policy which states that children cannot be taken 'into care' or be registered as being 'at risk' just because parents or carers are drug users.

   We will always try to work with you to get the best help for you and your children.

In this way, the service user is more able to see the value of concerns about children and a conflict of priorities is less likely to occur. Collaborative goals in the interest of children can be established, enabling disclosure of difficulties before a crisis.

The development of an awareness of the needs of children, the preliminary assessment of parenting capacity, and the child protection aspects of the care of young service users are therefore becoming core skills of the alcohol and drug work field.

Many substance users have had little experience of good enough parenting in their own childhood. Experience of physical, sexual and emotional neglect or abuse is common and a high proportion have spent some time in local authority care. A family history of problematic substance use is often found. It is also likely that the use of substances adversely affects the ability of individuals to mature emotionally. Substance use is associated with a raised prevalence of teenage pregnancy. Thus it is not surprising that many women find themselves emotionally unprepared for parenthood and with little understanding of what is required of them by their children. Their partners are likely to be similarly disadvantaged. They may, however, be very motivated, albeit with unrealistic expectations, to get things right and to provide what they were deprived of themselves.

Assessment and support of parents thus requires considerable skill and commitment on the part of professionals. In the course of working with mothers and their partners to develop their strengths and skills, there is the challenge of sometimes recognising and helping those mothers who, whatever help is provided, are unable to provide adequately for their children. There are several risk domains to consider:

- The focus of assessment often becomes inappropriately fixed on eliminating the substance use. Social workers and courts may give unwarranted emphasis to the results of laboratory urine or other tests of illicit drug use, and fall into the trap of allocating this greater importance in their assessment than parenting ability. Care planning meetings may repeatedly require the mother or partner to overcome their substance use as though the parenting difficulty will then be solved. Unrealistic targets may be set for detoxification or rehabilitation which the service user feels obliged to attempt, especially if required to do so by a court. Often, when placed under such pressure, the harder the woman strives towards this inappropriate target, the more severe the substance use problem may become. In such circumstances there is a risk of concealment of substance use or of a pregnancy.

- Patterns of use and the effects of those substances should be considered; chronic alcohol and stimulant use being characteristically associated with a higher risk of physical harm; sedative substances, including opiate use, being associated with physical neglect, and all being linked to risk of emotional neglect.
- Parental priorities, such as the physical care of the children, adequate food, and age-appropriate play are important.
- The nature of relationships with partners and friends and whether these support or detract from the care of children should be considered. Efforts should then be made to engage partners in substance use treatment if necessary as well as involving them as family members.
- Substance-related social behaviours, household violence and financial effects should all be assessed. Social behaviours should be specifically described and assessed in terms of their risks and care needs. Loose descriptions in terms of 'lifestyle' are to be avoided as this can give rise to false assumptions and poorly targeted care plans.
- Psychiatric co-morbidity issues of particular concern include delusional beliefs about the child, mental states producing disorganised behaviour, excitement states and depression with suicidal ideas.

Substance specialists have an important role in formulating realistic care plans, which often need to focus on parenting capacity, and substance-related behaviours rather than substance use itself (see SCODA guidelines, Appendix 12). Overemphasising the importance of urine tests because they are 'hard evidence' is unhelpful. Setting service users up to fail is a very unsatisfactory way of concluding child protection proceedings, which could more appropriately be managed by enabling the parent to recognise the limits of their abilities and the priorities for their children.

Children's need for emotional stability in early years is prompting courts to conclude custody issues in a relatively short timescale. It is vital that substance workers enable the most productive focus of care planning at all stages.

Older children who use substances may also be in need of protection within formal child protection procedures. Adolescents who use substances in a problematic way invariably have associated difficulties and may be severely vulnerable. Situations such as the effects of coercive adults, sexual exploitation, parental neglect or severe behaviour problems all indicate the need for a multiagency child protection intervention framework.

Constructive relationships with other agencies and services involved in childcare are essential for effective working (DH, 1999c; 2001b). The avoidance of conflict and the development of common understandings about the goals, priorities and resources of each component of care systems can be facilitated by shared training and regular meetings. Substance services should ensure participation in local child protection working parties, shared care planning forums for pregnant women, and develop as many liaison contacts as possible at managerial level as well as at practitioner level. Such contacts may include child and adolescent psychiatry, obstetric units, social services child protection teams and police family protection units.

Alcohol and drug workers should have the skills to contribute to child protection assessment. Attendance at formal child protection meetings and the preparation of reports can be stressful and requires a depth of knowledge which may not be appropriate for all team members. The identification of one team practitioner to provide advice and supervision is recommended. This can also assist in the important task of enabling individual workers to present difficult decisions to service users in a constructive and professional way.

Older women

The available data on substance use and dependency in older age is poor. To a great extent this reflects the hidden nature of problems as well as a lack of research interest. The rates of alcohol use above safe limits, estimated at about 5% in women over 65, are likely to rise with increased affluence and longevity. Illicit drug use is extending into older age, reflecting social changes. The use of

OTC medicines and analgesics can be major problems in this age group.

Women are vulnerable for many reasons linked to their traditional roles. Substance use can develop in the context of care giving, either to a substance-using partner, parent or child, or as the recipient of care from a substance user in advancing frail health. Older women have been seen as custodians of moral standards and thus may find it difficult to present for treatment. There may be professional failure to recognise problems for similar reasons. Older women have experienced many changes in social attitudes to substance use (Lender, 1986) and may have had many setbacks in seeking help in the past. Overcoming professional pessimism is a significant barrier for service users and providers. And yet they have many strengths to build on in therapy. These include coping strategies for distress, an inclination to socialisation and recognition of the value of the care of, and from, others (Rathbone-McCuan *et al.*, 1991).

Engagement in treatment requires sensitivity and special provision, allowing for difficulties of physical access. Recognition of associated physical health needs may be an important route. This and the treatment of common problems of underlying pain, depression and immobility are essential components of care plans (Crome & Day, 1999; Crome, 1999a).

Lesbian issues

The relatively neglected needs of lesbian women is reflected in the lack of targeted service components for gay and lesbian people in the substance use field. This is unfortunate as the evidence suggests that their vulnerability for substance use is higher than among other women (Adger, 1991). Studies also report different patterns of alcohol and drug use including higher rates of alcohol-related problems and more widespread use of marijuana and cocaine than among heterosexuals (McKirnan & Petersen, 1989).

Studies have found that lesbian women are less likely to have accessed cervical screening, breast screening and health care information (Diamont *et al.*, 2000). The National Household Survey of Drug Abuse found a raised prevalence of alcohol-related problems, with the same-sex partner group using alcohol more frequently and in larger amounts (Cochran *et al.*, 2000). The survey also found that homosexually active women were more likely than other women to be classified with drug dependency syndromes. They were also more likely to have used mental health services in the previous year, suggesting a small increased risk of psychiatric morbidity (Cochran & Mays, 2000).

Factors which may underlie these findings include stigma, isolation, lack of age-appropriate services and sexual harassment. Sexual harassment in the workplace has been demonstrated to have a more marked effect on the alcohol intake of lesbian women compared to its effect on other women staff (Nawyn *et al.*, 2000).

Ryan and Futterman (1998) propose that sexual orientation is an important aspect of assessment when working with young people and should be supported by psychological assessment including assessment of suicide risk and by the provision of appropriate counselling and information.

Ethnic minority women and families

Substance users from ethnic minorities are less likely to present to treatment services and are less likely to have their needs recognised in primary care. There are many barriers to treatment including traditional gender roles and expectations that are culturally linked. Some women, particularly recent immigrants whose residence is linked to their partner or who have not acquired local knowledge, linguistic skills or social confidence, will be deterred from approaching services. Their most likely sources of help will be through other routine contacts with primary care or obstetric services where it is important to have accessible information and a non-stigmatising and open attitude to the possibility of substance problems and related possibilities of psychiatric illness, domestic violence and physical illness.

Women and prison

Although the rate of criminality is comparable between male and female users of illicit drugs, the pattern of crime differs, with women more likely to be convicted of acquisitive crime and less likely to have convictions for violence. It has been suggested that a proportion of women drug users may be protected from prosecution because their partners collude to accept punishment in order to avoid the separation of a mother from her children (Parker & Chadwick, 1987). It has also been argued that the courts act more harshly towards substance-related women offenders because of notions of taboo and disapproval.

The criminal justice systems have contact with a large number of drug users and despite recent policy in the UK to use alternatives to custody, the proportion of imprisoned women who have substance problems is rising and the number of women sentenced for drug-related offences increased by 400% between 1979 and 1988 alone (Maden et al., 1990). In that large survey of women prisoners, 23% were identified as drug dependent, using either opiates or a combination including opiates. By 1999, 17% of males and 40% of females in UK prisons were sentenced for drug offences. Most prisoners in Maden's study had injected in the six months before arrest. The authors commented on the need for co-ordination between prison services and outside agencies.

In a US study of the needs of women in prison, Alemagno (2001) found that drug-using women were more likely to report a need for intensive mental health counselling, education, job training, medical care, family support and parenting assistance when released from jail, and concluded that referral for drug treatment may not break the cycle of drug use and incarceration if other needs cannot be addressed.

Conclusion

Services need to attract women substance users who are not only at high risk from the physical and emotional effects of their use but also have a high underlying morbidity which is likely to have a continuing effect on the likelihood of substance use.

Teams should ensure that the needs of women and families are advocated clearly by staff and service users in service planning and provision. Although a high proportion of staff are female, their experience will usually have been dominated by the preponderance of male service users. Women service users may require safer settings, alternative opening hours, the opportunity to see same gender staff and the option of home visits to facilitate a whole family approach. Family therapy skills and the care of women's physical health are key components. Liaison with other providers of specialist resources for women can facilitate appropriate and imaginative developments.

Women are in a pivotal position too, to enable their partners to make effective use of treatment and to influence the risk of substance use in subsequent generations. They require services which are able to identify substance needs and related mental health needs when women present with other issues. There is also a need for encouragement to engage without fear of stigmatisation or other disadvantages to their role as parents.

Issues relating to childhood trauma and separations need better responses and interventions to enable substance-using women to break the cycle of adverse consequences of their own experiences. Imaginative, rather than separate, services are generally appropriate, and the body of emerging research points to the benefits of targeted initiatives.

Chapter 19
Professionally Aided Self-Help, Twelve-Step Work and the Maintenance of Abstinence

Introduction

Most self-help interventions have been devised for drinkers rather than drug users. However, on the basis of the transferability of other interventions, we can expect them to be equally applicable to other substance users. In this book the discussion is limited to therapist-initiated interventions where professionals have an early role in facilitating self-help, such as Guided Self-Change and Behavioural Self-Control Training (BSCT), before handing over completely to the individual. Facilitated twelve-step work, Rational Recovery (RR) groups and a number of other professionally aided self-help groups (e.g. hepatitis C support groups) available in the substance use field are then considered.

Guided Self-Change for people with drink problems

The guided self-management approach for 'problem drinkers' devised by Sobell and Sobell (1993) falls halfway between self-help and treatment. Aided by professional help, people learn how to prevent the development of alcohol-related problems themselves.

Individuals should be carefully selected. The Guided Self-Change approach is not suitable for those who are severely alcohol dependent or who have major physical withdrawal symptoms. Although many will drink excessively at times, they should be able to moderate their drinking when required, and be able to have some days that are alcohol-free. It is most suitable for individuals at a relatively early stage of their drinking career, but who have developed problems relating to their alcohol consumption.

Such people are taught how to help themselves move away from problem alcohol use. Although research shows that about 25–30% of people with drink problems do deteriorate (Fillmore, 1988), the most common pattern is that they move in and out of problems with varying severity, with problem episodes separated by periods either of abstinence or drinking without problems (Pattison *et al.*, 1977). It is not clear whether the Guided Self-Change programme will help prevent the 25–30% who deteriorate or the larger group, but avoiding future problems and the harm they generate is important.

The emphasis of the approach is to help people identify their own strengths and resources and capitalise on these assets in situations when they are required. The Guided Self-Change approach intrudes in only a minimal way on a person's lifestyle. There is no defined number of treatment sessions.

The approach excludes learning new techniques for dealing with problems. For example, there is no place for skills training to help avoid relapse. The individual is forced to choose from a range of options within his or her current skills and strengths. Thus when confronted with social pressure to drink, a person might choose any one of the following:

- Resist the pressures by being appropriately assertive.
- Resist the pressures by being less assertive (e.g. 'my doctor told me that I shouldn't drink').
- Leave the situation.

- Enlist the help of others (e.g. spouse, friend) in resisting the pressures.
- Ignore the pressures.

If a skill is not used, this may be because the individual has a skills deficiency or he or she has decided not to use those skills because of a lack of motivation. The guiding themes of the approach are its emphasis on increasing clients' motivation and on finding ways to help people help themselves. Initially, guided self-management facilitates change by

- increasing motivation to avoid alcohol-related problems by encouraging people to identify reasons for changing;
- providing general strategies for achieving and maintaining change; and
- providing advice.

Because it relies on peoples' inherent strengths, Guided Self-Change is a relatively brief intervention. The basic strategy is

(1) learning how to identify high-risk situations;
(2) recognising their own strengths for dealing with risk situations (i.e. a person might possess the necessary skills but not realise how those skills can be used to avoid drinking excessively); and
(3) increasing the individual's motivation to avoid problems from drinking by identifying and emphasising the adverse consequences of heavy drinking, and helping the individual recognise the benefits derived from avoiding problems related to drinking.

For some people not drinking at all is the best way of preventing future drink problems, but at least 80% of those who use the Guided Self-Change approach opt for controlled drinking rather than abstinence. For such people it is important that realistic conservative drinking limits are set, e.g. three drinks on three days of the week, rather than reducing the number of drinks on any one occasion from seven to six. The approach must not be used to justify heavy drinking. This is one reason why guidance is helpful in the initial stages. The client needs to choose specific, well-thought-out rules about drinking limits and the circumstances under which he or she may drink (e.g. limit number of drinks on any one occasion, avoid spirits, never drink to aid emotional problems such as anxiety or depression, never drink alone and so on).

Although it is important that the individual chooses the rules, it is helpful if this is done in the presence of a professional, there is discussion about it and it is recorded. It is helpful to limit the rules to a specific time period and then reassess. A good technique for discussing goals is to ask a series of questions. If the goal is abstinence, ask the reasons for refraining from drinking. If the goal is to reduce drinking, ask about proposed limits and guidelines, whether the limits are realistic given their history, and whether they are consistent with the avoidance of high-risk drinking and of past problems. It is important to ascertain whether the individual has been able to drink at low levels and without problems, especially in the past year. If not, why does he or she believe that this could be achieved now? A useful question in helping people decide whether a non-abstinence goal is feasible is to ask whether they would feel it would be easier not to drink at all, or limit their drinking to one or two drinks per day. If the response is that it would be easier not to drink at all and that just one or two drinks would serve no purpose, then abstinence would be the most appropriate goal.

Although clients should be given the opportunity to change or revise their alcohol consumption goals, part of later professional guidance will be to ensure that the self-imposed rules and limits do not change with time as a way of rationalising behaviour that does not conform to previous intentions. Also goals should not be changed while the person is drinking or when a high-risk situation is imminent. People should be very careful about any changes which allow more drinking. Goals should only be modified after full consideration of the potential consequences of the change and ideally at the end of the assessment period.

Besides helping define realistic drinking goals, professionals also have a role as educators about the way the body handles alcohol, blood alcohol levels, standard drink conversions and tolerance. Oral advice should be backed up with educational pamphlets or other handouts. A discussion of known high-risk situations is important, but in some cases a high-risk situation can only be recognised in retrospect – another role for professional guidance. The desire to feel intoxicated often signals the presence of a high-risk situation and may be a warning sign. Although situations are generally regarded as high-risk because they tend to promote drug use or heavy or uncontrolled drinking, some situations are high-risk with problems arising even at low drinking levels. Driving skills can be impaired by cannabis and very low quantities of alcohol; and alcohol increases susceptibility to damage (see Chapter 17) but many drivers are unaware of this. Although most countries allow some drinking and impose legal limits regarding alcohol levels and driving, it is best not to drink alcohol at all when driving. People with a tendency to drink to excess and who have had any past problems related to drinking should be especially careful about drinking and driving.

In between professional consultations, various pieces of *homework* are useful. One of the most important of these is to keep a drinking diary or self-monitoring card outlining the quantities of alcohol consumed, the situation and timing. This should help pinpoint any previously unrecognised high-risk situations and other *triggers*, and ensure that if people do drink more than the agreed set limits, this is not overlooked. It also enables the professional involved to educate the drinker concerning a unit or standard drink, remembering that these vary from country to country. Monitoring cards normally allow space to record the number of standard drinks consumed.

Well-prepared reading material is also helpful, not only to consolidate and back up oral advice about the Guided Self-Change approach, but to educate the drinker about alcohol and its effects and to advertise local services. Some suggestions regarding useful supplementary reading material is given by the Canadians, Mark and Linda Sobell, in their book *Problem Drinkers: Guided Self-Change Treatment* (1993).

Behavioural Self-Control Training (BSCT)

Hester (1995) describes BSCT as involving 'goal setting, self-monitoring, managing consumption, rewarding goal attainment, functionally analysing drinking situations and learning alternative coping skills'. The teaching of coping skills by professionals is the main way in which this intervention differs from Guided Self-Change, although it is more structured and more firmly based in behavioural psychology. Like Guided Self-Change the substance user maintains primary responsibility for making decisions throughout. It can be completely self-directed using a self-help manual, but it can also be therapist-directed. Like the Guided Self-Change approach for people with drink problems, it is most often used when the consumption goal is moderation rather than abstinence.

Again those who are most likely to benefit from BSCT are those with less severe alcohol dependence or those who have drink problems but are not dependent. Several studies have shown that women are more successful than men in maintaining moderation following BSCT. It is not an effective approach for everyone. If failures of controlled drinking occur, sometimes they may be interpreted as an inappropriate match between the individual and the treatment goal and the goal rescheduled to abstinence, if this is acceptable to the individual. Miller suggests seeing those who are selected for BSCT for eight weekly programmes of 45–50 minutes each. The BSCT programme involves eight steps in the following order:

(1) setting limits on the number of standard drinks per day and on peak Blood Alcohol Concentrations (BACs)
(2) self-monitoring of drinking behaviours
(3) changing the rate of drinking
(4) practising assertiveness in refusing drinks
(5) setting up a reward system for achievement of goals
(6) learning which antecedents result in overdrinking and which in moderation
(7) learning other coping skills instead of drinking
(8) learning how to avoid relapsing back into heavy drinking

A self-monitoring card should ideally be used, and the information on the card should be completed before the drink is taken as this aids the monitoring process (Table 19.1). If people realise they are not self-monitoring when they are drinking, they

Table 19.1   Self-monitoring card

	Date	Day	Time	Drink type	Amount	Standard drinks	Where	With whom
1								
2								
3								
4								
5								
6								
7								
8								
9								
10								

should reconstruct their drinking pattern and then go on, rather than forget the monitoring process for the rest of the day. Some people express embarrassment at filling in cards or concern about the comments that others will make. Role-playing different situations can be a helpful way of rehearsing successful ways through this.

The first two sessions are usually devoted to mastering the self-monitoring process, and keeping to the limits set. Once this is achieved other strategies can be tackled. For example, peak BACs can still be adhered to when drinking more if the drinks are weaker. Switching to a less favoured drink, drinking in sips rather than gulps, monitoring the time between sips, spacing drinks out over, for example, a 4-hour period are all helpful ways of self-monitoring which explore new avenues of control.

The verbal and non-verbal elements of drink refusal skills are ideally first demonstrated. Clients will enjoy attempting to pressurise professionals to drink while they point out the various components of eye contact, body language, voice tone and volume, in addition to the verbal content.

Attention to various rewards are important. These should include congratulatory self-talk even after minor success. Tangible rewards should be given as soon as possible after goals have been achieved. Busy people sometimes give themselves rewards of doing absolutely nothing, or taking the time to read a favourite book. Some people feel so badly about themselves that they find it hard to give themselves rewards. Penalties for not achieving goals also help. However, penalties should never be imposed if there is no system in place for rewards.

Reviewing the self-monitoring card can also help highlight environmental and emotional triggers to alcohol use. These may relate to particular days of the week, times of the day, or situations, the amount of money the individual has at any one time or the presence of certain people.

BSCT has been extensively evaluated. A review by Hester (1995) shows that many, but not all, studies found that self-directed BSCT with minimal therapist contact is as effective as more intensive therapist-directed treatment.

Self-help manuals

Self-help manuals have an important place in the treatment of drink problems. Those who particularly favour a self-help approach may be especially sensitive to stigma and may wish to avoid contact with agencies. They have the potential to reach drinkers and drug users who are not in contact with services.

There are clear benefits of self-help manuals over other low-threshold interventions, such as the use of telephone helplines. One well-received manual was the DRAMS (Drinking Responsibly And Moderately with Self-control) scheme. It was adopted in Scotland (Heather, 1986) and has been successfully tested in other cultural contexts.

Miller and colleagues have shown that self-help manuals are an effective supplement to treatment. In a study designed to compare three different behavioural treatment modalities they randomly gave half the clients at the end of treatment a self-help manual as an afterthought, with the other half receiving it three months later. At the three-month follow-up the manual group continued to show therapeutic gains during the follow-up period and were significantly more improved. The non-manual group remained at the level reached at termination of treatment (Miller, 1978).

Following the success of DRAMS, Heather and colleagues (1987) devised and evaluated another self-help manual *Let's Drink to Your Health* for people with drink problems recruited via the media. Subjects were randomly allocated by mail either the manual or a booklet of general advice and information. At one-year follow-up, both groups had reduced their consumption by about a third. However, those who received the manual had significantly lower alcohol consumption than the control group. A number of other self-help manuals have been produced. Sanchez-Craig's (1993) manual, *Saying When: How to Quit Drinking or Cut Down*, formed the basis for the 'drinkwise programme'. There is no doubt that self-help manuals are not only useful in their own right, but also have the potential to help a sector of the population who would not otherwise come forward for help.

The twelve-step movement

The best known and most widely available self-help groups are the twelve-step groups Alcoholics Anonymous (AA) and Narcotics Anonymous (NA). The only requirement for membership to AA or NA is a desire to stop drinking or taking drugs. There are no membership fees. Each group is self-supporting and is not allied with any sect, denomination, political party, organisation or institution.

People in AA and NA believe they suffer from 'alcoholism' and drug addiction as a disease. They believe they have a progressive illness which can be arrested through complete abstinence and following the twelve steps of the AA/NA programme. However, a difficult area for some people is the association of twelve-step recovery with a spiritual awakening and the repeated emphasis on God and a higher power.

Meetings are locally accessible throughout the UK, the USA and almost everywhere. It should be possible to attend different meetings on a daily or even twice-daily basis and many people recommend that newcomers attend 90 meetings in 90 days. If there is that sort of commitment to the AA/NA programme, the result is likely to be successful. People know they will not be drinking while they attend the meetings and eke out the time in between each meeting. Slips are of course common but the AA/NA maxim of taking one day at a time is helpful. The days build up to become weeks, and then months. In the early stages cravings may be so great that taking a minute at a time may be what is required.

One of the great strengths of the twelve-step movement is the social support offered by other people attending the programme, some of whom have not had a drink for several years. Most AA/NA members freely hand out their telephone numbers so that people can ring them at times of difficulty. It is helpful for new attenders to ask to have a sponsor who will guide them and help them get to meetings and be there for times of crisis or if things go wrong. Sponsors should have been abstinent for a long period themselves, preferably several years, and should have achieved recovery through working the programme. AA and NA suggest the following ground rules:

- Sponsors should be of the same sex as the patient.
- Sponsors should be of the same age as, or older than, the patient.
- Sponsors should have at least a full year of sobriety and should be actively working the twelve-step programme, including going to

meetings, using the telephone and having their own sponsor.

Twelve-step publications recommend the following strategies to deal with urges and slips:

- calling an AA/NA friend
- going to an AA/NA social
- calling your sponsor
- calling the AA/NA hotline
- doing something different
- distracting yourself
- praying

THE SERENITY PRAYER

GOD grant me the serenity
To accept the things I cannot change;
The courage to change the things I can,
And the wisdom to know the difference.

Most AA/NA meetings are closed to outsiders, but at times open meetings are held when those who do not have a drink or drug problem are invited to attend. The format of most meetings is the same. One or more people will say 'My name is . . . and I am an alcoholic/addict.' He or she will then give a brief description of their life's story and how it became dominated and destroyed by drink or drugs. The others listen and most can identify with what is being said, understand how someone else managed to achieve success by working the twelve-step programme, and come to realise that they could do it for themselves.

Al-Anon, a programme for the families and significant others, Al-Ateen, a programme for the teenage children of alcoholics, NA and Families Anonymous (FA) for families of drug users all employ the same twelve steps as AA. It is important that families, friends and teenagers come to realise that they are just as powerless over alcohol or drugs as the drinker or drug user. Many become so deeply and obsessively entrenched in trying to stop the individual concerned from drinking or taking drugs that it totally dominates their lives and makes life unbearable for everyone else. By working the twelve-step programme such people are taught how to achieve detachment and start rebuilding their own lives back to normality.

THE TWELVE STEPS

(1) We admitted we were powerless over (alcohol) – that our lives had become unmanageable.

(2) Came to believe that a Power greater than ourselves could restore us to sanity.

(3) Made a decision to turn our will and our lives over to the care of God as we understand Him.

(4) Made a searching and moral inventory of ourselves.

(5) Admitted to God, ourselves, and to another human being the exact nature of our wrongs.

(6) Were entirely ready to have God remove all these defects of character.

(7) Humbly asked Him to remove our shortcomings.

(8) Made a list of all persons we had harmed, and became willing to make amends to them all.

(9) Made direct amends to such people wherever possible, except when to do so would injure them or others.

(10) Continued to take a personal inventory and when we were wrong, promptly admitted it.

(11) Sought through prayer and meditation to improve our conscious contact with God as we understood Him, praying only for knowledge of His will for us and the power to carry that out.

(12) Having had a spiritual awakening as the result of these steps, we tried to carry this message to (alcoholics) and to practise these principles in all our affairs.

Recovery is achieved by working through these 12 steps, one at a time, beginning with step 1. A sponsor can be an invaluable aid, facilitating this process by helping the individual understand and tackle each step in much the same way as Twelve-step Facilitation Therapy (TFT) for groups in a day care or residential rehabilitation facility as described below.

Twelve-step Facilitation Therapy (TFT)

Although each TFT programme must be adapted to the needs of the individual substance user, it is commonly undertaken in a group setting.

Twelve-step facilitators are nearly always people who have successfully achieved abstinence with the help of the programme and, like sponsors, most have been drink- or drug-free for several years. Some facilitators have simplified the 12 steps and made them less overtly dependent on religion.

The simple steps

- step 1: We admitted we had a problem, that our lives were in a mess.
- step 2: We realised we needed/could get help.
- step 3: We asked for help.
- step 4: We wrote a detailed description of ourselves, both positive and negative.
- step 5: We told someone else what we were like.
- step 6: We recognised personality traits that caused us pain.
- step 7: We asked other people how they changed.
- step 8: We made a list of people we had harmed.
- step 9: We made amends to these people always remembering to look after them and ourselves.
- step 10: We continued to look at our behaviour.
- step 11: We looked at ways we could improve our relationship with people, places and so on.
- step 12: We woke up, tried to help others and did our best.

(Courtesy of Chip Somers, Focus, Bury St Edmunds, Suffolk.)

Some TFT programmes address only step 1 but most programmes concentrate on the first five steps. Facilitators have a responsibility to ensure that the individuals attending the programme are internalising the material given. However, when TFT is done in a group setting it is the group who decide when to move on to the next step. Peer group evaluation is considered to be both accurate and powerful.

Step 1 facilitation: 'We admitted we were powerless over alcohol – that our lives had become unmanageable.' Or from the simple steps: 'We admitted we had a problem, that our lives were in a mess.'

This step concentrates on the concepts of powerlessness and unmanageability. Most people want to retain the *delusion* that they are still in control. Step 1 is the most important step. Without it twelve-step recovery is impossible. It necessitates total surrender. Step 1 proposes that, both consciously and unconsciously, people must accept that they are chemically dependent, and that their lives are unmanageable as long as they use mood-altering chemicals. Until this is achieved they cannot grow. While they feel they can somehow bring their lives back under control and learn to use alcohol or drugs normally, they have not accepted their disease and will not break free and progress.

Although acceptance of powerlessness can be made in a single leap, in practice it is sometimes helpful to see it as a process involving a series of stages:

- stage 1: 'I have a problem with alcohol and/or drugs.'
- stage 2: 'Alcohol and/or drug use is gradually making my life more difficult and causing problems for me.'
- stage 3: 'I have lost my ability to effectively control (limit) my use of alcohol/drugs, and the only alternative that makes sense is to give it up.'

Facilitators believe that the way to convince people to surrender is to show them, over and over again, that they get into trouble when they drink or use drugs. This is best done by writing down as many drink- and drug-related problems that have been experienced as possible. Chemically dependent people do things when they are intoxicated they would never do when they are sober. If people are to move on, they must be able to identify these problems, understand them and learn different ways for dealing with each problem.

Facilitators may ask people to write down how drinking or drug use affected the family, problems at work, and how substance use caused them to break their own moral code (e.g. neglecting the children). To help unearth as many problems as possible, examples from different problem areas may be requested. For example, the facilitator may request three written examples of protecting supplies (e.g. hiding bottles, sleeping with a dealer), ten ways in which life had become unmanageable (e.g. not eating properly), and previous attempts to control substance use when control had been lost.

Step 1 is time consuming because it involves written assignments, delineating past problems. This may then be rewritten and adapted as the person's life story to be presented and discussed in step 4. Here it will be used to help drinkers and drug users make rational decisions regarding their future substance use.

People do not get into trouble every time they drink or take drugs and they can never predict when trouble is going to occur. In a group others will prompt memories of past problems, e.g. drunk driving. Sometimes there are memory blackouts. It is scary to know that you were awake and doing things but have no recollection as to what these were. The facilitator may ask: 'Did you do something embarrassing when intoxicated?' 'How do you feel about not doing things with the family, at school, or at work because you were too intoxicated or hung over?' 'Is the family falling apart?' 'How did it feel being unable to keep promises?' Talking about their shame, depression, and anxiety which has been caused by substance use helps people come to terms with the fact that life has become unmanageable. Step 1 completion provides a solid foundation for moving on to step 2, but if step 1 is not completed properly, it is no use attempting to move on.

Step 2 facilitation: 'Came to believe that a Power greater than ourselves could restore us to sanity.' Or in the simple steps: 'We realised we needed/could get help.'

Step 2 involves the recognition that addiction is a form of insanity – a compulsive obsession. The essential ingredient of this step is a willingness by individuals to seek a power greater than themselves – to stop going it alone and accept help. It is accompanied by a recognition that other people have recovered with outside help. In AA the definition of sanity is soundness of mind and the ability to see and adapt to reality. The step 2 hypothesis is that those who are chemically dependent do not see things rationally. The substance takes precedence. Reality is perceived differently. It suggests that they live in an irrational deluded world of their own creation. Step 2 also involves looking at past failed approaches and the reasons why people have failed. There may be recognition that previously help has been blocked by defence mechanisms. Individuals may be asked to 'write a list of three "insane" things you did when you were using drugs that a rational person would never have considered doing (e.g. shared needles, took an overdose, drinking and driving)'. To complete step 2 people must conclude that they cannot continue their old ways of thinking. If they do, they will relapse into old behaviour.

Acceptance and handing over to a higher power and a spiritual awakening is difficult for many people. Sometimes it is easier to start with the idea that the group itself is a power that is greater than the individual. Physically if the other members of the group wished to stop someone leaving the room they would have the numbers and strength to do that. Handing over to a higher power involves trusting that power. Individual drug users and drinkers often have great difficulty in trusting others. Yet, if they cannot trust anyone else or themselves, if their lives are unmanageable, there is nowhere else to turn.

The way to start is by developing a group ethos which involves genuine interest and care about its members. This helps instil trust. Group members should be actively interested in each other's growth and help each other search for the right solutions. This involves being kind, encouraging and supportive, never hostile and aggressive. Aggression destroys trust. Any confrontations should be done in an atmosphere of positive regard for the individual concerned, so that trust in the group is maintained.

Step 3 facilitation: 'Made a decision to turn our will and our lives over to the care of God as we understood Him.' Or in the simple steps: 'We asked for help.'

For many people this is a very difficult step. For those working with the original steps, it involves active spiritual awakening. The world can no longer revolve around the drinker or drug taker.

Many substance users are narcissistic. If things do not go the way they want they may fly into a rage. They may care so deeply about themselves and the things they want that they are unable to empathise with others. Some may have had experiences which have led them to disregard the feelings of others as a way of coping. Step 3 involves overcoming this problem by developing empathy for others and asking people to turn their lives over to the care of a higher power. Many people who have been in the programme for years continue to have trouble with step 3. With the simple steps this is not such a problem. One simply has to ask for help.

Step 4 and step 5 facilitation
- *Step 4*: 'Made a searching and fearless moral inventory of ourselves.' Or in the simple steps: 'We wrote a detailed description of ourselves, both positive and negative.'
- *Step 5*: 'Admitted to God, ourselves, and to another human being the exact nature of our wrongs.' Or in the simple steps: 'We told someone else what we were like.'

Step 4 is where people identify past wrongs and their own character defects. Once these are identified people can work towards resolving them. For most people it is a relief to finally get everything off their chest. It is more difficult to share that information as is required in step 5. In TFT the life story is the main vehicle through which this is achieved.

The life story describes the way drink and/or drug use has affected the person's life, their family and other peoples' lives. It is a very helpful way forward. People must write exactly what happened. The good things are shared with the bad. This helps stop a slide into negativism, but it can be a very painful process. To do this successfully necessitates sharing difficulties and problems which have occurred in the past. In the original steps this involves sharing with God, ourselves and one other person. The one other person in step 5 is necessary because substance users need to see a human being respond to their wrongs. The person must be well

chosen, stable, with a knowledge of the world and forgiving.

Most day programmes and residential facilities expect the life history to be read out to the group in confidence. Other members of the group will identify with it, and it will help them overcome denial and delusion and face up to reality. The group facilitator will emphasise the importance of confidentiality and will ensure that the material contained within the life history will be used constructively and that no part of it is mentioned to anyone outside the group.

A written detailed life story helps drinkers and drug users make rational decisions regarding their future drink and drug use. Past blackouts and overdoses are discussed, aiding the recognition that it is not just a vague problem. Most people have a tendency to leave something out that is considered really bad. The 'Big Book', *Alcoholics Anonymous* (1976), refers to this in the following way: 'Time after time newcomers have tried to keep to themselves certain facts about their lives. Trying to avoid the humbling experience, they have turned to easier methods. Almost always they got drunk.' People are encouraged to share everything, however difficult that might be. Nothing is left to fester.

Sometimes material is presented which has been suppressed for years because it is so painful. Some individuals may become quite depressed on encountering events which they have suppressed for such a long time. They will need to know they are valuable people who deserve to be accepted and loved. This is why it is helpful that positive qualities and attributes are also recorded in the life history to help redress the balance and that the group is supportive. However, it is important to remember that some people with substance use problems are so vulnerable that further professional help may be required.

In between sessions, participating individuals are commonly asked to do some homework. This might involve reading printed material which has been handed out, and maintaining a journal or record. Reading material might include the three AA texts: *Alcoholics Anonymous* (1976), *Twelve Steps and Twelve Traditions* (1952) and *Living Sober* (1975) pamphlets and meditation books. In the journal they might be asked to record:

- all AA/NA meetings attended;
- personal reactions to, and thoughts about, meetings;
- reactions to suggested readings;
- 'slips' and what is done about them;
- reactions to recovery tasks; and
- cravings and urges to drink, and what was done about them.

Twelve-step facilitation, with the help of an experienced facilitator who has been through the programme and understands the difficulties that members of the group are facing, can be a remarkably useful way for some substance users to make progress. This includes those whose severity of dependence has led them and others to give up hope. No one is past redemption. Twelve-step programmes are particularly useful for those with a long history of substance use. For many people the welcoming atmosphere of a twelve-step group, and the support of the facilitator and group members can mark a turning point when all else has failed.

Rational Recovery (RR)

RR groups are self-help groups who achieve self-help with the aid of an adapted form of Rational–Emotive Therapy (RET). There is now a well-established network of RR groups throughout the USA, although they have yet to spread in a significant way to other countries. In addition to the groups some RR residential facilities have been established.

Instead of AA's Big Book, *Alcoholics Anonymous*, RR has *The Small Book* (Trimpey, 1989). It stresses that virtually all dependent drinkers in the USA are advised to go to AA even when it does not suit them. Although twelve-step programmes discourage this, sometimes AA/NA attendance is enforced through military and civil courts, or through social services. RR provides an effective alternative which is not dependent on a spiritual awakening – the most common reason given for rejecting AA/NA.

There are many other reasons apart from religious or spiritual ones why AA/NA is rejected. Some do not like to talk about themselves in front of a group. Others will not call themselves 'alcoholics', or they do not want to attend AA/NA because they want to pick their own friends, because they do not want to depend on a sponsor or on groups, or because they would prefer to help themselves independently.

Like AA and NA, RR agrees that the most reasonable solution to drug and alcohol dependence is usually lifetime abstinence from drugs and alcohol. *The Small Book* is like a primer to help significantly dependent substance users to become their own rational–emotive therapists and achieve what Trimpey has termed 'the "unmiracle" of NHP (No Higher Power) sobriety'. It also differs from twelve-step work in that it discourages the writing of life histories and the repeated telling of life stories of past struggles, mishaps and misdeeds that have occurred through drinking or drug use (Trimpey calls these 'drunkalogues'). Fearless moral inventories are not considered necessary in RR. As *The Small Book* says: 'We do not become sober to become good; we do so because we want some good out of life.'

The desire to be in control of one's life is discouraged by AA/NA. In contrast RR states, 'confidence, competence, and control of one's emotions and behaviour are hallmarks of maturity and mental health, rather than being sick or part of the disease of alcoholism'. The rational viewpoint of RR is that substance users can be empowered through sound mental health principles to achieve a healthy sobriety.

RR has its own techniques to help people avoid relapse. One of these is the acronym BEAST, which stands for:

Boozing opportunity
Enemy voice recognition
Accuse the voice of malice
Self-control and self-worth reminders
Treasure your sobriety

A boozing opportunity, or in other words *a high-risk situation*, will instigate cravings that may be difficult to control. Alcohol- and drug-dependent people hear these cravings or voices and are able to think both rationally and irrationally about them. Alcohol and drug users are powerfully conditioned to the 'quick fix' of another drink or hit because the results are so swift and usually so immediately gratifying. They live on a roller coaster of pain and pleasure. Almost all pleasure becomes associated with the intoxicant, even though it is the chief cause of the underlying pain. RR calls thoughts promoting substance use a 'beastly animal' (AA/NA call it 'stinking thinking'). The beast concept helps people prevent relapse by thinking rationally. Recognising the beast through addictive voice recognition training (AVRT) is an essential part of relapse prevention in RR. It involves: 'Any thinking that supports the use of drugs or alcohol in any amount, in any form – ever.' AVRT plays the same vital role in RR as the higher power does in AA/NA. Transforming the BEAST concept by utilising its acronym is a good defence against the first drink. Active and assertive distancing techniques are needed. Some occasions will be more difficult than others. Accusing the voice of malice is one way that is recommended in RR. Self-control and self-worth reminders are also helpful. Instead of drinking or taking drugs, people in RR learn to make themselves feel good at will just by thinking lovingly of themselves, and that they do not need to change in order to do so. 'We do not remain sober in order to think well of ourselves; it is because we like or value ourselves that we do not drink.' Another helpful part of the BEAST concept is to treasure sobriety and consciously reaffirm its intrinsic value when faced with a high-risk situation. It is clear that relapse is preceded by a great deal of premeditation and that drinking or drug use is a conscious decision. This gives all dependent drinkers and drug users an opportunity to take evasive action.

In spite of the BEAST concept or other relapse prevention techniques, relapses will inevitably occur, particularly in those who are beginning to adjust to sobriety as a way of life. If these are taken as learning opportunities, they will not be wasted. In the twelve-step alcoholism disease approach, confrontation is commonplace and people who are not ready to move forward to abstinence are said to be 'in denial'. In contrast RR, like other cognitive-based therapies, finds people to be in a state of ambivalence, simultaneously holding two opposing views about the same behaviour – the BEAST and the rational view. In RR it does not matter whether someone had two, five or eight beers or snorted cocaine ten times instead of five. The focus is always on rational sobriety. There are however a number of ground rules. RR group members make decisions for themselves and do not attempt to persuade others to abstain from drugs and alcohol. Several people who attend RR meetings continue to drink during their 'recoveries', giving recognition to their ambivalence. A continuing drinker or drug user is said to be 'all beast'. To help such people RR developed the concept of the idealised rational human being who is

(1) imperfect, fallible, yet having *intrinsic worth*;
(2) wanting, because of (1) to *survive*;
(3) emotionally *independent* from external events;
(4) thinking thoughts that stand the test of *reason*, i.e. to be 'right' or intelligent as opposed to 'wrong' or stupid;
(5) feeling good, and enjoying the *pleasures* of living; and
(6) able to *tolerate* frustration, pain and discomfort.

Instead of accusations of denial which are part of the twelve-step approach, discussions with individuals and within RR groups are aimed at establishing the above conditions as products of reasoning.

RR has generated some controversy, but it does provide a useful and potentially effective alternative to recovery through twelve-step programmes. It is also helpful for the families of substance users, who no longer need feel responsible for their loved one's drinking or drug-using, or believe they are suffering from 'the disease of co-dependence'.

Other self-help groups

A number of other self-help groups, such as support groups for families and friends, or support groups for those with hepatitis C, are useful adjuncts to treatment services. Access to self-help groups through the internet is becoming increasingly popular and can provide a level of support that is even more readily available than a traditional meeting (Nowinski, 1999). Self-help groups can provide support, insight and empathy that, when things go well, is unparalleled. They can also be a useful route by which to educate and help ensure constructive behaviour change both for substance users and their families or significant others.

For twelve-step groups there is a well-honed programme that enables each group to function without a specific leader. Those attending know precisely the nature of the group they are attending and, although individual groups do vary according to the membership present, anyone attending a group anywhere in the world will be presented with roughly the same format.

Other self-help groups do however need a great deal of support if they are to run well. Those who attend such groups often feel extremely vulnerable and may lurch from crisis to crisis. Adequate support for each group is vital. This can be achieved either by training special leaders or coordinators for each group, as is the case with RR groups, or by employing a professional to oversee and back up several groups. It can be extremely demanding both on time and emotional resources to do this, and those selected need to be very stable and committed people themselves. Not to give this point adequate attention is likely to dictate whether a group runs well or badly, whether it provides a useful function, or indeed whether the group survives.

Conclusion

Professionally aided self-help makes an important contribution to recovery for many people. Group work and supportive individual contact are the traditional methods of self-help. However, self-help through electronic information sharing, virtual groups and Internet-based networking are likely to make this form of help much more accessible in the future. It is an area ready for imaginative development.

Epilogue

Much progress has been made in recent years and most of the interventions described in this book are not new. In spite of this, many have yet to be incorporated into current routine service provision. Change can be threatening. It is perhaps easier to continue old ways of doing things, particularly when working under pressure. Thus many services are aware that progress has been made but have yet to accommodate it and incorporate any necessary changes to their working practice.

In 1990 the alcohol field was in a similar position to the drug field today. Much was known about many interventions which were helpful yet most drinkers were given unstructured alcoholism counselling and recommended to attend Alcoholics Anonymous (AA). Then an influential report, *Broadening the Base of Treatment for Alcohol Problems*, was published in the USA by the Institute of Medicine (IOM, 1990). In it the steering committee outlined their *vision* of the holistic way in which the multiple aspects of the subject could be integrated. It recognised that other groups and individuals might develop alternative views and welcomed such alternatives. Since that time further effective treatment options have been described and most have also been shown to apply to people with other chemical dependencies. In this book we have demonstrated the extensive evidence base for many different treatments that should now be available for all substance users and we have suggested a potential therapeutic framework which can be applied whatever the substance. One broad-based intervention has been shown to be particularly effective both in the prevention and treatment of alcohol and drug problems, and that is life skills training, comprising the acquisition of better social and coping skills. Botvin and colleagues (1995) have demonstrated that this is of great importance in the classroom for the prevention of future substance use problems and dependence. Three independent meta-analyses of '*alcoholism management*' comparing outcomes have ranked coping and social skills training as either the most effective (Holder *et al.*, 1991) or the second most effective (Finney & Monahan, 1996; Miller & Wilbourne, 2002) treatment intervention. Of the two types of training Monti and colleagues (2002) state that interpersonal (i.e. social) skills training is more likely to show significant results, but both coping and social skills training are useful.

We do not propose that the treatment framework we have suggested is the only way forward. Like the steering committee of the IOM, we welcome other innovations and modifications. Most local specialist services have developed their own way of doing things. The framework we have suggested can be easily incorporated into existing services. Expanding the interventions available in order to provide a fuller service will take time and significant training will be needed for many of those working with specialist services, but will reap major dividends.

In their report the steering committee of the IOM also highlighted another sense in which the base of treatment for alcohol problems has been broadened. Treatment was no longer seen to be exclusively the province of a specialised treatment sector. Although some people have multiple and complex substance use problems, most have a small number of such problems but as a consequence may encounter a wide range of professionals particularly those from health, social services and probation. Individuals may need help for physical health, childcare and mental health problems, or may encounter professionals working within the criminal justice system as a result of their substance use. It is essential that all professionals learn to work together from a broad base and in an integrated way when dealing with drug users and drinkers. Many generic professionals can learn to master brief structured interventions and incorporate them into their routine work. Others, particularly doctors, who are in a position to undertake a prescribing role, may share care with specialist drug and alcohol services. Many generic professionals might benefit from incorporating Motivational Interviewing (MI) into their professional working methods. The IOM report recommended the creation of a broad, community-wide network of assessment, referral and case managers who are to undertake differential diagnosis, match patients to appropriate treatment and monitor patient progress. However their vision entailed either giving a brief intervention and referring to specialist services where necessary. They did not see generic workers as providing treatment interventions themselves. With the development of tier 2 generic service providers who have special training in this area, we are now enabled to move to a new treatment framework, which has been outlined in Chapter 6. This involves a comprehensive spectrum of specialised treatment options that incorporates brief interventions, self-help, intensive outpatient care, medical detoxification, Minnesota Model inpatient treatment, and quarter and halfway houses, which is equally applicable to drug users as it is to drinkers.

When we talk of treatment in the substance use field we are in the main describing interventions which promote behaviour change rather than relating treatment to particular substances. With one or two exceptions, such as substitute prescribing, the interventions which are necessary are rarely dependent on specific mind-altering substances. To consider all substance types as having a universal need for treatment, rather than addressing a perceived need for separate interventions for alcohol and a wide range of different drugs, greatly enhances the number of possible useful treatment interventions. Most can be targeted to individual need and desired outcomes, and will also enhance the quality of people's lives. Unifying drug and alcohol service provision at a clinical level opens the door to potential cost savings, easier geographical access and joint training. It also enables professionals working in specialist services to more readily specialise, developing enhanced skills in one or two areas of their choice. Many will find this extremely rewarding. Thus it has the potential for greater efficiency of service provision as a whole to the benefit of substance users and their professional service providers.

In this book we recommend that all those working in specialist services familiarise themselves with the concepts of MI and use this as a style of counselling in day-to-day interactions with service users. We hope that service providers will diversify and develop different specialised areas of input to enable comprehensive coverage. When it is not possible to provide a specific skill from within a team, services should contract skills from outside. This will provide a full holistic service which will enable drinkers and drug users to become better integrated in mainstream society and move further along the recovery process than they might otherwise go.

From another viewpoint this book is about the stage of preparation. It involves an incremental process of recovery and in doing so is preparing people to change so that, if it is their chosen goal, they have the best possible chance of successful abstinence. Abstinence should not be a dirty word to be avoided, and for most people it is achievable if it is approached in the right way. The important thing is that it is the individual drinker or drug user who decides if and when abstinence is attempted. The care coordinator may advise differently, for instance, if a drinker or drug user is severely dependent, but the final say should rest with the substance user. In the reverse situation where the care coordinator is advising abstinence but the drinker or drug user does not feel ready for this, a trial period of abstinence for a defined period of time (in the words of the Community Reinforcement Approach 'sobriety sampling') can be a helpful way forward. It is less threatening than the prospect of stopping forever. Placing the substance user in control of decision-making on goals and interventions, with the professional acting as adviser, is the key to success.

When the goal chosen by a drinker or drug user is abstinence, the joy of a successful outcome for someone who is chemically dependent can be shared by all. But for many service providers that joy is relatively short-lived. Those who successfully achieve abstinence move away to a different life. Service providers thus work with those who do not attempt or achieve this goal. Some become disillusioned and cynical. If, when preparing for abstinence, we look for incremental improvement in outcome, the balance is readdressed and service providers can start to live with their successes.

In many cases people who attempt abstinence are not properly prepared for it and so they fail. If they fail repeatedly, they may come to believe that they are unable to stop drinking or taking drugs and will never succeed. This applies just as much to opiate users on substitute medication as to severely dependent drinkers. There are many reasons why people experience failure. Social support systems may be inadequate, individuals may have forgotten, or perhaps may never have learned, how to cope with difficult emotions in any other way apart from using drugs or drink. Homelessness, unemployment, poverty, social exclusion, low self-regard, poor self-efficacy, poor social and psychological functioning, complex drug- and drink-related problems, and a failure to utilise personal strengths that may be available all conspire to ensure failure.

With the help of a good assessment process and treatment framework, these difficulties can be gradually overcome. The role of the professional who wishes to give the best possible help is comparable to that of a good teacher. In some cases master craftsman/craftswoman might be a more appropriate word. Professionals must guide individual drinkers and drug users and help them harness those forces that are helpful and avoid or overcome those forces that hinder. Like sailing by harnessing fair winds, avoiding adverse currents, knowing when to reef your sail, plotting a course where you know the winds and tides will be more favourable, and avoiding rocks and shallows, there is great skill involved. Just as seasoned sailors respect the sea, we too must respect the forces of addiction. They are extremely powerful and not easily overcome.

With the right approach, the way forward can be found. It begins with a clear understanding of the issues involved that led to drink- or drug-related problems or dependency in the first place. It encompasses the current situation and it defines those interventions which are most needed and likely to be most helpful. It may take time – in some individuals several years – before someone is completely ready for abstinence. It is not just a case of detoxifying or putting an opiate user on a substitute prescription and waiting until he or she is ready to stop using drugs. That can be done, and when it is done people may slowly improve and integrate into mainstream society. Many, however, will never get there without professional help. Nevertheless, by including additional appropriate interventions targeted to individual need, much more is achievable and the process is speeded up.

Whether or not they choose abstinence as a goal, if there is an aim for incremental positive change, more people will successfully move further along the continuum away from drugs or drink. As they do this they will become more integrated in mainstream society, function better on both a social and psychological level, have more rewarding personal relationships, recognise their own abilities and regain their self-respect. All things then become possible and people may choose the life they wish, unencumbered by ambivalent thoughts and desires which give undue salience to matters relating to substance use. For most people the world simply becomes a better place.

Appendices

Appendices

Appendix 1

Diagnosis of Drug and Alcohol Dependence

Substitute prescribing should only be considered if there is proven drug dependence using criteria of the *Diagnostic and Statistical Manual of Mental Disorders*, 4th edn (DSM-IV). These criteria are satisfied when the answer is 'yes' to three or more of the following seven questions, if this is applicable within the same 12-month period:

(1) Do you find that you now need markedly increased amounts of alcohol or the drug you take in order to achieve the same effects?
or
Have the effects of alcohol or the drug you take markedly diminished if you take the same amount you originally used to take?

(2) Do you get alcohol/drug withdrawals?
or
Do you take the drug/alcohol to prevent withdrawals?

(3) Have you taken your drugs/alcohol in larger amounts over a longer period than you intended?

(4) Do you persistently wish to cut down or control your drug/alcohol use?
or
Have you had a number of unsuccessful attempts to cut down or control your drug/alcohol use?

(5) Is a great deal of time spent obtaining or taking your drugs/alcohol, or recovering from their effects?

(6) Are important social, occupational or recreational activities given up or reduced because of your drug/alcohol use?

(7) Do you continue to take drugs/alcohol even though you are aware that there are physical or psychological problems which are probably caused by your use of drugs? (e.g. amphetamine-induced depression)

If less than three 'yes' answers, substitute prescribing is not indicated.
If three or more 'yes' answers, substitute prescribing may be indicated.

Appendix 2

Model Initial Assessment Proforma

Record No: . . . .   **Date**: . . . .

Name: . . . .   **DOB**: . . . .

(1) Reason for referral (problem presented by client or other person):

(2) Current drug and alcohol use in last four weeks (to include both unprescribed and prescribed drugs):

    In what ways has this been a problem for you? (problem recognition):

(3) Drug and alcohol history:

(4) Infection injecting/BBV risk history:

    Sexual health:

    Injecting sites evident: Y/N

    Health screen needed: Y/N   Contemplating: Y/N

(5) Previous treatment/abstinence:

(6) Relapse factors:

(7) Physical health:

    Overdose history/overdose leaflet provided:

(8) Mental health:

    Previous or present treatment:

    Presentation during interview:

(9) Current social situation:

    Housing/accommodation:

    Employment:

    Relationship/family:

    Recreation interests:

(10) Forensic history:

    Court appearances pending:

    Current or past probation orders:

    Past imprisonment:

    Are criminal activities a consequence of drug use?

    Probation officer (obtain consent):

(11) Personal history:

    Childhood:

    Education:

    Major life events:

    Employment history:

(12) Relationships:

How does your drug or alcohol use affect these people? (problem recognition):

Do these people know about your drug use or drinking and how are they helping you?

Would these people be involved in your treatment? Obtain consent for involvement:

Information from parent/carer (if applicable):

(13) Motivating factors:

What do you imagine will happen if you don't make a change to your drug use or drinking? (concern):

What are the reasons that you see for making a change? (intention to change):

What encourages you that you can change if you want to? (optimism):

(14) Clients under the age of 18 years – competence (Gillick factors):

(i) Does the young person's intellectual development and emotional maturity enable him or her to

- present a thoughtful and accurate account?   Y/N

- understand the issues in assessing the problem?   Y/N

- understand the issues in formulating a care plan?   Y/N

- make a decision about his or her treatment?   Y/N

If 'No' is indicated, what service provision would lead to obtaining an accurate assessment, formulation of care plan and reduction of risk for the client?

(ii) Is there likely to be a significant difference between the staff opinion about the young person's needs and the expressed wishes or the known wishes of the parent/carer?

(15) Care plan for team discussion:

Identified problem/need:

Objective(s):

Intervention/action:

(16) Checklist: Date completed:

    Urine sample taken: Y/N

    Further appointment offered: Y/N

    Database form completed: Y/N

    Child protection assessment completed: Y/N

    Risk assessment completed: Y/N

    Consent to contact form completed: Y/N

    Health screen booked: Y/N

    Information on other agencies given: Y/N

    Overdose leaflet provided: Y/N

    Methadone handbook given: Y/N

    Information to parent/carer given
    (e.g. overdose leaflet, drug info, methadone handbook):   Y/N

    GP and client address checked: Y/N

    If prescription planned, pharmacy address checked: Y/N

(17) Name of interviewer:

    Discipline:

    Date:

(With permission from The Bure Centre, Norwich, UK.)

Appendix 3

Approximate Duration of Detectability of Selected Drugs in Urine

Substance	Duration	Substance	Duration
Amphetamines	48 hours	**Cocaine metabolites**	2–3 days
Methamphetamine	48 hours	**Methadone (maintenance dosing)**	7–9 days
Barbiturates		**Codeine/morphine/propoxyphene**	48 hours
Short-acting	24 hours	(heroin is detected in urine as morphine)	
Intermediate-acting	48–72 hours	**Norpropoxyphene**	6–48 hours
Long-acting	7 days or more	**Cannabinoids (marijuana)**	
Benzodiazepines (therapeutic dose)	3 days	Single use	3 days
Ultra-short-acting (e.g. midazolam)	12 hours	Moderate use (4 times per week)	4 days
Short-acting (e.g. triazolam)	24 hours	Heavy use	10 days
Intermediate-acting (e.g. temazepam)	40–80 hours	Chronic heavy use	21–27 days
Long-acting (e.g. diazepam)	7 days	**Methaqualone**	7 days or more
		Phencyclidine (PCP)	8 days (approx.)

(From Wolff, K., Welch, S., Marsden, J., *et al.* (1997) *Working Group on Identification and Management of Psychoactive Substance Use Problems in Primary Health Care Settings*. Geneva: WHO.)

Appendix 4

Drinkers/Drug Takers Diary

DAY	TIME	PLACE	WHY YOU STARTED	WHO WITH	TYPE OF DRINK/ DRUG	AMOUNT	WHAT HAPPENED
Monday							
Tuesday							
Wednesday							
Thursday							
Friday							
Saturday							
Sunday							

Appendix 5

Severity of Dependence Scale (SDS)

During the past year:

(1) Did you think your use of [named drug] was out of control?

(2) Did the prospect of missing a fix (or dose) or not chasing make you anxious or worried?

(3) Did you worry about your use of [named drug]?

(4) Did you wish you could stop?

(5) How difficult did you find it to stop, or go without [named drug]?

For questions 1–4 each item is scored on a four-point scale:

0 = never/almost never
1 = sometimes
2 = often
3 = always/nearly always

Question 5 is also scored on a four-point scale, but here:

0 = not difficult
1 = quite difficult
2 = very difficult
3 = impossible

The SDS has been validated to measure severity of dependence of opiate and stimulant users. A total SDS score is calculated. Higher scores indicate higher levels of dependence. It is primarily a measure of compulsive use, which is a central component of dependence. It does not measure tolerance, withdrawal or reinstatement.

(From Gossop, M., Darke, S., Griffiths, P., *et al.* (1995) The severity of dependence scale (SDS): psychometric properties of the SDS in English and Australian samples of heroin, cocaine and amphetamine users. *Addiction*, **90**, 607–14. With permission from Blackwell Publishing.)

Appendix 6

The Severity of Dependence Scale (SDS) Adaptation for High-Dose Non-Therapeutic Benzodiazepine Users

During the last month:

(1) Did you think your use of tranquillisers was out of control?

(2) Did the prospect of missing a dose make you anxious or worried?

(3) Did you worry about your use of tranquillisers?

(4) Did you wish you could stop?

(5) How difficult would you find it to stop or go without your tranquillisers?

For questions 1–4 each item is scored on a four-point scale:

0 = never/almost never
1 = sometimes
2 = often
3 = always/nearly always

Question 5 is also scored on a four-point scale, but here:

0 = not difficult
1 = quite difficult
2 = very difficult
3 = impossible

A total SDS score can be obtained by addition of the scores for all items with higher total scores indicating higher levels of dependence.

(From De las Cuevas, C., Sanz, E. J., De la Fuente, J. A., *et al.* (2000) The severity of dependence scale (SDS) as screening test for benzodiazepine dependence: SDS validation study. *Addiction*, **95**(2), 245–50. With permission from Blackwell Publishing.)

Appendix 7

The Leeds Dependence Questionnaire

A ten-item self-completion questionnaire designed to measure the severity of dependence on any drug including alcohol

In answering this questionnaire

- *think about the last week*
- *think about your main substance groups, please specify . . .*
- *tick the answer that is most appropriate to you*

	Never (0)	*Sometimes* (1)	*Often* (2)	*Nearly always* (3)

(1) Do you find yourself thinking about when you will next be able to have another drink or take drugs?

(2) Is drinking or taking drugs more important than anything else you might do during the day?

(3) Do you feel your need for drink or drugs is too strong to control?

(4) Do you plan your days around getting and taking drink or drugs?

(5) Do you drink or take drugs in a particular way in order to increase the effect it gives you?

(6) Do you drink or take drugs morning, afternoon and evening?

(7) Do you feel you have to carry on drinking or taking drugs once you have started?

(8) Is it getting the effect you want more important than the particular drink or drug you use?

(9) Do you want to take more drink or drugs when the effect starts to wear off?

(10) Do you find it difficult to cope with life without drink or drugs?

As can be seen answers to the ten questions are rated by scores of 0–3 giving a maximum score of 30. There is no specific cut-off points for low, moderate or severe dependence. Instead users of the scale are encouraged to view it as a continuum. However a score of 20 or more approximates to a score for severe dependence.

(From Raistrick, D., Bradshaw, J., Tober, G., *et al.* (1994) Development of the Leeds Dependence Questionnaire (LDQ): a questionnaire to measure alcohol and opiate dependence in the context of a treatment evaluation package. *Addiction*, 89, 563–72. With permission from Blackwell Publishing.)

Appendix 8

Readiness to Change Questionnaire

This questionnaire applies solely to excessive drinkers and not to drug users. It measures three stages: precontemplation (questions 1, 5, 10 and 12), contemplation (questions 3, 4, 8 and 9) and action (questions 2, 6, 7 and 11). Questions designed to measure maintenance were abandoned when it was found that they prevented the emergence of factors corresponding to the stages of change. All answers are scored in the following way:

Strongly disagree:	− 2
Disagree:	− 1
Unsure:	0
Agree:	+ 1
Strongly agree:	+ 2

The following questionnaire is designed to identify how you personally feel about your drinking right now. Please read each of the following questions carefully, and then decide whether you agree or disagree with the statements. Please tick the answer of your choice to each question.

	Strongly agree	Agree	Unsure	Disagree	Strongly disagree
(1) I don't think I drink too much.	☐	☐	☐	☐	☐
(2) I am trying to drink less than I used to.	☐	☐	☐	☐	☐
(3) I enjoy my drinking, but sometimes I drink too much.	☐	☐	☐	☐	☐
(4) Sometimes I think I should cut down on my drinking.	☐	☐	☐	☐	☐
(5) It's a waste of time thinking about my drinking.	☐	☐	☐	☐	☐

(6) I have just recently changed
my drinking habits.

□   □   □   □   □

(7) Anyone can talk about wanting to do
something about drinking, but I am
actually doing something about it.

□   □   □   □   □

(8) I am at the stage where I should think
about drinking less alcohol.

□   □   □   □   □

(9) My drinking is a problem sometimes.

□   □   □   □   □

(10) There is no need for me to think about
changing my drinking habits.

□   □   □   □   □

(11) I am actually changing my drinking
habits right now.

□   □   □   □   □

(12) Drinking less alcohol would be
pointless for me.

□   □   □   □   □

As there are four questions for each of the three stages measured, the total score for each stage will vary from -8 to $+8$. If one answer has not been completed, the sum of the other three answers for the same stage of change should be multiplied by 1.33. If two or more answers are missing, the questionnaire should be regarded as invalid. The stage of change with the highest score gives the stage of change designation. Increasing scores for precontemplation indicate *decreasing* readiness to change, whereas increasing scores for contemplation and action indicate *increasing* readiness to change. Where two of the three stages have equally high scores, the stage furthest is taken (i.e. if precontemplation and contemplation tie with the highest scores, contemplation is the designated stage of change, and if contemplation and action tie, action is the designated stage of change).

(From Rollnick, S., Heather, N., Gold, R., *et al.* (1992) Development of a short 'readiness to change' questionnaire for use in brief opportunistic interventions among excessive drinkers. *British Journal of Addiction*, **87**, 743–54. With permission from Blackwell Publishing.)

Appendix 9

The Decisional Balance

Advantages of using drugs/drinking	Disadvantages of using drugs/drinking
Advantages of stopping	Disadvantages of stopping

(From Janis, I. L. & Mann, L. (1977) *Decision Making: A Psychological Analysis of Conflict, Choice and Commitment*. New York: Free Press. Reprinted with permission from Free Press, a division of Simon and Schuster Adult Publishing Group. Copyright 1977 by Free Press. All rights reserved.)

Appendix 10

Injecting Questionnaire (Self-Completion)

All questions refer to the last four weeks only.

Have you injected in the last four weeks?　　　　　　　　**Yes/No**

If you have not injected in the last four weeks, do not answer the remaining questions.

If you have injected in the last four weeks, please circle the answer that applies to you or write in the number of people.

(1) During the last four weeks, how often have you shared injecting equipment?　　　Frequently : Sometimes : Hardly ever : Never

(2) During the last four weeks, with how many different people have you shared injecting equipment?　　　Number of people _____

During the last four weeks how often have you done any of the following things:

(3) given or lent used needles/syringes to a sexual partner?　　　Frequently : Sometimes : Hardly ever : Never

(4) given or lent used needles/syringes to a friend or acquaintance?　　　Frequently : Sometimes : Hardly ever : Never

(5) given or lent needles/syringes to a stranger?　　　Frequently : Sometimes : Hardly ever : Never

(6) injected with needles/syringes that had already been used by a sexual partner?　　　Frequently : Sometimes : Hardly ever : Never

(7) injected with needles/syringes that had already been used by a friend or acquaintance?　　　Frequently : Sometimes : Hardly ever : Never

(8) injected with needles/syringes that had already been used by a stranger?　　　Frequently : Sometimes : Hardly ever : Never

(9) filled your syringe from one that had already
     been used by someone else?

Frequently : Sometimes : Hardly ever : Never

(10) let someone else fill their syringe with a syringe
      you had already used?

Frequently : Sometimes : Hardly ever : Never

(11) drawn up from a container or spoon into which
      someone else had put a used syringe?

Frequently : Sometimes : Hardly ever : Never

(12) put a used needle into a container or spoon that
      was then used by someone else?

Frequently : Sometimes : Hardly ever : Never

(13) used a filter into which someone else had
      put a used syringe?

Frequently : Sometimes : Hardly ever : Never

(14) let someone else use a filter into which you
      had put a used syringe?

Frequently : Sometimes : Hardly ever : Never

(15) used the same water or bleach as someone else
      for flushing out or cleaning?

Frequently : Sometimes : Hardly ever : Never

(16) used old syringes that had been kept in the same
      container or 'sin bin' as someone else's syringes?

Frequently : Sometimes : Hardly ever : Never

(17) with how many *different* people have you done any
      of the things on this page?

Number of people_____

(Reproduced with permission from the Centre for Research on Drugs and Health Behaviour, London.)

Appendix 11

Hamilton Depression Rating Scale

For each item write in the box the number that best characterises the patient during the past week.

(1) **Depressed mood** (sad, hopeless, helpless, worthless)
    0   Absent
    1   Indicates these feeling states only on questioning
    2   Spontaneously reports these feeling states verbally
    3   Communicates these feeling states non-verbally, i.e. through facial expression, posture, voice and tendency to weep
    4   Spontaneously reports 'virtually only' these feeling states verbally and non-verbally

(2) **Feeling of guilt**
    0   Absent
    1   Self-reproach, feels he or she has let people down
    2   Ideas of guilt or rumination over past errors or sinful deeds
    3   Present illness is a punishment, has delusions of guilt
    4   Hears accusatory or denunciatory voices and/or experiences threatening visual hallucinations

(3) **Suicide**
    0   Absent
    1   Feels life is not worth living
    2   Wishes he or she were dead or any thoughts of possible death to self
    3   Suicide ideas or gesture
    4   Attempts at suicide (any serious attempt rates 4)

(4) **Insomnia early**
    0   No difficulty falling asleep
    1   Complains of occasional difficulty falling asleep, i.e. more than half hour
    2   Complains of nightly difficulty falling asleep

(5) Insomnia middle

   0   No difficulty falling asleep

   1   Complains of being restless and disturbed during the night

   2   Waking during the night (any getting out of bed rates 2) except for purposes of voiding

(6) Insomnia late

   0   No difficulty falling asleep

   1   Waking in early hours of the morning, but goes back to sleep

   2   Unable to fall asleep again if he or she gets out of bed

(7) Work and activities

   0   No difficulty

   1   Thoughts and feelings of incapacity, fatigue or weakness related to activities, work or hobbies

   2   Loss of interest in activity, hobbies or work, either directly reported by patient, or indirectly through listlessness, indecision and vacillation (feels the need to push self to work or activities)

   3   Decrease in actual time spent in activities or decrease in productivity (in hospital, rate 3 if patient does not spend at least 3 hours a day in activities (hospital job or hobbies) exclusive of ward chores)

   4   Stopped working because of present illness (in hospital, rate 4 if patient engages in no activities except ward chores, or if patient fails to perform ward chores unassisted)

(8) Retardation (slowness of thought and speech; impaired ability to concentrate; decreased motor activity)

   0   Normal speech and thought

   1   Slight retardation at interview

   2   Obvious retardation at interview

   3   Interview difficult

   4   Complete stupor

(9) Agitation

   0   None

   1   Fidgetiness

   2   Playing with hands, hair, etc.

   3   Moving about, cannot sit still

   4   Hand-wringing, nail-biting, hair-pulling, biting of lips

(10) Anxiety psychic

   0   No difficulty

   1   Subjective tension and irritability

   2   Worrying about minor matters

3   Apprehensive attitude apparent in face or speech
4   Fears expressed without questioning

☐

(11) **Anxiety somatic** (physiological concomitants of anxiety, such as gastrointestinal: dry mouth, wind, indigestion, diarrhoea, cramps, belching; cardiovascular: palpitations, headaches; respiratory: hyperventilation, sighing; urinary frequency: sweating)

0   Absent
1   Mild
2   Moderate
3   Severe
4   Incapacitating

☐

(12) **Somatic symptoms: gastrointestinal**

0   None
1   Loss of appetite, but eating without staff encouragement; heavy feeling in abdomen
2   Difficulty in eating without staff urging; requests or requires laxatives or medication for bowels or medication for gastrointestinal symptoms

☐

(13) **Somatic symptoms: general**

0   None
1   Heaviness in limbs, back or head; backache, headache, muscle aches; loss of energy and fatigability
2   Any clear-cut symptom rates 2

☐

(14) **Genital symptoms** (loss of libido, menstrual disturbances)

0   Absent
1   Mild
2   Severe

☐

(15) **Hypochondriasis**

0   Not present
1   Self-absorption (bodily)
2   Preoccupation with health
3   Frequent complaints, requests for help, etc.
4   Hypochondriacal delusions

☐

(16) **Loss of weight**

    (A) **When rating by history**:
        0   No weight loss
        1   Probable weight loss associated with present illness
        2   Definite (according to patient) weight loss

    or

    (B) **On weekly rating by ward psychiatrist, when actual weight changes are measured**:
        0   Less than 1 lb (500 g) weight loss in a week
        1   Greater than 1 lb (500 g) weight loss in a week
        2   Greater than 2 lb (1000 g) weight loss in a week

    ☐

(17) **Insight**
    0   Acknowledges being depressed and ill
    1   Acknowledges illness but attributes cause to bad food, climate, overwork, virus, need for rest, etc.
    2   Denies being ill at all

    ☐

TOTAL SCORE   ☐

(From *British Journal of Social and Clinical Psychology* (1967), **6**, 278–96.)

Short Beck Depression Inventory BDI-II

This is an alternative questionnaire which can also be used to diagnose depression. Qualified individuals may be able to purchase these Beck Scales through the London office of the Psychological Corporation Europe, 32 Jamestown Road, London, NW1 7BY Tel: 0207 424 4456 Fax: 0207 424 4457. The Short Beck Depression Inventory (Short BDI-II) is a 7-item questionnaire, rather than the full 21-item Beck Depression Inventory (BDI-II) and is therefore more user-friendly.

Appendix 12

Assessment of Risk Factors When Working with Drug-Using Parents

Drug use by parents does not automatically indicate child neglect or abuse. Automatic child abuse registration will deter parents from approaching drug dependence clinics or other professionals for help, and should be avoided in families where drug use is a factor, and a comprehensive assessment of the relationship between parental drug use and childcare is indicated. Each family should be assessed individually.

(1) The pattern of parental drug use:
   - Is there a drug-free parent or supportive partner?
   - Type, quantity and method of administration of drugs.
   - Whether drug use is relatively 'stable' or 'chaotic', i.e. swings between states of severe intoxication and periods of withdrawal and/or polydrug use, including alcohol.
   - Are there levels of care different from when the parent is a non-user?

(2) Accommodation and home environment:
   - Is accommodation adequate for children?
   - Are parents ensuring that rent and bills are paid?
   - Does the family remain in one locality or move frequently, and why?
   - Are other drug users sharing the accommodation?
   - Is the family living in a drug-using community?

(3) Provision of basic necessities:
   - Is there adequate food, clothing and warmth for the children?
   - Are the children attending school regularly?
   - Are the children engaged in age-appropriate activities?
   - Are the children's emotional needs being adequately met?
   - Are the children assuming parental responsibility?

(4) How the drugs are procured:
   - Are the children being left alone whilst the parents are procuring drugs?
   - Are the children being taken to places where they can be deemed to be at risk?
   - How much are the drugs costing, and how is the money obtained?
   - Are the premises being used for selling drugs, prostitution and so on?
   - Are the parents allowing their premises to be used by other drug users?

(5) Health risks:
- Where are the drugs normally kept?
- Are the parents injecting drugs? Are the syringes shared? How are they disposed of?
- Are the parents aware of the health risks attached to injecting or otherwise using drugs?

(6) Family's social network and support systems:
- Do parents and children associate primarily with other drug users, non-users or both?
- Are relatives aware of the drug use? Are they supportive?
- Will parents accept help from the relatives and other professional/voluntary agencies involved?

(7) When is intervention necessary:
- Automatic intervention deters contact.
- Are there grounds under one's own local authority care procedures? Are these appropriate for assessment?

(8) What are the parents' perception of the situation:
- Do the parents see their drug use as harmful to themselves or their children?
- Do the parents place their own needs before those of their children?

(From SCODA (1989) *Drug-Using Parents and Their Children*. Second report of the National Local Authority Forum on Drugs Misuse in conjunction with the Standing Conference on Drug Abuse, London.)

Appendix 13

Maudsley Addiction Profile (MAP)

A brief instrument for treatment outcome research

SECTION A: MANAGEMENT AND OPERATIONAL INFORMATION

Programme/setting

Community drug/alcohol team ☐	Inpatient programme ☐
Community detox. ☐	Residential rehabilitation ☐
General practitioner ☐	Prison programme ☐
Advice, counselling and information ☐	Other – describe ☐
Harm minimisation ☐	

Interview point

Intake	☐	Departure	☐
3 months	☐	+ 3 months	☐
6 months	☐	+ 6 months	☐
12 months	☐	+ 12 months	☐

Assessor:

Date of MAP interview

D D   M M   Y Y Y Y

☐☐   ☐☐   ☐☐☐☐

Referral details

Self	☐	HA	☐
CDT/CAT	☐	Vol. agency	☐
GP	☐	Probation	☐
SSD	☐	Other	☐

Non-attributable client identifiers

Initials   Sex   Age
        M F

☐☐   ☐☐   ☐☐

Date of birth

D D   M M   Y Y Y Y

☐☐   ☐☐   ☐☐☐☐

General practitioner

☐☐☐☐☐☐☐☐☐☐☐☐☐☐

First part of postcode   **Research ID**

☐☐☐☐   ☐☐☐

Ethnicity

White (UK)	☐	Black – African	☐
Irish	☐	Black – others	☐
White (EU)	☐	Bangladeshi	☐
Black – Caribbean	☐	Indian	☐
Chinese	☐	Pakistani	☐
Other	☐	*Specify*	☐

SECTION B: SUBSTANCE USE

(A) Enter whether used in the past 30 days

(B) [Card 2] Record number of days used in past 30 days

(C) Enter amount used on typical using day in past 30 days

(D) Record route(s) of administration

Note: Record grammes/money equivalent for amount consumed; probe fully for alcoholic drinks and record type(s), brand, size (e.g. small/large can; pint/half-pint; size measures for spirit).

FREQUENCY OF USE IN THE PAST 30 DAYS

1 day only	2 days only	3 days only	Once every week	2 days a week	3 days a week	4 days a week	5 days a week	6 days a week	Every day
1	2	3	4	9	13	17	21	26	30

Oral	Snort/sniff	Smoke/chase	Intravenous
1	2	3	4

Type	Yes/No	No of times past 30 days	Amount used on a typical day	Route(s) of administration

(1) Alcohol

(2) Heroin

(3) Illicit methadone

(4) Illicit benzodiazepine
    Specify

(5) Cocaine powder

(6) Crack/rock cocaine

(7) Amphetamines

SECTION C: HEALTH RISK BEHAVIOUR

Injected drugs in the past 30 days?   Yes/No

If no injecting in the past 30 days skip to sexual behaviour items

(1) Days in the past 30 days injected drugs (days)

(2) Times injected on a typical day in past 30 days (times)

(3) Times injected with a needle/syringe already used by someone else (times)

Had penetrative sex in the past 30 days and not used condom?   Yes/No

If no non-condom sex in the past 30 days skip to health items

(4) How many people had sex with and not used condom (people)

(5) Times had sex when not used condom (times)

SECTION D: HEALTH SYMPTOMS

(1) **Physical health symptoms**

Past 30-day frequency	Never	Rarely	Sometimes	Often	Always
(a) Poor appetite	☐	☐	☐	☐	☐
(b) Tiredness/fatigue	☐	☐	☐	☐	☐
(c) Nausea (feeling sick)	☐	☐	☐	☐	☐
(d) Stomach pain	☐	☐	☐	☐	☐
(e) Difficulty breathing	☐	☐	☐	☐	☐
(f) Chest pain	☐	☐	☐	☐	☐
(g) Joint/bone pain	☐	☐	☐	☐	☐
(h) Muscle pain	☐	☐	☐	☐	☐
(i) Numbness/tingling	☐	☐	☐	☐	☐
(j) Tremors (shakes)	☐	☐	☐	☐	☐

(2) Psychological health symptoms

Past 30-day frequency	Never	Rarely	Sometimes	Often	Always
(a) Feeling tense	☐	☐	☐	☐	☐
(b) Suddenly scared for no reason	☐	☐	☐	☐	☐
(c) Feeling fearful	☐	☐	☐	☐	☐
(d) Nervousness or shakiness inside	☐	☐	☐	☐	☐
(e) Spells of terror or panic	☐	☐	☐	☐	☐
(f) Feeling hopeless about the future	☐	☐	☐	☐	☐
(g) Feelings of worthlessness	☐	☐	☐	☐	☐
(h) Feeling no interest in things	☐	☐	☐	☐	☐
(i) Feeling lonely	☐	☐	☐	☐	☐
(j) Thoughts of ending your life	☐	☐	☐	☐	☐

SECTION E: PERSONAL/SOCIAL FUNCTIONING

In relationship with a partner in the past 30 days?   Yes/No

If no partner in the past 30 days skip to relatives items

(1) The number of days that you had contact with your partner
(i.e. saw them or talked to them on the telephone)

(2) On how many of these days was there conflict between you?
(i.e. had major arguments etc.)

Tick here if no relatives or no contact with any in the past month   ☐
(3) The number of days that you had contact with your relatives
(i.e. saw them or talked to them on the telephone)

(4) On how many of these days was there conflict between you?
(i.e. had major arguments etc.)

Tick here if no contact with any friends in past month ☐

(5) The number of days that you had contact with your friends
     (i.e. saw them or talked to them on the telephone)
     ☐

(6) On how many of these days was there conflict between you?
     (i.e. had major arguments etc.)
     ☐

(7) Days had paid work in past 30 days
     ☐

(8) Days missed from work because of sickness or unauthorised absence
     ☐

(9) Days formally unemployed in the past 30 days
     ☐

(10) Crime involvement in the past 30 days
      ☐

		Yes/No	Days in the past month	Number of times on a typical day
(a)	Selling drugs	☐	☐	☐
(b)	Fraud/forgery	☐	☐	☐
(c)	Shoplifting	☐	☐	☐
(d)	Theft from a property	☐	☐	☐
(e)	Theft from a person	☐	☐	☐
(f)	Theft from a vehicle	☐	☐	☐
(g)	Theft of a vehicle	☐	☐	☐

END OF INTERVIEW

(From Marsden, J., Gossop, G., Stewart, D., *et al.* (1998) The Maudsley Addiction Profile (MAP): a brief instrument for assessing treatment outcome. *Addiction*, **93**(12), 1857–67. With permission from Blackwell Publishing and author.)

Appendix 14

Christo Inventory for Substance-misuse Services (CISS)

With the permission of Dr George Christo, the CISS questionnaire is detailed below. Devised by George Christo, CISS is an acronym for the Christo Inventory for Substance-misuse Services. It is a short and easy-to-use audit toll to evaluate outcome, and many services use it on a three-monthly basis. As it is an audit assessing individuals rather than research tool for populations, the scores given cannot be absolutely relied upon. Nevertheless it gives a reasonably good indication as to what is happening from a holistic standpoint. It is scored on a three-point scale according to severity (0 = none; 1 = moderate; 2 = severe).

Christo Inventory for Substance-misuse Services

Assessor . . . .   Date . . . .

Client . . . .   DOB . . . .   M   F

Drugs of choice . . . .   (e.g. alcohol, opiates, etc.)

Intake assessment . . . .   or follow-up assessment. . . . .

Residence . . . .   (e.g. hostel, prison, residential treatment, home, hospital, NFA)

Service name . . . .   Date in . . . .   Date out . . . .   Reason left . . . .

This form is for evaluation/clinical audit purposes only and is a rough indicator of professional impression of recent drug-related/alcohol-related problems in the past month. Specific situations/behaviours are listed only as guiding examples and may not reflect the exact situations/behaviours of the client.
(Please ring a number under each heading.)

Social functioning
0 . . .   client has a stable place to live and supportive friends or relatives who are drug-free/alcohol-free
1 . . .   client's living situation may not be stable, or he or she may associate with drug users/heavy drinkers (Tick one)
2 . . .   living situation not stable, and he or she either claims to have no friends or their friends are drug users/heavy drinkers

General health

0 ...   client has reported no significant health problems

1 ...   moderate health problems, e.g. teeth/sleep problems, occasional stomach pain, collapsed vein, asymptomatic hepatitis B/C/HIV

2 ...   major problems, e.g. extreme weight loss, jaundice, abscesses/infections, coughing up blood, fever, overdoses, blackouts, seizures, significant memory loss, neurological damage, HIV symptoms

Sexual/injecting risk behaviour

0 ...   client claims not to inject or have unsafe sex (except in monogamous relationship with long-standing partner, spouse)

1 ...   may admit to occasional 'unsafe' sexual encounters, or suspected to be injecting but denies sharing equipment

2 ...   may admit to regular 'unsafe' sexual encounters, or has recently been injecting and sharing injecting equipment

Psychological

0 ...   client appears well adjusted and relatively satisfied with the way his or her life is going

1 ...   may have low self-esteem, general anxiety, poor sleep, may be unhappy or dissatisfied with their lot

2 ...   has a neurotic disorder, e.g. panic attacks, phobias, OCD, bulimia, recently attempted or seriously considered suicide, self-harm, overdose or may be clinically depressed. Or client may have psychotic disorders, paranoia (e.g. everybody is plotting against them), deluded beliefs or hallucinations (e.g. hearing voices)

Occupation

0 ...   client is in full-time occupation, e.g. homemaker, parent, employed or student

1 ...   has some part-time parenting, occupation or voluntary work

2 ...   is largely unoccupied with any socially acceptable pastime

Criminal involvement

0 ...   client has no criminal involvement (apart from possible possession of illicit drugs for personal use)

1 ...   suspected of irregular criminal involvement, perhaps petty fraud, petty theft, drunk driving, small-scale dealing

2 ...   suspected of regular criminal involvement, or breaking and entering, car theft, robbery, violence, assault

Drug/alcohol use

0 ...   client has no recent drug/alcohol use

1 ...   suspected of periodic drug/alcohol use, or else may be socially using drugs that are not considered a problem, or may be on prescribed drugs but not supplementing from other sources

2 ...   suspected of bingeing or regular drug/alcohol use

Ongoing support

0 ...   client regularly attends AA/NA, drug-free drop-in centre, day centre, counselling or treatment aftercare

1 ...   has patchy attendance, i.e. less than once-a-week contact with at least one of the above

2 ...   is not known to be using any type of structured support

Compliance

0...   client attends all appointments and meetings on time, follows suggestions or complies with treatment requirements

1...   is not very reliable, or may have been reported as having an 'attitude' problem or other difficulty with staff

2...   is chaotic, may have left treatment against staff advice or been ejected for non-compliance, e.g. drug use, attitude problem

Working relationship

0...   client is relatively easygoing, e.g. interviews easily, not time consuming or stressful to work with

1...   is moderately challenging, e.g. a bit demanding or time consuming, but not excessively so

2...   is quite challenging, e.g. very demanding, hard work, time consuming, emotionally draining or stressful to see

(From Christo, G., Spurrell, S. & Alcorn, R. (2000) Validation of the Christo Inventory for Substance-misuse Services (CISS). *Drug and Alcohol Dependence*, **59**, 189–97. Copyright 2000 Elsevier Ireland Ltd. Reprinted with permission.)

Appendix 15

Mesa Grande

Summary of evidence of comparative effectiveness of alcohol clinical treatment modalities

Treatment modality	N	% Clinical	MQS	Clinical CES
Brief intervention	31	48	12.68	+ 136
Social skills training	25	84	10.50	+ 125
GABA agonist medication (acamprosate)	5	100	11.6	+ 116
Opiate antagonist medication	6	100	11.33	+ 100
Community Reinforcement Approach	4	80	13.00	+ 68
Behaviour contracting	5	100	10.40	+ 64
Behavioural marital therapy	8	100	12.88	+ 60
Case management	6	100	10.20	+ 60
Motivational Enhancement Therapy	17	53	13.12	+ 37
Client-centred therapy	7	86	10.57	+ 28
Cognitive Therapy	88	10	10.00	+ 41
Disulfiram	24	100	10.75	+ 38
Self-help manual	5	60	12.00	+ 33
Covert sensitisation	8	100	10.88	+ 18
Acupuncture	3	100	9.67	+ 14
Self-monitoring	6	83	12.00	− 3
Family therapy	3	100	9.30	− 5
Behavioural Self-Control Training	35	63	12.80	− 8
Stress management	3	66	10.33	− 22
Antidepressant (SSRI)	15	53	8.60	− 22
Functional analysis	3	66	12.00	− 24
Lithium medication	7	100	11.43	− 32
Marital therapy (other than behavioural)	8	100	12.25	− 33
Hypnosis	4	100	10.25	− 41
Calcium carbimide	3	100	10.00	− 52
Relapse prevention	20	85	11.85	− 62
Alcoholics Anonymous (mandated)	7	86	10.71	− 80
Anti-anxiety medication	14	100	8.36	− 80
Videotape self-confrontation	8	88	10.50	− 84
Relaxation training	18	66	10.56	− 98
Antidepressant medication (non-SSRI)	6	100	8.67	− 104
Milieu therapy	12	100	10.58	− 107
'Standard' treatment	15	87	9.20	− 111
Confrontational counselling	11	73	10.73	− 129
Educational lectures/films	23	38	8.74	− 161
Psychotherapy	18	88	10.94	− 185
General alcoholism counselling	20	85	11.15	− 211

Modalities with two or fewer studies

Treatment modality	N	% Clinical	MQS	Clinical CES
Biofeedback	2	100	13.0	+ 38
Cue exposure	2	100	10.0	+ 32
Anticonvulsant medication	1	100	13	+ 26
Detoxification as treatment	1	100	13	+ 26
Significant other as treatment support	1	100	13	+ 26
Transcendental meditation	1	100	12.0	+ 24
Aversion therapy, negative emotion	1	100	22	+ 22
Hypnotic medication	1	100	11.0	+ 22
Problem-solving	2	100	13.5	+ 18
Affective contra-attribution therapy	1	100	9.0	+ 18
Systematic desensitisation	2	100	11.5	+ 13
Reminiscence therapy	1	100	10	+ 10
Therapeutic community	1	100	12	− 4
Community reinforcement – buddy system	1	100	8	− 8
Recreational therapy	1	100	8	− 8
Job finding	1	100	9	− 9
BAC surveillance	1	100	11	− 11
Occupational therapy	1	100	11	− 11
Twelve-step Facilitation Therapy	3	100	15.67	− 13
Dopamine agonist medication	1	100	8	− 16
Dopamine precursor	1	100	8	− 16
Serotonin precursor	1	100	8	− 16
Minnesota Model	3	33	11.33	− 22
Stress management	3	66	10.33	− 22
Functional analysis	3	66	12.00	− 24
BAC discrimination training	2	100	12	− 24
Beta-blocker medication	1	100	13	− 26
Group psychotherapy	2	100	10	− 30
Antipsychotic medication	2	100	9	− 36
Serotonin antagonist medication	3	66	11.33	− 46
Placebo medication	2	100	12	− 48

N = number of studies reviewed   % Clinical = percentage of those studies conducted in the clinical domain
MQS = methodological quality score   CES = cumulative evidence score

(Adapted from Miller, W. R. & Wilbourne, P. L. (2002) Mesa Grande: a methodological analysis of clinical trials of treatments for alcohol use disorders. *Addiction*, **97**, 265–77. With permission from Blackwell Publishing.)

Appendix 16

Mesa Grande Interventions with Negative Cumulative Evidence Score (CES)

Intervention	CES
Therapeutic community*	− 4
Family therapy	− 5
Moral reconation therapy*	− 7
Community reinforcement – buddy system*	− 8
Recreational therapy*	− 8
Self-control training	− 8
Job finding*	− 9
Legally sanctioned probation/rehabilitation*	− 9
Medical monitoring*	− 9
Blood alcohol concentration surveillance*	− 11
Occupational therapy*	− 11
Exercise	− 11
Tobacco cessation with nicotine gum*	− 12
Tobacco cessation with exercise*	− 12
Aversion therapy†	− 13
Twelve-step Facilitation Therapy	− 13
Dopamine agonist*	− 16
Serotonin precursor*	− 16
Minnesota Model	− 22
Stress management	− 22
Antidepressant	− 22
Blood alcohol concentration discrimination training*	− 24
Functional analysis	− 24
Beta blocker*	− 26
Client choice among options*	− 28
Psychotherapy, group process*	− 30
Lithium	− 30
Marital therapy	− 33
Electrical stimulation of the head*	− 34
Antipsychotic medication*	− 36
Psychedelic medication	− 44
Hypnosis	− 44
Serotonin antagonist	− 46
Placebo (non-blinded to provider)*	− 48
Calcium carbide	− 52
Relapse prevention	− 62

Intervention	CES
Anti-anxiety medication	− 80
Alcoholics Anonymous	− 80
Metronidazole	− 82
Video self-confrontation	− 84
Relaxation training	− 98
Non-SSRI antidepressant	− 104
Milieu therapy	− 107
Standard treatment	− 111
Confrontational counselling	− 129
Educational lectures, films and groups	− 161
Psychotherapy	− 185
General alcoholism counselling	− 211

*Treatment modalities with only 1–2 studies.

†Other aversion therapies have positive CES but interfere with the professional–client relationship and are no longer used.

(Adapted from Miller, W. R. & Wilbourne, P. L. (2002) Mesa Grande: a methodological analysis of clinical trials of treatments for alcohol use disorders. *Addiction*, **97**, 265–77. With permission from Blackwell Publishing.)

Appendix 17

Substance User's Recovery Checklist and Worksheet

NAME: . . . . DOB: . . . .

Please answer each question with an 'X' in the column to the right that best fits.
If a question does not pertain to you, place 'N/A' in the column headed 'NEVER'.

	NEVER	1	2	3	4	5	ALWAYS
I MANAGE/ELIMINATE SUBSTANCE USE							
(If you continue to use substances (drugs/alcohol), start here)							
(1) Able to place a limit on my use and not exceed that limit							
(2) Able to consistently reduce my use of substances							
(3) Able to eliminate my use for specific time periods							
(4) Able to avoid situations where I might abuse substances							
(If you have decided to stop, start here)							
(5) Able to avoid situations where I might be tempted to use substances again							
(6) Accepted my substance-free lifestyle							
(7) Able to enjoy life without substances							
(8) Able to recognise my substance-related lifestyle							
(9) Comfortable socialising where substances are available without using and/or							
(10) Able to leave situations (to protect my recovery) where substances are being used							
II EMOTIONAL, PSYCHOLOGICAL & PHYSICAL WELL-BEING							
(1) Able to practise personal hygiene skills							
(2) Able to relax without using substances							
(3) Able to attend to physical health problems							
(4) Able to put past problems in a positive perspective							
(5) Able to express my feelings appropriately							
(6) Able to admit mistakes to myself and others							
(7) Able to participate in regular exercise							
(8) Able to cope with stress (without substance use)							
(9) Able to experience a positive self-image							
III SOCIAL & FAMILY WELL-BEING							
(1) Able to maintain interest in welfare of others							
(2) Able to maintain interest in family members							
(3) Able to engage in social/family activities without substances							

	NEVER	1	2	3	4	5	ALWAYS
(4) Able to help with household chores							
(5) Able to participate in child-rearing chores							
(6) Able to communicate with significant other							
(7) Able to solve problems with people							
(8) Able to seek the support of family/friends							
IV JOB AND FINANCIAL WELL-BEING							
(1) Able to go to work							
(2) Able to improve job performance							
(3) Able to maintain a balanced household budget							
(4) Able to budget time to accomplish tasks							
(5) Able to use talents and abilities to better myself							
V SPIRITUAL WELL-BEING							
(1) Able to have interest in my own future							
(2) Able to experience a sense of peacefulness							
(3) Able to maintain a positive outlook on life							
(4) Able to experience and express gratitude							

GOAL WORKSHEET

Four or fewer areas (from the above left) where a little improvement will make a big difference:

(1) _____

(2) _____

(3) _____

(4) _____

How will improvement in these areas make a difference in your use of substances (drugs and alcohol)?

_____

_____

_____

_____

_____

_____

(From Berg, I. K. & Reuss, N. H. (1998) *Solutions Step by Step: A Substance Abuse Treatment Manual*, pp. 164–5. New York: W. W. Norton & Co. with permission from W. W. Norton & Co., Inc.)

Appendix 18

Objective Opiate Withdrawal Scale (OOWS)

Name: . . . .   Date: . . . .

                                                          Time: . . . .

Score
(Absent = 0
Present = 1)

Yawning
(one or more during observations)

Rhinorrhoea
(greater than three sniffs during observation)

Piloerection (gooseflesh – observe patient's arm)

Lacrimation

Mydriasis (dilated pupils)
Tremors (hands)

Hot and cold flushes
(shivering or huddling for warmth)

Restlessness
(frequent shifts in position)

Vomiting

Muscle twitches

Abdominal cramps (holding stomach)

Mild anxiety (scores one)
foot-shaking, fidgeting, finger-tapping
Moderate (scores two) to
severe anxiety (scores three)
Observable signs: agitation, unable to sit,
trembling, panicky
Symptoms: difficulty in breathing, choking
sensations, palpitations

TOTAL SCORE (maximum 14)

(Reprinted from Handelsman, L., Cochrane, K. J., Aronson, M. J., *et al.* (1987) Two new rating scales for opiate withdrawal. *American Journal of Drug and Alcohol Abuse*, **13** (3), 293–308. By courtesy of Marcel Dekker, Inc.)

Appendix 19

Approximate methadone equivalents of other opioids/opiates

Drug	Dose	Approximate methadone equivalent
Street heroin (variable purity)	*	
Pharmaceutical heroin	10 mg tablet (taken orally) 10 mg freeze dried ampoule 30 mg freeze dried ampoule	15 mg 20 mg 60 mg
Morphine	10 mg ampoule 10 mg MST continus tablets (taken orally) 15 mg, 30 mg MST continus tablets 60 mg, 100 mg MST continus tablets	10 mg 7.5 mg 11 mg, 22 mg 44 mg, 75 mg
Dipipanone (Diconal)	10 mg tablet	4 mg
Dihydrocodeine	30 mg tablet 60 mg continus tablet	3 mg 6 mg
Dextromoramide (Palfium)	5 mg tablet 10 mg tablet	5–10 mg 10–20 mg
Pethidine	25 mg or 50 mg tablet (taken orally) 50 mg ampoule	2.5 mg or 5 mg 8 mg
Buprenorphine (Temgesic) (Subutex)	200 μg tablet (taken sublingually) 300 μg ampoule 2 mg and 8 mg tablets (taken sublingually)	5 mg 8 mg †
Pentazocine	50 mg capsule 25 mg tablet	4 mg 2 mg
Codeine linctus	100 ml (300 mg codeine phosphate)	20 mg
Codeine phosphate tablets	15 mg, 30 mg and 60 mg tablets	1 mg, 2 mg and 4 mg
J. Collis Brown	100 ml (10 mg extract of opium)	10 mg
Gee's linctus	100 ml (16 mg anhydrous morphine)	10 mg

Note: If tablets are ground and injected, they will avoid partial metabolism in the first pass through the liver and their methadone equivalent will be about 30% greater.

*Cannot be accurately estimated because street drugs vary in purity, though 1 g of street heroin is roughly equivalent to 50–80 mg oral methadone. Titrate dose against withdrawal symptoms.

†Buprenorphine (Subutex) 2 mg and 8 mg tablets. An approximate methadone equivalent is not currently available. The relationship between dose of buprenorphine and methadone is not a linear one.

NB: Temgesic dose is in microgrammes (μg).
   Subutex dose is in milligrammes (mg).

Appendix 20

Cognitive–behavioural worksheet linking emotions and thoughts

Date	Emotion	Situation	Automatic thoughts	Rational response	Outcome
	What did you feel? How bad was it?	*What were you doing or thinking?*	*What exactly were your thoughts? How far did you believe each of them? (0–100%)*	*What are the rational answers to the automatic thoughts? How far do you believe each of them? (0–100%)*	*1. How far do you now believe the thoughts? 2. How do you feel (0–100%)? 3. What can you do now?*

(From Fennell, M. V. (1989) Depression. In: K. Hawton, P. M. Salkovskis, J. Kirk, *et al.* (Eds) *Cognitive Behaviour Therapy for Psychiatric Problems: A Practical Guide*, pp. 169–234. Oxford: Oxford Medical Publications. Reprinted with permission from Oxford University Press.)

Appendix 21

Beliefs about Substance Use

Name: . . . .   **Date:** . . . .

Listed below are some common beliefs about substance use. Please read each statement and rate how much you agree or disagree with each one.

1	2	3	4	5	6	7
Totally disagree	Disagree very much	Disagree slightly	Neutral	Agree slightly	Agree very much	Totally agree

Belief	Rating
(1) Life without using drugs/drinking is boring.	. . . . . .
(2) Using drugs is the only way to increase my creativity and productivity.	. . . . . .
(3) I can't function without it.	. . . . . .
(4) This is the only way to cope with pain in my life.	. . . . . .
(5) I'm not ready to stop using drugs/drinking.	. . . . . .
(6) The cravings/urges make me use drugs/drink.	. . . . . .
(7) My life won't get any better, even if I stop using drugs/drinking.	. . . . . .
(8) The only way to deal with my anger is by using drugs/drinking.	. . . . . .
(9) Life would be depressing if I stopped.	. . . . . .
(10) I don't deserve to recover from drug use/drink.	. . . . . .
(11) I'm not a strong enough person to stop.	. . . . . .
(12) I could not be social without using drugs/drinking.	. . . . . .
(13) Drug use and drinking are not problems for me.	. . . . . .
(14) The cravings/urges won't go away unless I use drugs/drink.	. . . . . .
(15) My drug use/drinking is caused by someone else (e.g. spouse, family, etc.).	. . . . . .
(16) If someone has a problem with drugs/drink, it's all genetic.	. . . . . .
(17) I can't relax without drugs/drink.	. . . . . .
(18) Having this drug/drink problem means I am fundamentally a bad person.	. . . . . .

Belief   **Rating**

(19) I can't control my anxiety without using drugs/drinking.   . . . . . .

(20) I can't make my life fun unless I use drugs/drink.   . . . . . .

(Adapted from Beck, A. T., Wright, F. D., Newman, C. F., *et al.* (1993) *Cognitive Therapy of Substance Abuse*, p. 311. New York: Guilford Press. With permission from Guilford Publications, Inc.)

NB: A similar questionnaire can be compiled for people with a drink problem.

Appendix 22

CRA Marriage Happiness Scale

This scale is intended to estimate your current happiness with your marriage in each of the ten areas listed below. Ask yourself the following question as you rate each area: How happy am I today with my partner in this area? Then circle the number that applies. Numbers towards the left indicate various degrees of unhappiness, while numbers towards the right reflect various levels of happiness. In other words, by using the proper number you will be indicating how happy you are with that particular marriage area.

Remember: You are indicating your current happiness, i.e. how you feel today. Also, try not to let your feelings in one area influence the ratings in another area.

	Completely unhappy									Completely happy
Household responsibilities	1	2	3	4	5	6	7	8	9	10
Raising the children	1	2	3	4	5	6	7	8	9	10
Social activities	1	2	3	4	5	6	7	8	9	10
Money management	1	2	3	4	5	6	7	8	9	10
Communication	1	2	3	4	5	6	7	8	9	10
Sex and affection	1	2	3	4	5	6	7	8	9	10
Job or school	1	2	3	4	5	6	7	8	9	10
Emotional support	1	2	3	4	5	6	7	8	9	10
Partner's independence	1	2	3	4	5	6	7	8	9	10
General happiness	1	2	3	4	5	6	7	8	9	10

(From Meyers, R. J. & Smith, J. E. (1995) *Clinical Guide to Alcohol Treatment*. Appendix 5A, p. 95. New York: Guilford Press. With permission from Guilford Publications, Inc.)

Appendix 23

The Perfect Marriage Form

Under each area listed below, write down what activities would occur in what would be for you an ideal marriage. Be brief, be positive, and state in a specific and measurable way what you would like to occur.

(1) In household responsibilities I would like my partner to:
    (a) _____
    (b) _____
    (c) _____
    (d) _____
    (e) _____

(2) In raising the children I would like my partner to:
    (a) _____
    (b) _____
    (c) _____
    (d) _____
    (e) _____

(3) In social activities I would like my partner to:
    (a) _____
    (b) _____
    (c) _____
    (d) _____
    (e) _____

(4) In money management I would like my partner to:
    (a) _____
    (b) _____
    (c) _____
    (d) _____
    (e) _____

(5) In communication I would like my partner to:

(a) _____

(b) _____

(c) _____

(d) _____

(e) _____

(6) In sex and affection I would like my partner to:

(a) _____

(b) _____

(c) _____

(d) _____

(e) _____

(7) In job or school I would like my partner to:

(a) _____

(b) _____

(c) _____

(d) _____

(e) _____

(8) In emotional support I would like my partner to:

(a) _____

(b) _____

(c) _____

(d) _____

(e) _____

(9) In partner's independence I would like my partner to:

(a) _____

(b) _____

(c) _____

(d) _____

(e) _____

(10) In general happiness I would like my partner to:

(a) _____

(b) _____

(c) _____

(d) _____

(e) _____

(From Meyers, R. J. & Smith, J. E. (1995) *Clinical Guide to Alcohol Treatment*. Appendix 9D, pp. 174–6. New York: Guilford Press. With permission from Guilford Publications, Inc.)

Glossary

Abbreviations and Acronyms

AA	Alcoholics Anonymous
ABV	Alcohol by volume
ACMD	Advisory Council on the Misuse of Drugs
ADHD	Attention-deficit/hyperactivity disorder
A&E	Accident and Emergency
AIDS	Acquired immune deficiency syndrome
ALDH	Aldehyde dehydrogenase
ALT	Alanine aminotransferase
AMI	Adaptations of Motivational Interviewing
ASI	Addiction Severity Index
AST	Aspartate aminotransferase
AUDIT	Alcohol Use Disorders Identification Test
AVE	Abstinence Violation Effect
BA	Brief Advice
BAC	Blood Alcohol Concentration
BBV	Blood-borne virus
BCC	Behaviour Change Counselling
BDI	Beck Depression Inventory
BSCT	Behaviour Self-Control Training
CA	Cocaine Anonymous
CAGE	Questionnaire to screen for alcohol problems
CAMHT	Child & Adolescent Mental Health Team
CARAT	Counselling, Assessment, Referral, Advice & Throughcare
CAT	Community Alcohol Team
CBT	Cognitive–Behavioural Therapy
CDT	Community Drug Team
CES	Cumulative evidence score
CET	Cue exposure treatment
CISS	Christo Inventory for Substance-misuse Services
CMHT	Community Mental Health Team
CNS	Central nervous system
CPA	Care Programme Approach
CPN	Community psychiatric nurse
CRA	Community Reinforcement Approach
CRAFT	Community Reinforcement And Family Training
CSO	Concerned significant other
CT	Cognitive Therapy

D(A)AT	Drug (& Alcohol) Action Team
DDU	Drug Dependency Unit
DH/DoH	Department of Health
DSM-IV	*Diagnostic and Statistical Manual of Mental Disorders*, 4th edition
DTTO	Drug Treatment and Testing Order
DVT	Deep vein thrombosis
FA	Families Anonymous
FAST	Fast Alcohol Screening Test
FBC	Full blood count
5-HT	Five-hydroxytryptamine
GABA	Gamma-aminobutyric acid
GGT	Gamma-glutamyltransferase
GHB	Gamma-hydroxybutyrate
GP	General practitioner
GUM	Genitourinary medicine
HAS	Health Advisory Service
HBV	Hepatitis B virus
HCV	Hepatitis C virus
HIV	Human immunodeficiency virus
HO	Home Office
ICD-10	*International Classification of Diseases*, 10th edition
IDU	Injecting drug user
IOM	Institute of Medicine
IQ	Intelligence quotient
ISDD	Institute for the Study of Drug Dependence
IV	Intravenous
LAAM	L-alpha acetylmethadol (long-acting methadone)
LFT	Liver function tests
LLR	Larger later rewards
LSD	Lysergic acid diethylamide
MAP	Maudsley Addiction Profile
MAST	Michigan Alcohol Screening Test
MCV	Mean corpuscular volume
MET	Motivational Enhancement Therapy
MI	Motivational Interviewing
MMT	Methadone maintenance treatment
MST	Multisystemic therapy
NA	Narcotics Anonymous
NEP	Needle Exchange Programme
NHS	National Health Service
NTA	National Treatment Agency
NTORS	National Treatment Outcome Research Study
OBI	Opportunistic Brief Intervention
OCD	Obsessive–compulsive disorder
ONS	Office of National Statistics
OOWS	Objective Opiate Withdrawal Scale
OTC	Over-the-counter
OTI	Opiate Treatment Index

PCR	Polymerase chain reaction
PEP	Post-exposure prophylaxis
PTSD	Post-traumatic stress disorder
RET	Rational–Emotive Therapy
RR	Rational Recovery
RTA	Road traffic accident
SADQ	Severity of Alcohol Dependence Questionnaire
SBNT	Social Behaviour and Network Therapy
SCODA	Standing Conference on Drug Abuse
SDS	Severity of Dependence Scale
SFT	Solution-Focused Therapy
SLT	Social Learning Theory
SODQ	Severity of Opiate Dependence Questionnaire
SOWS	Subjective Opiate Withdrawal Scale
SSR	Smaller sooner rewards
SSRI	Selective serotonin reuptake inhibitor
TFT	Twelve-step Facilitation Therapy
UKATT	United Kingdom Alcohol Treatment Trial
WHO	World Health Organization

References

ACMD (Advisory Council on the Misuse of Drugs) (1982) *Treatment and Rehabilitation*. London: HMSO.

ACMD (1984) *Prevention*. London: HMSO.

ACMD (1988) *AIDS and Drug Misuse*, Part I. London: HMSO.

ACMD (1989) *AIDS and Drug Misuse*, Part II. London: HMSO.

ACMD (1990) *Problem Drug Use: A Review of Training*. London: HMSO.

ACMD (1991) *Drug Misusers and the Criminal Justice System*, Part I: *Community Resources and the Probation Service*. London: HMSO.

ACMD (1996) *Drug Misusers and the Prison System*. London: HMSO.

ACMD (1998) *Drug Misuse and the Environment*. London: HMSO.

ACMD (2000) *Report on Drug-Related Deaths*. London: HMSO.

ACMD (2003) *Hidden Harm: Responding to the Needs of Children of Problem Drug Users*. London: Home Office.

Addington, J. & Duchak, V. (1997) Reasons for substance use in schizophrenia. *Acta Psychiatrica Scandanavica*, 96(5), 329–33.

Addington, J. & Addington, D. (1998) Effect of substance misuse in early psychosis. *British Journal of Psychiatry*, 172(Suppl. 33), 134–6.

Adesso, V. J. (1985) Cognitive factors in alcohol and drug use. In: M. Galizio & S. A. Maisto (Eds) *Determinants of Substance Abuse: Biological, Psychological, and Environmental Factors*. New York: Plenum Press.

Adger, H. (1991) Problems of alcohol and other drug use in adolescents. *Journal of Adolescent Health Care*, 12, 606.

Aertgeerts, B., Buntix, F., Ansoms, S., *et al.* (2001) Screening properties of questionnaires and laboratory tests for the detection of alcohol abuse or dependence in a general practice setting. *British Journal of General Practice*, 51(464), 206–17.

Agosti, V. (1995) The efficacy of treatment in reducing alcohol consumption: a meta-analysis. *International Journal of the Addictions*, 30, 1067–77.

Albee, G. (1985) The argument for primary prevention. *Journal of Primary Prevention*, 5(4), 238–41.

Alcohol Concern (1997) *Brief Intervention Guidelines. Information Briefing for Purchasers of Alcohol Services*. London : Alcohol Concern.

Alemagno, S. A. (2001) Women in jail: is substance abuse treatment enough? *American Journal of Public Health*, 91(5), 798–800.

Alexander, M. J. (1996) Women with co-occurring addictive and mental disorders: an emerging profile of vulnerability. *American Journal of Orthopsychiatry*, 66(1), 61–70.

Alford, B. A. & Beck, A. T. (1997) *The Integrative Power of Cognitive Therapy*. New York: Guilford Press.

Allsop, S. & Saunders, B. (1989) Relapse and alcohol problems. In: M. Gossop (Ed.) *Relapse and Addictive Behaviour*, pp. 11–40. London: Routledge.

Alter, M. J., Kruszon-Moran, D., Nainan, O. V., *et al.* (1999) The prevalence of hepatitis C virus infection in the United States, 1988 through to 1994. *New England Journal of Medicine*, 341, 556–62.

Amaro, H., Fried, L., Carbal, H., *et al.* (1990) Violence during pregnancy and substance use. *American Journal of Public Health*, 80, 575.

Amass, L., Bickel, W. K., Crean, J., *et al.* (1996) Preferences for clinic privileges, retail items and social activities in an outpatient buprenorphine treatment programme. *Journal of Substance Abuse Treatment*, 13, 43–9.

Anastopoulos, A. D., Shelton, T. L., DuPaul, G. J., *et al.* (1993) Parent training for attention deficit hyperactivity disorder: its impact on child and parent functioning. *Journal of Abnormal Child Psychology*, 21, 581–96.

Anderson, P. (1989) Health Authority policies for the prevention of alcohol problems. *British Journal of Addiction*, 84, 203–209.

Anderson, P. & Scott, E. (1992) The effect of general practitioners' advice on heavy drinking men. *British Journal of Addiction*, **87**, 891–900.

Anderson, P. (1993) Effectiveness of general practice interventions for patients with harmful alcohol consumption. *British Journal of General Practice*, **43**, 386–9.

Anderson, P., Cremona, A., Paton, A., *et al.* (1993) The risk of alcohol. *Addiction*, **88**, 1493–1508.

Anderson, S. & Sabatelli, R. (1993) *Family Interaction: A Multigenerational Developmental Perspective*. Needham Heights: Allyn & Bacon.

A New Life for You (1964) *Drug Abuse and the Criminal Justice System: A Survey of New Approaches in Treatment and Rehabilitation*, p. 83. Davis, CA: Staff Research Center.

Anglin, M. D., Hser, Y. I. & McGlothin, W. H. (1987) Sex differences in addict careers. II. Becoming addicted. *American Journal of Drug and Alcohol Abuse*, **13**(12), 59–71.

Annis, H. M., Graham, J. M. & Davis, C. S. (1987) *Inventory of Drinking Situations (IDS) Users Guide*. Toronto: Addiction Research Foundation.

Annis, H. M. & Graham, J. M. (1988) *Situational Confidence Questionnaire (SCQ-39) Users Guide*. Toronto: Addiction Research Foundation.

Annis, H. M. (1990) Relapse to substance abuse: empirical findings within a cognitive–social learning approach. *Journal of Psychoactive Drugs*, **22**, 117–24.

Annis, H. M., Turner, N. E. & Sklar, S. E. (1997) *Inventory of Drug-Taking Situations (IDTS) Users Guide*. Toronto: Addiction Research Foundation.

Anthony, J. C. & Helzer, J. E. (1991) Syndromes of drug abuse and dependence. In: L. N. Robins & D. A. Regier (Eds) *Psychiatric Disorders in America*, pp. 116–54. New York: Macmillan Free Press.

Anton, R. F., Moak, D. H., Waid, L. R., *et al.* (1999) Naltrexone and cognitive–behavioral therapy for the treatment of outpatient alcoholics: results of a placebo-controlled trial. *American Journal of Psychiatry*, **156**, 1758–64.

Antti-Poika, I. (1988) *Alcohol Intoxication and Abuse in Injured Patients* (Dissertationes *9, Commentationes Physico-Mathematicae). Helsinki, Finland: Finnish Society of Sciences and Letters.

Appleby, L. (2000) Drug misuse and suicide: a tale of two services. *Addiction*, **95**(2), 175–7.

Argeriou, M. & McCarty, D. (Eds) (1990) Treating alcoholism and drug abuse among homeless men and women: nine community demonstration grants. *Alcoholism Treatment Quarterly*, **7**(Special issue), 1.

Arnett, T. (1992) Reckless behaviour in adolescents: a developmental perspective. *Developmental Review*, **12**, 339–73.

Arseneault, L., Cannon, M., Poulton, R., *et al.* (2002) Cannabis use in adolescence and risk of adult psychosis: longitudinal study. *British Medical Journal*, **325**, 1212–13.

Ashton, H. (1991) Psychotropic drug prescribing and women. *British Journal of Psychiatry*, **158**(Suppl. 10), 30–35.

Atkinson, L., Paglia, A., Coolbear, J., *et al.* (2000) Attachment security: a meta-analysis of maternal mental health correlates. *Clinical Psychology Review*, **20**(8), 1019–40.

August, G. J., Stewart, M. A. & Holmes, C. S. (1983) A four-year follow-up of hyperactive boys with and without conduct disorder. *British Journal of Psychiatry*, **143**, 192–8.

Azrin, N. H., Sisson, R. W., Myers, R. W., *et al.* (1982) Alcoholism treatment by disulfiram and community reinforcement therapy. *Journal of Behavioral Therapy and Experimental Psychiatry*, **13**, 105–12.

Babor, T. F., Korner, P., Wilber, C., *et al.* (1987) Screening and early intervention strategies for harmful drinkers: initial lessons from the Amethyst Project. *Australian Drug and Alcohol Review*, **6**, 325–39.

Babor, T. F., Stephens, R. S. & Marlatt, G. A. (1987a) Verbal report methods in clinical research on alcoholism: response bias and its minimisation. *Journal of Studies on Alcohol*, **48**, 410–24.

Babor, T. F., Dolinsky, Z., Rounsaville, B., *et al.* (1988) Unitary versus multidimensional models of treatment outcome: an empirical study. *Journal of Studies on Alcohol*, **49**, 167–77.

Babor, T. F. & Grant, M. (1992) *Project on Identification and Management of Alcohol-Related Problems. Report on Phase II: A Randomized Clinical Trial of Brief Interventions in Primary Health Care*. Geneva: WHO.

Bacchu, L. B., Mezey, G. & Bewley, S. (2002) Women's perceptions and experience of routine enquiry for domestic violence in a maternity service. *British Journal of Obstetrics and Gynaecology*, **109**(1), 9–16.

Backmund, M., Meyer, K., Von Zielonka, M., *et al.* (2001) Treatment of hepatitis C infection in injecting drug users. *Hepatology*, **34**(1), 188–93.

Baer, P. E., Garmezy, L. B., McLaughlin, R. J., *et al.* (1987) Stress, coping, family conflict, and adolescent alcohol use. *Journal of Behavioural Medicine*, **10**, 449–66.

Bahr, S. J., Hawks, R. D. & Wang, G. (1993) Family and religious influences on adolescent substance abuse. *Youth and Society*, **24**, 443–65.

Baker, A. & Dixon, J. (1991) Motivational interviewing for HIV risk reduction. In: W. R. Miller & S. Rollnick (Eds) *Motivational Interviewing: Preparing People to Change Addictive Behavior*, pp. 293–302. New York: Guilford Press.

Baldwin, S. (Ed.) (1990) *Adult Education and Offenders*. London: Batsford.

Ball, J. C. & Ross, A. (1991) *The Effectiveness of Methadone Maintenance Treatment: Patients, Programs, Services, and Outcome*. New York: Springer-Verlag.

Ball, J. C., Lange, W. R., Myers, C. P., *et al.* (1998) Reducing the risk of AIDS through methadone maintenance treatment. *Journal of Health and Social Behaviour*, **29**, 214–26.

Bandura, A. (1969) *Principles of Behavior Modification*. New York: Holt, Rinehart & Winston.

Bandura, A. (1977) Self-Efficacy: toward a unifying theory of behaviour change. *Psychological Review*, **84**, 191–215.

Bandura, A. (1977a) *Social Learning Theory*. Englewood Cliffs, NJ: Prentice-Hall.

Bandura, A. (1982) Self-efficacy mechanism in human agency. *American Psychologist*, **37**, 122–47.

Bandura, A. (1986) *Social Foundations of Thought and Action: A Social Cognitive Theory*. Englewood Cliffs, NJ: Prentice-Hall.

Bandura, A. (1994) Social cognitive theory and exercise of control over HIV infection. In: R. J. DiClemente & J. L. Peterson (Eds) *Preventing AIDS: Theories and Methods of Behavioural Interventions*. London: Plenum Press.

Bandura, A. (1997) *Self-efficacy: The Exercise of Control*. New York: Freeman.

Bangert-Drowns, R. L. (1988) The effects of school-based substance abuse education – a meta-analysis. *Journal of Drug Education*, **18**, 243–65.

Banks, A. & Waller, T. A. N. (1988) *Drug Misuse: A Practical Handbook for GPs*, pp. 97–102. London: Blackwell Scientific Publications.

Barber, J. G. & Crisp, B. R. (1995) The 'pressures to change' approach to working with the partners of heavy drinkers. *Addiction*, **90**, 269–76.

Barnes, G. M. (1990) Impact of the family on adolescent drinking patterns. In: R. L. Collins, K. E. Leonard & J. S. Searles (Eds) *Alcohol and the Family: Research and Clinical Perspectives*, pp. 137–61. New York: Guilford Press.

Barnow, B. S. (1987) The impact of CETA programs on earnings: a review of the literature. *The Journal of Human Resources*, **22**(2), 157–93.

Barrett, M. E., Simpson, D. D. & Lehman, W. E. (1988) Behavioral changes of adolescents in drug abuse intervention programs. *Journal of Clinical Psychology*, **44**, 461–73.

Barrison, I. G., Viola, L., Mumford, J., *et al.* (1982) Detecting excessive drinking among admissions to a general hospital. *Health Trends*, **14**, 80–83.

Bauman, A. & Phongsavan, P. (1999) Epidemiology of substance use in adolescence: prevalence, trends and policy. *Drug and Alcohol Dependence*, **55** (Special issue: Young people and substance abuse), 187–208.

Beardsley, W. R. & Podorefsky, D. (1988) Resilient adolescents whose parents have serious affective and other psychiatric disorders: importance of self-understanding and relationships. *American Journal of Psychiatry*, **145**, 63–9.

Beardsley, W. R. (1989) The role of self-understanding in resilient individuals: the development of a perspective. *The American Journal of Orthopsychiatry*, **59**(2), 266–78.

Bearn, J., Gossop, M. & Strang, J. (1996) Randomised double-blind comparison of lofexidine and methadone in the inpatient treatment of opiate withdrawal. *Drug and Alcohol Dependence*, **43**, 87–91.

Bearn, J., Gossop, M. & Strang, J. (1998) Accelerated lofexidine treatment regimen compared with conventional lofexidine and methadone treatment for inpatient opiate detoxification. *Drug and Alcohol Dependence*, **50**(3), 227–32.

Beattie, M. (1987) *Co-dependent No More: How to Stop Controlling Others and Start Caring for Yourself*. New York: Harper/Hazelden.

Beautrais, A. L. (2000) Risk factors for suicide and attempted suicide among young people. *Australian and New Zealand Journal of Psychiatry*, **34**(3), 420–36.

Bebbington, P., Brewin, C. R., Marsden, L., *et al.* (1996) Measuring the need for psychiatric treatment in the general population: the community version of the MRC Needs for Care Assessment. *Psychological Medicine*, **26**(2), 229–36.

Beck, A. T., Ward, C. H., Mendelson, M., *et al.* (1961) An inventory for measuring depression. *Archives of General Psychiatry*, **4**, 561–71.

Beck, A. T., Rush, A. J., Shaw, B. F., *et al.* (1979) *Cognitive Therapy of Depression*. New York: Guilford Press.

Beck, A. T., Hollon, S. D., Young, J. E., *et al.* (1985) Treatment of depression with cognitive therapy and amitriptyline. *Archives of General Psychiatry*, **42**, 142–8.

Beck, A. T., Emery, G. & Greenberg, R. (1985a) *Anxiety Disorders and Phobias: A Cognitive Perspective*. Basic Books: New York.

Beck, A. T. (1993) Addictive set of beliefs. Presented at the Fourth Annual Symposium of the American Academy of Psychiatrists in Alcoholism Addiction, Palm Beach, FL.

Beck, A. T., Wright, F. D., Newman, C. F., *et al.* (1993) *Cognitive Therapy of Substance Abuse*. New York: Guilford Press.

Beck, A. T., Steer, R. A. & Brown, G. K. (1996) *Manual for Beck Depression Inventory-II*. San Ar, TX: Psychological Corporation.

Beich, A., Gannick, D. & Malterud, K. (2002) Screening and brief intervention for excessive alcohol use: qualitative interview study of the experiences of general practitioners. *British Medical Journal*, **325**, 870–72.

Bennett, G. A., Velleman, R. D., Carter, G., *et al.* (2000) Gender differences in sharing injecting equipment in England. *Aids Care*, **12**(1), 77–87.

Bennett, J. & O'Donovan, D. (2001) Substance use by doctors, nurses and other healthcare workers. *Current Opinion in Psychiatry*, **14**, 195–9.

Berg, I. K. & Reuss, N. H. (1998) *Solutions Step by Step: A Substance Abuse Treatment Manual*. New York: W. W. Norton.

Bergin, A. & Garfield, S. (1994) Overview, trends and future issues. In: A. Bergin & S. Garfield (Eds) *Handbook of Psychotherapy and Behavior Change*, 4th edn, pp. 821–30. New York: Wiley.

Bergmark, A. (1998) The relationship between alcohol and drug treatment systems. In: H. Klingeman & G. Hunt (Eds) *Drug Treatment Systems in an International Perspective*. Thousand Oaks, CA & London: Sage.

Berlin, R. & Davis, R. (1989) Children from alcoholic families: vulnerability and resilience. In: T. Dugan & R. Coles (Eds) *The Child in Our Times Studies in the Development of Resiliency*, pp. 81–105. New York: Brunner/Mazel.

Berne, E. (1964) *Games People Play*. New York: Grove Press.

Bernstein, D. A. & Borkovec, T. D. (1973) *Progressive Relaxation Training*. Champaign, IL: Research Press.

Berridge, K. C. & Robinson, T. E. (1998) What is the role of dopamine in reward: hedonistic impact, reward learning, or incentive salience? *Brain Research Reviews*, **28**, 309–69.

Berridge, V. (1993) Harm reduction and public health: an historical perspective. In: N. Heather, A. Wodak, E. Nadelman, *et al.* (Eds) *Psychoactive Drugs and Harm Reduction: From Faith to Science*, pp. 55–64. London: Whurr.

Best, D., Rawaf, S., Rowley, J., *et al.* (2000) Drinking and smoking as concurrent predictors of illicit drug use and positive attitudes in adolescents. *Drug and Alcohol Dependence*, **60**(3), 319–21.

Bickel, W. K., DeGrandpre, R. J. & Higgins, S. T. (1993) Behavioural economics: a novel experimental approach to the study of drug dependence. *Drug and Alcohol Dependence*, **33**, 173–92.

Biederman, J., Wilens, T., Mick, E., *et al.* (1999) Pharmacotherapy of attention deficit/hyperactivity disorder reduces risk for substance use disorder. *Paediatrics*, **104**(2), e20.

Bien, T. H., Miller, W. R. & Tonigan, J. S. (1993) Brief interventions for alcohol problems: a review. *Addiction*, **88**, 315–36.

Biernacki, P. (1986) *Pathways to Heroin Addiction: Recovery Without Treatment*. Philadelphia: Temple University Press.

Bigelow, G. E., Brooner, R. K. & Silverman, K. (1998) Competing motivations: drug reinforcement vs nondrug reinforcement. *Journal of Psychopharmacology*, **12**, 8–14.

Bigelow, G. E. (2001) An operant behavioural perspective on alcohol abuse and dependence. In: N. Heather, T. J. Peters & T. Stockwell (Eds) *Alcohol Dependence and Problems*. Chichester, UK: Wiley.

Billings, A. G., Kessler, M., Gomberg, C. A., *et al.* (1979) Marital conflict-resolution of alcoholic and non-alcoholic couples during drinking and non-drinking session. *Journal of Studies on Alcohol*, **40**, 183–95.

Billings, A. G. & Moos, R. H. (1983) Psychosocial processes of recovery among alcoholics and their families: implications for clinicians and program evaluators. *Addiction Behaviours*, **8**, 205–18.

Black, D. & Newman, N. (1996) Children and domestic violence: a review. *Clinical Child Psychology and Psychiatry*, **1**, 79–88.

Blackburn, I. M., Eunson, K. M. & Bishop, S. (1986) A two-year naturalistic follow-up of depressed patients treated with cognitive therapy, pharmacotherapy, and a combination of both. *Journal of Affective Disorders*, **10**, 67–75.

Blackwell, J. S. (1983) Drifting, controlling, and overcoming: opiate users who avoid becoming chronically dependent. *Journal of Drug Issues*, **13**, 219–35.

Blakey, R. & Baker, R. (1980) An exposure approach to alcohol abuse. *Behaviour Research and Therapy*, **18**, 319–25.

Blaxter, M. (1990) *Health and Lifestyles*. London: Tavistock/Routledge.

Blechman, E. (1982) Conventional wisdom about familial contributions to substance abuse. *American Journal of Drug and Alcohol Abuse*, **9**, 35–53.

Blow, F. C. & Barry, K. L. (2000) Patients with at-risk problem drinking patterns: new developments in brief interventions. *Journal of Geriatric Psychiatry* **13**(3), 115–23.

Blumenthal, L. M., Hunter, J. R. & Sawka, E. (1993) A comprehensive and integrated system for treating alcohol and drug problems in Alberta. In: J. S. Baer, G. A. Marlatt & R. J. McMahon (Eds) *Addictive Behaviours Across the Life Span: Prevention, Treatment and Policy Issues*, pp. 219–39. London: Sage.

Boffetta. P. & Garfinkel, L. (1990) Alcohol drinking and mortality among men enrolled in an American Cancer Society prospective study. *Epidemiology*, **1**, 342–8.

Bond, A. J., Lader, M. H. & Da Silveira, J. C. (1997) *Aggression: Individual Differences, Alcohol, and Benzodiazepines* (Maudsley Monographs 39). London: Psychology Press.

Booker, O. (1999) *Averting Aggression: Safety at Work with Adolescents and Adults*. Dorset, UK: Russell House.

Booth, P. G. (1990) Maintained controlled drinking following severe alcohol dependence – a case study. *British Journal of Addiction*, **85**, 315–22.

Borduin, C. M., Henggeler, S. W., Blaske, D. M., *et al.* (1990) Multisystemic treatment of adolescent sexual offenders. *International Journal of Offender Therapy and Comparitive Criminology*, **35**, 105–14.

Borduin, C. M., Mann, B. J., Cone, L. T., *et al.* (1995) Multisystemic treatment of serious juvenile offenders: long-term prevention of criminality and violence. *Journal of Consulting and Clinical Psychology*, **63**, 569–78.

Botvin, G. & Tortu, S. (1988) Preventing adolescent substance abuse through life skills training. In: R. Price (Ed.) *Fourteen Ounces of Prevention: A Casebook for Practitioners*, pp. 98–110. Washington, DC: American Psychological Association.

Botvin, G. J. & Botvin, E. M. (1992) Adolescent tobacco, alcohol, and drug abuse: prevention strategies, empirical findings, and assessment issues. *Journal of Developmental and Behavioral Pediatrics*, **13**, 290–301.

Botvin, G. J., Baker, E., Dusenbury, L., *et al.* (1995) Long-term follow-up results of a randomized drug abuse prevention trial in a white middle class population. *Journal of the American Medical Association*, **273**, 1106–12.

Bownes, I. T., O'Gorman, E. C. & Sayer, A. (1991) Assault characteristics and post-traumatic stress disorder in victims. *Acta Psychiatrica Scandanavica*, **83**(1), 27–30.

Bradley, B. P. & Moorey, S. (1988) Extinction of craving during exposure to drug-related cues: three single case reports. *Behavioural Psychotherapy*, **16**, 45–56.

Bradley, B. P. (1989) Heroin and the opiates. In: M. Gossop (Ed.) *Relapse and Addictive Behaviour*, pp. 73–85. London: Tavistock/Routledge.

Brady, K. T., & Sonne, S. C. (1995) The relationship between substance abuse and bipolar affective disorder. *Journal of Clinical Psychiatry*, **56**(Suppl. 3), 19–24.

Brady, K. T., Killeen, T. K., Brewerton, T., *et al.* (2000) Co-morbidity of psychiatric disorders and post-traumatic stress disorder. *Journal of Clinical Psychiatry*, **7** (Suppl.), 22–32.

Brady, M. (1993) Giving away the grog: ethnography of aboriginal drinkers who quit without help. *Drug and Alcohol Review*, **12**, 401–11.

Breslau, N., Kilbey, M. M. & Andreski, P. (1991) Nicotine dependence, major depression, and anxiety in young adults. *Archives of General Psychiatry*, **48**, 1069–74.

BMA (British Medical Association) (1995) *Alcohol: Guidelines on Sensible Drinking*. London: BMA.

Brizer, D. A., Hartman, N., Sweeney, J., *et al.* (1985) Effect of methadone plus neuroleptics on treatment resistant chronic paranoid schizophrenia. *American Journal of Psychiatry*, **142**(9), 1106–107.

Bromet, E. & Moos, R. (1977) Environmental resources and post-treatment functioning of alcoholic patients. *Journal of Health and Social Behaviour*, **18**, 326–38.

Brook, J. S., Brook, D. W., Gordon, A. S., *et al.* (1990) The psychosocial etiology of adolescent drug use: a family interactional approach. *Genetic, Social and General Psychology Monographs*, **116**, 111–267.

Broom, D. H. (1995) Rethinking gender and drugs. *Drug and Alcohol Review*, **14**, 411–15.

Brown, C., Madder, P. A., Palenchar, D. R., *et al.* (2000) The association between depressive symptoms and cigarette smoking in an urban primary care sample. *International Journal of Psychiatry Medicine*, **30**(1), 15–26.

Brown, J. M. & Miller, W. R. (1993) Impact of motivational interviewing on participation in residential alcoholism treatment. *Psychology of Addictive Behaviors*, **7**, 211–18.

Brown, S. & Lewis, V. (1999) *The Alcoholic Family in Recovery: A Developmental Model*. New York: Guilford Press.

Brown, S., D'Amico, E., McCarthy, D., *et al.* (2001) Four-year outcomes from adolescent alcohol and drug treatment. *Journal of Studies on Alcohol*, **62**, 381–8.

Brown, S. A., Mott, M. A. & Myers, M. G. (1990) Adolescent alcohol and drug treatment outcome. In: R. R. Watson (Ed.) *Drug and Alcohol Abuse Prevention: Drug and Alcohol Abuse Review*, pp. 373–403. Clifton, NJ: Humana Press.

Brown, V. B., Melchior, L. A. & Huba, G. J. (1999) Level of burden among women diagnosed with severe mental illness and substance abuse. *Journal of Psychoactive Drugs*, **31**(1), 31–40.

Brundtland, G. (2001) The People's Health Assembly. *British Medical Journal*, **7304**, 109–10.

Brunette, M. F. & Drake, R. E. (1998) Gender differences in patients with schizophrenia and substance abuse. *Comprehensive Psychiatry*, **38**(2), 109–16.

Brunk, M., Henggeler, S. W. & Whelan, J. P. (1987) A comparison of multisystemic therapy and parent training in the brief treatment of child abuse and neglect. *Journal of Consulting and Clinical Psychology*, **55**, 311–18.

Bruun, K., Edwards, G., Lumio, M., *et al.* (1975) *Alcohol Control Policies in Public Health Perspective. Finnish Foundation for Alcohol Studies*, vol. 25. Helsinki: FFAS.

Bryant-Jefferies, R. (2001) *Counselling the Person Beyond the Alcohol Problem*. London: Jessica Kingsley.

Buchanan, J. & Young, L. (1998) *The Impact of Second Chance Structured Day Programme for Recovering Drug Users: A Student Perspective*. Liverpool: Social Partnership, Transit.

Buchanan, J. & Young, L. (2000) The war on drugs – a war on drug users? *Drugs: Education, Prevention and Policy*, **7**(4), 409–22.

Budney, A. J., Higgins, S. T., Delaney, D. D., *et al.* (1991) Contingent reinforcement of abstinence with individuals abusing cocaine and marijuana. *Journal of Applied Behavior Analysis*, **24**, 657–65.

Bulik, C. M., Sullivan, P. F., Carter, F. A., *et al.* (1997) Lifetime co-morbidity of alcohol dependence in women with bulimia nervosa. *Addictive Behaviours*, **22**(4), 437–46.

Buning, E. (1990) The role of harm reduction programmes in curbing the spread of HIV by drug injectors. In: J. Strang & G. V. Stimson (Eds) *AIDS and Drug Misuse*, pp. 153–61. London: Routledge.

Buning, E. & van Brussel, G. H. A. (1995) The effect of harm reduction in Amsterdam. *European Addiction Research*, **1**(3), 92–8.

Bunton, R., Murphy, S. & Bennet, P. (1991) Theories of behavioural change and their use in health promotion: some neglected areas. *Health Education Research: Theory and Practice* (Special issue: Theory) **6**(2), 153–62.

Bunton, R., Baldwin, S., Flynn, D., *et al.* (2000) The 'Stages of Change' model in health promotion: science and ideology. *Critical Public Health*, **10**(1), 55–70.

Buntwal, N., Bearn, J., Gossop, M., *et al.* (2000) Naltrexone and lofexidine combination treatment compared with conventional lofexidine treatment for inpatient opiate detoxification. *Drug and Alcohol Dependence*, **59**(2), 183–8.

Bush, K., Kivlahan, D. R., McDonnel, M. B., *et al.* (1998) The AUDIT alcohol consumption questions (AUDIT-C): an effective brief screening test for problem drinking. *Archives of Internal Medicine*, **16**, 1789–95.

Buster, M. C. A., van Brussel, G. H. A. & van den Brink, W. (2002) An increase in overdose mortality during the first 2 weeks after entering and re-entering treatment in Amsterdam. *Addiction*, **97**, 993–1001.

Buydens-Branchey, L., Branchey, M. H., Noumair, D., *et al.* (1989) Age of alcoholism onset. *Archives of General Psychiatry*, **46**, 231–6.

Byrne, A. (2000) Nine-year follow-up of 86 consecutive patients treated with methadone in general practice, Sydney, Australia. *Drug and Alcohol Review*, **19**, 153–8.

Cadoret, R. J., Yates, W. R., Troughton, E., *et al.* (1995) Adoption studies demonstrating two genetic pathways to drug abuse. *Archives of General Psychiatry*, **52**, 42–52.

Campbell, S. B. (1991) Longitudinal studies of active and aggressive preschoolers: individual differences in early behavior and outcome. In: D. Cicchetti & S. L. Toth (Eds) *Internalizing and Externalizing Expressions of Dysfunction: Rochester Symposium on Developmental Psychopathology*, vol. 2, pp. 67–90. Hillsdale, NJ: Lawrence Erlbaum.

Cannon, D. S. & Baker, T. B. (1981) Emetic and electric shock aversion therapy: assessment of conditioning. *Journal of Consulting and Clinical Psychology*, **49**, 20–33.

Cantwell, R., Brewin, J., Glazebrook, C., *et al.* (1999) Prevalence of substance misuse in first episode psychosis. *British Journal of Psychiatry*, **174**, 150–53.

Capaldi, D. M. & Stoolmiller, M. (1999) Co-occurrence of conduct problems and depressive symptoms in early adolescent boys. III. Prediction to young-adult adjustment. *Development and Psychopathology*, **11**, 59–84.

Caplehorn, J. R. M., Dalton, S. Y. N., Cluff, M. C., *et al.* (1994) Retention in methadone maintenance and heroin addict's risk of death. *Addiction*, **89**, 203–207.

Carey, M. P., Maisto, S. A., Kalichman, S. C., *et al.* (1997) Enhancing motivation to reduce the risk of HIV infection for economically disadvantaged urban women. *Journal of Consulting and Clinical Psychology*, **65**, 531–41.

Carney, M. W. P., Bacelle, L. & Robinson, B. (1984) Psychosis after cannabis abuse. *British Medical Journal*, **288**(6423), 1047.

Carroll, K. M., Rounsaville, B. J. & Gawin, F. H. (1991) A comparative trial of psychotherapies for ambulatory cocaine abusers: relapse prevention and interpersonal psychotherapy. *American Journal of Drug and Alcohol Abuse*, **17**, 229–47.

Carroll, K. M., Power, M. D., Bryant, K., *et al.* (1993) One-year follow-up status of treatment-seeking cocaine abusers: psychopathology and dependence severity as predictors of outcome. *Journal of Nervous and Mental Disease*, **181**, 71–9.

Carroll, M. E. (1996) Reducing drug abuse by enriching the environment with alternative nondrug reinforcers. In: L. Green & J. Kagel (Eds) *Advances in Behavioral Economics*, vol. 3, *Substance Use and Abuse*, pp. 37–68. Norwood, NJ: Ablex.

Carver, C. S. & Dunham, R. G. (1991) Abstinence expectancy and abstinence among men undergoing inpatient treatment for alcoholism. *Journal of Substance Abuse*, **3**(1), 39–57.

Catalano, R. F., Hawkins, J. D., Wells, E. A., *et al.* (1990–91) Evaluation of the effectiveness of adolescent drug abuse treatment, assessment of risks for relapse, and promising approaches for relapse prevention. *International Journal of the Addictions*, **25**, 1085–140.

Centers for Disease Control and Prevention (2000) *HIV/AIDS Surveillance Report*, vol. 12(1). Washington, DC: National Center for HIV, STD, and TB Prevention.

Chaney, E. F., O'Leary, M. R. & Marlatt, G. A. (1978) Skill training with alcoholics. *Journal of Consulting and Clinical Psychology*, **46**, 1092–104.

Chaney, E. F., O'Leary, M. R. & Marlatt, G. A. (1978a) Skill training with alcoholics. *Journal of Consulting and Clinical Psychology*, **48**, 419–26.

Chang, G., Wilkins-Haug, L., Berman, S., *et al.* (1999) Brief intervention for alcohol use in pregnancy: a randomised trial. *Addiction*, **94**, 1499–508.

Chaoyang, L., Pentz, M. A. & Chou, C. (2002) Parental substance use as a modifier of adolescent substance use risk. *Addiction*, **97**, 1537–50.

Chapman, P. L. H. & Huygens, I. (1988) An evaluation of three treatment programmes for alcoholism: an experimental study with 6- and 18-month follow-up. *British Journal of Addiction*, **83**, 67–81.

CHAR (1992) *Four in Ten*. London: CHAR.

CHAR (1994) *Counted Out*. London: CHAR.

Charney, D. A., Paraherikas, A. M., Negrette, J. C., *et al.* (1998) The impact of depression on the outcome of addictions treatment. *Journal of Substance Abuse*, **15**(2), 123–30.

Chassin, L., Curran, P., Hussong, A., *et al.* (1996) The relation of parent alcoholism to adolescent substance use: a longitudinal follow-up study. *Journal of Abnormal Psychology*, **108**, 106–19.

Chein, I., Gerrard, D. L., Lee, R. S., *et al.* (1964) *Narcotics Delinquency and Social Policy: The Road to H.* New York: Basic Books.

Chen, W. J., Loh, E. W., Hsu, Y. P., *et al.* (1996) Alcohol-metabolising genes and alcoholism among Taiwanese Han men: independent effect of ADH2, ADH3, and ALDH2. *British Journal of Psychiatry*, **168**, 762–7.

Chick, J., Lloyd, G. & Crombie, E. (1985) Counselling problem drinkers in medical wards: a controlled study. *British Medical Journal*, **290**, 965–7.

Chick, J., Gough, K., Falkowski, W., *et al.* (1992) Disulfiram treatment of alcoholism. *British Journal of Psychiatry*, **161**, 84–9.

Chick, J. (1994) Alcohol problems in the general hospital. *British Medical Bulletin*, **50**(1), 200–10.

Childress, A. R., McLellan, A. T. & O'Brien, C. P. (1986) Abstinent opiate abusers exhibit conditioned craving, conditioned withdrawal, and reductions in both through to extinction. *British Journal of Addiction*, **81**, 655–60.

Childress, A. R., McLellan, A. T. & O'Brien, C. P. (1986a) Role of conditioning factors in the development of drug dependence. *Psychiatric Clinics of North America*, **9**, 413–25.

Childress, A. R., McLellan, A. T. & O'Brien, C. P. (1988) Classically conditioned responses in cocaine and opioid dependence: a role in relapse? In: *Learning Factors in Drug Dependence* (NIDA Research Monograph 84), pp. 25–43. DHHS publication no. (ADM) 88-1576. Washington: National Academic Press.

Christiansen, B. A., Goldman, M. S. & Inn, A. (1982) Development of alcohol-related expectancies in adolescents: separating pharmacological from social learning issues. *Journal of Consulting and Clinical Psychology*, **50**, 336–44.

Christo, G., Spurrell, S. & Alcorn, R. (2000) Validation of the Christo Inventory for Substance-misuse Services (CISS): a simple outcome evaluation tool. *Drug and Alcohol Dependence*, **59**, 189–97.

Churchill, A. C., Burgess, P. M., Pead, J., *et al.* (1993) Measurement of the severity of amphetamine dependence. *Addiction*, **88**, 1335–40.

Clark, D. M., Salkovskis, P. M. & Chalkley, A. J. (1985) Respiratory control as a treatment for panic attacks. *Journal of Behavioral Therapy and Experimental Psychiatry*, **16**, 23–30.

Clarke, K. & Formby, J. (2000) Feeling good, doing fine: a study of a pregnancy liaison clinic. *Druglink*, **15**(5), 10–13.

Cloninger, C. R., Bohman, M. & Sigvardsson, S. (1981) Inheritance of alcohol abuse: cross-fostering analysis of adopted men. *Archives of General Psychiatry*, **38**, 861–8.

Cloninger, C. R., Sigvardsson, S. & Bohman, M. (1988) Childhood personality predicts alcohol abuse in young adults. *Alcohol Clinical and Experimental Research*, **12**, 494–504.

Clore, G. & Byrne, D. (1974) A reinforcement-affect model of attraction. In: T. S. Huston (Ed.) *Perspectives on Interpersonal Attraction*. New York: Academic Press.

Cochran, S. D., Keenan, C., Schober, C., *et al.* (2000) Estimates of alcohol use and clinical treatment needs among homosexually active men and women in the US population. *Journal of Consulting and Clinical Psychology*, **68**(6), 1062–71.

Cochran, S. D. & Mays, V. M. (2000) Relation between psychiatric syndromes and behaviorally defined sexual orientation in a sample of the US population. *American Journal of Epidemiology*, **151**(5), 516–23.

Colby, S. M., Monti, P. M., Barnett, N. P., *et al.* (1998) Brief motivational interviewing in a hospital setting for adolescent smoking: a preliminary study. *Journal of Consulting and Clinical Psychology*, **66**, 574–8.

Colletti, G. & Brownell, K. D. (1982) The physical and emotional benefits of social support: application to obesity, smoking, and alcoholism. *Progress in Behaviour Modification*, **13**, 109–78.

Collinson, M. (1996) In search of the high life: a non-treatment paradigm. *British Journal of Criminology*, **36**, 428–43.

Commander, M. J., Odell, S. O., Williams, K. J., *et al.* (1999) Pathways to care for alcohol use disorders. *Journal of Public Health Medicine*, **21**(1), 65–9.

Connell, P. H. (1958) *Amphetamine Psychosis*. Oxford: Oxford University Press.

Connors, G. C., Donovan, D. M. & DiClemente, C. C. (2001) *Substance Abuse Treatment and the Stages of Change*. New York: Guilford Press.

Connors, G. J., Tarbox, A. R. & Faillace, L. A. (1993) Changes in alcohol expectancies and drinking behavior among treated problem drinkers. *Journal of Studies on Alcohol*, **53**, 676–83.

Cooney, N. L., Gillespie, R. A., Baker, L. H., *et al.* (1987) Cognitive changes after alcohol cue exposure. *Journal of Consulting and Clinical Psychology*, **55**, 150–55.

Cooney, N. L., Litt, M. D., Agupp, L., *et al.* (1989) Recent attempts to increase alcohol cue reactivity in alcoholics: the effects of negative moods. In: *Recent Advances in Cue Reactivity Research in the Addictions*. Symposium presented at the annual meeting of the Association for Advancement of Behavior Therapy, Washington, DC.

Cooper, M. L., Russell, M., Skinner, J. B., *et al.* (1992) Stress and alcohol use: moderating effects of gender, coping, and alcohol expectancies. *Journal of Abnormal Psychology*, **101**, 139–52.

Copello, A., Templeton, L., Krishnan, M., *et al.* (2000) A treatment package to improve primary care services for relatives of people with alcohol and drug problems. *Addiction Research*, **8**, 471–84.

Copello, A., Orford, J., Hodgsin, R., *et al.* (2002) Social behaviour and network therapy: key principles and early experiences. *Addictive Behaviours*, **27**, 345–66.

Cottler, L. B., Robins, L. E. & Helzer, J. E. (1989) The reliability of the CIDI-SAM: A comprehensive substance abuse interview. *British Journal of Addiction*, **84**, 801–14.

Cox, J., Holden, J. M. & Sagovsky, R. (1987) Detection of postnatal depression: development of the 10-item Edinburgh Postnatal Depression Scale. *British Journal of Psychiatry*, **150**, 782–6.

Crofts, N. & Aitken, C. K. (1997) Incidence of blood-borne virus infection and risk behaviours in a cohort of injecting drug users in Victoria, 1990–1995. *Medical Journal of Australia*, **167**, 17–20.

Crofts, N., Caruana, S., Bowden, S., *et al.* (2000) Minimising harm from hepatitis C virus needs better strategies (Letter). *British Medical Journal*, **321**, 899.

Croft-White, C. & Rayner, G. (1993) *Assessment and Care Management for People with Problem Drug or Alcohol Use: A National Study*. Report organised by SCODA and Alcohol Concern, London.

Crome, I. B. (1997) Alcohol problems in the older person. *Journal of the Royal Society of Medicine*, **90**(Suppl. 32), 16–22.

Crome, I. B. (1997a) Gender differences in substance misuse and psychiatric comorbidity. *Current Opinion in Psychiatry*, **10**(3), 194–8.

Crome, I. B. (1999) Substance misuse and psychiatric comorbidity: towards improved service provision. *Drugs: Education, Prevention and Policy*, **6**(2), 151–74.

Crome, I. B. (1999a) Treatment interventions – looking towards the millennium. *Drug and Alcohol Dependence*, 55(3), 247–63.

Crome I. B. & Day, E. (1999) Substance misuse and dependence: older people deserve better services. *Reviews in Clinical Gerontology*, 9, 327–42.

Crome, I. B., Christian, J. & Green, C. (2000) The development of a unique dedicated community drug service for adolescents: policy, prevention and education implications. *Drugs: Education, Prevention and Policy*, 7(1), 87–108.

Crowley, T. J., Chesluk, D., Dilts, S., *et al.* (1974) Drug and alcohol abuse among psychiatric admissions: a multi-drug clinical toxological study. *Archives of General Psychiatry*, 30(1), 13–20.

Cullen, W., Bury, G. & Langton, D. (2000) Experience of heroin overdose among drug users attending general practice. *British Journal of General Practice*, 50(456), 546–9.

Cunningham, R. M., Maio, R. F., Hill, E. M., *et al.* (2002) The effects of alcohol on head injury in the motor vehicle crash victim. *Alcohol and Alcoholism*, 37(3), 236–40.

Curran, H. V. & Monaghan, L. (2001) In and out of the K-hole: a comparison of the acute and residual effects of ketamine in frequent and infrequent ketamine users. *Addiction*, 96, 749–60.

Currie, E. (1993) *Reckoning: Drugs, the Cities and the American Future*. New York: Hill & Wang.

Daeppen, J. B., Yersin, B., Landry, U., *et al.* (2000) Reliability and validity of the Alcohol Use Disorders Identification Test (AUDIT) imbedded within a general health risk questionnaire: results of a survey in 332 primary care patients. *Alcoholism: Clinical and Experimental Research*, 24, 659–65.

Dakof, G. A. (2000) Understanding gender differences in adolescent drug abuse: issues of co-morbidity and family functioning. *Journal of Psychoactive Drugs*, 32(1), 25–32.

Daley, D. (1987) Relapse prevention with substance abusers: clinical issues and myths. *Social Work*, 45(2), 38–42.

Daley, D. (1988) *Relapse Prevention: Treatment Alternatives and Counseling Aids*. Bradenton, FL: Human Services Institute.

Darke, S., Hall, W., Wodak, A., *et al.* (1992) Development and validation of a multidimensional instrument for assessing outcome of treatment among opiate users: the Opiate Treatment Index. *British Journal of Addiction*, 87, 733–42.

Darke, S., Hall, W. & Swift, W. (1994) Prevalence, symptoms and correlates of antisocial personality dis-order among methadone maintenance clients. *Drug and Alcohol Dependence*, 34, 253–7.

Darke, S., Sunjic, S., Zador, D., *et al.* (1997) A comparison of blood toxicology of heroin-related deaths and current heroin users in Sydney, Australia. *Drug and Alcohol Dependence*, 60, 141–50.

Darke, S. & Ross, J. (2000) Fatal heroin overdoses resulting from non-injecting routes of administration. *Addiction*, 95, 569–73.

Darke, S., Ross, J., Zador, D., *et al.* (2000) Heroin-related deaths in New South Wales, Australia, 1992–96. *Drug and Alcohol Dependence*, 60, 141–50.

Darke, S., Hall, W., Kaye, S., *et al* (2002) Hair morphine concentrations of fatal heroin overdose cases and living heroin users. *Addiction*, 97, 977–84.

Davey Smith, G., Dorling, D., Gordon, D., *et al.* (1999) The widening health gap: what are the solutions? *Critical Public Health*, 9, 151–70.

Davis, R. M. & Pless, B. (2001) BMJ bans accidents. *British Medical Journal*, 332, 1320–21.

Davoli, M., Perucci, C. A., Forastiere, F., *et al.* (1993) Risk factors for overdose mortality a case control study within a cohort of intravenous drug users. *International Journal of Epidemiology*, 22, 273–6.

Dawe, S., Powell, J. H., Richards, D., *et al.* (1993) Does post-withdrawal cue exposure improve outcome in opiate addiction? A controlled trial. *Addiction*, 88, 1233–45.

Dawe, S. & Powell, J. H. (1995) Cue exposure treatment in opiate and cocaine dependence. In: D. C. Drummond, S. T. Tiffany, S. Glautier, *et al.* (Eds) *Addictive Behavior: Cue Exposure Theory and Practice*, pp. 197–209. New York: Wiley.

Deas, D. & Thomas, S. (2001) An overview of controlled studies of adolescent substance abuse treatment. *American Journal of Addiction*, 10, 178–89.

Deehan, A., Templeton, L., Drummond, C., *et al.* (1996) *The Detection and Management of Alcohol Misuse Patients in Primary Care: General Practitioners' Behaviour and Attitudes*. Report for the Department of Health. London: Institute of Psychiatry.

de Haes, W. & Schuurman, J. (1975) Results of an evaluation study of three drug education methods. *International Journal of Health Education*, 28(4) (Suppl.), 1–16.

De las Cuevas, C., Sanz, E. J., De la Fuente, J. A., *et al.* (2000) The severity of dependence scale (SDS) as screening test for benzodiazepine dependence: SDS validation study. *Addiction*, 95(2), 245–50.

de Lima, M. S., de Oliveira Soares, B. G., Reisser, A. A. P., *et al.* (2002) Pharmacological treatment of cocaine dependence: a systematic review. *Addiction*, 97, 931–9.

Denning, P. (2000) *Practicing Harm Reduction Psychotherapy*. New York: Guilford Press.

Dennis, M. L., Godley, S. H., Godley, M. D., *et al.* (1998) *Drug Outcome Monitoring System (DOMS): Developing a New Paradigm for Health Services Research*. Bloomington, IL: Chestnut Health Systems.

Des Jarlais, D. C. & Friedman, S. R. (1993) AIDS, injecting drug use and harm reduction. In: N. Heather, A. Wodak, E. Nadelman, *et al.* (Eds) *Psychoactive Drugs and Harm Reduction: From Faith to Science*, pp. 297–309. London: Whurr.

Des Jarlais, D. C., Hagan, H., Friedman, S. R., *et al.* (1998) Preventing epidemics of HIV-1 among injecting drug users. In: G. V. Stimson, D. C. Des Jarlais & A. Ball (Eds) *Social Aspects of AIDS: Drug Injecting and HIV Infection*, pp.183–200. London: University College London Press.

de Zwart, W. M. (1989) *Alcohol, tabak en drugs in cijfers* (Quantitative data on alcohol, tobacco, and drugs). Utrecht: Nederlands Instituut voor Alcohol en Drugs (NIAD) (Netherlands Institute of Alcohol and Drugs).

de Zwart, W. M. & Mensink, C. (1996) *Jaarboek verslaving 1995* (Addiction Year Report 1995). Utrecht/Houten: NIAD/Bohn Stafleu Van Lochum.

DH (Department of Health and Social Security, UK) (1981) *Drinking Sensibly*. London: HMSO.

DH (Department of Health, UK) (1992) *Report of the Confidential Inquiry into Homicides and Suicides by Mentally Ill People*. London: Departments of Health.

DH (Department of Health: Effective Health Care Team) (1993) Brief interventions and alcohol use: are brief interventions effective in reducing harm associated with alcohol consumption? In: *Effective Health Care Bulletin*, No 7. London: Departments of Health.

DH (Department of Health, UK) (1995) *Sensible Drinking: The Report of an Interdepartmental Working Group*. London: Departments of Health.

DH (Department of Health, UK) (1998) Statistics on smoking: England, 1976–1996. In: *Department of Health Bulletin* 1998/25. London: Departments of Health.

DH (Department of Health, UK) (1998a) Psychiatric causes: suicide and substance abuse (Ch. 12). In: *Why Mothers Die: Report on Confidential Enquiries into Maternal Deaths in the United Kingdom*. London: The Stationery Office.

DH (Departments of Health, UK) (1999) *Drug Misuse and Dependence – Guidelines on Clinical Management*. London: The Stationery Office.

DH (Departments of Health, UK) (1999a) *Reducing Health Inequalities: An Action Report*. London: Departments of Health.

DH (Departments of Health, Scottish Office) (1999b) *Towards a Healthier Scotland: A White Paper on Health*. Edinburgh: The Stationery Office.

DH (Departments of Health, UK) (1999c) *Working Together to Safeguard Children: A Guide to Interagency Working to Safeguard and Promote the Welfare of Children*. London: The Stationery Office.

DH (Departments of Health, UK) (2001) *Safety First: Five-Year Report of the Confidential Inquiry into Suicide and Homicide by People with Mental Illness*. London: Departments of Health.

DH (Departments of Health, UK) (2001a) *Hepatitis C – Guidance for Those Working with Drug Users*. London: Departments of Health.

DH (Departments of Health, UK) (2001b) *The Children Act Now: Messages from Research*. London: The Stationery Office.

Diamont, A. L., Schuster, M. A. & Lever, J. (2000) Receipt of preventive care by lesbians. *American Journal of Preventive Medicine*, **19**(3), 141–8.

Dickson, D. A., Saunders, C. & Stringer, M. (1993) *Rewarding People: The Skill of Responding Positively*. London: Routledge.

DiClemente, C. C., Prochaska, J. O. & Gibertini, M. (1985) Self-efficacy and the stages of self-change of smoking. *Cognitive Therapy and Research*, **9**(2), 181–200.

DiClemente, C. C., Prochaska, J. O., Fairhurst, S. K., *et al.* (1991) The processes of smoking cessation: an analysis of precontemplation, contemplation, and preparation stages of change. *Journal of Consulting and Clinical Psychology*, **59**, 295–304.

DiClemente, C. C. & Scott, C. W. (1997) Stages of change: interactions with treatment compliance and involvement. In: L. S. Onken, J. D. Blaine & J. J. Boren (Eds) *Beyond the Therapeutic Alliance: Keeping the Drug-Dependent Individual in Treatment* (NIDA Research Monograph 165). Washington, DC: DHHS.

Dixon, L. (1999) Dual diagnosis of substance abuse in schizophrenia: prevalence and impact on outcomes. *Schizophrenia Research*, **35**(Suppl.), S93–100.

Dixon, N. (1990) *Audit primer for allied health professionals*. Quest for Healthcare (UK).

Djukanovic, B., Milosavcevic, V. & Jovanovic, R. (1976) The social lives of alcoholics and their wives. *Journal of Studies on Alcohol*, **39**, Abstract no. 1141.

Dodge, K. A. & Coie, J. D. (1987) Social information processing factors in reactive and proactive aggression in children's peer groups. *Journal of Personality and Social Psychology*, **53**, 1146–58.

Dodge, K. A., Bates, J. E. & Petit, G. S. (1990) Mechanisms in the cycle of violence. *Science*, **250**, 1678–83.

Dolan, K., Wodak, A., Mattick, R., *et al.* (2000) A Randomized Controlled Trial of the NSW Prison Methadone Program. Presentation to the 11th International Harm Reduction Conference, Jersey.

Dole, V. P. & Nyswander, M. E. (1967) Heroin addiction – a metabolic disease. *Archives of Internal Medicine*, **120**, 19–24.

Dole, V. P. & Nyswander, M. (1976) Methadone maintenance treatment: a ten-year perspective. *Journal of the American Medical Association*, **235**, 2117–21.

Downing-Orr, K. (1996) *Alienation and Social Support: A Social Psychological Study of Homeless Young People in London and Sydney*. Aldershot, UK: Avebury.

Doyle, H., Delaney, W. & Trobin, J. (1994) Follow-up study of young attendees at an alcohol unit. *Addiction*, **89**, 183–9.

Drake, R. E., Bartels, S. J., Teague, G. B., *et al.* (1993) Treatment of substance abuse in severely mentally ill patients. *Journal of Nervous and Mental Disease*, **181**(10), 606–11.

Drake, R. E. & Mueser, K. T. (2000) Psychosocial approaches to dual diagnosis. *Schizophrenia Bulletin*, **26**(1), 105–18.

Driessen, F. M. H. M., van Dam, G. & Olson, B. (1989) De ontwikkeling van het cannabisgebruik in Nederland, enkele Europese landen en de VS sinds 1969 (Development of cannabis use in the Netherlands, several other European countries and the USA since 1969). *Tijdschrift voor Alcohol, Drugs en andere Psychotrope stoffen*, **15**, 2–14.

Drucker, E. (1992) US drug policy. Public health versus prohibition. In: P. A. O'Hare, R. Newcombe, A. Matthews, *et al.* (Eds) *The Reduction of Drug-Related Harm*, pp. 71–81. London: Routledge.

Drugscope (2001) *Drug Abuse Briefing*, 8th edn. London: Drugscope.

Drummond, D. C., Tiffany, S. T., Glautier, S., *et al.* (Eds) (1995) *Addictive Behaviour: Cue Exposure Theory and Practice*. Chichester, UK: Wiley.

Dunn, C., Deroo, L. & Rivara, F. P. (2001) The use of brief interventions adapted from motivational interviewing across behavioral domains: a systematic review. *Addiction*, **96**, 1725–42.

Dunne, F. J., Waller, T. A. N. & Paton, A. (1989) Alcohol and drug services: the case for combining. *Alcohol and Alcoholism*, **24**(2), 75–6.

D'Zurilla, T. & Goldfried, M. (1971) Problem solving and behaviour modification. *Journal of Abnormal Psychology*, **78**, 107–26.

Edlin, B. R., Seasl, K. H., Lorvick, J., *et al.* (2001) Is it justifiable to withhold treatment for hepatitis C from illicit drug users? *New England Journal of Medicine*, **345**, 211–14.

Edwards, G. & Gross, M. M. (1976) Alcohol dependence: provisional description of a clinical syndrome. *British Medical Journal*, **1**, 1058–61.

Edwards, G., Gross, M. M., Keller, M., *et al.* (1977) *Alcohol-Related Disabilities*. WHO Offset Publication No. 32. Geneva: WHO.

Edwards, G., Orford, J., Egert, S., *et al.* (1977a) Alcoholism: a controlled trial of "treatment" and "advice". *Journal of Studies on Alcohol*, **38**, 1004–31.

Edwards, G., Duckitt, A., Oppenheimer, E., *et al.* (1983) What happens to alcoholics? *Lancet*, **2**, 269–71.

Edwards, G. (1986) The alcohol dependence syndrome: a concept as stimulus to enquiry. *British Journal of Addiction*, **81**, 171–83.

Edwards, G. (1987) *The Treatment of Drinking Problems: A Guide for the Helping Professions*, 2nd edn. Oxford & Boston: Blackwell Scientific Publications.

Edwards, G., Anderson, P., Babor, T., *et al.* (1994) *Alcohol Policy and the Public Good*. Oxford: Oxford University Press.

Edwards, G. (1996) Doctors should stick with the independent medical advice. *British Medical Journal*, **312**, 1.

Eldred, C. & Washington, M. (1976) Interpersonal relationships in heroin use by men and women and their role in treatment outcome. *International Journal of Addictions*, **11**, 117–30.

El-Guebaly, N. (1990) Substance abuse and mental disorders: the dual diagnosis concept. *Canadian Journal of Psychiatry*, **35**(3), 261–7.

Elifson, K. W., Boles, J., Darrow, W. W., *et al.* (1999) HIV seroprevalence and risk factors among clients of female and male prostitutes. *Journal of Acquired Immune Deficiency Syndromes and Human Retrovirology*, **20**(2), 195–200.

Ellis, A., McInerney, J. F., DiGiuseppe, C., *et al.* (1988) *Rational–Emotive Therapy with Alcoholics and Substance Abusers*. Needham Heights, MA: Allyn & Bacon.

Ellis, A. & Dryden, W. (1999) *The Practice of Rational Emotive Therapy*, 2nd edn. London: Free Association Books.

Elvy, G. A., Wells, J. E. & Baird, K. A. (1988) Attempted referral as intervention for problem drinking in the general hospital. *British Journal of Addiction*, **83**, 83–9.

Emmelkamp, P. M. G. & deLange, I. (1983) Spouse involvement in the treatment of obsessive–compulsive patients. *Behaviour Research and Therapy*, **14**, 341–6.

Emrick, C. D., Tonigan, J.S., Montgomery, H., *et al.* (1993) Alcoholics Anonymous: what is currently known? In: B. S. McCrady & W. R. Miller (Eds) *Research on Alcoholics Anonymous: Opportunities and Alternatives*, pp. 41–76. New Brunswick, NJ: Rutgers Center of Alcohol Studies.

Engel, G. L. (1980) The clinical application of the biopsychosocial model. *American Journal of Psychiatry*, **137**, 535–44.

Engelsman, E. M. (1989) Dutch policy on the management of drug-related problems. *British Journal of Addiction*, **84**, 211–18.

Ennett, S. T., Tobler, N. S., Ringwalt, C. L., *et al.* (1994) How effective is drug abuse resistance education? A meta-analysis of project DARE outcome evaluations. *American Journal of Public Health*, **84**, 1394–401.

Epstein, E. & McCrady, S. (1998) Behavioural couples treatment of alcohol and drug use disorders: current status and innovations. *Clinical Psychology Review*, **18**, 689–711.

Epstein, S. & Meier, P. (1989) Constructive thinking: a broad coping variable with specific components. *Journal of Personality and Social Psychology*, **57**, 332–50.

Eriksen, L., Bjornstad, S. & Gotestam, K. G. (1989) Social skills training in groups for alcoholics: one-year treatment outcome for groups and individuals. *Addictive Behaviours*, **11**, 309–29.

Evans, D. M. (1987) Hand injuries due to glass. *Journal of Hand Surgery*, **123**, 284.

Evans, D. M. & Dunn, N. J. (1995) Alcohol expectancies, coping responses, and self-efficacy judgments: a replication and extension of Cooper *et al.*'s 1988 study in a college sample. *Journal of Studies on Alcohol*, **56**, 186–93.

Evans, J., Heron, J., Francom, H., *et al.* (2001) Cohort study of depressed mood during pregnancy and after childbirth. *British Medical Journal*, **323**, 257–60.

Evans, K. & Sullivan, J. S. (1990) *Dual Diagnosis: Counseling the Mentally Ill Substance Abuser*, pp. 130–31. New York: Guilford Press.

Evans, K. & Sullivan, M. (1995) *Treating Addicted Survivors of Trauma*. New York & London: Guilford Press.

Falloon, I. R., Coverdale, J. H., Laidlaw, T. M., *et al.* (1998) Early intervention for schizophrenic disorders: implementing optimal treatment strategies in routine clinical services, OTPP Collaborative Group. *British Journal of Psychiatry*, **172**(33)(Suppl.), 33–8.

Fals-Stewart, W. & Birchler, G. (2001) A national survey of the use of couples therapy in substance abuse treatment. *Journal of Substance Abuse Treatment*, **20**, 277–83.

Farrell, M. & Lewis, G. (1990) Discrimination on the grounds of diagnosis. *British Journal of Addiction*, **85**(7), 883–90.

Farrell, M., Ward, J., Mattick, R., *et al.* (1994) Methadone maintenance treatment in opiate dependence: a review. *British Medical Journal*, **309**, 991–1001.

Farrell, M., Neeleman, J., Griffiths, P., *et al.* (1996) Suicide and overdose among opiate addicts. *Addiction*, **91**, 321–3.

Farrell, M., Howes, S., Taylor, C., *et al.* (1998) Substance misuse and psychiatric co-morbidity: an overview of the OPCS National Psychiatric Morbidity Survey. *Addictive Behaviours*, **23**(6), 909–18.

Farrell, M., Howes, S., Bebbington, P., *et al.* (2001) Nicotine, alcohol and drug dependence and psychiatric co-morbidity: result of a national household survey. *British Journal of Psychiatry*, **179**, 432–7.

Farrell, M. & Marsden, J. (2002) Methamphetamine: drug use and psychoses becomes a major public health issue in the Asia Pacific region. *Addiction*, **97**, 771–2.

Farrell, M., Boys, A., Bebbington, P., *et al.* (2002) Psychosis and drug dependence: results from a national survey of prisoners. *British Journal of Psychiatry*, **181**, 393–8.

Farrington, D. P., Loeber, R. & Van Kammen, W. B. (1990) Long-term criminal outcomes of hyperactivity–impulsivity–attention deficit and conduct problems in childhood. In: L. Robins & M. Rutter (Eds) *Straight and Devious Pathways from Childhood to Adulthood*, pp. 62–81. New York: Cambridge University Press.

Faupel, C. E. (1988) Heroin use, crime, and employment status. *The Journal of Drug Issues*, **18**(3), 467–79.

Feachem, R. G. A. (1995) *Valuing the Past . . . Investing in the Future: Evaluation of the National HIV/AIDS Strategy 1993–94 to 1995–96*. Commonwealth Department of Human Services and Health. Canberra: Australian Government Publishing Service.

Felsman, J. K. (1989) Risk and resilience in childhood: the lives of street children. In: T. Dugan & R. Coles (Eds) *The Child in Our Times: Studies in the Development of Resiliency*. New York: Brunner/Mazel.

Fennel, M. V. (1989) Depression. In: K. Hawton, P. M. Salkovskis, J. Kirk, *et al.* (Eds) *Cognitive–Behaviour Therapy for Psychiatric Problems: A Practical Guide*, pp. 169–234. Oxford: Oxford Medical Publications.

Fergusson, D. M. (1993) Conduct problems and attention deficit behaviour in middle childhood and cannabis use by age 15. *Australian and New Zealand Journal of Psychiatry*, **27**, 673–82.

Fillmore, K. M. (1988) *Alcohol Use Across the Life Course: A Critical Review of 70 Years of International Longitudinal Research*. Toronto: Addiction Research Foundation.

Finney, J. W. & Monahan, S. C. (1996) The cost-effectiveness of treatment for alcoholism: a second approximation. *Journal of Studies on Alcoholism*, **29**, 229–43.

Fischer, G., Johnson, R. E., Eder, H., *et al.* (2000) Treatment of opioid-dependent pregnant women with buprenorphine. *Addiction*, **95**(2), 239–44.

Fischer, J. (1973) Is casework effective? A review. *Social Work*, **18**, 5–20.

Fischer, J. (1978) Does anything work? *Journal of Social Science Research*, **3**, 213–43.

Fleming, M. F., Barry, K. L., Manwell, L. B., *et al.* (1997) Brief physician advice for problem alcohol drinkers: a randomised controlled trial in community-based primary care practices. *Journal of the American Medical Association*, **277**, 1039–45.

Folkman, S. (1984) Personal control and stress and coping processes: a theoretical analysis. *Journal of Personality and Social Psychology*, **46**, 839–52.

Folkman, S. & Lazarus, R. S. (1988) *Manual for the Ways of Coping Questionnaire*. New York: Mind Garden.

Follette, V. M., Ruzek, J. I. & Abueg, F. R. (1998) *Cognitive–Behavioral Therapies for Trauma*. New York: Guilford Press.

Forgas, J. (1985) *Interpersonal Behaviour*. Oxford: Pergamon Press.

Forton, D. M., Allsop, J., Main, J., *et al.* (2001) Evidence of a cerebral effect of the hepatitis C virus. *Lancet*, **358**, 38–9.

Forton, D. M., Thomas, H. C., Murphy, C. A., *et al.* (2002) Hepatitis C and cognitive impairment in a cohort of patients with mild liver disease. *Hepatology*, **35**(2), 433–9.

Foster, J. (2000) Social exclusion, crime and drugs. *Drugs: Education, Prevention and Policy*, **7**(4), 317–30.

Fountain, J. & Howes, S. (2002) *Home and Dry? Homelessness and Substance Use*. London: Crisis.

Frances, A., Pincus, H. A. & First, M. B. (Eds) (1994) *Diagnostic and Statistical Manual of Mental Disorders*, 4th edn. Washington, DC: American Psychiatric Press.

Fraser, R. C. (1992) Setting the scene. In: R. C. Fraser (Ed.) *Clinical Method: A General Practice Approach*, 2nd edn. Oxford: Butterworth Heinemann.

Freeling, P., Rao, B. M., Paykel, E. S., *et al.* (1985) Unrecognised depression in general practice. *British Medical Journal*, **290**(6485), 1889–93.

Freeman, A. (1987) Cognitive therapy: an overview. In: A. Freeman & V. Greenwood (Eds) *Cognitive Therapy:*
Application in Psychiatric and Medical Settings, pp. 19–35. New York: Human Sciences Press.

Freemantle, N., Gill, P., Godfrey, C., *et al.* (1993) Brief interventions and alcohol use. *Effective Health Care Bulletin*, No. 7. Leeds: Nuffield Institute for Health.

Freud, S. (1954) *Origins of Psychoanalysis: Letters to Wilhelm Fliess, Drafts and Notes, 1887–1902*, M. Bonaparte (Ed. & Trans.). New York: Basic Books.

Fried, P. (1986) Marijuana and human pregnancy. In: I. J. Chasnoff (Ed.) *Drug Use in Pregnancy: Mother and Child*, pp. 64 –74. MTP Press.

Friedman, A. S., Schwartz, R. & Utada, A. (1989) Outcome of a unique youth drug abuse program: a follow-up study of clients of Straight. *Journal of Substance Abuse Treatment*, **6**, 259–68.

Fujii, E. T. (1974) Public investment in the rehabilitation of heroin addicts. *Social Science Quarterly*, **55**(1), 39–51.

Fulkerson, J. A., Harrison, P. A. & Beebe, T. J. (1999) DSM-IV substance abuse and dependence: are there really two dimensions of substance use disorders in adolescents? *Addiction*, **94**(4), 495–506.

Fuller, R. K., Branchey, L., Brightwell, D. R., *et al.* (1986) Disulfiram treatment in alcoholism: a Veterans Administration cooperative study. *Journal of Nervous and Mental Disease*, **256**, 1449–55.

Galanter, M. (1993) *Network Therapy for Alcohol and Drug Abuse: A New Approach in Practice*. New York: Basic Books.

Garbutt, J. C., West, S. L., Carey, T. S., *et al.* (1999) (Agency for Health Care Policy and Research, AHCPR) Evidence Report/Technology Assessment. No. 3: Pharmaco-therapy for alcohol dependence. Pharmacological treatment of alcohol dependence: a review of the evidence. *Journal of the American Medical Association*, **281**, 1318–25.

Garfein, R. S., Doherty, M. C., Monterrosso, E. R., *et al.* (1998) Prevalence and incidence of hepatitis C infection among young adult injection drug users. *Journal of Acquired Immune Deficiency Syndromes and Human Retrovirology*, **18**, S11–19.

Garland, R. J. & Dougher, M. J. (1991) Motivational intervention in the treatment of sex offenders. In: W. R. Miller & S. Rollnick (Eds) *Motivational Interviewing: Preparing People to Change Addictive Behavior*, pp. 303–13. New York: Guilford Press.

Gearing, F. R., D'Amico, D. A. & Thompson, F. (1978) Impact of the economic recession on the employment of heroin addicts in methadone maintenance treatment. In: A. Schechter, H. Alksre & E. Kaufman (Eds) *Critical Concerns in the Field of Drug Abuse*. New York: Marcel Dekker.

Gearon, J. S. & Bellack, A. S. (2000) Sex differences in illness presentation, course and level of functioning in substance-abusing schizophrenia patients. *Schizophrenia Research*, **43**(1), 65–70.

George, S. L., Gebhardt, J., Klinzman, D., *et al.* (2002) Hepatitis C virus viremia in HIV-infected individuals with negative HCV antibody tests. *Journal of Acquired Immune Deficiency Syndrome*, **31**(2), 154–62.

Gerstein, D. R. & Harwood, H. J. (1990) *Treating Drug Problems*, vol. 1. Washington, DC: National Academy Press.

Gerstein, D. R., Johnson, R. A., Harwood, H. J., *et al.* (1994) *Evaluating Recovery Services: The Califoria Drug and Alcohol Treatment Assessment (CALDATA)*. General Report submitted to the State of California Department of Alcohol and Drug Programs.

GG & GD (Municipal Public Health Service) (1996) *Dovend vuur. Jaarbericht Drugsafdeling 1994–1995* (Extinguishing fire. Year report drugs department 1994–1995). Amsterdam: Amsterdam Municipal Public Health Service.

GGHB (Greater Glasgow Health Board) (2000) Likely cause of injector outbreak in Glasgow identified. *GGHB Bulletin*, 15 July 2000.

Ghodse, A. H., Sheehan, M., Taylor, C., *et al.* (1985) Deaths from drug addicts in the United Kingdom 1967–81. *British Medical Journal*, **290**, 427–8.

Gibb, D. M., Goodall, R. L., Dunn, D. T., *et al.* (2000) Mother-to-child transmission of hepatitis C virus: evidence for preventable peripartum transmission. *Lancet*, **356**, 904–907.

Gieringer, D. H. (1988) Marijuana, driving and accident safety. *Journal of Psychoactive Drugs*, **20**, 93–101.

Gill, K., Nolimal, D. & Crowley, T. J. (1992) Antisocial personality disorder, HIV risk behaviour and retention in methadone maintenance therapy. *Drug and Alcohol Dependence*, **30**, 247–52.

Gilvary, E. (1998) Young drug users: early intervention. *Drugs: Education, Prevention, and Policy*, **5**(3), 281–92.

Glaser, F. (1980) The core shell model and the Matching Hypothesis. In: G. Edwards & M. Grant (Eds) *Alcoholism Treatment in Transition*. London: Croom Helm.

Glaser, F. B. (1999) The unsinkable Project MATCH. *Addiction*, **94**(1), 34–6.

Glass, I. & Jackson, P. (1988) Maudsley Hospital survey: prevalence of alcohol problems and other psychiatric disorders in a hospital population. *British Journal of Addiction*, **83**(9), 1105–11.

Glennerster, H., Noden, P. & Power, A. (1998) Poverty, Social Exclusion, and Place: Studying the Area Bases of Social Exclusion. Paper presented at SPA conference, Lincoln.

Gmel, G., Klingeman, S., Muller, R., *et al.* (2001) Revising the preventive paradox: the Swiss case. *Addiction*, **96**, 273–84.

Golding, J. F. & Cornish, A. M. (1987) Personality and lifestyle in medical students: psychological aspects. *Psychology and Health*, **1**, 287–301.

Gold-Steinberg, S. & Buttenheim, M. (1993) Telling one's story in an incest survivors group. *International Journal of Group Psychotherapy*, **43**(2), 173.

Goleman, D. (1996) *Emotional Intelligence*. London: Bloomsbury Publishing.

Gondoli, D. M. & Jacob, T. (1990) Family treatment of alcoholism. In: R. R. Watson (Ed.) *Drug and Alcohol Abuse Prevention*, pp. 245–62. New York: Humana Press.

Gordon, A. J. & Zrull, M. (1991) Social networks and recovery: one year after inpatient treatment. *Journal of Substance Abuse Treatment*, **8**, 143–52.

Gordon, J. R. & Barrett, K. (1993) The Codependency Movement: issues of context and differentiation. In: J. S. Baer, A. Marlatt & J. McMahon (Eds) *Addictive Behaviours Across the Life Span*. London: Sage.

Gore, S. M. & Bird, A. G. (1996) Prison rights: mandatory drug tests and performance indicators for prisons. *British Medical Journal*, **312**, 1411–13.

Gore, S. M. & Bird, A. G. (1998) Drugs in British prisons. *British Medical Journal*, **316**, 1256–7.

Gorman, J. & Rooney, J. (1979) The influence of Al-Anon on the coping behaviour of wives of alcoholics. *Journal of Studies on Alcohol*, **40**, 1030–38.

Gorski, T. & Miller, M. (1988) *Staying Sober Workbook*. Independence, MO: Independence Press.

Gossop, M., Green, L., Phillips, G., *et al.* (1990) Factors predicting outcome among opiate addicts after treatment. *British Journal of Clinical Psychology*, **29**, 209–16.

Gossop, M. (1993) *Living with Drugs*, 3rd edn. Aldershot, UK: Ashgate.

Gossop, M., Griffiths, P., Powis, B., *et al.* (1993) Severity of heroin dependence and HIV risk. I. Sexual behaviour. *AIDS Care*, **5**, 149–57.

Gossop, M., Griffiths, P., Powis, B., *et al.* (1993a) Severity of heroin dependence and HIV risk. II. Sharing injecting equipment. *AIDS Care*, **5**, 159–68.

Gossop, M., Darke, S., Griffiths, P., *et al.* (1995) The severity of dependence scale (SDS): psychometric properties of the SDS in English and Australian samples of heroin, cocaine, and amphetamine users. *Addiction*, **90**, 607–14.

Gossop, M., Marsden, J. & Stewart, D. (1997) *National Treatment Outcome Research Study*. London: Department of Health.

Gossop, M., Stewart, D., Rolfe, A., *et al.* (1999) NTORS: two-year outcomes. *The National Treatment Outcome Research Study*, 4th bulletin. London: Departments of Health.

Gossop, M., Marsden, J., Stewart, D., *et al.* (2000) Patterns of improvement after methadone treatment: 1-year follow-up results from the National Treatment Outcome Research Study (NTORS). *Drug and Alcohol Dependence*, **60**, 275–86.

Gossop, M. (2001) A web of dependence (Editorial). *Addiction*, **96**(5), 677–8.

Gossop, M., Marsden, J., Stewart, D., *et al.* (2001) Outcomes after methadone maintenance and methadone reduction treatments: two-year follow-up results from the National Treatment Outcome Research Study. *Drug and Alcohol Dependence*, **62**, 255–64.

Gossop, M., Stewart, D., Browne, N., *et al.* (2002) Factors associated with abstinence, lapse or relapse to heroin use after residential treatment: protective effect of coping responses. *Addiction*, **97**(10), 1259–67.

Gossop, M., Marsden, J. & Stewart, D. (2003) Methadone maintenance and reduction treatments: the need for clarity of goals and procedures. In: G. Tober & J. Strang (Eds) *Methadone Matters*, pp. 271–82. London: Martin Dunitz.

Graeven, D. B. & Graeven, K. A. (1983) Treated and untreated addicts: factors associated with participation in treatment and cessation of heroin use. *Journal of Drug Issues*, **13**, 207–18.

Graham, K. (1985) Determinants of heavy drinking and drinking problems: the contribution of the bar environment. In: E. Single & T. Storm (Eds) *Public Drinking and Public Policy*, pp. 71–84. Toronto: Addiction Research Foundation.

Graham, K., Wells, S. & West, P. (1997) A framework for applying explanations of alcohol-related aggression to naturally occurring aggressive behaviour. *Contemporary Drug Problems*, **24**(4), 625–66.

Grant, B. F. (1997) Barriers to alcoholism treatment: reasons for not seeking treatment in a general population. *Journal of Studies on Alcohol*, **58**(4), 365–71.

Grant, B. F. & Dawson, D. A. (1998) Age of alcohol onset and alcohol disorders: results from the national longitudinal alcohol epidemiological survey. *Journal of Substance Abuse*, **10**(2), 163–73.

Grant, M. & Hodgson, R. (Eds) (1991) *Responding to Drug and Alcohol Problems in the Community: A Manual for Primary Health Care Workers*. WHO: Geneva.

Gray, J. A. (1987) *The Psychology of Fear and Stress*, 2nd edn. New York: Academic Press.

Green, M., Setchell, J., Hames, P., *et al.* (1993) Management of alcohol-abusing patients in accident and emergency departments. *Journal of the Royal Society of Medicine*, **86**, 393–5.

Greenberg, J., Solomon, S., Pyszcynski, T., *et al.* (1992) Why do people need self-esteem? Converging evidence that self-esteem serves an anxiety-buffered function. *Journal of Personality and Social Psychology*, **63**, 913–22.

Greenberg, M. T., Kusche, C. A. & Speltz, M. (1991) Emotional regulation, self-control and psychopathology: the role of relationships in early childhood. In: D. Cicchetti & S. L. Toth (Eds) *Internalizing and Externalizing Expressions of Dysfunction: Rochester Symposium on Developmental Psychopathology*, vol. 2, pp. 21–66. Hillsdale, NJ: Lawrence Erlbaum.

Griffiths, R. R., Bigelow, G. E. & Henningfield, J. E. (1980) Similarities in animal and human drug-taking behavior. In: N. K. Mello (Ed.) *Advances in Substance Abuse: Behavioral and Biological Research*, pp. 1–90. Greenwich, CT: JAI Press.

Grimley, D. M., Riley, G. E., Bellis, J. M., *et al.* (1993) Assessing the stages of change and decision making for contraceptive use for the prevention of pregnancy, sexually transmitted diseases, and acquired immunodeficiency syndrome. *Health Education Quarterly*, **20**, 455–70.

Grove, W. M., Eckert, E. D., Heston, L., *et al.* (1990) Heritability of substance abuse and antisocial behavior: a study of monozygotic twins reared apart. *Biological Psychiatry*, **27**, 1293–304.

Gruen, R. J., Folkman, S. & Lazarus, R. S. (1989) Centrality and individual differences in the meaning of daily hassels. *Journal of Personality*, **56**, 743–62.

Gunn, J., Maden, A. & Swinton, M. (1991) Treatment needs of prisoners with psychiatric disorders. *British Medical Journal*, **303**(6798), 338–41.

Gunton, A., Thompson, L., Arnason, R. C., *et al.* (1995) Pregnant women and smoking. *The Canadian Nurse*, **91**(7), 26–30.

Haefely, W. (1986) Biological basis of drug-induced tolerance, rebound, and dependence. Contribution of recent research on benzodiazepines. *Pharmacopsychiatrica*, **19**, 353–61.

Hall, S. M., Loeb, P., LeVois, P., *et al.* (1981) Increasing employment in ex-heroin addicts. II. Methadone maintenance sample. *Behavioral Medicine*, **12**, 453–60.

Hall, W., Solowij, N. & Lemon, J. (1994) *The Health and Psychological Effects of Cannabis*. Report to the National Task Force on Cannabis, Melbourne, Australia.

Hall, W. (1996) Methadone maintenance treatment as a crime control measure. *Contemporary Issues in Crime and Justice*, **29**, 1–12.

Hall, W. & Farrell, M. (1997) Co-morbidity of mental disorders with substance misuse. *British Journal of Psychiatry*, **171**, 4–7.

Hall, W., Johnston, L. & Donnelly, N. (1999) The epidemiology of cannabis use and its consequences. In: H. Kalant, W. Corrigall, W. Hall, *et al.* (Eds) *The Health Effects of Cannabis*, pp. 69–125. Toronto: Addiction Research Foundation.

Hall, W., Lynskey, M. & Degenhartd, L. (2000) Trends in opiate-related deaths in the United Kingdom and Australia between 1985 and 1995. *Drug and Alcohol Dependence*, **57**(3), 247–54.

Handelsman, L., Cochrane, K. J., Aronson, M. J., *et al.* (1987) Two new rating scales for opiate withdrawal. *American Journal of Drug and Alcohol Abuse*, **13**(3), 293–308.

Hankin, J. R. (1994) FAS prevention strategies: passive and active measures. *Alcohol Health and Research World*, **18**, 62–6.

Hargreaves, W. (1983) Methadone dosage and duration for maintenance treatment. In: J. A. Cooper, A. Altman, B. Brown, *et al.* (Eds) *Research on the Treatment of Narcotic Addiction: State of the Art*, pp. 19–91. DHHS Publication No. ADM-83-1281. Washington, DC: Government Printing Office.

Harland, J., White, M., Drinkwater, C., *et al.* (1999) The Newcastle exercise project: a randomised controlled trial of methods to promote physical activity in primary care. *British Medical Journal*, **319**, 828–31.

Harrison, P. A., Beebe, T. J., Fulkerson, J. A., *et al.* (1996) The development of patient profiles from Minnesota's treatment outcomes monitoring system. *Addiction*, **91**, 687–99.

Harrison, P. A., Fulkerson, J. A. & Beebe, T. J. (1998) DSM-IV substance use disorder criteria for adolescents: a critical examination based on a statewide school survey. *American Journal of Psychiatry*, **155**, 486–92.

Harrison, R. (1986) The non-essential use of drugs, alcohol and cigarettes during pregnancy. *Irish Medical Journal*, **79**, 338–41.

Hartnoll, R. L., Mitcheson, M. C., Battersby, A., *et al.* (1980) Evaluation of heroin maintenance in controlled trial. *Archives of General Psychiatry*, **37**, 877–84.

Harwood, H., Fountain, D. & Livermore, G. (1998) *The Economic Costs of Alcohol and Drug Abuse in the United States 1992*. National Institutes of Health Publication No. 98-4327. Rockville, MD: DHHS.

HAS (Health Advisory Service) (1996) *Children and Young People Substance Misuse Services: The Substance of Young Needs*. London: HMSO.

HAS (Health Advisory Service) (2001) *The Substance of Young Needs: Review 2001*. London: HMSO.

Hawkins, J. D. & Weis, J. G. (1985) The social development model: An integrated approach to delinquency prevention. *Journal of Primary Prevention*, **6**, 73–95.

Hawkins, J. D., Catalano, R. F., Gillmore, M. R., *et al.* (1989) Skills training for drug abusers: generalisation, maintenance and effects on drug use. *Journal of Consulting and Clinical Psychology*, **57**, 559–63.

Hawton, K., Fagg, J., Plant, S., *et al.* (1993) Factors associated with suicide after parasuicide in young people. *British Medical Journal*, **306**(6893), 1641–4.

Hayes, S. C., Nelson, R. O. & Jarrett, R. B. (1987) The treatment utility of assessment: a functional approach to evaluating assessment quality. *American Psychologist*, **42**, 963–74.

Hayward, P. & Bright, J. (1998) Stigma and mental illness: a review critique. *Journal of Mental Health*, **6**, 345–54.

Heather, N. & Robertson, I. (1981) *Controlled Drinking*. London: Methuen.

Heather, N. (1986) Change without therapists. The use of self-help manuals by problem drinkers. In: W. R. Miller & N. Heather (Eds) *Treating Addictive Behaviors*, pp. 331–59. New York: Plenum Press.

Heather, N., Robertson, I., MacPherson, B., *et al.* (1987) Effectiveness of a controlled drinking self-help manual: one-year follow-up results. *British Journal of Clinical Psychology*, **26**, 279–87.

Heather, N., Wodak, A., Nadelmann, E., *et al.* (1993) *Psychoactive Drugs and Harm Reduction: From Faith to Science*. London: Whurr.

Heather, N. (1996) The public health and brief interventions for excessive alcohol consumption: the British experience. *Addictive Behaviours*, **21**, 857–68.

Heather, N. & Robertson, I. (1997) *Problem Drinking*, 3rd edn. Oxford: Oxford Medical Publications.

Heather, N. (2001) Brief interventions. In: N. Heather, T. J. Peters & T. Stockwell (Eds) *Alcohol Dependence and Problems*, pp. 605–26. Chichester, UK: Wiley.

Hedouin, V. & Gosset, D. (1998) Infection with hepatitis C virus in a prison environment: a prospective study in Loos-les-Lille, France. *Gastroenterologie Clinique et Biologique*, **22**, 55–8.

Henggeler, S. W., Melton, G. B. & Smith, L. A. (1992) Family preservation using multisystemic therapy: an effective alternative to incarcerating serious juvenile offenders. *Journal of Consulting and Clinical Psychology*, **60**, 953–61.

Henggeler, S. W., Melton, G. B., Brondino, M. J., *et al.* (1997) Multisystemic therapy with violent and chronic juvenile offenders and their families: the role of treatment fidelity in successful dissemination. *Journal of Consulting and Clinical Psychology*, **65**, 821–33.

Henggeler, S. W. (1998) Outcomes of MST: findings from controlled evaluations. In: S. W. Henggeler, S. K. Schoenwald, C. M. Borduin, *et al.* (Eds) *Multisystemic Treatment of Antisocial Behaviour in Children and Adolescents*, pp. 237–47. New York: Guilford Press.

Henggeler, S. W., Schoenwald, S. K., Borduin, C. M., *et al.* (1998) *Multisystemic Treatment of Antisocial Behavior in Children and Adolescents*. New York: Guilford Press.

Henningfield, J. E., Lukas, S. E. & Bigelow, G. E. (1986) Human studies of drugs as reinforcers. In: S. R. Goldberg & I. P. Stolerman (Eds) *Behavioral Analysis of Drug Dependence*, pp. 69–122. Orlando, FL: Academic Press.

Henry, J. A. (1996) Ecstasy and serotonin depletion. *Lancet*, **347**(9004), 833.

Hepburn, M. & Forrest, C. A. (1988) Does infection with HIV affect the outcome of pregnancy? *British Medical Journal*, **296**, 934.

Hepburn, M. (1993) Drug use in pregnancy. *British Journal of Hospital Medicine*, **49**, 51–5.

Herrstein, R. J. & Murray, C. (1994) *The Bell Curve: Intelligence and Class Structure in American Life*. New York: Free Press.

Hesselbrock, M. N., Meyer, R. E. & Keener, J. J. (1985) Psychopathology in hospitalised alcoholics. *Archives of General Psychiatry*, **42**, 1050–55.

Hester, R. K. (1995) Behavioral self-control training. In: R. K. Hester & W. R. Miller (Eds) *Handbook of Alcoholism Treatment Approaches: Effective Alternatives*, 2nd edn, pp. 149–59. Boston: Allyn & Bacon.

Higgins, S. T., Budney, A. J., Bickel, W. K., *et al.* (1993) Achieving cocaine abstinence with a behavioral approach. *American Journal of Psychiatry*, **150**, 763–9.

Higgins, S. T. & Budney, A. (1994) Participation of significant other in outpatient behavioral treatment predicts greater cocaine abstinence. *American Journal of Drug and Alcohol Abuse*, **201**, 47–56.

Higgins, S. T., Budney, A. J., Bickel, W. K., *et al.* (1994) Incentive improve outcome in outpatient behavioral treatment of cocaine dependence. *Archives of General Psychiatry*, **51**, 568–76.

Higgins, S. T. (1997) The influence of alternative reinforcers on cocaine use and abuse: a brief review. *Pharmacology Biochemistry and Behaviour*, **57**, 419–27.

Higgins, S. T. (1999) Potential contributions of the community reinforcement approach and contingency management to broadening the base of substance abuse treatment. In: J. A. Tucker, D. M. Donovan & G. A. Marlatt (Eds) *Changing Addictive Behavior: Bridging Clinical and Public Health Strategies*, pp. 283–306. New York: Guilford Press.

Higgins-Biddle, J. C. & Babor, T. F. (1996) *Reducing Risky Drinking: A Report on the Early Identification and Management of Alcohol Problems Through Screening and Brief Intervention*. Farmington, CT: University of Connecticut.

Hindler, C., Nazareth, I., King, M., *et al.* (1995) Drug users' views on general practitioners. *British Medical Journal*, **310**, 302.

Hobfoll, S. E., Ritter, C., Lavin, J., *et al.* (1995) Depression prevalence and incidence among inner-city pregnant and post-partum women. *Journal of Consulting and Clinical Psychology*, **63**(3), 445–53.

Hodgson, R. J., Alwyn, T., John, B., *et al.* (2002) The Fast Alcohol Screening Test. *Alcohol and Alcoholism*, **37**(1), 61–6.

Hoeksema, H. L. & De Bock, G. H. (1993) The value of laboratory tests for the screening and recognition of alcohol abuse in primary care patients. *Journal of Family Practitioners*, **37**, 268–76.

Holder, H., Longabaugh, R., Miller, W. R., *et al.* (1991) The cost-effectiveness of treatment for alcoholism: a first approximation. *Journal of Studies on Alcohol*, **52**, 517–40.

Holder, H. D., Miller, W. R. & Carina, R. T. (1995) *Cost Savings of Substance Abuse Prevention in Managed Care*. Berkeley, CA: Center for Substance Abuse Prevention.

Holder, H. D. (2000) Community prevention of alcohol problems. *Addictive Behaviours*, **25**(6), 843–59.

Holder, H. D., Gruenwald, P. J., Ponicki, W. R., *et al.* (2000) Effect of community-based interventions on high-risk drinking and alcohol-related injuries. *Journal of the American Medical Association*, **284**(18), 2341–7.

Hollon, S. D., DeRubeis, R. J., Evans, M. D., *et al.* (1992) Cognitive therapy and pharmacotherapy for depression: singly and in combination. *Archives of General Psychiatry*, **49**, 774–81.

Holmes, K. K., Johnson, D. W., Kvale, P. A., *et al.* (1996) Impact of a gonorrhea control program, including selective treatment, in female sex workers. *Journal of Infectious Diseases*, **174** (Suppl. 2), 230–39.

Holsen, D. S., Harthug, S., Myrmel, H., *et al.* (1993) Prevalence of antibodies to hepatitis C virus and association with intravenous drug abuse and tattooing in a national prison in Norway. *European Journal of Clinical Microbiological Infectious Diseases*, 12, 673–6.

Homel, R. & Clark, J. (1994) The prediction and prevention of violence in pubs and clubs. *Crime Prevention Studies*, 3, 1–46.

Home Office (1998) *Guidance on Good Practice (Drugs Prevention Initiative)*. London: Home Office.

Hope, V. D., Judd, A., Hickman, M., *et al.* (2001) Prevalence of hepatitis C among injection drug users in England and Wales: is harm reduction working? *American Journal of Public Health*, 91, 38–42.

Hover, S. & Gaffney, L. R. (1991) The relationship between social skills and adolescent drinking. *Alcohol and Alcoholism*, 26, 207–14.

Hoza, B., Molina, B. S. G., Bukowski, W. M., *et al.* (1995) Peer variables as predictors of later childhood adjustment. *Development and Psychopathology*, 7 (Special issue: Developmental processes in peer relations and psychopathology), 787–802.

Huba, G. J. & Bentler, P. B. (1982) A developmental theory of drug use: derivation and assessment of a causal modeling approach. In: P. B. Baltes & O. G. Brim, Jr (Eds) *Life Span Development and Behavior*, vol. 4, pp. 147–203. New York: Academic Press.

Hubbard, R. L., Marsden, M. E., Rachal, J. V., *et al.* (1989) *Drug Abuse Treatment: A National Survey of Effectiveness*. Chapel Hill: University of North Carolina Press.

Hughes, J. R., Hatsukami, D. K., Mitchell, J. E., *et al.* (1986) Prevalence of smoking among psychiatric outpatients. *American Journal of Psychiatry*, 143(8), 993–7.

Hull, J. G., Young, R. D. & Jouriles, E. (1986) Applications of the self-awareness model of alcohol consumption: predicting patterns of use and abuse. *Journal of Personality and Social Psychology*, 51, 790–96.

Hulse, G. K. & Basso, M. R. (2000) The association between naltrexone compliance and daily supervision. *Drug and Alcohol Review*, 19(1), 41–8.

Humenuik R., Ali, R., White, J., *et al.* (2000) *Induction and Stabilisation of Patients onto Methadone: Evidence-Based Guidelines*. Canberra: Commonwealth Department of Health and Aged Care.

Humphries, K. & Tucker, J. A. (2002) Towards more responsive and effective intervention systems for alcohol-related problems (Editorial). *Addiction*, 97(2), 126–32.

Hunt, G. M. & Azrin, N. H. (1973) A community-reinforcement approach to alcoholism. *Behaviour Research and Therapy*, 11, 91–104.

Hunt, N., Stillwell, G., Taylor, C., *et al.* (1998) Evaluation of a brief intervention to prevent initiation into injecting. *Drugs: Education, Prevention, and Policy*, 5(2), 185–94.

Hunt, W. A., Barnett, L. W. & Branch, L. G. (1971) Relapse rates in addiction programmes. *Journal of Clinical Psychology*, 27, 355.

Hunter, G. M., Stimson, G. V., Judd, A., *et al.* (2000) Measuring injecting risk behaviour in the second decade of harm reduction: a survey of injecting drug users in England. *Addiction*, 95, 1351–61.

Hurry, J. & Lloyd, C. (1997) A follow-up evaluation of Project Charlie. A life skills drug education programme for primary schools. Paper 16. Home Office Drugs Prevention Initiative.

Hutson, S. & Liddiard, M. (1994) *Youth Homelessness: The Construction of a Social Issue*. Basingstoke, UK: Macmillan Press.

Ikonomidou, C., Bittigau, P., Ishimaru, M. J., *et al.* (2000) Ethanol-induced apopoptic neurodegeneration and foetal alcohol syndrome. *Science*, 287(5455), 1056–60.

IOM (Institute of Medicine) (1990) *Broadening the Base of Treatment for Alcohol Problems*. Washington, DC: National Academy Press.

ISAD (Interdepartmental Steering Group on Alcohol and Drug Policy) (1985) *Drugbeleid in beweging, naar een normalisering van de drugproblematiek* (Drug Policy in Motion, toward the normalization of drug problems). Leidschendam, Netherlands: Ministry of Health.

ISDD (Institute for the Study of Drug Dependence) (1979) *Teaching About a Volatile Situation: Suggested Health Education Strategies for Minimising Casualties Associated with Solvent Sniffing*. London: ISDD.

Israel, Y., Hollander, O., Sanchez-Craig, M., *et al.* (1996) Screening for problem drinking and counselling by the primary care physician–nurse team. *Alcoholism: Clinical and Experimental Research*, 20, 1443–50.

Jackson, R., Scragg, R. & Beaglehole, R. (1991) Alcohol consumption and risk of coronary heart disease. *British Medical Journal*, 303, 553–6.

Jaeckel, E., Cornberg, M., Wedemeyer, H., *et al.* (2001) Treatment of acute hepatitis C with interferon alfa-2b. *New England Journal of Medicine*, 345(20), 1452–7.

James, W. (1983) *The Principles of Psychology* (originally published 1890). Cambridge, MA: Harvard University Press.

Jang, K. L., Livesley, W. J. & Vernon, P. A. (1997) Gender-specific etiological differences in alcohol and drug problems: a behavioural genetic analysis. *Addiction*, 92, 1265–76.

Janis, I. L. & Mann, L. (1977) *Decision Making*. New York: Free Press.

Jargowsky, P. A. (1996) *Poverty and Place*. New York: Russell Sage.

Jarvis, T. J., Tebbutt, J. & Mattick, R. P. (1995) *Treatment Approaches for Alcohol and Drug Dependence*. Chichester, UK: Wiley.

Jessor, R., Donovan, J. E. & Costa, F. N. (1991) *Beyond Adolescence: Problem Behavior and Young Adult Development*. Cambridge, MA: Cambridge University Press.

Johns, A. (1998) Substance misuse and offending. *Current Opinion in Psychiatry*, **11**, 669–73.

Johns, A. (2001) Psychiatric effects of cannabis. *British Journal of Psychiatry*, **178**, 116–22.

Johnson, M., Fisher, D. G., Fernaughty, A., *et al.* (1998) Hepatitis C virus and depression in drug users. *American Journal of Gastroenterology*, **93**, 785–9.

Johnson R. A., Gerstein, D. R., Pach, A., III *et al.* (2002) HIV risk behaviors in African-American drug injector networks: implications of injecton-partner mixing and partnership characteristics. *Addiction*, **97**, 1011–24.

Jones, B. T. & McMahon, J. (1994) Negative and positive alcohol expectancies as predictors of abstinence after discharge from a residential treatment program: a one-month and three-month follow-up study in men. *Journal of Studies on Alcohol*, **55**, 543–8.

Jones, K. L., Smith, D. W., Ulleland, C. N., *et al.* (1973) Pattern of malformation in offspring of chronic alcoholic mothers. *Lancet*, **1**, 1267–71.

Joseph, H. & Roman-Nay, H. (1990) The homeless intravenous drug abuser and the AIDS epidemic. In: C. G. Leukefeld, R. J. Battjes & Z. Amsel (Eds) *AIDS and Intravenous Drug Use: Community Intervention and Prevention*, pp. 210–53. New York: Hemisphere.

Judd, A., Hickman, M., Renton, A., *et al.* (1999) Hepatitis C virus infection among injecting drug users: has harm reduction worked? *Addiction Research*, **7**, 1–6.

Judd, A., Stimson, G. V., Hickman, M., *et al.* (2000) Low prevalence of HIV infection in a multi-site sample of injecting drug users not in contact with treatment services in England. *AIDS*, **14**, 2413–15.

Kadden, R., Carroll, K., Donovan, D., *et al.* (1995) *Cognitive–Behavioral Coping Skills Therapy Manual: A Clinical Research Guide for Therapists Treating Individuals with Alcohol Abuse and Dependence*. Rockville, MD: National Institute of Alcohol Abuse and Alcoholism.

Kadden, R. M., Cooney, N. L., Getter, H., *et al.* (1990) Matching alcoholics to coping skills or interactional therapies: post-treatment results. *Journal of Consulting and Clinical Psychology*, **57**, 698–704.

Kaempf, G., O'Donnell, C., Oslin, D. W., *et al.* (1999) The BRENDA model: a psychosocial addiction model to identify and treat alcohol disorders in elders. *Geriatric Nursing*, **20**, 302–304.

Kamali, M., Kelly, L., Gervin, M., *et al.* (2000) The prevalence of comorbid substance misuse and its influence on suicidal ideation among inpatients with schizophrenia. *Acta Psychiatrica Scandanavica*, **101**(6), 452–6.

Kaminer, Y. (1994) *Adolescent Substance Abuse: A Comprehensive Guide to Theory and Practice*. New York: Plenum Press.

Kandel, D. B., Johnson, J. G., Bird, H. R., *et al.* (1997) Psychiatric disorders associated with substance use among children and adolescents: findings from the Methods for the Epidemiological Child and Adolescent Mental Disorders (MECA) Study. *Journal of Abnormal Child Psychology*, **25**(2), 121–32.

Kandel, D. B. & Yamaguchi, K. (1987) Job mobility and drug use: an event history analysis. *American Journal of Sociology*, **92**(4), 836–78.

Kaner, E., McAvoy, B., Heather, N., *et al.* (1997) Report on Strand 1: the views and current practices of general practitioners regarding preventive medicine and early intervention for hazardous alcohol use. In: J. B. Saunders & S. Wutzke (Eds) *WHO Collaborative Study on Implementing and Supporting Early Intervention in Primary Health Care*. Copenhagen: WHO Regional Office for Europe.

Kaplan, R. F., Cooney, M. L., Baker, L. H., *et al.* (1985) Reactivity to alcohol-related cues: physiological and subjective responses in alcoholics and non-problem drinkers. *Journal of Studies on Alcohol*, **46**, 267–72.

Kaufman, E. (1992) Family therapy: a treatment approach with substance abusers. In: J. H. Lowinson, P. Ruiz & R. B. Millman (Eds) *Substance Abuse: A Comprehensive Textbook*, 2nd edn. Baltimore: Wilkins & Wilkins.

Kaufman, E. (1994) *Psychotherapy of Addicted Persons*. New York: Guilford Press.

Kaufman, E. (1994a) Family therapy: other drugs. In: M. Galanter & H. D. Kleber (Eds) *Textbook of Substance Abuse Treatment*, pp. 331–48. Washington, DC: American Psychiatric Press.

Kazdin, A. E. (1995) *Conduct Disorders in Childhood and Adolescence*, 2nd edn. Thousand Oaks, CA: Sage.

Keane, F. E., Young, S. M. & Boyle, H. M. (1996) The prevalence of previous sexual assault among routine female attenders at a department of genitourinary medicine. *International Journal of STD and AIDS*, **7**(7), 840–44.

Keene, J. (1998) Effective interventions for problem drinkers: is matching the answer? In: M. Bloor & F. Wood (Eds) *Addictions and Problem Drug Use: Issues in Behaviour, Policy, and Practice*, pp. 197–215. London: Jessica Kingsley.

Keene, J., Willner, P. & Love, A. C. (1999) The relevance of problems and models to treatment outcome: a comparative study of two agencies. *Substance Use and Misuse*, **34**(10), 1347–69.

Keene, J. (2001) *Clients with Complex Needs.* Oxford: Blackwell Science.

Kelly, T. M., Donovan, J. E., Kinnane, J. M., *et al.* (2002) A comparison of alcohol screening instruments among under-age drinkers treated in emergency departments. *Alcohol and Alcoholism*, **37**, 444–50.

Kendler, K. S., Karkowski, L. M., Corey, L. A., *et al.* (1999) Genetic and environmental factors in the aetiology of illicit drug initiation and misuse in women. *British Journal of Psychiatry*, **175**, 351–6.

Kendler, K. S., Bulik, C. M., Silberg, J., *et al.* (2000) Childhood sexual abuse and adult psychiatric and substance use disorders in women: an epidemiological and cotwin analysis. *Archives of General Psychiatry*, **57**(10), 953–9.

Kennedy, J. T., Petrone, J., Deisher, R. W., *et al.* (1990) Health care for famililess, runaway street kids. In: P. Brickner, L. Scharer & B. C. Scanlan (Eds) *Under the Safety Net*, pp. 15–31. New York: W. W. Norton.

Khantzian, E. J., Halliday, K. S. & McAuliffe, W. E. (1990) *Addiction and the Vulnerable Self.* New York: Guilford Press.

Klee, H., Faugier, J., Hayes, C., *et al.* (1990) Sexual partners of injecting drug users: the risk of HIV infection. *British Journal of Addiction*, **85**, 413–18.

Klee, H., Faugier, J., Hayes, C., *et al.* (1991) Risk reduction among injecting drug users. Changes in the sharing of injecting equipment and in condom use. *Aids Care*, **3**, 63–73.

Klee, H. & Reid, P. (1998) Drugs and youth homelessness: reducing the risk. *Drugs: Education, Prevention, and Policy*, **5**(3), 269–80.

Klevens, R. M., Fleming, P., Neal, J., *et al.* (1999) Is there really a heterosexual AIDS epidemic in the United States? Finding from a multisite validation study, 1992–95. *American Journal of Epidemiology*, **149**, 75–84.

Klingeman, H. (1994) Environmental influences which promote or impede change in substance behaviour. In: G. Edwards & M. Lander (Eds) *Addiction: Processes of Change*. Oxford: Oxford University Press.

Klingeman, H. & Hunt, G. (Eds) (1998) *Drug Treatment Systems in an International Perspective: Drugs Demons and Delinquents*. Thousand Oaks, CA: Sage.

Korf, D. J. (1994) Drug tourists and drug refugees. In: E. Leuw & I. H. Marshall (Eds) *Between Prohibition and Legalisation: The Dutch Experiment in Drug Policy*, pp. 119–43. New York: Kugler.

Korf, D. J. & Buning, E. C. (2000) Coffee shops, low-threshold methadone, and needle exchange: controlling illicit drug use in the Netherlands. In: J. A. Inciardi & L. D. Harison (Eds) *Harm Reduction: National and International Perspectives*, pp. 111–35. Thousand Oaks, CA: Sage.

Kozarickovacic, D., Folnegovicsmalc, V., Folnegovic, Z., *et al.* (1995) Influence of alcoholism on the prognosis of schizophrenic patients. *Journal of Studies on Alcohol*, **56**(6), 622–7.

Kranzler, H. R., Burleson, J. A., Del Boca, F. C., *et al.* (1994) Buspirone treatment of anxious alcoholics: a placebo-controlled trial. *Archives of General Psychiatry*, **51**(9), 720–31.

Kreitman, N. (1986) Alcohol consumption and the preventive paradox. *British Journal of Addiction*, **81**, 353–63.

Kristenson, H., Ohlin, H., Hulten-Nosslin, M., *et al.* (1983) Identification and intervention of heavy drinking in middle-aged men: results and follow-up of 24:60 months of long-term study with randomized control. *Alcoholism: Clinical and Experimental Research*, **20**, 203–209.

Kroenke, K. (2001) Studying symptoms: sampling and measurement issues. *Annals of Internal Medicine*, **134**, 844–55.

Kumpulainen, K. (2000) Psychiatric symptoms and deviance in early adolescence predict heavy alcohol use 3 years later. *Addiction*, **95**(12), 1847–57.

Kushner, M. G., Sher, K. J. & Beitman, B. D. (1990) The relation between alcohol problems and the anxiety disorders. *American Journal of Psychiatry*, **147**(6), 685–95.

Laberg, J. C. (1990) What is presented, and what prevented, in cue exposure and response prevention with alcohol-dependent subjects? *Addictive Behaviours*, **15**, 367–86.

Lader, M. (1988) The psychopharmacology of addiction – benzodiazepine tolerance and dependence. In: M. Lader (Ed.) *The Psychopharmacology of Addiction*. Oxford: Oxford Medical Publications.

Lader, M. H., Ron, M. & Petursson, H. (1984) Computed axial brain tomography in long-term benzodiazepine users. *Psychological Medicine*, **14** (1), 203–206.

Laga, M., Alary, M., Nzila, N., *et al.* (1994) Condom promotion, sexually transmitted diseases treatment, and declining incidence of HIV-1 infection in female Zairian sex workers. *Lancet*, **334**(8917), 246–8.

Larsen, T. F., Friis, S., Haahr, U., *et al.* (2001) Early detection and intervention in first-episode schizophrenia: a critical review. *Acta Scandanavica*, **103**(5), 321–2.

Lawner, K., Doot, M., Gausas, J., *et al.* (1997) Implementation of CAGE alcohol screening in a primary care practice. *Family Medicine*, **29**, 332–5.

Lazarus, A. A. (1984) *In the Mind's Eye*. New York: Guilford Press.

Lazarus, R. S. & Folkman S. (1984) *Stress, Appraisal and Coping*. New York: Springer-Verlag.

Lazarus, R. S. (1991) *Emotion and Adaptation*. New York: Oxford University Press.

Lazarus, R. S. (1999) *Stress and Emotion: A New Synthesis*. London: Free Association Books.

Leen, C. L. & Brettle R. P. (1991) Fungal infections in drug users. *Journal of Antimicrobial Chemotherapy*, **28**(Suppl. A), 83–96.

Leigh, B. C. (1990) The relationship of sex-related alcohol expectancies to alcohol consumption and sexual behaviour. *British Journal of Addiction*, **85**, 919–28.

Lemoine, P., Harousseau, H., Borteyru, J. P., *et al.* (1968) Les enfants des parents alcooliques: anomalies observées à propos 127 cas. *Quest Medicale*, **25**, 476–82.

Lender, M. E. (1986) A special stigma: women and alcoholism in the late 19th and early 20th centuries. In: D. L. Stug, S. Priyadarsini & M. M. Hyman (Eds) *Alcohol Interventions: Historical and Socio-Cultural Approaches*. New York: Haworth Press.

Lenton, S. & Single, E. (1998) The definition of harm reduction. *Drug and Alcohol Review*, **17**, 213–20.

Lester, D. (1988) Genetic theory: an assessment of the hereditability of alcoholism. In: C. D. Chaudron & D. A. Wilkinson (Eds) *Theories on Alcoholism*, pp. 1–28. Toronto: Addiction Research Foundation.

Levin, J. D. (1995) *Introduction to Alcoholism Counseling: A Bio-Psycho-Social Approach*, 2nd edn. New York: Taylor & Francis.

Levy, B. (1972) Five years later: a follow-up of 50 narcotic addicts. *American Journal of Psychiatry*, **7**, 102–106.

Lewin, K. (1951) *Field Theory in Social Science*. New York: Harper.

Lewinsohn, P. M., Sullivan, M. J. & Grosscup, S. J. (1982) Behavioral therapy: clinical applications. In: A. J. Rush (Ed.) *Short-Term Psychotherapies for Depression*, pp. 50–87. New York: Wiley.

Lewis, C. E., Smith, E., Kercher, C., *et al.* (1995) Assessing gender interactions in the prediction of mortality in alcoholic men and women: a twenty-year follow-up study. *Alcohol Clinical and Experimental Research*, **19**, 1162–72.

Lewis, O. (1961) *The Children of Sanchez*. New York: Random House.

Ley, A., Jeffrey, D. P., McLaren, S., *et al.* (2000) Treatment programmes for people with both severe mental illness and substance misuse. *Cochrane Database Systematic Review* (2), CD001088. Chichester, UK: Wiley.

Lilenfield, L. R., Kaye, W. H., Greeno, G. C., *et al.* (1997) Psychiatric disorders in women with bulimia nervosa and their first degree relatives: effects of comorbid substance dependency. *International Journal of Eating Disorders*, **22**(3), 253–64.

Lindstrom, L. (1992) *Managing Alcoholism: Matching Clients to Treatment*. Oxford: Oxford University Press.

Linehan, M. M., Schmidt III, H., Dimeff, L. A., *et al.* (1999) Dialectical behavior therapy for patients with borderline personality disorder and drug dependence. *American Journal of Addiction*, **8**(4), 279–92.

Linquist, C. M., Lindsay, T. S. & White, G. D. (1979) Assessment of assertiveness in drug abusers. *Journal of Clinical Psychology*, **35**, 676–9.

Lipsey, M. W. (1992) Juvenile delinquency treatment: a meta-analytic enquiry into the variability of effects. In: T. D. Cook, H. Cooper, D. S. Coudray, *et al.* (Eds) *Meta-analysis for Explanation: A Casebook*. New York: Russell Sage.

Lipsey, M. W. (1992a) The effect of treatment on juvenile delinquents: results from meta-analysis. In: F. Losel, T. Bliesener & D. Bender (Eds) *Psychology and Law: International Perspectives*. Berlin: de Gruyter.

Litten, R. Z., Croop, R. S., Chick, J., *et al.* (1996) International update: new findings on promising medications. *Alcoholism: Clinical and Experimental Research*, **20**, 216A–18A.

Little, B. B., Snell, L. M., Klein, V. R., *et al.* (1989) Cocaine abuse during pregnancy: maternal and fetal implications. *Obstetrics and Gynaecology*, **73**, 157–60.

Little, B. B., Snell, L. M., Gilstrap III, L. D., *et al.* (1990) Patterns of multiple substance abuse during pregnancy: implications for mother and foetus. *Southern Medical Journal*, **83**(5), 507–509, 518.

Lloyd, C. (1998) Risk factors for problem drug use: identifying vulnerable groups. *Drugs: Education, Prevention, and Policy*, **5**(3), 217–32.

Lloyd, G., Chick, J., Crombie, E., *et al.* (1986) Problem drinkers in medical wards: consumption patterns and disabilities in newly identified male cases. *British Journal of Addiction*, **81**, 789–95.

Lochman, J. E. (1992) Cognitive–behavioural interventions with aggressive boys: three-year follow-up and preventive effects. *Journal of Consulting and Clinical Psychology*, **60**, 426–32.

Lochman, J. E. & Wells, K. C. (1996) A social–cognitive intervention with aggressive children: prevention effects and contextual implementation issues. In: R. deV. Peters & R. J. McMahon (Eds) *Preventing Childhood Disorders, Substance Abuse, and Delinquency*, pp. 111–43. Thousand Oaks, CA: Sage.

Loeber, R. (1990) Development and risk factors of juvenile antisocial behaviour and delinquency. *Clinical Psychology Review*, 10, 1–42.

Loeber, R., Wung, P., Keenan, K., *et al.* (1993) Developmental pathways in disruptive child behavior. *Development and Psychopathology*, 5, 103–33.

Long, J., Knowler, W., Hanson, R., *et al.* (1998) Evidence for genetic linkage to alcohol dependence on chromosomes 4 and 11 from an autosome-wide scan in an American-Indian population. *American Journal of Medical Genetics*, 81, 216–21.

Longabaugh, R. & Morgenstern, J. (2000) Cognitive–behavioural coping skills therapy for alcohol dependence: current status and future directions. *Alcohol Research and Health*, 23, 78–87.

Luborsky, L., McLellan, A. T., Woody, G. E., *et al.* (1985) Therapist success and its determinants. *Archives of General Psychiatry*, 42, 602–11.

Ludwig, A. M. & Stark, L. H. (1974) Alcohol craving: subjective and situational aspects. *Quarterly Journal of Studies on Alcohol*, 35, 899–905.

Ludwig, A. M. & Wikler, A. (1974) Craving and relapse to drinking. *Quarterly Journal of Studies on Alcohol*, 35, 108–30.

Lurie, P. & Drucker, E. (1997) An opportunity lost: HIV infections associated with the lack of needle exchange programs in the United States. *Lancet*, 349, 604–608.

Luthar, S. (1991) Vulnerability and resilience: a study of high risk adolescence. *Child Development*, 62(3), 600–16.

MacGreggor, S. (1999) Medicine, custom, or moral fibre: policy responses to drug misuse. In: N. South (Ed.) *Drugs: Cultures, Controls, & Everyday Life*, pp. 67–85. London: Sage.

MacKenzie, D. M., Langa, A. & Brown, T. M. (1996) Identifying hazardous or harmful alcohol use in medical admissions: a comparison of AUDIT, CAGE and Brief MAST. *Alcohol and Alcoholism*, 31, 591–9.

Madden, G. J., Petry, R. C., Badger, G. J., *et al.* (1997) Impulsive and self-control choices in opioid-dependent patients and non-drug using control participants. *Experimental and Clinical Psychopharmacology*, 5, 256–63.

Maden, A., Swinton, M. & Gunn, J. (1990) Women in prison and use of illicit drugs before arrest. *British Medical Journal*, 301, 1133.

Magura, S., Rosenblum, A., Lovejoy, M., *et al.* (1992) Cocaine-using methadone patients show declines in cocaine use and dysphoria during cognitive–behavioral treatment. In: L. S. Harris (Ed.) *Problems of Drug Dependence* (NIDA Research Monograph No. 132), p. 316. Rockville, MD: National Institute on Drug Abuse.

Magura, S. & Rosenblum, A. (2001) Leaving methadone treatment: lessons learned, lessons forgotten, lessons ignored. *Mount Sinai Journal of Medicine*, 68, 62–74.

Maheswaran, R., Beevers, M. & Beever, D. G. (1992) Effectiveness of advice to reduce alcohol consumption in hypertensive patients. *Hypertension*, 19, 79–84.

Mahoney, M. J. (1987) Psychotherapy and the cognitive sciences: an evolving alliance. *Journal of Cognitive Psychotherapy: An International Quarterly*, 1, 39–59.

Maisto, S. A. & O'Farrell, T. J. (1985) Comments on the validity of Watson *et al.*'s "Do alcoholics give valid self-reports?" *Journal of Studies on Alcohol*, 46, 447–50.

Maisto, S. A., Carey, K. B. & Braddizza, C. M. (1999) Social learning theory. In: K. E. Leonard & H. T. Blane (Eds) *Psychological Theories of Drinking and Alcoholism*, 2nd edn. New York: Guilford Press.

Maisto, S. A., Carey, M. P., Carey, K. B., *et al.* (2000) Use of the AUDIT and the DAST-10 to identify alcohol and drug disorders among adults with a severe and persistent mental illness. *Psychological Assessment*, 12(2), 186–92.

Mallams, J. H., Godley, M. D., Hall, G. M., *et al.* (1982) A social-systems approach to resocialising alcoholics in the community. *Journal of Studies on Alcohol*, 43, 1115–23.

Mann, R. E., MacDonald, S., Stoduto, G., *et al.* (1998) Assessing the potential impact of lowering the legal blood alcohol limit to 50 mg% in Canada. *Transport Canada Publication No. TR 13321 E*. Ottawa: Transport Canada.

Margolin, A., Avants, S. K. & Kosten, T. R. (1995) Mazindol for relapse prevention to cocaine abuse in methadone-maintained patients. *American Journal of Drug Abuse*, 21, 469–81.

Margolis, R. D. & Zweben, J. E. (1998) *Treating Patients with Alcohol and Drug Problems: An Integrated Approach*. Washington, DC: American Psychological Association.

Marks, I. M. (1990) Behavioural (nonchemical) addictions. *British Journal of Addiction*, 85, 1389–94.

Marks, I. M. (1991) Self-administered behavioural treatment. *Behavioural Psychotherapy*, 19, 42–6.

Marlatt, G. A. (1978) Craving for alcohol, loss of control, and relapse: a cognitive–behavioral analysis. In: P. E. Nathan, G. A. Marlatt & T. Loberg (Eds) *Alcoholism: New Directions in Behavioral Research and Treatment*. New York: Plenum Press.

Marlatt, G. A. & Gordon, J. R. (1980) Determinants of relapse: implications for the maintenance of behavior change. In: P. O. Davidson & S. M. Davidson (Eds) *Behavioral Medicine: Changing Health Lifestyles*. New York: Brunner/Mazel.

Marlatt, G. A. (1985) Cognitive factors in the relapse process. In: G. A. Marlatt & J. R. Gordon (Eds) *Relapse Prevention: Maintenance Strategies in the Treatment of Addictive Behaviors*. New York: Guilford Press.

Marlatt, G. A. & Gordon, J. R. (1985) *Relapse Prevention: Maintenance Strategies in the Treatment of Addictive Behaviors*. New York: Guilford Press.

Marlatt, G. A. (1985a) Relapse prevention: Theoretical rationale and overview of the model. In: G. A. Marlatt & J. R. Gordon (Eds) *Relapse Prevention: Maintenance Strategies in the Treatment of Addictive Behaviors*. New York: Guilford Press.

Marlatt, G. A. (1985b) Lifestyle modification. In G. A. Marlatt & J. R. Gordon (Eds) *Relapse Prevention*, pp. 280–348. New York: Guilford Press.

Marlatt, G. A. (Ed.) (1998) *Harm Reduction: Pragmatic Strategies for Managing High-Risk Behaviors*. New York: Guilford Press.

Marlatt, G. A. (1999) From hindsight to foresight: a commentary on Project MATCH. In: J. A. Tucker, D. M. Donovan & G. A. Marlatt (Eds) *Changing Addictive Behavior: Bridging Clinical and Public Health Strategies*. New York: Guilford Press.

Marmot, M. G. & Brunner, E. J. (1991) Alcohol and cardiovascular disease: the status of the U-shaped curve. *British Medical Journal*, 303, 565–8.

Marmot, M. G. (1996) A not-so-sensible drinks policy. *Lancet*, 346, 1643–44.

Marsden, J., Gossop, G., Stewart, D., *et al.* (1998) The Maudsley Addiction Profile (MAP): a brief instrument for assessing treatment outcome. *Addiction*, 93(12), 1857–67.

Marsden, J., Gossop, M., Stewart, D., *et al.* (2000) Psychiatric symptoms among clients seeking treatment for drug dependence – intake data from the National Treatment Outcome Research Study. *British Journal of Psychiatry*, 176, 285–9.

Marselli, P. L., Principi, N., Tognoni, C., *et al.* (1973) Diazepam elimination in premature and full-term infants and children. *Journal of Perinatal Medicine*, 1, 133–41.

Marshall, L. F., Marshall, S. B., Klauber, M. R., *et al.* (1992) The diagnosis of head injury requires a classification system based on computed axial tomography. *Journal of Neurotrauma*, 9, S287–92.

Martin, C. E., Duncan, D. F. & Zunich, E. M. (1983) Students' motives for discontinuing illicit drug-taking. *Health Values*, 7(5), 8–11.

Mason, P. & Wilkinson, G. (1996) The prevalence of psychiatric morbidity OPCS survey of psychiatric morbidity in Britain. *British Journal of Psychiatry*, 168, 1–3.

Masten, A., Best, K. M. & Garmezey, N. (1990) Resilience and development: contributions from the study of children who overcome adversity. *Development and Psychopathology*, 2, 425–44.

Matthews, M., Meaden, J., Petrak, J., *et al.* (2000) Psychological consequences of sexual assault among female attenders at a genitourinary medicine clinic. *Sexually Transmitted Infections*, 76, 49–50.

Mattick, R. P. & Heather, N. (1993) Developments in cognitive and behavioural approaches to substance misuse. *Current Opinion in Psychiatry*, 6, 424–9.

McBride, A. J., Sullivan, G., Blewitt, A., *et al.* (1997) Amphetamine prescribing as a harm reduction measure: a preliminary study. *Addiction Research*, 5, 95–112.

McBride, A. J., Pates, R. M., Arnold, K., *et al.* (2001) Needle fixation, the drug user's perspective: a qualitative study. *Addiction*, 96, 1049–58.

McCarthy, J. E., Siney, C., Shaw, N. J., *et al.* (1999) outcome predictors in pregnant opiate and polydrug users. *European Journal of Paediatrics*, 158, 748–9.

McConnaughy, E. A., DiClemente, C. C., Prochaska, J. O., *et al.* (1983) Stages of change in psychotherapy: measurement and sample profiles. *Psychotherapy: Theory, Research and Practice*, 20, 368–75.

McConnaughy, E. A., DiClemente, C. C., Prochaska, J. O., *et al.* (1989) Stages of change in psychotherapy: a follow-up report. *Psychotherapy*, 26, 494–503.

McCrady, B., Stout, R., Noel, N., *et al.* (1991) Comparative effectiveness of three types of spouse involved alcohol treatment: outcomes 18 months after treatment. *British Journal of Addiction*, 86, 1415–24.

McCusker, M. (2001) Influence of hepatitis C status on alcohol consumption in opiate users in treatment. *Addiction*, 96(7), 1007–14.

McDermott, P. (2002) Flavour of the month: users in service provision. *Druglink*, 17(1), 18–21.

McIntosh, I. D. (1982) Alcohol-related disabilities in general hospital patients: a critical review of the evidence. *International Journal of the Addictions*, 17, 609–39.

McKay, J. R., McLellan, A. T., Durell, J., *et al.* (1998) Characteristics of recipients of Supplemental Security Income (SSI) benefits for drug addicts and alcoholics. *Journal of Nervous and Mental Disease*, 186, 172–80.

McKay, J. R., Alterman, A. I., Mulvaney, F. D., *et al.* (1999) Predicting proximal factors in cocaine relapse and near miss episodes: clinical and theoretical implications. *Drug and Alcohol Dependence*, **56**, 67–78.

McKirnan, D. J. & Petersen, P. L. (1989) Alcohol and drug use among homosexual men and women: epidemiology and population characteristics. *Addictive Behaviours*, **14**, 545.

McLellan, A. T., Luborsky, L., Erdlen, F. R., *et al.* (1980) The Addiction Severity Index: a diagnostic/evaluative profile of substance abuse patients. In: E. Gottheil, A. T. McLellan & K. A. Druley (Eds) *Substance Abuse and Psychiatric Illness*. Oxford: Pergamon Press.

McLellan, A. T., O'Brien, C. P., Kron, R., *et al.* (1980a) Matching substance abuse patients to appropriate treatment methods: a conceptual and methodological approach. *Drug and Alcohol Dependence*, **5**, 189–95.

McLellan, A. T., Luborsky, L., Woody, G. E., *et al.* (1981) Are the 'addiction-related' problems of substance abusers really related? *Journal of Nervous and Mental Disease*, **169**, 232–9.

McLellan, A. T., Woody, G. E., Luborsky, L., *et al.* (1983) Increased effectiveness of substance abuse treatment: a prospective study of patient–treatment 'matching'. *Journal of Nervous and Mental Disease*, **171**, 597–605.

McLellan, A. T., Luborsky, L., Woody, G. E., *et al.* (1983a) Predicting response to alcohol and drug abuse treatments: role of psychiatric severity. *Archives of General Psychiatry*, **40**, 620–25.

McLellan, A. T., Childress, A. R., Ehrman, R., *et al.* (1986) Extinguishing conditioned responses during opioid dependence treatment: turning laboratory findings into clinical procedures, *Journal of Substance Abuse Treatment*, **3**, 33–40.

McLellan, A. T., Kushner, H., Metzger, D., *et al.* (1992) The fifth edition of the Addiction Severity Index: historical critique and normative data. *Journal of Substance Abuse Treatment*, **9**, 199–213.

McLellan, A. T., Arndt, I. O., Metzger, D. S., *et al.* (1993) The effects of psychosocial services in substance abuse treatment. *Journal of the American Medical Association*, **269**(15), 1953–9.

McLellan, A. T., Alterman, A. I., Metzger, D. S., *et al.* (1997) Similarities of outcome predictors across opiate, cocaine, and alcohol treatments: role of treatment services. In: G. A. Marlatt & G. R. VandenBos (Eds) *Addictive Behaviors: Readings on Etiology, Prevention, and Treatment*. pp. 598–645. Washington, DC: American Psychological Association.

McLellan, A. T., Grissom, G. R., Zanis, D., *et al.* (1997a) Improved outcomes from problem service "matching". *Archives of General Psychiatry*, **54**(8), 730–35.

McLellan, A. T., Hagan, T. A., Levine, M., *et al.* (1999) Does clinical case management improve outpatient addictions treatment. *Drug and Alcohol Dependence*, **55**(1–2), 91–103.

McLellan, A. T., Lewis, D. C., O'Brien, C. P., *et al.* (2000) Drug dependence, a chronic medical illness: implications for treatment, insurance, and outcomes evaluation. *Journal of the American Medical Association*, **284**(13), 1689–95.

McMahon, R. J. (1994) Diagnosis, assessment, and treatment of externalizing problems in children: the role of longitudinal data. *Journal of Consulting and Clinical Psychology*, **62**, 901–17.

McMahon, T. J. & Rounsaville, B. J. (2002) Substance abuse and fathering: adding poppa to the research agenda. *Addiction*, **97**(9), 1109–15.

McMurran, M. (1994) *The Psychology of Addiction*. London: Taylor & Francis.

McPhillips, M., Strang, J. & Barnes, T. (1998) Hair analysis: new laboratory ability to test for substance use. *British Journal of Psychiatry*, **173**, 287–90.

McPhillips, M. A., Kelly, F. J., Barnes, T. R. E., *et al.* (1997) Detecting co-morbid substance misuse among people with schizophrenia in the community: a study comparing the results of questionnaires with analysis of hair and urine. *Schizophrenia Research*, **25**(2), 141–8.

McQueeney, D. A., Stanton, A. L. & Sigmon, S. (1997) Efficacy of emotion-focused and problem-focused group therapies for women with fertility problems. *Journal of Behavioral Medicine*, **20**, 313–31.

Mearns, D. & Thorne, B. (1988) *Person-centred Counselling in Action*. London: Sage.

Mensch, B. & Kandel, D. B. (1992) Drug use as a risk factor for premarital teen pregnancy and abortion in a national sample of young white women. *Demography*, **29**(3), 409–27.

Mental Health Act, (1983) London: HMSO.

Metzger, D. S. & Platt, J. J. (1990) Solving vocational problems for addicts in treatment. In: J. J. Platt, C. D. Kaplan & P. J. McKim (Eds) *The Effectiveness of Drug Abuse Treatment: Dutch and American Perspectives*, pp. 110–12. Malabar, FL: Krieger Publishing Co.

Meyer, A. T. (1995) Minimization of substance use: what can be said at this point? In: T. P. Gullotta, G. R. Adams & R. Montemayor (Eds) *Substance Misuse in Adolescence*. London: Sage.

Meyers, R. J. & Smith, J. E. (1995) *Clinical Guide to Alcohol Treatment: The Community Reinforcement Approach*. New York: Guilford Press.

Meyers, R. J., Smith, J. E. & Miller, E. J. (1998) Working through the concerned significant other. In: W. R. Miller & N. Heather (Eds) *Treating Addictive Behaviors*, pp. 149–61. New York: Plenum Press.

Mezey, G. S. & Bewley, S. (1997) Domestic violence in pregnancy. *British Journal of Obstetrics and Gynaecology*, **104**(5), 528–33.

Midanik, L., Tam, T., Greenfield, T., *et al.* (1994) *Risk Functions for Alcohol-Related Problems in a 1988 US National Sample*. Berkeley, CA: California Pacific Medical Center Research Institute, Alcohol Research Group.

Midanik, L. (1995) Alcohol consumption and consequences of drinking in general population surveys. In: H. Holder & G. Edwards (Eds) *The Scientific Rationale for Alcohol Policy*. Oxford: Oxford University Press.

Midanik, L., Tam, T., Greenfield, T., *et al.* (1996) Risk functions for alcohol-related problems in a 1988 US national sample. *Addiction*, **91**, 1427–38.

Milberger, S., Faraone, S. V., Bierderman, J., *et al.* (1999) Substance use disorders in high-risk adolescent offspring. *American Journal on Addictions*, **8**, 211–19.

Miller, P. & Eisler, R. (1977) Assertive behaviour of alcoholics: a descriptive analysis. *Behaviour Therapy*, **8**, 146–9.

Miller, W. R. (1978) Behavioural treatment of problem drinkers: a comparative outcome study of three controlled drinking therapies. *Journal of Consulting and Clinical Psychology*, **46**, 74–86.

Miller, W. R. & Hester, R. K. (1980) Treating the problem drinker: modern approaches. In: W. R. Miller (Ed.) *The Addictive Behaviours: Treatment of Alcoholism, Drug Abuse, Smoking, and Obesity*, pp. 11–141. Oxford: Pergamon Press.

Miller, W. R., Taylor, C. A. & West, J. C. (1980) Focused versus broad-spectrum behavior therapy for problem drinkers. *Journal of Consulting and Clinical Psychology*, **48**, 590–601.

Miller, W. R. (1983) Motivational interviewing with problem drinkers. *Behaviour Psychotherapy*, **11**, 147–72.

Miller, W. R. (1985) Motivation for treatment: a review with special emphasis on alcoholism. *Psychological Bulletin*, **98**, 84–107.

Miller, W. R. & Hester, R. K. (1986) The effectiveness of alcoholism treatment: what research reveals. In: W. R. Miller & N. Heather (Eds) *Treating Addictive Behaviors: Processes of Change*, pp. 121–74. New York: Plenum Press.

Miller, W. R. & Hester, R. K. (1986a) Inpatient alcoholism treatment: who benefits? *American Psychologist*, **41**, 794–805.

Miller, W. R., Sovereign, R. G. & Krege, B. (1988) Motivational interviewing with problem drinkers. II. The Drinkers Check-up as a preventive intervention. *Behavioral Psychotherapy*, **6**, 251–68.

Miller, W. R. & Sovereign, R. G. (1989) The check-up: a model for early intervention in addictive behaviours. In: T. Loberg, W. R. Miller, P. E. Nathan, *et al.* (Eds) *Addictive Behaviours: Prevention and Early Intervention*, pp. 219–31. Amsterdam: Swets & Zeitlinger.

Miller, W. R. & Rollnick, S. (1991) *Motivational Interviewing: Preparing People to Change Addictive Behavior*. New York: Guilford Press.

Miller, W. R., Zweben, A., DiClemente, C. C., *et al.* (1992) *Motivational Enhancement Therapy Manual: A Clinical Research Guide for Therapists Treating Individuals with Alcohol Abuse and Dependence*, vol. 2 (Project MATCH Monograph Series). Rockville, MD: National Institute on Alcohol Abuse and Alcoholism.

Miller, W. R. & Sanchez, V. C. (1993) Motivating young adults for treatment and lifestyle change. In: G. Howard (Ed) *Issues in Alcohol Use and Misuse by Young Adults*, pp. 55–79. Notre Dame, IN: University of Notre Dame Press.

Miller, W. R. & Cooney, N. D. (1994) Designing studies to investigate client–treatment matching. *Journal of Studies on Alcohol*, **12** (Suppl.), 38–45.

Miller, W. R. (1995) Increasing motivation for change. In: R. K. Hester & W. R. Miller (Eds) *Handbook of Alcoholism Treatment Approaches: Effective Alternatives*, 2nd edn, pp. 89–104. Boston: Allyn & Bacon.

Miller, W. R., Brown, J. M., Simpson, T. L., *et al.* (1995) What works? A methodological analysis of the alcohol treatment outcome literature. In: R. K. Hester & W. R. Miller (Eds) *Handbook of Alcoholism Treatment Approaches: Effective Alternatives*, 2nd edn. Boston: Allyn & Bacon.

Miller, W. R. & Tonigan, J. S. (1996) Assessing drinkers' motivation for change: the stages of change readiness and treatment eagerness scale (SOCRATES). *Psychology of Addictive Behaviors*, **10**, 81–9.

Miller, W. R., Andrews, N. R., Wilbourne, P., *et al.* (1998) A wealth of alternatives: effective treatments for alcohol problems. In: W. R. Miller & N. Heather (Eds) *Treating Addictive Behaviors*, 2nd edn, pp. 203–16. New York: Plenum Press.

Miller, W. R. & Rollnick, S. (2002) *Motivational Interviewing: Preparing People for Change*, 2nd edn. New York: Guilford Press.

Miller, W. R. & Wilbourne, P. L. (2002) Mesa Grande: a methodological analysis of clinical trials of treatments for alcohol use disorders. *Addiction*, **97**, 265–77.

Millstein, R. A. (1998) Gender and drug abuse research. *Gender Specific Medicine*, **1**(3), 44–7.

Milroy, C. M. & Forrest, A. R. W. (2000) Methadone deaths: a toxicological analysis. *Journal of Clinical Pathology*, **53**, 277–81.

Ministerial Council on Drug Strategy (1993) *National Drug Strategic Plan 1993–1997*. Canberra: AGPS.

Mitcheson, M. (1994) Drug clinics in the 1970s. In: J. Strang & M. Gossop (Eds) *Heroin Addiction and Drug Policy: The British System*. Oxford: Oxford University Press.

Mitcheson, M. C. & Hartnoll, R. L. (1978) Conflicts in deciding treatment within drug dependency clinics. In: D. J. West (Ed.) *Problems of Drug Abuse in Britain*, pp. 74–7. Cambridge: Cambridge University Institute of Criminology.

Moffitt, T. E. (1993) Adolescence-limited and life-course persistent antisocial behaviour: a developmental taxonomy. *Psychological Review*, **100**, 674–701.

Monti, P. M., Binkoff, J. A., Abrams, D. B., *et al.* (1987) Reactivity of alcoholics and non-alcoholics to drinking cues. *Journal of Abnormal Psychology*, **96**, 122–6.

Monti, P. M., Abrams, D. B., Kadden, R. M., *et al.* (1989) *Treating Alcohol Dependence: A Coping Skills Training Guide*. London: Cassell.

Monti, P. M., Abrams, D. B., Binkoff, J. A., *et al.* (1990) Communication skills training with family and cognitive–behavioural mood management training for alcoholics. *Journal of Studies on Alcohol*, **51**, 263–70.

Monti, P. M., Kadden, R. M., Rohsenow, D. J., *et al.* (2002) *Treating Alcohol Dependence: A Coping Skills Training Guide*, 2nd edn. London: Guilford Press.

Moos, R. H., Finney, J. W. & Cronkite, R. C. (1990) *Alcoholism Treatment: Context, Process, and Outcome*. Oxford: Oxford University Press.

Morgenstern, J. & Longabaugh, R. (2000) Cognitive–behavioural treatment for alcohol dependence: a review of evidence for its hypothesized mechanisms of action. *Addiction*, **95**(10), 1475–90.

Morris, P. (1999) A controlled trial of naltrexone for alcohol dependence: an Australian perspective. Presented at the 1999 Scientific Meeting of the Research Society on Alcoholism, June 26–July 1, 1999, Santa Barbara, CA.

Morrisson, C. L., Ruben, S. & Wakefield, D. (1994) Female street prostitution in Liverpool. *AIDS*, **8**(8), 1194–5.

Morrisson, C. L. & Ruben, S. (1995) The development of healthcare services for drug misusers and prostitutes. *Postgraduate Medical Journal*, **71**(840), 593–7.

Moskowitz, S. (1983) *Love Despite Hate*. New York: Schocken.

Moss, A. R. (1987) AIDS and intravenous drug use: the real heterosexual epidemic. *British Medical Journal*, **294**, 389–90.

Mueser, K. T. (1998) Dual diagnosis: a review of etiological theories. *Addictive Behaviours*, **23**(6), 717–34.

Mullender, A. & Morly, R. (Eds) (1994) *Children Living with Domestic Violence*. London: Whiting & Birch.

Murray, C. (1984) *Losing Ground: American Social Policy 1950–1980*. New York: Basic Books.

Murray, L., Sinclair, D., Cooper, P., *et al.* (1999) The socio-emotional development of 5-year-old children of post-natally depressed mothers. *Journal of Child Psychology and Psychiatry*, **40**(8), 1259–71.

Musselman, D. L. & Kell, M. J. (1995) Prevalence and improvement in psychopathology in opioid-dependent patients participating in methadone maintenance. *Journal of Addictive Diseases*, **14**, 67–82.

Myers, M. G. & Brown, S. A. (1990) Coping responses and relapse among adolescent substance abusers. *Journal of Substance Abuse*, **2**, 177–89.

Myles, J. (1997) Treatment for amphetamine misuse in the United Kingdom. In: H. Klee (Ed.) *Amphetamine Misuse: International Perspectives on Current Trends*, pp. 69–79. Netherlands: Harwood Academic Publishers.

NACAIDS (National Advisory Committee on AIDS) (1987–88) *The Recommendations of an IVDU Working Party*. Canberra: Australian Government Publishing Service.

Nace, E. P. (1982) Therapeutic approaches to the alcoholic marriage. *Psychiatric Clinics of North America*, **5**, 543–5.

Nace, E. P. (1987) *The Treatment of Alcoholism*. New York: Brunner/Mazel.

Nace, E. P. (1995) *Achievement and Addiction: A Guide to the Treatment of Professionals*. New York: Brunner/Mazel.

Najavits, L. M., Weiss, R. D. & Shaw, S. R. (1997) The link between substance abuse and post-traumatic stress disorder in women: a research review. *American Journal of Addiction*, **6**(4), 273–83.

Narcotics Working Party (1972) *Backgrounds and Risks of Drug Use*. The Hague: Government Publishing Office.

Nathan, P. E. (1989) Treatment outcomes for alcoholism in the US: current research. In: T. Lorberg, W. R. Miller, P. E. Nathan, *et al.* (Eds) *Addictive*

Behaviours: Prevention and Early Intervention, pp. 87–101. Amsterdam: Swets & Zeitlinger.

National Health and Medical Research Council (1992) *Is There a Safe Level of Daily Consumption of Alcohol for Men and Women?* Canberra: AGPS.

National Report into Youth Homelessness (1996) *The New Picture of Youth Homelessness*. London: Centrepoint.

National Treatment Agency (2003) *Injectable Heroin (and Injectable Methadone): Potential Roles in Drug Treatment*. London: NTA.

Nawyn, S. J., Richman, J. A., Rospenda, K. M., *et al.* (2000) Sexual identity and alcohol-related outcomes: contributions of workplace harassment. *Journal of Substance Abuse*, 11(3), 289–304.

Neaigus, A., Friedman, S., Goldstein, M., *et al.* (1995) Using dyadic data for a network analysis of HIV infection and risk behaviors among injecting drug users. In: R. H. Needle, S. L. Coyle, S. G. Genser, *et al.* (Eds) *Social Networks, Drug Abuse, and HIV Transmission*, pp. 20–37. Rockville, MD: National Institute on Drug Abuse.

Neale, J. (2000) Suicidal intent in non-fatal illicit drug overdose. *Addiction*, 95(1), 85–93.

Neale, J. (2001) Don't overdo it: overdose prevention and extent. *Druglink*, 16(4), 18–22.

Needle, R., McCubbion, H., Reineck, R., *et al.* (1986) Interpersonal influences in adolescent drug use – the role of older siblings, parents, and peers. *The International Journal of the Addictions*, 21, 739–66.

Neeleman, J. & Farrell, M. (1997) Fatal methadone and heroin overdoses: time trends in England and Wales. *Journal of Epidemiology and Community Health*, 51, 435–7.

Negrete, J. C. (2001) Harm reduction: quo vadis? (Editorial). *Addiction*, 96, 543–5.

Nelson-Jones, R. (1996) *Relating Skills*. London: Cassell.

Newcombe, R. (1992) The reduction of drug-related harm: a conceptual framework for theory, practice and research. In: P. A. O'Hare, R. Newcombe, A. Mathews, *et al.* (Eds) *The Reduction of Drug-Related Harm*. London: Routledge.

NIAAA (National Institute on Alcohol Abuse and Alcoholism) (1989) *Homelessness, Alcohol, and Other Drugs*. Rockville, MD: DHSS, Public Health Service, Alcohol, Drug Abuse and Mental Health Administration.

NIAAA (1993) *Alcohol and Health*. 8th Special Report to the US Congress: Publication No. 94-3699. Washington, DC: US Government Printing Office.

NICE (National Institute for Clinical Excellence) (2000) *Guidance on the Use of Ribavirin and Interferon Alpha for Hepatitis C*. www.nice.org.uk

NIDA (2000) *Community Drug Alert Bulletin – Hepatitis C* (May). National Institute on Drug Abuse, USA.

Nightingale, R. (2002) *Suffolk Drug-Related Deaths Research Project*. Ipswich, UK: Suffolk Blood-Borne Virus Project.

Nisbett, R. E. & Ross, L. (1980) *Human Inference: Strategies and Shortcomings of Social Judgement*. Englewood Cliffs, NJ: Prentice-Hall.

Norwood, R. (1986) *Women Who Love Too Much*. London: Arrow Books.

Nowinski, J. (1999) Self-help groups for addictions. In: B. S. McCrady & E. E. Epstein (Eds) *Addiction: A Comprehensive Guidebook*, pp. 328–46. Oxford: Oxford University Press.

NTA (National Treatment Agency) (2002) *Models of Care for Treatment of Adult Drug Misusers*. Part I. London: NTA.

Obadia, Y., Perrin, V., Feroni, I., *et al.* (2001) Injecting misuse of buprenorphine among French drug users. *Addiction*, 96, 267–72.

O'Brien, C., Childress, A., McLellan, A., *et al.* (1984) Use of naltrexone to extinguish opioid-conditioned responses. *Journal of Clinical Psychiatry*, 45, 53–6.

Odell, S. M., Surtees, P. G., Wainwright, N. W., *et al.* (1997) Determinants of general practitioner recognition of psychological problems in a multi-ethnic inner-city health district. *British Journal of Psychiatry*, 171, 537–41.

Oei, T. P. S. & Jackson, P. (1980) Long-term effects of group and social skills training with alcoholics. *Addictive Behaviours*, 5, 129–36.

Oei, T. P. S. & Jackson, P. R. (1982) Social skill and cognitive–behavioural approaches to the treatment of problem drinking. *Journal of Studies on Alcohol*, 43, 532–47.

O'Farrell, T. J., Cutter, H. S. G., Choquette, K. A., *et al.* (1992) Behavioral marital therapy for male alcoholics: marital and drinking adjustment during the two years after treatment. *Behavior Therapy*, 23, 529–49.

O'Farrell, T. J. (Ed.) (1993) *Treating Alcohol Problems*. New York: Guilford Press.

Offord, D. R., Alder, R. J. & Boyle, M. H. (1986) Prevalence and sociodemographic correlates of conduct disorder. *American Journal of Social Psychiatry*, 6, 272–8.

Olney, J. W., Wozniak, D. F., Farber, N. B., *et al.* (2002) The enigma of foetal alcohol neurotoxicity. *Annals of Medicine*, 34(2), 109–19.

Olweus, D. (1979) Stability of aggressive behaviour patterns in males: a review. *Psychological Bulletin*, 86, 852–975.

O'Malley, S. S., Jaffe, A. J., Chang, G., *et al.* (1996) Six-month follow-up of naltrexone and psychotherapy for alcohol dependence. *Archives of General Psychiatry*, **53**, 217–24.

ONS (Office for National Statistics) (2000) *Health and Well-Being Among Homeless People in Glasgow*. London: HMSO.

ONS (2002) *Tobacco, Alcohol and Drug Use, and Mental Health*. London: Departments of Health.

OPCS (1995) *Economic Activity and Social Functioning of Adults with Psychiatric Disorders*. Report 3. London: OPCS.

Oppenheimer, E. (1991) Alcohol and drug misuse among women. *British Journal of Psychiatry*, **158**(Suppl. 10), 36–44.

Oppenheimer, E. (1994) Women drug misusers: a case for special consideration. In J. Strang & M. Gossop (Eds) *Heroin Addiction and Drug Policy: The British System*. Oxford: Oxford University Press.

Orford, J., Guthrie, S., Nicholls, P., *et al.* (1975) Self-reported coping behaviour of wives of alcoholics and its association with drinking. *Journal of Studies on Alcohol*, **36**, 1254–67.

Orford, J., Oppenheimer, E., Egert, S., *et al.* (1976) The cohesiveness of alcoholism complicated marriages and its influence on treatment outcome. *British Journal of Psychiatry*, **128**, 318–39.

Orford, J. & Edwards, G. (1977) *Alcoholism: A Comparison of Treatment and Advice with a Study of the Influence of Marriage* (Maudsley Monographs No. 26). Oxford: Oxford University Press.

Orford, J., Oppenheimer, E. & Edwards, G. (1979) Abstinence or control: the outcome for excessive drinkers two years after consultation. *Behaviour, Research and Therapy*, **14**, 409–18.

Orford, J. (1985) *Excessive Appetites: A Psychological View of Addictions*. New York: Wiley.

Orford, J. & Keddie, A. (1986) Abstinence or controlled drinking in clinical practice: indications at initial assessment. *Addictive Behaviours*, **11**, 71–6.

Orford, J. (1990) Alcohol and the family: an international review of the literature with implications for research and practice. In: L. T. Kozlowski, H. M. Annis, H. D. Cappell, *et al.* (Eds) *Research Advances in Alcohol and Drug Problems*, vol. 10, pp. 81–4. New York: Plenum Press.

Ormel, J., Von Korff, M., Ustun, T. B., *et al.* (1994) Common mental disorders and disability across cultures: results from the WHO collaborative study on psychological problems in general health care. *Journal of the American Medical Association*, **272**, 1741–8.

Osei, T. P. S. & Jackson, P. (1980) Long-term effects of group and individual social skills training with alcoholics. *Addictive Behaviours*, **5**, 129–36.

Ossip-Klein, D. J. & Rychtarik, R. G. (1993) Behavioral contracts between alcoholics and family members to improve aftercare participation and maintain sobriety after inpatient alcohol treatment. In: T. J. O'Farrell (Ed.) *Treating Alcohol Problems: Marital and Family Interventions*, pp. 281–304. New York: Guilford Press.

Palmer, A. J., Neeser, K., Weiss, C., *et al.* (2000) The long-term cost-effectiveness of improving alcohol abstinence with adjuvant acamprosate. *Alcohol and Alcoholism*, **35**(5), 478–92.

Parker, H. & Chadwick, C. (1987) *Unattractive Alternatives: Dilemmas for Drug Services in Wirral: 1987*. Liverpool, UK: Sub-dept of Social Work Studies, University of Liverpool.

Parker, H., Aldridge, J. & Measham, F. (1998) *Illegal Leisure: The Normalization of Adolescent Recreational Drug Use*. London: Routledge.

Parsons, J., Hickman, M., Turnbull, P. J., *et al.* (2002) Over a decade of syringe exchange: results from the 1997 UK survey. *Addiction*, **97**, 845–50.

Patterson, C. H. (1984) Empathy, warmth and genuineness in psychotherapy: a review of reviews. *Psychotherapy*, **21**(4), 431–8.

Patterson, G. R. (1982) *Coercive Family Process*. Eugene, OR: Castalia.

Patterson, G. R. & Stouthamer-Loeber, M. (1984) The correction of family management practices and delinquency. *Child Development*, **55**, 1299–307.

Patterson, G. R. & Forgatch, M. S. (1985) Therapist behavior as a determinant for client non-compliance: a paradox for the behavior modifier. *Journal of Consulting and Clinical Psychology*, **53**, 846–51.

Patterson, G. R., Reid, J. B. & Dishion, T. J. (1992) *Antisocial Boys*. Eugene, OR: Castalia.

Pattison, E. M., Sobell, M. B. & Sobell, L. C. (Eds) (1977) *Emerging Concepts of Alcohol Dependence*. New York: Springer-Verlag.

Patton, G. C., Coffey, C., Carlin, J. B., *et al.* (2002) Cannabis use and mental health in young people: cohort study. *British Medical Journal*, **325**, 1195–8.

Pavlov, I. P. (1927) *Conditioned Reflexes*. Oxford: Oxford University Press.

Pederson, W. & Hegna, K. (2000) Children and adolescents selling sex. *Tidsskrift for den Norske Laegeforening*, **120**(2), 215–20.

Peele, S. (1991) *The Truth About Addiction and Recovery*. New York: Simon & Schuster.

Peele, S. (1998) All wet. *The Sciences*, **38**(2), 17–21.

Peters, R. deV. & Russell, C. C. (1996) Promoting development and preventing disorder: the Better Beginnings, Better Futures Project. In: R. deV. Peters & R. J. McMahon (Eds) *Preventing Childhood*

Disorders, Substance Abuse, and Delinquency (Banff International Behavioral Science Series). Thousand Oaks, CA: Sage.

Peterson, J. B., Rothfleish, J., Zelazo, P. D., *et al.* (1990) Acute alcohol intoxication and cognitive functioning. *Journal of Studies on Alcohol*, **51**, 114–22.

Petridou, E., Zavitsanos, X., Dessypris, N., *et al.* (1997) Adolescents in high-risk trajectory: clustering of risky behavior and the origins of socioeconomic health differentials. *Preventative Medicine*, **26**, 215–19.

Pettinati, H. M., Volpicelli, J. R., Pierce, J. D., Jr., *et al.* (2000) Improving naltrexone response: an intervention for medical practitioners to enhance medication in alcohol-dependent patients. *Journal of Addictive Diseases*, **19**, 71–83.

Pfeifer, R. W. & Oliver, J. (1997) A study of HIV prevalence in a group of homeless youth in Hollywood, California. *Journal of Adolescent Health*, **20**, 339–42.

PHLS (Public Health Laboratory Service) (1999) *Results of the collaborative survey of salivary antibodies to HIV, HBC and HCV in injecting drug users.* UK: PHLS.

Piccinelli, M., Tessari, E., Bartolomasi, M., *et al.* (1997) Efficacy of the alcohol use disorder identification test as a screening tool for hazardous alcohol intake and related disorders in primary care: a validity study. *British Medical Journal*, **314**, 420–27.

Pickens, R., Bigelow, G. & Griffiths, R. (1973) An experimental approach to treating alcoholism: a case study and one-year follow-up. *Behaviour Research and Therapy*, **11**, 321–5.

Pizzolongo, P. J. (1996) The Comprehensive Child Development Program and other early intervention program models. In: R. deV. Peters & R. J. McMahon (Eds) *Preventing Childhood Disorders, Substance Abuse, and Delinquency* (Banff International Behavioral Science Series). Thousand Oaks, CA: Sage.

Plant, M. & Miller, P. (2001) Young people and alcohol: an international insight. *Alcohol and Alcoholism*, **36**(6), 513–15.

Plant, M. A. & Plant, M. L. (1992) *Risk Takers: Alcohol, Drugs, Sex and Youth.* London: Tavistock/Routledge.

Plant, M. A., Miller, P., Plant, M. L., *et al.* (1994) No such thing as safe glass. *British Medical Journal*, **308**, 6–7.

Plant, M. A. & Plant, M. L. (2001) Heavy drinking by young British women gives cause for concern. *British Medical Journal*, **323**, 1183.

Platt, J. J., Perry, G. M. & Metzger, D. S. (1980) The evolution of a heroin addiction treatment program within a correctional environment. In: R. R. Ross & P. Gendreau (Eds) *Effective Correctional Treatment.* Toronto: Butterworth.

Platt, J. J. & Metzger, D. S. (1987) Cognitive interpersonal problem solving skills and the maintenance of treatment success in heroin addicts. *Psychology of Addictive Behaviour*, **1**, 5–13.

Pleace, N. & Quilgars, D. (1996) *Health and Homelessness in London.* London: King's Fund.

Police Foundation Report (2000) *Drugs and the Law: Report of the Independent Inquiry into the Misuse of Drugs Act 1971.* London: Police Foundation.

Pollock, V. E., Volavka, J., Goodwin, D. W., *et al.* (1983) The EEG after alcohol in men at risk for alcoholism. *Archives of General Psychiatry*, **40**(8), 857–64.

Polnay, L. & Ward, H. (2000) Promoting the health of looked after children (Editorial). *British Medical Journal*, **320**, 661–2.

Poole, R. & Brabbins, C. (1996) Drug-induced psychosis. *British Journal of Psychiatry*, **168**(2), 135–8.

Potter-Efron, R. T. & Potter-Efron, P. S. (1991) *Anger, Alcoholism and Addiction: Treating Individuals, Couples and Families.* London: W. W. Norton.

Powell, J., Bradley, B. & Gray, J. (1992) Classical conditioning and cognitive determinants of subjective craving for opiates: an investigation of their relative contributions. *British Journal of Addiction*, **87**, 1133–44.

Powell, J. H. (1990) *Cue Exposure in Opiate Addiction: Effects and Mechanisms* (Ph.D. thesis, University of London).

Powis, B., Griffiths, P., Gossop, M., *et al.* (1998) Drug use and offending behaviour among young people excluded from school. *Drugs: Education, Prevention, and Policy*, **5**(3), 245–56.

Poynard, T., Bedossa, P. & Opolon, P. (1997) The natural history of liver fibrosis progression in patients with chronic hepatitis C. *Lancet*, **349**, 825–32.

Prochaska, J. O. (1979) *Systems of Psychotherapy: A Transtheoretical Analysis.* Homewood, IL: Dorsey Press.

Prochaska, J. O. & DiClemente, C. C. (1982) Transtheoretical therapy: toward a more integrated model of change. *Psychotherapy: Theory, Research and Practice*, **19**, 276–88.

Prochaska, J. O. & DiClemente, C. C. (1984) *The Transtheoretical Approach: Crossing Traditional Boundaries of Therapy.* Homewood, IL: Dow Jones-Irwin.

Prochaska, J. O., DiClemente, C. C., Velicer, W. F., *et al.* (1985) Predicting change in smoking status for self-changers. *Addictive Behaviours*, **10**, 395–406.

Prochaska, J. O., Velicer, W. F., Rossi, J. S., *et al.* (1994) Stages of change and decisional balance for twelve problem behaviours. *Health Psychology*, **13**, 39–46.

Prochaska, J. O., Diclemente, C. C. & Norcross, J. (1997) In search of how people change: applications to addictive behaviors. In: G. A. Marlatt & G. R. VandenBos (Eds) *Addictive Behaviors: Readings on Etiology, Prevention, and Treatment*. Washington, DC: American Psychological Association.

Project MATCH Research Group (1997) Matching alcoholism treatment to client heterogeneity: Project MATCH post-treatment drinking outcomes. *Journal of Studies on Alcohol*, **58**, 7–29.

Project MATCH Research Group (1998) Matching alcoholism treatments to client heterogeneity: Project MATCH three-year drinking outcomes. *Alcoholism: Clinical and Experimental Research*, **22**, 1300–11.

Rado, S. (1960) The psychic effects of intoxicants: an attempt to evolve a psychoanalytic theory of morbid cravings. In: S. Rado (Ed.) *Psychoanalysis of Behavior*, pp. 25–39. New York: Grune & Stratton. (Original work published 1926)

Raistrick, D. (1988) The 'combined approach' – still an important debate. *British Journal of Addiction*, **83**, 867–9.

Raistrick, D., Bradshaw, J., Tober, G., *et al.* (1994) Development of the Leeds Dependence Questionnaire (LDQ): a questionnaire to measure alcohol and opiate dependence in the context of a treatment evaluation package. *Addiction*, **89**, 563–72.

Raistrick, D., Hodgson, R. & Ritson, B. (Eds) (1999) *Tackling Alcohol Together: The Evidence Base for a UK Alcohol Policy*. London: Free Association Books.

Ramsay, A., Vredenburgh, J., Gallagher, R. M., III, *et al.* (1983) Recognition of alcoholism among patients with psychiatric problems in a family practice clinic. *Journal of Family Practice*, **17**(5), 829–32.

Rankin, H. J. (1982) Cue exposure and response prevention in South London. In: P. Nathan & W. Hay (Eds) *Case Studies in the Behavioral Modification of Alcoholism*, pp. 227–48. New York: Plenum Press.

Ranson, J. H. C. (1984) Acute pancreatitis: pathogenesis, outcome and treatment. *Clinical Gastroenterology*, **13**(3), 343–63.

Raskin, N. (1974) Studies on psychotherapeutic orientation: ideology in practice (*American Academy of Psychotherapists Psychotherapy Research Monographs*). Florida: American Academy of Psychotherapists.

Ratcliffe, J., Ades, A. E., Gibb, D., *et al.* (1998) Prevention of mother-to-child transmission of HIV-1 infection: strategies and their cost effectiveness. *AIDS*, **12**(11), 1381–8.

Rathbone-McCuan, E., Dyer, L. & Wartman, J. (1991) Double jeopardy: chemical dependence and codependence in older women. In: N. Van den Burgh (Ed.) *Feminist Perspectives on Addiction*. New York: Springer-Verlag.

Rawson, R. A., McCann, M. J., Hasson, A. J., *et al.* (2000) Addiction pharmacotherapy 2000: new options, new challenges. *Journal of Psychoactive Drugs*, **32**(4), 371–8.

Reed, M. D. & Rountree, P. W. (1997) Peer pressure and adolescent substance use. *Journal of Quantitative Criminology*, **13**, 143–80.

Reed Report (1992) *A review of health and social services for mentally disordered offenders and others requiring similar services*. London: HMSO.

Regier, D. A., Farmer, M. E., Rae, D. S., *et al.* (1990) Comorbidity of mental disorders with alcohol and other drug abuse: results from the epidemiological catchment area (ECA) study. *Journal of the American Medical Association*, **264**, 2511–18.

Regier, D. A., Rae, D. S., Narrow, W. E., *et al.* (1998) Prevalence of anxiety disorders and their comorbidity with mood and addictive disorders. *British Journal of Psychiatry*, **34** (Suppl.), 24–8.

Rehm, J., Ashley, K. J., Room, R., *et al.* (1996) On the emerging paradigm of drinking patterns and their social and health consequences. *Addiction*, **91**, 1615–21.

Reich, T., Edenberg, H. J., Goate, A., *et al.* (1998) Genome-wide search for genes affecting the risk for alcohol dependence. *American Journal of Medical Genetics*, **81**, 207–15.

Reid, S., Wessely, S., Crayford, T., *et al.* (2001) Medically unexplained symptoms in frequent attenders of secondary health care: retrospective cohort study. *British Medical Journal*, **322**, 1–4.

Report of a Joint Working Group of Royal Colleges of Physicians, Psychiatrists & GPs (1995) *Alcohol and the Heart in Perspective: Sensible Limits Reaffirmed*. London: Royal Colleges of Physicians, Psychiatrists and General Practitioners.

Report of the Departmental Committee on Morphine and Heroin Addiction (1926) (Chaired by Sir Humphrey Rolleston). London: HMSO.

Restoin, A., Montagner, H., Rodriguez, D., *et al.* (1985) Chronologie des comportements de communication et profils de comportement chez le jeune enfant. In: R. E. Trimblay, M. A. Provost & F. F. Strayer (Eds) *Ethologie et Développement de l'Enfant*, pp. 93–130. Paris: Editions Stock/Laurence Pernoud.

Reuter, P. & MacCoun, R. (1995) Drawing lessons from the absence of harm reduction in American drug policy. *Tobacco Control*, **4**, S28–32.

Reynolds, W. (1991) *Reynolds Child Depression Scale Manual*. Odessa, FL: Professional Resources.

Rhodes, T. & Stimson, G. V. (1994) What is the relationship between drug taking and sexual risk? Social relations and social research. *Sociology of Health and Illness*, **16**, 210–28.

Richards, H. M., Reid, M. E. & Watt, G. (2002) Socio-economic variations in response to chest pain: qualitative study. *British Medical Journal*, **324**, 1308–10.

Richmond, R. L., Kehoe, L., Hailstone, S., *et al.* (1999) Quantitative and qualitative evaluations of brief interventions to change excessive drinking, smoking and stress in the police force. *Addiction*, **94**, 1509–21.

Ridenour, T. A., Fazzone, P. & Carter, L. (2002) Classification and assessment. In: C. A. Essau (Ed.) *Substance Abuse and Dependence in Adolescence: Epidemiology, Risk Factors and Treatment*. Hove, Sussex: Brunner-Routledge.

Rietmeijer, C. A., Wolitski, R. J., Fishbein, M., *et al.* (1998) Sex hustling, injection drug use, and non-gay identification by men who have sex with men: associations with high-risk sexual behaviors and condom use. *Sexually Transmitted Diseases*, **25**(7), 353–60.

Rist, F. & Watzl, H. (1983) Self-assessment of relapse risk and assertiveness in relation to treatment outcome of female alcoholism. *Addictive Behaviours*, **8**, 121–7.

Robins, L. N., Davis, D. H. & Goodwin, D. W. (1974) Drug users in Vietnam: a follow-up on return to the USA. *American Journal of Epidemiology*, **99**, 235–49.

Robins, L. N., Helzer, J. E. & Davis, D. H. (1975) Narcotic use in South East Asia and afterwards. *Archives of General Psychiatry*, **32**, 955–61.

Robins, L. N. & Przybeck, T. R. (1985) Age of onset of drug use as a factor in drug and other disorders. In: C. L. Jones & R. J. Battjes (Eds) *Etiology of Drug Abuse: Implications for Prevention* (NIDA Research Monograph No. 56), pp. 178–93. Rockville, MD: National Institute on Drug Abuse.

Robson, P. (1992) Opiate misusers: are treatments effective? In: K. Hawton & P. Cowen (Eds) *Practical Problems in Clinical Psychiatry*, pp. 141–58. Oxford: Oxford University Press.

Roche, A., Evans, K. R. & Stanton, W. R. (1997) Harm reduction: roads less travelled to the Holy Grail. *Addiction*, **92**(9), 1207–12.

Roche, A. (1998) Alcohol and drug education and training: a review of the key issues. *Drugs: Education, Prevention, and Policy*, **5**, 85–100.

Rogers, C. R. (1951) *Client-Centred Therapy: Its Practice, Implications and Theory*. Boston: Houghton Mifflin.

Rohsenow, D. J. & Marlatt, G. A. (1981) The balanced placebo design: methodological considerations. *Addictive Behaviours*, **6**, 107–22.

Rohsenow, D. J., Smith, R. E. & Johnson, J. (1986) Stress management as a prevention program for heavy social drinkers: cognitions, affect, drinking and individual differences. *Addictive Behaviours*, **10**, 45–54.

Rohsenow, D. J., Niaura, R. S., Childress, A. R., *et al.* (1990–91) Cue reactivity in addictive behaviours: theoretical and treatment implications. *The International Journal of the Addictions*, **25**, 957–93.

Rohsenow, D. J., Monti, P. M. & Abrams, D. B. (1995) Cue exposure treatment in alcohol dependence. In: D. C. Drummond, S. T. Tiffany, S. Glautier, *et al.* (Eds) *Addictive Behaviour: Cue Exposure Theory and Practice*, pp. 169–96. Chichester, UK: Wiley.

Rohsenow, D. J., Monti, P. M., Rubonis, A. V., *et al.* (2001) Cue exposure with coping skills training and communication skills training for alcohol dependence: six and twelve month outcomes. *Addiction*, **96**, 1161–74.

Roizen, R., Cahalan, D. & Shanks, P. (1978) Spontaneous remission among untreated problem drinkers. In: D. B. Kandel (Ed.) *Longitudinal Research on Drug Use: Empirical Findings and Methodological Issues*, pp. 197–221. Washington, DC: Hemisphere.

Rollnick, S., Heather, N., Gold, R., *et al.* (1992) Development of a short 'readiness to change' questionnaire for use in brief opportunistic interventions among excessive drinkers. *British Journal of Addiction*, **87**, 743–54.

Rollnick, S. (1996) Behaviour change in practice: targeting individuals. *International Journal of Obesity*, **20**(Suppl. 1), 22–6.

Rollnick, S. (2001) Enthusiasm, quick fixes and premature controlled trials. *Addiction*, **96**(12), 1769–70.

Rollnick, S., Allinson, J., Balliotes, S., *et al.* (2002) Variations on a theme: motivational interviewing and its adaptations. In: W. R. Miller & S. Rollnick (Eds) *Motivational Interviewing: Preparing People for Change*, 2nd edn, pp. 270–83. New York: Guilford Press.

Room, R., Bondy, S. & Ferris, J. (1995) The risk of harm to oneself from drinking, Canada 1989. *Addiction*, **90**, 499–513.

Rosenbaum, M. (1990) *Learned Resourcefulness: On Coping Skills, Self-Control, and Adaptive Behavior*. New York: Springer-Verlag.

Rosenberg, H. (1983) Relapsed versus non-relapsed alcohol abusers: coping skills, life events and social support. *Addictive Behaviours*, **8**, 183–6.

Rosenberg, S. D. (1979) Relaxation training and a differential assessment of alcoholism. *Dissertation Abstracts International*, University Microfilms No. 8004362. Ann Arbor, MI: University of Michigan.

Rosenthal, R. N. & Miner, C. R. (1997) Differential diagnosis of substance-induced psychosis and schizophrenia in patients with substance use disorders. *Schizophrenia Bulletin*, **23**(2), 187–93.

Rotgers, F., Keller, D. S. & Morgenstern, J. (1996) *Treating Substance Abuse: Theory and Technique*. New York: Guilford Press.

Rotily, M., Delorme, C., Obadia, Y., *et al.* (1998) Survey of French prison found that injecting drug use and tattooing occurred. *British Medical Journal*, **316**, 777.

Rotter, J. (1966) Generalised expectancies for internal vs external control of reinforcement. *Psychological Monograph*, **80**, 60.

Rounsaville, B. J. & Carroll, K. M. (1997) Individual psychotherapy. In: J. H. Lowinson, P. Ruiz, R. B. Millman, *et al.* (Eds) *Substance Abuse: A Comprehensive Textbook*, 3rd edn, pp. 430–39. New York: Williams & Wilkins.

Rounsaville, B. J. & Kosten, T. R. (2000) Treatment for opioid dependence: quality and access. *Journal of the American Medical Association*, **283**, 1337–9.

Roy, E., Haley, N., Leclerc, P., *et al.* (2000) Prevalence of HIV infection and risk behaviours among Montreal street youth. *International Journal of STD and AIDS*, **11**, 241–7.

Roy, E., Haley, N., Leclerc, P., *et al.* (2002) Drug injection among street youth: the first time. *Addiction*, **97**, 1003–1009.

Royal College of General Practitioners (1986) *Alcohol: A Balanced View*. London: RCGP.

Royal College of Physicians (1987) *A Great and Growing Evil: The Medical Consequences of Alcohol Abuse*. London: Tavistock.

Royal College of Psychiatrists (1979) *Alcohol and Alcoholism*. London: Tavistock.

Royal College of Psychiatrists (1986) *Alcohol: Our Favourite Drug*. London: Tavistock.

Rumball, D. & Williams, J. (1997) Rapid opiate detoxification: assessment is needed to exclude certain patients before detoxification. *British Medical Journal*, **314**(7091), 1365.

Rush, A. J., Beck, A. T., Kovacs, M., *et al.* (1977) Comparative efficiency of cognitive therapy versus pharmacotherapy in outpatient depression. *Cognitive Therapy and Research*, **1**, 17–37.

Russell, M. (1990) Prevalence of alcoholism among children of alcoholics. In: M. Windle & J. S. Searles (Eds) *Children of Alcoholics: Critical Perspectives*, pp. 9–38. New York: Guilford Press.

Russell, M. A. H., Wilson, C., Taylor, C., *et al.* (1979) Effect of general practitioners' advice against smoking. *British Medical Journal*, **283**, 231–5.

Russell, M. N. (1992) *Clinical Social Work*. Newbury Park: Sage.

Rutter, M. (1985) Resilience in the face of adversity: protective factors and resistance to psychiatric disorder. *British Journal of Psychiatry*, **147**, 598–611.

Rutter, S., Dolan, K., Wodak, A., *et al.* (2001) *Prison Syringe Exchange: A Review of International Research and Program Development*. Technical Report No. 112. Sydney: National Drug and Alcohol Research Centre.

Ryan, C. & Futterman, D. (1998) *Lesbian and Gay Youth: Care and Counselling*. Columbia: Columbia University Press.

Rychtarik, R. G., Prue, D. M., Rapp, S. R., *et al.* (1992) Self-efficacy, aftercare, and relapse in a treatment programme for alcoholics. *Journal of Studies on Alcohol*, **53**, 435–40.

Sanchez-Craig, M. & Lei, H. (1986) Disadvantages of imposing the goal of abstinence on problem drinkers: an empirical study. *British Journal of Addiction*, **81**, 505–12.

Sanchez-Craig, M. (1993) *Saying When: How to Quit Drinking or Cut Down*. Toronto: Addiction Research Foundation.

Saunders, B., Wilkinson, C. & Phillips, M. (1995) The impact of a brief motivational intervention with opiate users attending a methadone programme. *Addiction*, **90**, 415–24.

Saunders, J., Aasland, O., Babor, T., *et al.* (1993) Development of the alcohol use disorders identification test (AUDIT): WHO collaborative project on early detection of persons with harmful alcohol consumption. II. *Addiction*, **88**, 791–804.

Saunders, J. B., Wodak, A. D. & Williams, R. (1985) Past experience of advice and treatment for drinking problems of patients with alcoholic liver disease. *British Journal of Addiction*, **80**, 51–6.

Saunders, W., Wilkinson, C. & Allsop, S. (1991) Motivational intervention with heroin users attending a methadone clinic. In: W. R. Miller & S. Rollnick (Eds) *Motivational Interviewing: Preparing People to Change Addictive Behavior*, pp. 279–92. New York: Guilford Press.

Saunders, W. M. & Kershaw, M. D. (1979) Spontaneous remission from alcoholism – a community study. *British Journal of Addiction*, **74**, 251–65.

Scheier, M. F. & Carver, C. S. (1987) Dispositional optimism and physical well-being: the influence of generalised outcome expectancies on health. *Journal of Personality*, **55**, 169–210.

Schifano, F., Oyefeso, A., Webb, L., *et al.* (2003) Review of deaths related to taking Ecstasy, England and Wales, 1997–2000. *British Medical Journal*, **326**, 80–81.

Schuckit, M. A. (1995) Genetics and the risk for alcoholism. *Journal of the American Medical Association*, **254**(28), 2614–17.

Schuckit, M. A. (1995a) Ethanol-induced changes in body sway in men at high alcoholism risk. *Archives of General Psychiatry*, **42**, 375–9.

Schumacher, J. E., Milby, J. B., McNamara, C. L., *et al* (1998) Effective treatment of homeless substance abusers: the role of contingency management. In: S. T. Higgins & K. Silverman (Eds) *Motivating Behavior Change Among Illicit Drug Abusers*, pp. 77–94. Washington, DC: American Psychological Association.

Schwartz, G. E. (1982) Testing the biopsychosocial model: the ultimate challenge facing behavioural medicine? *Journal of Consulting and Clinical Psychology*, **50**, 1040–53.

Schwartz, J., Jacobson, A., Hauser, S., *et al.* (1989) Explorations of vulnerability and resilience: case studies of diabetic adolescents and their families. In: T. Dugan & R. Coles (Eds) *The Child in Our Times: Studies in the Development of Resiliency*, pp. 134–44. New York: Brunner/Mazel.

SCODA (1999) *Young People and Drugs: Policy Guidance for Drug Interventions*. The Standing Conference on Drug Abuse and The Childrens' Legal Centre, London.

Scott, H., Johnson, S., Menezes, P., *et al.* (1998) Substance misuse and the risk of aggression and offending among the severely mentally ill. *British Journal of Psychiatry*, **172**, 345–50.

Scott, J. (1993) Homelessness and mental illness. *British Journal of Psychiatry*, **162**, 314–24.

Scott, J., Gilvarry, E. & Farrell, M. (1998a) Managing anxiety and depression in drug and alcohol dependency. *Addictive Behaviours*, **23**(6), 919–31.

Scott, R. T. A., Gruer, L. D., Wilson, P., *et al.* (1995) Glasgow has an innovative scheme for encouraging GPs to manage drug misusers (Letter). *British Medical Journal*, **310**, 464–5.

Scott-Gliba, E., Minne, C. & Mezey, G. (1995) The psychological, behavioural and emotional impact of surviving an abusive relationship. *Journal of Forensic Psychiatry*, **6**(2), 343–58.

Seaman, S. R., Brettle, R. P. & Gore, S. M. (1998) Mortality from overdose among injecting drug users recently released from prison: database linkage study. *British Medical Journal*, **316**, 426–8.

Seivewright, N. & Daly, C. (1997) Personality disorder and drug use: a review. *Drug and Alcohol Review*, **16**, 235–50.

Sellers, E. M., Higgins, G. A., Tomkins, D. R., *et al.* (1991) Opportunities for treatment of psychoactive substance use disorders with serotonergic medications. *Journal of Clinical Psychiatry*, **52**, 12(Suppl.), 49–54.

Selzer, M. (1971) The Michigan Alcoholism Screening Test: the quest for a new diagnostic instrument. *American Journal of Psychiatry*, **127**, 1653–8.

Selzer, M. L., Vinokur, A. & Van Rooijen, L. A. (1974) A self-administered Short Michigan Alcoholism Screening Test (SMAST). *Journal of Studies on Alcohol*, **36**, 1653–8.

Seppa, K., Makela, R. & Sillanaukee, P. (1995) Effectiveness of the Alcohol Use Disorders Identification Test in occupational health screenings. *Alcohol Clinical and Experimental Research*, **19**, 999–1003.

Seppa, K., Makela, R. & Sillanaukee, P. (1998) Five-shot questionnaire on heavy drinking. *Alcohol Clinical and Experimental Research*, **22**, 1788–91.

Shaner, A., Douglas, E., Tucker, L. J., *et al.* (1998) Disability income, cocaine use, and contingency management among patients with cocaine dependence and schizophrenia. In: S. T. Higgins & K. Silverman (Eds) *Motivating Behavior Change Among Illicit Drug Abusers*, pp. 95–121. Washington, DC: American Psychological Association.

Shaper, A. G. (1990) Alcohol and mortality: a review of prospective studies. *British Journal of Addiction*, **85**, 837–47.

Shawcross, M., Robertson, S., Jones, A., *et al.* (1996) *Family and Alcohol Project: Report on a Pilot Project*. Edinburgh: Lothian Regional Council Social Work Department.

Shearer, J., Wodak, A., Mattick, R. P., *et al.* (2001) Pilot randomised controlled study of dexamphetamine substitution for amphetamine dependence. *Addiction*, **96**(9), 1289–96.

Sheehan, D. V., Lecrubier, Y., Sheehan, K. H., *et al.* (1998) The Mini-International Neuropsychiatric Interview (MINI): the development and validation of a structured diagnostic psychiatric interview for DSM-IV and ICD-10. *Journal of Clinical Psychiatry*, **59**(Suppl. 20), 22–33; quiz 34–57.

Sheehan, M., Oppenheimer, E. & Taylor, C. (1993) Opiate users and the first years after treatment: outcome analysis of the proportion of the follow-up time spent in abstinence. *Addiction*, **88**(12), 1679–89.

Shepherd, J. P., Price, M. & Shenfine, P. (1990) Glass abuse in urban licenced premises. *Journal of the Royal Society of Medicine*, **83**, 276–7.

Shepherd, J. P. (1994) Preventing injuries from bar glasses. *British Medical Journal*, **308**, 932–3.

Sheridan, J., Lovell, S., Turnbull, P., *et al.* (2000) Pharmacy-based needle exchange in South East

England: a survey of service providers. *Addiction*, 95(10), 1551–60.

Shiner, M. & Newburn, T. (1996) Young people, drugs and peers education. Paper 13, Home Office Drugs Prevention Initiative.

Shkolnikov, V., McKee, M. & Leon, D. A. (2001) Changes in life expectancy in Russia in the mid-1990s. *Lancet*, 357, 917–21.

Shoptaw, S., Rotheram-Fuller, E., Xiaowei, Y., *et al.* (2002) Smoking cessation in methadone maintenance. *Addiction*, 97(10), 1317–28.

Siegel, S. (1983) Classical conditioning, drug tolerance, and drug dependence. In: Y. Israel, F. B. Glaser, H. Kalant, *et al.* (Eds) *Research Advances in Alcohol and Drug Problems*, vol. 7, pp. 207–46. New York: Plenum Press.

Siegel, S. (1989) Pharmacological conditioning and drug effects. In: A. J. Goudie & M. W. Emmett-Oglesby (Eds) *Psychoactive Drugs: Tolerance and Sensitization*. Clifton, NJ: Humana Press.

Simpson, D. D., Joe, G. W., Fletcher, B. W., *et al.* (1999) A national evaluation of treatment outcomes for cocaine dependence. *Archives of General Psychiatry*, 56, 507–14.

Sinclair, J. D., Adkins, J. & Walker, S. (1973) Morphine-induced suppression of voluntary alcohol drinking in rats. *Nature*, 246, 425–7.

Sinclair, J. D. (1990) Drugs to decrease alcohol drinking. *Annals of Medicine*, 22, 357–62.

Sinclair, J. D., Scheinin, H. & Lammintausta, R. (1992) Method for treating alcoholism with nalmefene. USA patent 5 086 058.

Single, E. & Wortley, S. (1993) Drinking in various settings as it relates to demographic variables and level of consumption: findings from a national survey in Canada. *Journal of Studies on Alcohol*, 54, 590–99.

Single, E. (1995) A harm reduction approach for alcohol: between the lines of 'Alcohol Policy and the Public Good'. *Addiction*, 90(2), 195–9.

Single, E., Robson, L., Xie, X., *et al.* (1996) *The Costs of Substance Abuse in Canada*. Ottawa: Canadian Centre on Substance Abuse.

Singleton, N., Meltzer, H. & Gatward, R. (1998) *Psychiatric Morbidity Among Prisoners in England and Wales*. London: HMSO.

Sisson, R. W. & Azrin, N. (1989) Family members' involvement to initiate and promote the treatment of problem drinkers. *Journal of Behavior Therapy and Experimental Psychiatry*, 17, 15–21.

Sisson, R. W. & Azrin, N. H. (1993) Community reinforcement training for families: a method to get alcoholics into treatment. In: T. J. O'Farrell (Ed.) *Treating Alcohol Problems*, pp. 34–53. New York: Guilford Press.

Skinner, H. A., Holt, S., Schuller, R., *et al.* (1984) Identification of alcohol abuse using laboratory tests and a history of trauma. *Annals of Internal Medicine*, 101, 847–51.

Skog, O. J. (1999) Alcohol policy: why and roughly how? *Nordic Studies on Alcohol and Drugs*, 16, 21–34.

Smith, C., Lizotte, A., Thornberry, T., *et al.* (1995) Resilient youth: identifying factors that prevent high-risk youth from engaging in delinquency and drug use. In: J. Hagan (Ed.) *Delinquency and Disrepute in the Life Course*. Greenwich, CT: JAI Press.

Smith, E. M., North, C. S. & Spitznagel, E. L. (1993) Alcohol, drugs, and psychiatric comorbidity among homeless women: an epidemiologic study. *Journal of Clinical Psychiatry*, 54(3), 82–7.

Smith R. (2001) Social exclusion: old problem, new name. *British Medical Journal*, 323, 28 July (Editor's Choice).

SMMGP (Substance Misuse Management in General Practice) (2002) Primary care responds to the challenge. *Network*, 2, 1.

Snowden, P. (2001) Substance misuse and violence: the scope and limitations of forensic psychiatry's role. *Advances in Psychiatric Treatment*, 7, 189–96.

Snyder, C. R., Harris, C., Anderson, J. R., *et al.* (1991) The will and the ways: development and validation of an individual difference measure of hope. *Journal of Personality and Social Psychology*, 60, 570–85.

Snyder, J. J. & Patterson, G. R. (1995) Individual differences in social aggression: a test of a reinforcement model of socialization in the natural environment. *Behavior Therapy*, 26, 371–91.

Sobell, M. B., Sobell, L. C., Bogardis, J., *et al.* (1992a) Problem drinkers' perceptions of whether treatment goals should be self-selected or therapist-selected. *Behaviour Therapy*, 23, 43–52.

Sobell, L. C., Sobell, M. B. & Toneatto, T. (1992) Recovery from alcohol problems without treatment. In: N. Heather, W. R. Miller & J. Greeley (Eds) *Self-Control and the Addictive Behaviors*, pp. 198–242. New York: Maxwell/McMillan.

Sobell, M. B. & Sobell, L. C. (1993) *Problem Drinkers: Guided Self-Change Treatment*. New York: Guilford Press.

Sobell, M. B. & Sobell, L. C. (1993a) Treatment for problem drinkers: a public health priority (Ch. 7). In: J. S. Baer, G. A. Marlatt & R. J. McMahon (Eds)

Addictive Behaviors Across the Lifespan: Prevention, Treatment, and Policy Issues, pp. 138–57. Beverly Hills, CA: Sage.

Sobell, M. B. & Sobell, L. C. (1995) Controlled drinking after 25 years: how important was the great debate? *Addiction*, **90**(9), 1149–53.

Sonne, S. C. & Brady, K. T. (1999) Substance abuse and bipolar co-morbidity. *Psychiatric Clinics of North America*, **22**(3), 609–27.

Sood, B., Delaney-Black, V., Covington, C., *et al.* (2001) Low-dose prenatal alcohol exposure linked to behaviour problems. *Paediatrics*, **108**(2), 34–6.

Soyka, M. (2000) Substance misuse, psychiatric disorder and violent and disturbed behaviour. *British Journal of Psychiatry*, **176**, 345–50.

Spivack, G., Platt, J. J. & Shure, M. B. (1976) *The Problem-Solving Approach to Adjustment*. San Francisco: Jossey-Bass.

Stacey, A. W., Newcomb, M. D. & Bentler, P. M. (1992) Interactive and high-order effects of social influences on drug use. *Journal of Health and Social Behaviour*, **33**, 226–41.

Stall, R. (1983) An examination of spontaneous remission from problem drinking in the bluegrass region of Kentucky. *Journal of Drug Issues*, **13**, 191–206.

Stallings, M. C., Hewitt, J. K., Cloninger, C. R., *et al.* (1996) Genetic and environmental structure of the Tridimensional Personality Questionnaire: three or four temperament dimensions? *Journal of Personal and Social Psychology*, **70**, 127–40.

Stanton, M. D. (1982) Appendix A: review of reports on drug abusers' family living arrangements and frequency of family contact. In: M. D. Stanton and T. C. Todd (Eds) *The Family Therapy of Drug Abuse and Addiction*. New York: Guilford Press.

Stark, C., Scott, J., Hill, M., *et al.* (1989) *A Survey of the Long-Stay Users of DSS Resettlement Units: A Research Report*. London: Department of Social Security.

Stark, E. & Flitcraft, A. (1996) *Women at Risk: Domestic Violence and Women's Health*. London: Sage.

Steer, R. A., Emery, G. D. & Beck, A. T. (1980) Correlates of self-reported and clinically assessed depression in male heroin addicts. *Journal of Clinical Psychology*, **36**(3), 789–800.

Steinglass, P., Bennett, L., Wolin, S., *et al.* (1987) *The Alcoholic Family*. New York: Basic Books.

Steinglass, P. (1994) Family therapy: alcohol. In: M. Galanter & H. D. Kleber (Eds) *Textbook of Substance Abuse Treatment*, pp. 315–29. Washington, DC: American Psychiatric Press.

Stephens, R. S., Roffman, R. A. & Curtin, L. (2000) Comparison of extended versus brief treatments for marijuana use. *Journal of Consulting and Clinical Psychology*, **68**, 898–908.

Stewart, J., de Wit, H. & Eikelboom, R. (1984) Role of unconditioned and conditioned drug effects in the self-administration of opiates and stimulants. *Psychological Review*, **91**, 251–68.

Stimson, G. V. (1995) AIDS and injecting drug use in the United Kingdom, 1987–93: the policy response and the prevention of the epidemic. *Social Science and Medicine*, **41**, 699–716.

Stimson, G. V. (1996) Has the United Kingdom averted an epidemic of HIV-1 infection among drug injectors? *Addiction*, **91**(8), 1085–8.

Stimson, G. V., Hunter, G. M., Donoghue, M. C., *et al.* (1996) HIV-1 prevalence in community-wide samples of injecting drug users in London, 1990–93. *AIDS*, **10**, 657–66.

Stimson, G. V. & Fitch, C. (2000) What is the relationship between demand reduction and harm reduction? Presentation at the 3rd International Seminary on Drug Abuse – Challenges in Post-Modernity: Diversity and Perspectives, Rio de Janeiro, Brazil.

Stockwell, T., Hodgson, R., Edwards, G., *et al.* (1979) The development of a questionnaire to measure severity of alcohol dependence. *British Journal of Addiction*, **74**, 79–87.

Stockwell, T., Bolt, L., Milner, I., *et al.* (1990) Home detoxification for problem drinkers: acceptability to clients, relatives and general practitioners, and outcome after 60 days. *British Journal of Addiction*, **85**(1), 61–70.

Stockwell, T. (1991) Dealing with alcohol problems in the community. In: W. R. Miller & S. Rollnick (Eds) *Motivational Interviewing: Preparing People to Change Addictive Behavior*, pp. 272–8. New York: Guilford Press.

Stockwell, T., Hawks, D., Lang, E., *et al.* (1994) *Unravelling the Prevention Paradox*. Perth: National Centre for Research into the Prevention of Drug Abuse.

Stockwell, T., Norberry, J. & Solomon, R. (1995) Liquor laws and the prevention of violence in and around Australian pubs and clubs. Paper presented at the International Conference on Social and Health Effects of Different Drinking Patterns, Toronto, Canada.

Stockwell, T., Hawks, D., Lang, E., *et al.* (1996) Unravelling the preventive paradox for acute alcohol problems. *Drug and Alcohol Review*, **15**, 7–15.

Vaillant, G. E. (1988) What can long-term follow-up teach us about relapse and prevention of relapse in addiction? *British Journal of Addiction*, 83, 1147–57.

Vaillant, G. E. (1995) *The Natural History of Alcoholism Revisited*. Cambridge, MA: Harvard University Press.

Vaillant, G. A. (1996) A long-term follow-up of male alcohol abuse. *Archives of General Psychiatry*, 53, 243–9.

Valera, R. J., Sawyer, R. G. & Schiraldi, G. R. (2001) Perceived health needs of inner city prostitutes: a preliminary study. *American Journal of Health Behavior*, 25(1), 50–59.

Van Beek, I., Dwyer, R., Dore, G. J., *et al.* (1998) Infection with HIV and hepatitis C virus among injecting drug users in a prevention setting: retrospective cohort study. *British Medical Journal*, 317, 433–7.

van Bilsen, H. & van Emst, A. (1986) Heroin addiction and motivational milieu therapy. *International Journal of Addictions*, 21, 707–13.

van Brussel, G. & Buning, E. C. (1988) Public health management of AIDS and drugs in Amsterdam. In: L. S. Harris (Ed.) *Problems of Drug Dependence* (NIDA Research Monograph No. 90), pp. 295–301. Rockville, MD: DHHS.

Vaux, A. (1983) Variations in social support associated with gender, ethnicity, and age. *Journal of Social Issues*, 41(1), 89.

Velicer, W. F., DiClemente, C. C., Prochaska, J. O., *et al.* (1985) Decisional balance measure for assessing and predicting smoking status. *Journal of Personality and Social Psychology*, 48, 1279–89.

Velicer, W. F., DiClemente, C. C., Rossi, J. S., *et al.* (1990) Relapse situations and self-efficacy: an integrative model. *Addictive Behaviours*, 15, 271–83.

Velleman, R., Bennett, G., Miller, T., *et al.* (1993) The families of problem drug users: a study of 50 close relatives. *Addiction*, 88, 1281–9.

Velleman, R., Mistral, W. & Sanderling, L. (1997) Involving Parents in Drugs Prevention. Paper presented at the Drugs Prevention Initiative Research Conference, Liverpool.

Vento, S. & Cainelli, F. (2002) *Lancet Infectious Diseases*, 2, 303–309.

Verheul, R., van dem Brink, W. & Hartgens, C. (1995) Prevalence of personality disorders among alcoholics and drug addicts: an overview. *European Addiction Research*, 1, 166–77.

Verheul, R., Kranzler, H. R., Poling, J., *et al.* (2000) Co-occurrence of Axis I and Axis II disorders in substance abuse. *Acta Psychiatrica Scandanavica*, 101(2), 110–18.

Volpicelli, J. R., O'Brien, C. P., Alterman, A. I., *et al.* (1990) Naltrexone and the treatment of alcohol dependence: initial observations. In: L. D. Reid (Ed.) *Opioids, Bulimia, and Alcohol Abuse and Alcoholism*, pp. 195–214. New York: Springer-Verlag.

Volpicelli, J. R., Alterman, A. I., Hayashida, M., *et al.* (1992) Naltrexone in the treatment of alcohol dependence. *Archives of General Psychiatry*, 49, 876–80.

Volpicelli, J. R., Pettinati, H. M., McLellan, A. T., *et al.* (2001) *Combining Medication and Psychosocial Treatments for Addictions: The BRENDA Approach*. New York: Guilford Press.

Vuchinich, R. E. (1997) Behavioral economics of drug consumption. In: B. A. Johnson & J. D. Roache (Eds) *Drug Addiction and its Treatment: Nexus of Neuroscience and Behavior*, pp. 73–90. Philadelphia: Lippincott-Raven.

Vuchinich, R. E. & Simpson, C. A. (1998) Hyperbolic temporal discounting in social drinkers and problem drinkers. *Experimental and Clinical Psychopharmacology*, 6, 292–305.

Vuchinich, R. E. & Tucker, J. A. (1998) Choice, behavioral economics, and addictive behavior patterns. In: W. R. Miller & N. Heather (Eds) *Treating Addictive Behaviors*, 2nd edn. New York: Plenum Press.

Waldorf, D. (1983) The social–psychological processes of control and recovery from substance abuse. *Journal of Drug Issues*, 13, 189–90.

Walker, L. E. (1979) *The Battered Woman*. New York: Harper & Row.

Wallace, P., Cutler, S. & Haines, A. (1988) Randomised controlled trial of general practitioner intervention in patients with excessive alcohol consumption. *British Medical Journal*, 297, 663–8.

Waller, T. (1993) *Working with GPs: Drugs Work Booklet*, No 5. London: Institute for the Study of Drug Dependence.

Wanigaratne, S., Wallace, W., Pullin, J., *et al.* (1990) *Relapse Prevention for Addictive Behaviours: A Manual for Therapists*. Oxford: Blackwell Science.

Warburton, F. (1998) Tackling social exclusion: the work of NACRO. In: A. Marlow & J. Pitts (Eds) *Planning Safer Communities*, pp. 15–22. Lyme Regis: Russel House.

Ward, H., Day, S. & Weber, J. (1999) Risky business: health and safety in the sex industry over a 9-year period. *Sexually Transmitted Infection*, 75(5), 340–43.

Ward, H., Pallecaros, A., Green, A., *et al.* (2000) Health issues associated with increasing use of crack cocaine among female sex workers in London. *Sexually Transmitted Infection*, 76(4), 292–3.

Ward, M. & Applin, C. (1998) *The Unlearned Lesson: The Role of Alcohol and Drug Misuse in Homicides and Suicides Perpetrated by People with Mental Health Problems*. London: Wayne Howard Books.

Ward, S., Mattick, R. P. & Hall, W. (Eds) (1998) *Methadone Maintenance Treatment and Other Opioid Replacement Therapies*. Amsterdam: Harwood Academic Publishers.

Warner-Smith, M., Darke, S., Lynskey, M., *et al.* (2001) Heroin overdose: causes and consequences. *Addiction*, **96**, 1113–25.

Warner-Smith, M., Darke, S. & Day, C. (2002) Morbidity associated with non-fatal heroin overdose. *Addiction*, **97**, 963–7.

Washton, A. (Ed.) (1995) *Psychotherapy and Substance Abuse: A Practitioner's Handbook*. New York: Guilford Press.

Webb, G. R., Redman, S., Sanson-Fisher, R. W., *et al.* (1990) Comparison of quantity frequency method and a diary method of measuring alcohol consumption. *Journal of Studies on Alcohol*, **51**, 271–7.

Webster-Stratton, C. (1990) Stress: a potential disruptor of parent perceptions and family interaction. *Journal of Clinical Child Psychology*, **19**, 302–12.

Wedel, M., Pieters, J. E., Pikaar, N. A., *et al.* (1991) Application of a three-compartment model to a study of the effects of sex, alcohol dose and concentration, exercise and food consumption on the pharmacokinetics of ethanol in healthy volunteers. *Alcohol and Alcoholism*, **26**, 329–36.

Weild, A. R., Gill, O. N., Bennett, D., *et al.* (2000) Prevalence of HIV, hepatitis B and hepatitis C antibodies in prisoners in England and Wales: a national survey. *Communicable Disease and Public Health*, **3**(2), 121–6.

Weisner, C. & Schmidt, L. (1993) Alcohol and drug problems among diverse health and social service populations. *American Journal of Public Health*, **83**, 824–9.

Weller, B., Weller, M., Coker, E., *et al.* (1987) Crisis at Christmas 1986. *Lancet*, **1**, 553–4.

Werner, E. E. & Smith, R. S. (1982) *Vulnerable but Invincible: A Longitudinal Study of Resilient Children and Youth*. New York: McGraw-Hill.

White, I. R., Altmann, D. R. & Nanchahal, K. (2002) Alcohol consumption and mortality: modelling risks for men and women at different ages. *British Medical Journal*, **325**, 191–4.

White, R. (2000) Dexamphetamine substitution in the treatment of amphetamine abuse: an initial investigation. *Addiction*, **95**, 229–38.

White, R. K. & Wright, D. G. (1998) *Addiction Intervention: Strategies to Motivate Treatment-Seeking Behavior*. New York: Haworth Press.

Whitmore, E. A., Mikulich, S. K., Thompson, L. L., *et al.* (1997) Influences on adolescent substance dependence: conduct disorder, depression, attention deficit hyperactivity disorder, and gender. *Drug and Alcohol Dependence*, **47**, 87–97.

WHO (World Health Organization) Expert Committees on Mental Health and on Alcohol (1955) The 'craving' for alcohol. *Quarterly Journal of Studies on Alcohol*, **16**, 33–66.

WHO (1992) *Tenth Revision of the International Classification of Diseases* (ICD-10). Geneva: WHO.

WHO (1996) The Jakarta declaration on Health Promotion into the 21st Century. 4th International Conference on Health Promotion.

WHO Programme on Substance Abuse (1997) *Cannabis: A Health Perspective and Research Agenda*. Geneva: WHO.

WHO (1997a) *Amphetamine-Type Stimulants*. A report from the WHO meeting on amphetamine, MDMA, and other psychostimulants, Geneva, 12–15 November 1996. Geneva: WHO.

WHO (1997b) HIV/AIDS: the global epidemic. *Weekly Epidemiologic Record*, **72**, 17–24.

WHO (1997c) Hepatitis C. *Weekly Epidemiologic Record*, **72**, 65–72.

Wikler, A. (1948) Recent progress in research on the neurophysiological basis of morphine addiction. *American Journal of Psychiatry*, **105**, 328–38.

Wille, R. (1983) Processes of recovery from heroin dependence: relationship to treatment, social changes, and drug use. *Journal of Drug Issues*, Summer, **13**, 333–42.

Williams, M. L., Zhuo, Z., Siegal, H. A., *et al.* (1995) A comparison of drug use networks across three cities. In: R. H. Needle, S. L.Coyle, S. G. Genser, *et al.* (Eds) *Social Networks, Drug Abuse, and HIV Transmission*, pp. 109–30. Rockville, MD: National Institute on Drug Abuse.

Williams, R. & Morgan, H. (1994) *Suicide Prevention – The Challenge Confronted*. NHS Health Advisory Service. London: HMSO.

Wills, T. A. & Shiffman, S. (1985) Coping and substance use: a conceptual framework. In: S. Shiffman & T. A. Wills (Eds) *Coping and Substance Use*, pp. 3–24. New York: Academic Press.

Wills, T. A., Sandy, J. M. & Yaeger, A. (2000) Temperament and adolescent substance use: an epigenetic approach to risk protection. *Journal of Personality*, **68**, 1127–51.

Wilson, P. (1980) *Drinking in England and Wales*. London: HMSO.

Wilson, W. J. (1987) *The Truly Disadvantaged*. Chicago: University of Chicago Press.

Wilson, W. J. (1996) *When Work Disappears: The World of the New Urban Poor*. New York: Alfred A. Knopf.

Windle, M. (1990) A longitudinal study of antisocial behaviour in early adolescence as predictors of late adolescence substance use: gender and ethnic group differences. *Journal of Abnormal Child Psychology*, **99**, 86–92.

Windle, M. & Windle, R. C. (1996) Coping strategies, drinking motives, and stressful life events among adolescents: associations with emotional and behavioral problems, and academic functioning. *Journal of Abnormal Psychology*, **105**, 551–60.

Winkleby, M. A., Rockhill, B., Jatulis, D., et al. (1992) The medical origins of homelessness. *American Journal of Public Health*, **82**(10), 1394–8.

Winstock, A., Sheridan, J., Lovell, S., et al. (2000) Availability of overdose resuscitation facilities: a survey of drug agencies in England and Wales. *Journal of Substance Use*, **5**(2), 99–102.

Winters, K. C., Stinchfield, R. D., Opland, E., et al. (2000) The effectiveness of the Minnesota Model approach in the treatment of adolescent drug abusers. *Addiction*, **95**(4), 601–12.

Wolff, K., Welch, S., Marsden, J., et al. (1997) *Working Group on Identification and Management of Psychoactive Substance Use Problems in Primary Health Care Settings*. Geneva: WHO.

Wolkstein, E. & Hastings-Black, D. (1979) Vocational rehabilitation. In: R. L. DuPont, A. Goldstein & J. O'Donnell (Eds) *Handbook on Drug Abuse*, pp. 159–64. Rockville, MD: National Institute on Drug Abuse.

Woody, G. E., McLellan, A. T, Luborsky, L. et al. (1990) Psychotherapy and counselling for methadone maintained opiate addicts: results of research studies. *NIDA Research Monographs*, **104**, 9–23.

Woolley, P. D., Bowman, C. A. & Kinghorn, G. R. (1998) Prostitution in Sheffield: differences between prostitutes. *Genitourinary Medicine*, **64**(6), 391–3.

Wren, C. S. (1998) Alcohol or drugs tied up to 80% of inmates. *New York Times*, 9 January 1998, p. A14.

Xie, X., Rehm, J., Single, E., et al. (1996) *The Economic Costs of Alcohol, Tobacco, and Illicit Drug Abuse in Ontario: 1992*. Toronto: Addiction Research Foundation.

Yamaguchi, K. & Kandel, D. B. (1985) On resolution of role incompatability: a life event history analysis of family roles and marijuana use. *American Journal of Sociology*, **90**, 1284–325.

Zador, P. L. (1991) Alcohol-related relative risk of fatal driving injuries in relation to driver age and sex. *Journal of Studies on Alcohol*, **52**, 302–10.

Zador, D., Sunjic, S. & Darke, S. (1996) Heroin-related deaths in New South Wales, 1992: toxicological findings and circumstances. *Medical Journal of Australia*, **164**, 204–207.

Zeitlin, H. (1999) Psychiatric co-morbidity with substance misuse in children and teenagers. *Drug and Alcohol Dependence*, **55**(3), 225–34.

Zekoski, E. M., O'Hara, M. W. & Wills, K. E. (1987) The effects of maternal mood on mother–infant interaction. *Journal of Abnormal Child Psychology*, **15**(3), 361–78.

Zinberg, N. E. (1984) *Drug, Set, and Setting: The Basis for Controlled Intoxicant Use*. New Haven, CT: Yale University Press.

Zucker, R. A. & Gomberg, E. S. L. (1986) Etiology of alcoholism reconsidered. *American Psychologist*, **41**, 783–93.

Zucker, R. A., Fitzgerald, H. E. & Moses, H. D. (1995) Emergence of alcohol problems and the several alcoholisms: a developmental perspective on etiologic theory and life course trajectory. In: D. Cicchetti & D. J. Cohen (Eds) *Developmental Psychopathology*, vol. 2: *Risk, Disorder, and Adaptation*, pp. 677–711. New York: Wiley.

Further Reading

Alcoholics Anonymous, 3rd edn (1976) New York: Alcoholics Anonymous World Services.

Alcohol Use Among Adolescents (1999) Windle, M. Thousand Oaks, CA, London & New Delhi: Sage.

Children and Young People Substance Misuse Services: The Substance of Young Needs (1996) (updated 2001) Health Advisory Service (HAS) Thematic Review. London: HMSO.

Clinical Guide to Alcohol Treatment: The Community Reinforcement Approach (1995) Meyers, R. J. & Smith, J. E. New York: Guilford Press.

Coexisting Problems of Mental Disorder and Substance Misuse (Dual Diagnosis): An Information Manual – 2002. S. Banerjee, C. Clancy & I. Crome (Eds). London: The Royal College of Psychiatrists Research Unit.

Cognitive Therapy of Substance Abuse (1993) Beck, A. T., Wright, F. D., Newman, C. F., *et al.* New York & London: Guilford Press.

Counselling for Stress Problems (1995) Palmer, S. & Dryden, W. London: Sage.

Drug Abuse Briefing, 8th edn (2001) Drugscope. London: Drugscope.

Drug Addiction Research and the Health of Women (A compilation of papers covering a wide range of topics) (1998) C. L. Wetherington & A. B. Roman (Eds). Rockville, MD: National Institute on Drug Abuse.

Drug Misuse and Dependence – Guidelines on Clinical Management (1999) England, Wales, Scotland & N. Ireland: HMSO, Departments of Health.

Drug Misuse and Motherhood (2002) Klee, H., Jackson, M. & Lewis, C. London & New York: Routledge.

Drugs, Pregnancy and Childcare: A Guide for Professionals (1999) Mountney, J. London: ISDD (Drugscope).

International Handbook of Alcohol Dependence and Problems (2001) N. Heather, T. J. Peters & T. Stockwell (Eds). Chichester, UK & New York: Wiley.

Living Sober (1975) New York: Alcoholics Anonymous World Services.

Motivational Enhancement Therapy Manual (1995) National Institute on Alcohol Abuse and Alcoholism. Rockville, MD: DHHS.

Motivational Interviewing: Preparing People for Change, 2nd edn (2002) W. R. Miller & S. Rollnick (Eds). New York: Guilford Press.

Multisystemic Treatment of Antisocial Behavior in Children and Adolescents (1998) Henggeler, S. W., Schoenwald, S. K., Borduin, C. M., *et al.* New York: Guilford Press.

Problem Drinkers: Guided Self-Change Treatment (1993) Sobell, M. B. & Sobell, L. C. London & New York: Guilford Press.

Relapse Prevention (1985) Marlatt, G. A. & Gordon, J. R. New York: Guilford Press.

Relapse Prevention for Addictive Behaviours: A Manual for Therapists (1990) Wanigaratne, S., Wallace, W., Pullin, J., *et al.* Oxford: Blackwell Science.

Solutions Step by Step (1998) Berg, I. K. & Reuss, N. H. London & New York: W. W. Norton.

The Alcoholic Family in Recovery (1999) Brown, S. & Lewis, V. New York: Guilford Press.

The Transtheoretical Approach: Crossing Traditional Boundaries of Therapy (1984) Prochaska, J. O. & DiClemente, C. C. Homewood, IL: Dow Jones-Irwin.

Treating Alcohol Dependence: A Coping Skills Training Guide, 2nd edn (2002) Monti, P. M., Kadden, R. M., Rohsenow, D. J., *et al.* London: Cassell.

Treating Alcohol Problems: Marital and Family Interventions (1993) T. J. O'Farrell (Ed.). New York: Guilford Press.

Twelve Steps and Twelve Traditions (1952) New York: Alcoholics Anonymous World Services.

Twelve-Step Facilitation Therapy Manual (1995) National Institute on Alcohol Abuse and Alcoholism. Rockville, MD: DHHS.

Working with Drug Family Support Groups (1996) Lockley, P. London & New York: Free Association Books.

Index